Professional JSP

Karl Avedal
Danny Ayers
Timothy Briggs
Carl Burnham
Ari Halberstadt
Ray Haynes
Peter Henderson
Mac Holden
Sing Li
Dan Malks
Tom Myers
Alexander Nakhimovsky
Stéphane Osmont
Grant Palmer
John Timney
Sameer Tyagi
Geert Van Damme
Mark Wilcox
Steve Wilkinson
Stefan Zeiger
John Zukowski

Wrox Press Ltd. ®

Professional JSP

First Published	May 2000
Reprinted	August 2000

Published by Wrox Press Ltd
Arden House, 1102 Warwick Road, Acock's Green, Birmingham B27 6BH, UK
Printed in USA
ISBN 1-861003-62-5

Trademark Acknowledgements

Credits

Authors
Karl Avedal
Danny Ayers
Timothy Briggs
Carl Burnham
Ari Halberstadt
Ray Haynes
Peter Henderson
Mac Holden
Sing Li
Dan Malks
Tom Myers
Alexander Nakhimovsky
Stéphane Osmont
Grant Palmer
John Timney
Sameer Tyagi
Geert van Damme
Mark Wilcox
Steve Wilkinson
Stefan Zeiger
John Zukowski

Technical Editors
Richard Huss
Greg Pearson

Development Editor
Timothy Briggs

Managing Editor
Paul Cooper

Project Manager
Chandima Nethisinghe

Technical Reviewers
Thomas Bishop
Jason Bock
Michael Boerner
Carl Burnham
Cosmo DiFazio
Matthew Ferris
Ethan Henry
David Hudson
Jim Johnson
Rod Johnson
Andrew Jones
Jim MacIntosh
Stephen Potts
David Schultz
John Timney
Krishna Vedati
Paul Warren
Andrew H. Watt
Mark Wilcox

Production Project Manager
Mark Burdett

Design / Layout
Tom Bartlett
William Fallon
Jonathan Jones
Laurent Lafon

Index
Alessandro Ansa

Cover Design
Shelley Frazier

Cover Photographs

Left to right:

Danny Ayers, Carl Burnham, Ari Halberstadt, Ray Haynes
Sing Li, Dan Malks, Tom Myers, Alexander Nakhimovsky
Stéphane Osmont, Grant Palmer, John Timney, Geert van Damme
Mark Wilcox, Steve Wilkinson, Stefan Zeiger, John Zukowski

About the Authors

Karl Avedal

Karl Avedal has been a Java developer since the language was publically launched in 1995. With the advent of Java server side technologies like servlets he quickly turned his attention to the server and worked a lot with CORBA before his first contacts with EJB in 1998. He is now a developer with the Orion Application Server team (http://www.orionserver.com). He is also taking part in the development of the the J2EE 1.3 specification as well as the JSP 1.2 and Servlet 2.3 specifications as a member of the expert groups for these standards.

Danny Ayers

Since going freelance, Danny Ayers divides his time unequally between network consultancy and contract work, woodcarving, and creating dance-floor crazes. Contact: danny_ayers@yahoo.com

To Mary, my mother (because she grumbled when Caroline got the last dedication).

Carl Burnham

Carl is a web developer, Internet consultant, and founder of Southpoint.com, a popular U.S. travel portal. He has 15 years of experience working as an IT professional in the private and public sectors, and was recently a senior network administrator for a leading Internet company. His interests include developing web sites, writing, photography, and using the full potential of the Web. He travels extensively via RV, with his wife Rhonda, golden retriever Gus, blind mutt Rocky, and Peewee, the cat. He can be reached at burnhamc@southpoint.com.

Dan Malks

Dan Malks is an Enterprise Java Architect with Sun Microsystems, working in the Sun Java Center in McLean, VA. He received a Master of Science degree in Computer Science from Johns Hopkins University in 1996 after having earned a Bachelor of Science in Computer Science from The College of William and Mary in 1987. While focusing on Object-Oriented technologies, he has developed in a variety of environments, including Smalltalk and most recently Java. He has published a number of articles about Java in leading industry periodicals, in addition to being a contributing author to *Professional JSP*, Wrox, 2000. Currently he has been focusing on Distributed, Service-based architectural designs, patterns and implementations.

Thanks to the helpful group of editors and reviewers at Wrox Press and most of all to Beth, my wonderful wife.

Ray Haynes

I have been programming ASP using JavaScript for 3 years now. I discovered JSP about 6 months ago and have been intrigued since. As the Lead Web Developer of an Internet start-up company in Kansas City, MO, I have been told that I am the ultimate geek when it comes to web development. My full time job is as a web programmer, and when I get home, I work on my own web sites. I am also attending college, working for my Bachelor of Science in Computer Information Systems, and should graduate around October 2001. My girlfriend, while feeding and watering me so that I don't wither away, keeps my heart warm, and my cat keeps my feet warm on late nights.

Peter Henderson

Peter is a senior developer at Oyster Partners, a Web Consultancy in London. Since graduating in mathematics he moved back into computing. He has been having fun working with web technologies for the last 4 years.

Mac Holden

Mac Holden has over 15 years experience in the Information Technology Industry. For the last 10 years he has been running his own software house based in South East Asia. The company initially concentrated on development and implementation of Client Server systems and then moved increasingly into web-based applications written in Java. He first became interested in Java in its alpha days as a means of connecting remote locations such as mines and oil rigs to their head offices. Mac is also the chief designer and developer of a pure Java application development tool called JdJ Servlet Builder which creates database aware servlets from HTML forms.

Sing Li

First bitten by the computer bug in 1978, Sing has grown up with the microprocessor revolution. His first 'PC' was a $99 do-it-yourself COSMIC ELF computer with 256 bytes of memory and a 1 bit LED display. For two decades, Sing has been an active author, consultant, speaker, instructor, and entrepreneur. His wide-ranging experience spans distributed architectures, multi-tiered Internet/Intranet systems, computer telephony, call center technology, and embedded systems. Sing has participated in several Wrox projects in the past, and has been working with (and writing about) Java and Jini since their very first alpha release. He is an active participant in the Jini community.

Tom Myers

Tom has a BA (cum laude), St. John's College, Santa Fe, New Mexico ("Great Books" program), 1975 and a PhD in computer science from the University of Pennsylvania, 1980. He taught computer science at the University of Delaware and Colgate before becoming a full-time consultant and software developer. He is the author of "Equations, Models, and Programs: A Mathematical Introduction to Computer Science" Prentice-Hall Software Series, 1988, several articles on theoretical computer science, and two joint titles with Alexander Nakhimovsky: *Javascript Objects*, Wrox, 1998, and *Professional Java XML Programming with Servlets and JSP*, Wrox, 1999.

Alexander Nakhimovsky

Alexander Nakhimovsky received an MA in mathematics from Leningrad University in 1972 and a PhD in general linguistics from Cornell in 1978, with a graduate minor in computer science. He taught general and slavic linguistics at Cornell and SUNY Oswego before joining Colgate's computer science department in 1985. He published a book and a number of articles on theoretical and computational linguistics, several Russian language textbooks, a dictionary of Nabokov's Lolita, and, jointly with Tom Myers, *Javascript Objects*, Wrox, 1998, and *Professional Java XML Programming with Servlets and JSP*, Wrox, 1999.

Stéphane Osmont

Stéphane Osmont is a Software Engineer at Netscape Communications. Stéphane worked on the team that developed the JSP engine for Netscape Enterprise Web Server 4.0, and has recently been working on the Online Procurement ecommerce solutions for the Sun-Netscape Alliance. Stéphane, whose interests include traveling to South of France to visit his family and hanging out with friends and his wife Karen around the sunny San Francisco Bay Area, will be starting a new adventure by joining the greenlight.com team. He can be reached at sosmont@seolan.com.

Grant Palmer

Grant has worked as a scientific programmer in the Space Technology Division at the NASA Ames Research Center for the past 15 years. He has worked with Java since 1996 developing programs for scientific applications as well as converting older FORTRAN and C codes to the Java platform.

Grant lives in Chandler, Arizona with his wife, Lisa, and his two sons, Jackson and Zachary. In his spare time, Grant enjoys skiing and gardening, and is a competitive swimmer. He also likes to watch movies and read historical fiction.

John Timney

John lives in the UK with his wife Philippa in a small town called Chester-le-Street in the north of England. He is a postgraduate of Nottingham University having gained an MA in Information Technology following a BA Honours Degree from Humberside University. John currently works for Syntegra at their Newcastle office and specialises in Internet development. John's hobbies include Martial Arts and he has black belts in two different styles of Karate. His computing expertise has gained him a Microsoft MVP (Most Valuable Professional) award.

Sameer Tyagi

Sameer writes regularly for online and print publications.He has over four years of experience in software design and development and specializes in server side Java based distributed applications. (N-tier architectures, JDBC, JNDI, EJB, JMS, RMI, JSP, Servlets *et al.*) He has a Bachelors in Electronic Engineering and numerous other certifications.

He is a Java addict who gets his fix by jumping head on into almost anything that compiles into bytecodes and is known to blame that newly discovered area of the brain called the Javasphere for such stimuli.

When he's not going through another latte flavor, he can be found flying around at 15000 ft in a small Cessna.

Geert van Damme

I live in Leuven (Belgium) with my wife Sofie and my little son Jules. I studied Mathematical Psychology and Philosophy but ended up working in the IT business after a short while. In 1997 I started my own development and consulting company Darling, currently focussing on server side Java. Since then I work as an independant consultant on a number of projects, mainly from my home office. I can be reached at geert.vandamme@darling.be.

You can leave your name on my Graffiti wall at http://www.gojasper.be/wall.jsp

Mark Wilcox

Mark is the Web Administrator for the University of North Texas. He's also a frequent author and speaker on a variety of Internet topics. You can reach him at mark@mjwilcox.com.

To my lovely wife, Jessica. Thanks to our parents for bringing us up right.

Steve Wilkinson

Steven is a hands-on software developer with over 13 years experience. Steven is currently a Principal with Elkhorn Creek Software, Incorporated were he concentrates on design and implementation of web based applications using Java Technologies.

Steven has been using Java Technologies since 1996. He has worked on projects for companies that range from start-ups to fortune 500 companies like Sun Microsystems, MCI, BellSouth and IBM. In these previous positions, Steven has used Java Technologies as RMI, Java Servlets, JHTML, JavaServer Pages, Java Applications, and Java Applets.

Steven has a degree in Electrical Engineering from the University of Kentucky, and is currently finishing his Master's of Science in Computer Information Systems from Regis University in Denver, Colorado.

Steven is also a contributing author to *Developing Java Servlets* by James Goodwill were he developed two chapters on Servlets and Object Databases and Servlets as Distributed Clients using RMI and CORBA.

Steven would like to thank his partner Diana for her patience, understanding, proof reading, and encouragement during his writing experiences.

Stefan Zeiger

Stefan Zeiger has been working as a freelance Java programmer since 1997 and studying computer science at the Technical University of Darmstadt since 1996. He is the author of the *NetForge* web server software and the popular online servlet tutorial *Servlet Essentials.*

John Zukowski

John Zukowski is the Content Director with jGuru.com. He received a B.S. in computer science and mathematics from Northeastern University and M.S. in computer science from Johns Hopkins University. He is the author of *John Zukowski's Definitive Guide to Swing for Java 2* from APress, *Java AWT Reference* from O'Reilly & Associates, as well as *Borland's JBuilder: No Experience Required* and *Mastering Java 2* from Sybex. In addition, John has authored numerous Java technologies articles and serves on the Senior Advisory Board of JavaWorld. John also serves as the vice-chairman of ACM's WebTech user group and the *Focus on Java* guide for About.com (http://java.about.com).

Congratulations to my wife Lisa for completing her Masters.

J2EE
JSP

Table of Contents

J2EE
JSP

Introduction

Welcome

Welcome to Professional JSP. This book shows how JavaServer Pages (JSP) and the Java 2 Enterprise Edition (J2EE) can help you develop great web applications – delivering dynamic content to web clients in a portable, secure, and well-designed way.

Because your web applications are only as good as the functionality they provide we also survey the Java Enterprise APIs that interface with JSP. And to show the practice of programming Java applications, we present seven case studies of JSP in action.

Who is this Book For?

Java, the language, needs no introduction. It's not been out of the news since it was released. The JavaServer Pages specification extends the Java Servlet API to provides web developers with a framework for creating dynamic content on the server using HTML and XML templates, and Java code, which is secure, fast, and independent of server platform.

Both JSP and Servlets form part of the Java 2 Platform Enterprise Edition, which supports and provides ready-built functionality for all manner of application domains.

Over the last two years, Java's support for applications has expanded enormously. You can now develop dynamic web server applications which:

- Serve HTML and XML, and stream data to the client
- Separate presentation, logic and data
- Track client sessions
- Scale better than CGI
- Interface to databases, other Java applications, CORBA, directory and mail services
- Make use of application server middleware to provide transactional support

The APIs in question have very broad industry support, having been developed by JavaSoft in wide consultation with expert partners. In consequence, the Java revolution of portable code and open APIs is married with an evolution in existing products (whether database, application, mail or web servers). The wide availability of products to run Java applications on the server has made this a fast-moving and very competitive market, but the essential compatibility through specifications, standard APIs and class libraries has held. This makes server-side Java a very exciting area.

This book is aimed at professional developers with some experience of programming for the Web. A quick start Java tutorial can be found at http://www.wrox.com. For an in-depth Java tutorial, see *Beginning Java 2, JDK 1.3 Edition* (Ivor Horton, ISBN 1-861003-66-8), or some other tutorial book that covers similar ground. We'll review key areas that crop up again and again in server-side programming.

What's Covered in this Book

The book has the following structure:

- An introduction to JSP, explaining how they relate to servlets, showing the tags, and creating beans to encapsulate business logic and keep the page simple.
- Further chapters cover database access and connection pooling, JSP debugging, and web application architecture using JSP and servlets.
- Having covered the basics, the next few chapters look at the design and implementation of some sample JSP web applications.
- After considering security issues in JSP and web applications, further case studies cover E-Commerce, J2EE and Enterprise JavaBeans, streaming data to the client, and using JSPs and XSLT to target data at both desktop WAP clients. A final case study considers a project where an ASP-based application was re-targetted to JSP.

Appendices give advice on installing the Tomcat JSP/Servlet engine, detailed references to JSP, the Servlet API, HTTP, and finally JSP for ASP programmers.

What You Need to Use this Book

The code in this book was tested with the Java 2 Platform Standard Edition SDK (JDK 1.3). For the JSP and Servlet engine we used both Tomcat 3.1 and JSWDK 1.0.1.

We also used the following software:

- Web Server – we used Apache 1.3.12
- Databases – any JDBC/ODBC compliant database. We used both Access and MySQL
- Sun's JNDI SDK, which is included with JDK 1.3
- LDAP server – Netscape Directory Server version 4.11
- iPlanet Web Server 4.1
- J2EE Application Server –Orion Application Server, http://www.orionserver.com
- Sun's Java Media Framework (JMF) API and Java API for XML Parsing (JAXP)
- WAP phone simulator – we used that available from phone.com, http://updev.phone.com/
- XSLT engine – xt from James Clark, http://www.jclark.com/xml

The code in the book will work on a single machine, provided it is networked (that is, it can see http://localhost through the local browser).

The complete source code from the book is available for download from:

http://www.wrox.com

Conventions

To help you get the most from the text and keep track of what's happening, we've used a number of conventions throughout the book.

For instance:

> **These boxes hold important, not-to-be forgotten information which is directly relevant to the surrounding text.**

While the background style is used for asides to the current discussion.

As for styles in the text:

When we introduce them, we **highlight** important words.

We show keyboard strokes like this: *Ctrl-A*.

We show filenames and code within the text like so: `doGet()`

Text on user interfaces and URLs are shown as: Menu.

We present code in three different ways. Definitions of methods and properties are shown as follows:

```
protected void doGet(HttpServletRequest req, HttpServletResponse resp)
                     throws ServletException, IOException
```

Example code is shown:

```
In our code examples, the code foreground style shows new, important,
    pertinent code
while code background shows code that's less important in the present context,
    or has been seen before.
```

J2EE
JSP

1

Introducing JavaServer Pages

In this chapter, we will set the scene, looking at:

- Integrating applications with web services
- The Java 2 Enterprise Edition
- Comparisons with other technologies
- A first JSP and what's happening under the covers
- The future development of JSP

The Internet needs no introduction. The success of the HTTP protocol, in its simplicity, scalability and ubiquity, is obvious.

The current push is to put more of business processes on the web, whether in business-to-consumer (B2C) or business-to-business (B2B) markets (BEA recently forecast a $billion market for B2C, and $trillion market for B2B applications). These applications show up some drawbacks in conventional web site design, using CGI for instance. The main problems facing developers seeking to develop web applications are:

- Scalability – a successful site will have more users than the biggest corporation intranet. And the number of users is rising all the time, so your solutions have to scale.
- Integration of backend data and business logic – the web is just another way to conduct business, and so it should be able to use the same middle-tier and data-access code. Interfacing web-based requests to backend systems can be a big headache.
- Manageability – sites just keep getting bigger, and we need some way to manage the content and its interaction with business systems. Object-oriented programming techniques have proven their worth in client-server systems and they should help us in web application development.

- Personalization – Adding a personal touch to the page isn't just cosmetic, it's essential to keeping your customer. Knowing their preferences, allowing them to configure the information they see, remembering past purchases or frequent search terms are all important in providing feedback and interaction from what is otherwise a fairly one-sided conversation.

These points all depend on the right application architecture – get that wrong and you're fighting a losing battle. And architecture can be greatly aided by a good framework for providing a web view on your business.

The Java 2 Enterprise Edition

The official Java framework for enterprise application development is the Java 2 Enterprise Edition (http://java.sun.com/j2ee). There are other solutions, notably WebObjects from Apple, but J2EE has the backing of Sun, IBM, Oracle, BEA, the Apache Group and a host of application server vendors.

J2EE provides:

- A platform for enterprise applications, with full API support for enterprise code and guarantees of portability between server implementations
- A clear division between code which deals with presentation, business logic, and data

J2EE consists of the following APIs, ordered roughly by where in a three-tier app they're used:

- JavaServer Pages
- Servlets
- Java support for XML
- Enterprise JavaBeans (EJBs)
- Java Messaging
- Java Transaction support
- JavaMail
- Java Naming and Directory Interface (JNDI)
- JDBC
- Java support for CORBA

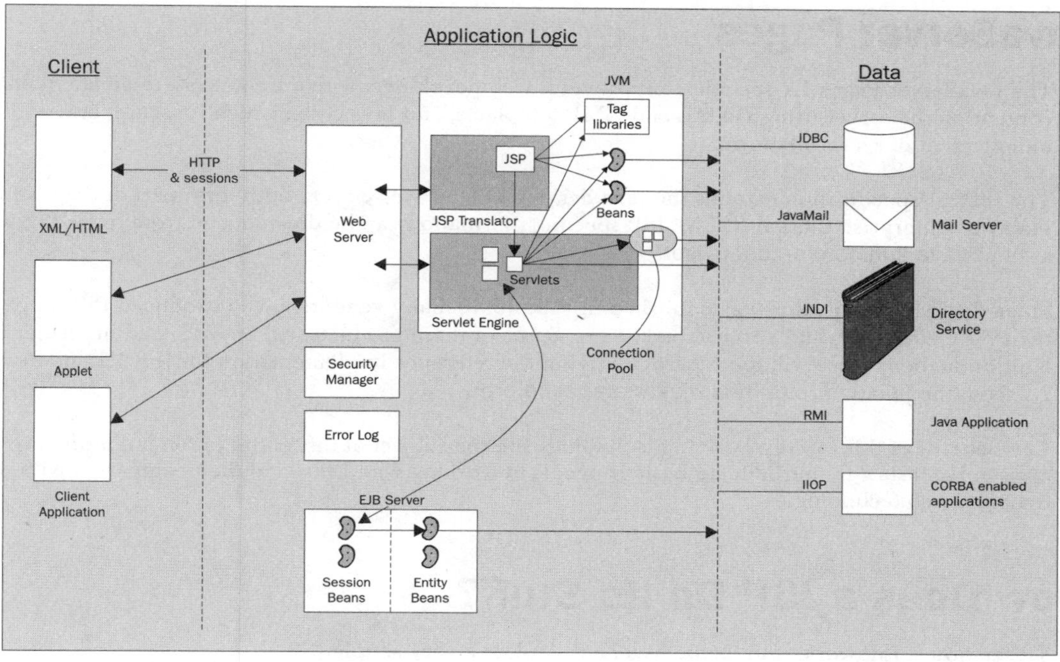

The J2EE specification meets the needs of *web* applications because it provides:

- Rich interaction with a web server via Servlets, which provide objects representing the elements of an HTTP request and response
- Built-in support for sessions, both in Servlets and EJBs
- The use of EJBs to mirror the user interaction with data by providing automatic session and transaction support to EJBs operating in the EJB server
- Entity EJBs to represent data as an object
- Seamless integration with the Java data access APIs
- Flexible template-based output using JSP and XML

This family of APIs mean that the final web page can be generated from a user request, which was processed by a servlet or JSP and a session EJB (representing the user's session with the server), using data extracted from a database and put into an entity EJB.

We'll see more of EJBs in Chapter 17, JDBC in Chapter 7, JNDI in Chapters 15 and 16, and XML in Chapters 17 and 19.

JavaServer Pages

The JavaServer Pages 1.1 specification provides web developers with a framework to create dynamic content on the server using HTML and XML templates, and Java code, which is secure, fast, and independent of server platform.

The JSP 1.1 specification extends the Java Servlet API. As we've seen, both form part of the Java 2 Platform Enterprise Edition (J2EE). JSP-specific information can be downloaded from Sun's JSP web site at http://java.sun.com/products/jsp/.

Since the JSP specification was published in June 1999, many vendors have introduced JSP support in their Servlet engines and application servers. Some of these products will be discussed in further detail later in the book – we will focus particularly on the reference implementation for JSP 1.1 and Servlets 2.2 from the Jakarta group (http://jakarta.apache.org).

The benefits of this rapidly evolving technology are the subject of this entire book, but in the present chapter we'll start by introducing basic concepts in working with JSPs, and then compare it with other dynamic web technologies.

How Does a JSP Do Its Stuff?

To see how a JSP works and its lifecycle, let's look at a very simple JSP.

We create a simple HTML form, `SimpleJSP.html`, which allows a user to type a number into a form in their web browser, and submit the form to the server. The server will respond with "Hello, world!" repeated that number of times followed by a standard footer at the bottom of the page.

The contents of `SimpleJSP.html` are:

```
<HTML>
<HEAD>
<TITLE>Simple JSP Example</TITLE>
</HEAD>

<BODY>

<P>How many times?</P>

<FORM METHOD="GET" ACTION="SimpleJSP.jsp">
<INPUT TYPE="TEXT" SIZE="2" NAME="numtimes">
<INPUT TYPE="SUBMIT">
</FORM>

</BODY>
</HTML>
```

When viewed in a web browser, it looks like this:

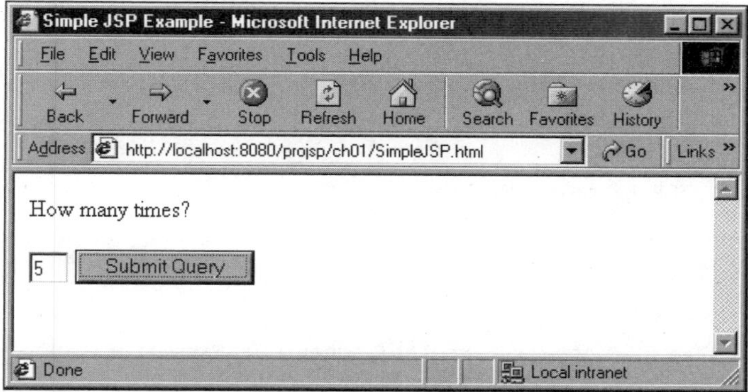

When the user clicks the Submit Query button, the browser sends a **request** to the web server for `SimpleJSP.jsp`, and includes with its request the value entered by the user. The server interprets the JSP code and creates a **response** HTML code, which is sent back to the browser. We will look into this process in more detail in a moment, but first let's look at the response itself and the JSP that generated it.

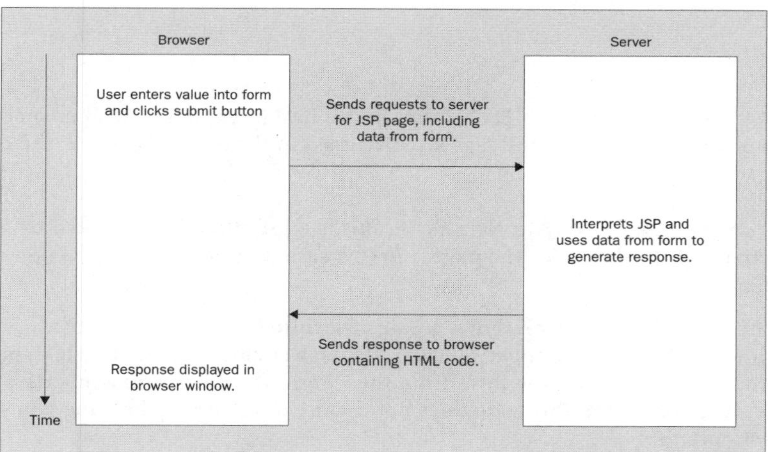

For the screenshot just shown, the response from the server will be displayed as follows:

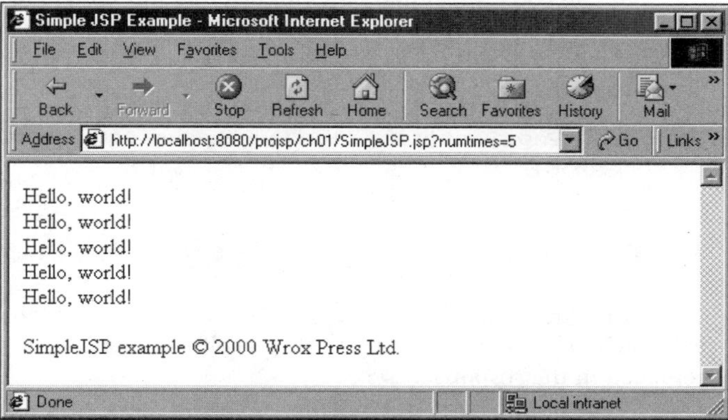

The file `SimpleJSP.jsp` contains the following code:

```
<%@ page language="java" %>

<HTML>
<HEAD>
<TITLE>Simple JSP Example</TITLE>
</HEAD>

<BODY>

<P>
  <% int numTimes = Integer.parseInt(request.getParameter("numtimes"));
     for (int i = 0; i < numTimes; i++) {
  %>
       Hello, world!<BR>
  <% }
  %>
</P>

<%@ include file="PageFooter.html" %>

</BODY>
</HTML>
```

As you can see, most of this is plain HTML but it also has, interspersed with it, special JSP tags (highlighted above). The possible JSP tags are discussed in detail in Chapter 2; the ones you can see here are:

- `<%@ page language="java" %>` – This is a JSP **directive** (denoted by `<%@`). The page directive sets attributes for the page – in this case it indicates that the code on the page is written in Java.
- The next highlighted block shows a pair of **scriptlets** (indicated by `<% ... %>` tags) either side of a line of plain HTML code. The scriptlet tags enclose Java code which gets the value entered by the user into the form from the `request` object, and converts it into an integer value. (For simplicity, this code does not do any of the error checking you would normally expect here.)

  The code then enters a loop, printing out the HTML code (`Hello, world!<BR>`) the requisite number of times. Notice that this HTML code is *not* included inside the `<% ... %>` tag – it is not to be processed itself, but passed straight to the browser.
- `<%@ include file="PageFooter.html" %>` – This directive includes the contents of the file `PageFooter.html` in the response at that point. `PageFooter.html` contains one line of HTML:

```
<P>SimpleJSP example &copy; 2000 Wrox Press Ltd.</P>
```

That's our simple JSP page. The HTML code received by the browser is shown below; by comparing it with the contents of `SimpleJSP.jsp` itself, you can see how the JSP tags have been interpreted and replaced in the response.

```
<HTML>
<HEAD>
<TITLE>Simple JSP Example</TITLE>
</HEAD>

<BODY>

<P>

       Hello, world!<BR>

       Hello, world!<BR>

       Hello, world!<BR>

       Hello, world!<BR>

       Hello, world!<BR>

</P>

<P>SimpleJSP example &copy; 2000 Wrox Press Ltd.</P>


</BODY>
</HTML>
```

To get this working, we've used the Tomcat JSP engine (for instructions on installing Tomcat see Appendix A). Tomcat contains its own built-in web server, which can be accessed by going to http://localhost:8080/.

To test this code, put the `projsp` WAR file (available from the Wrox web site) in the `/webapps` folder. It will be expanded on startup.

What's Happening?

So, what happens when the browser requests our JSP page?

First, as we said, the browser sends its request to the server, asking for http://localhost:8080/projsp/ch01/SimpleJSP.jsp?numtimes=5. This specifies the value of `numtimes` (the number entered into the form by the user) as a `GET` parameter.

The web server (Tomcat's built-in server, in this case) recognizes the `.jsp` file extension in the URL requested by the browser, indicating that the requested resource is a JavaServer Page, and therefore that this request must be handled by the JSP engine.

The JSP page is then translated into a Java class, which is then compiled into a Servlet. This translation and compilation phase occurs only when the JSP file is first called, or when it subsequently changes. You will notice a slight delay the first time that a JavaServer Page is run because of this.

> **For each additional request of the JSP page thereafter, there is no delay because the request goes to the Servlet byte code already in memory.**

We'll learn more about the Servlet lifecycle in the next two chapters, but for now, just remember that an `init()` method is called when the Servlet is first loaded into the virtual machine, to perform any global initialization that every request of the Servlet will need. Then the individual requests are sent to a `service()` method, where the response is put together.

The Servlet creates a new thread to run `service()` for each request. The request from the browser is converted into a Java object of type `HttpServletRequest`, which is passed to the Servlet along with an `HttpServletResponse` object that is used to send the response back to the browser. This whole process is illustrated below. (We'll see this figure again in Chapter 3.)

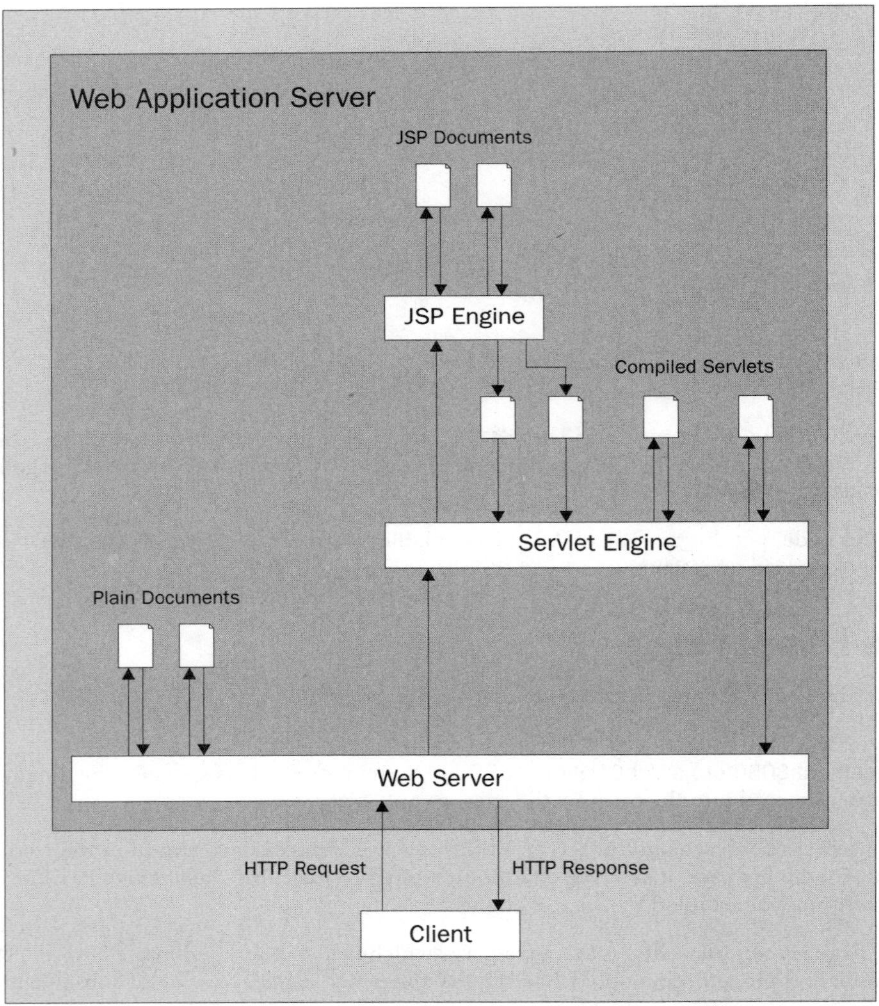

The Servlet code performs the operations specified by the JSP elements in the `.jsp` file. In our example above, the generated Servlet will have a `_jspService()` method that contains Java code to output the required HTML code. In our case, the Java source for the compiled servlet looks like this (cleaned up somewhat):

```
package ch_00030_00031;

import javax.servlet.*;
import javax.servlet.http.*;
import javax.servlet.jsp.*;
import javax.servlet.jsp.tagext.*;
import java.io.PrintWriter;
import java.io.IOException;
import java.io.FileInputStream;
import java.io.ObjectInputStream;
import java.util.Vector;
import org.apache.jasper.runtime.*;
import java.beans.*;
import org.apache.jasper.JasperException;

public class _0002fch_00030_00031_0002fSimpleJSP_0002ejspSimpleJSP_jsp_0
                                                     extends HttpJspBase {

    static {
    }
    public _0002fch_00030_00031_0002fSimpleJSP_0002ejspSimpleJSP_jsp_0( ) {
    }

    private static boolean _jspx_inited = false;

    public final void _jspx_init() throws JasperException { }

    public void _jspService(HttpServletRequest request,
                            HttpServletResponse  response)
        throws IOException, ServletException {

        JspFactory _jspxFactory = null;
        PageContext pageContext = null;
        HttpSession session = null;
        ServletContext application = null;
        ServletConfig config = null;
        JspWriter out = null;
        Object page = this;
        String  _value = null;
        try {

            if (_jspx_inited == false) {
                _jspx_init();
                _jspx_inited = true;
            }
            _jspxFactory = JspFactory.getDefaultFactory();
            response.setContentType("text/html");
            pageContext = _jspxFactory.getPageContext(this, request,
                                  response, "", true, 8192, true);

            application = pageContext.getServletContext();
            config = pageContext.getServletConfig();
            session = pageContext.getSession();
            out = pageContext.getOut();
```

```
            out.write("\r\n\r\n<HTML>\r\n<HEAD>\r\n<TITLE>" +
                      "Simple JSP Example</TITLE>\r\n</HEAD>\r\n\r\n" +
                      "<BODY> \r\n\r\n<P>\r\n  ");
            int numTimes = Integer.parseInt(
                           request.getParameter("numtimes"));
            for (int i = 0; i < numTimes; i++) {
                out.write("\r\n       Hello, world!<BR>\r\n  ");
            }
            out.write("\r\n</P>\r\n\r\n");

            out.write("<P>SimpleJSP example &copy;" +
                      " 2000 Wrox Press Ltd.</P>");
            out.write("\r\n\r\n</BODY>\r\n</HTML>\r\n");
        } catch (Exception ex) {
            if (out.getBufferSize() != 0)
                out.clear();
            pageContext.handlePageException(ex);
        } finally {
            out.flush();
            _jspxFactory.releasePageContext(pageContext);
        }
    }
}
```

Generated code is rarely pretty to look at, but in the highlighted block above you can see the Java code which creates the response to send to the browser. It writes the unchanged sections of HTML code, and loops `numtimes` to print out the message, to the `out` stream. We'll see more on the remainder of the generated code in the next few chapters.

Hopefully, you should now have a better idea of what JSPs are, and how they work to generate dynamic content within a web server. It's time to compare them to other dynamic web content technologies.

Comparison with Existing Technologies

How do JSPs compare with existing technologies for dynamic content generation on the server?

CGI

The Common Gateway Interface (CGI) is the simplest and oldest way to use an HTTP request to control the HTTP output of a server-side application. When a request is sent from a browser to a web site, an external script (often written in PERL, C++, or Python) is run on the server so that the page can be created. In the simplest implementations, each request involves creating a new process into which the script (and runtime, if one is necessary) is loaded, run, and unloaded once the response has been sent. CGI can therefore take up valuable system resources. Newer implementations use threads for each request and keep code in memory to improve performance and scalability.

There's one further problem: CGI only requires the server to pass request information to the script and to be prepared for receiving the output to be returned to the client. There's no further support for building web applications – you have to roll your own session support to remember a user's state between requests, for a sequence of pages needed to complete an order, for example.

By comparison:

- JSP can maintain state on the server between requests (since it can use Servlet sessions)
- Spawns a new thread for each request
- Does not have to be loaded each time, once it has been initiated
- Runs in a ready-loaded JVM as an extension to the web server

Web Server APIs

Many web servers have their own built-in APIs for creating dynamic content, examples including ISAPI for Microsoft IIS and NSAPI for Netscape web servers. These work well, but at the expense of portability – when using a server API, the code is written specifically for that web server and particular platform. The lack of web server choice is a source of concern for some developers.

ASP

The main competing technology for JSPs is Active Server Pages (ASP), from Microsoft. The technologies are quite similar in the way they support the creation of dynamic web pages, using HTML templates, scripting code and components for business logic. Both also interface to enterprise application frameworks, J2EE and Microsoft DNA, respectively.

The table here provides a comparison:

	JSP	ASP
Platforms	All major web platforms	Microsoft only (see below)
Base Language	Java	JScript or VBScript
Components	JSP Tags, JavaBeans, or Enterprise JavaBeans	COM/DCOM
Code Interpretation	Once	Each instance

ASP is usually used on Microsoft IIS or PWS web servers. Two third parties, Chili!Soft (http://www.chilisoft.com) and Halcyonsoft (http://www.halcyonsoft.com), sell software (Chili!Soft ASP and Instant ASP, respectively) that allows ASPs to be used with other platforms. The main problem these companies face is in porting the COM components to the new platform – Halcyonsoft convert them to JavaBeans, or employ a JavaBeans-ActiveX bridge.

JSPs score over ASP in that:

- JSPs are interpreted only once, to Java byte-code, and re-interpreted only when the file is modified
- JSPs run on all the main web servers
- JSPs provide better facilities for separation of page code and template data by means of JavaBeans, Enterprise JavaBeans and custom tag libraries.

But don't be complacent, ASP+ is in the works.

Client-Side Scripting (JavaScript, JScript, VBScript)

Using client-side scripting languages such as JavaScript, JScript, and VBScript brings into play the issue of varying interpretations by different browser versions; a user can also decide to disable scripting altogether. Since JSP runs on the server as such, the browser is not an issue (unless, of course, the JSP produces HTML code which contains client side scripting code).

Servlets

The JSP specification is built on top of the Java Servlet API. Servlets provide the ability to build dynamic content for web sites using the Java language, and are supported on all major web server platforms. Why then, the need for JSPs, if Java already has an API for answering HTTP requests?

Whilst anything that can be done with a JSP can be done with a Servlet, JSPs provide a much cleaner separation of presentation from logic, and are simpler to write. Servlets and JSPs are work well together, as we will see in later chapters.

Many web-hosting companies, however, do not yet include Servlets as a standard feature of their service. Most currently support only add-on CGI scripting or perhaps ASP. But look around and ask for it.

The Future of the Platform

> **"Make everything as simple as possible, but no simpler." Albert Einstein**

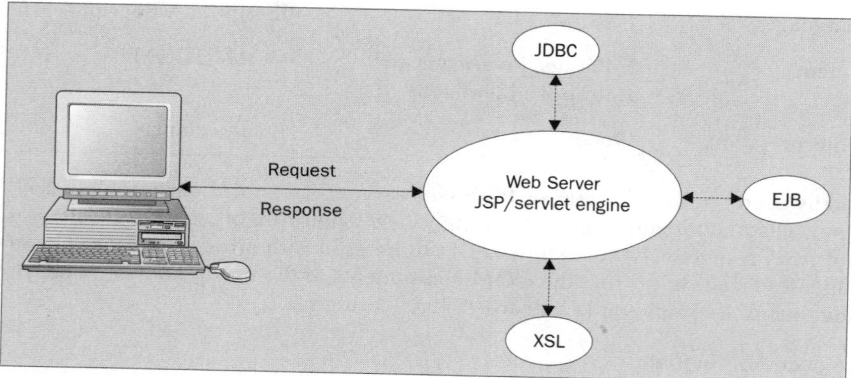

JSP and Servlets are gaining rapid acceptance as means to provide dynamic content on the Internet. With full access to the Java platform, running from the server in a secure manner, the application possibilities are almost limitless. When JSPs are used with Enterprise JavaBeans technology, e-commerce and database resources can be further enhanced to meet an enterprise's needs for web applications providing secure transactions in an open platform.

J2EE technology as a whole is as easy, if not easier, to develop for, deploy and use than comparable technologies, such as CGI and ASP. At the time of writing, tools are becoming available to allow quick web application development, and to easily convert existing server-side technologies to JSP and Servlets.

JSP technology is continuing to develop rapidly to include new features. As this book was being finalized, a new Java Specification Request was being prepared for new versions of the Java Servlet (2.3) and JSP (1.2) technologies. The main changes are:

- Better support for application localization
- Proper support for including JSP pages, without forcing flushing of buffers
- Application event support
- Improved debugging and tool support
- Improved XML support
- Improved tag library support, with standard tags
- Improved JSP authoring support
- Better support for component composition
- Enabling of WebDAV and WAP requests

Many companies, such as IBM, are aggressively deploying JSP within a wide range of products, such as WebSphere Application Server and WebSphere Studio. BEA uses JSP heavily in its portal server, and provides support for JSP in its spin-off company WebGain's tools.

E-commerce will greatly benefit from the new JSP version, with its XML functionality, and scalability. With recent e-commerce web sites in the spotlight from security attacks, it is apparent that active network management along with more scalable implementations need to be pursued to ensure robust enterprise platforms.

By providing a clear separation between content and coding, JSP offers what companies are seeking. With access to the full Java API, and the ability to operate securely on all leading server platforms, JSP is and will continue to be an attractive technology for enterprise development.

Summary

In this chapter, we've introduced JSP, seen how it fits in with the J2EE framework for enterprise web application development and deployment. We've looked at a simple JavaServer Page, and seen how it's translated, compiled and run when a user requests it. We'll look at lifecycle and JSP tags a lot more in the next few chapters. We've also compared JSPs with its competitors, and looked a little into the future.

Time to start going into the JSP syntax in more detail.

J2EE
JSP

2

The Basics

What do JSPs contain?

JavaServer Pages are, on the whole, text files that combine standard HTML and new scripting tags. JSPs look like HTML, but they get compiled into Java servlets the first time they are invoked. The resulting servlet is a combination of the HTML from the JSP file and embedded dynamic content specified by the new tags. That is not to say that JSPs must contain HTML. Some of them will contain only Java code; this is particularly useful when the JSP is responsible for a particular task like maintaining application flow. (See chapter 12.)

Everything in a JSP page can be broken into 2 categories:

- **Elements** that are processed on the server .
- **Template data**, or everything other than elements, that the engine processing the JSP ignores.

Before we look into the intricacies of elements, let us examine the JSP model a little to see what these elements actually do.

A JSP page is executed by a **JSP engine** or **container**, which is installed on a web server, or on an application server. When the client asks for a JSP resource the engine wraps up that **request** and delivers it to the JSP along with a response object. The JSP processes the request and modifies the response object to incorporate the communication with the client. The container then wraps up the **responses** from the JSP page and delivers it to the client. It is imperative to keep in mind that the underlying layer for a JSP is that of a servlet implementation. The abstractions of the request and response are the same as the `javax.servlet.ServletRequest` and `javax.servlet.ServletResponse` (or `HttpServletRequest` and `HttpServletResponse` for the HTTP protocol) respectively.

Keep in mind that the basic servlet architecture is not protocol specific, and the `javax.servlet.http` package is just one implementation of this architecture. A JSP container or engine must support HTTP, but is free to support additional protocols.

> *WebLogic application server, for example, provides a JSP implementation which supports HTTP and its own proprietary t3 protocol.*

The first time the engine intercepts a request for a JSP, it compiles this **translation unit** (the JSP page and other dependant files) into a class file that implements the servlet protocol. If the dependent files are other JSPs they are compiled into their own classes. This is shown in the figure below:

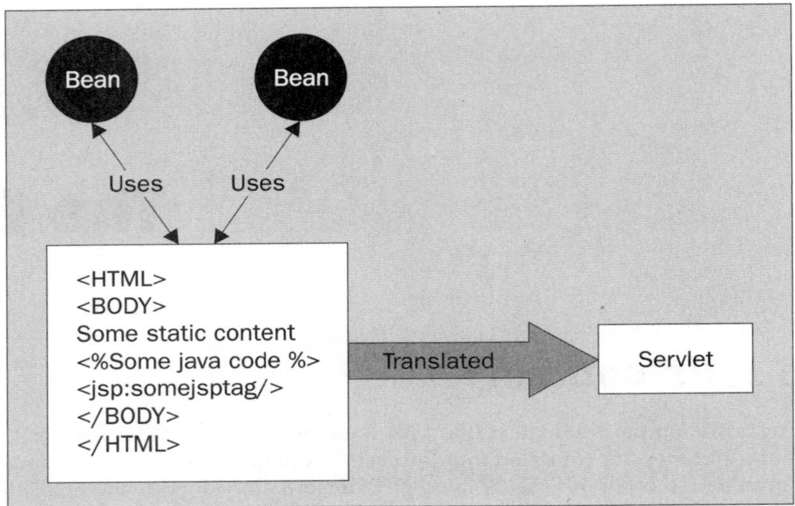

Generated Implementation Class and the JSP Life Cycle

The servlet class generated at the end of the translation process must extend a superclass that is either:

- specified by the JSP author through the use of the `extends` attribute in the `page` directive as we shall see in a while, or
- is a JSP container specific implementation class that implements the `javax.servlet.jsp.JspPage` interface and provides some basic page specific behavior. (Since most JSP pages use HTTP their implementation classes must actually implement the `javax.servlet.jsp.HttpJspPage` interface, which is a sub interface of `javax.servlet.jsp.JspPage`.)

The `javax.servlet.jsp.JspPage` interface contains 2 methods:

Method	Usage
`public void jspInit()`	This is invoked when the JSP is initialized. This is similar to the `init()` method in servlets. Page authors are free to provide initialization of the JSP by implementing this method in their JSPs.
`public void jspDestroy()`	This is invoked when the JSP is about to be destroyed by the container. This is similar to the `destroy()` method in servlets. Page authors are free to provide cleanup of the JSP by implementing this method in their JSPs

The `javax.servlet.jsp.HttpJspPage` interface contains 1 method:

Method	Usage
`public void _jspService (HttpServletRequest request, HttpServletResponse response) throws ServletException, IOException`	This method corresponds to the body of the JSP page and is used for threaded request processing, just like the `service()` method in servlets. This implementation for this method is generated by the JSP container and should never be provided by page authors.

How these 3 methods work together in a JSP can be seen in the figure below, which summarizes the 3 major life events in a JSP.

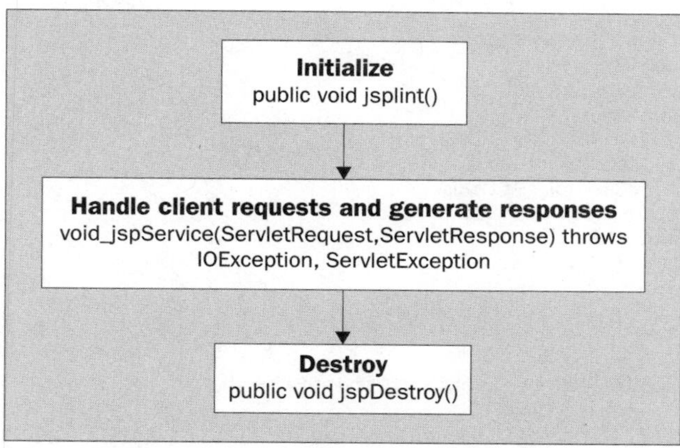

- The page is initilized by invoking the `jspInit()` method, which may be user defined. This initializes the JSP much in the same way as servlets are initialised.
- Every time a request comes to the JSP, the container generated `_jspService()` method is invoked, the request is processed, and the JSP generates the appropriate response. This response is taken by the container and passed back to the client.
- When the JSP is destroyed by the server (for example at shut down), the `_jspDestroy()` method, which can be user defined, is invoked to perform any clean up.

It is worth noting that in most cases the `jspInit()` and `jspDestroy()` methods don't need to be provided by the JSP author and can be omitted. Unlike servlets, the essence of the Java code should be tucked inside beans with the right scope.

Note: For explanatory purposes, this chapter shows code that is generated by Sun's JSP 1.0 and Servlet 2.1 reference implementation, the JavaServer Web Development Kit (JSWDK). Other containers might use a different implementation approach, though the basic premise is the same: the JSP specification and the JSP interfaces. The reader should keep this in mind. For example JSWDK reads the JSP, extracts the HTML and makes a temporary file, while BEA WebLogic doesn't.

Tomcat is the combined JSP 1.1 and Servlets 2.2 reference implementation being developed under the Apache process. As stated by Sun (http://java.sun.com/products/jsp/tomcat/), this Reference Implementation will be the only reference implementation available. Both Tomcat and JSWDK can be downloaded from http://java.sun.com/products/jsp/download.html

Consider a very simple JSP called `hello.jsp` that actually contains no Java and is simple HTML:

```
<html>
<body>
<h1>Hello World</h1>
</html>
```

This JSP gets translated into a Java source file by the server, which looks like:

```
// Generated pacakage statement
package C_0003a.Jswdk.examples;

// Generated import statements
import javax.servlet.*;
import javax.servlet.http.*;
import javax.servlet.jsp.*;
import java.io.PrintWriter;
import java.io.IOException;
import java.io.FileInputStream;
import java.io.ObjectInputStream;
import java.util.Vector;
import com.sun.jsp.runtime.*;
import java.beans.*;
import com.sun.jsp.JspException;


public class hello_jsp_1 extends HttpJspBase {

    static char[][] _jspx_html_data = null;

    public hello_jsp_1( ) {
    }

    private static boolean _jspx_inited = false;
// Internally generated implememtation initialization.
// Not to be confused with the user defined jspInit() method
    public final void _jspx_init() throws JspException {
        ObjectInputStream oin = null;
```

```
        int numStrings = 0;
        try {
            FileInputStream fin = new FileInputStream
              ("work\\%3A8080%2Fexamples\\C_0003a.Jswdk.exampleshello.dat");
            oin = new ObjectInputStream(fin);
            _jspx_html_data = (char[][]) oin.readObject();
        } catch (Exception ex) {
            throw new JspException("Unable to open data file");
        } finally {
            if (oin != null)
                try { oin.close(); } catch (IOException ignore) { }
        }
    }

// Generated method
public void _jspService(HttpServletRequest request,
                        HttpServletResponse response)
  throws IOException, ServletException {

        JspFactory _jspxFactory = null;
        PageContext pageContext = null;
        HttpSession session = null;
        ServletContext application = null;
        ServletConfig config = null;
        JspWriter out = null;
        Object page = this;
        String  _value = null;
        try {

            if (_jspx_inited == false) {
                _jspx_init();
                _jspx_inited = true;
            }
            _jspxFactory = JspFactory.getDefaultFactory();
            response.setContentType("text/html");
            pageContext = _jspxFactory.getPageContext(this, request,
                response, "", true, 8192, true);

            application = pageContext.getServletContext();
            config = pageContext.getServletConfig();
            session = pageContext.getSession();
            out = pageContext.getOut();

            out.print(_jspx_html_data[0]);

        } catch (Throwable t) {
            if (out.getBufferSize() != 0)
                out.clear();
            throw new JspException("Unknown exception: ", t);
        } finally {
            out.flush();
            _jspxFactory.releasePageContext(pageContext);
        }
    }
}
```

The implementation class shown above is taken from Sun's JSWDK. It is worth noticing that there are no `jspInit()` or `jspDestroy()` methods, and the class extends a server specific base class (which actually implements `javax.servlet.jsp.HttpJspPage`). The `init()` in the code is a server generated internal initialization mechanism for the class.

Element basics

JSP syntax is similar to XML syntax and is actually based on XML. The following general rules are applicable to all JSP tags.

- Tags have either a start tag with optional attributes, an optional body, and a matching end tag:

```
<somejsptag attributename="attribute value">
   body
</somejsptag>
```

  or they have an empty tag (possibly with attributes: see example below):

```
<somejsptag attributename="attribute value"/>
```

- Attribute values in the tag always appear quoted. (Either single or double quotes can be used). The special strings `'` and `"` can be used (just as in HTML) if quotes are a part of the attribute value itself.

- Any whitespace within the body text of a document is not significant, but is preserved, which means that any whitespace in the JSP being translated is read and preserved during translation into a servlet.

- The character \ (backslash) can be used as an escape character in a tag, for example to use the `%` character, `\%` can be used.

- URLs used by JSPs follow servlet conventions and a URL starting with a /, called a context-relative path, is interpreted with reference to the **application** (available as an implicit object, see later) or the `ServletContext` to which the JSP page belongs. If the URL does not start with a / it is interpreted relative to the current JSP. It is a good practice to use context-relative URLs.

> **A URL specified in a JSP can use relative URL specifications, as in the Servlet 2.1 specification, and as defined in RFC 2396 (no scheme or authority) available at http://www.ietf.org/rfc/rfc2396.txt**

Element data, or that part of the JSP which is processed on the server, can be classified into the following categories:

- Directives
- Declarations
- Scriptlets
- Expressions
- Standard actions

Let us now move on to look at these in turn.

Directives

JSP **directives** serve as messages to the JSP container from the JSP. They are used to set global values such as class declaration, methods to be implemented, output content type, etc. They do not produce any output to the client. All directives have scope of the entire JSP file. In other words, a directive affects the whole JSP file, and only that JSP file. Directives are characterized by the `@` character within the tag, and the general syntax is:

```
<%@ directivename attribute="value" attribute="value" %>
```

The three directives are:

- The `page` directive
- The `include` directive
- The `taglib` directive

The page Directive

The `page` directive defines a number of important attributes that affect the whole page. A single JSP can contain multiple `page` directives, and during translation all the `page` directives are assimilated and applied to the same page together. However, there can be only one occurrence of any attribute/value pair defined by the `page` directive in a given JSP. (An exception is the `import` attribute, since there can be multiple imports.)

```
<%@ page ATTRIBUTES %>
```

Attribute	Description	Default
`language`	Defines the scripting language to be used. For future use if the JSP engine supports multiple languages.	`"Java"`
`extends`	The value is a fully qualified class name of the superclass that the generated class (into which this JSP page is compiled) must extend. This attribute should be used with extreme caution because the engines usually provide specialized superclasses with a lot of functionality that the generated classes extend.	Attribute omitted by default.
`import`	Comma separated list of packages or classes just like `import` statements in usual Java code.	Attribute omitted by default.
`session`	Specifies if the page participates in an HTTP session.	`"true"`

Table continued on following page

Attribute	Description	Default
buffer	Specifies the buffering model for the output stream to the client. If the value is "none", then no buffering occurs and all output is written directly through to the ServletResponse by a PrintWriter. If a buffer size is specified (e.g. 24kb) then output is buffered with a buffer size not less than that.	The default is buffered with an implementation buffer size of not less than 8kb. (The server can choose a value more than 8kb, depending on its implementation)
autoFlush	If "true", the output buffer to the client is flushed automatically when it is full. If "false", a runtime exception is raised to indicate buffer overflow.	"true"
isThreadSafe	Defines the level of thread safety implemented in the page. If "false" then the JSP processor queues up client requests sent to the page for processing. It processes them one at a time, in the order they were received. This is the same as implementing the javax.servlet.SingleThreadModel interface in a servlet.	"true"
info	Defines an informative string that can subsequently be obtained from the page's implementation of Servlet.getServletInfo() method.	Omitted by default.
isErrorPage	Indicates if the current JSP page is intended to be the URL target of another JSP page's errorPage. If "true", then the implicit variable exception is available, and refers to the instance of the java.lang.Throwable thrown at runtime by the JSP causing the error.	"false"
errorPage	Defines a URL to another JSP that is invoked if an unchecked runtime exception is thrown. The page implementation catches the instance of the Throwable object and passes it to the error page processing. See the isErrorPage attribute above.	Omitted by default.

Attribute	Description	Default
`contentType`	Defines the character encoding for the JSP and the MIME type for the response of the JSP page. This can have either of the form `"TYPE=MIME type"` or `"TYPE=MIME type; charset=CHARSET"`, with an optional white space after the `;`. `CHARSET`, or character encoding if specified, must be the IANA value for a character encoding. IANA is the Internet Assigned Numbers Authority. The names, and other details, of the different character encodings can be found at http://www.iana.org/	The default value for the `TYPE` is `"text/html"`; the default value for the `CHARSET` is `ISO-8859-1`.

The `extends` attribute should be used with extreme caution, since it restricts some of the decisions that a JSP container can make. For example, the container looks for `javax.servlet.Servlet` as being the contract agreement between itself and the page. Implicit variables like `request`, `response`, `application`, etc. (covered later) would not be available to the JSP if some other class were extended.

Example

Consider the following JSP `pagedirective.jsp` with a detailed page directive:

```
<%@ page  language="java" import="java.rmi.*,java.util.*"
 session="true"  buffer="12kb"  autoFlush="true"
 info="my page directive jsp"  errorPage="Error.jsp"
 isErrorPage="false" isThreadSafe="false"%>

<html>
<body>
<h1>done</h1>
THIS is a JSP to test the page directive
<body>
</html>
```

The container translates the above JSP into a class that looks like:

```
package C_0003a.Jswdk.examples.lowestloan;

import javax.servlet.*;
import javax.servlet.http.*;
import javax.servlet.jsp.*;
import java.io.PrintWriter;
import java.io.IOException;
import java.io.FileInputStream;
import java.io.ObjectInputStream;
import java.util.Vector;
import com.sun.jsp.runtime.*;
import java.beans.*;
```

```
import com.sun.jsp.JspException;
import java.rmi.*;
import java.util.*;

public class pagedir_jsp_1 extends HttpJspBase implements SingleThreadModel {

    static char[][] _jspx_html_data = null;
        public String getServletInfo() {
            return "my page directive jsp";
        }

    public pagedir_jsp_1( ) {
    }

    private static boolean _jspx_inited = false;

    public final void _jspx_init() throws JspException {
        ObjectInputStream oin = null;
        int numStrings = 0;
        try {
            FileInputStream fin = new FileInputStream
("work\\%3A8080%2Fexamples\\C_0003a.Jswdk.examples.lowestloanpagedir.dat");
            oin = new ObjectInputStream(fin);
            _jspx_html_data = (char[][]) oin.readObject();
        } catch (Exception ex) {
            throw new JspException("Unable to open data file");
        } finally {
            if (oin != null)
                try { oin.close(); } catch (IOException ignore) { }
        }
    }

    public void _jspService(HttpServletRequest request,
                            HttpServletResponse  response)
        throws IOException, ServletException {

        JspFactory _jspxFactory = null;
        PageContext pageContext = null;
        HttpSession session = null;
        ServletContext application = null;
        ServletConfig config = null;
        JspWriter out = null;
        Object page = this;
        String  _value = null;
        try {

            if (_jspx_inited == false) {
                _jspx_init();
                _jspx_inited = true;
            }
            _jspxFactory = JspFactory.getDefaultFactory();
            response.setContentType("text/html");
            pageContext = _jspxFactory.getPageContext(this, request,
               response, "Error.jsp", true, 12288, true);

            application = pageContext.getServletContext();
            config = pageContext.getServletConfig();
            session = pageContext.getSession();
            out = pageContext.getOut();
            out.print(_jspx_html_data[0]);
```

```
                out.print(_jspx_html_data[1]);

            } catch (Throwable t) {
                if (out.getBufferSize() != 0)
                    out.clear();
                throw new HandleErrorPageException("Error.jsp", t, out);
            } finally {
                out.flush();
                _jspxFactory.releasePageContext(pageContext);
            }
        }
    }
```

Of course, most parts of this translation to Java source are JSP container dependant. For example, WebLogic application server allows you to configure the package name, and has a different mechanism than that used by the JSWDK in the `_jspx_init()` method to read and verify if the JSP has been modified. (`_jspx_init()` is not to be confused with the user defined `jspInit()` method.)

The include Directive

This directive notifies the container to include the content of the resource in the current JSP, inline, at the specified place. Of course the file specified should be accessible and available to the JSP container.

It is important to note that the content of the included file is parsed by the JSP and this happens only at translation time. (The include *action* is used to include resources at runtime, as we will see later.) The included file should not be another dynamic page. Most JSP containers usually keep track of the included file and recompile the JSP if it changes.

```
<%@ include file="Filename" %>
```

Attribute	Description
`file`	The static filename to include

Example

The following tag example requests the inclusion, during compilation, of a copyright file containing HTML legal disclaimers.

```
<%@ include file="/examples/myfile.html" %>
```

The server may choose whatever mechanism it prefers to read the included file. The generated code below for Sun's JSWDK shows how that container reads HTML in the JSP and the included resources into a single file and then writes it to the output stream. Another server may implement it differently.

```
package C_0003a.Jswdk.examples;

import javax.servlet.*;
import javax.servlet.http.*;
import javax.servlet.jsp.*;
import java.io.PrintWriter;
import java.io.IOException;
import java.io.FileInputStream;
```

```
import java.io.ObjectInputStream;
import java.util.Vector;
import com.sun.jsp.runtime.*;
import java.beans.*;
import com.sun.jsp.JspException;


public class inittest_jsp_1 extends HttpJspBase {

    static char[][] _jspx_html_data = null;

        private int i=4;
        public void myMethod(){
          // do some work here
            }

    public inittest_jsp_1( ) {
    }

    private static boolean _jspx_inited = false;

    public final void _jspx_init() throws JspException {
        ObjectInputStream oin = null;
        int numStrings = 0;
        try {
            FileInputStream fin = new FileInputStream
("work\\%3A8080%2Fexamples\\C_0003a.Jswdk.examplesinittest.dat");
            oin = new ObjectInputStream(fin);
            _jspx_html_data = (char[][]) oin.readObject();
        } catch (Exception ex) {
            throw new JspException("Unable to open data file");
        } finally {
            if (oin != null)
                try { oin.close(); } catch (IOException ignore) { }
        }
    }

    public void _jspService(HttpServletRequest request,
                            HttpServletResponse response)
        throws IOException, ServletException {

        JspFactory _jspxFactory = null;
        PageContext pageContext = null;
        HttpSession session = null;
        ServletContext application = null;
        ServletConfig config = null;
        JspWriter out = null;
        Object page = this;
        String  _value = null;
        try {

            if (_jspx_inited == false) {
                _jspx_init();
                _jspx_inited = true;
            }
```

```
                _jspxFactory = JspFactory.getDefaultFactory();
                response.setContentType("text/html");
                pageContext = _jspxFactory.getPageContext(this, request,
                    response, "", true, 8192, true);

                application = pageContext.getServletContext();
                config = pageContext.getServletConfig();
                session = pageContext.getSession();
                out = pageContext.getOut();

                out.print(_jspx_html_data[0]); // The text in the included file
                out.print(_jspx_html_data[1]);

            } catch (Throwable t) {
                if (out.getBufferSize() != 0)
                    out.clear();
                throw new JspException("Unknown exception: ", t);
            } finally {
                out.flush();
                _jspxFactory.releasePageContext(pageContext);
            }
        }
    }
```

The taglib Directive

This directive allows the page to use custom user defined tags. It also names the tag library (a compressed file) that they are defined in. The engine uses this tag library to find out what to do when it comes across the custom tags in the JSP. The tag library concept was recognized to be very powerful, however in the JSP 1.0 version of the specification the implementation mechanism to enable tag libraries was not clearly defined.

The JSP 1.1 specification is actually a lot clearer on tag libraries and their usage.

```
<%@ taglib uri="tagLibraryURI" prefix="tagPrefix" %>
```

Attribute	Description	Default
`uri`	A URI (Uniform Resource Identifier) that identified the tag library descriptor. A tag library descriptor is used to uniquely name the set of custom tags and tells the container what to do with the specified tags.	No value causes compilation error.
`tagPrefix`	Defines the prefix string in `<prefix>:<tagname>` that is used to define the custom tag. Note: The prefixes `jsp`, `jspx`, `java`, `javax`, `servlet`, `sun`, and `sunw` are reserved. For example if this value is `"mytag"` then when the container comes across any element that starts like `<mytag:tagname ... />` in the JSP, it references the tag library descriptor specified in the URI.	No value causes compilation error.

Example

In the following example, a tag library is used. The container is instructed that if, during the JSP translation phase, it comes across any tag with the `sameer` prefix , it should refer to the tag library for the set of elements and the actions needed to be taken So if the JSP looks something like:

```
<%@ taglib uri="http://www.myserver.com/mytags" prefix="sameer" />
...
<sameer:processElement>
...
</sameer:processElement>
```

This convention is similar to the standard JSP action tags definition:

```
<jsp:element "some attributes go here" >
</jsp>
```

The only difference is that now when the engine comes across a tag with the prefix `sameer` (instead of the standard `jsp` prefix), it refers to the tag library defined in the tag library directive (instead of the built-in `jsp` prefix handler) to get the elements and actions that need to be performed for those elements.

> **Tag libraries are a very powerful, and often misunderstood, concept. Chapter 8 explores tag libraries further.**

Scripting Elements

Scripting elements are used to include scripting code (normally Java code) within the JSP. They allow you to declare variables and methods, include arbitrary scripting code, and evaluate an expression.

The three types of scripting element are:

- Declarations
- Scriptlets
- Expressions

Declarations

A **declaration** is a block of Java code in a JSP that is used to define class-wide variables and methods in the generated class file. Declarations are initialized when the JSP page is initialized and have "class" scope. Anything defined in a declaration is available throughout the JSP, to other declarations, expressions or code. A declaration block is enclosed between `<%!` and `%>`.

```
<%! Java variable and method declaration(s) %>
```

Example

Consider a simple JSP, `declarations.jsp`, containing the declaration:

```
<html>
<body>
<h1> Hello World </h1>
</html>

<%!
private int i=4; // my counter
public void myMethod(){
  // do some work here
}
%>
```

This gets translated into a servlet that looks something like this:

```
package C_0003a.Jswdk.examples;

import javax.servlet.*;
import javax.servlet.http.*;
import javax.servlet.jsp.*;
import java.io.PrintWriter;
import java.io.IOException;
import java.io.FileInputStream;
import java.io.ObjectInputStream;
import java.util.Vector;
import com.sun.jsp.runtime.*;
import java.beans.*;
import com.sun.jsp.JspException;


public class hello_jsp_1 extends HttpJspBase {

    static char[][] _jspx_html_data = null;
        private int i=4; // my counter
        public void myMethod(){
          // do some work here
            }

    public hello_jsp_1( ) {
    }

    private static boolean _jspx_inited = false;

    public final void _jspx_init() throws JspException {
        ObjectInputStream oin = null;
        int numStrings = 0;
        try {
            FileInputStream fin = new FileInputStream
("work\\%3A8080%2Fexamples\\C_0003a.Jswdk.exampleshello.dat");
            oin = new ObjectInputStream(fin);
            _jspx_html_data = (char[][]) oin.readObject();
        } catch (Exception ex) {
            throw new JspException("Unable to open data file");
        } finally {
            if (oin != null)
                try { oin.close(); } catch (IOException ignore) { }
```

```
        }
    }

    public void _jspService(HttpServletRequest request,
                            HttpServletResponse response)
        throws IOException, ServletException {

        JspFactory _jspxFactory = null;
        PageContext pageContext = null;
        HttpSession session = null;
        ServletContext application = null;
        ServletConfig config = null;
        JspWriter out = null;
        Object page = this;
        String  _value = null;
        try {

            if (_jspx_inited == false) {
                _jspx_init();
                _jspx_inited = true;
            }
            _jspxFactory = JspFactory.getDefaultFactory();
            response.setContentType("text/html");
            pageContext = _jspxFactory.getPageContext(this, request,
                response, "", true, 8192, true);

            application = pageContext.getServletContext();
            config = pageContext.getServletConfig();
            session = pageContext.getSession();
            out = pageContext.getOut();

            out.print(_jspx_html_data[0]);
            out.print(_jspx_html_data[1]);

        } catch (Throwable t) {
            if (out.getBufferSize() != 0)
                out.clear();
            throw new JspException("Unknown exception: ", t);
        } finally {
            out.flush();
            _jspxFactory.releasePageContext(pageContext);
        }
    }
}
```

Scriptlets

A **scriptlet** is a block of Java code that is executed at request-processing time. A scriptlet is enclosed between `<%` and `%>`. What the scriptlet actually does depends on the code, and it can produce output into the output stream to the client. Multiple scriptlets are combined in the compiled class in the order in which they appear in the JSP. Scriptlets, like any other Java code block or method, can modify objects inside them as a result of method invocations.

A simple analogy would be to assume that a JSP gets compiled into a servlet and all the code appearing between the `<%` and `%>` in the JSP, gets put into the `service()` method of this servlet, as is, in the order it appeared. Hence it is processed for every request that the servlet processes.

```
<% Java code statements %>
```

Example

Consider the simple JSP, `scriptlets.jsp`, below:

```
<html>
<body>

<h1> This is a scriptlet example </h1>

<%
for(int i=0;i< 10;i++){
    out.println(" <b> Hello World This is a loop test "+i +"</b>");
    System.out.println("This goes to the system.out stream "+i);
}

%>

</html>
```

The above JSP after compilation gets translated into a Java source file that looks something like this:

```
package C_0003a.Jswdk.examples;

import javax.servlet.*;
import javax.servlet.http.*;
import javax.servlet.jsp.*;
import java.io.PrintWriter;
import java.io.IOException;
import java.io.FileInputStream;
import java.io.ObjectInputStream;
import java.util.Vector;
import com.sun.jsp.runtime.*;
import java.beans.*;
import com.sun.jsp.JspException;

public class hello_jsp_1 extends HttpJspBase {

    static char[][] _jspx_html_data = null;

    public hello_jsp_1( ) {
    }

    private static boolean _jspx_inited = false;

    public final void _jspx_init() throws JspException {
        ObjectInputStream oin = null;
        int numStrings = 0;
        try {
            FileInputStream fin = new FileInputStream
("work\\%3A8080%2Fexamples\\C_0003a.Jswdk.exampleshello.dat");
            oin = new ObjectInputStream(fin);
            _jspx_html_data = (char[][]) oin.readObject();
        } catch (Exception ex) {
            throw new JspException("Unable to open data file");
        } finally {
            if (oin != null)
                try { oin.close(); } catch (IOException ignore) { }
        }
    }
```

```
    public void _jspService(HttpServletRequest request,
                            HttpServletResponse response)
        throws IOException, ServletException {

        JspFactory _jspxFactory = null;
        PageContext pageContext = null;
        HttpSession session = null;
        ServletContext application = null;
        ServletConfig config = null;
        JspWriter out = null;
        Object page = this;
        String  _value = null;
        try {

            if (_jspx_inited == false) {
                _jspx_init();
                _jspx_inited = true;
            }
            _jspxFactory = JspFactory.getDefaultFactory();
            response.setContentType("text/html");
            pageContext = _jspxFactory.getPageContext(this, request,
                response, "", true, 8192, true);

            application = pageContext.getServletContext();
            config = pageContext.getServletConfig();
            session = pageContext.getSession();
            out = pageContext.getOut();

            out.print(_jspx_html_data[0]);
             for(int i=0;i< 10;i++){
               out.println(" <b> Hello World This is a loop test "+i +
                          "</b><br>");
               System.out.println("This goes to the system.out stream "+i);
                 }
            out.print(_jspx_html_data[1]);

        } catch (Throwable t) {
            if (out.getBufferSize() != 0)
                out.clear();
            throw new JspException("Unknown exception: ", t);
        } finally {
            out.flush();
            _jspxFactory.releasePageContext(pageContext);
        }
    }
}
```

(The avid reader would quickly spot that there is a mix of `out.print()` and `out.println()` statements in the generated servlets. As mentioned before, just like in XML, whitespace is preserved. Because our JSP file contains a line break after the HTML, the container generates a `println()`. Of course, for browsers to actually start a new line, a <BR> tag is needed since whitespace is ignored by the web browser.) The output of this JSP is shown opposite:

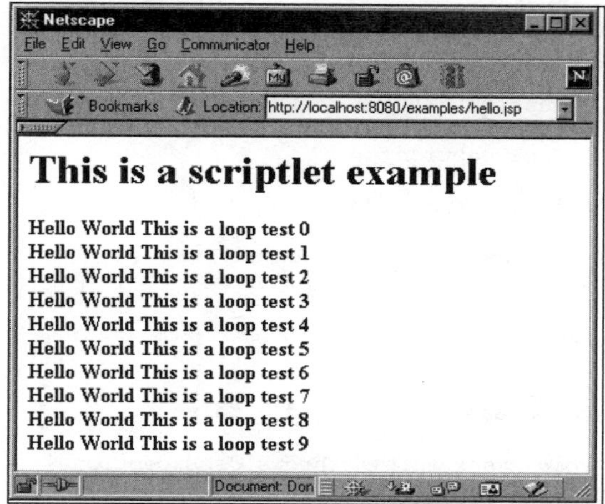

Expressions

An **expression** is a shorthand notation for a scriptlet that outputs a value in the response stream back to the client. When the expression is evaluated, the result is converted to a string and displayed.
An expression is enclosed within `<%=` and `%>`. If any part of the expression is an object, the conversion is done by using the `toString()` method of the object.

```
<%= Java expression to be evaluated %>
```

Example

Consider the example JSP, `counter.jsp`, below that sets up a simple counter and shows declarations, scriptlets, and expressions together.

```
<html>
<body>
<h1> This is a counter example </h1>

<%! int i=0 ; %>

<%
    i++;
%>
Hello World !  <%= "This JSP has been accessed " +i +" times" %>
</body>
</html>
```

The above JSP gets translated into a Java class that looks like this:

```
package C_0003a.Jswdk.examples;

import javax.servlet.*;
import javax.servlet.http.*;
import javax.servlet.jsp.*;
import java.io.PrintWriter;
import java.io.IOException;
```

```
import java.io.FileInputStream;
import java.io.ObjectInputStream;
import java.util.Vector;
import com.sun.jsp.runtime.*;
import java.beans.*;
import com.sun.jsp.JspException;

public class hello_jsp_5 extends HttpJspBase {

    static char[][] _jspx_html_data = null;
         int i=0 ;

    public hello_jsp_5( ) {
    }

    private static boolean _jspx_inited = false;

    public final void _jspx_init() throws JspException {
        ObjectInputStream oin = null;
        int numStrings = 0;
        try {
            FileInputStream fin = new FileInputStream
("work\\%3A8080%2Fexamples\\C_0003a.Jswdk.exampleshello.dat");
            oin = new ObjectInputStream(fin);
            _jspx_html_data = (char[][]) oin.readObject();
        } catch (Exception ex) {
            throw new JspException("Unable to open data file");
        } finally {
            if (oin != null)
                try { oin.close(); } catch (IOException ignore) { }
        }
    }

    public void _jspService(HttpServletRequest request,
                            HttpServletResponse response)
        throws IOException, ServletException {

        JspFactory _jspxFactory = null;
        PageContext pageContext = null;
        HttpSession session = null;
        ServletContext application = null;
        ServletConfig config = null;
        JspWriter out = null;
        Object page = this;
        String  _value = null;
        try {

            if (_jspx_inited == false) {
                _jspx_init();
                _jspx_inited = true;
            }
            _jspxFactory = JspFactory.getDefaultFactory();
            response.setContentType("text/html");
            pageContext = _jspxFactory.getPageContext(this, request,
                response, "", true, 8192, true);

            application = pageContext.getServletContext();
            config = pageContext.getServletConfig();
            session = pageContext.getSession();
            out = pageContext.getOut();
```

```
            out.print(_jspx_html_data[0]);
            out.print(_jspx_html_data[1]);

                i++;
            out.print (_jspx_html_data[2]);
                out.print ( "This JSP has been accessed " +i +" times" );
            out.print(_jspx_html_data[3]);

        } catch (Throwable t) {
            if (out.getBufferSize() != 0)
                out.clear();
            throw new JspException("Unknown exception: ", t);
        } finally {
            out.flush();
            _jspxFactory.releasePageContext(pageContext);
        }
    }
}
```

Notice how the expression is sent to the output stream as a string. Every time the page is accessed, the counter variable `i` is incremented by the scriptlet, and the expression evaluated and sent to the client.

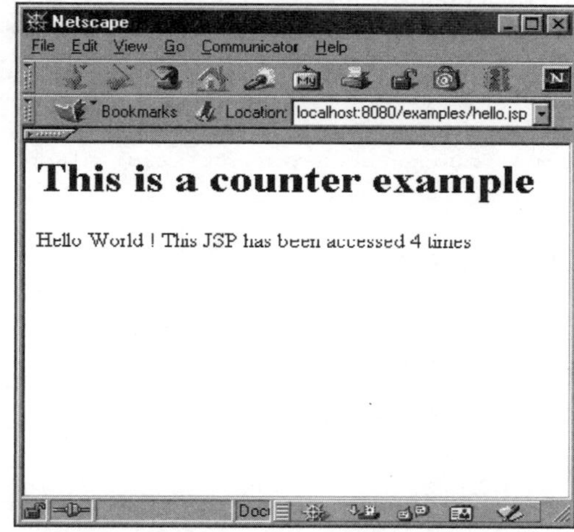

Standard Actions

Actions are specific tags that affect the runtime behavior of the JSP and affect the response sent back to the client. The JSP specification lists some action types that are standard, and these have to be provided by all containers, irrespective of the implementation. Standard actions provide page authors with some basic functionality to exploit; the vendor is free to provide other actions to enhance behavior. The standard action types are:

- `<jsp:useBean>`
- `<jsp:setProperty>`
- `<jsp:getProperty>`

- <jsp:param>
- <jsp:include>
- <jsp:forward>
- <jsp:plugin>

The `<jsp:useBean>`, `<jsp:setProperty>`, and `<jsp:getProperty>` tags are used in connection with JavaBeans. JavaBeans are software components - Java classes - which can be used to encapsulate Java code and separate presentation from content within your JSPs. JavaBeans are covered in detail in Chapter 4.

jsp:useBean

A `jsp:useBean` action is used to associate a JavaBean with the JSP. It ensures that the object is available for the appropriate scope specified in the tag. The bound object can be referenced from the JSP using the id it is associated with (or even from other JSPs, depending on the scope).

Internally, the container first tries to locate the object using the `id` and `scope` and, if it is not found, uses the name of the bean as an argument to the `instantiate()` method of the `java.beans.Beans` using the current class loader. (If this instantiation fails, a request-time exception due to the `instantiate()` is thrown.)

```
<jsp:useBean  id="name"  scope="page|request|session|application"
 beandetails />
```

Where *beandetails* is one of:

- `class="className"`
- `class="className" type="typeName"`
- `beanName="beanName" type="typeName"`
- `type="typeName"`

Attribute	Description
id	The case sensitive name used to identify the object instance.
scope	The scope within which the reference is available. The default value is page.
class	The fully qualified class name.
beanName	The name of a Bean, as you would supply to the `instantiate()` method in the `java.beans.Beans` class. This attribute can also be a request time expression. It is permissible to supply a `type` and a `beanName`, and omit the `class` attribute. The `beanName` follows the standard bean specification and can be of the form `"a.b.c"`, where `"a.b.c"` is either a class, or the name of a serialized resource in which case it is resolved as `"a/b/c.ser"` (see the JavaBeans specification).

Attribute	Description
`type`	This optional attribute specifies the type of the class, and follows standard Java casting rules. The type must be a superclass, an interface, or the class itself. Just like any casting operation, if the object is not of this type then `java.lang.ClassCastException` can be thrown at request time. The default value is the same as the value of the class attribute.

Let us examine the underlying semantics that occur because of this tag, in the order they occur:

1. The container tries to locate an object that has this `id`, in the specified scope.
2. If the object is found, and a type has been specified in the tag, the container tries to cast the found object to the specified type. A `java.lang.ClassCastException` is thrown if the cast fails.
3. If the object is not found in the specified scope, and no `class` or `beanName` is specified in the tag, a `java.lang.InstantiationException` is thrown.
4. If the object is not found in the specified scope, and the class specified is a non-abstract class with a public no argument constructor, then that class is instantiated. A new object reference is associated with the variable, in the specified scope. If any of the conditions specified in this step are not met then a `java.lang.InstantiationException` is thrown.
5. If the object is not found in the specified scope, and a `beanName` is specified, then the `instantiate()` method of `java.beans.Beans` is invoked (with the `beanName` as an argument). If the method succeeds, the new object reference is associated with the variable, in the specified scope.
6. If the `jsp:useBean` element has a non-empty body, the body is processed. At this point the variable is initialized and available within the scope of the body. The body is processed like any other part of the JSP, and any template text is sent to the output stream. Additional scriptlets, or the `jsp:setProperty` standard action, can be used to further initialize the bean instance.

Consider the example JSP, `simpleusebean.jsp`:

```
<jsp:useBean id="mparam" scope="session" class="java.lang.String">
This is used to initialize the bean...
</jsp:useBean>

<html>
<body>
 Hello World !
</body>
</html>
```

This gets compiled into something that looks like:

```
// preceeding code not shown here for brevity

public void _jspService(HttpServletRequest request,
                        HttpServletResponse  response)
        throws IOException, ServletException {

        JspFactory _jspxFactory = null;
        PageContext pageContext = null;
        HttpSession session = null;
        ServletContext application = null;
        ServletConfig config = null;
        JspWriter out = null;
        Object page = this;
        String  _value = null;
        try {

            if (_jspx_inited == false) {
                _jspx_init();
                _jspx_inited = true;
            }
            _jspxFactory = JspFactory.getDefaultFactory();
            response.setContentType("text/html");
            pageContext = _jspxFactory.getPageContext(this, request,
                response, "", true, 8192, true);

            application = pageContext.getServletContext();
            config = pageContext.getServletConfig();
            session = pageContext.getSession();
            out = pageContext.getOut();

            out.print(_jspx_html_data[0]);
            java.lang.String mparam = null;
            boolean _jspx_specialmparam  = false;
            synchronized (session) {
                mparam= (java.lang.String)
                pageContext.getAttribute("mparam",PageContext.SESSION_SCOPE);
                if ( mparam == null ) {
                    _jspx_specialmparam = true;
                     try {
                    mparam =
(java.lang.String) Beans.instantiate(getClassLoader(),"java.lang.String");
                         } catch (Exception exc) {
                        throw new ServletException
                            (" Cannot create bean of class "
                                                + "java.lang.String");
                         }
            pageContext.setAttribute("mparam", mparam, PageContext.SESSION_SCOPE);
                    }
               }
                if(_jspx_specialmparam == true) {
            out.print(_jspx_html_data[1]);
                }
            out.print(_jspx_html_data[2]);

        } catch (Throwable t) {
            if (out.getBufferSize() != 0)
                out.clear();
            throw new JspException("Unknown exception: ", t);
```

```
        } finally {
            out.flush();
            _jspxFactory.releasePageContext(pageContext);
        }
    }
```

JSP actually uses contexts for much of its "scope" abstraction. (This is also discussed in Chapter 5.)

> **A context is actually a Java interface that serves as the communication point between a container and the resource running in the container. For example consider the `ServletContext`. When a servlet is deployed, it runs or lives in a particular context (defined by hostname and port). Everything that the servlet needs to know about its server it can extract from this context, and everything the server wants to communicate to the servlet goes via the context. By using interfaces to define contexts, the vendor has flexibility in implementing the interface, while the developer is assured that the contract represented by the context between the server and the resource will always be fulfilled.**

For the purpose of understanding the scope in a bean tag, think of the bean having a different life duration, depending on the context to which it is bound. An abstract class called a `PageContext` is introduced in JSP (`javax.servlet.jsp.PageContext`), which delegates this context level binding.

Scope in tag	Description
`page`	The object reference is discarded upon completion of the current `Servlet.service()` invocation. The servlet engine, when generating the servlet, creates an object in the `service()` method, which follows the usual object scope convention in Java. The object exists for every client request to the resource.
`request`	The object reference is available as long as the `HttpRequest` object is not discarded, even if the request is passed/chained to different pages. The underlying generated servlet relies on binding the object to the `HttpServletRequest` using the `setAttribute(String key,Object value)` method in the `HttpServletRequest` This however is transparent to the user. The object is distinct for every client request.

Table continued on following page

Scope in tag	Description
`session`	In the pre Servlet 2.1 specifications, a session always ran under a session context. (Though deprecated in Servlet 2.1, an implementation for an `HttpSessionContext` is still available in most servers.) The underlying generated servlet relies on binding the object to the `HttpSession` using the `putValue(String key,Object value)` method in the `HttpServletSession`. This however is transparent to the user. The object is distinct for every client, and is available as long as the client's session is valid.
`application`	This is the most persistent. The underlying generated servlet relies on binding the object to the `ServletContext` using the `setAttribute(String key,Object value)` method in the `ServletContext`. This is not unique for clients, and consequently all clients access the same object.

jsp:setProperty

This standard action is used in conjunction with the `useBean` action described in the preceding section, and sets the value of simple and indexed properties in a bean.

The properties in a bean can be set either:

- at request time from parameters in the request object,
- at request time from an evaluated expression, or
- from a specified string (or hard coded in the page).

Bean introspection is used to discover what properties are present, their names, if they are simple or indexed, their type, and the accessor and mutator methods.

```
<jsp:setProperty name=" beanName" propertydetails />
```

Where *propertydetails* is one of:

- `property="*"`
- `property="propertyName"`
- `property="propertyName" param="parameterName"`
- `property="propertyName" value="propertyValue"`

and `propertyValue` is a string or a scriptlet.

Attribute	Details
`name`	The name of a bean instance defined by a `<jsp:useBean>` tag.
`property`	The name of the bean property whose value is being set. If this is set to `"*"` then the tag iterates over all the parameters in the `ServletRequest`, matching parameter names and value types to bean properties, and setting each matched property to the value of the matching parameter. If a parameter has a value of `""`, the corresponding property is not modified.
`param`	It is not necessary that the bean have the same property names as the names in the name-value pairs in the request. This attribute is used to specify the name of the request parameter whose value you want to assign to a bean property. However if the `param` value is not specified, then the request parameter name is assumed to be the same as the bean property name. If the parameter is not set in the `ServletRequest`, or has the value of `""`, the `jsp:setProperty` standard action has no effect on the bean.
`value`	The value to assign to the bean property. This can be a string or a request-time expression. A tag cannot have both `param` and `value` attributes.

While setting the properties, the container uses bean introspection to discover details about the bean, such as what properties are present, their names, whether they are simple or indexed, their type, and setter/getter methods.

When properties are assigned from `String` constants or request parameter values, conversion is applied using the methods shown below:

Property type	Conversion using
`boolean` or `Boolean`	`java.lang.Boolean.valueOf(String)`
`byte` or `Byte`	`java.lang.Byte.valueOf(String)`
`char` or `Character`	`java.lang.Character.valueOf(String)`
`double` or `Double`	`java.lang.Double.valueOf(String)`
`int` or `Integer`	`java.lang.Integer.valueOf(String)`
`float` or `Float`	`java.lang.Float.valueOf(String)`
`long` or `Long`	`java.lang.Long.valueOf(String)`

However, request-time expressions can be assigned to properties of any type, and the container performs no conversion. Also note that for indexed properties the value must be an array.

Example

Consider the bean `SpellCheck.java` shown below. It has one simple property, `word`, and two methods, one to reverse the word and the other to check the spelling.

```
package projsp;

/**
 * This bean encapsulates the functionality to spell check a String
 */
public class SpellCheck {
  private String word;

  public SpellCheck() {}

  /**
   * Method to reverse the string uses
   * @return the reversed String
   */
  public String reverse() {
    return (new StringBuffer(word).reverse()).toString();
  }

  /**
   * Checks the spelling of the word. This method has no body, and just
   * returns true for the example
   * @return boolean, true if the spelling is right
   */
  public boolean check() {
    return true;
  }

  /**
   * Access method for the word property.
   *
   * @return   the current value of the word property
   */
  public String getWord() {
    return word;
  }

  /**
   * Sets the value of the word property.
   *
   * @param aWord the new value of the word property
   */
  public void setWord(String aWord) {
    word = aWord;
  }
}
```

An HTML form, shown below, obtains input from the user to be processed by our JSP:

```
<html>
<head>
<title>Untitled Document</title>
</head>

<body bgcolor="#FFFFFF">
<form action="wordpro.jsp" method="POST">
Enter word:
<input type="text" name="word">
<select name="mode">
  <option value="1" selected>Reverse</option>
  <option value="2">Spellcheck</option>
</select>
<input type="submit" name="Go" value="Submit">
</form>

</body>
</html>
```

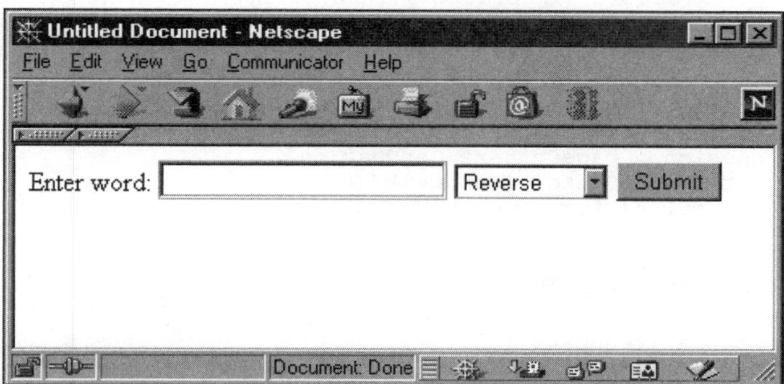

We use the bean from within a JSP, `wordpro.jsp`, which takes the input from the form:

```
<jsp:useBean id="help" scope="request" class="projsp.SpellCheck" />
<jsp:setProperty name="help" property="*"/>

<html>
<body>
You entered the input, <b> <%= request.getParameter("word") %></b><br>
The processed output is:<br>
<%= Integer.parseInt(request.getParameter("mode"))==1
  ? help.reverse() :""+help.check() %>
</body>
</html>
```

The `useBean` tag specified a request scope. In other words, the instance of the bean will be available for the duration of a single request. (A session scope would be more appropriate if the same instance needed to be used elsewhere during a user's visit.)

The code below shows an excerpt of how this tag might be implemented in the generated servlet.

```
//  imports and preceeding init code are not shown here for brevity

public void _jspService(HttpServletRequest request,
                        HttpServletResponse response)
        throws IOException, ServletException {

        JspFactory _jspxFactory = null;
        PageContext pageContext = null;
        HttpSession session = null;
        ServletContext application = null;
        ServletConfig config = null;
        JspWriter out = null;
        Object page = this;
        String  _value = null;
        try {

            if (_jspx_inited == false) {
                _jspx_init();
                _jspx_inited = true;
            }
            _jspxFactory = JspFactory.getDefaultFactory();
            response.setContentType("text/html");
            pageContext = _jspxFactory.getPageContext(this, request,
                response, "", true, 8192, true);
            application = pageContext.getServletContext();
            config = pageContext.getServletConfig();
            session = pageContext.getSession();
            out = pageContext.getOut();
            out.print(_jspx_html_data[0]);

    // begin bean initialization
       projsp.SpellCheck help = null;
       boolean _jspx_specialhelp  = false;
       synchronized (request) {
          help= (projsp.SpellCheck)
          pageContext.getAttribute("help",PageContext.REQUEST_SCOPE);
          if ( help == null ) {
             _jspx_specialhelp = true;
             try {
                help = (projsp.SpellCheck)
                       Beans.instantiate(getClassLoader(),"projsp.SpellCheck");
             } catch (Exception exc) {
                throw new ServletException (" Cannot create bean of class"+"
                                            projsp.SpellCheck");
             }
             pageContext.setAttribute("help", help, PageContext.REQUEST_SCOPE);
          }
       }
       if(_jspx_specialhelp == true) {}
    // End bean initialization

            out.print(_jspx_html_data[1]);

 // Container sets the bean properties
            JspRuntimeLibrary.introspect(help, request);
            out.print(_jspx_html_data[2]);
            out.print( help.getWord() );
            out.print(_jspx_html_data[3]);
```

```
            out.print( Integer.parseInt(request.getParameter("mode"))==1 ?
                      help.reverse() :""+help.check() );
            out.print(_jspx_html_data[4]);
        } catch (Throwable t) {
            if (out.getBufferSize() != 0)
                out.clear();
            throw new JspException("Unknown exception: ", t);
        } finally {
            out.flush();
            _jspxFactory.releasePageContext(pageContext);
        }
    }
```

The JSP uses the standard action `<jsp:setProperty name="help" property="*"/>`. You could also choose to explicitly set the single property by `<jsp:setProperty name="help" property="word"/>`, in which case the generated servlet would differ slightly, since it doesn't need to do any bean introspection.

The JSP code below, `wordproint.jsp`, shows how a body could be included in the bean tag to provide additional initialization of the bean

```
<jsp:useBean id="help" scope="request" class="projsp.SpellCheck">
<%
   System.out.println("Explicitly doing some work on the bean...");
   help.setWord(request.getParameter("word"));
%>
</jsp:useBean>

<html>
<body>
You entered the input, <b> <%= help.getWord() %></b><br>
The processed output is:<br>
<%= Integer.parseInt(request.getParameter("mode"))==1 ? help.reverse()
:""+help.check() %>
</body>
</html>
```

The end result is still the same, although the generated implementation class differs slightly, taking the code in the body of the `useBean` tag into account.

```
// Imports and preceeding init code are not shown here for brevity

public void _jspService(HttpServletRequest request,
                        HttpServletResponse response)
        throws IOException, ServletException {

        JspFactory _jspxFactory = null;
        PageContext pageContext = null;
        HttpSession session = null;
        ServletContext application = null;
        ServletConfig config = null;
        JspWriter out = null;
        Object page = this;
        String  _value = null;
        try {

            if (_jspx_inited == false) {
                _jspx_init();
```

```
                _jspx_inited = true;
            }
            _jspxFactory = JspFactory.getDefaultFactory();
            response.setContentType("text/html");
            pageContext = _jspxFactory.getPageContext(this, request,
                response, "", true, 8192, true);

            application = pageContext.getServletContext();
            config = pageContext.getServletConfig();
            session = pageContext.getSession();
            out = pageContext.getOut();

            out.print(_jspx_html_data[0]);
    // Start bean initialization
    projsp.SpellCheck help = null;
    boolean _jspx_specialhelp  = false;
    synchronized (request) {
    help= (projsp.SpellCheck)
    pageContext.getAttribute("help",PageContext.REQUEST_SCOPE);
    if ( help == null ) {
       _jspx_specialhelp = true;
       try {
          help = (projsp.SpellCheck)
          Beans.instantiate(getClassLoader(), "projsp.SpellCheck");
       } catch (Exception exc) {
          throw new ServletException (" Cannot create bean of class
             "+"projsp.SpellCheck");
       }
       pageContext.setAttribute("help",help,PageContext.REQUEST_SCOPE);
    }
 }
 if(_jspx_specialhelp == true) {
    out.print(_jspx_html_data[1]);
    System.out.println("Explicitly doing some work on the bean...");
    help.setWord(request.getParameter("word"));
 }
 // End bean initialization

            out.print(_jspx_html_data[3]);
            out.print( help.getWord() );
            out.print(_jspx_html_data[4]);
            out.print( Integer.parseInt(request.getParameter("mode"))==1
               ? help.reverse() :""+help.check() );
            out.print(_jspx_html_data[5]);
        } catch (Throwable t) {
            if (out.getBufferSize() != 0)
                out.clear();
            throw new JspException("Unknown exception: ", t);
        } finally {
            out.flush();
            _jspxFactory.releasePageContext(pageContext);
        }
    }
```

jsp:getProperty

The `jsp:getProperty` action is complementary to the `jsp:setProperty` action and is used to access the properties of a bean. It accesses the value of a property, converts it to a `String`, and prints it to the output stream.

To convert the property to a `String`, the `toString()` method is invoked on the property value if it is an object, or it is converted directly if it is a primitive value, just like Java's `System.out.println()` method.

```
<jsp:getProperty name=" name" property=" propertyName" />
```

Attribute	Description
name	The name of the bean instance from which the property is obtained. The bean must already have been found or created using `<jsp:useBean>`.
property	The name of the property to retrieve.

Example

The preceding example shown in the section describing the `jsp:setProperty` action could be modified to use this action, as follows:

```
<jsp:useBean id="help" scope="session" class="projsp.SpellCheck" />
<jsp:setProperty name="help" property="*"/>

<html>
<body>
You entered the input, <b>
<jsp:getProperty name="help" property="word"/> </b><br>
The processed output is:<br>
<%= Integer.parseInt(request.getParameter("mode"))==1
      ? help.reverse() :""+help.check() %>
</body>
</html>
```

jsp:param

The `jsp:param` action is used to provide other tags with additional information in the form of name-value pairs. This action is used in conjunction with `jsp:include`, `jsp:forward`, and `jsp:plugin` actions, and is described in the relevant following sections.

```
<jsp:param name="paramname" value="paramvalue" />
```

Attribute	Description
name	The key associated with the attribute. (Attributes are key-value pairs.)
value	The value of the attribute.

jsp:include

This action allows a static or dynamic resource to be included in the current JSP at request time. The resource is specified using the URL format described in the earlier section on the `include` directive. An included page has access only to the `JspWriter` object, and it cannot set headers or Cookies. A request-time exception will be thrown if this is attempted. The constraint is equivalent to the one imposed on the `include()` method of the `javax.servlet.RequestDispatcher` class.

If the page output is buffered then the buffer is flushed prior to the inclusion. The `jsp:include` action pays a small penalty in efficiency, and precludes the included page from containing general JSP code.

```
<jsp:include page=" filename" flush="true"/>
```

or

```
<jsp:include page=" urlSpec" flush="true">
   <jsp:param name="paramname" value="paramvalue" />
   ...
</jsp:include>
```

A `jsp:include` action may have one or more `jsp:param` tags in its body, to provide additional name-value pairs. The included page can access the original request object, with both the original and the new parameters. If the parameter names are same, the old values are kept intact, but the new values take precedence over existing values. For example, if the request has a parameter `param1=myvalue1` and a parameter `param1=myvalue2` is specified in the `jsp:param` tag, the request received on the second JSP will have `param1=myvalue2, myvalue1`. The augmented attributes can be extracted from the request using the `getParameter(String paramname)` method in the `javax.servlet.ServletRequest` interface.

Attribute	Description
`filename`	The resource to include. The URL format is the same as described in the include directive earlier.
`flush`	In JSP 1.1 this value must always be `"true"`, and `"false"` is not supported. If the value is `"true"`, the buffer in the output stream is flushed.

It is important to understand the difference between the include *directive* and this include *action.* This difference is summarized in the table.

Include	Syntax	Done when	Included content	Parsing
directive	`<%@ include file="filename" %>`	Compilation time	Static	Parsed by container
action	`<jsp:include page="filename" />`	Request processing time	Static or Dynamic	Not parsed but included in place.

Example

Consider the JSP `include.jsp`, which shows how the include directive and include action work:

```
<html>
<body>

<h2>This example shows how the includes work: </h2><br>

Including a jsp and html with the include directive...<br><br>
```

```
<%@ include file="two.html" %><br>
<%@ include file="two.jsp" %> <br>

<hr><br>
Including a jsp and html with the include action..<br><br>

<jsp:include page="two.html" flush="true"/> <br>
<jsp:include page="two.jsp" flush="true"/>

</body>
</html>
```

The included files are `two.jsp`:

```
<!--
  This is some comment in the second JSP
-->
<%@ page import="java.util.Date"%>
<%= "The current date is " +new Date() %>
```

and `two.html`:

```
<a href="two.html"> This is text in two.html </a>
```

The figure below shows the screen shot of the output when `include.jsp` is invoked.

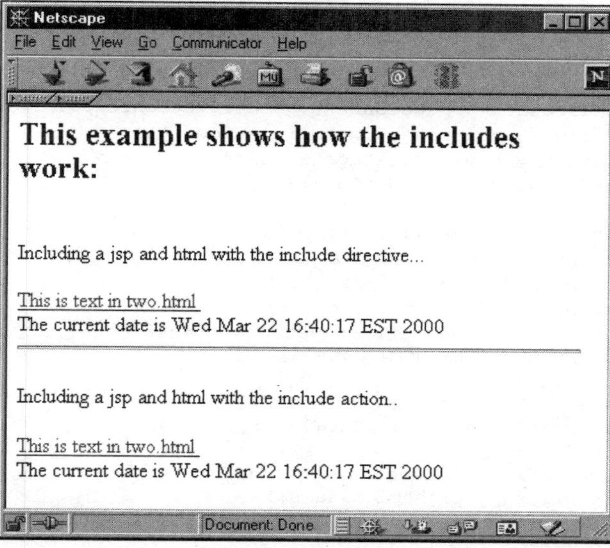

The output looks identical! So what is the difference? The difference is in how the two includes are evaluated and included. If you look carefully while loading this page, the second part takes a fraction of a second longer. This is because it is being computed at request time (hence the slight performance penalty mentioned earlier).

Let us look at the code of the generated servlet class to see the internal semantics of this inclusion. See how the code for the `include` *directive* actually parses (or inlines) the content of the included files into the current JSP while compiling it. The directive does not lead to compilation of the included JSP.

The `include` *action* actually takes the content or output from the included JSP at request time, and compiles the included JSP if necessary. (The reader can verify compilation of the included JSP by using the includes in `include.jsp` one at a time.)

```
// imports and previous code not shown here.

public void _jspService(HttpServletRequest request,
                        HttpServletResponse response)
        throws IOException, ServletException {

        JspFactory _jspxFactory = null;
        PageContext pageContext = null;
        HttpSession session = null;
        ServletContext application = null;
        ServletConfig config = null;
        JspWriter out = null;
        Object page = this;
        String  _value = null;
        try {

            if (_jspx_inited == false) {
                _jspx_init();
                _jspx_inited = true;
            }
            _jspxFactory = JspFactory.getDefaultFactory();
            response.setContentType("text/html");
            pageContext = _jspxFactory.getPageContext(this, request,
               response, "", true, 8192, true);

            application = pageContext.getServletContext();
            config = pageContext.getServletConfig();
            session = pageContext.getSession();
            out = pageContext.getOut();

            out.print(_jspx_html_data[0]);
            out.print(_jspx_html_data[1]);
            out.print(_jspx_html_data[2]);
            out.print(_jspx_html_data[3]);
            out.print( "The current date is " +new Date() );
            out.print(_jspx_html_data[4]);
            out.flush();
            pageContext.include("two.html");
            out.print(_jspx_html_data[5]);
            out.flush();
            pageContext.include("two.jsp");
            out.print(_jspx_html_data[6]);

        } catch (Throwable t) {
            if (out.getBufferSize() != 0)
                out.clear();
            throw new JspException("Unknown exception: ", t);
        } finally {
            out.flush();
            _jspxFactory.releasePageContext(pageContext);
        }
    }
```

The code below shows an alternate form of the `include` directive, where additional name-value pairs can be added while including the page. This allows the attributes to be accessible in the included JSP through the `request` object.

```
<html>
<body>
<h2>This example shows how the includes work: </h2><br>
Including a jsp and html with the include directive...<br><br>

<jsp:include page="two.jsp" flush="true">
<jsp:param name="attribute1" value="value1"/>
<jsp:param name="attribute2" value="value2"/>
</jsp:include>

</body>
</html>
```

In this code, `two.jsp` can access the values of `attribute1` using `request.getParameter("attribute1")`.

A practical use of this include action could be a 'Today's news' page. Every time the headlines change, authors need only to update the headline files and can leave the main JSP page unchanged.

jsp:forward

The `jsp:forward` action allows the request to be forwarded to another JSP, a servlet, or a static resource.

```
<jsp:forward page="url" />
```

or

```
<jsp:forward page="urlSpec">
   <jsp:param name="paramname" value="paramvalue" />
   ...
</jsp:forward>
```

The resource to which the request is being forwarded must be in the same context as the JSP dispatching the request. Execution in the current JSP stops when it encounters a `jsp:forward` tag. The buffer is cleared, and the request is modified to augment any additionally specified parameters in the same way as described for the `jsp:include` tag above.

If the output stream was not buffered and some output has been written to it, a `jsp:forward` action will throw a `java.lang.IllegalStateException`.

Example

Consider a JSP responsible for searching a database. Once the results have been obtained, they can be stored in a bean, and the request forwarded to another JSP that is responsible for displaying these results.

```
// Get the results from the search.
// store them in the session or a bean
// And forward the request..
<jsp:forward page="/search/advanced/results.jsp" />
```

This approach is very useful in the designs described in Chapter 12.

jsp:plugin

The `jsp:plugin` action is used to generate client browser specific HTML tags (`OBJECT` or `EMBED`) that ensures that the Java Plug-in software is available, followed by execution of the applet or JavaBean component specified in the tag.

The `jsp:plugin` tag can have two optional additional support tags:

- `<jsp:param>` elements, to pass additional parameters to the Applet or JavaBean component.
- A `<jsp:fallback>` element, to specify the content to be displayed in the client browser if the plugin cannot be started because the generated tags are not supported. The `<jsp:fallback>` tag does the same thing as the HTML "`ALT`" or "`NOFRAMES`" attributes.

```
<jsp:plugin type="bean|applet"  code="objectCode"  codebase="objectCodebase"
      align="alignment" archive="archiveList" height ="height" hspace="hspace"
      jreversion="jreversion"  name="componentName"  vspace="vspace"
      width="width"  nspluginurl="url"  iepluginurl="url" >
   <jsp:params>
      <jsp:param name=" paramName" value=" paramValue" />
      <jsp:param name=" paramName" value=" paramValue" />
      ...
   </jsp:params>
   <jsp:fallback> Alternate text to display </jsp:fallback>
</jsp:plugin>
```

Attribute	Details	Required
`type`	Identifies the type of the component; a Bean, or an Applet.	Yes
`code`	Same as HTML syntax	Yes
`codebase`	Same as HTML syntax	No
`align`	Same as HTML syntax	No
`archive`	Same as HTML syntax	No
`height`	Same as HTML syntax	No, but some browsers do not allow an object of zero height due to security issues
`hspace`	Same as HTML syntax	No
`jreversion`	The Java runtime environment version needed to execute this object. The default is `"1.1"`	No
`name`	Same as HTML syntax	No

Attribute	Details	Required
vspace	Same as HTML syntax	No
title	Same as HTML syntax	No
width	Same as HTML syntax	No, but some browsers do not allow an object of zero width due to security issues.
nspluginurl	URL where JRE plugin can be downloaded for Netscape Navigator, default is implementation defined.	Only if the Java Plugin software needs to be installed on the client.
iepluginurl	URL where JRE plugin can be downloaded for Internet Explorer, default is implementation defined.	Only if the Java Plugin software needs to be installed on the client.

Although the syntax of this tag is specific, the semantics depend on how the application server traps the user agent and decides on how to handle it. See the example below.

> **The latest version of the HTML specifications can be downloaded from the W3C site at http://www.w3.org/TR/REC-html40/. HTML4.01 deprecates the `<applet>` tag in favor of the more generic `<object>` tag.**

Example

Consider the JSP below:

```
<html>
<body>
<h2>This example shows how the plugin tag works: </h2><br>

<jsp:plugin type="applet" code="projsp.TestApplet" codebase="/classes/applets"
height="100" width="100">
    <jsp:params>
    <jsp:param name="color" value="black"/>
    <jsp:param name="speed" value="fast"/>
    <jsp:param name="sound" value="off"/>
    </jsp:params>
  <jsp:fallback>Your browser cannot display this applet text </jsp:fallback>
</jsp:plugin>
</body>
</html>
```

The Sun JSWDK, for example, compiles the JSP in to a servlet that generates the following HTML for both Netscape and Internet Explorer, and prompts the user to download the Java Plugin software:

```
<html>
<body>

<h2>This example shows how the plugin tag works: </h2><br>


<OBJECT classid="clsid:8AD9C840-044E-11D1-B3E9-00805F499D93" width="100"
height="100" codebase="http://java.sun.com/products/plugin/1.2.2/jinstall-1_2_2-
win.cab#Version=1,2,2,0">
<PARAM name="java_code" value="projsp.TestApplet">
<PARAM name="java_codebase" value="/classes/applets">
<PARAM name="type" value="application/x-java-applet;">
<PARAM name="color" value="black">
<PARAM name="sound" value="off">
<PARAM name="speed" value="fast">
<COMMENT>
<EMBED type="application/x-java-applet;"  width="100"  height="100"
  pluginspage="http://java.sun.com/products/plugin/" java_code="projsp.TestApplet"
  java_codebase="/classes/applets" color="black" sound="off" speed="fast">
<NOEMBED>
</COMMENT>
Your browser cannot display this applet text
</NOEMBED></EMBED>
</OBJECT>

</body>
</html>
```

The results of using this page in Netscape and Internet Explorer are shown below.

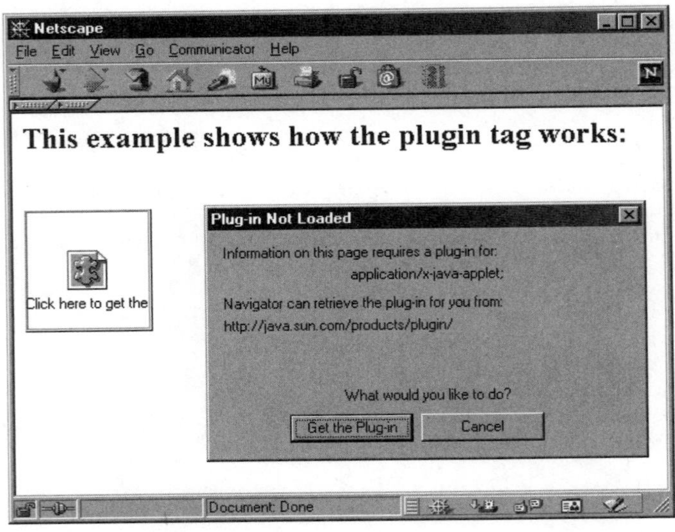

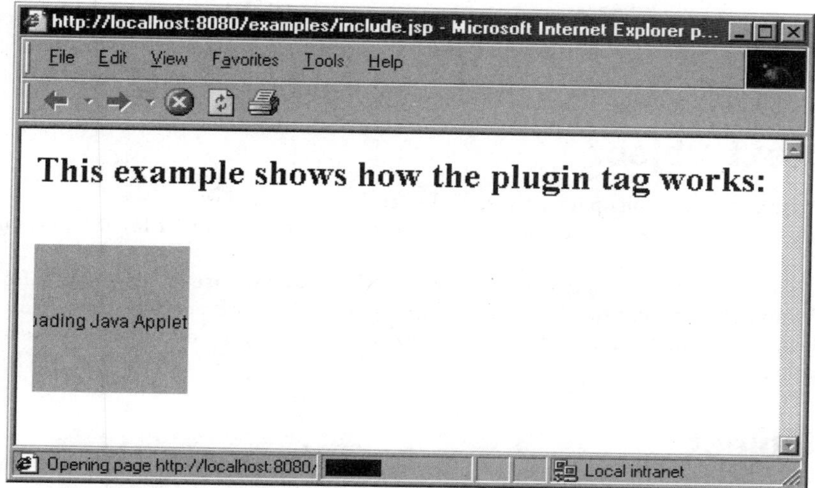

The generated servlets in Weblogic application server (5.0) and Orion server, for example, generate different HTML for Netscape and Internet Explorer (using the `EMBED` and `OBJECT` tags respectively). They do not prompt the user for the Java Plugin unless a `jreversion` and plugin URL for the browser (`iepluginurl` or `nspluginurl`) are specified *and* the browser Java version is not the same as the `jreversion` specified in the `jsp:plugin` tag.

Implicit Objects

JSP tries to simplify page authoring, and provides certain implicit objects accessible within the JSP. These objects do not need to be declared or instantiated by the JSP author, but are provided by the container in the implementation class.

All the implicit objects are available *only* to scriptlets or expressions, and are *not* available in declarations. This is logical since, as mentioned before, declarations translate into class variables (or method declarations), whereas the implicit objects are only available in the `_jspService()` method of the generated servlet and, in Java, variables declared within a method are not available outside that method.

request Object

The `request` object has request scope, and is an instance of `javax.servlet.ServletRequest`. It encapsulates the request coming from the client and being processed by the JSP. It is passed to the JSP by the container, as a parameter to the `_jspService()` method.

response Object

The `response` object has page scope, and is an instance of class `javax.servlet.ServletResponse`. It encapsulates the response generated by the JSP, to be sent back to the client in response to the request. It is generated by the container and passed to the JSP as a parameter to the `_jspService()` method, where it is modified by the JSP.

Since the output stream to the client (see `out` below) is buffered in JSPs, it *is* legal to set HTTP status codes and response headers, even though this is not permitted in regular servlets once any output has been sent to the client.

pageContext Object

The `pageContext` object has page scope, and is an instance of class `javax.servlet.jsp.PageContext`. It encapsulates the page context for the particular JSP page.

JSP introduced a new class, called `PageContext`, to encapsulate use of server specific features (like higher performance `JspWriters`), the reason being that if the JSP accesses these features through a standard class, rather than directly, the JSP can execute in any JSP container, irrespective of its implementation.

session Object

The `session` object has session scope, and is an instance of class `javax.servlet.http.HttpSession`. It represents the session created for the requesting client, and is only valid for HTTP requests. Sessions are created automatically, so this variable exists even if there was no incoming session reference. The one exception is if you use the `session` attribute of the `page` directive to turn sessions off, in which case attempts to reference the session variable cause translation (compilation) errors for the JSP. Sessions are covered in more detail in Chapter 5.

application Object

The `application` object has application scope, and is an instance of class `javax.servlet.ServletContext`. It represents the context within which the JSP is executing (the servlet context).

out Object

The `out` object has page scope, and is an instance of class `javax.servlet.jsp.JspWriter`. It represents the output stream opened back to the client. This is the `PrintWriter` used to send output to the client. However, in order to make the `response` object useful, this is a buffered version of `PrintWriter` called `JspWriter`. Note that you can adjust the buffer size, or even turn buffering off, through use of the `buffer` attribute of the `page`.

config Object

The `config` object has page scope, and is an instance of class `javax.servlet.ServletConfig`. It represents the servlet configuration.

page Object

The `page` object has page scope, and is an instance of class `java.lang.Object`. It refers to the instance of the JSP implementation class, in other words the JSP itself, and can be accessed using the `this` reference.

exception Object

The `exception` object has page scope, and is an instance of class `java.lang.Throwable`. It refers to the runtime exception that resulted in the error page being invoked, and is available only in an error page (a page that has the `isErrorPage=true` attribute in the page directive).

The container is free to choose how to expose this, though most use the standard mechanism of catching the runtime exception in the JSP then adding it as an attribute to the `request` object (using `ServletRequest.setAttribute()`), and finally forwarding the request to the error JSP, where it is extracted using the `request.getAttribute(String name)` method.

How Implicit Objects Work

Most of these variables are available through methods in the abstract `javax.servlet.jsp.PageContext` class. The container provides the implementation for the methods in its subclass, and is actually free to choose whatever mechanism it desires to make these objects available.

A look at any of the generated code shown earlier shows clearly how the JSWDK container makes the implicit objects available. A code excerpt is shown below:

```
// Preceding and succeeding code is not shown for brevity.
public void _jspService(HttpServletRequest request,
                        HttpServletResponse  response)
        throws IOException, ServletException {

        JspFactory _jspxFactory = null;
        PageContext pageContext = null;
        HttpSession session = null;
        ServletContext application = null;
        ServletConfig config = null;
        JspWriter out = null;
        Object page = this;
        String  _value = null;
        try {

            if (_jspx_inited == false) {
                _jspx_init();
                _jspx_inited = true;
            }
            _jspxFactory = JspFactory.getDefaultFactory();
            response.setContentType("text/html");
            pageContext = _jspxFactory.getPageContext(this, request,
                response, "", true, 8192, true);

            application = pageContext.getServletContext();
            config = pageContext.getServletConfig();
            session = pageContext.getSession();
            out = pageContext.getOut();
            ...
```

And the code below shows how the exception object is made available in an error page:

```
// Preceding and succeeding code is not shown for brevity
public void _jspService(HttpServletRequest request,
                        HttpServletResponse response)
        throws IOException, ServletException {

        JspFactory _jspxFactory = null;
        PageContext pageContext = null;
        HttpSession session = null;
        Throwable exception=
          (Throwable)request.getAttribute("javax.servlet.jsp.jspException");
        ...
```

Revisiting jspInit() and jspDestroy()

At the beginning of the chapter, I mentioned that the lifecycle of a JSP included these two methods. Now that we are familiar with JSP declarations, let's revisit these methods and see how to actually use them.

The interface `javax.servlet.jsp.JspPage` defines these two methods, and the generated servlet class must provide implementations of these methods. Though this is not necessary in most cases, the user is free to provide their own implementation of these methods if the JSP needs to do some initialization and cleanup. To satisfy the interface requirement, containers provide an empty implementation in the base class they use. When the user specifies implementations for these methods, the base class implementations are overridden.

Let's take a look at an example. When the JSP is loaded, it must do some initialization, like opening a new log file and logging the IP address of each request that it is servicing, and the log file must be closed when the server is shut down. (Not the most elegant solution, but it serves our demonstration purposes.) Of course, the server must be shutdown gracefully using its shutdown mechanism to ensure that the `jspDestroy()` method is invoked.

These methods should be used in a JSP only when there is no other alternative since their use leads to excessive Java code in the JSP. Whenever possible, code which provides the same functionality should be tucked inside a bean.

The JSP below, `logtest.jsp`, shows this:

```
<%@ page import="java.io.*,java.util.Date" %>
<%!
// Instance variable declaration so that it can be accessed
// anywhere in the JSP.
private PrintWriter logger;
```

```
/**
  * This method starts a log file on initialization
  * Invoked by the container when the JSP is loaded
  */
public void  jspInit() {
  try{
    logger= new PrintWriter(new FileWriter("JSPLogfile.txt"));
    logger.println("Log file opened on" + new Date());
  } catch(Exception e) {
    System.out.println(">>> Could not start log "+e);
  }
}

/**
  * This method closes the log file
  * Invoked by the container when the JSP is unloaded.
  */
public void jspDestroy(){
  logger.println("Log file closed on" + new Date());
  logger.flush();
  logger.close();
}

%>

<html>
<body>
 <h2>Init and destroy example.</h2>
 The information <%= request.getRemoteAddr()+" and " + new Date() %> have been
logged in the file JSPLogfile.txt <br>

</body>
</html>
<% // Since this is a scriptlet it goes in the container generated
   // _jspService() method.
   logger.println("Request received from "+ request.getRemoteAddr() +
                  " at " + new Date());
%>
```

Summary

This chapter has covered most of the nuts and bolts required in effective JSP authoring. The different kinds of tags, their syntax, and usage have been covered. The reader is encouraged to try everything out by running actual examples. A very powerful concept in JSPs, tag libraries and extensions, has been only briefly touched upon in this chapter (under the tag library directive) and is explored at greater length in Chapter 8.

In the next chapter, we'll look in more detail under the covers, at the Servlet architecture on which JSP is built.

J2EE
JSP

3

Beneath JSP

JSP is built on top of the Java Servlets technology. This chapter shows what is happening under the covers of a web application server and which important features of JSP are provided by the Servlet engine. We will discuss web application server architecture, the Servlet environment, and scalability and distributed server issues, followed by a number of important Servlet features that can be used in JSP documents:

- Session tracking
- Form data parsing
- Shared data
- Internationalized character I/O
- Init parameters
- Request delegation
- Logging

We will be looking at aspects the Servlet API and the HTTP specification; these are covered in more detail in Appendices C and D.

Web Application Server Architecture

The first time a Web Application Server receives a request for a JSP page, the JSP engine compiles the page source to a Servlet. Basically, a JSP page which consists of an HTML or XML page with embedded Java commands is turned into a Servlet class with a method which contains commands to print the page plus the commands from the JSP source. This also happens whenever a JSP page is changed, so the intermediate step of using Servlets is completely transparent to the JSP author.

The temporary Servlet is then executed by the Servlet engine to create the response message, which will be returned to the client.

The figure below shows a Web Application Server, composed of three basic layers: Web Server, Servlet engine and JSP engine.

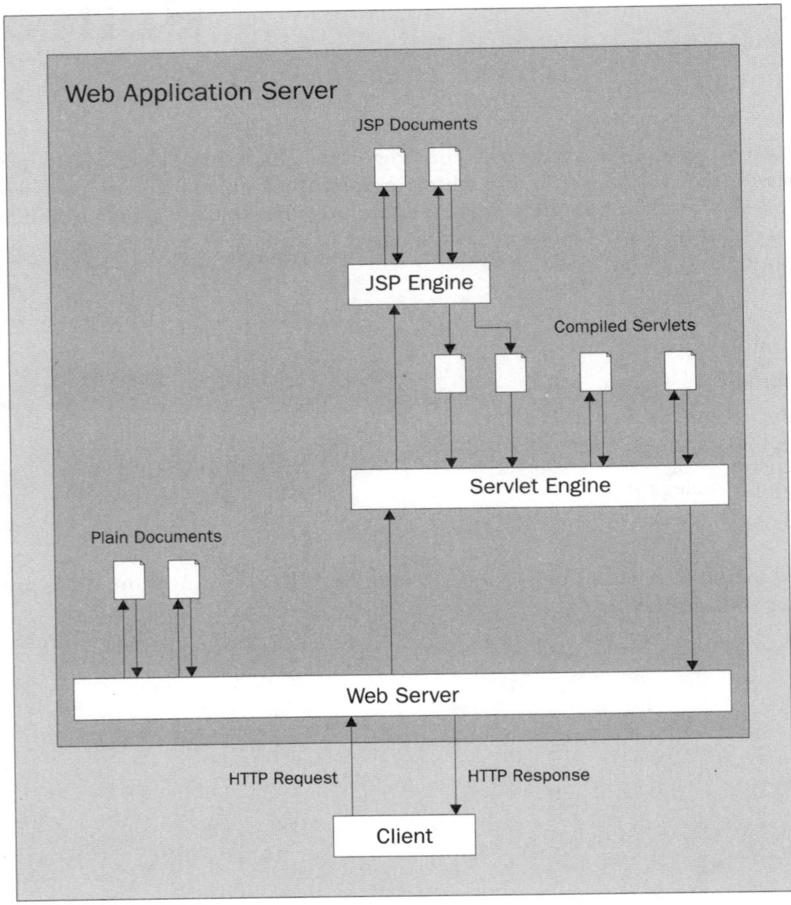

Using a Servlet engine as the middle layer between the JSP engine and the web server has several advantages:

- **Common API**

  Web application developers have to learn only a single core API, namely the Servlet API. The JSP API is a relatively small extension, which can be learned quickly and allows a Servlet developer to get acquainted with JSP in a short time.

- **Layer separation**

  A JSP engine can be built entirely based on the Servlet API: It does not need to reproduce any code from the Servlet engine. This reduces the complexity of implementing a JSP engine and allows the JSP and Servlet layers of a Web Application Server to be developed and tested independently.

- **Code reuse**

  Web application developers can reuse code from Servlets and other classes in JSPs, and vice versa, with low effort.

Once a JSP has been compiled to a Servlet it goes through the usual Servlet lifecycle. The byte code which was created from the Servlet source code is loaded by a custom `ClassLoader` which belongs to the web application. If an older version of the Servlet is already loaded, it needs to be destroyed first, together with the entire web application. All Servlets are put out of service and shut down by calling their `destroy()` method (which will call `jspDestroy()` in a JSP-generated Servlet). The application is then removed from the server (by assuring that there are no references left to objects of the application) and left to the garbage collector, which will eventually reclaim the memory used by the code and objects.

Once the new version of the web application's code has been loaded, instances of all Servlets are created and initialized by calling their `init()` methods, which in turn call `jspInit()` in JSP-generated Servlets.

Now the Servlets are ready to service requests. When a Servlet should answer an HTTP request its `service()` method is called. In an `HttpServlet` (the usual superclass of hand-written Servlets) the call is dispatched to one of the `doGet()`, `doPost()`, etc. methods depending on the HTTP request method. In a JSP-generated Servlet, the `service()` method calls `_jspService()`, the method which is created automatically from the HTML or XML code and the scriptlets and expressions in the JSP page.

The Servlet Environment

All Servlets of a web application can access a common `ServletContext` object, which allows them to share data. This equals the application scope in JSP, discussed in detail in Chapter 5. In fact, all application scope objects are stored as attributes of the Servlet context.

The `ServletContext` object has some more methods of interest:

- `getServerInfo()` returns the name and version number of the Web Application server.
- `getMajorVersion()` and `getMinorVersion()` return the version of the Servlet API which is supported by the server.
- `getResource()` and `getResourceAsStream()` enable a Servlet to access static resources in the web server's document space.

It is important to note that these methods will not invoke active resource like an external request would. If, for example, one of these methods is used to request a JSP page, the JSP source code is returned and not the processed page which is normally created by that JSP.

Several other `ServletContext` methods are discussed later on in this chapter.

Scalability

Unlike CGI scripts, Servlets and JSP pages are kept alive between requests and can carry on data from one request to another instead of initializing and freeing resources again each time they are are invoked. They also run in separate threads which are usually stored in a thread pool instead of creating a new process for each request which further minimizes the overhead associated with invoking a Servlet. These advantages make Servlets inherently more scalable than the CGI scripts which are traditionally used to build web applications.

Furthermore, Servlets are not limited to running only within a single JVM or on a single physical machine. They can be marked as distributable which allows them to run concurrently on several JVMs with only a few restrictions. This feature makes Servlets (and therefor JSPs) ideal for building large systems. If a single machine is not powerful enough to run a web application, it can be replaced by a distributed server which keeps instances of all Servlets on several machines and dispatches incoming request to these separate instances.

The major limitation of distributed Servlets is the separation of `ServletContext` attributes. Each JVM has its own context, so the Servlet context can no longer be used to share data. However, data can be shared with the session tracking mechanisms that are offered by the Servlet API, by using Enterprise JavaBeans, or storing shared data in an external database.

The API and the basic structure is always the same, no matter if you are running a simple standalone Servlet with the servlet runner or building a large distributed web application.

Important Servlet API features

Having looked at web application server architecture, the Servlet environment, and scalability issues, we can move on to consider important features that are provided by the Servlet engine and can be used directly or indirectly in JSP documents.

Session tracking

In a Servlet, sessions are created and maintained explicitly by calling the `ServletRequest` method `getSession()`. The Servlet engine manages a table of sessions, each identified by a unique string, the session key. For creating a new session upon a request, an `HttpSession` object and a session key are created and stored in the session table. The response message is used to send the session key to the client, which sends it back with future requests so that the server can identify the client and retrieve the `HttpSession` object associated with that client.

If a client does not continue session within a specified time, the server will expire the session and delete all data associated with that session. The session key is invalidated, so that the next request by the client, which may still include the old session key, is not associated with any session.

There are two common ways of passing session keys from the server to the client and back: Cookies and URL rewriting. Cookies are used by default; URL rewriting comes into play if cookies are not supported by the browser.

Cookies

A Cookie is a name-value pair which is sent to a client in a `Set-Cookie` HTTP header. The server can also specify a timeout after which the Cookie is deleted on the client side, or delete a Cookie explicitly with a zero timeout. Note that the client-side timeout is distinct from the server-side session timeout. Sessions without an explicit client-side timeout end when the client-side session ends; in case of a web browser this happens when the browser application gets closed.

Once the Cookie has been accepted by the client (which may ask the user for confirmation) it is sent back to the server from which it originated with all subsequent requests. This is done with the HTTP request header `Cookie` that is similar to the `Set-Cookie` response header.

URL rewriting

All URLs which are included in the server response are encoded to contain the session key. When the client follows a redirection automatically or the user selects a link, the URL requested is not the regular URL but a modified one like http://myserver.com/servlet/MyServlet&12345, from which the server can extract the session key ('12345' in this example).

This method has two major shortcomings: It requires more work on the server side because additional processing has to be applied to all responses to include the session keys. Even static resources which would normally be written directly in HTML or XML have to be created dynamically be Servlets or JSP pages in order to include the session keys. The second disadvantage is the lack of control on the client side. For example, when a user pushes the web browser's 'back' button or selects a bookmark to go to a page that was not part of the current session the session key is lost.

URL rewriting is useful mainly when the client does not support Cookies or has them disabled. With URL rewriting it is also possible to carry a session over from one server to another in a distributed server environment.

Using Sessions

We now look at an example to illustrate what happens on the HTTP level when a session is created, carried on, and destroyed. For more details of the HTTP protocol, see Appendix D.

A user goes to the starting page of a server (http://myserver/), which replies with a redirection to the login Servlet. The browser sends a header similar to the following one (all bodies and unnecessary header lines are left out in this example):

```
GET / HTTP/1.0
```

The server responds with the redirection:

```
HTTP/1.0 302 Moved Temporarily
Location: http://myserver/servlet/LoginServlet
```

The client follows the redirection and requests:

```
GET /servlet/LoginServlet HTTP/1.0
```

The server responds with a login form which leads back to the login Servlet. From now on the session should be tracked, so the `LoginServlet` calls `getSession()`, which leads to the inclusion of a session Cookie in the response:

```
HTTP/1.0 200 OK
Set-Cookie: SessionKey="12345"; Version="1"
```

The session key is also contained in the form's `ACTION` URL because the server can't know whether or not the client will accept the Cookie. Let's assume it will and the user entered a valid login name and password. Now the request includes the session key twice, in the URL and a Cookie:

```
POST /servlet/LoginServlet$SessionKey=12345 HTTP/1.0
Cookie: $Version="1"; SessionKey="12345"
```

Now the server knows that the Cookie was accepted and does not encode the session key in URLs anymore. Neither does the `Set-Cookie` header need to be sent again unless the Cookie should be modified or deleted, so the server sends a plain response:

```
HTTP/1.0 200 OK
```

The Servlet has probably stored the user's login name in a session attribute. Note that this attribute is kept only on the server side: the client never gets to see any data associated with a session except the session key.

Let's assume that the client now makes a request to the `MainServlet`, which is part of the same web application as the `LoginServlet`, and thus uses the same session data. The browser still includes the session Cookie in the request header:

```
GET /servlet/MainServlet HTTP/1.0
Cookie: $Version="1"; SessionKey="12345"
```

After some more requests the user wants to log out of the system. This is handled by the `LogoutServlet`. The browser sends a normal request:

```
GET /servlet/LogoutServlet HTTP/1.0
Cookie: $Version="1"; SessionKey="12345"
```

The `LogoutServlet` destroys the session by calling the `HttpSession` object's `invalidate()` method. Even if the client sent another request with the session key '12345' it would not be considered a part of any session because the key has been invalidated. In addition, the session Cookie is deleted by setting its timeout to zero:

```
HTTP/1.0 200 OK
Set-Cookie: SessionKey=""; Version="1"; Max-Age=0
```

Further requests by the client will not include the `SessionKey` Cookie anymore, so they are again stateless.

Form data parsing

When a client sends data with a GET or POST request it is often encoded in the `application/x-www-form-urlencoded` format. Most notably, this format is used for HTML form data sets. The format can be used for all kinds of name-value pairs.

All names and values are encoded separately in the following way: space characters are replaced by +; other non-alphanumeric characters are replaced by a `%HH` triplet, where `HH` is the hexadecimal ASCII code of the character. The encoded tokens are then combined to `encoded-name=encoded-value` pairs which in turn are joined with `&` characters (`encoded-pair&encoded-pair&encoded-pair&...`).

When a client issues a GET request, it can append form-urlencoded data to a URL with a leading `?` character. For example, when user John Doe enters his name and age into an HTML form with two fields named `full name` and `age`, and sends the form to http://myserver/page.jsp, the client would actually request the URL http://myserver/page.jsp?full+name=John+Doe&age=42. The request header could look like this:

```
GET /page.jsp?full+name=John+Doe&age=42 HTTP/1.0
```

If the form is sent using the POST method, the data is encoded in the say way and sent as the body of the HTTP message. The complete message (minus some additional headers) looks like this:

```
POST /page.jsp HTTP/1.0
Content-Type: application/x-www-form-urlencoded
Content-Length: 27

full+name=John+Doe&age=42
```

Note that the content length includes the line feed (a Carriage Return and Line Feed pair) which ends the form-urlencoded message body.

The Servlet engine knows how to parse data encoded in this format. No matter if the data was transmitted in a GET or POST request, you can always access the elements of the form with the `HttpServletRequest` method `getParameter()`.

In our example, the following code could be used in `/page.jsp` to print the decoded data:

```
Hello, <%= request.getParameter("full name") %>,
you are <%= request.getParameter("age") %> years old.
```

Shared data

We've already discussed some of the `ServletContext` methods. Now let's look at one important aspect of the Servlet context in more detail: The management of shared data.
All application scope (in JSP terms) objects of a web application are attributes of the servlet context and can be accessed manually with the following `ServletContext` methods:

- `getAttribute()` returns a stored object, given the attribute name.
- `getAttributeNames()` returns a list of all available attributes.
- `setAttribute()` stores a new object or replaces an existing one; this is useful for passing information between Servlets.
- `removeAttribute()` removes a stored attribute.

The web application server may also make additional attributes available, which contain server-dependant information that is not otherwise available through the Servlet API.

Internationalized character I/O

Internally, Java always uses the 16 bit Unicode character encoding which contains characters for almost all languages of the world. When a JSP page or Servlet returns a text page to the client it will not generally use Unicode, because most clients do not support the full character range. Some do not understand the Unicode encoding at all, but only older and more limited character sets.

Besides that, it would also be a waste of bandwidth. HTML and XML pages generally use only a very limited number of different languages and characters and, by choosing a more appropriate encoding, one character can be represented by less than 16 bits. For example, most encodings for European languages use a fixed size of only 8 bits per character.

The Unicode text which is returned by a Servlet is automatically encoded by the Servlet engine. Clients may provide information about their support for different character encodings through the `Accept-Charset` request header, for example:

```
Accept-Charset: iso-8859-2, unicode-1-1
```

The ISO-8859-1 encoding (also known as 'Latin 1', the standard encoding for western European languages) must be accepted by all clients. A Servlet engine which receives the above header could select one of the three acceptable encodings (including Latin 1) by looking at the Servlet response body. If it contains only characters from ISO-8859-1 or ISO-8859-2, these 8 bit encodings would be used, otherwise the 16 bit Unicode (version 1.1) encoding.

The automatic selection can be avoided by specifying a character set explicitly:

```
<% response.setContentType
  ("text/html; charset=unicode-1-1"); %>
```

Initialization parameters

When a Servlet is initialized it is passed a `ServletConfig` object containing the initialization parameters for the Servlet. These parameters are `String` objects associated with an attribute name; they can be defined by a web application server with custom configuration files, or in a standardized Web Application package.

Do not confuse initialization parameters with `ServletContext` attributes: the former are specific to a single Servlet or JSP page, while the latter are shared by all Servlets and JSP pages in a web application.

In a JSP page, the `ServletConfig` object can be accessed through the predefined `config` variable or, like in all Servlets, through the `getServletConfig()` method. The following methods can be used on `ServletConfig` objects:

- `getInitParameter()` returns the value of a named init parameter.
- `getInitParameterNames()` returns a list of all defined init parameters.
- `getServletContext()` returns the `ServletContext` object associated with the Servlet to which the configuration belongs. This method is used by the `GenericServlet` class to find the Servlet context; it is generally not used directly by web application developers. In Servlets which extend `GenericServlet` (or `HttpServlet`), the Servlet's `getServletContext()` method is used instead. In JSP pages you can use the predefined `application` variable.

Request delegation

The JSP actions `<jsp:include>` and `<jsp:forward>` can be used to forward a request to another JSP page or Servlet, or to include the output produced by such a resource in the JSP page's response. These actions have counterparts on the Servlet level, which can also be invoked directly in JSP scriptlets.

Request delegation is handled by `RequestDispatcher` objects. Such an object can be obtained for a specified destination path by calling the Servlet context's `getRequestDispatcher()` method; then, the request dispatcher's `include()` and `forward()` methods can be called to get a response from the resource associated with the dispatcher.

The following example illustrates how a Servlet `/servlet/ItemServlet` would set a request attribute and then redirect the request to a second Servlet `/servlet/HelpServlet`, which will read the attribute and create the requested help page. In a regular Servlet the code looks like this:

```
RequestDispatcher dispatcher =
  getServletContext().getRequestDispatcher("/servlet/HelpServlet");

dispatcher.forward(request, response);
```

In a JSP page, which uses a different superclass than `HttpServlet`, the following code can be used instead:

```
RequestDispatcher dispatcher =
  application.getRequestDispatcher("/servlet/HelpServlet");

dispatcher.forward(request, response);
```

The resource to which the request is forwarded has full control over the response. Of course, this is only possible if the Servlet has not started writing the response itself. That be done by calling the `include()` method which allows the output of several Servlets to be combined. Note that included resources cannot modify the response headers.

Logging

A web server has one or more log files where errors and other short messages are stored for the server administrator. Messages can be written to the appropriate Servlet log file in Servlets and JSP pages by using one of the `log()` methods defined in the servlet context:

- `log(String)` writes the string to the Servlet log file, whereas
- `log(String, Throwable)` writes a string and a stack trace of the supplied `Throwable` (that is, an `Exception` or `Error` object) to the Servlet log file.

In Servlets which extend `GenericServlet` or `HttpServlet` (which is usually not the case for JSP pages) the `log()` methods of the `GenericServlet` class can be used instead. They work like the `ServletContext` methods except they automatically add the Servlet class names to the logged messages.

Summary

JSP pages are compiled to temporary Servlets by the JSP engine, and can therefore use all of the features provided by the Servlet engine. Some of these features also have counterparts at the JSP level which use the Servlet engine to do the actual work.

In this chapter we have looked at the basic architecture of a web application server consisting of web server, Servlet engine and JSP engine, and the following Servlet engine features:

- Session tracking
- Form data parsing
- Shared data
- Internationalized character I/O
- Init parameters
- Request delegation
- Logging

In the next chapter we will learn how to use JavaBeans components with JavaServer Pages, to encapsulate Java code and separate presentation from logic within your JSPs.

J2EE
JSP

4

JSP and JavaBeans

Introduction

One of the most powerful aspects of using JSP is the ability to use the JavaBeans component architecture. The JavaBeans specification allows software components to be written in Java (or reused or bought in), which encapsulate the logic behind your web application and remove the bulk of the scriptlet code that would otherwise clutter up your JSPs. The result is JSP code that is simpler, easier to maintain, and which is more readily accessible to non-programmers.

With Java as the language underlying the JSP technology, we have access to a very varied range of APIs that can be easily plugged into any code and used to enhance the application. Additionally, unlike many scripting languages, we can make full use of object orientation. This means reusable bean classes can be defined, greatly reducing future maintenance requirements by allowing us to extend those classes and tailor them to organizational requirements.

JavaBeans is Sun's answer to the increasing demand in the software industry for a set of standards to define software components. Components are used in many industries to simplify distribution, enhancement, and maintenance. For example, to replace a broken headlight in your car, you would expect to be able to buy a readily available part from any distributor. Imagine the inconvenience and the cost if you had to get the manufacturer to build a special part just for your car every time a bulb blew. A minor change in system functionality is generally a costly and time-consuming affair. Software components are an attempt to rectify this and replace custom code with generic, reusable black boxes wherever possible.

Chapter 2 covered the `<jsp:useBean>`, `<jsp:setProperty>`, and `<jsp:getProperty>` tags used within JSPs to access JavaBeans; in this chapter, we will take a look at the basics of creating Java Beans, and will also walk through some of the core techniques of JDBC, the Java API for accessing databases. Armed with this knowledge, we will then create a pair of beans based on those concepts. These beans will allow JSP developers to create applications that act as a middleman between the web based user and a database, updating database tables with details entered by the user from a browser, and creating web pages based on queried output data. The designer will be able to change the source database, the SQL statements that are to be run and the text the user will see by adding or editing a few lines of code in the JSP documents. For example, a simple customer details form could be created allowing a Customer Service Representative to query customer details. A selection list with customer names can be presented allowing the rep to quickly click on a customer, as in the figure below:

When the Submit button is clicked the application queries the database for matching information and shows it to the user, as shown in the next figure.

Customer Details

Customer	DD Electrical
Contact	Lydia Summo
Tel	3839954
Address 1	19 North Bridge Road
Address 2	#05-02 Dixan Centre
Address 3	Singapore 179097
EMail	ddelect@singnet.com.sg
Industry	IT supplies

JavaBeans

As previously mentioned, Java uses the Beans specification to allow the creation of software components that can be used by other developers and designers to build specialist applications. Java's cross-platform nature means that the same JavaBean should be reusable across any machine, we are likely to use to support JSP. This really frees us from dependence on any particular platform (provided the beans do not use any native code). If an IT department decides to migrate their online systems from an NT based architecture running, say, Microsoft IIS, to an Apache Web Server running on Linux, we should be able to drop any legacy beans we have already created onto the Linux box. We may need to set some configuration parameters, but we should be able to carry on using the beans without a major re-development effort. The point about reconfiguring parameters is critical here; it is one of the fundamental aspects of the component model. While there are many definitions of what comprises a component; most of these definitions include the following features:

- Editable fields or properties for storing data.
- Methods or functions for performing processes and logical operations.
- Events for communication amongst beans and other objects.
- State persistence for storage of a bean's condition.

Bean Properties

A bean uses properties to describe internal data that affects how it works or what it shows. In Java, the actual bean property data is usually a private or protected field which can be edited by publicly available methods. In other words, beans allow access to internal data via public 'get' and 'set' methods. This conforms to Object Orientation norms, which hide internal data from users and expose it only through accessor methods. It also conforms to the black-box concept of the component model. For example, with a user-interface component we can set the text size by telling the bean to use a font size of '10' but we have no idea of what is going on inside the bean. We know that the 'set' method sets the font size, but we don't know how, and we probably don't care. The data item that the property represents could be based on any Java primitive such as an `int`, `boolean`, or any Java object such as a `String`, a `Locale`, or any custom user defined object.

The previous example was concerned with appearance. However, properties may also be used to define the behavior of a component. In many cases, most of the properties are server-based attributes that a user will never see. In that case, we are be defining behavioral properties.

For a designer who wants to make use of a bean but doesn't really want to be writing source code, many bean activities can be determined purely by setting properties. Most Java Integrated Development Environments (IDEs) available on the market (and many free ones) are aware of the Java Beans standard, and allow beans to be imported and edited. Most of these tools will provide a 'property sheet' where entering some text or selecting an option from a drop down list sets the property value.

Sun provides the Bean Development Kit (BDK) as a simple example of a user-interface design tool using Beans. Download a copy from the Java web site (http://www.java.sun.com/beans/software/bdk_download.html) if you want to try out some of the standard bean design features. This screenshot shows the `Juggler` bean with its property sheet. Changing the values in the property sheet updates the property values of the bean. If you want Duke to change the speed of juggling, enter a new number in the animation Rate box. If you want debug features enabled, select true in the debug combo. Almost all IDEs allow the editing of properties in a similar way.

Creating Accessor Methods for Properties

Accessor methods are used to set and retrieve internal bean property data. However, before accessor methods are created, we need to define a class we are going to use as a bean and add fields that will act as properties:

```
import java.beans.*;

class TestBean {
  private int  height;
  private String description;
  protected boolean debug = false;
}
```

The simple class TestBean now has three fields that can be used as bean properties. Each is a different type. Two are primitive types; the boolean field debug, and the int field height, and one is an object type, the String field description. Note that when declaring fields, a default value can be set. In this example, debugging options will not be available when we instantiate the bean, and will have to be specifically turned on. As these fields are not publicly accessible (they are all either private or protected), we will need some means of changing their values. This is done by accessor methods. The Java Beans specification states that accessor methods use the following patterns:

- public void set<*Property Name*>(<*Property Type*> value);
- public <*Property Type*> get<*Property Name*>();
- public boolean is<*Property Name*>();

There is one method formula for setting bean properties, and two for retrieving them. Methods for passing values to bean properties have names are prefixed with 'set', followed by the name of the property. They return a void, and use a parameter of the same type as the property.

Methods for retrieving the value of a property traditionally start with 'get' or, if the property is a boolean, 'is'. They return a value that is the same type as the property, and have no parameters. Bean designer tools look inside the beans for properties that match these signature patterns by using a technique called introspection. Properties that follow the rules are then presented on the property sheet ready for editing. To create assessor methods for our int property, we write:

```
public void setHeight (int i){
  height = i;
}

public int getHeight (){
  return height;
}
```

The important thing to notice in creating these methods is the symmetry. Both methods use 'Height' with an initial capital letter, and both deal with an int type variable. (If the getHeight() method returned a long instead of an int, this would not generate a compiler error, but the property would not show up in any property sheet.)

Repeating the process for the String property, description:

```
public void setDescription(String s) {
  description = s;
}

public String getDescription (){
  return description;
}
```

Again note the symmetry, same core name of 'Description'. The set method takes a String object and passes its value to the description property and the get method gives us access to whatever value is held in this private field.

Finally, defining the accessors for the boolean property, debug:

```
public void setDebug (boolean b){
  debug = b;
}

public boolean isDebug (){
  return debug;
}
```

Here the return method uses the 'is' prefix, in fact getDebug() probably sounds better and would be a perfectly legal way of defining the method – isDebug() and getDebug() are inter-changeable.

> **A point to remember is that when creating beans to use with JSP, we don't necessarily need to create both a get and a set method. We may only be interested in one of these processes, and therefore only need to bother with the one that is to be used.**

Indexed Properties

The JSP 1.1 specification also allows the setting of indexed properties. What are indexed properties? They are exactly the same as single value properties except that the properties consist of arrays. The signature patterns:

```
public <Property Type> get<Property Name>(int index)
public void set<Property Name>(int index, <Property Type> value)
public <Property Type>[] get<Property Name>()
public void set<Property Name>(<Property Type>[] value)
```

If we add an array property to our TestBean:

```
private String[] partNo;
```

we could put a new part number called 'widget3' into the partNo array at array index number 3 as follows:

```
setPartNo(3, "widget3");
```

If we wanted to find out what the value was in array index 7, we could use:

```
String s = getPartNo(7);
```

At the moment the JSP 1.1 specification only supports certain indexed property types, namely `boolean`, `Boolean`, `byte`, `Byte`, `char`, `Character`, `double`, `Double`, `int`, `Integer`, `float`, `Float`, `long`, and `Long`.

Bean Methods

If you already know how to write a Java method then you already know how to write a method for a bean. There is nothing inherently different about methods within Java Beans. If for example, we wanted to print out the current status of the bean to the console window, then we could set up a simple method to do that:

```
public void printStatus() {
  System.out.println("Height is " + height);
  System.out.println("Description is " + description");
  System.out.println("Debug is " + debug);
}
```

As you can see, this is just standard Java code.

Bound Properties and Bean Events

Another of aspect of a component is that it should be able to communicate with other objects or beans. JavaBeans accomplish this by firing events and listening for them. A bean that is interested in what happens to an object external to itself can register itself as a listener for various events in that object. Conversely, an external object can register itself to listen to that bean. This concept is really the key to providing standalone software components. The individual objects can all take an interest in each other without having to be aware of anything other than events that are fired out. This is known as 'Loose Coupling' as opposed to Strong or 'Direct Coupling'. While Loose Coupling requires more effort and planning, it is greatly preferable to hard-coding interactions between objects, and offers a much higher level of flexibility and maintainability.

Bound Properties

One way of exporting events is to use bound properties. When a property value changes, a bound property can inform other parts of the application that its value has changed. One example of this would be the `ConnectionManager` bean which we will create later. Every time a database connection is made or lost, other beans that need to put information into the database or get data from it using that connection will need to be informed of the current status. Another example may be a bean that is dedicated to informing the user of any problems that may have arisen. When we handled the error setting the height earlier, we sent the error message to the standard output stream for the machine. Most users would never see this, and carry on without knowing their selection was rejected. If instead, we fired an event with an error description to any listeners, we could have a dialog type object that would pick it up and pop up to inform the user.

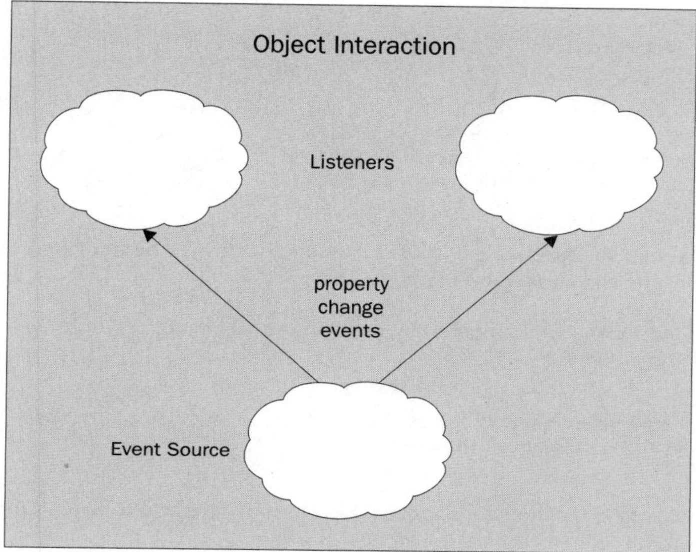

Adding listeners for bound property changes will be familiar to anyone who has worked with the Java Delegation Event Model. As expected, there is a method to add a listener, and one to remove a listener:

- `public void addPropertyChangeListener (PropertyChangeListener pcl);`
- `public void removePropertyChangeListener (PropertyChangeListener pcl);`

A Beans support class, `PropertyChangeSupport`, comes in very handily at this point. We can use this class to manage the listener list and inform those listeners of any property changes. `PropertyChangeSupport` has only three methods:

- `public void addPropertyChangeListener (PropertyChangeListener pcl);`
- `public void removePropertyChangeListener (PropertyChangeListener pcl);`
- `public void firePropertyChange(String propertyName, Object oldValue, Object newValue);`

The constructor needs the parent object as a parameter:

- `public PropertyChangeSupport(Object source);`

The first two methods handle the adding and removal of listeners. The third method helps us to fire the events to those listeners. Note that we can fire the name plus the old and new values of the property. If we then want to make our `TestBean` fire events when the `String` property `description` changes, we first need to declare and instantiate the support class:

```
Class TestBean {
  //  other declarations
  ...

  PropertyChangeSupport pcs;

  public TestBean(){
    pcs = new PropertyChangeSupport(this);
  }
```

Then we need to set up the listener methods. Listeners wanting to be informed of property changes are sent directly to the support class to be managed there:

```
public void addPropertyChangeListener(PropertyChangeListener l){
  pcs.addPropertyChangeListener(l);
}

public void removePropertyChangeListener(PropertyChangeListener l ){
  pcs.removePropertyChangeListener(l);
}
```

All that now remains to do is to change the setDescription() method to fire a property change event to the listeners before the value is updated.

```
public void setDescription(String s){
  pcs.firePropertyChange("description", description, s);
  description = s;
}
```

What happens here is that before the property is reset, we have a record of the current value in `description` (this now becomes the old value) and the new value in the `s` parameter. Using the `PropertyChangeSupport` class method `firePropertyChange()` creates a `PropertyChangeEvent`, and sends it all the registered listeners to do what they want with it.

The `PropertyChangeEvent` class is an extension of `Event` with a number of additional methods, among them:

- `public String getPropertyName();`
- `public Object getNewValue();`
- `public Object getOldValue();`

The methods can be used to test what property has changed and to retrieve the new and old values. The values are passed as `Objects` rather than any specific type, so in general a test will need to be made to ensure the `Object` is the correct type, avoiding a `ClassCastExceptions`. As far as `TestBean` is concerned, that is the end of the matter, and what any of the listeners now do with the new information is completely up to them. You can see how this can greatly simplify application maintenance. Most complexity in applications involves writing code to make different parts of it work together properly. If we can use a standard to achieve that, we can really improve development efficiency.

Now let's say we wanted a text field class that listens for changes in the `description` property in the `TestBean`, and sets the text of the field to the newly changed value. To do this, all classes that want to be listeners for property changes in the `TestBean` will need to implement the `PropertyChangeListener` interface. To be a `PropertyChangeListener`, we only need to implement one method:

- `public void propertyChange(PropertyChangeEvent evt);`

We create the listener class by extending the Swing text field class `JTextField`:

```
import java.beans.*;
import javax.swing.*;

class DescriptionField extends JTextField
  implements PropertyChangeListener {

  public void propertyChange(PropertyChangeEvent evt) {
    if (evt.getPropertyName().equals("description")) {

      // store the new value
      Object o = evt.getNewValue();

      // test for correct type
      if (o instanceof String) {
        setText((String) o);
      }
    }
  }
}
```

We now go back to the `TestBean`, create and instantiate a `DescriptionField` object, then add it to the `TestBean` as a property change listener:

```
DescriptionField field = new DescriptionField();
addPropertyChangeListener(field);
```

What will happen now is that any time `setDescription()` is invoked in `TestBean`, a `PropertyChangeEvent` will be fired at any listeners, including the new `DescriptionField` object. Within the `DescriptionField`, the `propertyChange()` method will be invoked, which will check for the property name. If the name matches '`description`', the text displayed will be set to the new value.

You may want to be able to revoke a property change if, for example, an attempt is made to set an illegal value. To do this, you can make use of **Constrained Properties**. Constrained properties are very similar to bound properties, but throw an exception under certain conditions. There are four methods to consider:

- `public <Property Type> getPropertyName();`
- `public void set<Property Name>(<Property Type> param) throws PropertyVetoException;`
- `public void addVetoableChangeListener (VetoableChangeListener v);`
- `public void removeVetoableChangeListener (VetoableChangeListener v);`

Like Property Change Listeners, Vetoable Change Listeners need to implement an interface `VetoableChangeListener` with the method:

- `public void vetoableChangeListener(PropertyChangeEvent evt) throws PropertyVetoException;`

Bean Events

The PropertyChangeSupport class should cater for most of our needs, it certainly will in the case of our mini application later in the chapter. However, on many occasions beans will still need to communicate, even though no property change activity has occurred. We may also need to create specific events and listeners for certain conditions. This is done by exporting events. The events may be one of the standard Java events, such as an ActionEvent, or they may be custom events designed to handle a unique set of circumstances. Remember that if the goal is to be able to communicate with any bean out there in the world, it is highly unlikely that the other bean will be aware of your own custom events.

Bean development tools and IDEs use introspection to look for events that a bean may export. They will only be successful in locating exportable events if they conform exactly to the conventions of the delegation event model.

Bean Persistence and Storage

For a component to be really useful, it must be possible to save it, and any values it may contain, and then reload it to the same state at a later date. No matter how wonderful the component we create, it will not be used much if it has to be reset every time it is retrieved. Java Beans use the Serializable interface to address this issue.

The Serializable interface has no methods to implement; it is simply an indicator to the compiler that an object may be made persistent by serialization. Any attempts to serialize objects that do not implement the interface will generate a NotSerializableException. In practice, serialization generally means saving the bean to a file using the ObjectOutputStream class. To restore the bean we then read the same file using ObjectInputStream. If our TestBean is to be serializable then all we need to do is add the Serializable interface in the class declaration:

```
class TestBean implements Serializable {
```

We can then decide whether to create serialization within the TestBean, or use a utility type object to save and reload the whole object as we require. If we look at TestBean at this stage of its development, it is easy to see that the only things that would ever need saving are the values of its 3 properties. We could, therefore, write methods that write the values of those items to a file and reload and set the values when reload is invoked. Here, for the sake of the example, we'll put together a little utility class that serializes the whole TestBean object:

```
import java.io.*;

public class Saver {

  public boolean save(Object o, String file) {
    boolean status = true;
    FileOutputStream fos;
    ObjectOutputStream os;
    try {
      fos = new FileOutputStream(file);
      os = new ObjectOutputStream(fos);
      os.writeObject(o);
      os.close();
    } catch (Exception ex) {
      status = false;
      System.out.println("Save Error: " + ex);
    }
```

```
      return status;
    }

    public Object load(String file) {
      FileInputStream fis;
      ObjectInputStream ois;
      Object o = null;
      try {
        fis = new FileInputStream(file);
        ois = new ObjectInputStream(fis);
        o = ois.readObject();

        ois.close();
      } catch (Exception ex) {
        System.out.println("Load Error: " + ex);
      }
      return o;
    }
  }
```

Saving or loading the `TestBean` (or any other serializable object) is now one line of code using this utility. Once the `Saver` class has been declared and instantiated, say as `saver`, to store the current state of `TestBean` into a file called `TestBean.ser` we would just use:

```
boolean saved = saver.save( testBean, "TestBean.ser");
```

and to load it again,

```
TestBean testBean = (TestBean)saver.load("TestBean.ser");
```

When serializing data, remember that methods, static fields and any field declared as `transient` are not saved.

JavaBeans and JDBC

Java uses a set of classes and interfaces called Java Database Connectivity (JDBC) to interact with databases. While JDBC is a relatively large package (known as `java.sql`) with some very large classes, for our mini application, we only really need to understand a small subset of its capabilities. In fact, most developers are only really concerned with connecting to databases, and getting data in or out using Select, Insert, Update or Delete SQL statements. In this section, we'll take a quick look at how JDBC performs those basic functions – JDBC will be covered in a lot more detail in Chapter 7.

After this, we will put together a `ConnectionManager` bean that will manage database connection activities for our example application. This bean will be reusable, so it will be available to provide that functionality for other beans we may create in the future.

Connecting to the Database

We need to establish a database connection to a database before we can do anything else. To connect, we typically need four elements:

- Database driver
- Database URL
- User Id
- Password

As noted at the beginning there are a large number of drivers available, each with their own little idiosyncrasies. For now, we will use the JDBC-ODBC driver, which is supplied with the JDK, connecting to an Access database.

To prepare the driver, we need to load its class and instantiate it:

```
Class.forName("sun.jdbc.odbc.JdbcOdbcDriver").newInstance();
```

You will need to catch any exceptions, such as `ClassNotFoundException` and `InstantiationException`, that are generated by this call.

Since we are going to use a Microsoft Access database, we need to setup an ODBC Data Source Name (DSN) to be able to connect to the database. If you are using a Windows machine, this is done in the Data Sources (ODBC) section in the Control Panel. Select the System DSN tab and click on the Add button to create a new data source. Then select the Microsoft Access driver. In the Data Source Name text field, enter Sales and enter a free text description in the Description field. Next, in the database section, use the Select button to bring up the Select Database dialog. Get this to point to the database you want to use, in this case `Sales.mdb`.

The next step is to locate and connect to the database: this is done using a URL string in the format `jdbc:`*`subprotocol`*`:`*`subname`*. If we are using an ODBC DSN named `Sales`, the URL for that connection would be `jdbc:odbc:Sales`. (Each driver has its own syntax for URLs, so it is worth looking through the accompanying documentation to see exactly how to create the string.) Once the driver is loaded and we know how to create the database URL, we need a User Id and a Password. We can then connect to the database using the one of a number of methods in the `java.sql.DriverManager` class:

- `getConnection(String url, Properties info);`
- `getConnection(String url, String user, String password);`

Both methods require the URL as a parameter. The first method uses a `Properties` parameter containing the username and password; the second simply puts the them in the second and third parameters respectively. Assuming a User Id of `admin` and a Password of `admin`, to connect in our example, remembering to handle the `SQLException` that may be thrown, we use the following:

```
Connection con;
try {
  con = DriverManager.getConnection("Jdbc:Odbc:Sales", "admin", "admin" );
} catch(SQLException ex){}
```

Running SQL Statements

Once we obtain a Connection object, we can use it for a variety of purposes, including creating SQL Statements. The Connection object can return both `Statement` and `PreparedStatement` objects. For a `Statement` object, we use:

```
try {
  Statement st = con.createStatement();
} catch(SQLException se){}
```

For a Statement to do anything, we have to provide it with some SQL to run. Do this by passing the SQL as a String parameter, and then calling one of the execute methods, execute(), executeQuery(), and executeUpdate(). executeQuery() returns a ResultSet object containing the result of the SQL query. If we want to create a result set of employee id's and names from a database table that contains those columns, we could use:

```
try {
  ResultSet rs = st.executeQuery("Select id, name from employee");
} catch(SQLException se){}
```

If we want to insert, update, or delete database information, we use the executeUpdate() method, and this time a ResultSet is not returned. An int variable telling us how many records have been changed comes back:

```
try{
  int count = st.executeQuery("Insert into employee values ('1','Smith')");
} catch(SQLException se){}
```

The PreparedStatement object provides us with more capability. It pre-compiles and stores a SQL statement, and as the PreparedStatement does not have to be recompiled every time it is used, it is a more efficient way to run a SQL statement that is to be run more than one time. Another aspect of the PreparedStatement is that we can use placeholders for parameters we may want to pass to the statement. This means we can define more generic statements at design time when we have no idea what parameters a user may want to use. At runtime, we can then pass real data to those placeholders. A '?' character is used as the placeholder, and can be used in the SQL 'Where', 'Set', and 'Values' clauses. The Insert statement above would then become:

```
("Insert into employee values (?,?)");
```

Or a Select statement using placeholders could be:

```
"Select from employee where id = ? "
```

When we get around to running our SQL, we replace those question marks with real values using the PreparedStatement setXXX() methods. There are about 20 setXXX() methods, each catering for a primitive or reference type. All share a similar format:

- set<*Type*>(int index>, <*Type*> value);

The first parameter is a reference to the question mark placeholder position: 1 for the first placeholder, 2 for the second, etc., and the second parameter is the value to be set. Using the above Select statement, if we want the where = ? to be where id = 'abc123', we would inform the PreparedStatement object ps using:

```
ps.setString(1, "abc123");
```

Or if, for example, we wanted to use an int as the third parameter and we wanted to set its value to 5:

```
ps.setInt(3, 5);
```

PreparedStatement is an extension of Statement and uses the same execute methods. One significant difference is that a SQL string is passed to a Connection object when creating the PreparedStatement, for example:

```
try {
  PreparedStatement ps = con.prepareStatement
    ("Select from employee where id = ? ");
  ps.setString(1, "abc123");
  ResultSet rs = ps.executeQuery();
} catch(SQLException se){}
```

Result Sets

As we have just seen, `Statements` and `PreparedStatements` return a `ResultSet` object. The `ResultSet` interface contains a whole list of `getXXX()` methods that are the mirror image of the `setXXX()` methods found in the `PreparedStatement` interface; there is also a list of `getXXX()` methods that use the database column name as the parameter:

- `<Type> get<Type>(int index);`
- `<Type> get<Type>(String columnName);`

Thus for the `"Select id, name from employee"` query, if we want to retrieve the data by their order in the statement, we could use:

```
String id = rs.getString(1);
String name = rs.getString(2);
```

or alternatively, using the column name:

```
String id = rs.getString("id");
String name = rs.getString("name");
```

A `ResultSet` consists of rows of data, and initially is positioned before the first row. To move it to the first row, we can invoke the `ResultSet`'s `next()` method. If there is a first row, `next()` will return `true`. Invoking it again will move it to the second row, and so on until no more rows are found and `false` is returned. To send a list of data to the console, we could use:

```
try {
  while (rs.next()){
    System.out.print( rs.getString(1) + " : ");
    System.out.print( rs.getString(2) + "\n");   }
} catch(SQLException se){}
```

Creating our Sample Application

At this point, we have enough knowledge to begin creating our sample application using JavaBeans and JDBC. Before jumping straight into any code writing however, let's think through what functionality we would like the our application to address, and we should also set some development goals. Finally, as we are serving data to and from JSP's, we should handle as much processing as possible in the bean, itself as we don't want to be writing large amounts of scriptlet code in the JSP files.

What do we want it to do? Well, we need a way of connecting to the database and we need to be able to tell the server what SQL statements to run.

Looking into connecting to a database and then managing that connection, it is easy to envisage this as a standalone activity. It is also easy to see how a connection manager object can be reusable for other applications we may build in the future. We should therefore, consider a good object oriented approach and split the bean into 2 separate beans, one handling database connections and the other managing SQL activity. Once this decision has been made, we then know that we will have to address how to connect the beans, and some form of event generation and listening mechanism will have to be built.

As the SQL statements themselves should be user defined, our application must be able to set criteria for finding and updating the database. This immediately suggests using `PreparedStatements` and setting parameters either directly with property accessor methods, or via the `request` object. The same ideas can be used for the JSP to retrieve data. Anyone who has dealt with relational databases (or for that matter JSP), has had difficulty in tracing errors and debugging problems that occur at runtime. To make life easy for us in the future, we should build in some logging facilities to help us pinpoint any errors we come across. Since logging tends to be disk and processor intensive, we ought to have an on/off switch attached to it. And as we are talking about reusability, why not make any logging capability we create a generic process that can also be used by other apps?

As the web is becoming increasingly international, it would be useful to offer some form of definable text output that can be edited for different languages, or even for different applications.

The goals of any modern project should include object-oriented design aspects like reusability, flexibility, maintainability, and portability. We have already considered reusability by breaking the development up into 2 separate bean objects, and making our connection manager a standalone object which could be employed by other apps. Writing the code in Java will go a long way to delivering platform portability. Application portability, flexibility, and maintainability are all related: we will try to address these aspects of design using the tools and techniques provided by the Java Beans API.

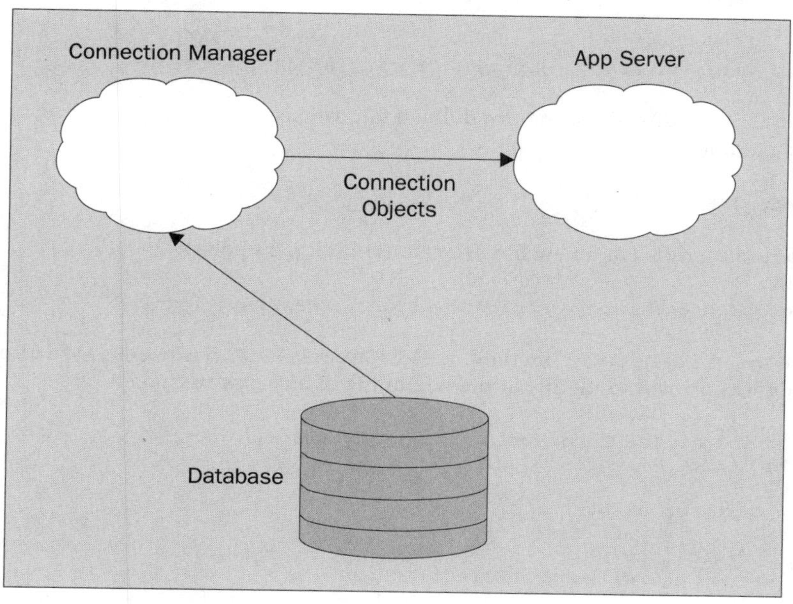

Logging the Application

Now we can begin to build the application. If we begin by creating logging capabilities, we can plug that ability straight into other beans as they are created. While logging is not really a substitute for a debugger, having some form of indication of what the application is doing should prove to be very useful, very few professional IDEs give much debugging capability for JSP development.

Our logger will output string data to a user-defined file; we must also create a default file name in case our user forgets to provide a filename. A set method will do the job:

```
public void setDebugFileName(String s){
  debugFile = s;
}

private String debugFile = "errors.log";
```

Now let's assume that on some occasions, we may want to place some data in a completely different file but carry on placing the bulk of the data into the `debugFile` property. No need to disappoint our user, we can achieve this with some simple overloading:

```
package com.wrox.projsp.ch06;

import java.io.*;
import java.util.Date;

public class DebugWriter {

  public void writeDebug(String s){
    writeDebug(s, debugFile);
  }

  public void writeDebug(String s, String sFile){
```

So if we want to write directly to the pre-defined file, we just use the `writeDebug()` method with only one `String` parameter:

```
writeDebug("Error");
```

but if we want to send this to a new file, we can use both parameters:

```
writeDebug("A completely separate error", "sepError.log");.
```

To complete the `writeDebug()` method, a `FileOutputStream` is needed. We also write the time the logging string was printed to the file at the beginning of any new message.

```
  public void writeDebug(String s, String sFile){
    FileOutputStream fos = null;
    try{
      //test for existence of file
      File f = new File(sFile);
      if (!f.exists()) {
        fos = new FileOutputStream( f );
      } else {
        //we want to append to the end of the file
        fos = new FileOutputStream( sFile, true);
      }
```

```
      s += "\n";
      //pre-pend a date time string
      fos.write((new Date( System.currentTimeMillis() ).toString() +
              " : " + s).getBytes() );
    } catch(Exception ex) {
      System.out.println("Error writing debug log in writeDebug : "+ex);
    } finally {
      try {
        fos.close();
      } catch(Exception ex){}
    }
  }
```

That's about it for our logger. To use it, all we have to do is instantiate it, give it a log file name and print our debugging messages through it:

```
DebugWriter debugger = new DebugWriter();
debugger. SetDebugFileName("OurDebugFile.log");
debugger.writeDebug( "Error at line 14");
```

Defining Constants

An interface offers a very simple solution to sharing `String` and `int` constants across different classes; it is much more effective than re-defining constants each time a new class is created. All a new class need do is implement the interface to make use of any of the interface fields. If for example, we are firing properties, each class can use a constant defined in the interface as a reference to the property name. This has three advantages:

- Firstly, we can change the value of the property right across the application by changing the text in one place; the interface.
- Secondly, we are not re-declaring the same variables in each class that needs to use the property.
- Thirdly, by using an interface constant, we can get some help from the compiler. If a typo is entered when writing out the property name as a string in one of the classes, the compiler can't help at all. However, if the typo is made when entering the constant name, the compiler will force its correction.

Here the interface is simply a list of constants:

```
package com.wrox.projsp.ch06;

public interface AppConstants {
  public static final String driverClass = "driverClass";
  public static final String connection = "connection";
  public static final String conError = "conError";
  public static final String paramBase = "param";
  public static final String userId = "UserId";
  public static final String password = "PassWd";
  public static final String selectType = "select";
}
```

Creating the Connection Manager

The Connection Manager is a bean that will control access to the various databases we wish to use, and pass connections onto other beans that need to work with a database. We've got a good idea what we need to do to put together this bean. A `Connection` needs a driver, a URL, a User Id and a Password. We can confidently assume that the URL and driver will change much less regularly than the User Id and Password. For those two properties then, we use 'set' type methods, and for the User Id and Password, we use HTTP request parameters. There is no hard and fast way of doing this; any combination of accessor methods and/or HTTP parameters should work just as well.

A little more complex to manage will be the export of any database connections once we've logged on. Our bean may have a long list of listening beans all waiting for connections in order to go about their specified tasks. If we define a `Connection` object as just another property of this bean, then the `PropertyChangeSupport` class can be used to send off information about database connections to those waiting classes. The `PropertyChangeSupport` and `DebugWriter` are both instantiated in the constructor, as they are required as class variables:

```
package com.wrox.projsp.ch06;

import java.io.*;
import java.util.*;
import java.beans.*;
import java.sql.*;

public class ConnectionManager implements AppConstants {
  /** The debug boolean - default is false */
  private boolean debug = false;
  protected Connection con;
  protected String driver;
  protected String passwd;
  protected String url;
  protected String user;
  protected DebugWriter writer;
  PropertyChangeSupport pcs;

  public ConnectionManager() {
    pcs = new PropertyChangeSupport(this);
    writer = new DebugWriter();
  }
```

When the `ConnectionManager` is informed of what driver to use, there is no reason why an attempt to load it should not be made immediately. We use the `PropertyChangeSupport` object to inform any of our listeners if an error has been made loading the driver. Note that the parameters for the `firePropertyChange()` method include the `driverClass` constant from the `AppConstants` interface as the name of the property, and the error message as the new value. It would also make sense to allow for a logging capability if the `debug` property is set to `true`:

```
  public void setDriverClass(String s) {
    driver = s;
    try {
      Class.forName( driver ).newInstance();
    } catch (Exception ex) {
      pcs.firePropertyChange(driverClass, null, ex);
      if (debug) {
        writer.writeDebug("Error setting driver: " + ex);
      }
    }
  }
```

We complete the `setXXX()` methods to enable setting of debug status and the database connection URL:

```
public void setConnectionUrl(String s) {
  url = s;
}

public void setDebug(String b) {
  debug = b.equals("true");
}
```

Then our `Connection` Manager needs some methods that other objects interested in any property change events it may fire out can hook up to and be informed:

```
public void addPropertyChangeListener(PropertyChangeListener l){
  pcs.addPropertyChangeListener( l );
}

public void removePropertyChangeListener(PropertyChangeListener l){
  pcs.removePropertyChangeListener( l );
}
```

If User Id and Password are to be passed as HTTP parameters, we need a method for retrieving that info from the HTTP request. Again, notice that the `user` and `passwd` variables are from `AppConstants`:

```
public void processRequest(HttpServletRequest req){
  user = req.getParameter(userId);
  passwd = req.getParameter(password);
  if (debug) {
    if (user == null || user.equals("") ) {
      writer.writeDebug("Empty user id parameter");
    }
    if (passwd == null || passwd.equals("") ) {
      writer.writeDebug("Empty password parameter");
    }
  }
}
```

All that now remains to be done to complete the `ConnectionManager` is to give it some instructions on how to log on to a database and then send the results to all interested listeners. No properties are set when running the logon method; it is assumed that this has already been done. If `debug` is set, the values that the driver uses to attempt a logon will be sent to the log file. On successful connection, a `PropertyChangeEvent` with a property name of the `AppConstants` string `connection`, and a new value of the `Connection` object, is fired to listeners. On failure, the property name will be the `AppConstants` string `conError`, with the `Exception` object in the new value.

```
public void logon() {
  try {
    con = DriverManager.getConnection( url, user, passwd );
    pcs.firePropertyChange(connection, null, con);
    if (debug) {
      writer.writeDebug("Connection succeded! URL: " + url +
        " Driver: " + driver + "  User: " + user + " Pwd: " + passwd);
    }
  } catch(Exception ex) {
    pcs.firePropertyChange( conError, null, ex);
```

```
      if (debug) {
        writer.writeDebug("Connection failed! URL: " + url +
          " Driver: " + driver + "  User: " + user + " Pwd: " + passwd +
          ex.getMessage());
      }
    }
  }
```

Ok! Our `ConnectionManager` class is ready for testing. We can use the `setConnectionUrl()` and `setDriverClass()` methods to set their respective properties, then pass User Id and Password as HTTP request parameters. Make sure any objects wanting database connections hookup via `addPropertyChangeListener()` and listen for a '`connection`' property. Whenever a logon attempt is to be made, all we then need to do is invoke the `logon()` method.

Building the Main Bean

Our final bean-building task is to create the bean that will transmit SQL data to and from the JSPs. This bean will have work between the JSP and the database passing information as required. It will also need to make use of the `ConnectionManager` to get the database connection. This means it has to be a `PropertyChangeListener` in order to be able to hook up to the `ConnectionManager` and pick up those connections as they are made. In the constructor, the `DebugWriter` is instantiated. Don't worry for the moment about the reference to the `currentLocale` and the `updateBundle()` call, as they will be discussed shortly. Let's create a class called `JspApp` as the main bean class:

```
package com.wrox.projsp.ch06;

import java.io.*;
import java.util.*;
import java.beans.*;
import java.sql.*;
import javax.servlet.http.*;
import javax.servlet.jsp.JspWriter;

public class JspApp implements PropertyChangeListener, AppConstants {
  public JspApp() {
    writer = new DebugWriter();
    //set the default locale and get its bundle text
    currentLocale = Locale.getDefault();
    updateBundle();
  }
```

If you remember, in order for a `PropertyChangeListener` to compile it has to implement the `propertyChange()` method. We need to know about database connections and handle them according to whether they or not were successful. When the `ConnectionManager` invokes this method by firing a property change, we can test what happened by checking the property name. If we get a successful connection, all that is needed is to set the local connection variable `con` so that it can be referenced at a later time. It would also be possible to provide the user with information on what is wrong with the database connection.

```
  public void propertyChange(PropertyChangeEvent evt) {
    String prop = evt.getPropertyName();

    //see if we got a connection
    if (prop.equals(connection)) {
      //ok so update the local connection
```

```
      try {
        //make sure it really is a connection
        con = (Connection)evt.getNewValue();
      } catch(Exception ex) {
        handleConError(ex);
      }
    } else if (prop.equals(conError)) {
      //no good connection
      try {
        if (debug) {
          handleConError( (Exception)evt.getNewValue() );
        }
      } catch(Exception ex) {
        //not an exception in the obj handle anyway
        if (debug) {
          handleConError( ex );
        }
      }
    }
  }

  protected void handleConError(Exception ex) {
    writer.writeDebug("Error connecting to database: "+ ex.getMessage() );
  }
```

Next, we need a way of adding the `ConnectionManager` and telling it we want to be informed of any property changes. This `public` method can be called by other objects (in our case, a JSP script) to give us a `ConnectionManager`. Before doing that, we remove any existing `ConnectionManagers` to avoid confusing the bean:

```
  public void setConnectionManager(ConnectionManager cm) {
    if (cm != null) {
      cm.removePropertyChangeListener( this );
      conMan = cm;
      cm.addPropertyChangeListener( this );
      if (debug) {
        writer.writeDebug("JspApp; Set connection manager "
                          + cm.toString());
      }
    } else {
      if (debug) {
        writer.writeDebug("JspAPP; Tried to set a null connection manager");
      }
    }
  }
```

We have to be able to pass information into the bean, so a number of `setXXX` methods are required. `setQueryType()` needs a little explanation. When we come to running a SQL statement, the server has to know whether this is a query or an update type. Remember that the `PreparedStatement` object uses different methods to perform these activities. Here we use an `AppConstants` field select to set the underlying `boolean` property. `setQueryType("select");` will mean that a query is run, whereas anything else will run an update:

```
    public void setQueryType(String s) {
      selectQuery = (s.equalsIgnoreCase(selectType) );
    }

  public void setSqlString(String s) {
    sql = s;
  }
```

Before attempting to run any queries, it would be useful to know if our JspApp bean has a current database connection. We can supply that information with a simple boolean method:

```
    public boolean isConnected() {
      return (con != null);
    }
```

In order for our app to run the SQL statements we give it, it will need to set the question mark parameters to any values a user may specify. If we envisage that a user will probably be entering values into an HTML form (which may or may not be combined with JSP commands), we then need to set up some naming framework for the HTML form items, which will have to extract HTTP request object parameters in a standard way. As with many other aspects of writing code, a large number of alternatives are available. For this example, we can use a naming convention for the parameters. If we name the first HTML form item as `param1`, the second as `param2`, the third as `param3` and so on, we can write some logic to set those parameters values to `PreparedStatement` parameters. As with other constant type names, we can define the core name in the `AppConstants` interface. The `processRequest()` method will provide the core functionality of the bean by handling the HTTP request. This is a large method, so we need to look at individual sections to understand what is happening:

```
    public void processRequest(HttpServletRequest req, JspWriter out) {
```

First thing to do is test if there is a SQL string to run. If not inform the user:

```
      if (sql == null || sql.equals("")) {
        try{
          out.write( bundle.getString( "NoSQL") );
        } catch(Exception ex){
          //don't need to send to debug msg - obvious
          return;
        }
      }
      PreparedStatement ps = null;
      try {
        ps = con.prepareStatement(sql);
      } catch(Exception ex) {
        if (debug) {
          handleException(ex);
        }
        return;
      }
```

Once we are sure there is a SQL statement to run and that the string has been prepared, we can then try to extract the parameter values from the request object. As we don't know how many parameters there are likely to be, we need a while loop which will continue as long as there are still parameters in the format `param1`, `param2`, etc. As each parameter is retrieved it will be set as the next parameter for the `PreparedStatement`.

```
      //now try to set the sql parameters with the req params
      int count = 0;
      String sqlParam, paramValue;
      boolean set = true;
      while (set) {
        count++;
        sqlParam = paramBase + String.valueOf( count );
        if (sqlParam == null) {
          set = false;
          continue;
        }
        paramValue = req.getParameter( sqlParam );
        if (paramValue == null){
          set = false;
          continue;
        } else {
          //clean any excess spaces
          paramValue = paramValue.trim();
        }
        try {
          ps.setString( count, paramValue );
        } catch(Exception ex) {
          //handle ex
          set = false;
          continue;
        }
      }
```

If we get this far, the `PreparedStatement` is ready to be run. The value of the `boolean` `selectQuery` will determine whether a query or an update will be run. If a query has been selected, the `ResultSet` from the database will be handled by the `updateResults()` method. For an update, the number of database records that are stored are placed in the `edited` variable. Errors can be handled by the `handleException()` method, which tests for error type and handles it accordingly.

```
      //run the sql
      try {
        if (selectQuery) {
          ResultSet rs = ps.executeQuery();
          updateResults( rs );
        } else {
          //store number of records changed in edited var

          //reset the edited so that -1 is stored in case of error
          edited = -1;
          //then set edited to new number
          edited = ps.executeUpdate();
        }
      } catch(Exception ex) {
        if (debug) {
          handleException(ex);
        }
      }
    }
```

If `processRequest()` completes successfully for a query type SQL statement, the result set is handled by the `updateResults()` method, which takes the first row of the results set and places the data into the `resultsVector` variable. This `Vector` will be used later so that a JSP document can request query values. An `int` value `resultElement` will be used to track the current object to deliver.

A better option here would be to make use of a queue type data structure. The JGL class library (available from http://www.objectspace.com*) contains some very powerful data management objects.*

One last detail. We need to know how many columns there are in the result set. As the SQL statement is set at runtime, there is no way we can know this in advance. The `ResultSetMetaData` object, returned by the `ResultSet` itself, supplies the information.

```
private void updateResults(ResultSet rs) {
  //reset the vector and its tracker element
  resultElement = 0;
  resultsVector.removeAllElements();
  try {
    ResultSetMetaData rsmd = rs.getMetaData();
    int count = rsmd.getColumnCount();
    while (rs.next() ){
      for (int i=0; i <= count ; i++)
      resultsVector.addElement( rs.getString( i+1 ) );

      //only handle the first row - ignore any other data
      //if using jdk1.2 - use the following lines
      //if (rs.isFirst() )
      //break;
      //if using jdk1.1 we've got first data so just break
      break;
    }
  }
  catch(Exception ex) {
    if (debug) {
      handleException(ex);
    }
  }
}
```

The easiest and most generic way to get the results of a SQL query to a JSP document is to provide a method that returns each column value in sequence. Each time the `getNext()` method is invoked, it moves on to the next column until there are no more columns to return. The returned strings are wrapped in double quotes. This is necessary for specific types of HTML form item. Without quotations, strings tend to break at the first space. For example, a string `"hello there"` typically only shows '`hello`' if not contained within the double quotes. When there are no more results, a blank string is returned.

```
public String getNext(){
  try {
    //wrap the result as a string
    //result element will be incremented for next use
    String result = (String)resultsVector.elementAt(resultElement++);
    result = (result == null) ? "" : result;
    return "\"" + result + "\"";
  } catch(Exception ex) {
    if (debug) {
      writer.writeDebug("Error getting data at " +
        String.valueOf( resultElement) +
        " in resultsVector: " + ex.getMessage() );
    }
    return "";
  }
}
```

Our bean is now ready for use, but before continuing and creating the JSP scripts to use the beans, how about considering a little refinement. As direct output of text to users will occur and I said it would be a good idea to allow text customization, let's take a quick look at how Java can helps us.

Customizing Textual Output

Since the JDK 1.1 release, a number of techniques have been included in the standard API libraries that can be used for the customization of textual output depending on factors such Locales. A `Locale` is an object defined in the `java.util` package that represents geographical political or cultural regions, and can be used to format data when presented to users in a way that they will understand it better.

Currency and date strings are good examples. Where an American may see a currency as $3,909.99, the correct format for a German user would be DM3.909,99. Formatting is handled by classes in the `java.text` package, such as `NumberFormat` and `DateFormat`, in combination with the `Locale` object.

Our bean is not yet going to offer that capability, but it will offer the ability to change certain text strings based on Locale and, if required, on application. To do this, it will read text strings from a property file, which will then be used to populate a `ResourceBundle`. The bundle in turn will be used to send text to the user application. Our bean is going to use the `PropertyResourceBundle` class to hold the external text. `PropertyResourceBundles` are loaded from property files that are just like any other property file, combining a name with a value. The file used for this example, `JspAppBundle.properties`, looks like this:

```
Logon=Logged on to Database
LogonFail=Logon Failed - Try Again!
NoSQL=SQL String not set or null
editedUpdate= Records
editedNone=No Records Changed
```

When the bundle is loaded, and we request the text for the 'Logon' property, '`Logged on to Database`' will be returned. `JspAppBundle.properties` is just an ASCII file. Any text editor like Notepad, vi, emacs, etc. can be used to change the value the user will see.

Bundles are not only used to store external text but also to select the correct text for a specific Locale. The Locale constructor contains up to 3 strings that it uses to uniquely define itself. The first string represents the language, the second the country and the third the variant. The English language is represented by '`en`', French by '`fr`', German by '`de`' and so on. Countries also have their own strings; '`US`' for the United States, '`GB`' for the United Kingdom, '`ES`' for Spain and so on. Variants are used to define subsets of groupings of the first 2 items. These strings are based on the ISO standards, and more complete lists and pointers to more information can be found the Java online documentation.

Bundle naming can be based on the strings that make up a Locale. For example, if we create a bundle for the French language, we would name the bundle `JspAppBundle_fr.properties`. A bundle for French Canadian would be called `JspAppBundle_fr_CA.properties`. When looking to load a bundle, Java starts at the most specific level for a given Locale and works up until it finds the most relevant properties file. If nothing is found, the default file is selected, in our case `JspAppBundle.properties`.

For our bean, we would like to be able to reset the Locale and then load the relevant text bundle for that Locale so that the correct text for the language can be used. The `setLocale()` method can manage the `currentLocale` variable, and then get `updateBundle()` to do the rest of the work:

```
public void setLocale(Locale loc) {
  currentLocale = loc;
  updateBundle();
}

private void updateBundle() {
  //get the bundle
  try {
    bundle = PropertyResourceBundle.getBundle(defaultBundle,
                                              currentLocale);
  } catch(Exception ex) {
    if (debug) {
      writer.writeDebug("Error getting bundle " + ex.getMessage() );
    }
  }
}
```

If we then want to give our user some information in their own language, we just query the bundle. For example, to show a connection status:

```
public String getConStatus() {
  if (isConnected()) {
    return bundle.getString( "Logon" );
  } else {
    return bundle.getString( "LogonFail" );
  }
}
```

While this example looks at providing different text for different languages, there is no reason why core bundle files cannot be different for each application. Alternatively, a `setBundle()` type method could be used to tell the bean to look for a specific bundle file at runtime.

Creating the JSP Documents

Now that we have the beans, we can create some applications using standard HTML and JSP documents. If we want to create the Customer Services Representative example mentioned at the start of this chapter, we need to picture a basic workflow for the rep:

- Logon to the Database
- Select a Customer from a List
- Run a Query on the Customer to Access the Details

Then we need to look at implementing each aspect.

Managing Database Logon

While there are many techniques that can be employed to create an interesting logon box to a user, here we will content ourselves with a basic HTML form that contains a text field and a hidden field to allow users to enter a User Id and Password – see the figure below:

Please Logon

User Id	admin
Password	*****

Logon

The form tag should send the output to `logonCustomer.jsp`, which we are now going to create:

```
<FORM ACTION="logonCustomer.jsp" METHOD="POST"
 ENCTYPE="application/x-www-form-urlencoded">
```

`logonCustomer.jsp` creates a drop down list of customers, with **Submit** and **Reset** buttons as shown back at the beginning of the chapter. It is worth noting that the data in the drop down is entered manually. It would not be too difficult a process to extend our bean to also offer List and Combo population functionality using columns from a database.

The `ConnectionManager` and `JspApp` beans have to be found or instantiated, and the scope set to session. Once ready, the `ConnectionManager` will require a JDBC driver and a connection URL. We use the property setter methods to do that:

```
<HTML>

<jsp:useBean id="con" scope="session" class="ConnectionManager" />
<jsp:useBean id = "app" scope="session" class="JspApp" />
<jsp:setProperty name="con" property="driverClass"
 value="sun.jdbc.odbc.JdbcOdbcDriver" />
<jsp:setProperty name="con" property="connectionUrl"
 value="Jdbc:Odbc:Sales" />
```

If debug output would be helpful, we can also set it at the start of the document:

```
<jsp:setProperty name="con" property="debug" value="true" />
```

A few scriptlet lines complete the logon process. The `JspApp` bean needs to listen for database connection details, so add it as a property change listener using the `setConnectionManager()` method we created earlier. The User Id and Password can then be accessed when the HTTP request is processed, and our `ConnectionManager` can proceed to logon to the database, informing the `JspApp` of the outcome.

```
<%
   app.setConnectionManager( con );
   con.processRequest(request);
   con.logon();
%>
```

What happens next is dependent on the results of the logon process. If our JspApp bean has picked up a successful connection, just include the drop down list (Customer.html), otherwise loop the user back to a cut down version of the original logon form.

```
<% if (app.isConnected() ) {  %>
     <P> <%@ include file ="Customer.html" %>
<% } else { %>
          <%@ include file ="LogonCustomerAgain.html" %>
<% } %>
```

Selecting the Customer

At this stage, we want our rep to be able to select a Customer, and then present the details of that customer in another HTML form when the **Submit** button is pressed. To do this we'll use custDetails.jsp, which can be called by the Customer.html form tag action:

```
<FORM ACTION="custDetails.jsp" METHOD="POST"
 ENCTYPE="application/x-www-form-urlencoded">
```

This will post the value selected in the drop down to custDetails.jsp. If you remember, it was decided to use a naming framework for the parameters that are to be passed to the SQL statement. Here, only the customer name will be used as a parameter in the search query:

```
<SELECT NAME="param1" SIZE="6">
```

Populating the HTML Form with SQL Data

To retrieve the required customer details data and populate the HTML, we have to inform the JspApp bean of what SQL statement is to be run. It also needs to know whether to run a select or update statement. Therefore, add these instructions to the start of to custDetails.jsp:

```
<HTML>

<jsp:useBean id = "app" scope="session" class="JspApp" />
<jsp:setProperty name="app" property="queryType" value="select" />
<jsp:setProperty name="app" property="sqlString"
 value="SELECT NameofCustomer, ContactName, TelNo, Add1, Add2, Add3, Email,
 Industry FROM Customer WHERE NameofCustomer = ?" />
```

Then process the HTTP request to run the SQL query. At the same time, hand the JspPrintWriter to the method. This can be used output any error messages directly to the user.

```
<% app.processRequest(request, out); %>
```

Each item retrieved by the SQL call can then be placed in an HTML text field in turn, by invoking the getNext() method in JspApp. Repeat the following process for each item that requires data population.

```
<TR>
  <TD WIDTH="26%">Customer</TD>
  <TD WIDTH="74%"><INPUT TYPE="TEXT" NAME="Customer" SIZE="40"
  VALUE=<jsp:getProperty name="app" property="next" /> >
  </TD>
</TR>
<TR>
  <TD WIDTH="26%">Contact</TD>
  <TD WIDTH="74%"><INPUT TYPE="TEXT" NAME="Contact" SIZE="40"
  VALUE=<jsp:getProperty name="app" property="next" /> >
  </TD>
</TR>

...
```

Preparing the Server

The only remaining task is to place the files in the correct directories on the JSP Engine. (All the required files, including a Microsoft Access database, are included with the code download for this chapter.) If you are using the Access database, don't forget to set up the ODBC DSN.

A Registration Form Example

If a further example is needed and we want to test the flexibility of our beans, we can quickly put together a Registration Form. Here, we'll use the `JspApp` class to insert that data into a database table. The user workflow is:

- Logon
- Complete Registration Form
- Get Confirmation

For the first 2 items, very little work needs to be done: we can just about copy what was done in the last example. There are only a couple of differences. Our logon HTML file Form Action has to point to `logonRegister.jsp`:

```
<FORM ACTION="logonRegister.jsp" METHOD="POST"
 ENCTYPE="application/x-www-form-urlencoded">
```

`logonRegister.jsp` is exactly the same as `logonCustomer.jsp`, except that a successful logon sends us to a different HTML file:

```
<% if (app.isConnected() ) {  %>
      <%@ include file ="Signup.html" %>
<% } else { %>
      <%@ include file ="LogonRegisterAgain.html" %>
<% } %>
```

`Signup.html` is simply an HTML form with name, address etc. fields for a user to complete, as shown below:

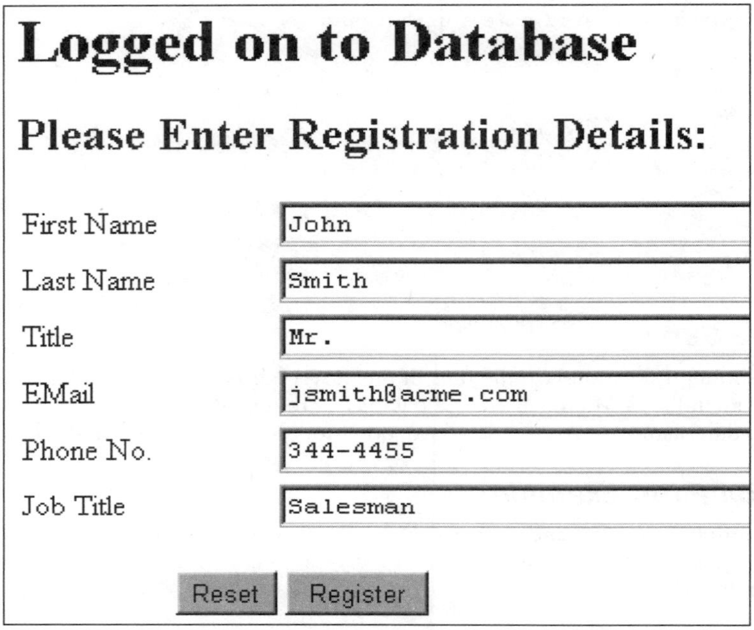

Logged on to Database

Please Enter Registration Details:

First Name John
Last Name Smith
Title Mr.
EMail jsmith@acme.com
Phone No. 344-4455
Job Title Salesman

Reset Register

To use this form with our `JspApp` bean, again only a couple of things need to be done. First point the form to `registered.jsp`:

```
<FORM ACTION="registered.jsp" METHOD="POST"
 ENCTYPE="application/x-www-form-urlencoded">
```

Secondly, we have to get hold of what the user has entered in order to insert it into the database. As this will come in the HTTP request object as parameters, we have to use our naming framework for the names of the textfields in the HTML file; param1, param2 and so on:

```
<TR>
  <TD WIDTH="29%">First Name</TD>
  <TD WIDTH="71%"><INPUT TYPE="TEXT" NAME="param1" SIZE="37"></TD>
</TR>
<TR>
  <TD WIDTH="29%">Last Name</TD>
  <TD WIDTH="71%"><INPUT TYPE="TEXT" NAME="param2" SIZE="37"></TD>
</TR>

...
```

That was easy! The only real work comes in defining the JSP document that will put that data into the database and inform users of the status. This is not really as difficult as it sounds. It can be achieved in a few lines in `registered.jsp`. As before, use the `JspApp` bean and give it a SQL statement to run. However, this time we are not running a query, we are inserting data. Tell the `JspApp` bean by setting the `queryType` property to `'insert'`. Then process the request:

```
<HTML>

<jsp:useBean id="app" scope="session" class="JspApp" />
<jsp:setProperty name="app" property="queryType" value="insert" />
<jsp:setProperty name="app" property="sqlString"
 value="INSERT INTO Registration ( FName, LName, Title, EMail, PhoneNo,
 JobTitle ) values (?,?,?,?,?,?)" />

<% app.processRequest(request, out); %>
```

To give our user some feedback on what happened, we can output one of the text bundle strings from `JspAppBundle.properties`. Use the `updatedString` property to get those details.

```
<H2><FONT COLOR="#000099"><jsp:getProperty name="app"
 property="updatedString" /> </FONT></H2>
```

That seems fairly flexible! Once the basic concepts are established, there really is not much work involved in creating new applications. If you want to try this out, the `Registration` table is in the included Access database. No new files need to be added to the class directory.

Possible Enhancements

We now have a functioning application that can provide data from SQL databases to JSP documents and vice-versa. While this is already a very useful tool, what are the other things we may like it to do? Once you get started on wish lists, the problem is stopping them! However, a number of ideas are fairly self-evident. Currently, our `JspApp` bean only handles string (or char/varchar columns in database talk) data. Any self-respecting database connection bean would also have to take care of dates and numbers, at the very least. As soon as dates and numbers are added, there will then be a requirement to localize that data, so that, for example, a user sees the date in the expected format. The best way to achieve that would probably to create a whole new bean class dedicated solely to presentation.

Another shortcoming is that when a database query is performed, only one row of data is returned. The rest is thrown away. Users generally want a list type selection of database results, which can form a basis for a drill down. To achieve this, a grid or table type component is required. The query results would have to populate an HTML table.

Once a table component is added, we can see that other types of component are also necessary; list boxes, combos, checkboxes, and radio buttons.

The beauty of object oriented coding in Java is that all these requests are possible. Extending any of the classes that have been written should not prove problematical. If we need to create new beans to address requests for additional functionality, we can easily make use of the Java Beans standard to link them to our existing work.

Summary

In this chapter, we have looked at the JavaBeans component architecture and how to create beans. Having had a quick look at JDBC, we went on to create some JavaBeans for accessing databases from within JSPs.

Within our web applications, we need to be able to store beans, so that they can be used by multiple JSP pages requested by the same user. This is **session management**, and we'll look at it in the next chapter.

J2EE
JSP

5

JSP Sessions

The Hyper Text Transfer Protocol (HTTP) is a stateless protocol. We take a more in-depth look at the HTTP protocol in Appendix D, but it is important to know what this statement actually means in order to understand why we need server-side sessions at all.

HTTP is the network protocol used to deliver resources on the web to the client, whether they're HTML files, image files, dynamically generated query results, the output of a servlet or JSP, or any CGI scripts. HTTP is a communication protocol that allows a server and client to understand each other, assuming an underlying TCP/IP connection. A good analogy is two people talking on the telephone, where the conversation is like HTTP and the telephone connection is like TCP/IP.

Like most network protocols, HTTP uses the client-server model: an HTTP client connects to the server over TCP/IP and sends a request message to the HTTP server. The server then returns a response message, usually containing the resource that was requested. After delivering the response, the server can close the connection, as the server's work is done – the conversation is over, the question has been answered. It treats the next request as independent from any previous request, and serves the requested resource. HTTP is therefore a stateless protocol.

In this chapter, we'll review the support Java provides to support state between the client and the server. Specifically we'll introduce:

- How HTTP works, including network optimizations like 'Keep-alive'
- Using hidden fields, cookies, and URL-rewriting to identify the client to the server
- Session support and lifecycle in JSP and servlets
- Contexts, and the way they declare an object's scope and how it interacts with sessions
- How to listen for session events
- Sessions and secure connections

A Sample HTTP Exchange

To retrieve `HelloWorld.jsp` at the URL http://www.somehost.com/path/HelloWorld.jsp, the client first opens a TCP/IP socket to the host www.somehost.com on port 80. Then, it communicates with the server over HTTP by sending something like the following over the socket:

```
GET /path/HelloWorld.jsp HTTP/1.0
User-Agent: Mozilla/4.0
[some other HTTP headers here ]
[a blank line here]
```

The server should respond with a header and the requested resource, something like the following, sent back over the same socket:

```
HTTP/1.0 200 OK
Date: Fri, 31 Dec 1999 23:59:59 GMT
Content-Type: text/html
Content-Length: 1354

<html>
<body>
<h1> Hello World </h1>
</body>
</html>
```

After sending the response, the server closes the socket.

Persistent Connections

In HTTP 1.0 and earlier versions, TCP connections are closed after each request and response, so each resource to be retrieved requires its own connection. Opening and closing TCP connections takes a substantial amount of CPU time, bandwidth, and memory. In practice, most Web pages consist of several files on the same server so time and resources can be saved by allowing several requests and responses to be sent through a single persistent connection, a concept introduced with HTTP 1.0 but made the default behavior in HTTP 1.1.

A further optimization is made by browsers, which store a copy of the resource locally in the cache once it is retrieved. Although the exact caching algorithm is browser specific, the browser basically compares the cache with the copy on the server and will use the cached copy rather than downloading the same file again if they're identical.

So if everyone uses persistent socket connections then how exactly is HTTP stateless? The answer is simple. Persistent connections are there only for network optimization and are transparent to the HTTP protocol. A server can close the connection at any time and it is the browser's responsibility to recover from this, and open a new connection.

The key to building effective web-based applications, therefore, lies in being able to identify a series of requests from a remote client as being from the same client.

For example, consider a common three-step user interaction with a web site:

- The user browses a catalog on a web site, and chooses something from it to put in the shopping basket
- The user continues to use other tools and utilities on the site
- The user decides to complete the order selected in the first step

The application needs to uniquely identify that client from 10000 simultaneous users of the site when this particular user decides to go to the third step, and also needs to know which items were chosen earlier by this user.

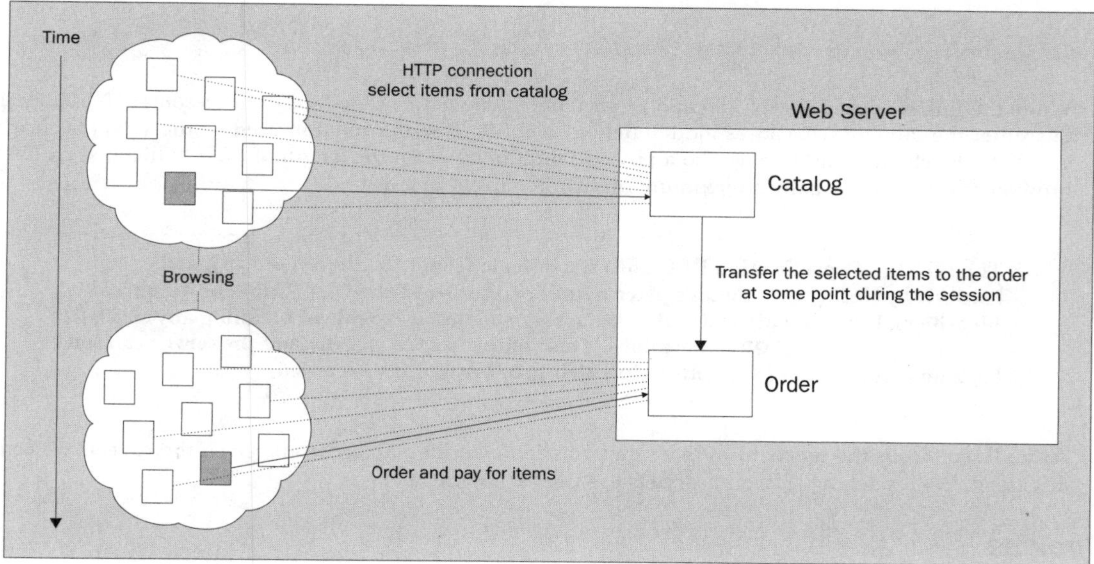

Techniques for Maintaining User Information across Pages

The idea of maintaining state between different requests is known as **session tracking**. JSP and servlets may be new, but session tracking is not. Here are some of the techniques used in web applications. We'll see how they apply to Java in the rest of the chapter.

HTTP Information

This included trapping HTTP headers, like the email header and the IP information. The technique quickly became obsolete with the sprouting of proxy servers and privacy issues.

Hidden Fields

This method is still popular and uses the HTML `HIDDEN` tag to embed information in each page:

```
<INPUT TYPE = HIDDEN NAME="MYKEY" VALUE="MYVALUE">
```

However this requires each page to be generated and a complex sequence mapping mechanism between page flows. This technique is also prone to security problems since all information is visible to the user with a simple View | Source in the browser.

Extended Path Info and URL-rewriting

This involves appending identification information to the end of every link on the page and uses the PATH-INFO header to extract it. For example, a normal link like:

```
<a href="/mypage.jsp"> Next </a>
```

would be modified to:

```
<a href="/mypage.jsp?login=james&item=book1"> Next </a>
```

When the link is clicked the login and item name-value pairs are passed to the resource. Not only does this suffer the same drawbacks as hidden fields – identification information used by the server is clearly visible to the client – but there is also a physical limit in bytes on the length of a URL, dictated by the browser and server. (Usually a maximum of 2Kb in current browsers.)

> **The HTTP 1.1 specification RFC 2616 is available from http://www.w3.org and http://www.ietf.org. It doesn't place a limit on the size of the URI (Uniform Resource Identifier), but explicitly states that the server should be capable of handling any size URIs if they support HTTP GET operations. This value is server specific and the server can send back an error code, 414 (Requested URI too long), if it's exceeded.**

As we'll see, this is the mechanism that's guaranteed to work on all browsers, given the caveats we've just discussed. We'll see how JSPs and servlets use this technique later.

Cookies

Cookies are small pieces of information deposited on the client by the server. A server, when returning an HTTP resource to a client, may also send a cookie containing some state information, which the client will then store. Included in that state information is a description of the range of URLs for which that state is valid. Any future HTTP requests made by the client, which fall in that range of URLs, will include a transmission of the current value of the cookie from the client back to the server.

> **Cookies were originally specified by Netscape (http://home.netscape.com/newsref/std/cookie_spec.html), but are now part of an Internet standard (RFC 2109, the HTTP State Management Mechanism).**

A cookie is introduced to the client by including a Set-Cookie HTTP header as part of an HTTP response:

```
Set-Cookie: NAME=VALUE; expires=DATE; path=PATH; domain=DOMAIN_NAME; secure
```

where the *NAME=VALUE* is a name-value pair containing the information and `expires=DATE` specifies a date string that defines the valid lifetime of that cookie. Consider the earlier example where a client requests a resource on the server and receives this in the response:

```
Set-Cookie: CUSTOMER=JAMES_M;
            path=/;
            expires=Wednesday, 09-Nov-99 23:12:40 GMT
```

This is stored in the browser in one of two ways depending on its age.

- If the cookie has a well-defined age, it is either written to a permanent storage (that is, appended to the `cookies.txt` file in Netscape Navigator or stored as an individual text file in the Temporary Internet Files directory for Internet Explorer)
- If the cookie is not assigned a particular age, it is stored in memory while the browser program is running. Once the browser is closed the cookie is lost. This type of cookie tracks a user session.

In both cases when the client requests any other resource on the server, a part of the request includes an HTTP header containing details of the cookie, which can be parsed by the server:

```
Cookie: CUSTOMER=JAMES_M
```

The servlet API has a `javax.servlet.http.Cookie` class that allows server applications to set cookies from JSP in order to maintain state:

```
Cookie uid = new Cookie("uid","112kkjk222kjj989c");
response.addCookie(uid);
```

There are two drawbacks to cookies:

- Users can choose not to accept them. This is really related to privacy issues. With the increased use of cookies to store and pass information between groups and associated vendors, people are becoming more sensitive to cookies and declining to accept them.
- The browser may not work with cookies. Almost all current web browsers, however, accept cookies.

Cookies are harmless and can greatly improve the user experience when used appropriately. People who don't accept cookies should be treated as the special case, not vice-versa.

A good example of cookies in action is where they are used to store an encrypted database key on the client. The next time the browser sends a request to the same web site, it includes the cookie. The server can then uses the cookie value to retrieve the appropriate information (for example, personalized home page, previous ordering history) from a database table

It is important to remember that cookies have a size limitation in terms of the total bytes per cookie (usually 4 Kb), and number of cookies per domain that can be stored in a browser (no more than 20 cookies from a particular domain).

Working with Cookies and Java

Developing applications that use cookies is simple in Java because of the object-based abstraction that the `javax.servlet.http.Cookie` class provides.

Here are the public methods in the `javax.servlet.http.Cookie` class that can be used from servlets or JSPs.

Method	Description
`Object clone()`	Overrides the standard `java.lang.Object.clone()` method to return a copy of this cookie.
`void setComment (String purpose)`	Set a comment that describes a cookie's purpose.
`String getComment()`	Returns the comment, or `null` if there is no comment.
`void setDomain (String pattern)`	Set the domain, the URLs for which this cookie should be presented to the server as part of any request.
`String getDomain()`	Returns the domain name for this cookie.
`void setMaxAge (int expiry)`	Set the maximum age of the cookie in seconds. A default return value of `-1` indicates that the cookie will last until the browser shutdowns.
`int getMaxAge()`	Returns the maximum age of the cookie in seconds.
`String getName()`	Returns the name of the cookie.
`void setPath (String uri)`	Set a path on the server to which the client should return the cookie.
`String getPath()`	Returns the path on the server to which the browser returns this cookie.
`void setSecure (boolean flag)`	Indicates to the browser whether the cookie should only be sent using a secure protocol, such as HTTPS or SSL.
`boolean getSecure()`	Returns `true` if the browser only sends the cookie over a secure protocol, or `false` if the browser can use a standard protocol.
`void setValue (String newValue)`	Set a value for the cookie.
`String getValue()`	Returns the value of the cookie.
`void setVersion(int v)`	Set the version of the cookie protocol.
`int getVersion()`	Returns the version of the protocol with which the cookie complies.

The example below illustrates how to use cookies in a JSP to print the last time the user visited that page.

```
<%@ page language="java" import="java.text.DateFormat,java.util.Date" %>

<%
  boolean found = false;
  Cookie info = null;
  String msg = "This is the first time you've visited this page.";

  // Get all the cookies that came with the request
  Cookie[] cookies = request.getCookies();

  for(int i = 0; i < cookies.length; i++) {
    info = cookies[i];
    if (info.getName().equals("MyCookie")) {
      found = true;
      break;
    }
  }

  String newValue = "" + System.currentTimeMillis();

  if (!found) {
    // Create a new Cookie and set its age.
    info = new Cookie("MyCookie", newValue );
    info.setMaxAge(60*1);
    info.setPath("/");

    response.addCookie(info);
  } else {
    long conv = new Long(info.getValue()).longValue();
    msg = "You last visited this site on " + new Date(conv);

    // Set the new value of the cookie, and add it to the response
    info.setValue(newValue);
    info.setMaxAge(10*24*60*60); // keep the cookie for 1 month.

    // Set the path so that the cookie is available everythere on the server
    info.setPath("/");
    response.addCookie(info);
  }
%>

<html>
<body>

<h2><%= msg %></h2>
<h2> Current system date is <%= new Date().toString() %> </h2>

</body>
</html>
```

In the JSP code, we use the `request.getCookies()` method to retrieve the cookies that have been sent as part of the request. Unfortunately, there's no method to extract a named cookie, so we need to iterate over the array of cookies searching for `MyCookie`. If there's no such cookie (it's the first time we've visited the page, or it's over a month since we were last there) we create a new one, otherwise we update the cookie and display the last time we visited and the current time.

In a practical application, cookie-handling code would be packed into a bean so that other JSPs can reuse the code.

In summary, simple applications frequently use a combination of hidden fields and cookies. The major problems with these two approaches are:

- The security of any information you store in plain text
- Clients not accepting cookies for reasons of privacy

One last point is that these techniques prove very useful when JSP and servlets are not the only server-side technology in use, but where information has to be shared.

Sessions

The noticeable fact among all the session-tracking mechanisms that we've seen so far is that they rely on plain text to store state. It hardly fits with the object-oriented paradigm and modeling a complex object-oriented business application would be hard within these constraints.

Consider the example of an ordering system. After analysis, you come up with a set of objects (an `Item`, a `Catalog`, an `Order` class, for example). It's clearly impossible to store a `java.util.Vector` object containing a set of `Item` objects in a cookie. A more robust, secure, and object-based mechanism is needed, which should interface cleanly to the web application code that generates the dynamic pages.

So What is a Session?

To recap, a session can be defined as a series of related interactions between a single client and the server, which take place over a period of time. In terms of objects, a session can be thought of as an object, resident and exposed to applications on the server (servlets and JSPs), that can be used for storing and retrieving objects.

Once a session object is created on the server, a unique identifier called a **session ID** is associated with it and this ID is the only information that is given to the client (by one of the mechanisms we saw in the last section).

Every time the client accesses a resource on the server, the client provides the session ID that it was assigned. Using this session ID, servlets can obtain the associated session object and retrieve any stored information. The simplest analogy would be to imagine a big hash table of hash tables living on the server with strings (session IDs) as keys. The key is mapped to a hash table that is created for a client, as shown in the following figure.

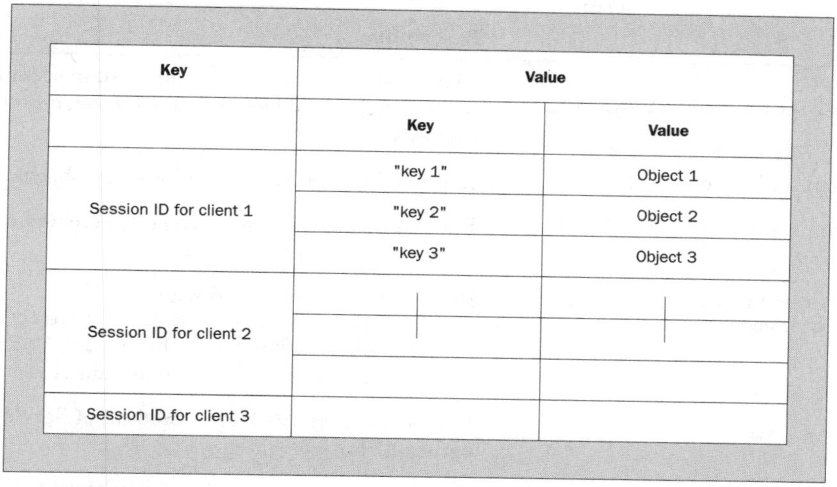

Key	Value	
	Key	Value
Session ID for client 1	"key 1"	Object 1
	"key 2"	Object 2
	"key 3"	Object 3
Session ID for client 2		
Session ID for client 3		

Two things should be noted:

- Since a session ID is generated by the server it will physically look quite different from server to server. (For example a BEA WebLogic session ID will be different from Tomcat's.)
- It is important to know that a session has a one-to-one association between a client and the server. That is, if a user is visiting a site that uses many servlets or JSPs and JavaBeans, there will be one session ID and one session that is shared among all of these resources.

Servlet Support for Sessions and Session Lifecycle

The Servlet API provides the `javax.servlet.http.HttpSession` interface and it is left to the servlet container to provide the implementation that represents the server's view of the session.

Some of the methods that this object must support are:

Method	Description
`long getCreationTime()`	Returns the time when this session was created, measured in milliseconds since midnight January 1, 1970 GMT or UTC. For example, 954131730850 for March 26 2000, 23:41:25
`String getId()`	Returns a string containing the unique identifier assigned to this session.
`long getLastAccessedTime()`	Returns the last time the client sent a request associated with this session, as the number of milliseconds since midnight January 1, 1970 GMT UTC.
`void setMaxInactiveInterval (int interval)`	Specifies the maximum length of time, in seconds, that the servlet engine keeps this session open if no user requests have been made of the session.

Table continued on following page

Method	Description
`int getMaxInactiveInterval()`	Returns the maximum time interval, in seconds, that the servlet engine will keep this session open between client requests.
`void invalidate()`	Expires this session and unbinds any objects bound to it.
`boolean isNew()`	Returns `true` if the web server has created a session but the client has not yet joined.
`Object getAttribute (String name)`	Returns the object bound with the `setAttribute(String name, Object value)` method and associated with the specified *name* in this session, `null` if no object of that name exists. Replaces the `getValue()` method of Servlet 2.1 and earlier APIs.
`String[] getAttributeNames()`	Returns an array containing the names of all the objects bound to this session. Replaces the deprecated `getValueNames()` in earlier APIs.
`void setAttribute (String name,Object value)`	Binds an object to this session, using the name specified. Replaces the deprecated `putValue()` method.
`void removeAttribute (String name)`	Removes the object bound with the specified name from this session. Replaces the `removeValue()` method of Servlet 2.1 and earlier APIs.

JSPs and servlets store the session ID on the client either by sending a cookie (the default mechanism) or by URL-rewriting. URL-rewriting involves appending the session ID to each link on the page.

More on URL Rewriting

In order to support URL rewriting you should avoid writing a URL straight to the output stream from the JSP or servlet and use the `HttpServletResponse.encodeURL()` method instead. This method does two things; it determines if the URL needs to be rewritten, and if so, it rewrites it, by including the session ID in the URL. For example,

```
<a href="/mydir/mypage.jsp">Click here </a>
```

should instead be coded as:

```
<a href=<%=response.encodeURL("/mydir/mypage.jsp") %> > Click here </a>
```

In addition you will also need to encode URLs that send redirects, for example,

```
response.sendRedirect("/mydir/mypage.jsp")
```

should instead be coded as:

```
response.sendRedirect(response.encodeRedirectUrl("/mydir/mypage.jsp"));
```

As an example of this in action, the WebLogic application server sends http://www.myserver.com:7001/mydir/mypage.jsp?AppId=*some_long_string_of_characters* to the client instead of http://www.myserver.com:7001/mydir/mypage.jsp. The name AppId in the URL above is configurable on the server.

Session Lifecycle

The `HTTPServletRequest` interface contains certain methods that are useful when using sessions.

Method	Description
`HttpSession getSession()`	Returns the current session associated with this request, or if the request does not have a session, creates one.
`HttpSession getSession(boolean create)`	Returns the current `HttpSession` associated with this request or, if `create` is `true`, creates a new session for the request.
`boolean isRequestedSessionIdFromCookie()`	Checks whether the session ID this request submitted came in as a cookie, if it does, it returns `true`.
`boolean isRequestedSessionIdFromUrl()`	Checks whether the session ID this request submitted came in as part of the request URL, if it does, it returns `true`.
	Replaces the deprecated method of the same name that ends `URL` instead of `Url`.
`boolean isRequestedSessionIdValid()`	Checks whether this request has a valid session associated with it, if it does, it returns `true`.

The figure overleaf illustrates the lifecycle of a session.

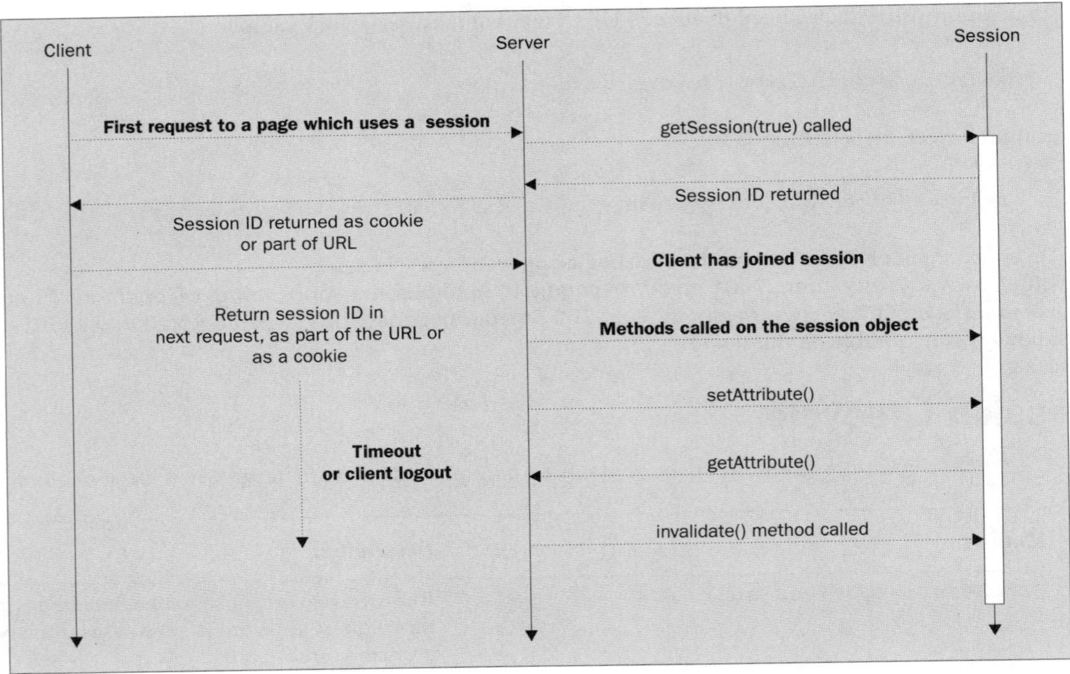

A session lifecycle is fairly simple. It is created on the server as a result of a client request and assigned a unique session ID and this ID is then passed to the client (as a cookie or a hidden variable). The session itself, is however considered 'new' until the client returns the session ID to the server (through a cookie or as a part of the requested URL) indicating that a session has been established. This associates the client with that particular session object. If the client doesn't support cookies (or rejects them) and URL rewriting has not been enabled on the server, no session ID will be returned to the server and the session will continue to be treated as new. A session exists on the server until it is invalidated or the server is stopped.

Session persistence is not used for storing long-term data between sessions. In other words, you should not rely on a session being active when client returns to a site at some later time. Instead the application should store any long-term information in a database. For example, you should not attempt to use the user's old session in an auto-login feature, but rather use a cookie, which doesn't expire for an extended period, to retrieve the user information from the database. Then you can create a new user session.

Sessions behave like any directory service and can store any object reference by binding it with a given string name. However, some servlet engine implementations will persist session data or distribute it amongst clustered machines. An example is BEA WebLogic 4.51 (see http://www.weblogic.com/docs/classdocs/API_servlet.html#sessionpersistence). Sessions that have not been invalidated on these servers will survive a server restart, and therefore require that objects within the session and their superclasses must implement the `java.io.Serializable` interface.

The table below illustrates how to store data in and read data from a session.

Storing Data in Servlet 1	Retrieving Data in Servlet 2
`HttpSession session = request.getSession(); MyObject m = new MyObject(); session.setAttribute("james", m);`	`HttpSession session = request.getSession(); MyObject n = (MyObject)session.getAttribute ("james");`

The Servlet 2.2 API also supports the concept of binding objects to the request object itself. This is similar to storing the object in a session, the difference being the life of the binding. An object bound to a request is available only for the life of that particular request, whereas bound to a session it is available until the session is invalidated. Binding objects to requests is particularly useful when the request is passed from one resource to another on the server, through the JSP forwarding mechanism, or directly by using the servlet `RequestDispatcher`. An object can be bound using the `setAttribute(String key, Object o)` in the `HttpRequest` interface and retrieved using the `getAttribute(String key)` method.

```
<%
  // Some code

  request.setAttribute("userid", "styagi");

  // Some more code
%>

<jsp:forward page="second.jsp" />
```

In the `second.jsp` the object can be retrieved:

```
// Some code here
String str = (String)request.getAttribute("userid");
```

Contexts

JSP is designed to be portable between different servers. It therefore needs to abstract information held by the web server from the JSPs and Java objects involved in creating the response. The JSP specification relies on contexts to provide that abstraction and bridge the gap between server-specific implementations and portable JSP code.

A context provides an invisible container for resources and an interface for them to communicate with their environment. For example, a servlet executes in a context (`javax.servlet.ServletContext`). Everything that the servlet needs to know about its server can be extracted from this context and everything the server wants to communicate to the servlet goes through the context. By using interfaces to define contexts, the vendor has flexibility in implementing the interface, while the developer is assured that the contract represented by the context between the server and the resource will always be fulfilled.

> **A rule of thumb is that everything in JSP is associated with a context, and every context has a scope.**

There's another context interface for JSPs, `javax.servlet.jsp.PageContext`, to which objects can be bound with different scopes.

Consider the following tag:

```
<jsp:useBean id="catalog"
             scope="page|request|session|application"
             class="projsp.Catalog"/>
```

What happens when this tag is compiled for the different values of the scope can be seen below. An object instance of the `com.wrox.projsp.Catalog` class is created and bound according to the details below:

Page Scope

`page` scope is interpreted as `PageContext.PAGE_SCOPE`. The object is bound to the `javax.servlet.jsp.PageContext`.

This is relatively simple – the object reference is discarded upon completion of the current `Servlet.service()` invocation. When generating the servlet, the servlet engine creates an object in the `service()` method which follows the usual object scope convection in Java. The object exists for every client request to the resource.

Request Scope

`request` scope is interpreted as `PageContext.REQUEST_SCOPE`, and the object bound to the `javax.servlet.jsp.PageContext`.

The object reference is available as long as the `HttpRequest` object exists, even if the request is passed/chained to different pages. The underlying, generated servlet relies on binding the object to the `HttpServletRequest` using the `setAttribute(String key, Object value)` method in the `HttpServletRequest`. This is transparent to the user. The object is distinct for every client request.

Session Scope

`session` scope is interpreted as `PageContext.SESSION_SCOPE` and the object bound to the `javax.servlet.jsp.PageContext`.

In earlier implementations of the servlet API, a session always ran under a separate session context. (Though deprecated for security reasons, an implementation for the `HttpSessionContext` interface is still available on most servers. It allows you to get a list of sessions or a particular session by its ID – and that's not really that secure.) These days, the only session ID you can get at is the one that's part of the request from the client, passed to the `PageContext` and made available to the JSP.

The generated servlet relies on binding the object to the `HttpSession` using the `setAttribute(String key, Object value)` method. This too is transparent to the user. The object is distinct for every client and is available as long as the client's session is valid.

Application Scope

`application` scope is interpreted as `PageContext.APPLICATION_SCOPE` and the object bound to the `javax.servlet.ServletContext`.

This is the most persistent scope. The generated servlet relies on binding the object to the `ServletContext` using the `setAttribute(String key, Object value)` method in the `ServletContext`. This is not unique to individual clients and, consequently, all clients access the same object.

By defining the available scopes as `"page|request|session|application"`, the JSP model simplifies things for the developer, who can now concentrate on the logic and implementation of the Bean/object, assured that with proper scope definition the object will still be accessible when needed.

One thing to bear in mind is that using a Bean means that an instance will be created if it doesn't exist, no matter what the scope. Using correct scope is important. If used carelessly it can cause unexpected results. For example, in a shopping cart, the items that the user chooses need to have session scope. If an application scope is specified then all users will share the same cart. (See `cart.jsp` in the next example.)

Listening for Changes to the Session Object

To provide objects with the ability to trap session-related events, the servlet API provides an event model similar to the listener-based AWT model. Objects that need to be told when they are being added or removed from a session can implement the `HttpSessionBindingListener` interface. When an application layer stores or removes data from the session, the session layer checks whether the object implements `HttpSessionBindingListener`. If it does, then the object is notified by calling the corresponding method. This is particularly useful in making sure that appropriate action and cleanup occurs before the object is discarded.

The figure below shows how the server invokes the listener methods:

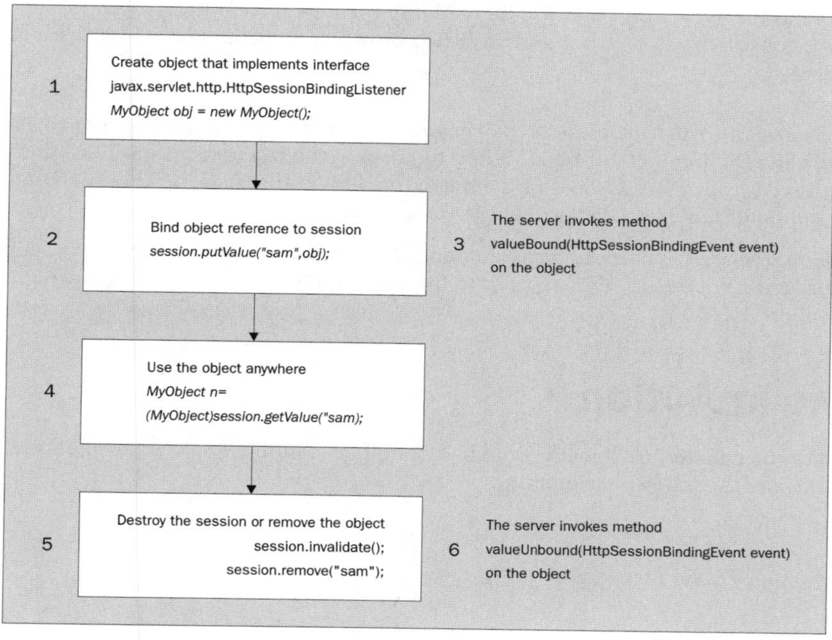

In the above figure it is worth noting that after the object is created, it resides in memory and only its reference is passed around.

Listeners can be used effectively when the application design is based on objects that are responsible for saving their own state. Consider a simple scenario of saving user settings. It's fairly straightforward to populate this object state from the database when the user logs in and then place this object in the session so that it is available throughout the user's visit. The converse of saving the object's state to the database when the user logs out is also fairly straightforward. It involves retrieving the object from the session and writing SQL code that saves its instance variables (or the object itself as a blob).

What happens, though, when the user doesn't log out by clicking on a logout button, but just closes the browser? The object still needs to be saved to the database. If the object implements the listener, it's pretty simple – you just need code in the `valueUnbound()` method to save the object to the database. When the user's session times out, the server will invalidate the session but not before invoking the `valueUnbound()` method so that the object can clean up.

```
public void valueBound(HttpSessionBindingEvent event) { }

public void valueUnbound(HttpSessionBindingEvent event) {
  // Save the state in the database.
  // using direct SQL code or by moving the code into another class
  // and saving the object there.
  MyDatabaseUtils.saveobject(this);
}
```

A closer look at the above solution will reveal a referential integrity problem. What happens when the user logs in, changes his preferences, then closes the browser and logs back in to the site, before his last session has timed out. The stale session has the preferences that were changed but have not been saved yet, while the database has his old settings that will be read into the new session upon login. In other words, you've got a major inconsistency. Users can also have two browsers open at once. There are a couple of solutions to this problem.

- One design would maintain some caching and checking mechanism. For example, the code handling the login could be modified to check if the last session was alive and the object retrieved from there instead of the database. This could be done simply by maintaining a mapping of the user ID to session ID in a hashtable.
- Alternatively, if your users have a unique ID and the new preferences information (or some other data) must not be lost, don't bind it to the session, bind it to the ID in some database instead.

Sessions in Action

For the rest of the chapter, we'll work through a complete example application to illustrate the use of sessions. Consider the following situation.

You need to build an application allowing users to buy a commodity on the net, where users have the ability to browse a catalog, choose items, and finally place an order. A user must be registered and logged in with the application. With a console you should be able to view details about all users logged in at any one time, including:

- User details, like IP address and user ID
- Number of users currently on the site
- Also we need to log user habits like which items they browse but do not place an order for. This is used to give feedback to the vendors.

Application Architecture

This can be implemented in many ways, but our solution looks like that in the following figure:

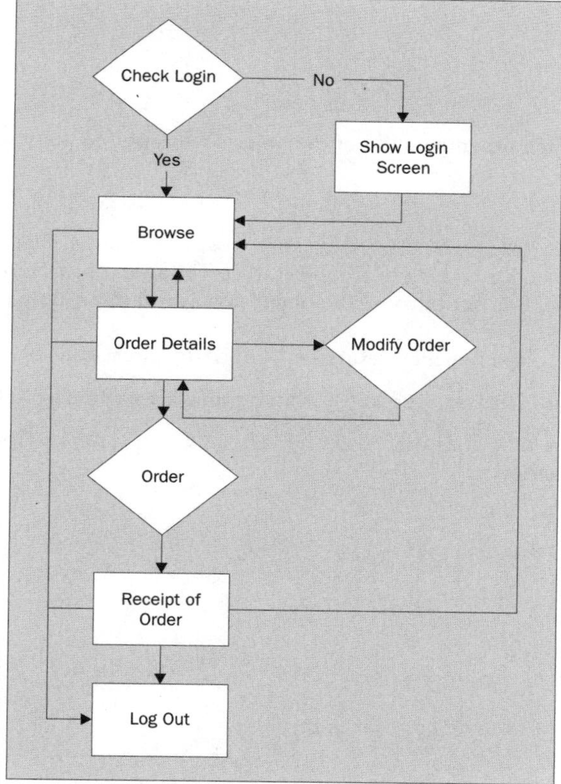

It's pretty simple – all the pages require the user to be logged in, and will push you to the login page if this is not the case. Then the application allows you to browse the catalog, make a selection, modify that selection and place the order, which is then confirmed. You can log out at any time.

The modeling of this problem is based on breaking it into the following objects/beans, belonging to the usual three categories that separate the presentation from the logic and all other code. (These categories are covered in Chapter 12):

- Business objects or Beans
- JSPs and servlets to maintain application flow
- JSPs to generate HTML

The important part is trying to figure what is going in a Bean and what is going in a JSP. This can be as simple as using a little intuition (changing everything that interacts with the client into a JSP and everything else into a Bean), or more than that (involving some object modeling, creating use cases, state, sequence, and class diagrams). This latter will be used to some extent in detail in Chapter 12 but for now we can use the former and think about object abstractions that this application might be broken into. A look at the vocabulary of the problem and the nouns used intuitively points us to the creation of a *User*, a *Catalog*, an *Item* and an *Order* of items. The verb login and the login process can be captured in another class *LoginBean*.

The JavaBeans

We start off by writing the implementation of the objects we captured above as the Beans used in the application.

The Catalog Class

This bean abstracts the vendor catalog in an object. It serves as an object representation and cache of the inventory in the database. For our purpose the object consists of three simple methods:

- `Vector getItems()`, which returns a `Vector` of `Item` objects
- `Item getItem(String itemId)`, which returns a particular item
- `void setItem(Item item, String itemId)`, to reset a particular item retrieved with the previous method

```
package com.wrox.projsp.ch04;

import java.util.Vector;

public class Catalog {
  private Vector items = new Vector();

  synchronized public Vector getItems() {
    return items;
  }

  synchronized public Item getItem(String itemId) {
    int index = Integer.parseInt(itemId);
    return (Item)items.elementAt(index);
  }
```

```
    synchronized public void setItem(Item item, String itemId) {
      int index = Integer.parseInt(itemId);
      items.set(index, item);
    }

    public Catalog() {
      /**
       * This could be the place for some JDBC code to connect and retrieve
       * inventory information, create Item objects and store them here
       */
      items.addElement(new Item("0", "Toothbrush", (float)10, true, 100));
      items.addElement(new Item("1", "Comb", (float)1, true, 100));
      items.addElement(new Item("2", "Razor", (float)13, true, 1000));
      items.addElement(new Item("3", "After shave", (float)10, true, 900));
      items.addElement(new Item("4", "Cologne", (float)25, true, 133));
      items.addElement(new Item("5", "Shaving cream", (float)12, true, 353));
      items.addElement(new Item("6", "Razor blades", (float)9, true, 333));
      items.addElement(new Item("7", "Pen stand", (float)0.99, true, 222));
      items.addElement(new Item("8", "Duke beanie", (float)19, true, 343));
      items.addElement(new Item("9", "Elec Razor", (float)100, true, 884));
    }
  }
```

The Item Class

This bean abstracts an item in the vendor catalog. Each `Item` has the following attributes:

- `String itemId`, the ID of the item in the catalog.
- `float price`, the price of the item.
- `String description`, the textual detail about the item.
- `boolean available`, `true` if it is available in stock.
- `int quantity_in_stock`, the quantity in stock.

Not all these attributes have mutator (set) methods. For example, the ID of an item can never change.

```
  package com.wrox.projsp.ch04;

  public class Item {

    private String itemId;
    private float price;
    private String description;
    private boolean available;
    private int quantity_in_stock;

    public Item(String itemId, String description,
                float price, boolean available,
```

```
                int quantity_in_stock) {
      this.itemId = itemId;
      this.description = description;
      this.available = available;
      this.price = price;
      this.quantity_in_stock = quantity_in_stock;
    }

    public String getItemId() {
      return itemId;
    }

    public void setItemId(String aItemId) {
      itemId = aItemId;
    }

    public float getPrice() {
      return price;
    }

    public String getDescription() {
      return description;
    }

    public boolean getAvailable() {
      return available;
    }

    public void setAvailable(boolean aAvailable) {
      available = aAvailable;
    }

    public int getQuantity_in_stock() {
      return quantity_in_stock;
    }

    public void setQuantity_in_stock(int aQuantity_in_stock) {
      quantity_in_stock = aQuantity_in_stock;
    }
  }
```

The Order Class

This bean abstracts the concept of a client order. Every such order has an assigned ID, a user, and some `Items` in it.

- `String itemIds[]`, which holds an array of Item IDs in an order
- `long orderId`, the ID for that order
- `User user`, the user placing the order
- `boolean processed`, denotes whether the order has been completed or not

Again not all these attributes can be changed for an order. For example the `User` cannot be changed once associated with an order.

The `Order` class implements the session listener and appends to a file the values of the user and `itemIds[]` attributes for an unprocessed order before it is destroyed when the session is unbound.

We also override the `Object.toString()` method to provide an informative string about the order.

```
package com.wrox.projsp.ch04;

import java.util.Date;
import javax.servlet.http.*;
import java.io.*;

public class Order implements HttpSessionBindingListener {

  private String itemIds[];
  private long orderId;
  private User user;
  private boolean processed = false;

  public Order(User user) {
    orderId = System.currentTimeMillis();
    this.user = user;
  }

  public void setItemIds(String itemIds[]) {
    this.itemIds = itemIds;
  }

  public String[] getItemIds() {
    return itemIds;
  }

  public long getOrderId() {
    return orderId;
  }

  public boolean isProcessed() {
    return processed;
  }

  public void complete(Catalog catalog) {
    // Alter catalog details
    for (int i = 0; i < itemIds.length; i++) {
      Item item = catalog.getItem(itemIds[i]);
      item.setQuantity_in_stock(item.getQuantity_in_stock() - 1);
      catalog.setItem(item, itemIds[i]);
    }

    // Send to shipping department
    processed = true;
  }

  public User getUser() {
    return user;
  }
```

```
  public void valueBound(HttpSessionBindingEvent event) {}

  public void valueUnbound(HttpSessionBindingEvent event) {
    if (!processed) {
      doLog();
    }
  }

  private void doLog() {
    try {
      PrintWriter log = new PrintWriter(
                          new FileWriter("../logs/shopping.txt"),
                                         true);
      log.println("Incomplete order  number " + orderId +
                  " for user " + user.getUserId());
      log.close();
    } catch(IOException e) {}
  }

  public String toString() {
    String temp = "";

    for (int i = 0; i < itemIds.length; i++) {
      temp += " , " + itemIds[i];
    }

    return "order id :" + orderId + "<br>Items ids : " + temp;
  }
}
```

The User Class

This bean represents the user on the system. Every user in the application must be unique and thus has a unique user ID describing the user (like the SSN or email address). Also, for security purposes, we need to capture the IP address for the machine from which the user is logging on. In effect this means that our user bean has two attributes – an ID and an IP address:

- `String userId`, the users ID
- `String ipAddr`, the IP address from where the user is logging on

```
package com.wrox.projsp.ch04;

public class User implements Comparable {

  private String userId;
  private String ipAddr;

  public User() {}

  public User(String userId) {
    this.userId = userId;
  }
```

```
  public String getUserId() {
    return userId;
  }

  public String getIpAddr() {
    return ipAddr;
  }

  public void setIpAddr(String ipAddr) {
    this.ipAddr = ipAddr;
  }

  public String toString() {
    return userId;
  }

  public int hashCode() {
    // Improve hashcode calculation using member variables of this class
    return 13*userId.hashCode() + 7*ipAddr.hashCode();
  }

  public boolean equals(Object user) {
    // Return true if the result of the compareTo() method is zero
    return compareTo(user) == 0;
  }

  public int compareTo(Object user) {
    // Compare the user IDs of the two user objects -
    // result is zero if they're identical
    int result = userId.compareTo(((User)user).getUserId());

    // If result is zero from previous method, return the comparison
    // of IP addresses. Otherwise, return the result.
    return result == 0 ? ipAddr.compareTo(((User)user).getIpAddr())
                       : result ;
  }
}
```

The User bean implements the `Comparable` interface and overrides the `hashCode()` and `equals()` methods of `Object`, so that `User` objects can be used as unique keys in the `monitor` hashmap. We'll use this to recover and complete uncompleted orders from a client session when the client connection has gone down and the user has logged back in.

The Login Bean

This bean is fairly simple. Its purpose in life is to take two attributes (a username and a password) and authenticate them. If authenticated, it returns a `User` object. Again there are no accessor methods, only set method for these two variables:

- `String username`, the username
- `String password`, the password

The class also has one simple method, `User authenticate()`, which returns the user.

```
package com.wrox.projsp.ch04;

public class Login {

  private String username = "";
  private String password = "";

  public Login() { }

  public void setUsername(String username) {
    this.username = username;
  }

  public void setPassword(String password) {
    this.password = password;
  }

  public User authenticate() {
    if (username.equals("duke") && password.equals("jsp")) {
      return new User("duke");
    } else if (username.equals("wrox") && password.equals("jsp")) {
      return new User("wrox");
    } else {
      return null;
    }
  }
}
```

A HashMap

Remember the referential integrity problem mentioned earlier? What happens when the user doesn't log out but closes the browser? We use an instance of a `java.util.HashMap`, called `monitor` to hold references to user sessions. There is one map for the entire application (not per user) that holds a user to session mapping. We need to do this because there is no way to access all the sessions on the server without using the deprecated `HttpSessionContext`.

That's it for our business objects or beans. Now that we have defined our objects, let's look at the JSPs.

The JSPs

Having covered the Beans used in the application, we can move on to the JSPs themselves. We'll follow a typical order flow in looking at the code here.

checkLogin.jsp

This is the main gateway that the user encounters, and it uses the `Login` bean.

```
<%@ page language="java"
         import="com.wrox.projsp.ch04.*, java.util.*"
         errorPage="error.jsp" %>
```

```
<jsp:useBean id="loginBean" scope="page" class="com.wrox.projsp.ch04.Login">
  <jsp:setProperty name="loginBean" property="*"/>
</jsp:useBean>

<jsp:useBean id="monitor" scope="application" class="java.util.HashMap"/>

<%
  String display = "showLogin.html";

  User user = loginBean.authenticate();

  if (user != null) {
    user.setIpAddr(request.getRemoteHost());

    // Got user. Do they already have a session?
    if (monitor.containsKey(user)) {
      // There's an old session for this user - invalidate it
      HttpSession oldSession = (HttpSession)monitor.get(user);
      oldSession.invalidate();
    }

    session.setAttribute("user", user);
    monitor.put(user, session);
    System.out.println("Assigned new session for: " + user);

    session.setMaxInactiveInterval(900);

    display = "browse.jsp";
  }
%>

<jsp:forward page="<%= display %>"/>
```

Notice the scope: since we don't need the `Login` bean outside this JSP we define it at page scope. The `monitor` object, however, has an application scope. This means that all other JSPs and servlets running within the same context have access to the monitor.

The bean invokes the `authenticate()` method which returns a `User` object capturing the user specific information from the database. The state of the `User` object is then modified (to capture the IP address since the IP can change every time the user logs in and is not stored in the database).

Next comes some code to check whether the user already has a session (which wasn't invalidated before the user logged back in). If there's a pre-existing session, we get a reference to it from `monitor` and invalidate it. If we wanted, here would be a good place to get outstanding order information from the old session and pass it into this session:

```
boolean recoverOrder = false;

if (monitor.containsKey(user)) {
  HttpSession oldSession = (HttpSession)monitor.get(user);
  Order oldOrder = (Order)oldSession.getAttribute("anOrder");
  if (oldOrder != null && oldOrder.isProcessed() == false) {
    session.setAttribute("anOrder", oldOrder);
    recoverOrder = true;
```

```
    }

    oldSession.invalidate();
  }

  session.setAttribute("user", user);
  monitor.put(user, session);
  session.setMaxInactiveInterval(900);

  display = recoverOrder ? "processOrder.jsp?action=1" : "browse.jsp";
```

The user is added to a new user session, thus signaling to the application that the user is now logged in. Any application on the server can then determine if the user is logged in by querying the session for this user object.

The authenticated user's session time-out period is set to 30 minutes, and a handle to the object and session are also kept in the monitor. It is important to note that an object, once added to a session, stays there until removed, and retrieval of the object returns a reference to the object, not the actual object itself.

If the login is successful, the user is forwarded to the `browse.jsp`, or otherwise is prompted to log in again via `ShowLogin.html`:

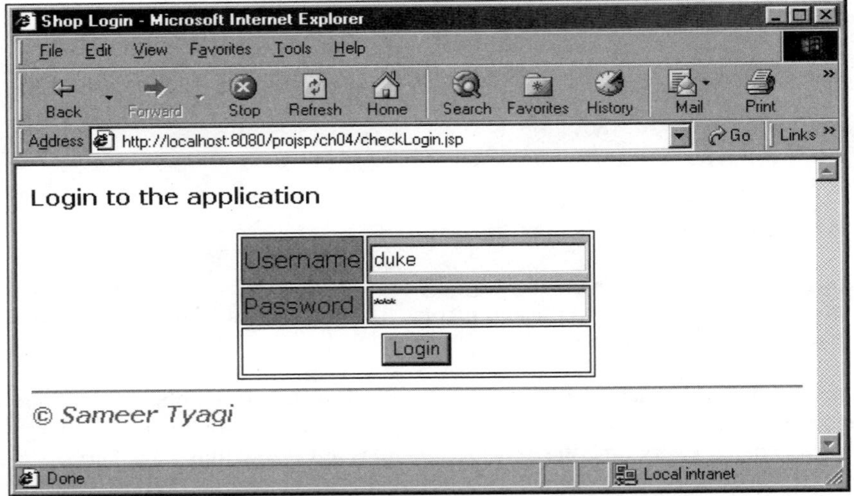

browse.jsp

This is the main page for the application.

```
<%@ page import="com.wrox.projsp.ch04.*" session="true" errorPage="error.jsp" %>

<html>
<title>Browse the Catalog</title>
<body>

<%
  if(session.getValue("user") == null)
```

```
    response.sendRedirect("showLogin.html");
  %>

  <jsp:useBean id="catalog" scope="application"
  class="com.wrox.projsp.ch04.Catalog"/>

  <body bgcolor="#FFFFFF">
  <table width="100%" border="1" bordercolor="#000000">
  <form action="processOrder.jsp" method=GET>

    <input type=hidden name=action value=0>
    <tr bgcolor="#9999FF">
      <td><b></b></td>
      <td><b><font face="Verdana, Arial, Helvetica, sans-serif" size="2">
        Item Description</font></b></td>
      <td><b><font face="Verdana, Arial, Helvetica, sans-serif" size="2">
        Price</font></b></td>
      <td><b><font face="Verdana, Arial, Helvetica, sans-serif" size="2">
        In Stock</font></b></td>
      <td><b><font face="Verdana, Arial, Helvetica, sans-serif" size="2">
        Quantity in stock</font></b></td>
    </tr>

  <%
    // Get the catalog entries
    Vector items = catalog.getItems();

    for (int i = 0; i < items.size(); i++) {
      Item myitem = (Item)items.elementAt(i);
  %>

   <tr>
     <td><input type=checkbox
                name=itemId
                value=<%= myitem.getItemId() %> ></td>
     <td><%= myitem.getDescription()%></td>

     <td><%= myitem.getPrice() %></td>
     <td><%= myitem.getAvailable() %></td>
     <td><%= myitem.getQuantity_in_stock() %></td>
    </tr>

  <%
    }
  %>

    <tr colspan=5>
      <td><input type=submit value="Add selected items"></td>
    </tr>
  </form>
  </table>

  <%@ include file="footer.html"%>

  </body>
  </html>
```

The page first checks if the user is logged in or not by querying the session for the `"user"` attribute. This will only be available if the user had successfully completed the login process.

`browse.jsp` then creates a `Catalog` bean. Again the scope is defined as `application`, so once the catalog is created, it will be available throughout the application and the object will only need to be created when the first user logs into the system for the first time.

If the catalog was one that changes frequently, like stock quotes, or was customized for individual users, then a page or session scope would be better suited for the object. For example if the scope was session, then the catalog would only last for the duration of the user's session on the site.

`browse.jsp` then queries the catalog for all the items and displays the relevant attributes for each item as a row in an HTML table. You can see that in the following screenshot, along with the `footer.html`.

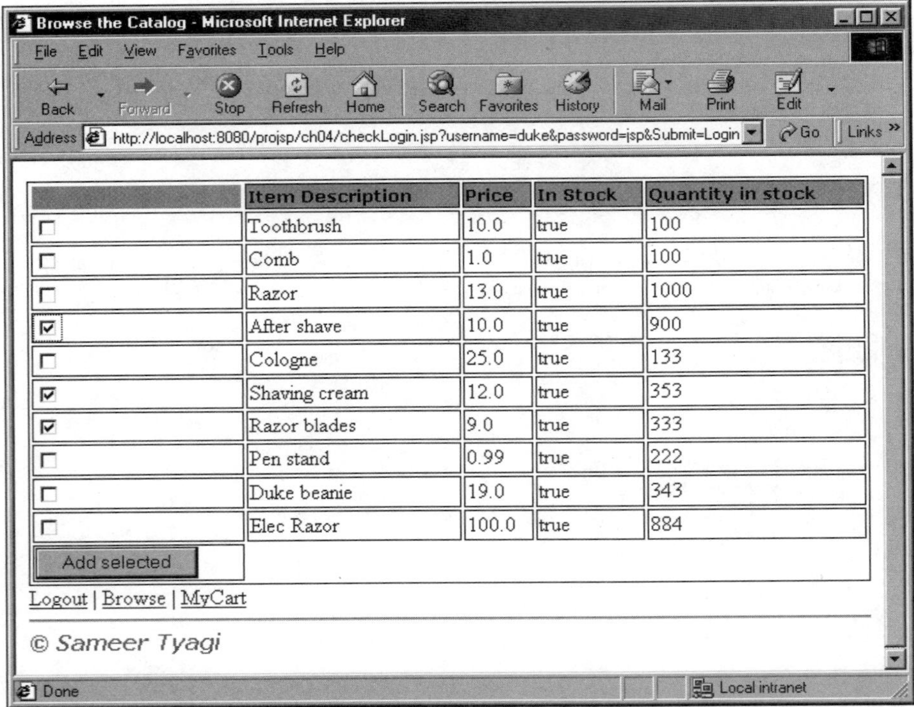

processOrder.jsp

This JSP controls the main flow of the application. It is responsible for maintaining the different states of a user's order. The parameter `"action"` tells the JSP what it needs to do. When prompted to complete the order, it retrieves the `Order` object and invokes the `complete()` method, passing in a reference to the `catalog` instance, so any ordered items can be deducted from the in-stock figures.

```
<%@ page import="com.wrox.projsp.ch04.*" errorPage="error.jsp" %>

<html>
<title>Process the Order</title>
```

```
<body>

<%
  if(session.getValue("user") == null) {
    response.sendRedirect("showLogin.html");
  }

  User user = (User)session.getValue("user");
  String display = "showDetails.jsp";
  int mode = (new Integer(request.getParameter("action"))).intValue();
  System.out.println("Action" + mode);
  Order order = null;

  switch(mode) {

    /* 0 = add / modify
       1 = complete
       2 = clear
       3 = display
     */

    case(0):
    case(2):
      // This is either a new order, a modified order or needs clearing...
      String itemIds[] = request.getParameterValues("itemId");

      if (itemIds != null && itemIds.length != 0) {
        order = new Order(user);
        order.setItemIds(itemIds);
        session.setAttribute("anOrder", order);
      } else
        session.removeAttribute("anOrder");

      break;
    case(1):
      // Complete the order here
      order = (Order)session.getAttribute("anOrder");
      System.out.println("Order: " + order);
      order.complete((Catalog)pageContext.getAttribute("catalog",
                                      pageContext.APPLICATION_SCOPE));

      System.out.println("Order placed");

      display = "receipt.html";
      break;
  }

  response.sendRedirect(display);
%>
```

showDetails.jsp

This JSP shows the details for an order. It simply retrieves the order object from the session and displays its attributes in a formatted manner. The order does not store the actual items, but item IDs. It retrieves the `Item` object for that ID from the `Catalog` object.

Notice here that the catalog object was created in the `browse.jsp` and bound to the application context. The catalog is thus available to all servlets as an application attribute. This is an alternative to the `pageContext.getAttribute("catalog", pageContext.APPLICATION_SCOPE)` method, used to retrieve the catalog in the previous example.

```
<%@ page import="com.wrox.projsp.ch04.*" errorPage="error.jsp" %>

<html>
<title>Order Details</title>
<body>

<%
  if(session.getValue("user") == null)
    response.sendRedirect("showLogin.html");

  Order order = (Order)session.getValue("anOrder");
  if (order == null) {
    out.println("There are no items in your cart<br>");
    out.println("<a href=browse.jsp>Browse catalog</a>");
    return;
  }
%>

<body bgcolor="#FFFFFF">
<table width="100%" border="1" bordercolor="#000000">
  <form action="processOrder.jsp" method=GET>

    <input type=hidden name=action value=0>
    <tr bgcolor="#9999FF">
      <td><b></b></td>
      <td><b><font face="Verdana, Arial, Helvetica, sans-serif" size="2">
        Item Description</font></b></td>
      <td><b><font face="Verdana, Arial, Helvetica, sans-serif" size="2">
        Price</font></b></td>
      <td><b><font face="Verdana, Arial, Helvetica, sans-serif" size="2">
        In Stock</font></b></td>
      <td><b><font face="Verdana, Arial, Helvetica, sans-serif" size="2">
        Quantity in stock</font></b></td>
    </tr>

<%
  Catalog catalog = (Catalog)application.getAttribute("catalog");
  String ids[] = order.getItemIds();
  for (int i = 0; i < ids.length; i++) {
%>

    <tr>
      <td>
        <input type=checkbox checked name=itemId value=
               <%= catalog.getItem(ids[i]).getItemId()%> checked>
      </td>
      <td><%= catalog.getItem(ids[i]).getDescription()%></td>
      <td><%= catalog.getItem(ids[i]).getPrice() %></td>
      <td><%= catalog.getItem(ids[i]).getAvailable() %></td>
```

```
        <td><%= catalog.getItem(ids[i]).getQuantity_in_stock() %></td>
      </tr>

  <%
    }
  %>

      <tr>
        <td colspan=5>
          <input type=submit value="Modify Order"> |
          <a href="processOrder.jsp?action=1">Place Order now</a>
         </td>
      </tr>
    </form>
  </table>
  <p>
  <font face="Verdana, Arial, Helvetica, sans-serif" size="2"><b>You may remove
  items by un-checking them.</b></font>
  <p>

  <%@ include file="footer.html"%>

  </body>
  </html>
```

And here's how it looks in the browser:

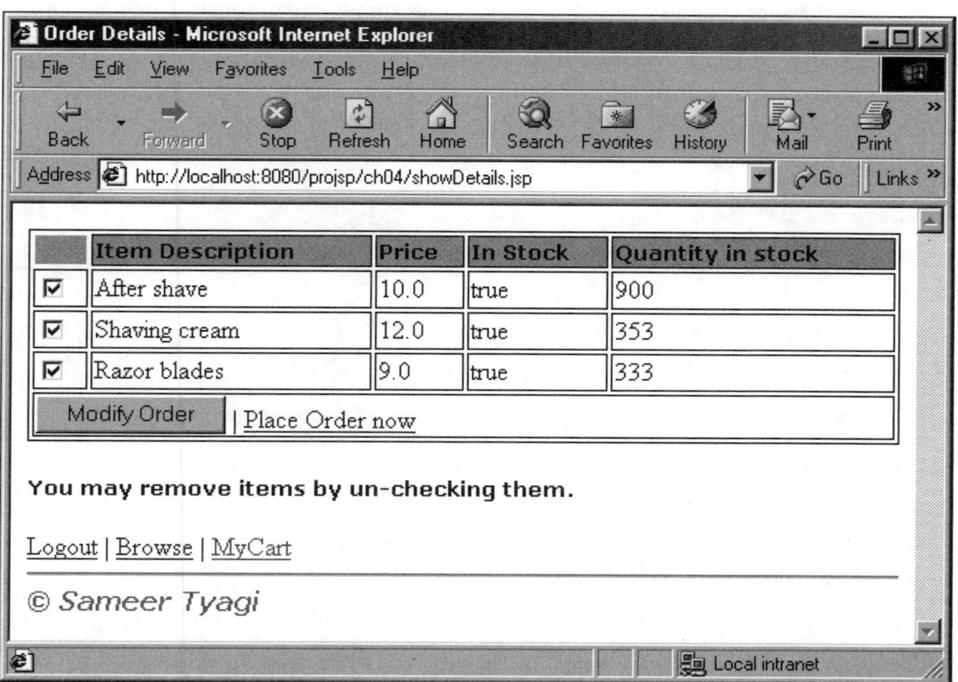

logOut.jsp

This is a simple JSP that logs out the user by removing the user handle in the monitor and killing their session by calling `invalidate()`. It does some error checking first, to make sure there are user and session objects to remove.

```
<%@ page import="com.wrox.projsp.ch04.*, java.util.HashMap"
         errorPage="error.jsp" %>

<%
  if (session != null) {
    User user = (User)session.getValue("user");
    if (user != null) {
      HashMap hash =(HashMap)application.getAttribute("monitor");
      hash.remove(user);
      session.invalidate();
    }
  }

  response.sendRedirect("showLogin.html");
%>
<%@include file="showLogin.h
```

console.jsp

This is the console that displays information about all the users present in the application to the administrator at any given point in time. It does so by querying the `monitor HashMap` that was bound to the application. A handle to a user and their session was stored here during the login process.

All this JSP does is to query the monitor object for both these objects and display the information about them using various accessor methods.

The generated HTML uses a `META` refresh tag to repeatedly retrieve information from the server.

```
<%@ page import="java.util.*, com.wrox.projsp.ch04.*" errorPage="error.jsp" %>

<html>
<body>
<META HTTP-EQUIV="refresh" content="1"; URL=console.jsp">

<table width="69%" border="1">
  <tr bgcolor="#9999FF">
    <td height="22" width="10%"><b><font face="Verdana, Arial, Helvetica,
                    sans-serif" size="2">UserId</b></td>
    <td height="22" width="10%"><b><font face="Verdana, Arial, Helvetica,
                    sans-serif" size="2">From IP</b></td>
    <td height="22" width="11%"><b><font face="Verdana, Arial, Helvetica,
                    sans-serif" size="2">Login at</b></td>
    <td height="22" width="36%"><b><font face="Verdana, Arial, Helvetica,
                    sans-serif" size="2">Last activity at</b></td>
    <td height="22" width="18%"><b><font face="Verdana, Arial, Helvetica,
                    sans-serif" size="2">Seconds before logout</b></td>
```

```
    <td height="22" width="25%"><b><font face="Verdana, Arial, Helvetica,
                    sans-serif" size="2">Order Details</b></td>
    <td height="22" width="25%"><b><font face="Verdana, Arial, Helvetica,
                    sans-serif" size="2">Order Processed ?</b></td>
    <td height="22" width="25%"><b><font face="Verdana, Arial, Helvetica,
                    sans-serif" size="2">Session Id</b> </td>
  </tr>

 <%
   HashMap hash = (HashMap)pageContext.getAttribute("monitor",
                                     pageContext.APPLICATION_SCOPE);
   // Get iterator for keys in HashMap
   Iterator keyIter = hash.keySet().iterator();

   while(keyIter.hasNext()) {
     User user = (User)keyIter.next();
     HttpSession user_sess = (HttpSession)hash.get(user);
     Order order = (Order)user_sess.getValue("anOrder") ;
     Date current_time = new Date();
 %>
   <tr>
     <td width="5%"><%= user %></td>
     <td width="11%"><%= user.getIpAddr() %></td>
     <td width="11%"><%= user_sess.getCreationTime() %></td>
     <td width="36%"><%= user_sess.getLastAccessedTime() %></td>
     <td width="18%"><%= ((user_sess.getMaxInactiveInterval()*1000 +
                          user_sess.getLastAccessedTime() -
                          current_time.getTime() )/1000) %></td>
 <%
     if (order != null) {
 %>
     <td width="25%"><%= order %></td>
     <td width="25%"><%= order.isProcessed() %></td>
 <%
     } else {
 %>
     <td width="25%"><%= "" %></td>
     <td width="25%"><%= "" %></td>
 <%
 }
 %>
     <td width="25%"><%= user_sess.getId() %></td>
   </tr>

 <%
 }
 %>

 </table>

 </body>
 </html>
```

The output is slightly complicated by the need to check that an `Order` object exists and provide blank entries if none has been bound to the session.

The Seconds before Logout column shows the time left on the session, using the current time, maximum inactive interval and the last time the session was accessed.

The screenshot of the console shows two user sessions, one without an order object, the other with an order that's been processed.

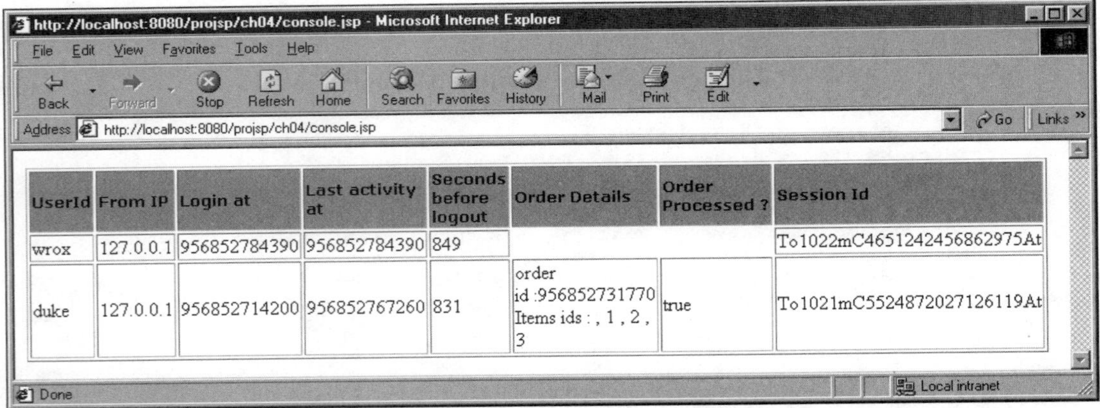

UserId	From IP	Login at	Last activity at	Seconds before logout	Order Details	Order Processed ?	Session Id
wrox	127.0.0.1	956852784390	956852784390	849			To1022mC4651242456862975At
duke	127.0.0.1	956852714200	956852767260	831	order id :956852731770 Items ids : , 1 , 2 , 3	true	To1021mC5524872027126119At

Although clearly this application leaves a lot to be desired in terms of functionality it does nevertheless show two ways in which JSP simplifies web application development: using a healthy mix of objects or beans declared with the right scope, and saving objects directly in sessions.

Sessions, HTTPS, and SSL

An interesting final discussion is how sessions work with HTTPS or SSL, and, more importantly, what happens to sessions when the JSPs are split between those running under HTTP and HTTPS. Consider the case of two JSPs: the JSP under normal HTTP (http://myhost/Jsp1.jsp) puts something in the session, which the second JSP (https://myhost/JSP2.jsp) tries to access. Although there is a lot of flexibility for the engine implementers, this is a tricky situation because the JSPs are running under two different servlet contexts, one of which is secure and one isn't.

A servlet can run in only one servlet context, but different servlets can have different views of the servlet engine by existing in different contexts. If a servlet engine supports virtual hosts, each virtual host has a servlet context, and a servlet context cannot be shared across virtual hosts. Different protocol and port numbers constitute a different servlet context, as they can be construed as a different virtual host.

So how do we deal with this? It depends on a couple of things.

- First it depends on how the server implements sessions. If it explicitly maintains different contexts for secure and non-secure protocols, you will have to persist your session object and then pass a key that uniquely identifies this newly created 'record' as a hidden HTML variable or cookie, and retrieve that persisted object using that key.

- If the server uses just one context (most servers do), then using default ports on the server will suffice. As usual, the server places a cookie identifying the session ID on the client. The cookie is marked for the domain for which it is valid (to which the browser must return it in a request). If you switch between HTTP and HTTPS, the browser will first try and match the domain on the cookies and then send it back to the server. If the cookie is the same between this switching, the server will still identify the same session for the client. However if the cookie is not returned, a new session will be started.

For example a server running on 7001 for HTTP and 7002 for HTTPS would have two different cookies To the browser the domain http://www.myserver.com:7001 is not the same as https://www.myserver.com:7002 and it will not return a cookie the second time to the server. However http://www.myserver.com appears the same as https://www.myserver.com (the default ports are 80 and 443) to browsers and they return the same cookie that was set for HTTP when the protocol switches to HTTPS.

If you need to run on non-default ports, the simplest way around the whole problem is to make sure that there are no integration points between HTTP and HTTPS, especially between different domains, where session information needs to be shared: it's all HTTP or all HTTPS.

Summary

In this chapter, we've looked at how to add state to a sequence of HTTP request/response pairs, in order to allow clients and web servers to conduct 'conversations'. The use of client identification, by cookies or URL rewriting, to access server-side sessions, which hold data about user transactions with the server for some suitable time, allows many of the problems with using a stateless protocol to be overcome.

The Java Servlet and JSP APIs provide strong support for cookies and URL rewriting. Also, by using application, session, request and page contexts to define scope for and hold instances of objects on the server-side, the servlet container can differentiate between objects that provide:

- Global data to all servlets in a servlet context
- Data for a user session
- Objects that last as long as it takes to answer a request or create a page

We've also seen something of the session lifecycle, and how it can interact with objects bound to it.

In the next chapter, we'll look at that most important of topics – error handling, and what JSP adds to Java's exception-handling scheme.

J2EE
JSP

6

Error Handling with JSP

Having looked at the basics of using JSPs, what's going on behind the scenes, and how session management works, we need to consider what happens when something goes wrong and an error occurs.

You need to make sure your web applications handle these situations, using the facilities built into JSP. If you don't, your users will see some ugly looking web pages, looking something like the following figure. (The exact message is dependent on the particular exception thrown, and your JSP run time container.)

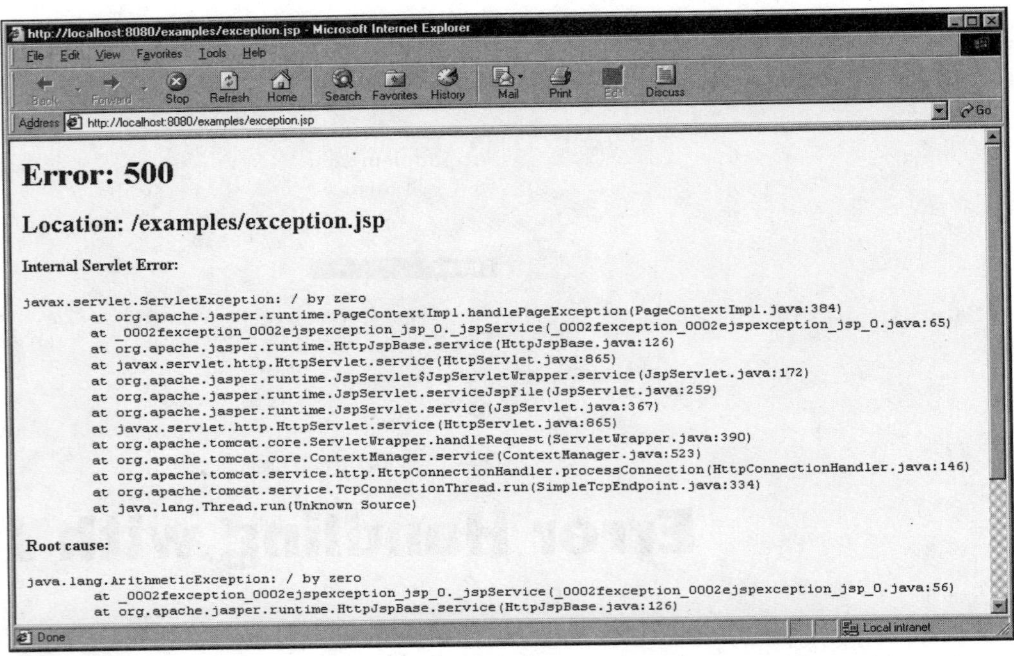

With JSP, errors and exceptions can happen at different times each of which requires a different mechanism to handle it.

Types of Errors and Exceptions

There are two primary types of exceptions you can run into when processing with JSP pages:

- Translation time errors
- Run time exceptions

We'll look at these in more detail shortly. In short, if a translation error occurs during page compilation, this results in an Internal Servlet Error (error code 500). An exception, on the other hand, occurs once the page is compiled and the servlet is running. Exceptions can be dealt with within the JSP, using the standard Java exception-handling mechanism, but if they are not then it is possible, using the special error-handling JSP directives and JSP error pages, to ensure a more pleasurable user experience instead of showing a stack dump of where the exception was thrown.

Handling Translation Time Errors

Compilation errors in JSP files result in translation time errors. Assuming your web application is properly tested, an end user should never see one of these: they should only appear during development, where you are creating the JSP files. Common translation time errors are caused by missing semicolons, forgetting to import a package, or using the wrong JSP directives. There are tools available with most JSP environments that let you precompile your JSP files, without waiting for users to access them, which can help you prevent this problem. For instance, with the reference implementation Tomcat, you can use the JspC compiler to precompile your files.

You'll need to examine the documentation for your specific JSP implementation for instructions on how to do this. For example, to see how to do this with the WebLogic JSP compiler, see http://www.weblogic.com/docs45/classdocs/API_jsp.html#compiler.

The specific error message displayed for a translation-time error is dependent on your JSP run time container. If you were using the Tomcat 3.1 reference implementation as your server then a page similar to the one shown in the figure below would be seen if you missed a semi-colon somewhere. Other servers could display different messages:

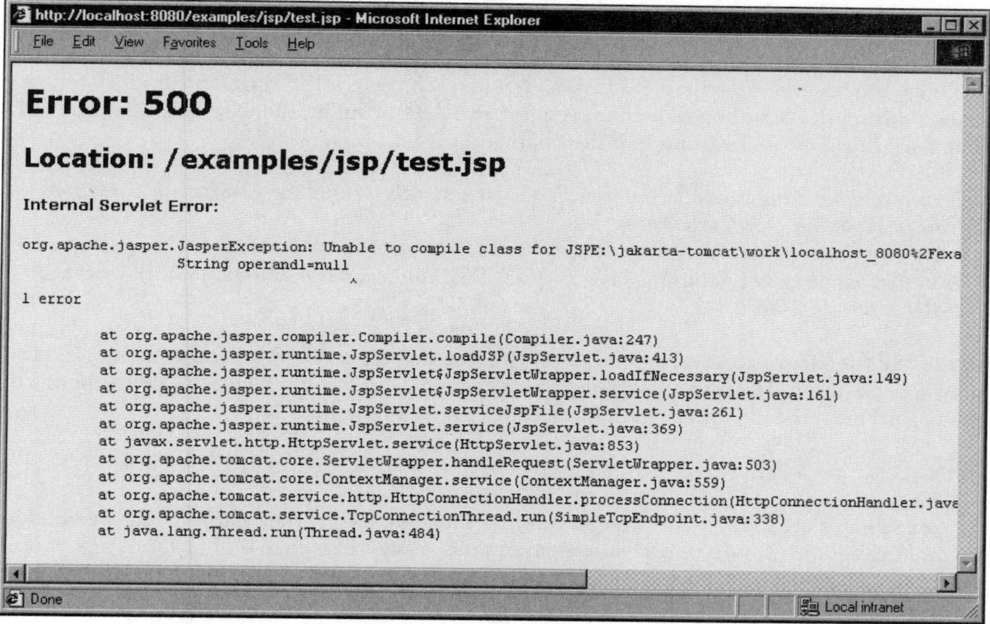

The top of the page shows the filename where the compilation error happened (Location: /examples/jsp/test/jsp) and displays the actual compilation error. On the bottom you'll find a stack dump indicating the compiler failed.

> **It is important to mention here that the line numbers do not refer to the line numbers in your original JSP file. Instead, they refer to the servlet source code generated from the JSP file. While some development environments might let you view/edit the `.java` file directly, remember to go back to the original JSP file to make the actual changes, or else the next time the servlet is generated from the JSP file you'll lose your changes.**

A translation error can also happen in the actual error-handling page. The same type of compilation error message is displayed; however, you'll need to watch the Location: line to see the name of the error-handling file. You'll learn more about error handling pages shortly. Another form of translation-time error can happen trying to get or set JavaBean properties using the special JSP tags discussed in Chapter 4.

With the Tomcat reference implementation, the compile-time error messages go into the `tomcat.log` file in the `logs` directory, under your Tomcat installation directory.

Handling Run Time Exceptions

Like Java programs, JSP files may catch exceptions that occur during execution:

```
<%
    try {
      URL url = new URL(param);
    } catch (MalformedURLException e) {
      response.sendRedirect(BAD_URL_PAGE);
    }
%>
```

`try-catch` blocks are perfectly legal Java source to include in a JSP scriptlet. If, however, an exception is thrown during the handling of a client request and is not caught, the user will again see a screen similar that shown at the beginning of the chapter.

If exception handling is new to you, you should see either the "Handling Errors with Exceptions" trail in the online Sun tutorial at http://java.sun.com/docs/books/tutorial/essential/exceptions/index.html, or read up on exception handling in Beginning Java 2 - JDK 1.3 Edition *by Ivor Horton, from Wrox Press, ISBN 1-861-003-66-8.*

With the JSP file already converted into a servlet, the default action when an exception is thrown is to display a stack dump. However, the JSP `page` directive provides the facility to override this default behavior and have the exception handling redirected to a new JSP file:

```
<%@ page ... errorPage="/error.html" %>
```

If the `errorPage` attribute is specified within the page directive, the *relative* URL specified is displayed when an uncaught `Throwable` object is encountered – any `Throwable` object, not just an `Error` or an `Exception`. The relative URL can be a fixed HTML file or another JSP file.

If an exception occurs, the output buffer is cleared before the error page is displayed. If, however, the `autoFlush` attribute of the page directive is set to `"true"`, then the dispatching of an uncaught exception could result in an error (HTTP error code 500 - Internal Server Error) if the `ServletResponse` has already received some output.

Writing the Error Page

The error page can be used to display a more user-friendly error message, maybe to provide you, the developer, with useful information while you are creating your application or maybe, once the application has been deployed, apologizing to the user for the problem and inviting them to contact a systems administrator if the problem persists.

If the error page is another JSP file, the error page should explicitly set the `isErrorPage` attribute to `"true"` in its `page` directive:

```
<%@ page ... isErrorPage="true" %>
```

While any page can be an error page without `isErrorPage` set, when `isErrorPage` is `"true"`, you have access to an implicit variable `exception`, of type `java.lang.Throwable`, which represents the `Throwable` object that caused the JSP runtime container to display the error page. The variable exists only for the lifetime of the page, so if you wish to use it beyond the lifetime of the single error page, you would need to save its value: `application.setAttribute("MyError", exception)`.

The `exception` variable can be used, if desired, display the message associated with the exception (optionally in a localized form), or to print the stack trace to standard error (the console) or to your own `PrintWriter`:

```
<%= exception.getMessage() %>
<%= exception.getLocalizedMessage() %>
<% exception.printStackTrace(PrintWriter); %>
```

The following example shows a very simple error page that just displays the exception along with these three pieces of information. The stack trace is saved into a `StringWriter` to avoid being sent to standard error.

```
<%@ page isErrorPage="true" import="java.io.*" %>
<html>
<head>
<title>Error Page</title>
</head>
<body>

<table border="1">
<tr>
<td>Exception</td>
<td><%= exception %></td>
</tr>
<tr>
<td>Message</td>
<td><%= exception.getMessage() %></td>
</tr>
<tr>
<td>Localized Message</td>
<td><%= exception.getLocalizedMessage() %></td>
</tr>
<tr>
<td>Stack Trace</td>
<td><pre>
<%
StringWriter sw = new StringWriter();
PrintWriter pw = new PrintWriter(sw);
exception.printStackTrace(pw);
out.println(sw);
%>
</pre></td>
</tr>
</table>

</body>
</html>
```

The screenshot below shows what the output would look like if the exception were an arithmetic division by zero exception:

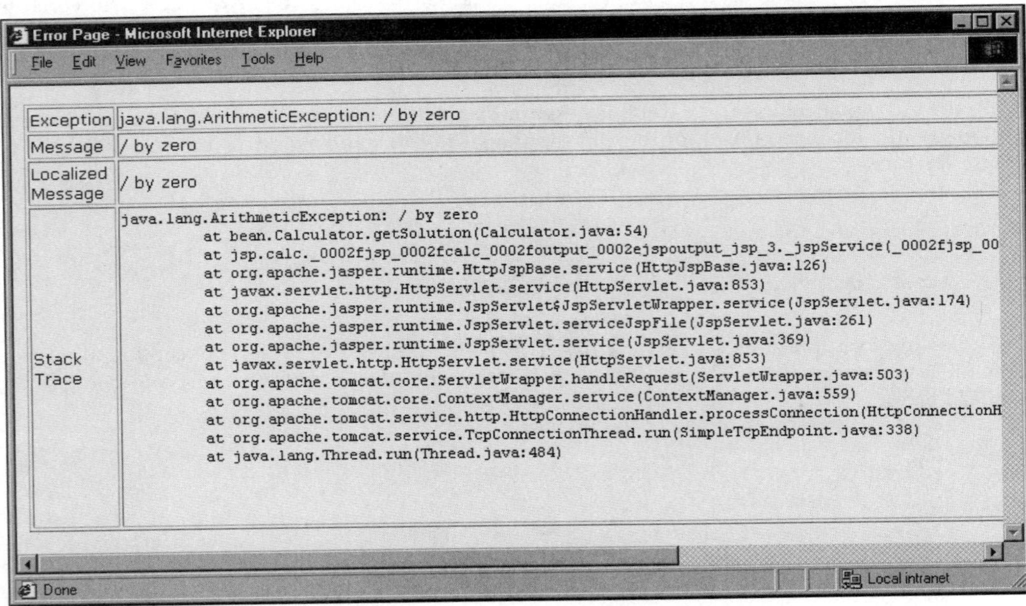

If the error page were saved in the file `error1.jsp`, the following would be necessary to cause this error page to be called:

```
<%@ page errorPage="error1.jsp" %>
<%= 1/0 %>
```

Since you are providing a custom error page for a reason, you probably don't want to display a stack trace to a user. However, it may be helpful during development, and you can log (or email) the stack trace in a production environment.

Besides using the implicit `exception` variable on the error page, the `"javax.servlet.jsp.jspException"` attribute of the servlet request contains the same contents:

```
<%
  Object attribute = request.getAttribute("javax.servlet.jsp.jspException");
  out.println("Attribute: " + attribute);
%>
```

You can use this attribute to have your own servlets use the JSP error-handling page, as in the following code fragment. By creating the following `gotoJSPErrorPage()` method, you can activate a JSP error handling page called from within a `catch` clause in your servlet. The only restriction is that the error page URL string would need to be a relative URL:

```
void gotoJSPErrorPage(HttpServletRequest request, HttpServletResponse response,
                      String errorPageURLString, Throwable throwable)
    throws ServletException, IOException {
```

```
    request.setAttribute ("javax.servlet.jsp.jspException", throwable);
    getServletConfig().getServletContext().getRequestDispatcher(errorPageURLString).
      forward(request, response);
  }
```

JSP-Specific Exception Classes

The JSP 1.1 specification added two `java.lang.Exception` subclasses into the mix; the figure below shows the class hierarchy for these classes. If you aren't writing JSP tag extensions or creating a JSP runtime container, you'll probably never need to use them:

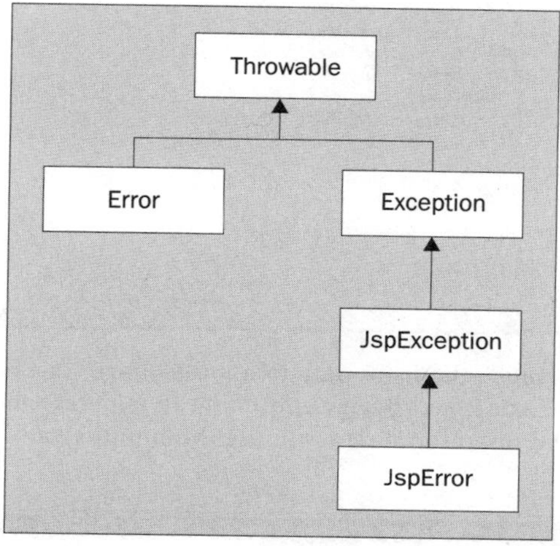

JspException

The `JspException` class represents a generic exception for the JSP packages. It can be found in the `javax.servlet.jsp` package.

JspError

The `JspError` class in the `javax.servlet.jsp` package is the only predefined subclass of `JspException`. It is meant to represent an unrecoverable error, as opposed to an exception. Why it doesn't subclass `java.lang.Error` is unknown, but it is a subclass of `Exception`.

An Example Web Application

Let's try out a simple example, demonstrating the use of an error-handling page for a `JSP` file. The example presents a simple calculator-like form, with two input fields to get the operands, and a set of radio buttons to select which mathematical operation to perform. Addition, subtraction, multiplication, division, and modulo operations are supported; the next figure shows what the input form looks like.

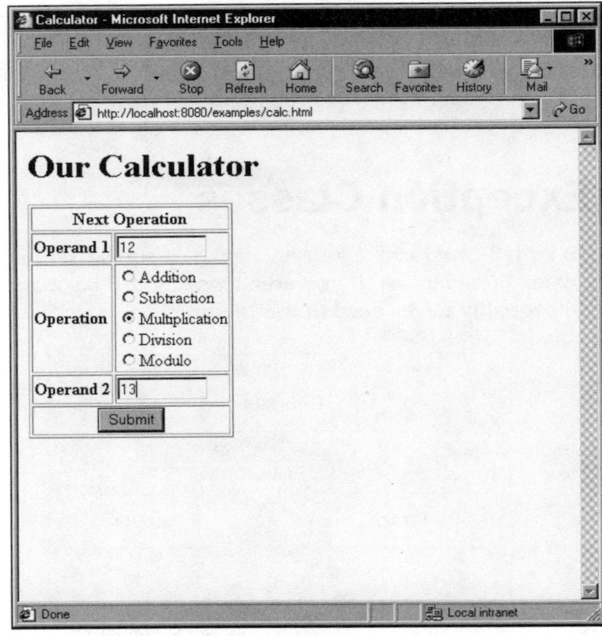

Pressing the Submit button sends the form data to another page, `output.jsp`, for processing; `output.jsp` uses a `Calculator` JavaBean component to generate the output. The operands are combined as specified by the operator and, assuming the input is valid, a results page will be seen, as shown below:

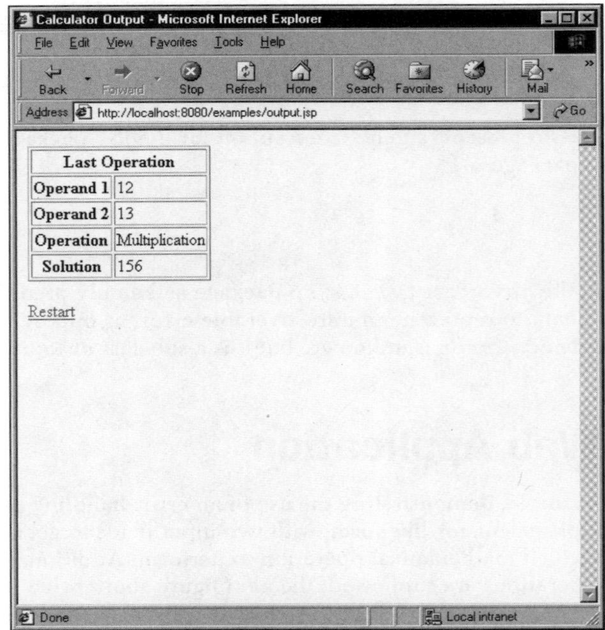

If, however, you specified invalid input, the web server would display the error page specified by the `errorPage` attribute of the `page` directive in the JSP file. Invalid input could be a floating point number entered (this calculator only supports integer arithmetic), an invalid character entered like a letter, or possibly division by zero, among other possibilities. If invalid input were entered, you would see the error page displayed, as below:

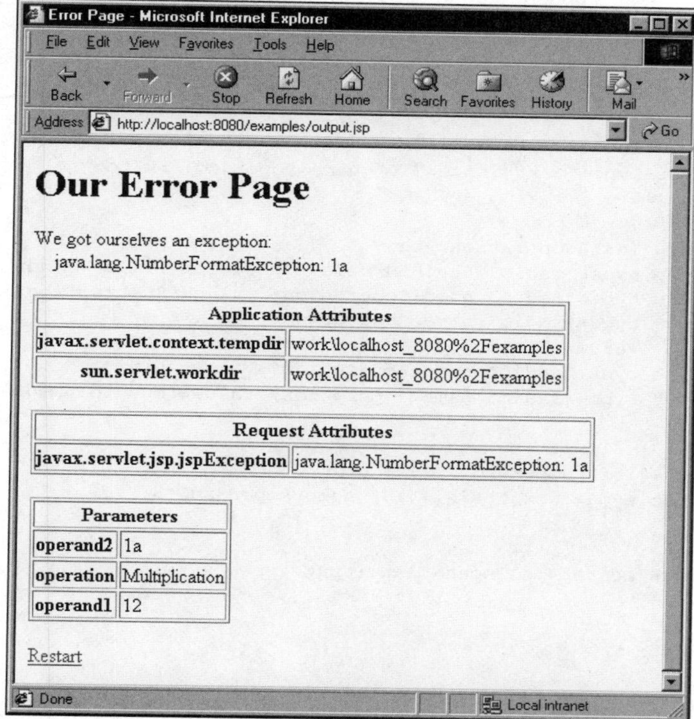

While the error page could definitely be made to look prettier, or more helpful for an end user, it displays the necessary information: basically, what caused the problem. In addition, there is also a link to restart a calculation. It is always a good idea to include a link to restart after the error has happened.

> **Notice in the figure above that even though the error page is displayed, the URL for the main page is displayed. This effectively hides the specific URL for the error page (as the source for the JSP file is never visible).**

Main Page

The source for the main calculator page, `calc.html`, is shown below; this page displays the input form for getting the operands and operator. The form data is sent to `output.jsp` for processing:

```
<html>
<head>
<title>Calculator</title>
```

```
</head>
<body>

<h1>Our Calculator</h1>

<form method="POST" action="output.jsp" >
<table border="1">
  <tr>
    <th colspan="2">Next Operation</th>
  </tr>
  <tr>
    <th align="left">Operand 1</th>
    <td><input type="text" size="10" name="operand1"></td>
  </tr>
  <tr>
    <th align="left">Operation</th>
    <td><input type="radio" checked name="operation" value="Addition">Addition<br>
        <input type="radio" name="operation" value="Subtraction">Subtraction<br>
        <input type="radio" name="operation"
               value="Multiplication">Multiplication<br>
        <input type="radio" name="operation" value="Division">Division<br>
        <input type="radio" name="operation" value="Modulo">Modulo</td>
  </tr>
  <tr>
    <th align="left">Operand 2</th>
    <td><input type="text" size="10" name="operand2"></td>
  </tr>
  <tr>
    <td align="center" colspan="2"><input type="submit" value="Submit"></td>
  </tr>
</table>
</form>

</body>
</html>
```

Output Page

`output.jsp` takes the form data sent from `calc.html`, performs the necessary calculation, and displays the results. Note the `page` directive at the top of the JSP, specifying that if an unhandled exception occurs (such as would happen if there are no parameters), the error page `error.jsp` should be used.

The actual calculations are performed by the `Calculator` bean:

```
<%@ page errorPage="error.jsp" %>

<html>
<head>
<title>Calculator Output</title>
</head>
<body>
```

```
<jsp:useBean id="calc" scope="page" class="bean.Calculator" />
<jsp:setProperty name="calc" property="*" />

<table border="1">
  <tr>
    <th colspan="2">Last Operation</th>
  </tr>
  <tr>
    <th>Operand 1</th>
    <td><jsp:getProperty name="calc" property="operand1" /></td>
  </tr>
  <tr>
    <th>Operand 2</th>
    <td><jsp:getProperty name="calc" property="operand2" /></td>
  </tr>
  <tr>
    <th>Operation</th>
    <td><jsp:getProperty name="calc" property="operation" /></td>
  </tr>
  <tr>
    <th>Solution</th>
    <td><jsp:getProperty name="calc" property="solution" /></td>
  </tr>
</table>

<p>
<a href="calc.html">Restart</a>

</body>
</html>
```

Calculator Bean

`output.jsp` uses the `Calculator` JavaBean component to do the actual calculations. It has three read-write properties: `operand1`, `operand2`, and `operation`, to match the HTML form names on the `calc.jsp` page. A fourth, read-only, property `solution` is the calculated answer. Using the bean reduces the amount of Java code needed in the JSP file. The source code for this bean, which should be contained in a file called `calculator.java`, is as follows:

```
package bean;

public class Calculator {
  String operand1;
  String operand2;
  String operation;

  public void setOperand1(String op1) {
    operand1 = op1;
  }

  public String getOperand1() {
    return operand1;
  }
```

```
    public void setOperand2(String op2) {
      operand2 = op2;
    }

    public String getOperand2() {
      return operand2;
    }

    public void setOperation(String op) {
      operation = op;;
    }

    public String getOperation() {
      return operation;
    }

    public String getSolution() {
      int intOp1 = 0;

      if ((operand1 != null) &&
          (operand1.trim().length() != 0))
        intOp1 = Integer.parseInt(operand1);

      int intOp2 = 0;

      if ((operand2 != null) &&
          (operand2.trim().length() != 0))
        intOp2 = Integer.parseInt(operand2);

      int solution = 0;

      if (operation.equals("Addition")) {
        solution = intOp1 + intOp2;
      } else if (operation.equals("Subtraction")) {
        solution = intOp1 - intOp2;
      } else if (operation.equals("Multiplication")) {
        solution = intOp1 * intOp2;
      } else if (operation.equals("Division")) {
        solution = intOp1 / intOp2;
      } else if (operation.equals("Modulo")) {
        solution = intOp1 % intOp2;
      }
      return new Integer(solution).toString();
    }
  }
```

Error Page

Finally, we come to the error page, `error.jsp`. This displays is the thrown exception, along with a complete list of application and servlet request parameters and attributes. Remember that it is the main page which sets the `errorPage` attribute, while the error page sets the `isErrorPage` attribute:

```
<%@ page import="java.util.Enumeration" isErrorPage="true" %>
<html>
<head>
<title>Error Page</title>
</head>
<body>
```

```
<h1>Our Error Page</h1>

<!-- Print Exception -->

We got ourselves an exception:<BR>
    <%= exception %>

<!-- Print Application Attributes -->
<p>

<table border="1">
  <tr>
    <th colspan="2">Application Attributes</th>
  </tr>
<%
  // Obtain the application attributes
  Enumeration appAttributeEnum = application.getAttributeNames();

  // Go through them one at a time and print them out
  while (appAttributeEnum.hasMoreElements()) {
    String name = (String)appAttributeEnum.nextElement();
%>

  <tr>
    <th><%= name %> </th>
    <td><%= application.getAttribute(name) %> </td>
  </tr>

<%
  }
%>
</table>

<!-- Print Request Attributes -->

<p>

<table border="1">
  <tr>
    <th colspan="2">Request Attributes</th>
  </tr>
<%
  // Obtain the request attributes
  Enumeration attributeEnum = request.getAttributeNames();

  // Go through them one at a time and print them out
  while (attributeEnum.hasMoreElements()) {
    String name = (String)attributeEnum.nextElement();
%>

  <tr>
    <th><%= name %> </th>
    <td><%= request.getAttribute(name) %> </td>
  </tr>

<%
  }
%>
</table>

<!-- Print Parameters -->
```

```
<p>

<table border="1">
  <tr>
    <th colspan="2">Parameters</th>
  </tr>
<%
  // Obtain the request parameters
  Enumeration parameterEnum = request.getParameterNames();

  // Go through them one at a time and print them out
  while (parameterEnum.hasMoreElements()) {
    String name = (String)parameterEnum.nextElement();
%>

  <tr>
    <th><%= name %> </th>
    <td><%= request.getParameter(name) %> </td>
  </tr>

<%
  }
%>
</table>

<p>

<a href="calc.html">Restart</a>

</body>
</html>
```

Keep in mind that not all the JSP files for a site have to use the same error-handling page. Each JSP file could have its own error-handling page, with common code in a library they shared.

Configuration

To run the example, save the three JSP files to the same directory on your JSP-enabled web server. Also, save the `.java` file for the JavaBean component, compile it, and place the class file in your `CLASSPATH`. (Since the `Calculator` class is in a package called `bean`, it must be contained in a directory called `bean`.) Once everything is ready, request the `calc.jsp` file.

Summary

In this chapter, we discussed how to configure your JSP files to display error pages. The important points included:

- How to configure a JSP page to use an error-handling page when a run time exception happens.
- How to configure a JSP to be an error-handling page.
- How an error-handling page accesses the implicit `exception` object.
- How to let a Servlet access a JSP error page.

Now we move on to look at connecting to databases from within JSP, using JDBC.

J2EE
JSP

7

Java Database Connectivity and Connection Pooling

Before the arrival of the web, most applications working with a significant amount of data had been using a database system to ease the burden of storage, retrieval, and management of data. By delegating this work to a 'database engine', the application engineer can focus on the complex problem domain at hand. The usage pattern of a web application implies that many more users may now use the very same application. This further compounds the need for a reliable and capable delegate for the database management task.

In this chapter, we will examine a technology that enables JSP based applications to interact directly with database engines. It is called **Java Database Connectivity** (JDBC), and is an integral part of the Java Platform (in both Standard and Enterprise editions).

We will implement an employee directory system using a production quality database. In particular, we will be working with JSP code that searches through a database, updates information in the database, and even removes records in a database.

JDBC/JSP based web applications access a database through a finite number of database connections. These connections must be managed carefully by the application, especially if a large number of concurrent users may be accessing them. We will study the common practices for managing databases, note some of the pitfalls and clear up common misconceptions. Furthermore, we will learn about a very useful performance optimization mechanism for JDBC called connection pooling. This 'trick of the trade' will improve system performance when working with high traffic JSP/JDBC sites.

Relational Database Management Systems

There are many classifications of databases available, we have heard of hierarchical databases, network databases, relational databases, object databases, etc. Due to their flexibility, relational database management systems, **Relational Database Management Systems** (**RDBMSs**) are the most successful breed of database in the history of computing. Most of us would have heard of ORACLE, IBM DB2, or Microsoft SQL Server – just to name a few major RDBMS products.

Relational databases store data in tables. Each table can have many rows of data, called records. Each record has a fixed number of fields. Fields are essentially data items, and can be of almost any data type (such as a string, a number, a float number, binary representing a GIF picture, etc.). As an example, an "employees" table may contain records with the following fields:

- employee ID
- firstname
- lastname
- phone extension
- department
- city of residence

As one can imagine, an employee table for a large corporation may contain tens of thousands of rows (records). If it is a frequent requirement to search through this table based on the value of certain fields (i.e. show me all employees living in a particular city), the RDBMS can help by allowing "indexes" to be created on those fields. Indexes are essentially ordered lists of pointers, and can speed up searches substantially.

Fields of a record that are indexed are called keys. For some fields, the key values can contain duplicates (for example, more than one employee can live in the same city). Most tables should have a 'primary key', which must be unique (contains a different value for each row). For example, an employee ID can be a primary key in an employee table.

RDBMSs yield most of their power from the 'join' operation. When a 'join' occurs, two or more tables are virtually merged together during a search based on their keys. This 'join' operation allows related data to be kept in separate tables without duplication (called the normalized form). When there is a need to query the database, the tables are dynamically 'joined' together to satisfy the query/search. We will perform some rather complex 'joins' later on in our JSP coding.

The *de facto* standard for querying, modifying, and updating an RDBMS is through the Structured Query Language or SQL. It is a 'common language' that can be used to access and manipulate data on most RDBMS products. Due to its heritage, and the widespread support for SQL across all commercial RDBMSs, almost all current day client/server database implementations use SQL somewhere amongst the layers of code.

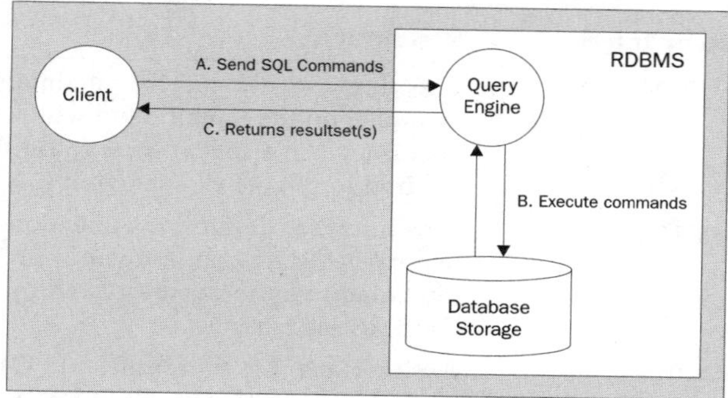

The figure above illustrates how a typical RDBMS system works. Basically:

- A client submits an SQL query statement to the RDBMS for execution.
- The server executes the SQL statement and optionally returns one or more resultsets.

A resultset is conceptually, rows of data extracted from one or more tables.

Note that a resultset is not a new RDBMS table, and is not persistent. However, executing the same query with the same database content should always return the same resultset.

When the resultset is large (for example, a listing of all the government employees in the United States), downloading all the database records from the server is both inefficient and impractical. In this case, the management of the resultset is shared between the client and server. Using something called a 'cursor' in RDBMS lingo, the resultset essentially provides a 'window' into the data within the actual table stored in the RDBMS.

Alien Object Model

Surprisingly, the premier Java Database interconnect technology is not really object oriented – it is not even a high level interface. It is a rather procedural and low-level interface. JDBC provides an X/OPEN SQL Call Level Interface (CLI) implementation. Its primary goal is to rid Java programs of vendor-specific database coding. JDBC provides a single interface, making applications independent of the underlying RDBMS and connectivity mechanism.

The higher level, 'more noble' action of translating between the actual Java objects that represent the data, to the actual rows of data that are contained in tables within the RDBMS (and vice versa) is still an art rather than a science.There are current leading-edge attempts to formalize and automate this process, SUN's Objectblend product is one such example.

Instead of providing a solution to the objects to RDBMS mapping problem, the object model of JDBC is that of the legacy yet popular SQL query mechanism. To illustrate how blatantly non-object oriented the JDBC mechanism is, there is even a `Statement` class that represents the line of SQL code that will be submitted to the DB engine for processing. Here is a tabulation of the most frequently used JDBC support classes and interfaces. They can all be found in the `java.sql` package.

JDBC Support Class or Interface	Description
`java.sql.DriverManager`	This singleton service class maintains a list of JDBC drivers available on the system, and will load and unload drivers as necessary. An application will use the `getConnection()` method to obtain a connection to a database.
`java.sql.Connection`	This interface defines a connection to a database. It is a factory for `Statement` objects, provides information (metadata) on the database, and manages transactions if the RDBMS supports it.
`java.sql.Statement`	An interface that represents an SQL statement. It can be used to execute a static SQL statement through its `executeQuery()` or `executeUpdate()` method.
`java.sql.PreparedStatement`	An interface extending the `Statement` interface, and representing a prepared SQL statement. A prepared statement provides some form of pre-compilation of a frequently used and parameterized SQL statement. RDBMSs that use 'query plans' typically support this with their JDBC driver to enhance query performance.
`java.sql.CallableStatement`	An interface extending the `PreparedStatement` interface, and representing stored procedures within the RDBMS. These procedures execute within the database engine and may return status code, or one or more resultsets. These statements are typically executed via the `execute()` method.
`java.sql.ResultSet`	A 'mini-table' abstraction of the resulting rows returned from a query. It provides many methods for easy programmatic navigation through the returned data rows and sets.
`java.sql.SQLException`	Wraps and reports any database access errors.
`java.sql.SQLWarning`	Extends `SQLException`, provides extra information on database access errors.

We will see shortly how we can use many of these classes in the JSP code that we will construct to access our database.

Why All the Driver Types?

Long before the conception of Java, RDBMSs already ruled the database world. To make custom client development feasible, vendors have come up with all sorts of proprietary schemes. Most frequently, an RDBMS vendor will provide a client component that offers a certain level of programmability (via the vendor's own version of a computer language, often presented as the next Fourth Generation Language 4GL). In time, after the 4GL excitement subsided, developers and users alike realized the proprietary 'vendor lock-in' nature of these 4GL schemes and demanded more open access to the databases. In the early days, these 'improved access mechanisms' most frequently manifested themselves as C or (later) C++ interfaces to the database. Still, a vendor's 'super code generator', compiler 'plug-ins', and/or proprietary libraries are often required to make this all work.

During this evolution, the architecture of how a SQL statement is sent from the client side to the server, and how a resultset travels back from the server to the client varied. With all the competing vendors vying for the same user base, many possible architectural variations have been tried.

Finally, when 'open' schemes such as JDBC and a closely related Win32 cousin ODBC (Open Database Connectivity from Microsoft) came along, the database vendors realized that the days of their proprietary 4GL and development environments were over. For obvious business reasons, many RDBMS vendors opted for a slow transition to open access instead of adopting JDBC/ODBC immediately. Meanwhile, the JDBC and ODBC mechanics were left tinkering with each vendor's client side programming technology to implement their drivers. The various types of driver are a perfect testament to how the various vendors have chosen their client communications architecture, and what the JDBC driver implementers have done to accommodate them.

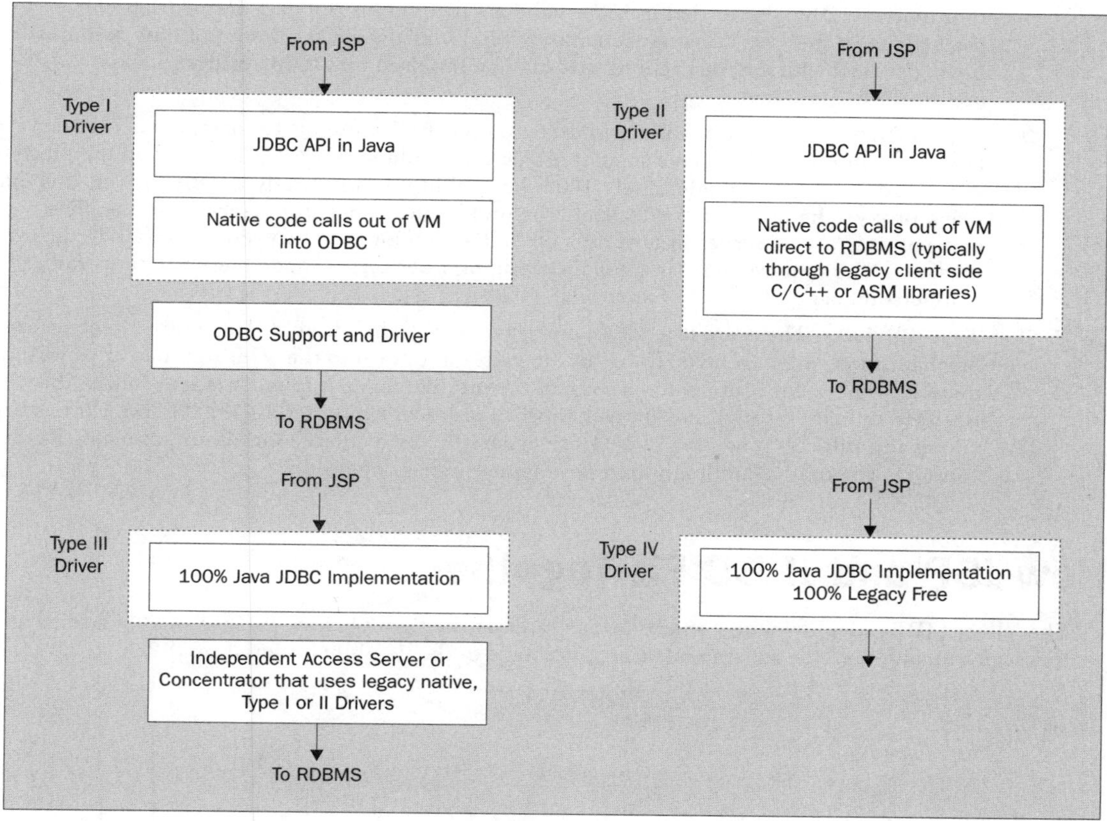

For smooth operation under Java, the most flexible, and most desirable architecture is Type 4. It was not until recently before Type 4 drivers were beginning to surface for many of the major databases. RDBMS vendors are starting to embrace the new open interconnection technologies in a big way – many are creating their own optimized JDBC drivers to showcase the capabilities of their RDBMS engines.

The checkered history and evolution of open database access technology has led to a myriad of driver architectures:

- **Type 1 Drivers.** This is how JDBC was bootstrapped. When JDBC started, there were many ODBC drivers already available. Instead of waiting for a complete design/development cycle for robust JDBC drivers, the Java community adopted the 'bridge' concept – enabling them to utilize the abundance of existing ODBC drivers. Even today, the J2SE and J2EE JDKs include the JDBC-ODBC bridge Type 1 driver as part of their distribution. Type 1 drivers are by definition not 100% Java. Having a 100% Java driver will not only enhance performance (no transition out of the Java VM necessary), but also allow for deterministic application tuning that is difficult with non-100% Java implementations.
- **Type 2 Drivers.** These are veneers over the existing native code drivers from the database vendors. They are 'quick and easy' implementations. Type 2 drivers enable a RDBMS vendor to provide a JDBC driver that uses the vendor's own optimized data access protocol (embedded in their exisiting native code drivers) in the shortest amount of time, without having to deal with any restrictions that may be imposed by ODBC bridging. Type 2 drivers are not 100% pure Java.
- **Type 3 Drivers.** These are really non-drivers: they are front-ends for database access servers and concentrators. Many have suggested that these solutions are 100% Java, and the piece that downloads to the client is definitely 100% Java – but it is not strictly a JDBC driver, it is more like a proxy. The proxy 'driver' talks to the middle-tier concentrator/access server. The concentrator/access server in turn uses ODBC or vendor specific protocol to talk to the actual database. The requirement for a collaborating mid-tier server made these solutions rather cumbersome (and often very expensive).
- **Type 4 Drivers.** These are true 100% pure Java, real JDBC drivers. The entire client access mechanism is coded in Java. There are no calls out of or into the VM from native code, and there is no need for some costly server-in-the-middle. Some implementations talk to the RDBMS directly through the 'native' network protocol supported by the RDBMS. It has been a long and difficult road, but Type 4 drivers are finally available for almost all major RDBMS vendors. The days of midnight reverse-engineering are over.

How JSP and JDBC Fit Together

The 'classic' JDBC deployment scenario is illustrated in the figure below. JSP can readily accommodate this scenario, although the scheme takes no advantage of the flexibility offered by JSP.

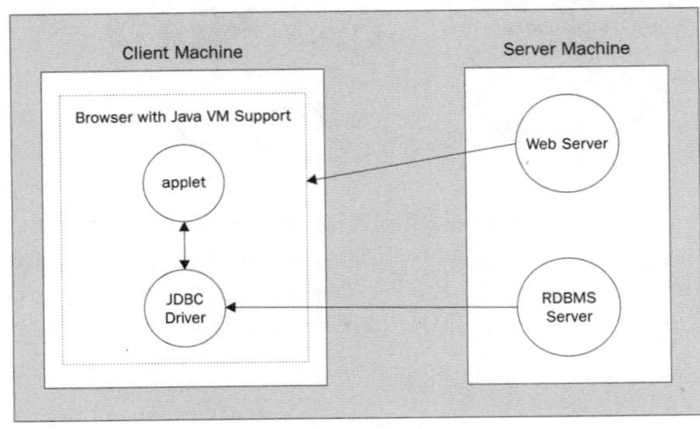

Note that the JDBC driver is downloaded with the applet embedded on the web page. The applet can then use JDBC to directly query and manipulate the data source. Some advantages cited for this architecture include:

- No installation of the application and the database driver is needed on the client; they are downloaded on-demand.
- Any updates or revision of the application and database driver is automatically taken care of.
- Only a browser supporting Java is needed at the client end.

While these advantages are an improvement on the alternate solution of creating a monolithic application executable using vendor supplied technology, embedding the database driver and application logic can give you major problems when used in the web application scenario:

- Download time of the applet (application logic) and JDBC driver can be substantial if the client is accessing the server over the Internet via a slow link or a heavily loaded network.
- We are assuming that all client browsers must support Java, otherwise they will have no access to the database.
- Every single client using the application will create his/her own JDBC server connection, that lasts an entire session. (In other words, with 500 users using the application simultaneously, you'll need to support 500 connections!)
- This solution cannot work through a firewall unless the JDBC driver to RDBMS protocol is explicitly routable through the firewall.

More in tune with the JSP/Servlet way of design, the next figure illustrates how a JSP page may interact with JDBC.

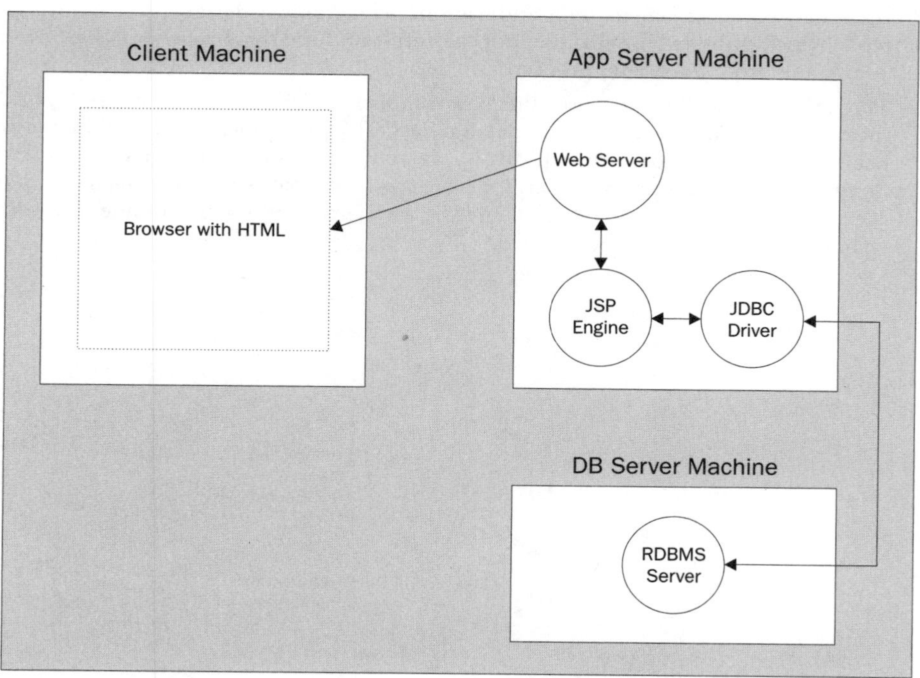

Now, compare this list of features with the shortcomings of the previous solution:

- There is no applet or JDBC driver to download to the client.
- The browser using the web application is not required to support Java at all.
- The JSP has full control over how many JDBC connections are made to the server, the client never makes direct JDBC connection to the server.
- This solution can work readily through a firewall, only standard HTTP is used between the web server and the client.
- As a bonus, this solution lends itself to an easily secured implementation, simply by adding secure socket layer support to the web server.

Because of the separation of the presentation from the business logic, which is separated from the database logic, this sort of system is often called a three-tier system, although, the application server and the database server can often be running on the same server machine.

There is still one minor nagging problem with this scenario. Project personnel accessing the JSP page containing the embedded JDBC code (such as a web graphics designer) can easily and inadvertently modify the database access code, and this may result in an erroneous application or even corrupted database. There are at least two solutions:

- Create JavaBeans or Java classes that encapsulate all JDBC operations

  This is a significantly better solution, but instantiation, initialization, and parameterization of the Java classes/beans can still represent a significant amount of embedded Java code within the JSP.
- Create a tag extension set to 'push down' all the database access logic. The data access logic programmers write the set of custom tags. The JSP application logic designers will then use the set of custom tags to create their applications. The graphics designer can in turn use layout tools, which provide 'visualization' for the result of these custom tag, and hide them completely from the layout process.

  The figure below illustrates how this is accomplished. This is the most desirable solution, since there is almost no chance that the database access logic can be corrupted. In addition, the decision of using (or not using) JDBC for database access is totally separated from the page designer or even JSP programmer. One can easily substitute another mechanism for data access into the tag implementation, and the web application will continue to work without changing a single line of the JSP code.

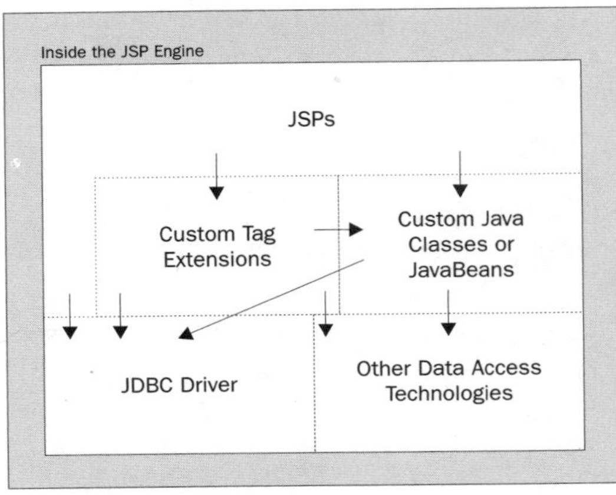

The Bigger J2EE Picture

By the J2EE definition, a web application consists of servlets and JSPs executing on their own engine on an application server, potentially using local Java classes and Java Beans, as well as Enterprise Java Beans if an EJB server is available. The primary interface from JSPs, servlets, or EJBs to any relational databases is JDBC.

In this bigger picture, one quickly realizes the importance of the potent combination of JSP and JDBC within the context of J2EE. In practice, JSP coupled with JDBC can provide:

- quick prototyping of new data driven application concepts and ideas using JSP,
- a means for non-technical personnel to design and deploy highly functional data driven applications (likely through a J2EE IDE tool supporting JSP and custom tag extensions), and
- a secure, highly customizable gateway to legacy data that forms the core asset of an enterprise.

Now that we have good grasp of how JDBC and JSP work together in various application context, we will move on and start working with some actual code.

Creating Our Own mySQL Database

We will start coding JSPs that will access our own database shortly. The example that we will use is an employee directory for a company called MyCo. The database will be stored in the very popular mySQL RDBMS.

mySQL is a multi-platform, industrial grade, relational database engine that can be, and has been, used for huge database applications including tables with millions of rows of data. While it is missing many of the features of the large and expensive commercial database servers (including transactions and stored procedures), it has proven itself again and again as more than adequate for most web based applications, which tend to be fairly simple in their database needs. It is developed and maintained by T.C.X DataKonsult AB of Stockholm, Sweden. You also cannot beat the mySQL price on Linux, UNIX and OS/2 platforms… it is FREE. In addition, mySQL is also available for platforms such as Windows NT at very competitive licensing fees.

If you have a site hosted somewhere on a UNIX based system, there is a good chance that your hosting company already supports mySQL. If you need to download the latest version of mySQL for your Linux, Unix, or Windows based system, go to http://www.mysql.com/.

We will now proceed assuming that you have DB administrative privileges (table create, add, drop, etc.) on your system. If you do not, your hosting company may have already created a database for you, and you can add the tables to the database immediately.

If you do have administrative privileges, you can create a new mySQL database using the command:

```
mysqladmin create wroxjsp
```

The MyCo directory database will consist of three tables:

- `employee`
- `depts`
- `city`

The employee table will have the following fields:

Fieldname	Description	Type	Length
empid	Unique employee ID.	int	11
lastname	Lastname of employee.	char	30
firstname	Firstname of employee.	char	30
extension	Phone extension.	char	4
cityofres idence	City where employee lives.	int	11
dept	The department that employee belongs to	int	11

The cityofresidence field contains the unique city ID associated with a row in the city table. The dept field contains the unique ID associated with a row in the dept table. Here is the city table:

Fieldname	Description	Type	Length
cid	Unique city ID	int	11
name	Actual city name	char	25

Finally, the dept table has the following structure:

Fieldname	Description	Type	Length
dpid	Unique department ID	int	11
name	Name of department	char	30
secretary	The employee ID of the secretary of this department.	int	11
phone	Outside accessible phone number for the department	char	15

The primary key of each table is the unique ID field. We can see quite clearly the relationships between the tables. For example, one relationship may be: each employee belongs to one department, and the department ID in he employee table links to the information on that department. Another relationship is: each department has one secretary, the employee ID in the secretary field of the department table links to a record in the employee table that has more information on the secretary. Later, we will be using these relationships in some complex join operations within our JSPs.

To create these tables in our mySQL database, we can use the commands in the createdb.sql file, using this command.

```
mysql -u<userid> -p wroxjsp < createdb.sql
```

where you will substitute your own user id and enter the associated password when prompted.

The command file createdb.sql contains SQL commands for creating the three related tables:

```
create table employee (
empid int(11) not null auto_increment,
lastname varchar(30) not null,
firstname varchar(30) not null,
extension varchar(4),
cityofresidence int(11) not null,
dept int(11) not null,

primary key(empid),
key city(cityofresidence),
key indept(dept)
);

create table city (
cid int(11) not null,
name varchar(25) not null,
primary key(cid)
);

create table dept (
dpid int(11) not null,
name varchar(30) not null,
secretary int(11) not null,
phone varchar(15),
primary key(dpid),
key secs(secretary)
);
```

To add data to the tables, use the `adddat.sql` file. This file contains the required SQL commands to add rows to the tables that were created earlier:

```
INSERT INTO city VALUES (1, 'London');
INSERT INTO city VALUES (2, 'Birmingham');
INSERT INTO city VALUES (3, 'New York');
INSERT INTO city VALUES (4, 'Boston');
INSERT INTO city VALUES (5, 'Toronto');

INSERT INTO dept VALUES (1, 'Sales', 5, '234-2234');
INSERT INTO dept VALUES (2, 'Engineering', 8, '322-1112');

INSERT INTO employee (lastname,firstname,extension,cityofresidence,dept) VALUES
('Campbell','Joshua','3432',2,1);
INSERT INTO employee (lastname,firstname,extension,cityofresidence,dept) VALUES
('Lieberman','Rosanna','3212',4,1);
INSERT INTO employee (lastname,firstname,extension,cityofresidence,dept) VALUES
('Ganz','Jack','2765',3,2);
INSERT INTO employee (lastname,firstname,extension,cityofresidence,dept) VALUES
('Wong','Diane','7662',2,2);
INSERT INTO employee (lastname,firstname,extension,cityofresidence,dept) VALUES
('Glutz','Nancy','3332',1,1);
INSERT INTO employee (lastname,firstname,extension,cityofresidence,dept) VALUES
('Helverson','Leslie','3787',2,1);
INSERT INTO employee (lastname,firstname,extension,cityofresidence) VALUES
('Land','Norman','3111',2,2);
INSERT INTO employee (lastname,firstname,extension,cityofresidence) VALUES
('Morris','Maggie','1132',2,2);
```

Our database and tables are now populated with data, and ready to roll. Next, we will need to configure the JDBC driver and make sure that Tomcat can access it when executing our JSP pages. If you are using another JSP engine other than Tomcat, you will need to visit its documentation to ensure that the JDBC drivers can be loaded during JSP execution time.

About Our Server Configuration

All of the code presented in this chapter has been developed on and tested with the following two-machine configuration:

Machine	Operating System/Software
Windows Client Machine	Windows 98 2nd Edition
	HyperTerminal for Telnet Access to Linux Server
	Internet Explorer 5.0 that comes with Windows 98
Linux Server Machine	RedHat Linux 6.2
	Blackdown JDK 1.2.2 RC 4 for Linux (JDK 1.1.8 should also work)
	Tomcat JSP Engine 3.0
	mySQL Server 3.22
	mm Type 4 JDBC Driver 1.2b
	PoolMan Connections Pool Manager 1.3.5

Most of the code can be readily used in all other Win32 or all UNIX configurations as well. For those with access to an RDBMS, but are not working on UNIX systems, you will have to adopt the database creation script to your own needs.

For readers who are running on Win32 systems but do not have access to mySQL, we have supplied an MS Access database that one can use with the JDBC-ODBC bridge driver to explore some of the samples. We will provide more details in a later section. Please bear in mind, however, that the JDBC-ODBC to MS Access database scenario is **not** a client/server scenario and most of the optimization issues that we will discuss later – including connections pooling – will have very little relevance to such a system.

Type 4 JDBC Driver for mySQL and Tomcat Configuration

A high performance Type 4 JDBC driver is available under the Gnu General Public License. It is being developed by Mark Matthews of Purdue University. It is affectionately known as the mm driver. You can always download the latest version from http://www.worldserver.com/mm.mysql/

To configure the mm driver for use with JSPs, you simply have to add it to Tomcat's CLASSPATH variable. The distribution of the driver comes with JDBC 1.0 and 2.0 versions, and in compressed and uncompressed JAR formats. For JDK 1.2.2, we can use the JDBC 2.0 compressed version. This is named `mysql_2_comp.jar`.

In the tomcat.sh file in your Tomcat installation directory, locate and add the following line:

```
oldCP=$CLASSPATH

CLASSPATH=${TOMCAT_HOME}/webserver.jar
CLASSPATH=${CLASSPATH}:${TOMCAT_HOME}/lib/servlet.jar
CLASSPATH=${CLASSPATH}:${TOMCAT_HOME}/lib/jasper.jar
CLASSPATH=${CLASSPATH}:${TOMCAT_HOME}/lib/xml.jar
CLASSPATH=${CLASSPATH}:${TOMCAT_HOME}/examples/WEB-INF/classes
CLASSPATH=${CLASSPATH}:${JAVA_HOME}/lib/tools.jar
CLASSPATH=${CLASSPATH}:~sing/mysql/mysqljdbc/mysql_2_comp.jar
```

You will need to replace the path above with your actual installation directory of the mm driver. You can install the mm driver in any directory that the Tomcat server will have access to. That is all you need to do to get JDBC driver installed for JSP operation.

While we are adding lines to the Tomcat configuration file, we should also add a web application declaration in the server.xml configuration file. You can substitute your own deployment directory instead of mine.

```
<Context path="/examples" docBase="examples"
   defaultSessionTimeOut="30" isWARExpanded="true"
   isWARValidated="false" isInvokerEnabled="true"
   isWorkDirPersistent="false"/>

<Context path="/wroxjdbc" docBase="wroxjdbc"
   defaultSessionTimeOut="30" isWARExpanded="true"
   isWARValidated="false" isInvokerEnabled="true"
   isWorkDirPersistent="false"/>

<Connector className="org.apache.tomcat.server.HttpServerConnector">
   </Connector>
```

Under the wroxjdbc/WEB-INF directory, place a web.xml file containing the following:

```
<?xml version="1.0" encoding="ISO-8859-1"?>

<!DOCTYPE web-app
    PUBLIC "-//Sun Microsystems, Inc.//DTD Web Application 2.2//EN"
    "http://java.sun.com/j2ee/dtds/web-app_2.2.dtd">

<web-app>
</web-app>
```

This will be enough preparation for Tomcat to run all of our sample JSP and connection pooling examples.

Alternative Setup for Type 1 Driver with Win32 JDBC-ODBC Bridging

For readers on Win32 system without access to mySQL, we have included EMPDIR.MDB. You can use this MS Access database file and the JDBC-ODBC bridge Type I driver that is included with JDK 1.1.x and 1.2.x to work through the example. This is provided as a convenience. Most of the optimization techniques mentioned later, including connection pooling, will not apply to this file-based database implementation.

To get the JSP code running on your machine, you must have:

Machine	Operating System and other Software
Single Intel Machine with 128 MB or more memory	Windows 98, Windows NT 4 SP3 or later, or Windows 2000 JDK 1.1.8 or later tested and installed Tomcat 3.0 installed and tested MS ODBC Support installed Microsoft Access ODBC Driver 4.00.3711.08 or later

To setup your system for the JSP pages:

1. Create an ODBC datasource (User DSN) called `projspdb` using the ODBC 32 Datasource applet in the control panel, point this datasource to the MSAcess database that we have provided, called `EMPDIR.MDB`.

2. Follow the instruction in the previous section for setting up the `Server.xml` and `Web.xml` files for Tomcat

3. Copy the files from the `\msdbjsps` directory into your Tomcat `\wroxjdbc\jsp` directory. Use these versions of the JSP files to explore the source code. The primary difference, you will find, are the following statements that load the JDBC-ODBC bridge driver instead of the mySQL mm driver:

```
Class.forName("sun.jdbc.odbc.JdbcOdbcDriver");
Connection myConn = DriverManager.getConnection("jdbc:odbc:projspdb");
```

Our narration throughout this chapter will be focused on the client/server mySQL database, but you can use the setup detailed here to work through most of the examples.

Coding a Simple JSP using JDBC

Now that Tomcat is configured, we are ready to create our first JSP that uses JDBC to access our MyCo database on the Linux mySQL server.

We will create a very simple and straightforward query page to start, which will clearly illustrate the complete anatomy of a JSP using JDBC. Note that there are better designs than this all JSP approach (i.e. using JavaBeans and custom tags) to data access, but using such approaches at this time will 'hide' the code anatomy from us. Be assured that these are the steps that must take place, whether you're coding them explicitly using JSP or that a JavaBean or Custom Tag is taking care of them for you.

Here are the general steps:

1. Create an instance of a JDBC driver.

2. Create a connection to an RDBMS through the JDBC driver instance.

3. Create one or more statements using the RDBMS connection.

4. Execute the statement, optionally obtaining one or more resultsets.
5. If the statement has no resultset, go to 7.
6. Iterate through the rows of the resultset and extract the needed information.
7. Perform processing and/or work with the data.
8. Repeat from 3 if more work is to be done with this connection.
9. Release the resultset.
10. Release the statement.
11. Disconnect from the database.

The JSP page we will look at is `dbquery.jsp`. For the sake of simplicity, this page displays only the contents of the employee table. It also does not lookup the actual value corresponding to the ids in the `cityofresidence` or the `dept` field. We have numbered each of the above steps in-line with the code for easy identification.

```
<html>
<head>
<title>
MyCo Directory
</title>
</head>
<%@ page language="java" import="java.sql.*" %>
<body>
<h1>MyCo Employees</h1>
<table border="1" width="400">
<tr>
     <td><b>ID</b></td><td><b>Last Name</b></td>
     <td><b>First Name</b></td><td><b>Extension</b></td>
</tr>
<%
  // Step 1
  Class.forName("org.gjt.mm.mysql.Driver");

  // Step 2
  Connection myConn =
DriverManager.getConnection("jdbc:mysql:///wroxjsp?user=sing&password=apple");

  // Step 3
  Statement stmt = myConn.createStatement();

  // Step 4
  ResultSet myResultSet = stmt.executeQuery("select * from employee");

  // Step 6
  if (myResultSet != null) {
    // Step 7
```

```
    while (myResultSet.next()) {
      String eid = myResultSet.getString("empid");
      String last = myResultSet.getString("lastname");
      String first = myResultSet.getString("firstname");
      String ext = myResultSet.getString("extension");
%>
<tr>
      <td><%= eid %></td>
      <td><%= last %></td>
      <td><%= first %> </td>
      <td><%= ext %> </td>
</tr>
<%
      // Step 8
    } /* of while */
  }  /* of if */

  // Steps 9 and 10
  stmt.close();

  // Step 11
  myConn.close();
%>
</table>
<a href="control.html">Go back to admin control</a>
</body>
</html>
```

In (1), note the use of the `forName()` method of the `Class` class to load an instance of the JDBC driver.

In (2), notice the JDBC URI syntax for the mm driver, and how the userid and password are passed to the database server to create a connection. We are accessing a local (to Tomcat) mySQL server instance in this case; if we were to access a mySQL server on a host with an IP address of `192.168.23.55` instead, we would have the URI jdbc:mysql://192.168.23.55/wroxjsp?user=sing&password=apple

Note also how the closing of a statement also closes all the resultsets associated with the statement, therefore step (9) and (10) are accomplished with one statement here.

If you execute this JSP page, you will receive the following listing of the employees in MyCo.

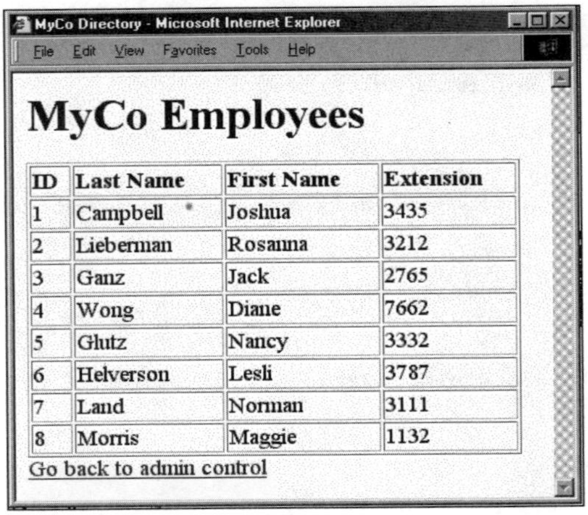

MyCo Directory - Microsoft Internet Explorer

File Edit View Favorites Tools Help

MyCo Employees

ID	Last Name	First Name	Extension
1	Campbell	Joshua	3435
2	Lieberman	Rosanna	3212
3	Ganz	Jack	2765
4	Wong	Diane	7662
5	Glutz	Nancy	3332
6	Helverson	Lesli	3787
7	Land	Norman	3111
8	Morris	Maggie	1132

Go back to admin control

All JSP pages that work with and process data using JDBC will perform all these eleven steps. It is possible, however, that some optimization may hide some of the steps. For example, a Java class or JavaBean may be used to 'fold up' some commonly used queries.

Using JavaBeans to 'Fold Up' Commonly Used Code

We have mentioned the use of Java classes (beans) to 'fold up' some of the more frequently used code in JSP to JDBC operations. We will show a general idea of how to do this by building upon our simple `dbquery.jsp` file.

First, we create a `sqlBean.java` file that encapsulates the basic connection and takedown of a JDBC connection. Note that it is an abstract class. All of our JDBC "beans" will derive from this class since they must all make a connection. There is one abstract method called `cleanup()` that all subclasses must implement. This provides the subclasses a chance to close statements, resultsets, etc. before the actual disconnection.

```
import java.sql.*;
import java.io.*;

public abstract class sqlBean {
  private String myDriver = "org.gjt.mm.mysql.Driver";
  private String myURL =
    "jdbc:mysql:///wroxjsp?user=sing&password=apple";

  protected Connection myConn;

  public sqlBean() {}

  public void makeConnection() throws Exception {
    Class.forName(myDriver);
    myConn = DriverManager.getConnection(myURL);
  }
  public abstract void cleanup() throws Exception;

  public void takeDown() throws Exception {
    cleanup();
    myConn.close();
  }

}
```

For our `dbquery.jsp` situation, we are working with a query to the employee table. We encapsulate much of the query work using `empQBean.java`, which derives from the `sqlBean` abstract class. Here, we hide the actual query and the resultset handling from the JSP programmer.

```
import java.sql.*;
import java.io.*;

public class empQBean extends sqlBean {
  String myEmpSQL = "select * from employee";
  ResultSet myResultSet = null;
  Statement stmt = null;
  public empQBean() {
```

```
    super();
  }

  public boolean getNextEmployee() throws Exception {
    return myResultSet.next();
  }
  public String getColumn(String inCol) throws Exception {
    return myResultSet.getString(inCol);
  }

  public boolean getEmployees() throws Exception {
    String myQuery = myEmpSQL;
    stmt = myConn.createStatement();
    myResultSet = stmt.executeQuery(myQuery);
    return (myResultSet != null);
  }
  public void cleanup() throws Exception {
    stmt.close();
  }
}
```

Using these two Java classes, we can now simplify the `dbquery.jsp` file significantly. You can find the new source code in the `dbqueryJB.jsp` file, under the `\javabeans` directory of the distribution.

```
<html>
<head>
<title>
MyCo Directory
</title>
</head>
<%@ page language="java" import="java.sql.*" %>
<jsp:useBean id="empbean" class="empQBean" scope="page" />

<body>
<h1>MyCo Employees</h1>
<table border="1" width="400">
<tr>
     <td><b>ID</b></td><td><b>Last Name</b></td>
     <td><b>First Name</b></td><td><b>Extension</b></td>
</tr>
<%
  empbean.makeConnection();  // connect up
  if (empbean.getEmployees())     // perform query
   {
    while (empbean.getNextEmployee())
     {
            String eid = empbean.getColumn("empid");
            String last = empbean.getColumn("lastname");
            String first = empbean.getColumn("firstname");
            String ext = empbean.getColumn("extension");
%>
<tr>
            <td><%= eid %></td>
            <td><%= last %></td>
            <td><%= first %> </td>
            <td><%= ext %> </td>
</tr>
<%
            } /* of while */
   }  /* of if */
```

```
    empbean.takeDown();
  %>
  </table>
  <a href="control.html">Go back to admin control</a>
  </body>
  </html>
```

By using `empQBean` in the JSP file, we have saved considerable Java coding within the JSP file – making it easier to maintain and understand.

To test this, you must create a `\wroxjdbc\WEB-INF\classes` directory under your Tomcat directory tree. Copy the `sqlBean.class` and `empQBean.class` file into this directory so that Tomcat can find it. Next, copy the `dbqueryJB.jsp` file into the `\wroxjdc\jsp` directory. Start Tomcat, and try out `dbqueryJB.jsp` – it is indistinguishable from the original `dbquery.jsp`.

In the rest of the chapter, we will not use this technique, as we want to show precisely what is going on between JSP and JDBC without hiding any details. In your production work, feel free to encapsulate frequently used JSP coding using this technique (or even use custom tags if you're using the JSP 1.1 platform).

More Advanced JDBC

Having seen the basics of using JDBC from within JSP, we can move on to examine some of the more advanced features of JDBC.

Querying a Database

While the previous example illustrates clearly the anatomy of a JSP using JDBC, we will now examine a more involved example that leverages the power of an RDBMS system. Instead of using one single table, we will now create a query JSP page that works with the 'join' of all three tables in the `wroxjsp` database.

In this JSP, we will iterate through all the departments in MyCo, and for each department:

- print its name and phone number,
- print out all the employees belonging to the department (in employee ID order),
- put an asterisk (*) next to the employee ID for the employee who is also the secretary of the department, and
- decode and show the city of residence for each employee.

In SQL terms, this translates to the following 'join' of the three tables using the `SELECT` command:

```
SELECT * FROM DEPT,EMPLOYEE,CITY WHERE DEPT.DPID=EMPLOYEE.DEPT AND
EMPLOYEE.CITYOFRESIDENCE=CITY.CID ORDER BY DEPT.DPID,EMPID
```

This is precisely the SQL statement that is used by the `dptquery.jsp` file to accomplish the above.

```
<html>
<head>
<title>
MyCo Departments
</title>
```

```
</head>
<%@ page language="java" import="java.sql.*" %>
<body>
<h1>MyCo Departments</h1>
<%
// Step 1
  Class.forName("org.gjt.mm.mysql.Driver");
  // Step 2
Connection myConn =
DriverManager.getConnection("jdbc:mysql:///wroxjsp?user=sing&password=apple");

 // Step 3
 Statement stmt = myConn.createStatement();
 // Step 4
 ResultSet myResultSet = stmt.executeQuery("select * from dept,employee,city where
dept.dpid=employee.dept and employee.cityofresidence=city.cid  order by
dept.dpid,empid");
```

The resultset from this query will have been ordered first by department IDs, we store the department ID of the current record in the resultset (in the variable `curDeptID`) in order to detect when there is a change in department. We will create a new HTML table to contain the employees of each department.

When a change of department is detected, the employee ID of the department secretary is stored into the `deptSec` variable for later use. The `secMark` variable will either contain a null string `""` or the asterisk `"*"`, depending on whether the current employee is the secretary of the department. `secMark` is always printed next to the ID.

```
    int curDeptID = 0;
    int deptSec = 0;
    String secMark = "";
    // Step 6
    if (myResultSet != null)
      {
         // Step 7
         while (myResultSet.next()) {
           int tpDeptID = myResultSet.getInt("dpid");
            if (tpDeptID != curDeptID)
              {
              if (curDeptID != 0)
                 {
%>
               </table>
 <%              }
              String tpDept = myResultSet.getString("dept.name");
              deptSec = myResultSet.getInt("dept.secretary");
              String tpPhone = myResultSet.getString("dept.phone");
 %>
               <H2><%= tpDept %> Department</H2>
               Direct Phone: <%= tpPhone %>, secretary marked with '*' below
               <table border="1" width="600">
               <tr>
                   <td><b>ID</b></td><td><b>Last Name</b></td>
                   <td><b>First Name</b></td><td><b>Extension</b></td>
                   <td><b>City</b></td>
               </tr>
<%
               curDeptID = tpDeptID;
             }
```

```
            int eid = myResultSet.getInt("empid");
            if (eid == deptSec)
             secMark = "*";
            else
             secMark = "";
            String last = myResultSet.getString("lastname");
            String first = myResultSet.getString("firstname");
            String ext = myResultSet.getString("extension");
            String city = myResultSet.getString("city.name");
%>
<tr>
            <td><%= eid %><%= secMark %></td>
            <td><%= last %></td>
            <td><%= first %> </td>
            <td><%= ext %> </td>
            <td><%= city %> </td>
</tr>
<%  // Step 8
            } /* of while */
    }  /* of if */
  // step 9,10
  stmt.close();
  // step 11
 myConn.close();
%>
</table>
<a href="control.html">Go back to admin control</a>
</body>
</html>
```

One thing that should become obvious is how similar in structure this is to the simple query JSP that we looked at. In fact, you will find that **all** JSPs that perform queries will have the exact general structure. Here is how the department listing will look.

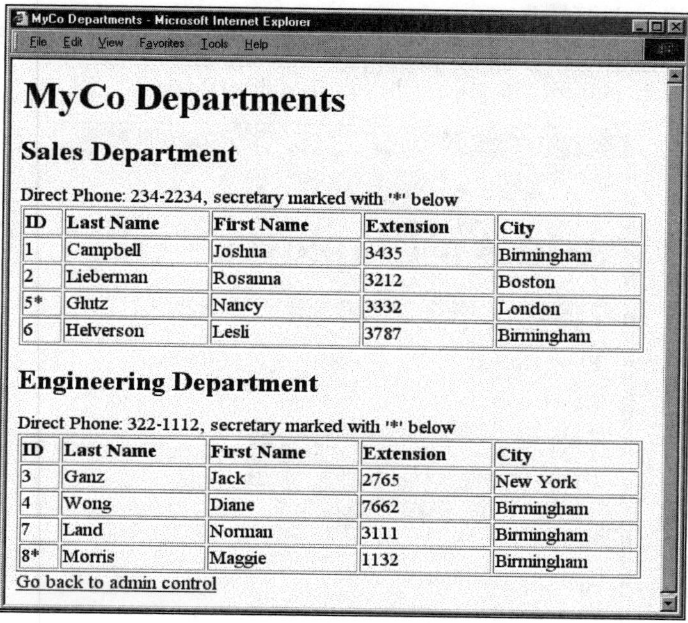

MyCo Departments

Sales Department

Direct Phone: 234-2234, secretary marked with '*' below

ID	Last Name	First Name	Extension	City
1	Campbell	Joshua	3435	Birmingham
2	Lieberman	Rosanna	3212	Boston
5*	Glutz	Nancy	3332	London
6	Helverson	Lesli	3787	Birmingham

Engineering Department

Direct Phone: 322-1112, secretary marked with '*' below

ID	Last Name	First Name	Extension	City
3	Ganz	Jack	2765	New York
4	Wong	Diane	7662	Birmingham
7	Land	Norman	3111	Birmingham
8*	Morris	Maggie	1132	Birmingham

Go back to admin control

Adding Records to a Database

Displaying database records and complex joins are relatively simple with JSPs, thanks to the incredible amount of work performed by the RDBMS engine, based on the embedded SQL statements. It turns out that adding records into the database is also quite straightforward.

To add a record into the employee table, the following SQL statement can be used:

```
INSERT INTO EMPLOYEE (LASTNAME, FIRSTNAME, EXTENSION, CITYOFRESIDENCE, DEPT)
VALUES (<value of lastname>,<value of firstname>,<value of extension>,<value of
cityofresidence>,<value of dept>)
```

We do not insert the value of the employee ID because this is automatically generated by the DB engine (mySQL) when the record is actually inserted. This 'auto_increment' feature is essential for a situation where there may be multiple administrators adding new employee records to the database at the same time. It guarantees that all new employees will have unique employee IDs.

Instead of one single JSP handling the record addition, we choose to use a two-JSP design. The next figure illustrates how the two pages work together.

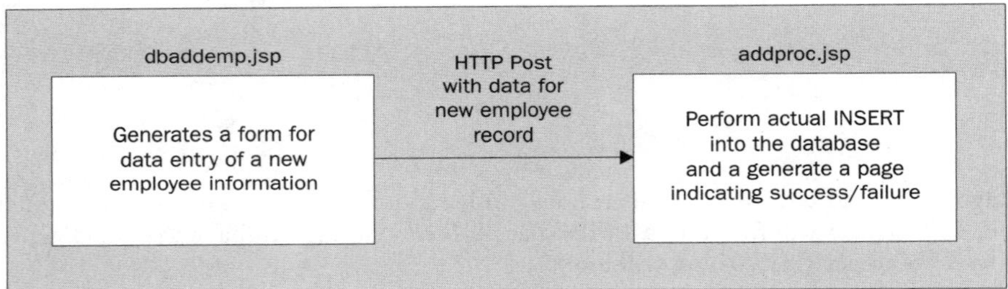

The `dbaddemp.jsp` presents a form, which allows entry of all the relevant fields of the new record. This form is dynamically generated by the JSP, allowing the user to select from all the current cities of residence and departments for the new employee via a drop down list.

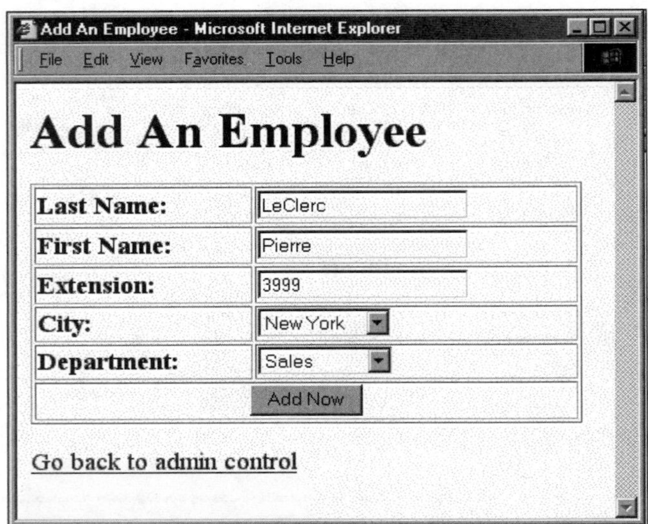

The code for `dbaddemp.jsp` is presented below. Notice how the `<select>` choice list for the `cityofresidence` and `dept` fields are generated from two SQL queries, to the `city` and `dept` tables respectively.

```
<html>
<head>
<title>
Add An Employee
</title>
</head>
<%@ page language="java" import="java.sql.*" %>
<body>
<h1>Add An Employee</h1>
<form method="post" action="addproc.jsp">
<table border="1" width="400">
<tr>
     <td><b>Last Name:</b></td><td><input name="inplast" type="text"
     width="30"></td>
</tr>
<tr>
     <td><b>First Name:</b></td><td><input name="inpfirst" type="text"
     width="30"</td>
</tr>
<tr>
     <td><b>Extension:</b></td><td><input name="inpext" type="text"
     width="11"</td>
</tr>
```

Both the `cityofresidence` and the `dept` fields need decoding. We create the list of choices in the `<select>` HTML tag by querying the actual tables. The user will select a choice based on the name of the city and name of the department. However, the value associated with the selection will be the actual city ID and dept ID that will be inserted into the table.

```
<tr>
     <td><b>City:</b></td><td><select name="inpcity">
<%

  Class.forName("org.gjt.mm.mysql.Driver");
  Connection myConn = DriverManager.getConnection
    ("jdbc:mysql:///wroxjsp?user=sing&password=apple");

  Statement stmt = myConn.createStatement();
  ResultSet myResultSet = stmt.executeQuery("select * from city");

  if (myResultSet != null)
    {
       while (myResultSet.next()) {
          String cid = myResultSet.getString("cid");
          String cname = myResultSet.getString("name");
%>
          <option value='<%= cid %>'><%= cname %>
<%
          } /* of while */
   }  /* of if */

%>
  </select> </td>
</tr>
<tr>
     <td><b>Department:</b></td><td><select name="inpdept">
```

```
<%

  myResultSet = stmt.executeQuery("select * from dept");

  if (myResultSet != null)
    {
        while (myResultSet.next()) {
           String dpid = myResultSet.getString("dpid");
           String dpname = myResultSet.getString("name");
%>
           <option value='<%= dpid %>'><%= dpname %>
<%
           } /* of while */
    }  /* of if */

%>
  </select> </td>
</tr>
<tr>
     <td colspan="2">
         <center>
            <input name="pagemode" type="hidden" value="submit">
            <input type="submit" value="Add Now">
         </center>
     </td>
</tr>
<%
  stmt.close();
  myConn.close();
%>
</table>
</form>
<a href="control.html">Go back to admin control</a>
</body>
</html>
```

After the administrator has completed the entry of the employee information, they click on the Add Now button, and the form sends an HTTP POST request to the second collaborating JSP, `addproc.jsp`. It is in `addproc.jsp` that the actual `INSERT` SQL statement is executed.

```
<html>
<head>
<title>
Add Employee Processing
</title>
</head>
<%@ page language="java" import="java.sql.*" %>
<body>

<%

  Class.forName("org.gjt.mm.mysql.Driver");
  String ilast = request.getParameter("inplast");
  String ifirst = request.getParameter("inpfirst");
  String iext = request.getParameter("inpext");
  String icity = request.getParameter("inpcity");
  String idept = request.getParameter("inpdept");
```

The parameters (fields from the submitted form) are extracted from the HTTP POST request, and provide the data that will be used in constructing the `INSERT` SQL statement.

```
    Connection myConn = DriverManager.getConnection
      ("jdbc:mysql:///wroxjsp?user=sing&password=apple");

    Statement stmt = myConn.createStatement();
    int rowsAffected = stmt.executeUpdate("insert into employee
  (lastname,firstname,extension,cityofresidence,dept) values('"
      + ilast +"','" + ifirst + "','" + iext + "'," + icity + "," + idept
      + ")");
```

Note the use of `executeUpdate()` method instead of the `executeQuery()` method. This is because the `INSERT` command is not expected to return any resultset. Instead, commands such as `INSERT` return a number indicating the actual number of rows affected by the operation. Since we are inserting precisely one record, a successful `INSERT` should return the number `1`. Note also the simplistic way we have opted to build the `INSERT` statement; we are assuming that the input fields from the user will not contain the escape character (single quote in this case). In production, you will want to parse and escape each field individually.

```
    if (rowsAffected == 1)
      {
%>
     <h1>Successful Addition of Employee</h1>
      Thank you for adding a new employee.
     <p>
      <a href="dbquery.jsp">See all employees</a><br>
      <a href="dptquery.jsp">See departments</a><br>
      <a href="control.html">Go back to control center</a>

<%    }
     else
      {
%>
      <h1>Sorry, addition has failed.</h1>
      <a href="control.html">Go back to control center</a>
<%
       }
   stmt.close();
   myConn.close();
%>
</body>
</html>
```

The `addproc.jsp` form processor will generate an HTML page that indicates a successful addition, or a failed one. For example, if a record addition is successful, the following page will be returned.

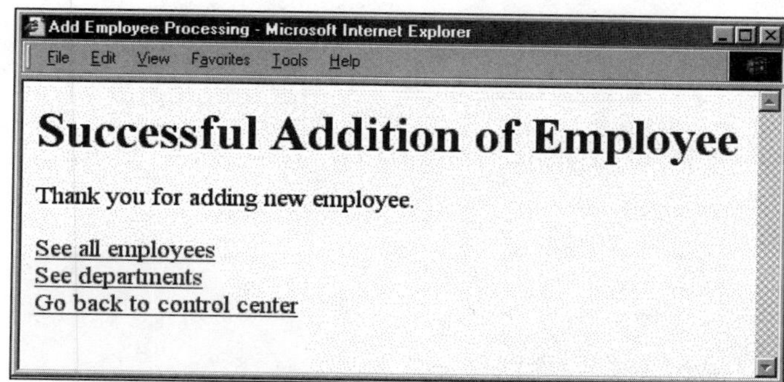

One can easily verify the record is added by viewing one of the query pages again.

Deleting Database Records

Non-query (that is, not `SELECT` command) JSP pages that use JDBC are quite similar in structure. We will see this pattern when we examine how to delete a record from the database using JSP.

To delete an employee record from our employee table, the SQL statement that is involved takes the following form:

```
DELETE FROM EMPLOYEE WHERE EMPID=<employee number to delete>
```

Again, we will use a two-JSP approach to provide the user interface. The first page we will present the user with is a selection page. This selection page tabulates all the employees that are currently in the database table.

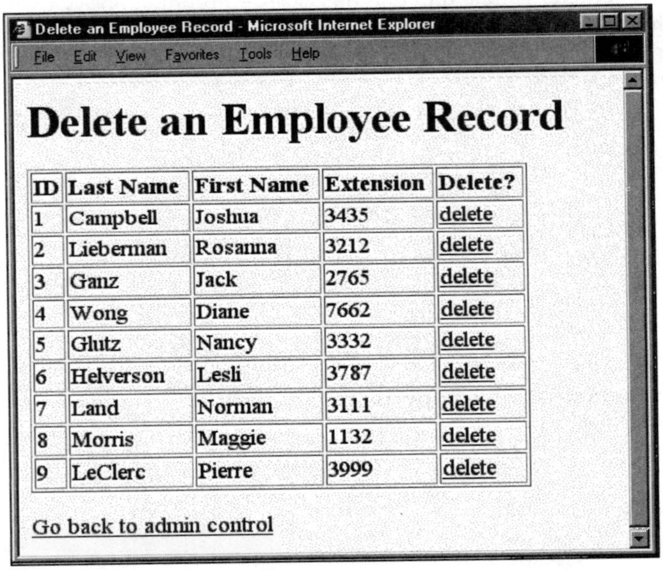

Delete an Employee Record - Microsoft Internet Explorer

File Edit View Favorites Tools Help

Delete an Employee Record

ID	Last Name	First Name	Extension	Delete?
1	Campbell	Joshua	3435	delete
2	Lieberman	Rosanna	3212	delete
3	Ganz	Jack	2765	delete
4	Wong	Diane	7662	delete
5	Glutz	Nancy	3332	delete
6	Helverson	Lesli	3787	delete
7	Land	Norman	3111	delete
8	Morris	Maggie	1132	delete
9	LeClerc	Pierre	3999	delete

Go back to admin control

The code for this page is contained in the `dbdelemp.jsp` file, and is an adaptation of the closely related `dbquery.jsp` that we have seen earlier:

```
<html>
<head>
<title>
Delete an Employee Record
</title>
</head>
<%@ page language="java" import="java.sql.*" %>
<body>
<h1>Delete an Employee Record</h1>
<table border="1" width="400">
<tr>
     <td><b>ID</b></td>
     <td><b>Last Name</b></td>
     <td><b>First Name</b></td>
     <td><b>Extension</b></td>
     <td><b>Delete?</d></td>
</tr>
```

Each row in the table has an additional **Delete?** field with a hyperlink in it. The user can click any of the links to delete the corresponding employee record. The target of the link is actually a fabricated HTTP GET request to the collaborating `delproc.jsp` handler, with the employee ID to be deleted as a parameter.

```
<%

   Class.forName("org.gjt.mm.mysql.Driver");
   Connection myConn = DriverManager.getConnection
     ("jdbc:mysql:///wroxjsp?user=sing&password=apple");

   Statement stmt = myConn.createStatement();
   ResultSet myResultSet = stmt.executeQuery("select * from employee");

   if (myResultSet != null)
     {
          while (myResultSet.next()) {
               String eid = myResultSet.getString("empid");
               String last = myResultSet.getString("lastname");
               String first = myResultSet.getString("firstname");
               String ext = myResultSet.getString("extension");
%>
<tr>
               <td><%= eid %></td>
               <td><%= last %></td>
               <td><%= first %> </td>
               <td><%= ext %> </td>
               <td><a href='delproc.jsp?eid=<%= eid %>'>delete</a></td>
</tr>
<%
               } /* of while */
    }  /* of if */
   stmt.close();
   myConn.close();
%>
</table>
<p>
<a href="control.html">Go back to admin control</a>
</body>
</html>
```

Now, when the user sees the output from `dbdelemp.jsp`, they may click on the **delete** link associated with one of the employee records. When this link is clicked, an HTTP GET request is sent to `delproc.jsp` for the actual deletion. The following figure illustrates how these two JSP pages work together:

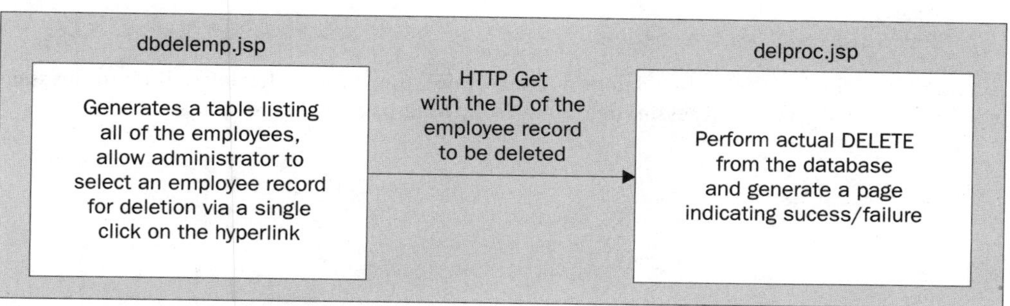

Here is the code for the delproc.jsp file:

```
<html>
<head>
<title>
Delete Employee Processing
</title>
</head>
<%@ page language="java" import="java.sql.*" %>
<body>

<%

  Class.forName("org.gjt.mm.mysql.Driver");
  String eid = request.getParameter("eid");
  Connection myConn =
DriverManager.getConnection("jdbc:mysql:///wroxjsp?user=sing&password=apple");

  Statement stmt = myConn.createStatement();
  int rowsAffected = stmt.executeUpdate("delete from employee where empid="+ eid);
```

We use the executeUpdate() method instead of the executeQuery() method here, as we have done previously in the INSERT case.

```
    if (rowsAffected == 1)
      {
%>
    <h1>Successful Deletion of an Employee Record</h1>
     The record has been deleted.
    <p>
     <a href="dbquery.jsp">See all employees</a><br>
     <a href="dptquery.jsp">See departments</a><br>
     <a href="control.html">Go back to control center</a>

<%    }
    else
     {
%>
     <h1>Sorry, deletion has failed.</h1>
     <a href="control.html">Go back to control center</a>
<%
       }
   stmt.close();
   myConn.close();
%>
</body>
</html>
```

Depending on whether the record deletion is successful, the JSP will display a different message on the output HTML page. For a successful delete, the following page will be displayed:

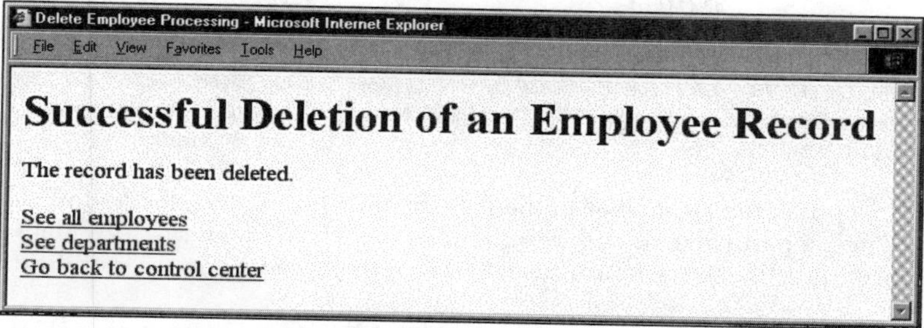

Modifying Records in a Database

We will implement a three-JSP solution to support modification of records. The figure below shows how the three JSPs collaborate.

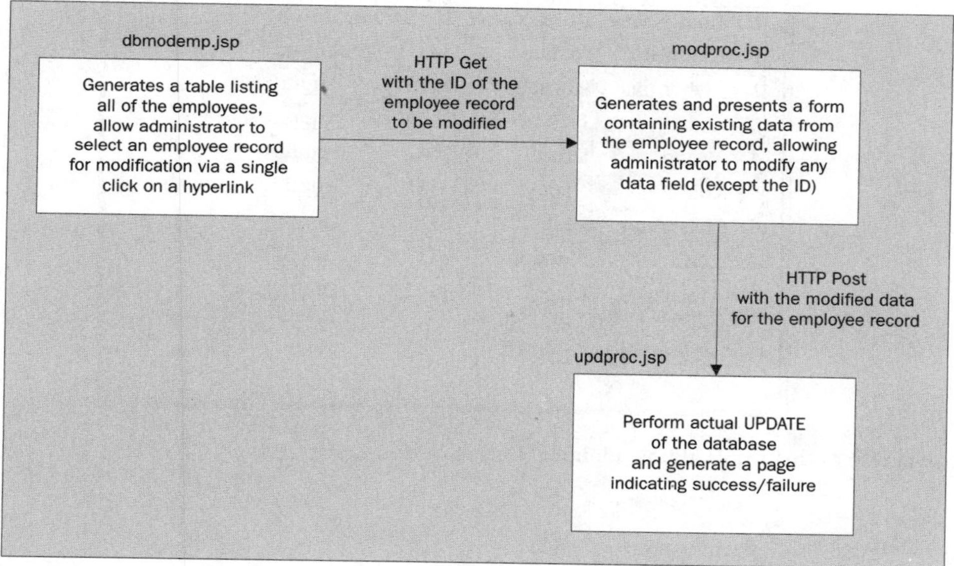

- `dbmodemp.jsp` will provide the user with the list of employee records available for modification, the user can click on any record for modification.
- `modproc.jsp` will display a data entry form; this form will be pre-filled with all the field values from the selected record. `city` and `dept` values should be fully decoded. The user can modify any of the field values, and submit the form for actual modification.
- `updproc.jsp` will process the modification form and make the actual change in the database.

The SQL command used in modifying an employee record is:

```
UPDATE EMPLOYEE SET LASTNAME=<lastname value>, FIRSTNAME=<firstname value>,
EXTENSION=<extension value>,CITYOFRESIDENCE=<cityofresidence value>,DEPT=<dept
value> WHERE EMPID=<the ID of the employee record to change>
```

The `updproc.jsp` file, the last player in the JSP chain, will actually execute this statement. But first, the user must select a particular record for modification. The `dbmodemp.jsp` file will present a list of employee records, just like the deletion case, for the user to select one for modification:

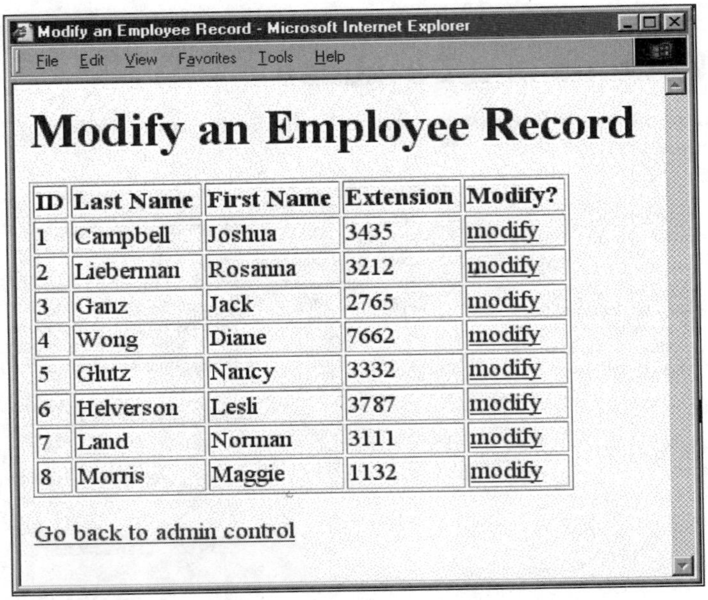

Modify an Employee Record - Microsoft Internet Explorer

File Edit View Favorites Tools Help

Modify an Employee Record

ID	Last Name	First Name	Extension	Modify?
1	Campbell	Joshua	3435	modify
2	Lieberman	Rosanna	3212	modify
3	Ganz	Jack	2765	modify
4	Wong	Diane	7662	modify
5	Glutz	Nancy	3332	modify
6	Helverson	Lesli	3787	modify
7	Land	Norman	3111	modify
8	Morris	Maggie	1132	modify

Go back to admin control

The structure of this JSP is almost identical to that of `dbdelemp.jsp`.

```
<html>
<head>
<title>
Modify an Employee Record
</title>
</head>
<%@ page language="java" import="java.sql.*" %>
<body>
<h1>Modify an Employee Record</h1>
<table border="1" width="400">
<tr>
     <td><b>ID</b></td>
     <td><b>Last Name</b></td>
     <td><b>First Name</b></td>
     <td><b>Extension</b></td>
     <td><b>Modify?</d></td>
</tr>
<%
```

```
   Class.forName("org.gjt.mm.mysql.Driver");
   Connection myConn = DriverManager.getConnection
     ("jdbc:mysql:///wroxjsp?user=sing&password=apple");

   Statement stmt = myConn.createStatement();
   ResultSet myResultSet = stmt.executeQuery("select * from employee");

   if (myResultSet != null)
     {
          while (myResultSet.next()) {
             String eid = myResultSet.getString("empid");
             String last = myResultSet.getString("lastname");
             String first = myResultSet.getString("firstname");
             String ext = myResultSet.getString("extension");
%>
<tr>
             <td><%= eid %></td>
             <td><%= last %></td>
             <td><%= first %> </td>
             <td><%= ext %> </td>
             <td><a href='modproc.jsp?eid=<%= eid %>'>modify</a></td>
</tr>
<%
             } /* of while */
    }  /* of if */
  stmt.close();
  myConn.close();
%>
</table>
<p>
<a href="control.html">Go back to admin control</a>
</body>
</html>
```

After the user has selected a record for modification, an HTTP GET submit is made to `modproc.jsp`. This JSP will display a form, which will be pre-filled with current field values from the employee record.

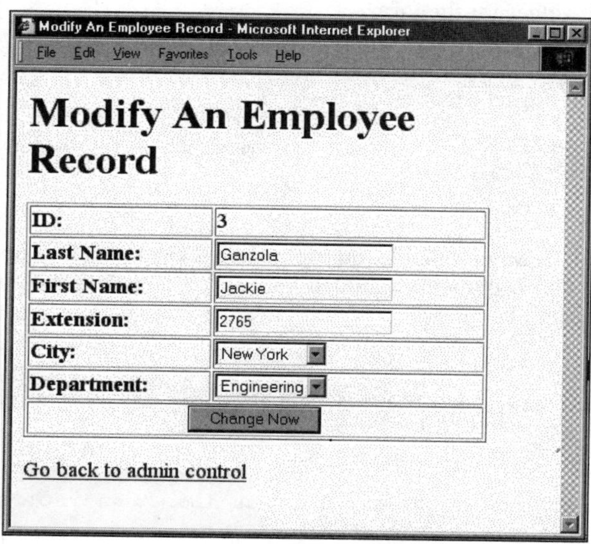

The code for `modproc.jsp` is listed here:

```
<html>
<head>
<title>
Modify An Employee Record
</title>
</head>
<%@ page language="java" import="java.sql.*" %>
<body>
<h1>Modify An Employee Record</h1>
<%

  String eid = request.getParameter("eid");
  Class.forName("org.gjt.mm.mysql.Driver");
  Connection myConn =
DriverManager.getConnection("jdbc:mysql:///wroxjsp?user=sing&password=apple");

  Statement stmt = myConn.createStatement();
  ResultSet myResultSet = stmt.executeQuery
    ("select * from employee where empid=" + eid);
  String optionSelected = "";
  if (myResultSet != null)
   myResultSet.next();   // should be one and only record

  String elast = myResultSet.getString("lastname");
  String efirst = myResultSet.getString("firstname");
  String eext = myResultSet.getString("extension");
  int ecity = myResultSet.getInt("cityofresidence");
  int edept = myResultSet.getInt("dept");
%>
```

The first thing we do here is to query the employee table for the existing field values. These will be used to generate the default values for the form.

```
<form method="post" action="updproc.jsp">
<table border="1" width="400">
<tr>
     <td><b>ID:</b></td><td><%= eid %><input name="inpeid" type="hidden"
     value="<%= eid %>"></td>
</tr>
```

The employee ID field is non-modifiable, but we need a way to pass it to `updproc.jsp` during the HTTP POST request. This is done via a hidden field called `inpeid`. The rest of the form fields are filled with field value from the query:

```
<tr>
     <td><b>Last Name:</b></td><td><input name="inplast" type="text"
     width="30" value="<%= elast %>"></td>
</tr>
<tr>
     <td><b>First Name:</b></td><td><input name="inpfirst" type="text"
     width="30" value="<%= efirst %>"></td>
```

```
  </tr>
  <tr>
       <td><b>Extension:</b></td><td><input name="inpext" type="text"
       width="4" value="<%= eext %>"></td>
  </tr>
  <tr>
       <td><b>City:</b></td><td><select name="inpcity">
  <%

    myResultSet = stmt.executeQuery("select * from city");

    if (myResultSet != null)
       {
            while (myResultSet.next()) {
                int cid = myResultSet.getInt("cid");
                String cname = myResultSet.getString("name");
                if (ecity == cid)
                      optionSelected = "selected";
                else
                      optionSelected = "";
%>
                <option value='<%= cid %>' <%= optionSelected %>><%= cname %>
<%
                } /* of while */
     }  /* of if */

%>
   </select> </td>
 </tr>
```

For both the cityofresidence and dept fields, we must mark the decoded choice with the selected attribute within the HTML <option> tag. This is done by comparing the city ID (or dept ID) from the old record against each value retrieved from a direct city table (or dept table) query:

```
  <tr>
       <td><b>Department:</b></td><td><select name="inpdept">
  <%

    myResultSet = stmt.executeQuery("select * from dept");

    if (myResultSet != null)
       {
            while (myResultSet.next()) {
                int dpid = myResultSet.getInt("dpid");
                String dpname = myResultSet.getString("name");
                if (edept == dpid)
                      optionSelected = "selected";
                else
                      optionSelected = "";
%>
                <option value='<%= dpid %>' <%= optionSelected %>><%= dpname %>
<%
                } /* of while */
     }  /* of if */
```

```
%>
  </select> </td>
</tr>
<tr>
     <td colspan="2">
          <center>
              <input type="submit" value="Change Now">
          </center>
     </td>
</tr>
<%
  stmt.close();
  myConn.close();
%>
</table>
</form>
<a href="control.html">Go back to admin control</a>
</body>
</html>
```

After the user has made the appropriate modification, the form is submitted to `updproc.jsp`, where the actual modification is performed:

```
<html>
<head>
<title>
Modify Employee Record Processing
</title>
</head>
<%@ page language="java" import="java.sql.*" %>
<body>

<%

  Class.forName("org.gjt.mm.mysql.Driver");
  String ieid = request.getParameter("inpeid");
  String ilast = request.getParameter("inplast");
  String ifirst = request.getParameter("inpfirst");
  String iext = request.getParameter("inpext");
  String icity = request.getParameter("inpcity");
  String idept = request.getParameter("inpdept");
```

As previously, this JSP needs to obtain the new values to update from the HTTP POST parameters. These are the form field values from `modproc.jsp`.

```
  Connection myConn =
DriverManager.getConnection("jdbc:mysql:///wroxjsp?user=sing&password=apple");

  Statement stmt = myConn.createStatement();
  int rowsAffected = stmt.executeUpdate("update employee  set lastname='" +
ilast + "', firstname='" + ifirst + "', extension='" + iext + "',
cityofresidence=" + icity +",dept=" + idept + "  where empid=" + ieid);
```

The actual modification is performed using `executeUpdate()`, and it should only affect one single row since the employee ID is always unique.

```
   if (rowsAffected == 1)
     {
%>
     <h1>Successful Modification of Employee Record</h1>
      The employee record has been modified.
     <p>
      <a href="dbquery.jsp">See all employees</a><br>
      <a href="dptquery.jsp">See departments</a><br>
      <a href="control.html">Go back to control center</a>

<%    }
     else
      {
%>
      <h1>Sorry, modification has failed.</h1>
      <a href="control.html">Go back to control center</a>
<%
       }
   stmt.close();
   myConn.close();
%>
</body>
</html>
```

Upon successful modification, this page will be presented to the user:

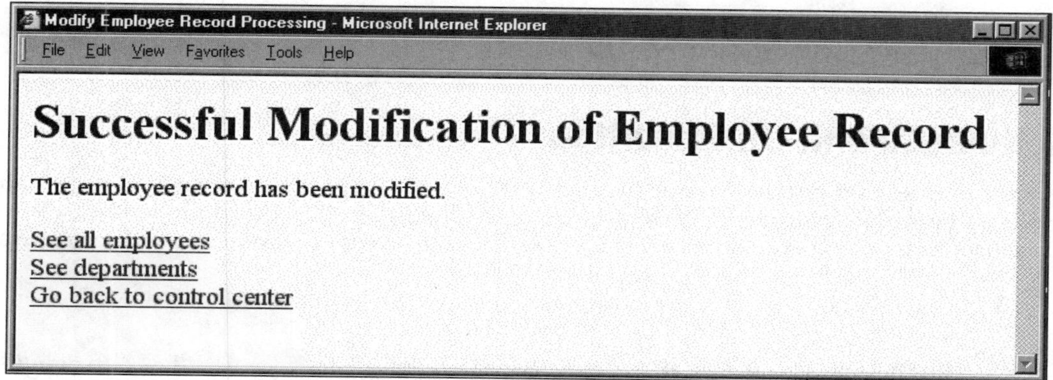

One interesting note to make is that for all of the multiple JSP solutions we have demonstrated above, the separate JSPs in a set can be easily combined together into one single JSP with a dispatching `if...then...else` statement. Conditional branching can then be made based on hidden field values generated into the forms that are being submitted. We did not do this because it will unnecessarily obfuscate the code. Even in production, keeping the JSPs separate will keep the logic on each page simple and ease the maintenance effort.

Completing the MyCo Administrative System

We add the following `control.html` file to complete the system. This system can be easily adapted to maintain an employee directory for a company:

```
<html>
<head></head>
<body>
<H1>MyCo Administrative Control</H1>
<P>
<a href="dbaddemp.jsp">Add An Employee</a><br>
<a href="dbdelemp.jsp">Delete An Employee</a><br>
<a href="dbmodemp.jsp">Modify Employee Record</a><br>
<a href="dbquery.jsp">See all employees</a><br>
<a href="dptquery.jsp">See all departments</a>
</body>
</html>
```

This simple page provides a common gateway to all the features of the web application.

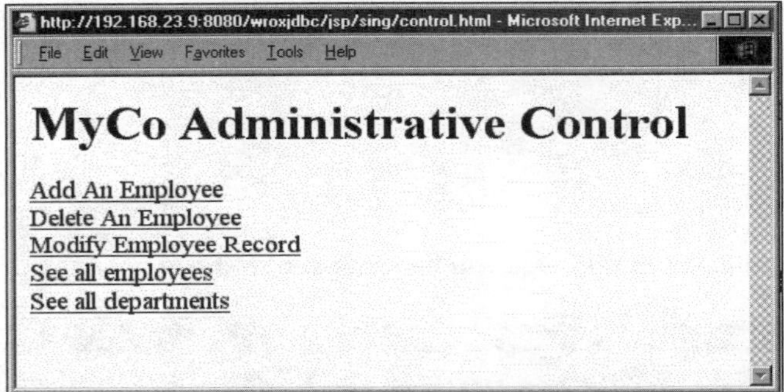

Modularity and Optimization

In the interests of clarity, we have not presented the code for the MyCo system in the most suitable manner for a production environment. In fact, we can readily observe several shortcomings. We will enumerate the issues here, and give some suggestions as to how they may be resolved or improved.

1. Code that is frequently used (such as connection and disconnection, frequently used static queries, etc.) are repeated throughout the JSP.

   Resolution: Create Java classes or beans to encapsulate this code. Use the `<jsp:useBean>` directive to include these classes/beans in the JSP to reduce and reuse code.

2. HTML formatting code is quite hopelessly mingled with embedded scripting code (in Java).

   Resolution: Create sets of custom tag extensions to hide the database operations from the HTML page developer, and to greatly reduce the need for embedded scripting code. Custom tag extensions are introduced in JSP 1.1 specifically for this reason.

3. Identical static and parameterized SQL statements that are static are repeatedly executed, from scratch.

   Resolution: Use JDBC prepared statements for repeated execution of the static or parameterized SQL statements. We will cover prepared statements in the next section.

4. Each page loads the database driver and creates a new connection to the database for every single request.

   Resolution: Use connection pooling to alleviate the need to create a new connection for every request. We will cover connection pooling in detail later in this chapter.

Other JDBC Features: Prepared Statements and Callable Statements

Prepared statements are an optimization offered by certain (but not all) RDBMS vendors for frequently executed queries. Most large commercial RDBMS engines separate the action of a complex query into multiple steps. One of the very first steps is to come up with a 'plan' on how to execute the query on the engine for the best possible performance. The strategy used in this optimization is proprietary, and for a complex query can be quite time consuming. Since it can represent a large percentage of the total query transaction time, it would be ideal if the output of this stage could be saved somehow whenever the same query is executed repeatedly, but with different parameters

This is the rationale behind prepared statements. Prepared statements work just like the statements we're used to, but we keep them around for repeated use by substituting different parameters. The execution 'plan' is kept around (usually in the DB engine) until the prepared statement is closed. Not all database engines support this optimization; on the engines that do not support it, there is no harm (or benefit) in using prepared statements. Notably, the current version of mySQL does not make use of this optimization.

You can use the `prepareStatement()` method of the `Connection` interface to obtain a `PreparedStatement`. This call will prepare the database engine for pre-compiling the statement. The SQL string passed in should contain `?` where parameterization is required. Execution of the statement is done via the same `execute()`, `executeUpdate()`, and `executeQuery()` methods that we are already used to. However, before the `PreparedStatement` is executed, it should be parameterized via the many `set<datatype>()` methods.

Callable statements are used to call into stored procedures for DB engines that support them. Stored procedures are essentially programs that you can write that are executed internally by the DB engine itself and can be stored in the database themselves. These procedures are usually written in some sort of vendor-proprietary language, although Java is becoming popular now with some DB engines. Stored procedures, because they are executed within the DB engine, have extremely efficient access to the data. Furthermore, behavior of the DB engine can also be 'customized' to your application using stored procedures.

Calling a stored procedure is actually the action to provide it (the procedure) with parameters. Use the `prepareCall()` method of the `Connection` interface to fabricate a `CallableStatement` instance. The stored procedure is parameterized via the same set of `set<datatype>()` methods as `PreparedStatement`. (`CallableStatement` actually extends `PreparedStatement`.). Callable statements are typically executed using the `execute()` method. We've mentioned a couple of times before that executing a statement may return more than one resultset. Stored procedures (and therefore callable statements) under most DB engines are allowed to return multiple resultsets. Since stored procedures are typically written in some proprietary language that is supported by the database engine internally, the database vendor is free to define their calling and data return conventions.

Multiple users and the Need for Connection Pooling

Web application access, especially when deployed over the Internet, lends itself to concurrency problems. With increasing number of users, the probability of a request coming in before the previous request finishes is increased. It is unrealistic to plan applications that can entertain only one database request at a time.

As mentioned earlier in the critique of our MyCo example, we opted for the simple approach of creating a new database connection for each and every request coming in. The figure below illustrates this approach:

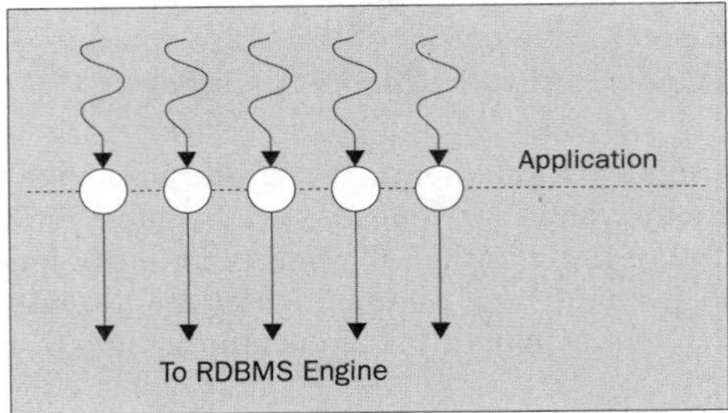

While rather simplistic, this approach does have the advantage that multiple requests to the database can be entertained at anytime. In fact, there may be no limit to the number of concurrent requests that can be made when the server is heavily loaded. As seen in the above figure, each thread executing the JSP instance will create its own database connection and talk directly to the RDBMS engine. In reality, the maximum number of connections may be imposed by a number of external factors:

- the licensing for the RDBMS
- concurrency limit of the JSP engine
- the exhaustion of the system's memory, and communications resources in sustaining the number of connections.

The last is especially nasty, since it may result in a system crash when it is least desirable (when the system is being accessed by many users).

Obviously, this is not a good outcome. One often sees, even in production code, a naïve attempt to fix this. The idea is to create a single database connection at the initialization of the JSP (which is guaranteed by the JSP engine to execute only once). Supposedly, this approach will eliminate the overhead of creating and destroying the database connection with every request. While that's true, this approach completely eliminates the possibility of request concurrency. See the next figure to understand what is happening:

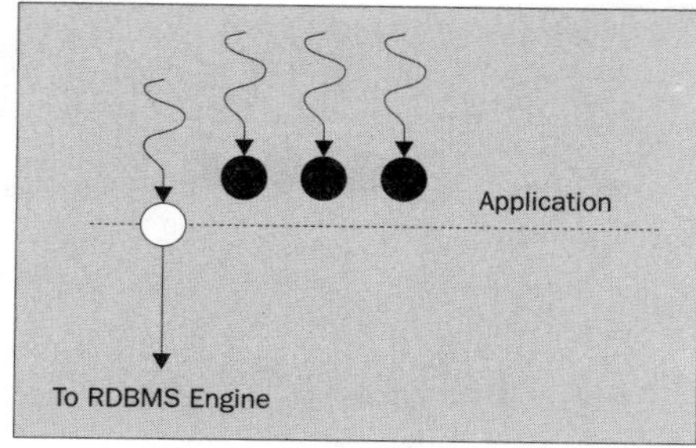

What is happening here is that all threads executing the JSP instance will be sharing the very same physical database connection. All of the requests through this connection will be processed serially. This means that when there are multiple concurrent requests arriving at the server, only one request will be processed at a time. The rest of the pending requests will **not** be blocked by any application level mechanism that may accommodate a large number of waiting clients, but instead by the lower level socket or networking protocol implementation. Most lower level blocking mechanisms are buffer size dependent. Translated, this approach practically guarantees resource exhaustion and system crashes when a system is overloaded. During lightly loaded situations, even the inefficient one-connection-per-request approach will offer some level of concurrent execution. Therefore, this single-connection-at-initialization approach has all the problems and none of the benefits of the other alternatives.

Finally, we examine what is currently deemed as the 'proper' way of handling database connections with JSPs. It is called connection pooling, and as with everything else in computing architectures, reflects a compromise in design catering to conflicting requirements. In this case, performance and efficiency are balanced against complexity and resource utilization. The idea of connection pooling is fairly simple.

A singleton (one instance only per JSP engine) 'Pool Manager' creates and maintains pools of database connections. All connections in any one specific pool are connections to the same JDBC URI (same host, database instance, and login ID). When a thread executing a JSP instance requires a database connection, it obtains the connection through the 'Pool Manager'. The database connection will then be made unavailable to any other requesting threads. Once the JSP thread has finished using the connection, it is responsible for returning the connection to the 'Pool Manager', which can then make the returned connection available to any other requesting threads (potentially blocked waiting). Therefore, in a very lightly loaded system, we have a situation very similar to the one-connection-per-request scenario. This is illustrated below:

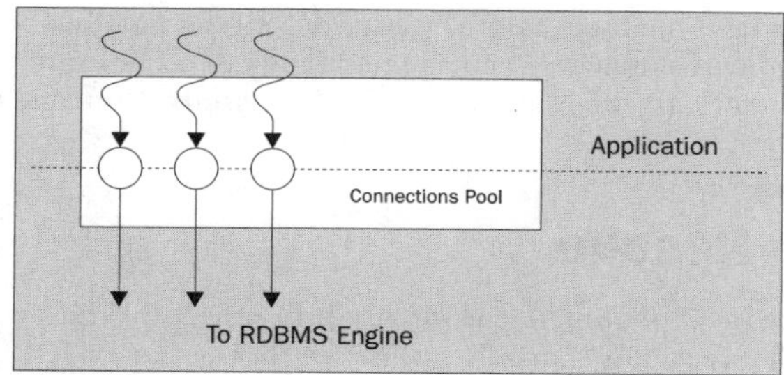

In fact, the above figure shows that there can be database connections that are open, but remain unused by any request in a lightly loaded system. This may be viewed as an **inefficiency** if connection pooling is used on very lightly loaded system. However, as the number of requests arriving increases, the benefit of the connection pooling approach is evident. See the next figure:

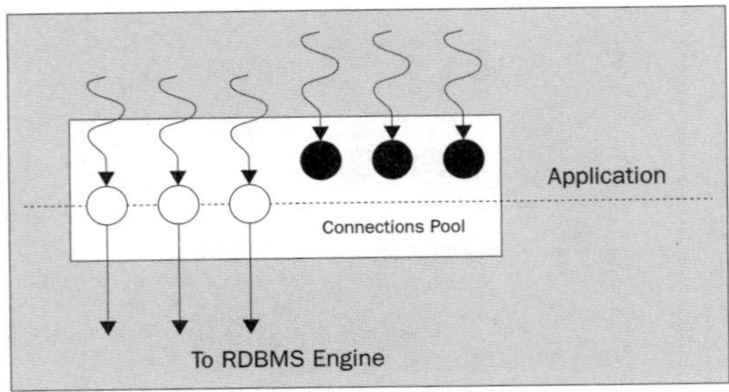

In this scenario, the maximum number of connections configured in the 'pool manager' controls how many concurrent database requests may be executing at the same time. All the remaining requests are programmatically blocked (typically at a queue) **by the pool manager**! This blocking of request threads is done via high level application code, and can arbitrarily support a large number of incoming requests without exceeding some low level buffer size limit.

Once a JSP frees a connection and returns it to the pool, the pool manager will immediately hand the freed connection to one of the blocked requests.

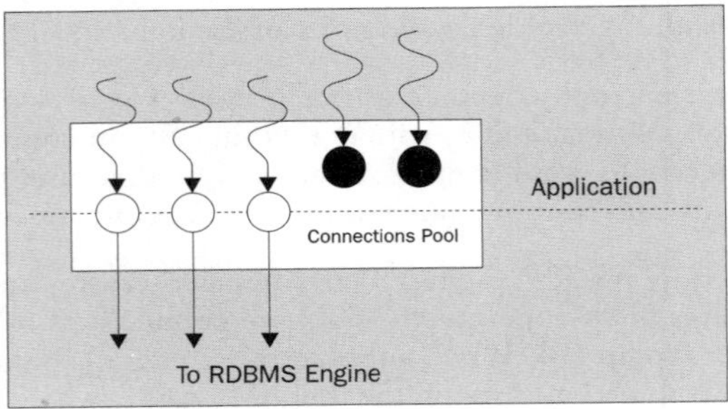

Therefore, in a highly loaded system, the connection pooling approach can be configured to work with better efficiency for a particular system.

Now that we understand how connection pooling works, we should examine how we may modify the MyCo database example to take advantage of connection pooling. Implementing a good connection pool manager is non-trivial. One must carefully consider all the possible concurrency issues before writing deadlock-free, concurrent access management code to orchestrate the distribution of the connections in the pool amongst the request threads. Thankfully, someone else has already done the hard work.

PoolMan to the Rescue

PoolMan is a 100% pure Java 'pool manager for any Java objects'. While you can use the manager software to pool any resources, it is specially optimized for pooling of JDBC. It is created by Code Studio and is distributed as free software, with an LGPL license. This means that complete source code is available, if you'd like to know how to write a production-grade connection pool manager yourself.

You can find the most recent version of PoolMan for download at http://www.codestudio.com/PoolMan/index.shtml

PoolMan works beautifully with the mm Type 4 JDBC driver and mySQL. In fact, integration is so smooth, you'd almost think they were created by the same commercial company.
To add PoolMan capability to Tomcat, add the following line to the `tomcat.sh` file:

```
oldCP=$CLASSPATH

CLASSPATH=${TOMCAT_HOME}/webserver.jar
CLASSPATH=${CLASSPATH}:${TOMCAT_HOME}/lib/servlet.jar
CLASSPATH=${CLASSPATH}:${TOMCAT_HOME}/lib/jasper.jar
CLASSPATH=${CLASSPATH}:${TOMCAT_HOME}/lib/xml.jar
CLASSPATH=${CLASSPATH}:${TOMCAT_HOME}/examples/WEB-INF/classes
CLASSPATH=${CLASSPATH}:${JAVA_HOME}/lib/tools.jar
CLASSPATH=${CLASSPATH}:~sing/mysql/mysqljdbc/mysql_2_comp.jar
CLASSPATH=${CLASSPATH}:~sing/poolman/lib/PoolMan.jar:~sing/poolman/lib
```

You need to replace my PoolMan installation directory with your own. Now, Tomcat will be able to access the PoolMan classes, and its properties file. When the pool manager starts, it will parse the properties file to determine the connection pools that it needs to create.

The properties file is called `pools.prop`, and is located in the `poolman/lib` directory (now in Tomcat's `CLASSPATH`). To add our database connection to the pool, you can add the following entry into the `pools.prop` file:

```
db_name.1=wroxjdbc
db_driver.1=org.gjt.mm.mysql.Driver
db_url.1=jdbc:mysql:///wroxjsp
db_username.1=sing
db_password.1=apple
maximumsize.1=5
```

We can see how the database name, JDBC driver to use, the JDBC URI, user name, and password is passed into the pool manager. The final entry, `maximumsize`, specifies how many connections should be in the pool – in our case, it is 5.

This will set up PoolMan to share 5 database connections across all our MyCo JSPs. To utilize PoolMan, we will need to make some very minor modifications to the JSPs that we have created. Namely, instead of creating and destroying a database connection with each request, we will need to ask the pool manager for a connection at the start, and return the connection to the pool manager when we finish.

The `com.codestudio.util` package has all the classes that make this possible. For JDBC pooling, we will be using the singleton `SQLManager` class exclusively.

Here is the simple `dbquery.jsp`, modified to use connection pooling. The new source is found in `dbqueryP.jsp`.

```
<html>
<head>
<title>
MyCo Directory
</title>
</head>
<%@ page language="java" import="java.sql.*,com.codestudio.util.*" %>
```

```
<body>
<h1>MyCo Employees</h1>
<table border="1" width="400">
<tr>
     <td><b>ID</b></td><td><b>Last Name</b></td>
     <td><b>First Name</b></td><td><b>Extension</b></td>
</tr>
<%
  SQLManager myMan = SQLManager.getInstance();
  Connection myConn = myMan.requestConnection();
  //Class.forName("org.gjt.mm.mysql.Driver");
  //Connection myConn = DriverManager.getConnection
  //   ("jdbc:mysql:///wroxjsp?user=sing&password=apple");

  Statement stmt = myConn.createStatement();
  ResultSet myResultSet = stmt.executeQuery("select * from employee");

  if (myResultSet != null)
    {
        while (myResultSet.next()) {
           String eid = myResultSet.getString("empid");
           String last = myResultSet.getString("lastname");
           String first = myResultSet.getString("firstname");
           String ext = myResultSet.getString("extension");
%>
<tr>
           <td><%= eid %></td>
           <td><%= last %></td>
           <td><%= first %> </td>
           <td><%= ext %> </td>
</tr>
<%
           } /* of while */
    }  /* of if */
  stmt.close();
  myMan.returnConnection(myConn);
//  myConn.close();
%>
</table>
<a href="control.html">Go back to admin control</a>
</body>
</html>
```

The changes above are both intuitive and simple. We can easily perform the same changes to every one of our JSP files to start enjoying the benefit of connection pooling.

The first JSP that calls the static method `SQLManager.getInstance()` will start the pool manager. Any other JSP that subsequently calls the same method will retrieve the same pool manager instance. Connections are created as they are needed up to the maximum number specified in the `pool.props` file.

A Word on JDBC 2.0 Standard Extension for Database Pooling

The JDBC 2.0 specification (Dec 1998) has specified a set of optional Standard Extensions (SE) for designers of JDBC drivers to support. Amongst them are three new interfaces:

- `javax.sql.DataSource`
- `javax.sql.ConnectionPoolDataSource`
- `javax.sql.PooledConnection`

An application that uses these three interfaces to obtain their data connections will enjoy connection pooling transparency feature. It can effectively defer the decision about whether to use a connection pool until application configuration/deployment time: the compiled byte code will not have to be changed.

In time, vendor specific JDBC drivers will evolve to support this extension. But due to the specification's tight binding with other J2EE services such as JNDI (Java Naming Directory Interface) – essentially to replace the need for an equivalent `pool.props` file – adoption by database vendors is relatively slow. A complete "buy-in" to the J2EE platform is required by the database vendor for this extension to function harmoniously. At the time of writing, there are no commercial vendors offering JDBC drivers that support this extension fully. In the meantime, general-purpose connection poolers such as PoolMan can provide a highly functional interim solution.

Limitations, Implementation Caveats and Gotchas

You may have noticed cautionary language used earlier when we describe connection pooling as the 'proper' way of managing database connections for JSPs. The reality is that connection pooling is far from the 'ideal' solution to manage database connections for any particular system running a web application. It represents only one workable approach to the significantly more complex problem of overall system tuning. In fact, there is probably no optimal way to solve the problem for all situations. To appreciate this, we need to look outside of the JSP context to the database engine scenario, and see the bigger picture. The figure below illustrates this:

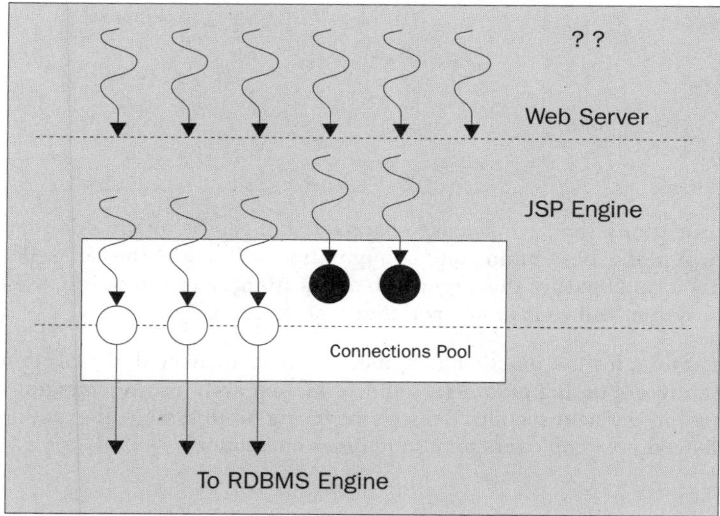

Here, we see clearly that the web server that is handling the incoming requests may have its own concurrency handling limitation and policies. In fact, its policy may be in conflict (or inconsistent) with those set up by the JSP engine, or those imposed by the connection pool manger or the RDBMS engine. Depending on the architecture of the system, there may be even more variations and limitations. For example, even our simplistic Tomcat, mySQL based MyCo system can be configured in at least three ways – some configurations lends itself more to experimentation, other to production scenarios.

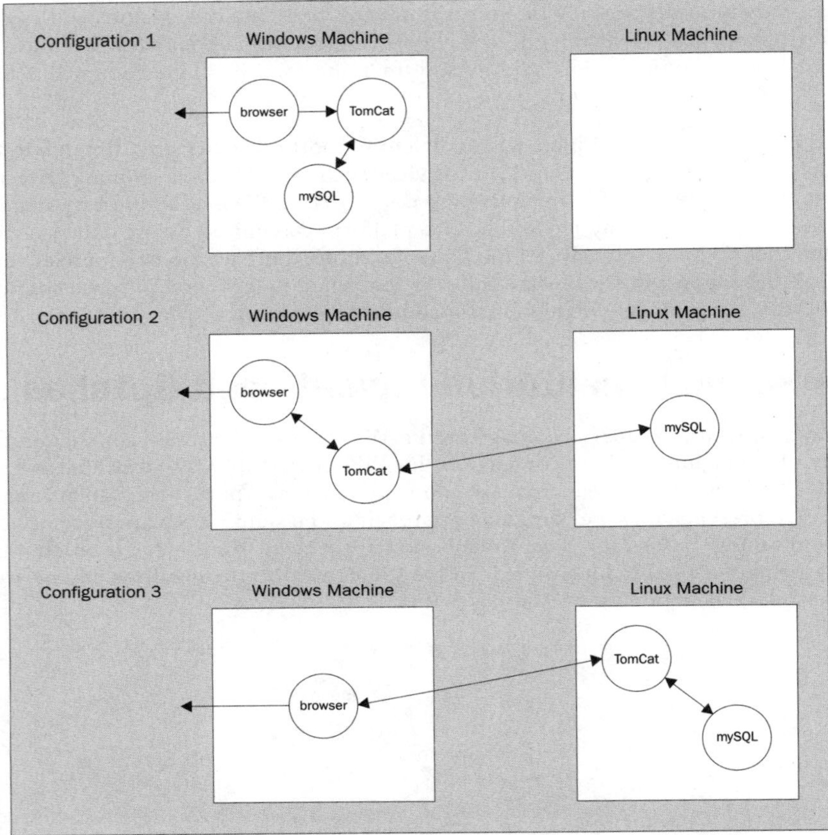

In each of these situations, the performance characteristics can be totally different; different sets of constraints apply, and the 'best' tuning and configuration will not be the same. Because JSP/JDBC connection is only a small part of the larger web application/system scenario, the tuning and optimization of a system will remain an art rather than a science.

It is essential, therefore, for the practicing engineer to have an arsenal of tools to test the performance of a system against different tuning parameters and/or system architecture changes. We will examine how to build such a tool in the next section. Before embarking on this, we will examine a frequent "gotcha" that even experienced Java engineers may sometimes encounter.

The "froggie in the well" Syndrome and Mysterious JVM Seizures

A frog in the bottom of a well can only view the world through the tiny distant opening, and therefore can have a very narrow view of what the world may be like. JSP experts working within the JVM that hosts the JSP engine can occasionally suffer from this problem. Here is an example scenario to illustrate the point:

A JSP guru is configuring a JSP web application where the JSP engine is co-located on the same machine as the database server. Using some super Java VM 'xray' debug tools, the JSP guru starts to engineer the connection pooling mechanism for a web application to maximally use the available heap and stack memory, balancing it carefully by tuning the garbage collection scheme. As a result, the guru concluded a connection pool size of 150 is best for the application on hand, and configured the system accordingly.

During production, the Java VM hosting the JSP engine seized up completely before the 28th database connection has been utilized. Panic sets in on the 'make-or-break product launch' day, the frazzled Java guru performs a post-mortem dump on the constantly crashing system. Seeing that both heap and stack space is vastly under-utilized, and that the finely tuned garbage collector didn't even get a chance to run, he/she is totally puzzled by the misfortune and retreats back to a world of C/C++ programming.

What happened?

Simply put, the view of memory and resource consumption within only the Java VM 'well' is totally non-indicative of the actual memory and resource consumption on the physical machine. In fact, a relatively 'small' footprint database connection data structure may in turn tie up huge memory and communication resources *outside* of the Java VM! This effect can easily exhaust the system of resource, long before any symptomatic failure within the VM.

The following figure illustrates this effect. Notice the small amount of memory inside the Java VM that is tying up the significantly larger pools of memory outside of the VM, but on the same physical machine. There is no way for the VM to know that this is happening.

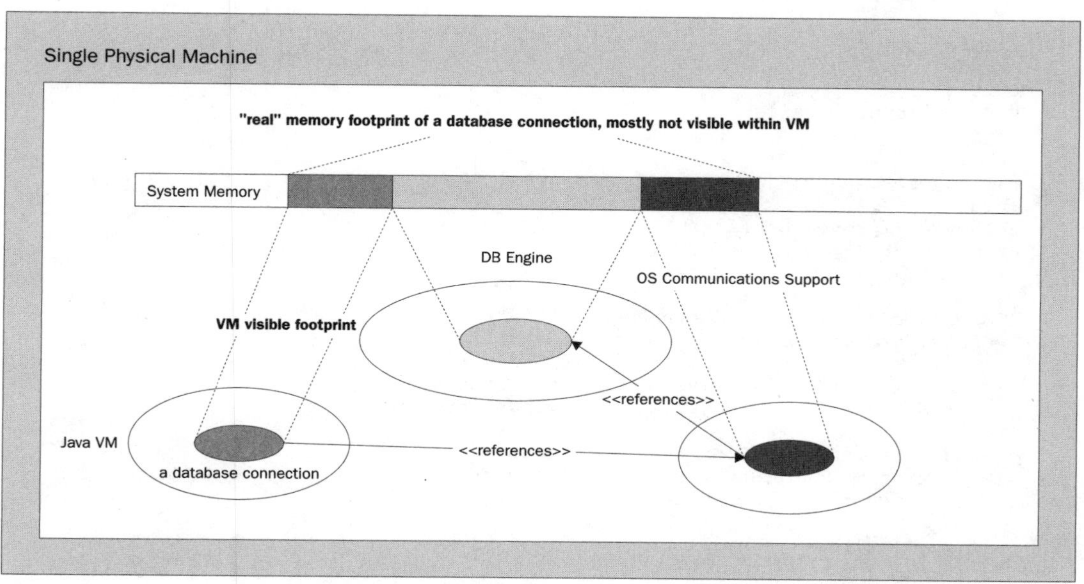

To be effective, one must adopt a "bigger picture" system approach to configuration and tuning of production JSP/JDBC web applications.

Testing and Improving Performance

Since there is no 'best way' to configure or tune any particular JSP/JDBC system, the use of a load test tool is essential to tuning any implementation and for gaining insight into potential problems that may occur during intensely concurrent operation.

Designing and coding such a tool is a non-trivial effort. We will give the reader a head start by presenting the skeleton for a tool that will satisfy some of the requirements. Of course, there are also commercially available load tools that can be used for such a purpose.

This tool, which we will call bench, does the following:

- takes a parameterized URL as parameter
- repeatedly accesses this URL on multiple threads and increments an internal counter
- discards any returned information from the URL
- stops all threads once a pre-set count is reached
- performs timing of the overall operation.

The parameterization of the URL is rather trivial. Bench will generate a random number and substitute it into the URL before using it each time.

One example of where bench is of value is for testing the concurrent performance of a JSP/JDBC application that can be accessed via HTTP GET operations. For example, consider this page, `dbinfemp.jsp`. This query page retrieves one employee record and displays it in detail.

```
<html>
<head>
<title>
MyCo Employee Details
</title>
</head>
<%@ page language="java" import="java.sql.*" %>
<body>
<h1>MyCo Employee Detail</h1>
<table width="350"  border="0">
<%

  String eid = request.getParameter("eid");
  Class.forName("org.gjt.mm.mysql.Driver");

  Connection myConn = DriverManager.getConnection
    ("jdbc:mysql:///wroxjsp?user=sing&password=apple");

  Statement stmt = myConn.createStatement();
  ResultSet myResultSet = stmt.executeQuery
    ("select * from employee where empid=" + eid);

  if (myResultSet != null)
    {
        myResultSet.next(); // one record only
        String last = myResultSet.getString("lastname");
        String first = myResultSet.getString("firstname");
        String ext = myResultSet.getString("extension");
%>
<tr>
```

```
            <td><b>Employee ID:</b></td> <td><%= eid %></td>
</tr>
<tr>
            <td><b>Lastname:</b></td><td><%= last %></td>
</tr>
<tr>
            <td><b>Firstname:</b></td><td><%= first %> </td>
</tr>
<tr>
            <td><b>Extension:</b></td><td><%= ext %> </td>
</tr>
<%
      }  /* of if */
  stmt.close();
  myConn.close();
%>
</table>
</body>
</html>
```

On our servers, the URL to access the page is:

http://127.0.0.1:8080/wroxjdbc/jsp/sing/dbinfemp.jsp?eid=5

This URL will produce the following details page:

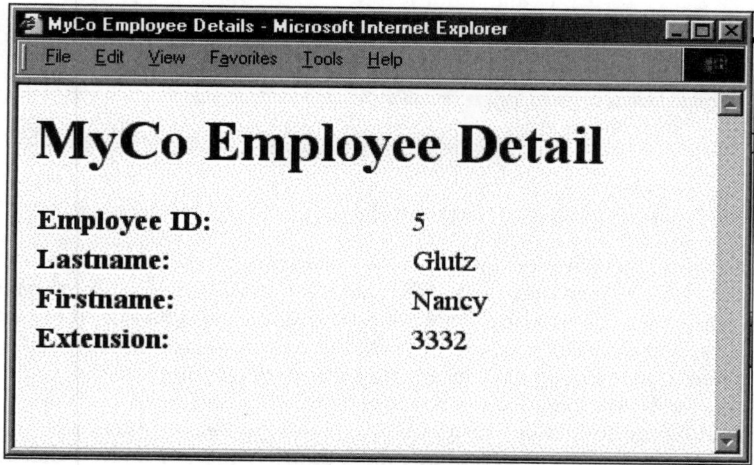

Bench can be used to measure the time to access this query JSP page 1,000 (or more) times; each time fetching a random employee record. While rather superficial for our sample database consisting of only a handful of records, bench can be used in the same way to test complex queries on very large tables. The effect of different database connection strategies can also be observed using bench. The usage syntax of bench is:

```
java bench <URL> <randomize range> <number of hits> <number of threads>
```

The randomize range indicates the range to substitute into the URL for varying the query. In our case, we choose 8, since we have only 8 employee records in the database.

Here is the sample output from the bench program:

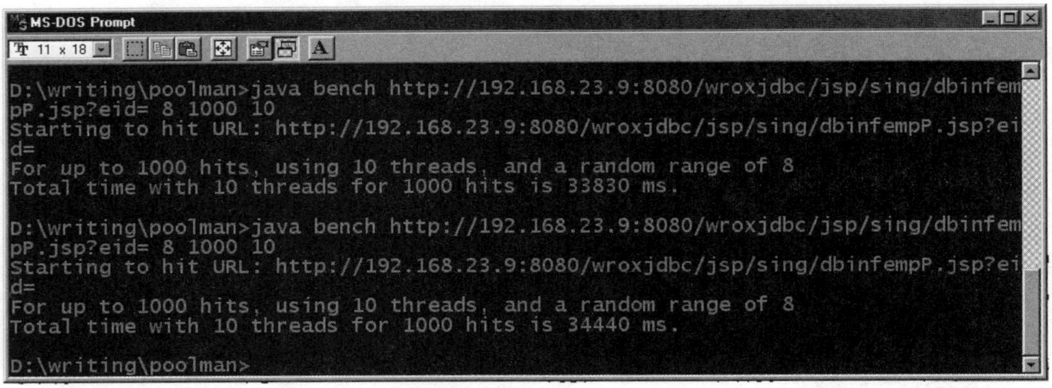

```
MS-DOS Prompt
D:\writing\poolman>java bench http://192.168.23.9:8080/wroxjdbc/jsp/sing/dbinfem
pP.jsp?eid= 8 1000 10
Starting to hit URL: http://192.168.23.9:8080/wroxjdbc/jsp/sing/dbinfempP.jsp?ei
d=
For up to 1000 hits, using 10 threads, and a random range of 8
Total time with 10 threads for 1000 hits is 33830 ms.

D:\writing\poolman>java bench http://192.168.23.9:8080/wroxjdbc/jsp/sing/dbinfem
pP.jsp?eid= 8 1000 10
Starting to hit URL: http://192.168.23.9:8080/wroxjdbc/jsp/sing/dbinfempP.jsp?ei
d=
For up to 1000 hits, using 10 threads, and a random range of 8
Total time with 10 threads for 1000 hits is 34440 ms.

D:\writing\poolman>
```

The source code of bench is fairly concise. The threads that the program will create perform the core work. The bench class itself implements the `Runnable` interface that is required for parameterizing a thread's constructor. The `run()` method of the `Runnable` interface is where the work of the thread will be performed.

```
import java.util.*;
import java.net.URL;
import java.io.*;
public class bench implements Runnable {
  static  String TESTURL =
    "http://192.168.23.9:8080/wroxjdbc/jsp/sing/dbinfemp.jsp?rid=";
  static int MAXRESID = 8;
  static int MAXTHREADS = 3;
  static int myCounter =0;

  static int MAXHITS = 1000;
  static boolean terminate = false;
```

All the static variables above are instance variables and shared by all threads. The `myCounter` variable will store the count of how many times the URL has been hit. The `boolean terminate` flag is polled by each thread while they are working. This allows one thread to signal the termination of all other threads. In fact, the first thread to discover that the counter has reached the specified number of hits will set this flag to `true`. Other threads will terminate naturally once they see this flag turned `true`. The other alternative would have been for the discovery thread to perform a `System.exit()` call. However, terminating multi-threaded program in this way can leave system resources used by the program in an inconsistent state. For example, the TCP/IP communications stack and sockets can have problems recovering from an indeterminate state when aborted in the middle of an operation.

```
  String hitURL;
  URL myURL;
  BufferedReader myReader;
  String testStr;
  Random myRnd;
  InputStream myStream;
  long myStart;

  public bench() {
    myStart = System.currentTimeMillis();
    myRnd = new Random();
  }
```

myStart stores the time when the instance is first created, before even the first work thread has been created. The run() method below contains the work for the thread.

```
    public void run() {
      while(true) {

        try {
          hitURL = TESTURL + (myRnd.nextInt(MAXRESID) + 1);
          myURL = new URL(hitURL);
          myStream = myURL.openStream();
          myReader = new BufferedReader(new   InputStreamReader(myStream));
          testStr = myReader.readLine();
          while (testStr != null) {
            testStr = myReader.readLine();
          }
        } catch (Exception e) {
          e.printStackTrace();
        } finally {
          try {
            myStream.close();
          }
          catch(Exception e) {
            e.printStackTrace();
          }
        }

        addOne();
          if (terminate) break;
      } // of while
    }
```

The addOne() method may be used by multiple threads. The synchronized keyword ensures that only one thread will be incrementing the counter at any time. Note that it is entirely possible, and occasionally may happen, that a thread may be waiting to enter addOne() while another is inside and changes the value of terminate. In this case, the threads will still all terminate gracefully, but you may get multiple lines if output.

```
    public synchronized void addOne() {
      if (!terminate) {
        myCounter++;
        if (myCounter >= MAXHITS) {
          System.out.println("Total time with " + MAXTHREADS + " threads for "
            + MAXHITS + " hits is " + (System.currentTimeMillis() - myStart)
            + " ms.");
        terminate = true;
      }
    }
  }
```

The main() method simply parses the command line arguments and creates the number of threads required by bench.

```
    public static void main (String args[]) {
      if (args.length < 4) {
        System.out.println
          ("Usage: bench <URL> <subst range> <max hits> <max threads>");
        System.exit(1);
      }
```

```
        try {
          TESTURL = args[0];
          MAXRESID = Integer.parseInt(args[1]);
          MAXHITS = Integer.parseInt(args[2]);
          MAXTHREADS = Integer.parseInt(args[3]);
          System.out.println("Starting to hit URL: " + TESTURL);
          System.out.println("For up to " + MAXHITS + " hits, using " +
            MAXTHREADS + " threads, and a random range of " + MAXRESID);

          for (int i=0; i<MAXTHREADS; i++) {
            new Thread(new bench()).start();
          }
        } catch(Exception e) {
          e.printStackTrace();
          System.exit(1);
        }

    }
  }
```

For the sample dbinfemp.jsp file, using the MyCo database hosted on our systems, we have obtained the following timings using bench:

Concurrent Loading	Connection Allocation Strategy	Max Size of Pool	Time for 1,000 random Queryies
5	One connection per request	N/A	51.19 sec
10	One connection per request	N/A	44.30 sec
10	Connection Pooling	2	33.83 sec
10	Connection Pooling	5	34.44 sec

Your own results will definitely vary. The way that various methods of tuning and optimization affect the overall throughput of your system will mostly likely also vary. One can extend bench in many meaningful ways. Here is a sampling of potential extensions:

- Add more application specific ways to randomly vary the query URL.
- Add analysis capability to examine the data returned from the URL.
- Co-ordinate startup and running of bench across a bank of client machines.
- Dynamically adjust the concurrency loading over time to discover the "sweet spot" loading for any single configuration.

Summary

The ease of programming afforded by JSP enables the rapid creation of database web applications. The Java Database Connectivity technology, an integral part of J2SE and J2EE, provides flexibility in accessing a large variety of RDBMSs.

In this chapter, we have seen how JSPs can be written to:

- perform simple and complex queries
- add records to a database
- delete records from a database
- modify record contents in a database.

The nature of web applications involves concurrent, simultaneous access by potentially many users. We examined how we can allocate database connections when dealing with concurrent access. Our exploration took us through several options, ending in the most flexible: database connection pooling. Subsequently, we have learned how connection pooling works, and concluded that it can significantly boost system throughput if used judiciously.

In the last part of the chapter, we have re-iterated the importance of taking a 'global system view' when tuning and optimizing web application systems based on JSP/JDBC. Simply tuning the JSP engine, web server, or the associated JVM is a rather pointless task. True performance and throughput needs to be tuned individually for each configuration. Tools are required to gather and tabulate metrics that can be used in such an activity. We presented the Java coding for a simple 'bench' tool that can be used on client computers for gathering such metrics.

The next chapter looks at Tag Extensions, which allow you to define your own JSP action tags.

J2EE
JSP

8

Introducing Tag Extensions and Libraries

You've created your first set of JavaServer Pages, and the output looks great. It's an improvement over servlets in its use of templates for the output, and it keeps the integration of servlets with databases and Beans. You're convinced, but it's time to sell JSPs and their part in J2EE to your colleagues and your boss.

There are two problems:

- The source is a depressing mix of HTML and Java scriptlets, and with every passing day, its meaning is getting murkier. It's going to be more difficult to maintain and debug than Servlets were.
- There's not the clean separation between presentation and logic, so it's difficult to split up the development roles of Java developer and web designer. How will you ever convince the website designers to roll up their sleeves and use JSPs to interface to your Java backend code?

In order to solve these problems, you need a template mechanism that's as close to HTML or XML as possible, but which interfaces with and controls generalized business logic. This code is configured by attributes in a tag and data is transferred between the template and the code in a manner that's transparent to the page designer.

Help is at hand, in the form of the tag extension mechanism introduced in JSP 1.1. It's relatively new and immature, but it has the potential to solve these two problems. It's a simple and flexible system with which to create your own tags for a page that call some code (perform an action, in the parlance) to influence the output in some way.

You may have some of the following questions now. If so, you'll get further towards the answers in this chapter:

- How do I get from scriptlets and beans to tags? Do I have to start from scratch?
- How do custom tags work? Are they difficult?
- How do I link tags together?
- What ways are there of getting information into and out of a tag?
- Are tags first class citizens of the compiled page?
- Should I work on the tags first, or create a messy page and then extract the code to tags?

In this chapter, we'll look at how JSP 1.1 and the reference implementation, Tomcat, support tag extensions, what help they provide, where some of the difficulties lie, and how we distribute them. More specifically, we'll:

- Examine what tag extensions offer
- Convert a standard JSP page to one that uses custom tags
- Introduce simple, body and nested tags, and the method frameworks for using them
- Look at how to initialize a tag
- See how tags support control logic
- Access implicit objects from tags
- Create `TagExtraInfo` classes to define variables set by the tag for the scope of the tag and the rest of the page
- Review how scope works
- Look at how to use pre-existing tag libraries – is the promise fulfilled yet?

The Need for a Tag Extension Mechanism

Let's first look at the split between presentation and business logic in more detail.

As we've seen in earlier chapters, JSP has supported the use of JavaBeans to provide server-side components since the first official release. The tags for using JavaBeans are fixed and rather limiting; you can only access properties, and have to use method calls from scriptlets for more involved initialization and so forth.

If you want to apply the Model-View-Controller (MVC) pattern to web applications, with the backend data (in the database or the entity EJB) providing the model, the business logic acting as the controller, then JSPs should provide the view on the data. It would be a big improvement to be able to separate the view and controller, something that JSP 1.0 and earlier versions didn't make easy.

Web applications often want to provide multiple views on the same data to different channels – generating, for example, WML and HTML, or different pages for devices with different abilities. It's important in these applications to separate the view from the controller so that the same controller code can create different views of the same data. (This topic is the subject of Chapter 12.)

Simplifying the page is important too, so that it can be written, customized and tested quickly, by people whose principle interest is not in the mechanics of the system, but in getting information onto a page in a form that's useful and aesthetic.

It's not a new idea; there are several other dynamic web solutions that are tag led, and there's even something of a Java precedent – the Java applet. The tags to insert an applet, though complicated by the use of the Java Runtime Environment (JRE), use attributes to set any parameters for the applet. As the page designer you set the attributes that you want the applet to use, but how it does this is none of your concern. The code in an applet is controlled by the set of framework methods (`init()`, `start()`, `stop()` and so on) called by the browser, but it can affect its environment too, with simple calls like `setStatus()` and more complicated communication between beans and applets via the InfoBus.

What is a Custom Tag?

A Tag Extension is, guess what, a Java class – in fact it's a JavaBean which implements one of two interfaces, the details of which we'll look at in a minute. The JSP specification states, in section 5.4, that tags have a richer run-time protocol than vanilla JavaBeans, for these reasons:

- Initialization can involve properties, without which the tag won't run. Compare this with the empty constructor in a JavaBean
- Setting and getting properties doesn't cover all bases – there's little control logic available within the bean. You have to control the bean externally, and you could do that with another bean, but that wouldn't be a very general component – it would need to be rewritten, compiled and tested for each JSP.
- Beans aren't as aware by default of their context in the JSP page as they need to be – there's no default concept of a parent or `pageContext` object within a bean

Tag classes remedy these omissions, as we'll see in the next section.

How Pages and Tags Sit Together

Given that we want to separate the view of the data from the controller in our JSPs, we want to decouple the page and the tags. That is, we want the JSP to initialize, set conditions for the operation of, and help format the output of the tag code, but for that to be encapsulated somewhere. The tags will affect the page, and vice versa, but the coupling is limited by the tag extension mechanism and the tag's design.

When a tag is read, and an action started (that is, a tag instance created), the `PageContext` object is passed to the tag object so that its environment can be initialized. You saw the start of a typical `_jspService()` method in a translated JSP in Chapter 1. Here's the usual setup code and then the bit where the tag instance is created, for an example we'll see later in the chapter:

```
public void _jspService(HttpServletRequest request,
                        HttpServletResponse response)
        throws IOException, ServletException {

  ...

  pageContext = _jspxFactory.getPageContext(this, request, response,
                                            "", true, 8192, true);
```

```
application = pageContext.getServletContext();
config = pageContext.getServletConfig();
session = pageContext.getSession();
out = pageContext.getOut();

com.wrox.projsp.ch07.AlphabetTag2 _jspx_th_test_alphabet2_0 = new
                              com.wrox.projsp.ch07.AlphabetTag2();
_jspx_th_test_alphabet2_0.setPageContext(pageContext);
_jspx_th_test_alphabet2_0.setParent(null);
...
```

The pageContext object is the first property to be set in the new tag instance, followed by the parent of the tag. The pageContext object is the central class for the page – where the JSP and the web server interact. The pageContext object:

- Sets the application, session, and out implicit objects – page, request, and response having already been set in the _jspService() method.
- Allows access to these implicit objects and to ServletConfig, and Exception objects.
- Also provides access to objects bound as attributes to any scope
- Provides methods to forward requests and include files

The parent of a tag is the JSP tag within which it's nested – in this case, there isn't one, so it's set to null. We'll look at nested tags later in the chapter.

Conversely, we can output data to the page in a variety of ways:

- Writing directly to the output stream
- Setting attributes in the page, session or other shared, 'bulletin-board' objects
- Using scope rules to provide data to nested tags via references to parent tags and get methods

This introduction has looked at why we need the tag extension mechanism, and a little about how the JSP container supports tag extensions. It's now time to look at some examples of custom tags, to see the details of how they work.

The Simplest Tag

For a really simple, "Hello World" tag, we borrow the code from cookie.jsp in Chapter 5 and put it into an empty tag with no attributes or output variables – to make the personalized equivalent of a page counter.

Here's the new JSP with the custom tag highlighted:

```
<%@ page language="java" import="java.util.Date" %>

<html>
<title>Simplest tag</title>
<body>

<%@ taglib uri="http://localhost:8080/projsp/projsp-taglib" prefix="test" %>
```

```
<h2><test:pageVisit/></h2>
<h2>Current system date is <%= new Date().toString() %> </h2>

</body>
</html>
```

We've removed all the code from the original, and replaced it with two new tags – the taglib directive and a `test:pageVisit` tag. We'll look first at the taglib directive, and then at the code behind the tag.

The taglib Tag

The taglib directive (section 5.2.3 of the JSP specification) references an XML document that defines the tag's operation. Here's the file for this first example:

```
<?xml version="1.0" encoding="ISO-8859-1" ?>
<!DOCTYPE taglib
        PUBLIC "-//Sun Microsystems, Inc.//DTD JSP Tag Library 1.1//EN"
        "http://java.sun.com/j2ee/dtds/web-jsptaglibrary_1_1.dtd">

<!-- a tag library descriptor -->

<taglib>
  <tlibversion>1.0</tlibversion>
  <jspversion>1.1</jspversion>
  <shortname>projsp</shortname>
  <uri>http://www.wrox.com</uri>
  <info>
    A simple tag library for examples from Professional JSP
  </info>

  <!-- Simple tags -->
  <tag>
    <name>pageVisit</name>
    <tagclass>com.wrox.projsp.ch07.PageVisitTag</tagclass>
    <bodycontent>empty</bodycontent>
    <info>
      This tag outputs the last time you've visited the page in the last month.

      The tag is meant to be very simple. Empty body and no attributes.
    </info>
  </tag>
</taglib>
```

We first define a tag library for the examples in this chapter, using the `<taglib>` tag. Then for each custom tag, we need a `<tag>` entry. Our `pageVisit` tag is very simple – it has:

- A name (which we use in the JSP)
- A tagclass that maps the name to a fully-qualified Java class, which implements the Tag interface
- A bodycontent that specifies the content type of the tag, if any. We've declared an empty tag – this will be checked when the JSP is translated to a servlet, so that the tag is used correctly
- Optional information on the tag

Apart from that it's rather boring. There are other elements used to describe the tag, and we'll look at them later in the chapter.

> **The taglib file is conventionally given the `.tld` extension. Note also that the file doesn't have to be at the URL specified in the JSP – Tomcat maps the URL to a local file, we'll see that in Appendix A.**

The taglib forms the central description for your tag library. It:

- Maps the tag name on the page to the implementing class
- Defines inputs to the class
- References the helper class that provides details of any output variables set by the tag class

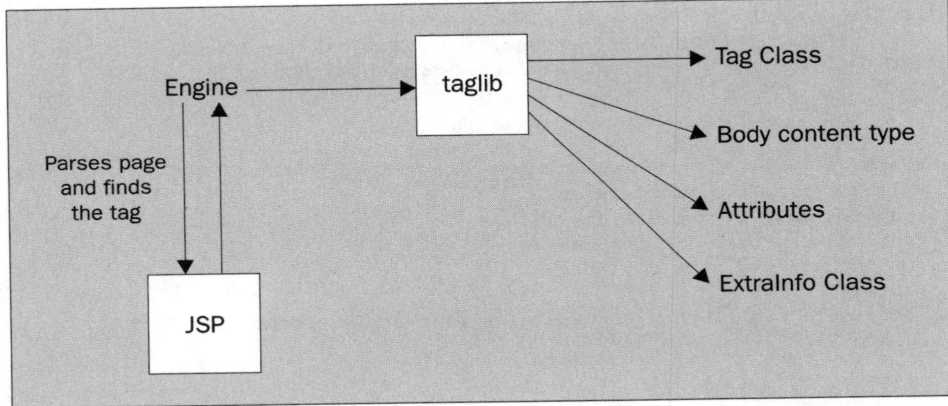

Let's take a look at the tag class itself.

The pageVisit Tag

This is very similar to the code in the original JSP in Chapter 5 – the changes are highlighted.

```
package com.wrox.projsp.ch07;

import javax.servlet.http.*;
import javax.servlet.jsp.*;
import javax.servlet.jsp.tagext.*;
import java.util.Date;
import java.io.IOException;

public class PageVisitTag extends TagSupport {

  public int doStartTag() throws JspTagException {
    Cookie info = null;
    String msg = "This is the first time you've visited this page.";
```

```
      // Get all the cookies that came with the request
      Cookie[] cookies =
   ((HttpServletRequest)pageContext.getRequest()).getCookies();

      for(int i = 0; i < cookies.length; i++) {
        info = cookies[i];
        if (info.getName().equals("MyCookie")) {
          found = true;
          break;
        }
      }

      String newValue = "" + System.currentTimeMillis();

      if (!found) {
        // Create a new Cookie and set its age.
        info = new Cookie("MyCookie", newValue );
        info.setMaxAge(60*1);
        info.setPath("/");

        ((HttpServletResponse)pageContext.getResponse()).addCookie(info);
      } else {
        long conv = new Long(info.getValue()).longValue();
        msg = "You last visited this site on " + new Date(conv);

        // Set the new value of the cookie, and add it to the response
        info.setValue(newValue);
        info.setMaxAge(10*24*60*60); // keep the cookie for 1 month.

        // Set the path so that the cookie is available everywhere on the server
        info.setPath("/");
        ((HttpServletResponse)pageContext.getResponse()).addCookie(info);
      }

      try {
        JspWriter out = pageContext.getOut();
        out.write(msg);
      } catch(IOException e) {
        throw new JspTagException("JspWriter not there: " + e);
      }

      return SKIP_BODY;
    }

    public int doEndTag() throws JspTagException {
      if (!found) {
        // Don't compare current and Cookie time this time
        return SKIP_PAGE;
      } else
        return EVAL_PAGE;
    }

    boolean found = false;
  }
```

The PageVisitTag class extends the helper class, javax.servlet.jsp.tagext.TagSupport, which implements the Tag interface. We need only override the two methods, doStartTag() and doEndTag().

The doStartTag() method is called by the container immediately after the initialization we saw earlier. Into this method, we've added the code from the JSP. The only changes we've had to make to the code are to the request and response objects (and I wish the code was a little more elegant than this, but the PageContext class returns the generic ServletRequest and ServletResponse objects, which don't support cookies – they're an HTTP feature).

Having sorted out the msg text, we get a reference to the JspWriter object, out, and write msg to it. Lastly we return SKIP_BODY, the default return, and the only sensible one when your tag has no body. If anything goes wrong, the method will throw a JspTagException, derived from JspException.

At the end of the tag, the doEndTag() method is called by the container. It returns EVAL_PAGE by default, allowing the container to continue evaluating the page. For this example, if there is no cookie, we return SKIP_PAGE to stop processing after the tag. A new cookie is created and the text telling you that is displayed, but the current date won't be.

The TagSupport class provides an implementation of the release() method called by the JSP container after the tag's work is complete, so we don't need to override this.

Setting Page Variables from Your Tag

As a slight modification to the first tag, we can set an attribute in the PageContext object with the msg text. The changes to the PageVisitTag class are trivial. Simply replace the try-catch block for the JspWriter with the following line:

```
pageContext.setAttribute("msg", msg);
```

In order for the JSP code to be able to access this variable (bearing in mind it doesn't necessarily have to be a String), we need to provide a helper class to describe "msg" for the container, PageVisitTagExtraInfo. This extends the TagExtraInfo base class and overrides the getVariableInfo() method:

```
package com.wrox.projsp.ch07;

import javax.servlet.jsp.tagext.*;

public class PageVisitTag2ExtraInfo extends TagExtraInfo {

  public VariableInfo[] getVariableInfo(TagData data) {
    return new VariableInfo[]
      {
        new VariableInfo("msg",
                         "String",
                         true,
                         VariableInfo.AT_END)
      };
  }
}
```

The TagExtraInfo (TEI) class provides a way to deal with the potential complexities of setting variables. It has four methods:

Method	Description
TagInfo getTagInfo()	TagInfo is the Java class that's instantiated from the taglib descriptions.
void setTagInfo(TagInfo ti)	Set the TagInfo for this class
VariableInfo[] getVariableInfo(TagData td)	Returns information on the variables that will be set from the tag
boolean isValid(TagData td)	Used for checking translation-time validity of information

The one that's interesting to us here is getVariableInfo() which returns an array of VariableInfo objects. A VariableInfo object, as you can see has four member variables that are set in the constructor:

Variable	Description
String ID	Name of the scripting variable
String Class	Fully qualified class name (except for classes that belong to the java.lang package)
boolean declare	Whether this variable will be new
int scope	Declares the scope of the variable, relative to the tag. One of the three defined scopes in VariableInfo – NESTED, AT_BEGIN, and AT_END. NESTED means that the variable is only available between the start and end tags, AT_BEGIN, that the variable is available after the start tag to the end of the page, and AT_END, which we've used in this example, initializes the variable after the end tag. It remains in scope for the rest of the page.

The TEI class is referenced in the taglib file, something which is easy to forget – if your carefully described variables are ignored by the JSP translator, check that the TEI file is referenced like so:

```
<tag>
  <name>pageVisit2</name>
  <tagclass>com.wrox.projsp.ch07.PageVisitTag2</tagclass>
  <teiclass>com.wrox.projsp.ch07.PageVisitTag2ExtraInfo</teiclass>
  <bodycontent>empty</bodycontent>
  <info>
    This tag outputs the last time you've visited the page in the last month.

    The tag is meant to be very simple. Empty body and no attributes.
    It does set a variable for use later in the page.
  </info>
</tag>
```

We also need to change the JSP to use the msg variable to output the data stored in the cookie:

```
<%@ page language="java" import="java.util.Date" %>

<html>
<title>Simplest tag</title>
<body>

<%@ taglib uri="http://localhost:8080/projsp/projsp-taglib" prefix="test" %>

<test:pageVisit2/>

<h2><%= msg %></h2>
<h2> Current system date is <%= new Date().toString() %> </h2>

</body>
</html>
```

Before we move on, it's worth a quick look at the generated code from Tomcat:

```
/* ----  test:pageVisit2 ---- */
com.wrox.projsp.ch07.PageVisitTag2 _jspx_th_test_pageVisit2_0 = new
                    com.wrox.projsp.ch07.PageVisitTag2();
_jspx_th_test_pageVisit2_0.setPageContext(pageContext);
_jspx_th_test_pageVisit2_0.setParent(null);

try {
  int _jspx_eval_test_pageVisit2_0 = _jspx_th_test_pageVisit2_0.doStartTag();
  if (_jspx_eval_test_pageVisit2_0 == BodyTag.EVAL_BODY_TAG)
    throw new JspTagException("Since tag handler class com.wrox.projsp.ch07.
                          PageVisitTag2 does not implement BodyTag, it
                          can't return BodyTag.EVAL_BODY_TAG");
  if (_jspx_eval_test_pageVisit2_0 != Tag.SKIP_BODY) {
    do {
      // end
      // begin [file="C:\\ch07\\simple_tag2.jsp";from=(8,0);to=(8,18)]
    } while (false);
  }
  if (_jspx_th_test_pageVisit2_0.doEndTag() == Tag.SKIP_PAGE)
    return;
  } finally {
    _jspx_th_test_pageVisit2_0.release();
  }
  String msg = null;
  msg = (String) pageContext.getAttribute("msg");

  ...
```

The msg variable is set and available to the rest of the page at the end of the tag, because we set its scope to AT_END in the VariableInfo class.

We'll get to understand more of the error checking in the next section. For now, it's worth re-emphasizing that the lifecycle for a tag that implements the Tag interface, is doStartTag(), doEndTag(), and release().

Evaluating the Body of a Tag

With tags based on the `Tag` interface, you can include body text (that is, content between the beginning and end of the tag) in the output stream, which can either be included or skipped (the default). If you want to include the body of the tag, return `EVAL_BODY_INCLUDE` after the `doStartTag()`, instead of the usual `SKIP_BODY`. This is most useful for printing explanatory or supplementary text to the action.

To illustrate this, we'll make a third version of the `PageVisitTag` example that has the following changes:

- In the taglib descriptor, the `<bodycontent>` tag allows `JSP` content
- The tag class returns `EVAL_BODY_INCLUDE` at the end of the `doStartTag()` method
- The TEI class makes `msg` available from the start of the `pageVisit` tag

Those simple changes mean that the following JSP code will work:

```
<%@ page language="java" import="java.util.Date" %>

<html>
<title>Simplest tag</title>
<body>

<%@ taglib uri="http://localhost:8080/projsp/projsp-taglib" prefix="test" %>

<test:pageVisit3>
This should show how the EVAL_BODY_INCLUDE return works. <br>
I can evaluate single-pass JSP too - for example: <br>
<%= msg %>
</test:pageVisit3>

<h2> Current system date is <%= new Date().toString() %> </h2>

</body>
</html>
```

This is a single-pass evaluation of any JSP expressions within the body of the tag. Note that you can't manipulate the body in the way that's possible with the `BodyTag` interface, which allows you to do multiple evaulations of the contents of the tag. We're going to meet the `BodyTag` interface next.

To summarize the different files we've seen in this section:

- The basic interface that a custom tag must implement is the `Tag` interface
- The `TagSupport` class provides a default implementation, so you only need to override `doStartTag()` and possible `doEndTag()` for your `Tag` implementation.
- The name of the tag, class name, optional `TagExtraInfo` implementation, body content type, attributes, and other descriptive information are stored in a `<tag>` entry in the taglib.
- The `TagExtraInfo` class describes, among other things, variables that the tag sets for use within the tag or in the page

Actions Implementing the BodyTag Interface

To look more closely at body tags and then at how tags can interwork, we'll use a fairly trivial JSP 1.0 example, which overdoes the code in the page. Here's the code for `color_alphabet.jsp`, the simple JSP which is our starting point:

```
<html>
<head>
<title>
Demo of a JSP with declarations and scriptlets only
</title>
</head>
<body>

<!-- This page generates a series of rainbow-colored letters -->
<%@ page language="java" import="java.awt.Color" %>

<!-- Declare constants -->
<%! int ALPHABET_LENGTH = 26; %>
<%! int ROW_REPEAT = 26; %>

<!-- Declare the character variable -->
<%! char c = 0; %>

<!-- Declare color variables -->
<%! float h = 0.0f; %>
<%! float s = 0.9f; %>
<%! float b = 0.9f; %>

<!-- Little helper method to format colors for HTML -->
<%! String formatHTMLColor(int rgbColor) {
      StringBuffer htmlColor = new StringBuffer(
                           Integer.toHexString(rgbColor
                                                 & 0x00ffffff));
      // toHexString() won't preserve leading zeros, so need to add them back in
      // if they've gone missing...
      if (htmlColor.length() != 6) {
         htmlColor.insert(0, "\"#00");
      } else
         htmlColor.insert(0, "\"#");

      htmlColor.append("\"");

      return htmlColor.toString();
   }
%>

<!-- Scriptlet - Java code -->
<%
   for(int i = 0; i < ROW_REPEAT; i++)
   {
      for(int j = 0; j < ALPHABET_LENGTH; j++)
      {
         int increment = (ALPHABET_LENGTH - i + j);
```

```
            // Output capital letters of the alphabet with their associated color
            c = (char)('A' + increment%ALPHABET_LENGTH);
            float h = (float)increment/ALPHABET_LENGTH;
%>
            <font color=<%= formatHTMLColor(Color.HSBtoRGB(h, s, b)) %> >
               <%= c %>
            </font>
<%
        }
%>
<BR>
<%
   }
%>

</body>
</html>
```

The code displays a series of characters with their associated color. A black and white screenshot doesn't do justice to the example so you'll have to run it to see it.

As you can see from the source listing, there's far too much code on the page – it's really no better than a servlet, apart from the obvious advantage of not having to worry explicitly about the output stream. But it's not a page you can show to your web designers.

Using a Bean

The solution in JSP 1.0 was to use a Bean to hide some of the computation behind a series of properties. It removed some code from the page, but not that much.

Also, we've added a class to the system – the development process now consists of compiling the Bean and retrying the JSP, rather than working with a JSP and pressing **Refresh** on your browser. Things have improved in the JSP 1.1 reference implementation with `ant`, the Jakarta project's Java/XML make tool, automatically updating and compiling changed files, and Tomcat's ability to reload updated Beans.

You have a choice of how to hide the code – do you create a component for the whole interaction or one that just knows about characters and their associated colors? For better or worse, we'll make the component a simple one, with lots of property interactions with the JSP page. Otherwise it would be rather boring, and its job could be done by redirecting the JSP to a servlet. It's more interesting to look at the situation where each row output was different.

Here's the 'improved' code with the Bean, from `color_alphabet2.jsp`:

```
<html>
<head>
<title>
Demo of a JSP using a Bean and its properties
</title>
</head>
<body>

<!-- This page generates a series of rainbow-colored letters -->
<%@ page language="java" %>
```

```
<!-- Declare constants (for this page) -->
<%! int ALPHABET_LENGTH = 26; %>
<%! int ROW_REPEAT = 26; %>
<%! char FIRST_LETTER = 'A'; %>

<!-- Declare the character variable -->
<%! char c = 0; %>

<jsp:useBean id="letterColor"
             scope="page"
             class="com.wrox.projsp.ch07.AlphabetCode" >
    <jsp:setProperty name="letterColor"
                     property="startLetter"
                     value="<%= FIRST_LETTER %>" />
    <jsp:setProperty name="letterColor"
                     property="alphabetLength"
                     value="<%= ALPHABET_LENGTH %>" />
    <% letterColor.initMap(); %>
</jsp:useBean>

<%
   for(int i = 0; i < ROW_REPEAT; i++)
   {
      for(int j = 0; j < ALPHABET_LENGTH; j++)
      {
         c = (char)(FIRST_LETTER + (ALPHABET_LENGTH - i + j)%ALPHABET_LENGTH);
%>

         <jsp:setProperty name="letterColor"
                          property="character"
                          value="<%= c %>" />

         <font color=<jsp:getProperty name="letterColor"
                                      property="color" /> >
            <jsp:getProperty name="letterColor"
                             property="character" />
         </font>

<%
      }
%>
<BR>
<%
   }
%>

</body>
</html>
```

How the Page has changed from the First Example

The two for loops still need to be in the page, as the component handles each character individually. However, we've lost all reference to color code from the page, and hidden the arcane details in our component.

Most of the code we've lost has ended up pretty much unchanged in the Bean, which we'll see in a moment. There's a `HashMap` class to handle the mapping between colors and characters, as this will be used by every call to the Bean instance from the page.

Additions to the Page

We've used the JSP Bean tags in this example. Firstly we set the variables that we'll use on this page, including the Bean. This could equally well have been done using request parameters. Next we instantiate the `AlphabetCode` Bean with the `<jsp:useBean>` tag. The empty constructor requirement for JavaBeans is a pain when we want to use the JSP to initialize some variables in the Bean. In this example, we need to use the JSP values for start letter and alphabet length in the Bean, which the Bean will use those values to initialize its map of color/character pairs. (This models a more complex example where these variables are the input for a query on some data.)

So how do we solve initialization without having to compile the information into the Bean (the big no-no)? Here we use the fact that a `useBean` tag can contain a body that will be evaluated only if the bean instantiation succeeds (see the JSP Specification, section 2.13.1), to put in some initializing properties, and a scriptlet to call the `initMap()` afterwards. As you'll see in a moment, `initMap()` won't allow itself to create the map twice.

```
<jsp:useBean id="letterColor"
             scope="page"
             class="com.wrox.projsp.AlphabetCode" >
    <jsp:setProperty name="letterColor"
                     property="startLetter"
                     value="<%= FIRST_LETTER %>" />
    <jsp:setProperty name="letterColor"
                     property="alphabetLength"
                     value="<%= ALPHABET_LENGTH %>" />
    <% letterColor.initMap(); %>
</jsp:useBean>
```

Making this kind of initialization more intuitive and declarative is one advantage of the tag extensions, as we'll see later.

The other point to note is that the properties may take in `Strings`, but they cast those to the right methods. Only with `getColor()`, do we have to be careful to return a `String` as HTML needs a string Hex representation.

Here's the complete code for AlphabetCode:

```
package com.wrox.projsp.ch07;

import java.awt.Color;
import java.util.HashMap;

public class AlphabetCode
{
   private HashMap map;
   char c = 0;

   // For initialization
   int startLetter = 0;
   int alphabetLength = 0;

   // Color variables
   float s = 0.9f;
   float b = 0.9f;
```

```
    public AlphabetCode() {}

    public void setStartLetter(char startLetter)
    {
       this.startLetter = startLetter;
    }

    public void setAlphabetLength(int length)
    {
       alphabetLength = length;
    }

    public void initMap()
    {
       if (map!=null)
          // If this has been called twice, by accident,
          //  and we have a map object, return
          return;
       else
          // Create and fill the map with character and color pairs
          map = new HashMap(alphabetLength*2);

       for(int i = 0; i < alphabetLength; i++)
       {
          this.c = (char)(startLetter + i);
          float h = (float)i/alphabetLength;
          this.map.put(new Character(c), Color.getHSBColor(h, s, b));
       }
    }

    public void setCharacter(char nextChar)
    {
       c = nextChar;
    }

    public char getCharacter()
    {
       return c;
    }

    public String getColor()
    {
       Color rgb = (Color)map.get(new Character(this.c));
       StringBuffer htmlColor = new StringBuffer(
                              Integer.toHexString(rgb.getRGB()
                                                  & 0x00ffffff));
       // toHexString() won't preserve leading zeros, so need to add them back in
       // if they've gone missing...
       if (htmlColor.length() != 6) {
          htmlColor.insert(0, "\"#00");
       } else
          htmlColor.insert(0, "\"#");

       htmlColor.append("\"");

       return htmlColor.toString();
    }
 }
```

Nothing that surprising here – just some property methods for setting initial variables and then the character, the public no-args constructor and an `initMap()` method. The `initMap()` method checks that `map` is `null` before it creates a new one, so that random calls to `initMap()` don't waste time.

One last point before we move onto using custom tags for this example. With the `useBean` *standard action, most of the development work in the specification has been on creating a mechanism that can respond to request parameters, rather than page designers. Tag libraries, on the other hand, are most definitely aimed at web designers, with inputting request parameters a secondary focus.*

Supporting Actions with Body

We have two objectives in this section; to hide the alphabet control code from the JSP, and introduce classes that support the `BodyTag` interface.

The `BodyTag` interface extends the `Tag` interface to provide the means to iterate through the contents of a tag any number of times. The contents of the tag can be:

- `JSP` – in which case the tag can manipulate shared variables and, each time the tag is iterated, output the new value to the response stream. The typical example is a `ResultSet` tag where the body content is the output of a row. The tag controls the iteration over the `ResultSet`, updating the returned row each time through.
- `tagdependent` – the body content is specific to the tag, you can read it in, and use it as configuration information. We can see this in the `QueryTag` class that's one of the JSP 1.1 examples from Sun.

Without further ado, then, let's take the `AlphabetCode` Bean we saw in the last section and convert it into a tag. Here's the code for the `AlphabetTag` class:

```
package com.wrox.projsp.ch07;

import java.awt.Color;
import java.util.HashMap;
import java.io.*;

import javax.servlet.jsp.*;
import javax.servlet.jsp.tagext.*;

public class AlphabetTag extends BodyTagSupport {
  HashMap map;
  char c = 0;

  // For initialization
  int startLetter = 0;
  int alphabetLength = 0;
  int rowRepeat = 0;

  // Color variables
  float s = 0.9f;
  float b = 0.9f;

  // Position
  int row = 0;
  int column = 0;
```

```
public void setStartLetter(String start) {
  startLetter = start.charAt(0);
}

public void setAlphabetLength(String length) {
  alphabetLength = Integer.valueOf(length).intValue();
}

public void setRowRepeat(String repeat) {
  rowRepeat = Integer.valueOf(repeat).intValue();
}

public int doStartTag() throws JspTagException {
  // Create and fill the map with character and color pairs
  map = new HashMap(alphabetLength*2);

  for(int i = 0; i < alphabetLength; i++) {
    this.c = (char)(startLetter + i);
    float h = (float)i/alphabetLength;
    this.map.put(new Character(c), Color.getHSBColor(h, s, b));
  }

  return EVAL_BODY_TAG;
}

public void doInitBody() {
  setOutputAttributes();
}

public int doAfterBody() throws JspTagException {
  try {
    // We're in a row, and have to sort out the next letter.
    if (column < alphabetLength) {
      setOutputAttributes();
      return EVAL_BODY_TAG;
    } else if (column == alphabetLength && row < rowRepeat) {
      // Need a new row
      column = 0;
      setNewLine();
      setOutputAttributes();

      return EVAL_BODY_TAG;
    } else { // if (column == alphabetLength && row == rowRepeat) {
      // We're finished - write the output to the enclosing out
      BodyContent body = getBodyContent();
      body.writeOut(getPreviousOut());

      return SKIP_BODY;
    }
  } catch (IOException ex) {
    throw new JspTagException(ex.toString());
  }
}

public int doEndTag() throws JspTagException {
  return EVAL_PAGE;
}

public void release() {
  map = null;
}

public void setOutputAttributes() {
```

```
      setCharacter((char)(startLetter +
                        (alphabetLength - row + column)%alphabetLength));

      pageContext.setAttribute("character",
                               new Character(getCharacter()).toString());
      pageContext.setAttribute("color", getColor());

      column++;
      if (column == alphabetLength)
        row++;
    }

    public void setNewLine() throws JspTagException {
      try {
        // Used the nested out
        BodyContent body = getBodyContent();

        body.println("<BR>");
        body.newLine();
      } catch(IOException e) {
        throw new JspTagException("Problems with BodyContent: " + e);
      }
    }

    // setCharacter(), getCharacter() and getColor() are unchanged

  }
```

Our tag extends `BodyTagSupport`, which implements the `BodyTag` interface, and provides some convenience methods we use here, `getBodyContent()` and `getPreviousOut()`.

The `doStartTag()`, `doEndTag()`, and `release()` methods don't appear much different from previous examples, except for one thing. You can see how we return `EVAL_BODY_TAG` in the `doStartTag()` method when we want to evaluate the body of the tag. This is the default behavior for body tags. `SKIP_BODY` is still available, but it's used for breaking out of loops, rather than ignoring the body – after all, if you're using a `BodyTag`, you're expecting to see a body.

> **Note that returning `EVAL_BODY_INCLUDE` in `doStartTag()` will cause a runtime error.**

`EVAL_BODY_TAG` isn't just for show. As the JSP specification outlines at the end of section 5.4.2, a `BodyTag` gets its own `BodyContent` object to help handle the body. `BodyContent` is derived from `JspWriter`, which provides the implicit `out` object in a JSP. The `BodyContent` object forms a nested output stream that you can write to, and which can be output to the enclosing stream once you're done. This seems like a lot of work, but it's there so that you can use a `tagdependent` `<bodycontent>` tag in the taglib. `tagdependent` will be interpreted by the tag and can be anything you need, but it has to be output to the nested stream first, read into and dealt with in the `doAfterBody()` or `doEndTag()` methods. The nested stream can then be cleared, and then any output for the user written to the stream.

After the `doStartTag()` method, the default output stream is stored away by the `pageContext`, a new `BodyContent` stream is created as a scratchpad for the body. Once you're finished with the body, you need to write the contents of this nested stream to the enclosing stream. We use the following code in `doAfterBody()` the last time it runs:

```
    } else { // if (column == alphabetLength && row == rowRepeat) {
      BodyContent body = getBodyContent();
      body.writeOut(getPreviousOut());
      return SKIP_BODY;
    }
```

You can write out the contents of the stream to the enclosing stream periodically if you want, and then call `body.clearBody()` to empty the stream so you don't repeat yourself. You can see from the `setNewLine()` method that you can write to the stream programmatically too.

We use the `doInitBody()` method to initialize the variables for the body which is about to be evaluated. Since this is the same code as that used in `doAfterBody()`, we've put it in the common method, `setOutputAttributes()`. It sets the attributes for the body and increments the column count.

The `doAfterTag()` controls the loop logic, allowing you to change the value of the attributes that the body evaluates, as long as you continue to return `EVAL_BODY_TAG`. To stop, just return `SKIP_BODY`. It's a bit strange moving from for loops to initialized do-while loops with lots of conditional logic, but it's grown on me, and the results are worth it.

An easy mistake to make, which took me a while to uncover when I made it, is that the two new methods for handling the body of the tag are,

- `void doInitBody()`
- `int doAfterBody()`

not `doInitTag()` and `doAfterTag()` as I used inadvertently. Note also that no return value is expected from `doInitBody()`, unlike its three companion methods.

Lastly we should mention that the three set methods at the start of the class match the entries in the taglib:

```
<!-- alphabet tag -->
<tag>
  <name>alphabet</name>
  <tagclass>com.wrox.projsp.ch07.AlphabetTag</tagclass>
  <teiclass>com.wrox.projsp.ch07.AlphabetTagExtraInfo</teiclass>
  <bodycontent>JSP</bodycontent>
  <info>
    Output character and color variables starting at the startLetter, continuing
    for the alphabetLength and repeating rowRepeat times.

    Uses 3 mandatory attributes
  </info>

  <attribute>
    <name>startLetter</name>
    <required>true</required>
  </attribute>
  <attribute>
    <name>alphabetLength</name>
    <required>true</required>
  </attribute>
  <attribute>
    <name>rowRepeat</name>
    <required>true</required>
  </attribute>
</tag>
```

The `AlphabetTagExtraInfo` class returns two nested `String` variables, `character` and `color`.

And the JSP? Well `AlphabetTag3.jsp` is rather insignificant-looking now:

```
<html>
<head>
<title>
Color and tags demo with custom tag
</title>
</head>
<body>

<!-- This page generates a series of rainbow colored letters -->

<%@ taglib uri="http://localhost:8080/projsp/projsp-taglib" prefix="test" %>

<test:alphabet startLetter="A" alphabetLength="26" rowRepeat="26" >
  <font color=<%= color %> >
    <%= character %>
  </font>
</test:alphabet>

</body>
</html>
```

Here's what we've just covered, in an edited version of the translated JSP:

```
/* ----  test:alphabet ---- */
com.wrox.projsp.ch07.AlphabetTag _jspx_th_test_alphabet_1 = new
                                        com.wrox.projsp.ch07.AlphabetTag();
_jspx_th_test_alphabet_1.setPageContext(pageContext);
_jspx_th_test_alphabet_1.setParent(null);

JspRuntimeLibrary.introspecthelper(_jspx_th_test_alphabet_1, "startLetter", "A",
                                  null, null, false);
JspRuntimeLibrary.introspecthelper(_jspx_th_test_alphabet_1, "alphabetLength",
                                  "26", null, null, false);
JspRuntimeLibrary.introspecthelper(_jspx_th_test_alphabet_1, "rowRepeat", "26",
                                  null, null, false);
try {
  int _jspx_eval_test_alphabet_1 = _jspx_th_test_alphabet_1.doStartTag();
  if (_jspx_eval_test_alphabet_1 == Tag.EVAL_BODY_INCLUDE)
    throw new JspTagException("Since tag handler class com.wrox.projsp.ch07.
                           AlphabetTag implements BodyTag, it can't return
                           Tag.EVAL_BODY_INCLUDE");
  if (_jspx_eval_test_alphabet_1 != Tag.SKIP_BODY) {
    try {
      if (_jspx_eval_test_alphabet_1 != Tag.EVAL_BODY_INCLUDE) {
        out = pageContext.pushBody();
        _jspx_th_test_alphabet_1.setBodyContent((BodyContent) out);
      }
      _jspx_th_test_alphabet_1.doInitBody();
      do {
        String character = null;
        character = (String) pageContext.getAttribute("character");
        String color = null;
        color = (String) pageContext.getAttribute("color");

        out.write("\r\n  <font color=");
```

```
        out.print( color );
        out.write(" > \r\n     ");
        out.print( character );
        out.write("\r\n   </font>\r\n");
      } while (_jspx_th_test_alphabet_1.doAfterBody() == BodyTag.EVAL_BODY_TAG);
    } finally {
      if (_jspx_eval_test_alphabet_1 != Tag.EVAL_BODY_INCLUDE)
        out = pageContext.popBody();
    }
    ...
```

To summarize, in the code above you can see how:

- The attributes are set
- The container checks that you're aware it's a `BodyTag`, after the `doStartTag()` method
- The `BodyContent` nested stream replaces the default stream, that is placed on a stack in the `pageContext` object
- The `doInitBody()` and `doAfterBody()` form a `do-while` loop for the body of the tag
- The `pageContext` holds the attributes defined in the `AlphabetTagExtraInfo` class
- The enclosing stream is replaced after the body has been evaluated. By then, you should have written out the `BodyContent` content to the enclosing stream from within the tag – that's your responsibility.

Nested Tag Extensions

In the previous section we used custom tags to banish unsightly code from the JSP. But the example was simple, and didn't reflect the intention behind the original Bean code – to keep the color/character mapping general and the control code for the alphabet separate. It seems that some of the more interesting things you can use tags for require nested tags to divide up responsibility and share data effectively for components on the page. For example, JDBC rows require `ResultSets`, a query and a live connection. The question is how best to share information between these tags.

To see how tags cooperate, we're basically going to take the two for loops in the original JSP and make the `AlphabetTag2` responsible for the first and a `RowTag` class for the second. This mimics the double loop in the `ResultSet` example, where the outer loop iterates over the `ResultSet`, while the inner loop extracts column data. Given this, the JSP we want to end up with is:

```
<html>
<head>
<title>
Demo of a JSP using tag extensions
</title>
</head>
<body>

<!-- This page generates a series of rainbow colored letters -->

<%@ taglib uri="http://localhost:8080/projsp/projsp-taglib" prefix="test" %>
```

```
<test:alphabet2 startChar="A" rowLength="26" rowRepeat="26" >
   <test:row2>
      <font color=<%= color %> >
         <%= character %>
      </font>
   </test:row2>
</test:alphabet4>

</body>
</html>
```

Cooperating Tags

What information do we need to pass to the `AlphabetTag2` from the page, and then what data do the `RowTag` objects need from the `AlphabetTag`, and how will we provide that?

- The `AlphabetTag`, as ever, needs to know the start character, the length of the row, and the number of times to loop. This is specified using tag attributes as before.
- The `RowTags` need the row number, first letter, and row length. So we need to pass the attributes in `AlphabetTag` through to the `RowTag` – not the cleanest separation of functionality.

Here's the TEI class for the `AlphabetTag2`:

```
package com.wrox.projsp.ch07;

import javax.servlet.jsp.tagext.*;

public class AlphabetTag2ExtraInfo extends TagExtraInfo {

    public VariableInfo[] getVariableInfo(TagData data) {
        return new VariableInfo[]
            {
                new VariableInfo("rowNumber",
                                 "String",
                                 true,
                                 VariableInfo.NESTED),

                new VariableInfo("startChar",
                                 "String",
                                 true,
                                 VariableInfo.NESTED),

                new VariableInfo("rowLength",
                                 "String",
                                 true,
                                 VariableInfo.NESTED)
            };
    }
}
```

In its turn, the RowTag sets the color and character attributes for its body, as for the previous example.

The RowTags (of which there will be as many instances during the life of the enclosing AlphabetTag as there are rows) each need to have the color/character mapping. The AlphabetTag2 is the obvious place to calculate and hold that, as that's where the row length and start character are specified, and the mapping needs to last over all the instances of RowTag. But how will the map be made available to the RowTags?

There are several options here:

- Use a named variable for the AlphabetTag2, and a getAlphabet() method to return the map of colored characters
- Use the findAncestorWithClass() method defined in the BodyTag interface to get hold of the AlphabetTag2 instance, and then call getAlphabet()
- Make the map an attribute of pageContext

We've seen how to set attributes in the pageContext object, so here we'll create a public getAlphabet() method in AlphabetTag2 for the map.

Changes to AlphabetTag

The doInitBody() method gains a call, to set the startChar attribute for the row tag. This only needs to be set once, so we do it here, rather than in setRowAttributes() or doAfterBody().

```
public void doInitBody() throws JspTagException {
  setRowAttributes();
  pageContext.setAttribute("startChar", new Character(startChar).toString());
}
```

The doAfterBody() method is much simplified, as its logic is now concerned only with rows:

```
public int doAfterBody() throws JspTagException {
  BodyContent body = getBodyContent();

  try {
    if (row < rowRepeat) {
      setRowAttributes();
    } else { // if (row == rowRepeat) {

      body.writeOut(getPreviousOut());
      return SKIP_BODY;
    }
  } catch (IOException ex) {
    throw new JspTagException(ex.toString());
  }

  return EVAL_BODY_TAG;
}
```

As promised, here's the getAlphabet() method that makes the color/character mapping available to the RowTag.

```
public HashMap getAlphabet() {
  return map;
}
```

`setOutputAttributes()` has moved to the `RowTag`, and been replaced with `setRowAttributes()`:

```
public void setRowAttributes() {
  // Set these in the pageContext so that the nested tags can get them
  pageContext.setAttribute("rowNumber", new Integer(row).toString());
  pageContext.setAttribute("rowLength", new Integer(rowLength).toString());
  // Increment the row number for next time
  row++;
}
```

The RowTag Class

The `RowTag` has no attributes to set, relying instead either on its position in relation to the `AlphabetTag2` class or attributes in the `pageContext` (whose scope is limited to the `AlphabetTag2` tags).

The first interesting method is `doStartTag()`:

```
public int doStartTag() throws JspTagException {

  rowLength = Integer.parseInt((String)(pageContext.getAttribute("rowLength")));
  startChar = ((String)pageContext.getAttribute("startChar")).charAt(0);
  row = Integer.parseInt((String)(pageContext.getAttribute("rowNumber")));

  // Is alphabetMap bound to the pageContext?
  map = (HashMap)pageContext.getAttribute("alphabetMap");

  if (map == null) {
    AlphabetTag2 tag = (AlphabetTag2)TagSupport.findAncestorWithClass(this,
                                        AlphabetTag2.class);
    if (tag == null) {
      throw new JspTagException("A RowTag without an alphabet attribute" +
                               " must be nested within an AlphabetTag2");
    }

    // Need to borrow this alphabet or construct it every time...
    map = tag.getAlphabet();
  }

  if (map == null) {
    throw new JspTagException("could not find alphabet object");
  }

  return EVAL_BODY_TAG;
}
```

First, we try to read the attributes we need from the `pageContext`. If that fails for the `alphabetMap`, we use a technique borrowed from the JSP example classes. We use the fact that the `RowTag` instance should be nested within an `AlphabetTag2` instance to get hold of `AlphabetTag2`. The `findAncestorWithClass()` method returns the enclosing tag, or throws a friendly exception about the need to read the documentation. It is implemented in the `TagSupport` (from which the `BodyTagSupport` class derives) and returns the parent tag (which the JSP container always sets with the `PageContext` at the start of the tag) if it matches the class.

Then we use the `getAlphabet()` method to get a reference to the map for this `RowTag` instance, before giving the thumbs-up to evaluating the tag's body.

```
public int doAfterBody() throws JspTagException {
  try {
    if (column < rowLength) {
      setOutputAttributes();
    } else { // if (column == rowLength) {
      column = 0;
      BodyContent body = getBodyContent();

      body.println("<br>");
      body.newLine();
      body.writeOut(getPreviousOut());
      return SKIP_BODY;
    }
  } catch (IOException e) {
    throw new JspTagException(e.toString());
  }

  return EVAL_BODY_TAG;
}
```

The `doAfterBody()` method is interesting because the `RowTag` has its own nested `BodyContent` stream, on top of the one that `AlphabetTag` looks after. We need to output the `RowTag` stream to the `AlphabetTag` before closing the `RowTag`. We don't need to output the `AlphabetTag` stream on each row, though, not unless you want to see everything repeated.

Finally there's the taglib entry for the `RowTag`:

```
<tag>
  <name>row</name>
  <tagclass>com.wrox.projsp.ch07.RowTag</tagclass>
  <teiclass>com.wrox.projsp.ch07.RowTagExtraInfo</teiclass>
  <bodycontent>JSP</bodycontent>
  <info>
     Nested inside the alphabet2 tag, this tag outputs color and
     character variables

     Takes the row number and row length from the pageContext object, set by the
     alphabet2 tag.
  </info>
</tag>
```

We can make a change to `RowTag` to make it more obvious to the tag user what attributes need to be set. But they can stay bound to the `pageContext`. In order to do this, we have to add the attributes to the taglib and make sure they can be set dynamically, with the `<rtexprvalue>` tag. Make the following changes to the taglib:

```
<tag>
  <name>row2</name>
  <tagclass>com.wrox.projsp.ch07.RowTag2</tagclass>
  <teiclass>com.wrox.projsp.ch07.RowTag2ExtraInfo</teiclass>
  <bodycontent>JSP</bodycontent>
  <info>
    Nested inside the alphabet2 tag, this tag outputs color and
    character variables
```

```
      Requires the alphabet attribute.
    </info>

    <attribute>
      <name>rowLength</name>
      <required>false</required>
    </attribute>
    <attribute>
      <name>startChar</name>
      <required>false</required>
    </attribute>
    <attribute>
      <name>rowNumber</name>
      <required>true</required>
      <rtexprvalue>true</rtexprvalue>
    </attribute>
  </tag>
```

Then we can write the JSP as follows:

```
<test:alphabet2 startChar="A" rowLength="26" rowRepeat="26" >
   <test:row2 rowNumber="<%= rowNumber %>" >
      <font color=<%= color %> >
         <%= character %>
      </font>
   </test:row2>
</test:alphabet2>
```

We already output the `rowNumber` as a variable between the alphabet tags, so `AlphabetTag2` needs no changes. The `RowTag2` class needs some set methods:

```
  public void setRowLength(String length) {
    this.rowLength = Integer.parseInt(length);
  }

  public void setStartChar(String startChars) {
    this.startChar = startChars.charAt(0);
  }

  public void setRowNumber(String row) {
    this.row = Integer.parseInt(row);
  }

  public int doStartTag() throws JspTagException {
    // Need to check this has been set somehow, or we'll get a divide
    // by zero error
    if (rowLength == 0) {
      rowLength = Integer.parseInt((String)
                     (pageContext.getAttribute("rowLength")));
    }
  // Rest of method as before
```

There are any number of combinations of shared objects and attributes, from the simple attributes we've used here, to passing the AlphabetTag as a reference to the RowTag, and providing get/set methods to reduce the use of the `pageContext`. The decision depends on how coupled the operation of the tags is.

Recipes for Tags

We've now seen a number of examples of custom tags. It's worth summarizing the main points:

For Empty Tags, or Tags with No Body

The `doStartTag()` method is evaluated once the `Tag` object has been initialized with any attributes and page context information. Its default implementation in the `TagSupport` class is to return `SKIP_BODY`, so that the body of the tag is not evaluated. If you want to evaluate the body of the tag, return `EVAL_BODY_INCLUDE` from this method. The body of the tag is output to the same stream as the rest of the page.

Similarly in all tags the `doEndTag()` will be called. Its default action is to return `EVAL_PAGE` and allow Java to continue with the rest of the page. If you want to halt the JSPs output, because of an error, for example, return `SKIP_PAGE` here.

You can declare that your tag is empty in the tag descriptor using the `<bodycontent>` tag:

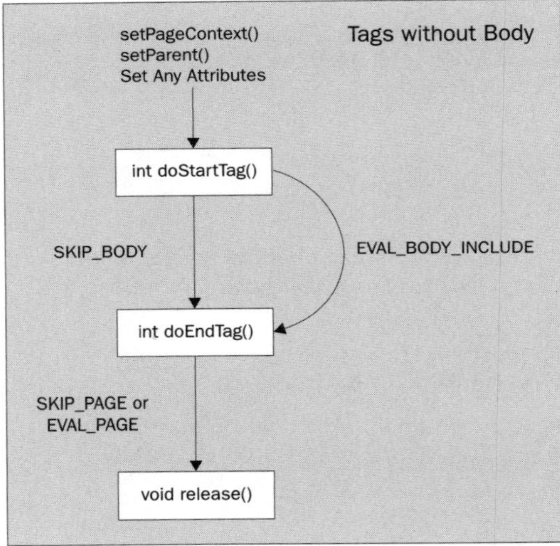

Tags with Actions within their Body

For tags with a body that needs more than just ignoring or transferring to the output stream, use the `BodyTag` interface, which defines two additional methods `doInitBody()` and `doAfterBody()`.

For body tags, the `doStartTag()` returns `EVAL_BODY_TAG` to evaluate the body, the container creates a nested stream of type `BodyContent` and passes it to the tag, and finally `doInitBody()` is invoked. The default implementation is empty.

The body between the tags is written to the `BodyContent` stream, then the `doAfterBody()` method is called. Its default implementation is to return `SKIP_BODY`, so that `doEndTag()` is called. But, as we've seen this method allows us to repeatedly output the body, so long as the method returns `EVAL_BODY_TAG`. And since the body can contain JSP variables, the output can change. Alternatively, for `<bodycontent>` marked as `tagdependent`, the `BodyContent` can also be used to read in content to configure the tag.

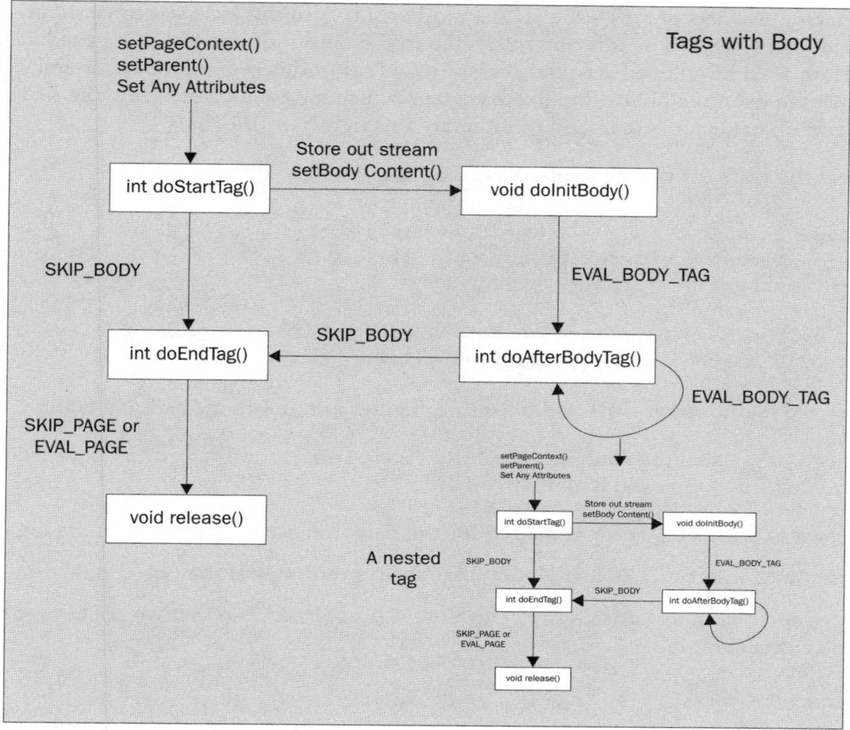

Using Other People's Work

One of the big promises of custom tags is the creation and widespread use of tag libraries in web application development. How easy is it to use these tag libraries?

Let's say we want to put together an example for part of charity bookstore site where donated first editions are advertised to the widest audience, not just those who can visit the local shop. The home page needs a search facility, and one search term is the bookstore town. Getting the list of towns into a select HTML tag is not a job one would relish doing by hand, and the bookstore list will grow over time.

Let's say that we also want to play with the database tags in the Sun JSP examples and have heard of Joe Ottinger's Form tag library on a newsgroup (see http://cupid.suninternet.com/~joeo/). Can we work up a simple database-driven `select` tag to show the list of bookstores towns from these two tag libraries?

Both the Sun and the Forms tag libraries are relatively immature, but it was instructive to try this to see what tag library developers need to provide. Initially we'll just work from the taglibs, which tell you the basics. But the way the Form family of tags works together with a JavaBean that represents the input data is made clear only by looking at examples and documentation for those classes. I suspect this will always be true because of how nested tags work together. Having strong error checking on your implicit references in a nested tag, as we've seen in `RowTag` and other tags is very important if the page is going to compile correctly.

Also interfacing two sets of tags – the JDBC and Form tags in this case – is never likely to be without friction, and you'll have to handle any mismatch in the output of one tag being used as the input of another. Here we'll often need scriptlets or our own tags (if this is going to be a regular pairing of the libraries). In the example below, the database tags return a `ResultSet`, while the `select` tag needs a `Collection` object (as it is intended to integrate this tightly with EJBs).

Let's look at the code for this example. First the JSP:

```
<%@ page language="java"
         import="com.wrox.projsp.ch07.*, java.util.*"
         errorPage="ErrorPage.jsp" %>

<%@ taglib uri="http://localhost:8080/projsp/projsp-taglib" prefix="test" %>
<%@ taglib uri="http://localhost:8080/form/taglib" prefix="form" %>
```

We import two tag libraries – the taglib for this chapter and the Form package taglib.

Now we need to get a connection. I've used the `examples.ConnectionTag` class from Sun as the basis for my tag, but I changed it so that:

- The `ref`, `userid`, and `password` for the database are all attributes to the tag
- `getConnection()` is a singleton (that always returns just the one connection object)
- Moved code out of `doEndTag()` to the `doStartTag()` so that we could nest queries within the connection tag

```
package com.wrox.projsp.ch07;

import javax.servlet.jsp.*;
import javax.servlet.jsp.tagext.*;
import java.io.*;
import java.sql.*;

/**
 * Example: A connection/password/userid/query set of tags.
 * Adapted from the JSP 1.1 examples from Sun
 *
 * This is the runtime representation of a connection tag
 *
 * ConnectionTag supports the following programming paradigm.
 *
 * Implicitly define a connection that is available within the start/end tag
 * <connection ref="connection"
 *             password="pwd"
 *             userid="uid" >
 * <query....> </query>
 * </connection>
 */

public class ConnectionTag extends BodyTagSupport {

  /**
   * Attributes for this action:
   *   id (inherited)
   *   ref
   *   userId and password
   */
```

```
  /**
   * ref is a reference to some connection
   */
  public void setRef(String s) {
    this.ref = s;
  }

  public String getRef() {
    return this.ref;
  }

  public void setUserId(String uid) {
    userId = uid;
  }

  public void setPassword(String pass) {
    password = pass;
  }

  public int doStartTag() throws JspTagException {
    ref = getRef();
    if (ref == null) {
      throw new JspTagException("missing ref attribute");
    }
    String tagId = getId();
    if (tagId != null) {
      if (userId == null) {
        throw new JspTagException("userId has not been defined yet");
      }
      if (password == null) {
        throw new JspTagException("password has not been defined yet");
      }
      if (connection == null) {
        getConnection();
      }
      pageContext.setAttribute(tagId, connection);
    }

    return EVAL_BODY_TAG;
  }

  public int doEndTag() throws JspTagException {
    connection = null;
    return EVAL_PAGE;
  }

  /**
   * Get the SQL connection Object.
   * A connection object needs both the userid and the password
   * Trying to get the connection object before the data is
   * available will produce an error
   */
  public Connection getConnection() throws JspTagException {
    // Want to return the connection if there's one already. Keep it a singleton.
    // If you want another connection use another tag...
    if (connection == null) {
      if (userId == null) {
        throw new JspTagException("userId has not been defined yet");
      }
      if (password == null) {
        throw new JspTagException("password has not been defined yet");
      }
```

```
        try {
          // get the connection object
          Class.forName("sun.jdbc.odbc.JdbcOdbcDriver");

          // String database =
          connection = DriverManager.getConnection(ref,
                                                   userId,
                                                   password);
        } catch (ClassNotFoundException e) {
          throw new JspTagException("Error loading driver: " + e);
        } catch (SQLException ex) {
          connection = null;
          throw new JspTagException("Connection failed " + ex);
        }
      }
      return connection;
    }

    // For completeness
    public String getUserId() { return userId; }
    public String getPassword() { return password; }

    private Connection connection;  // the sql connection object
    private String password;        // password for the connection
    private String userId;          // userid for the connection
    private String ref;             // the ref attribute; assumed to be some JDBC
  URL
  }
```

This code is fairly simple, setting the attributes for the connection, checking those in `doStartTag()` and then calling `getConnection()` if everything's present and correct. The corresponding JSP looks like:

```
<test:connection ref="jdbc:odbc:Books"
                 id="conn01" userId="guest" password="guest" >
  <test:bookStoreSearch/>
</test:connection>
```

Assuming that this will eventually get connection objects from some connection pool, we don't want to hang onto the connection any longer than we need, so we use `page` scope in setting the connection attribute bound to the `PageContext`. We close that `ConnectionTag` as soon as the `BookStoreSearch` tag has been created, as there's no need for the connection to hang around while the `form:select` tag is created.

If the connection fails we throw an exception, but on a commercial site, it might be better to return `SKIP_PAGE`, and use some "Contact the sys admin" text in the body of the tag.

> *I've not worried about security too much, as these files should always be translated, but more involved use of the tag would make some configuration files useful, which would make the system more secure. Some ways to accomplish this are mentioned in the JSP specification in section 5.8.3.*

The `BookStoreSearchTag` class is a mix of `java.sql.PreparedStatement` and data processing to create a collection for the `<form:select>` tag. The idea is that this search would run once per session, and that the collection would be available to all the objects in that session – as it's unlikely to change in that time. The data returned in the `ResultSet` is used to construct a `Vector` of `BookStore` objects whose `Town` property will be read by the tag.

Here's the code for the class:

```
package com.wrox.projsp.ch07;

import javax.servlet.jsp.*;
import javax.servlet.jsp.tagext.*;
import java.sql.*;
import java.util.*;

public class BookStoreSearchTag extends TagSupport implements Tag {

  public void setConnId(String id) {
    connection = id;
  }

  public int doStartTag() throws JspTagException {

    Connection dbConnect = (Connection)pageContext.getAttribute("connection");

    if (dbConnect == null) {
      ConnectionTag tag = (ConnectionTag)TagSupport.findAncestorWithClass(this,
                                                       ConnectionTag.class);
      if (tag == null) {
        throw new JspTagException("A BookStoreSearchTag without a connection" +
                                  " attribute must be nested within" +
                                  " a ConnectionTag");
      }

      // This returns the connection for this page
      dbConnect = tag.getConnection();
    }

    if (dbConnect == null) {
      throw new JspTagException("could not get connection");
    }

    ResultSet rs;

    try {
      PreparedStatement mystatement = dbConnect.prepareStatement(
                              "SELECT * FROM bookshop ORDER BY Town");
      rs = mystatement.executeQuery();
    } catch(SQLException e) {
      throw new JspTagException("Have you got the right DB - " +
                              "query on bookshop table failed " + e);
    }

    // Convert ResultSet to a Collection for our form:select tag to use
    // Want the town for the select
    bookStores = new Vector();

    int contactColumnNumber;
    int townColumnNumber;
    int addressColumnNumber;
    int phoneColumnNumber;

    try{
      contactColumnNumber = rs.findColumn("Contact");
      townColumnNumber = rs.findColumn("Town");
      addressColumnNumber = rs.findColumn("Address");
      phoneColumnNumber = rs.findColumn("Phone");
```

```
    } catch(SQLException e) {
      throw new JspTagException("Have you got the right DB - " +
                                "bookshop table with town column not there " + e);
    }

    try{
      while(rs.next()) {
        // Use this to create a BookStore bean...
        BookStore bookStore = new BookStore();
        // Set the details...
        bookStore.setContact(rs.getString(contactColumnNumber));
        bookStore.setTown(rs.getString(townColumnNumber));
        bookStore.setAddress(rs.getString(addressColumnNumber));
        bookStore.setPhone(rs.getString(phoneColumnNumber));

        bookStores.add(bookStore);
      }
    } catch(SQLException e) {
      throw new JspTagException("Bookshop resultset not happy " + e);
    }

    pageContext.setAttribute("bookstores", bookStores);

    // All well, then let's do the rest of the page...
    return EVAL_PAGE;
  }

  public void release() {
    super.release();
  }

  String statementText;
  String connection;
  String path;
  Vector bookStores;
}
```

The `BookStoreSearchTag` has the following taglib entry:

```
<!-- bookStoreSearch tag -->
<tag>
  <name>bookStoreSearch</name>
  <tagclass>com.wrox.projsp.ch07.BookStoreSearchTag</tagclass>
  <teiclass>com.wrox.projsp.ch07.BookStoreSearchTagExtraInfo</teiclass>
  <bodycontent>empty</bodycontent>
  <info>
    This tag prepares a Collection of the available bookstores.

    There is an optional connection attribute, which, when provided,
    must be the id for some connection tag.
  </info>

  <attribute>
    <name>connId</name>
    <required>false</required>
  </attribute>
</tag>
```

The TEI class is:

```
package com.wrox.projsp.ch07;

import javax.servlet.jsp.tagext.*;
import java.util.Vector;

public class BookStoreSearchTagExtraInfo extends TagExtraInfo {

    public VariableInfo[] getVariableInfo(TagData data) {
        return new VariableInfo[]
            {
                new VariableInfo("bookstores",
                                 "java.util.Vector",
                                 true,
                                 VariableInfo.AT_END)

            };
    }
}
```

In a more complete system the BookStore bean would form part of a Book bean that would be the data for a search term. This has the benefit that the Bean can represent the most-recent search data for the duration of a session. It's as much for the user's benefit as for the DB interaction

Here's that declaration of the BookStore bean in the JSP:

```
<jsp:useBean id="bookstore" class="BookStore" scope="session" />
```

The Bean itself is very simple, consisting of the public no-args constructor and the set and get methods for the `BookStore` info.

Finally, then, here's the compete JSP code:

```
<%@ page language="java"
         import="com.wrox.projsp.ch07.*, java.util.*"
         errorPage="ErrorPage.jsp" %>

<%@ taglib uri="http://localhost:8080/projsp/projsp-taglib" prefix="test" %>
<%@ taglib uri="http://localhost:8080/form/taglib" prefix="form" %>

<test:connection ref="jdbc:odbc:Books"
                 id="conn01" userId="guest" password="guest" >

<test:bookStoreSearch/>

</test:connection>


<html>
<body>

<jsp:useBean id="bookstore" class="com.wrox.projsp.ch07.BookStore" scope="page" />
<%
    Vector vector = (Vector)pageContext.getAttribute("bookstores");
%>
```

```
Contact Name: <form:text name="bookstore" property="contact" />
Town: <form:select name="bookstore"
                   list="<%= vector %>"
                   value="town"
                   property="town" />

</body>
</html>
```

As you can see from the `BookStoreSearchTag` class, the `bookstores` attribute is defined at `page` scope in the `doStartTag()`, but it's not directly available to the `form:select` tag's `list` attribute. Instead, we have to extract the `Vector` into a scriptlet, and pass that reference into the tag.

The Form tags are very easy to use, once you have the Bean to manipulate. The `text` and `select` tags use the `BookStore` bean on this page to store the selected entries on the form. Both tags use the `property` attribute to name the property to get and set in that bean. The `value` attribute in the `select` tag names the property in the objects returned by the `list Vector`. Take a look at the `doEndTag()` method in the `Select` tag class to see how these properties interact.

The Form library also shows us how to package up a tag library. The source tree is present, and the `build.xml` file compiles it to the class package (which starts at the top-level). The `taglib.tld` for the library is kept in the `/meta-inf` directory. `build.xml` also creates the JAR file. See Appendix A for the details of setting up tag libraries on the Tomcat server.

Resources

Here are some useful resources:

- The Jakarta project – http://jakarta.apache.org/taglibs/index.html
- JSP at Sun – http://java.sun.com/products/jsp/ and the examples from which we've developed the `ConnectionTag` class are available at http://java.sun.com/products/jsp/examples1_1.zip
- Joe Ottinger's Form library – http://cupid.suninternet.com/~joeo/Form.html and other JSP information at http://cupid.suninternet.com/~joeo/
- Go to Sourceforge.net and search on JSP to find, amongst others, the `in16` project, http://sourceforge.net/project/?group_id=1282
- A good portal site for JSP tag extensions can be found at http://jsptags.com/tags/
- Extensive prepackaged tag libraries are available from BEA for their WebLogic server – http://edocs.beasys.com/wlac/portals/docs/tagscontents.html
- The Orion server site has a good custom tag tutorial – http://www.orionserver.com
- Resin open source JSP tag libraries with XSL – http://www.caucho.com/

Summary

This chapter has introduced the tag extensions mechanism recently released with JSP 1.1, and shown some ways in which it can work. I hope it has shown that, while developing tags isn't without its problems, they provide a far more flexible method of abstracting code from a JavaServer Page into a component, than ordinary JavaBeans.

At the time of writing, tag libraries are in their early days, but the pace is heating up – watch the usual suspects for open source projects, and the tool and middleware vendors for their support in the very near future.

In this chapter we've:

- Reviewed where simple JSPs and bean tags are insufficient
- Met the different types of tags – simple, empty, with body, with attributes, defining scripting variables, nested
- Seen the lifecycle of a translated tag and how this affects the response output
- Written `tld` file entries to name the tag, map it to its class, hint at its body content and set its attributes.
- Created TEI classes to return the variables that the tag will make available, and in what scope
- Used third-party tag libraries to put JSPs together

We will now go on to look at generating dynamic web GUIs using JSP.

J2EE
JSP

9

Dynamic GUIs

Introduction

Have you ever wondered how you can let users define what they see on your site? If you have been building web pages for any length of time, you will probably have considered this idea. Most of the popular web sites or Internet portals allow users to customize their experience with their site either by changing the layout, colors or fonts of the site, or by changing and personalizing the information that is presented to them on a home page.

In this chapter we will discuss first what a Dynamic GUI is, and its uses. Next, we will build a mini-solution for each concept. We will be building the framework for a real web site called http://www.jspCafe.com. You will be able to visit this site to see how it works, and download any source code presented here.

What is a Dynamic GUI?

A Dynamic GUI can be defined in two different ways, each significantly different from the other.

- **Co-Branding** - customizing the look
- **Web Portal Model** - customizing the content

We will discuss the two definitions in turn.

Co-Branding Model (Customizing the Look)

The first definition can be best described through a Co-Branding model. Have you ever seen web sites that allow you to customize the look on the fly? Those sites are built on a model that allows them to Co-Brand their service to be used by subscribers. Each subscriber is assigned an account, which they can access in order to alter the way their Co-Branded site looks. One simple example would be the addition of your own logo to the Co-Branded page. This model is limited to allowing a subscriber to change the sites appearance but not the content presented. However, some Co-Branded site services do allow you to customize some of the site content.

The image below is a Co-Branded bookstore, which I created for one of my web sites. I signed up for this free service from vStore (http://www.vstore.com) and was able to customize the way the site looked. They offered several templates and font choices; this is an excellent example of the Co-Branding model.

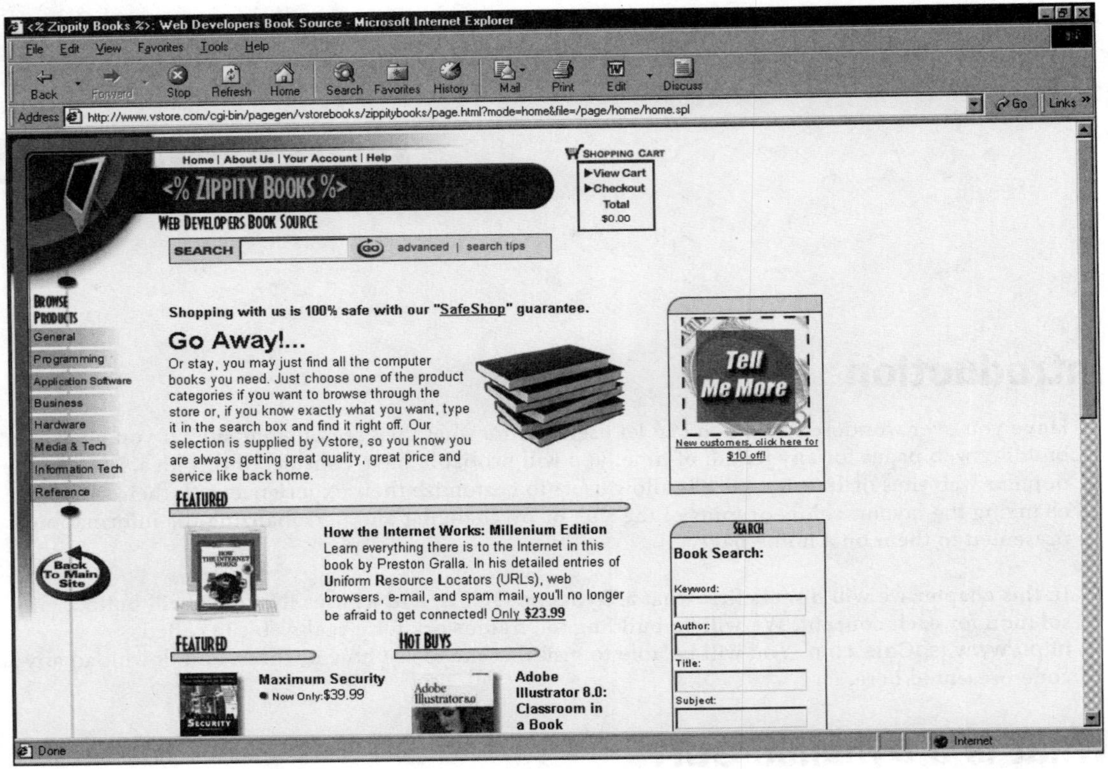

Web Portal Model (Customizing the Content)

The second definition is the most widely used Dynamic GUI system employed by Web Portals. The best example of this would be Netscape's (http://www.netscape.com) home page or Yahoo's My Yahoo! Page (http://my.yahoo.com). Excite and Yahoo both allow you to change the information that is displayed on the page, as opposed to the Co-Branding model that allows you to change only the look of a page.

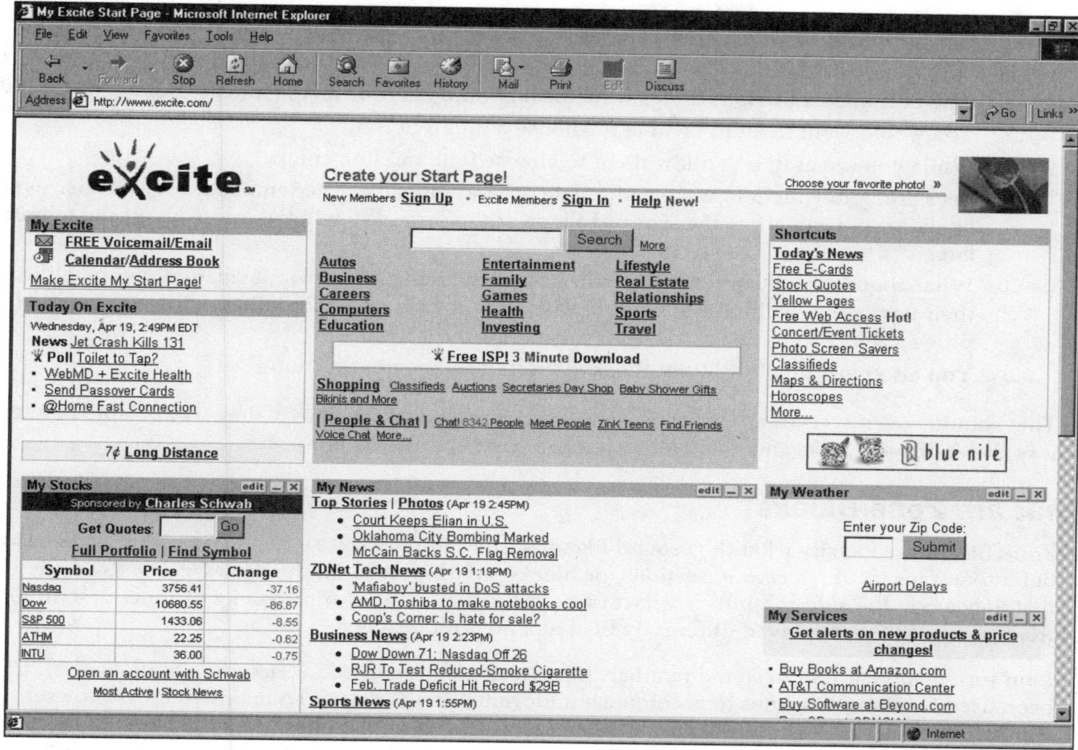

Obviously, the most powerful thing to do would be to allow visitors to change both the look (Co-Brand Model) and information (Portal Model) for their personal home page; this will be discussed in the second part of this chapter.

Creating a Co-Branding Modeled Web Site

Our first discussion will center on the Co-Branding model. There are three important factors to consider when you are building this type of site. First you need to decide if you want your subscribers to change the HTML layout (the position of the navigation menu, etc.) of the page, or just change colors, fonts and logos. Next, you must decide which elements of your page you want to allow people to change (paragraph headings, but not page headings). Last, you need to decide what kind of limits you want to place on the customization (only shades of blue and no red colors).

What will be customized?

For your web site, you will want to allow people to link to your pages from another site and make it look like their site visitors never left their site. To do this, your subscribers will need to register and customize their version of your site. They will then link to it and pass a subscriber ID in the query string:

```
http://www.mysite.com/default.jsp?myID=1000
```

To start off with, let's define some of the things you would want your site subscribers to be able to customize.

- One of the most obvious things is the background color or image for the site.
- You would want them to be able to choose a different font.
- While you are at it, let's allow them to choose font and link colors.
- Let's also allow them to wrap a template around the page. The template can be either dynamic or static, and can affect the size and shape of the page. We will talk more about the template later.
- What about the navigation? Let's allow them to create their own navigation design, although their navigation will have to comply with certain rules you will define in the construction process.
- You also need to allow 'Zone Block' definitions. (See next section.)

That should cover everything. If you allow subscribers to alter the above, they will be able to alter the way the entire site looks and enjoy a much more personalized experience.

What are Zone Blocks?

Zone Blocks are exactly what they sound like. Consider http://www.amazon.com, whose site has very definitive ways in which certain sections (or blocks) are displayed on the browser. For example, the text that appears in the side columns is very distinct from the text that appears in a product description. Also, a page title is displayed differently than a paragraph header.

I am sure this is starting to sound familiar. If it doesn't, consider CSS (Cascading Style Sheets). CSS has been used by many web sites to accomplish uniformity across pages. To maintain cross browser compatibility, we are not going to use CSS: we are going to use what I like to call Cascading JSP (CJSP) to mimic some of the features and functions of CSS.

To do this, we will define CJSP tags (which are nothing more than expressions to write a page variable) to wrap around your Zones and supply your template parameters. CJSP tags are used in a similar way to XML. Each tag will have a Start and End version. For example:

```
<%= paragraphStart %>My paragraph text...<%= paragraphEnd %>
```

Where:

```
String paragraphStart = '<p align=justify><font face="verdana,arial" size=2>';
String paragraphEnd = '</font></p>';
```

Doing this will produce the following HTML, once the server has processed the script and sent it to the browser:

```
<p align=justify><font face="verdana,arial" size=2>My paragraph text…</font></p>
```

Of course your tags can be much more complex than this simple representation. You could wrap a table around your paragraphs to achieve alignments, borders, background colors, or background images.

It has been brought to my attention several times that this could be accomplished more easily though XML/XSLT. The reason I am doing it this way is to allow for cross-browser compatibility. Not all browsers support XML, but they all support basic HTML tags. CJSP wraps plain HTML around your text: there is no need for browser tests and custom pages for each browser type. In my opinion, using a system that is not browser dependant makes for a web site that is much easier to maintain.

How do we store and retrieve the template data?

There are several ways to make your pages with dynamic templates. One way is to store all of your templates in JavaBeans. To use them, you would call the bean with a `session` scope and call properties from the Bean for each tag and/or zone block. The only problem with doing it this way is that whenever you need to change part of your template, you will need to recompile the Bean.

Another way would be to use include files for each template and include only the file that you want to use as your template. This method is even more limiting than the Bean method, because you would have to alter the include files' source code each time you change your template. And, depending on the changes you made, you might have to alter every include template to match the structure of the one you changed. This would get very tedious.

The most flexible way would be to store all of the CJSP tag definitions in a database and load the template data into a global include file, which you include in every page that you want to be affected by the CJSP tags. By storing your template parameters in a database, you have quick and easy access to them. All you need to do to alter a template is open the database and make changes to the appropriate tag values. The next time the page loads, the changes are instantly available.

If you needed to add a new tag type, the only file you would need to alter would be the template include file to retrieve the new tag(s) and add the field to the database. Once the altered page is saved, and the appropriate changes have been made to the database, your new tag type would be instantly available for use within your templated pages.

How do we Decide what the "Template Template" looks like?

"Template Template?" That's a strange term. What does it mean? A Template Template, or TT as we will call it, is a layout for how your information will be surrounded by the template code. The position you put the information, relative to the zone blocks and template tags, is crucial. If you do not arrange your TT in an efficient manner, your templating system will not be very flexible.

There really is no rule on this matter. The way you layout your TT is entirely dependent on the content of your site. For this project, let's choose a simple layout I like to call the "4 paned window". Below is a diagram describing this layout.

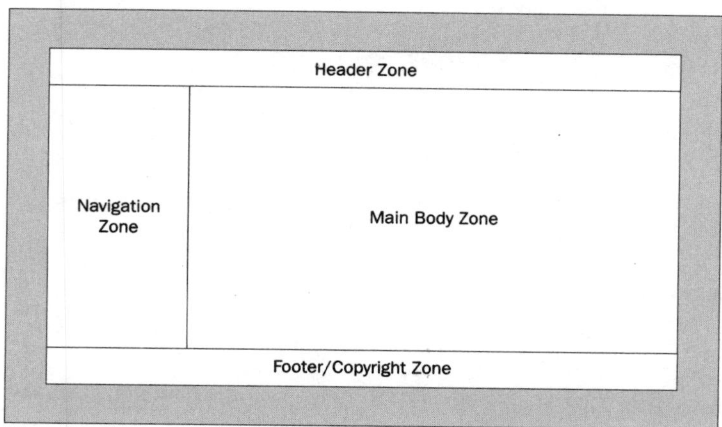

As you can see, we have 4 distinct areas or Zones

- **Header Zone** - the header for logos, banners, etc.
- **Navigation Zone** - left side navigation panel
- **Main Body Zone** - the main body
- **Footer/Copyright Zone** - footer, copyright, contact, terms, and special links area

Each one of these zones can be put into cells in a table:

```
<table width="100%" height="100%" border=5 cellspacing=0 bordercolor=black>
<tr>
  <td colspan=2 align=center valign=center>
    Header Zone
  </td>
</tr>
<tr height="90%">
  <td align=center valign=center>
    Navigation Zone
  </td>
  <td align=center valign=center width="90%">
    Main Body Zone
  </td>
</tr>
<tr>
  <td colspan=2 align=center valign=center>
    Footer/Copyright Zone
  </td>
</tr>
</table>
```

Next, we can easily break down the zones to specific start and end HTML tags:

Header Zone Start:

```
<table width="100%" height="100%" border=5 cellspacing=0 bordercolor=black>
<tr>
  <td colspan=2 align=center valign=center>
```

Header Zone End:

```
  </td>
</tr>
```

Navigation Zone Start:

```
<tr height="90%">
  <td align=center valign=center>
```

Navigation Zone End:

```
  </td>
```

Main Body Zone Start:

```
  <td align=center valign=center width="90%">
```

Main Body Zone End:

```
    </td>
  </tr>
```

Footer/Copyright Zone Start:

```
  <tr>
    <td colspan=2 align=center valign=center>
```

Footer/Copyright Zone End:

```
    </td>
  </tr>
  </table>
```

Now let's replace the HTML start and end tags for each Zone with a CJSP tag:

```
  <%= zone_Header_Start %>
    Header Zone
  <%= zone_Header_End %>

  <%= zone_Navigation_Start %>
    Navigation Zone
  <%= zone_Navigation_End %>

  <%= zone_Body_Start %>
    Main Body Zone
  <%= zone_Body_End %>

  <%= zone_Footer_Start %>
    Footer/Copyright Zone
  <%= zone_Footer_End %>
```

Now that we have accomplished this, we can create the database based on these zones.

SQL Server Enterprise Manager - [3:Design Table 'SUBSCRIBER_THEME']

Console Window Help

Column Name	Datatype	Length	Precision	Scale	Allow Nulls	Default Value	Identity	Identity Seed	Identity Increment	Is RowGuid
SUBSCRIBER_THEME_ID	int	4	10	0			✓	1	1	
ZONE_NAVIGATION_START	varchar	500	0	0	✓					
ZONE_NAVIGATION_END	varchar	500	0	0	✓					
ZONE_BODY_START	varchar	500	0	0	✓					
ZONE_BODY_END	varchar	500	0	0	✓					
ZONE_HEADER_START	varchar	500	0	0	✓					
ZONE_HEADER_END	varchar	500	0	0	✓					
ZONE_FOOTER_START	varchar	500	0	0	✓					
ZONE_FOOTER_END	varchar	500	0	0	✓					

That's not all we will need in the database. We should also define the regular tag types. We will need at least the following (we can always add more later):

- Background Color
- Background Image
- Font Face
- Font Color
- Link Color
- Header Start & Header End
- Paragraph Start & Paragraph End

Let's add these new tag types to the database:

SQL Server Enterprise Manager - [3:Design Table 'SUBSCRIBER_THEME']

Console Window Help

Column Name	Datatype	Length	Precision	Scale	Allow Nulls	Default Value	Identity	Identity Seed	Identity Increment	Is RowGuid
SUBSCRIBER_THEME_ID	int	4	10	0			✓	1	1	
BACKGROUND_COLOR	char	7	0	0	✓					
BACKGROUND_IMAGE	varchar	50	0	0	✓					
FONT_FACE	varchar	20	0	0	✓					
FONT_COLOR	char	7	0	0	✓					
LINK_COLOR	char	7	0	0	✓					
HEADING_START	varchar	500	0	0	✓					
HEADING_END	varchar	500	0	0	✓					
PARAGRAPH_START	varchar	500	0	0	✓					
PARAGRAPH_END	varchar	500	0	0	✓					
ZONE_NAVIGATION_START	varchar	500	0	0	✓					
ZONE_NAVIGATION_END	varchar	500	0	0	✓					
ZONE_BODY_START	varchar	500	0	0	✓					
ZONE_BODY_END	varchar	500	0	0	✓					
ZONE_HEADER_START	varchar	500	0	0	✓					
ZONE_HEADER_END	varchar	500	0	0	✓					
ZONE_FOOTER_START	varchar	500	0	0	✓					
ZONE_FOOTER_END	varchar	500	0	0	✓					

How do we Allow People to Change their Template?

Once you have your zone blocks and tag types defined, you need to design a system to allow the subscriber to change the templates.

The most obvious and probably the easiest way to allow your subscribers to change their template is to give them a web-based administration page. We could easily load the template fields from the database into HTML text areas. They could then alter the template data, preview the new tags, submit the changes, and make them available right away.

This administrative page would be kept in a password-protected directory on your web site. Once a subscriber successfully signs up for an account, they will use their chosen username and password to enter the administration area. If you do not already have some sample code for this type of process, I have provided some below.

The following code is for the login verification process. This is not the most secure method of user authentication, but for this implementation, we don't need to highest security. The user enters their username and password, which is submitted via the `POST` method and then used to check the database for a valid login.

On every page that needs to be authenticated, check for a user ID in the session object - if it does not exist, redirect the user to a login page, passing the URL the user was trying to access as a parameter.

On the login page, if the user successfully logs in, create a session for them, and add their user ID to the session. After this, redirect the user back to the original page they had tried to access. This way, even if the user bookmarks a page, they will be asked to login once the session has become invalid.

On every page include the following (either as code or an include file):

```
HttpSession session = request.getSession(true);
if (session.getValue("UID") == null) {
  response.sendRedirect(response.encodeRedirectUrl
     ("Login.jsp?Origin=thispage.jsp"));
}
```

In `Login.jsp` once the user has provided the correct login credentials, we do the following:

```
session.putValue("UID", UID);
response.sendRedirect(response.encodeRedirectUrl(request.getParameter("Origin")));
```

Creating a Web Portal Modeled Site

As seen in the previous example, we were able to dynamically create a template for the web site from a database. But, what if you want to be the next Yahoo? What if you want to allow visitors to customize the content that is displayed to them on their home page? This section talks about what is needed in order to accomplish this task.

Database-Driven Content

One of the first, and probably the most important factors to consider when deciding to make your site content customizable, is the database factor. In order to allow maximum flexibility within your web site, your content must be database-driven. By this I mean your content must exist in a database, and your pages must dynamically generate themselves from that database.

The reason this is important is that we are going to need to assign content zones to your pages so that we can pull only the content for those zones when needed. We also need these zone definitions so that we can allow a user to define which Zones they want to see on their home page.

Storing the Layout Information

Next, we need to decide how we want to store users' layout information. Two options come to mind when approaching this subject. The first is to use a database, and the second is to use cookies.

Using a database would mean that you would have to do one of two things to allow the visitor to see their specialized content format when they come to your site:

1. Use a single unique identifier (database generated) in a cookie placed on the user's machine to identify them to the server, with the data stored in the database.
2. Use a member login process to require a user to identify themselves manually, with the data stored in the database.

Using cookies would require that we store all of the customization data in cookies on the client machine. This would eliminate the need to build any database tables and maintain that data. From a database administration point of view, this is great.

You could also use a combination of the two. A cookie can be used to store a key from the database. You could allow the login script to create the key cookie if it is not found. This will provide for people using several computers and the loss of the cookie via the user deleting it in some manner. One last advantage would be that is a user does not accept cookies they can still persist the layout info.

In this day of convenience and user-friendliness, I prefer the non-login, or all-cookie approach. The major factor in making this decision is that none of the information we are going to store on the users machine is confidential or sensitive in any way. You will see what I mean by this later.

In writing this chapter, I have received a lot of feedback regarding my use of cookies. With that in mind, I feel I should explain to you why I am doing it this way. In this chapter, I am merely explaining the concept of Co-Branding and Portals. I think it would be unfair to the concept if I attempted to sum up every possible way to accomplish this extremely complicated task in one chapter. The models and concepts I am talking about would require an entire book by themselves to really delve into all of the possibilities.

What are Content Objects?

Take a look at excite.com and you will see each content type is more or less blocked in by a table or some other formatting method. Each one of these content zones is specialized to hold specific content. For example, there is a News Object, an Astrology Object, a Weather Object, a People Object and many others.

Each one of these Content Objects can be described with certain properties and methods. Let's examine the `News` Object.

Object Name:	News
Properties:	NewsCategories NumberofItems ShowExcepts
Methods:	showNews()

Using the above conceptual model, we can ascertain that the `showNews()` method causes the `News` object to return the news to be displayed to the user. The way in which the news is displayed is determined by how the properties are set.

- The `NewsCategories` property determines which categories will be displayed (i.e. World News, Sports, Local News, etc.).
- The `NumberOfItems` property determines how many headlines will be returned for each category.
- The `ShowExcerpts` property will tell the object whether to return a short exerpt of each headline.

Every content area on a web site can be described in this manner. Now that we know how to describe a content area, all we need to do is adjust the properties of the Content Objects for each user.

As discussed earlier, we are going to use cookies to store how a user wants to see their page. To maintain a simple approach to this, we are going to use only the method for displaying the news. Once you see how this works, it should be a short stretch to integrate display parameters for your Content Objects. To allow users to re-arrange the content we are going to create generic Content Zones for users to arrange their content into.

What are Content Zones?

Most Internet portal sites use a two-column layout for arranging their content. They put a column on the left side, usually the larger one, and a column on the right side for shorter content. For ease of use, and simplicity, we are going to define columns of equal width so that we can easily move content from one column to the other.

Each column is then broken down further into rows. Each row in a column is a content area. Below is a simple illustration of this:

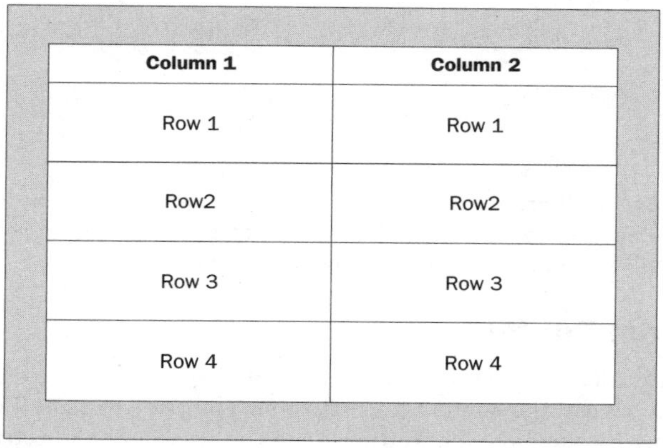

Column 1	**Column 2**
Row 1	Row 1
Row2	Row2
Row 3	Row 3
Row 4	Row 4

And here is the HTML:

```
<html>
<head>
<title>
  Two Column Layout Example
</title>
</head>
<body>

<table width="100%" height="100%" cellspacing=0 border=2>
<tr>
  <td width="50%" align=center valign=top>
    <b>Column 1</b>
    <table width="100%" height="100%" cellspacing=0 border=2>
    <tr>
      <td height="50%" align=center valign=center>
        Row 1 (c1r1)
```

```
        </td>
      </tr>
      <tr>
        <td height="50%" align=center valign=center>
          Row 2 (c1r2)
        </td>
      </tr>
      </table>
    </td>
    <td width="50%" align=center valign=top>
      <b>Column 2</b>
      <table width="100%" height="100%" cellspacing=0 border=2>
      <tr>
        <td height="50%" align=center valign=center>
          Row 1 (c2r1)
        </td>
      </tr>
      <tr>
        <td height="50%" align=center valign=center>
          Row 2 (c2r2)
        </td>
      </table>
    </td>
  </tr>
  </table>

  </body>
  </html>
```

As you can see, we have 4 different areas, or Content Zones to put content in this example. Our site visitors will customize each of the Content Zones. You can use forms that set cookies with the values we need to do this. We will talk about setting cookies this way later.

Building the Custom Content

Each content area will call a method from an include file (we will create this shortly) and pass to it the parameters needed to present the content for that zone. The page will get the cookie values from the visitor. Here is a listing for the page that retrieves the cookie values and retrieves the content for each zone:

```
<%@ include file="cookieMonster.jsp" %>
<%@ include file="myCafeContent.jsp" %>

<html>
<head>
<title>
  myCafe
</title>
</head>
<body>

<center>

<p>
  <a href=myCafeCustomizerForm.jsp>
    Click here to customize this page
  </a>
</p>
```

```
<table width="80%" height="80%" cellspacing=0 border=2>
<tr>

  <% for (int c = 1; c <= 2; c++) { %>

  <td width="50%" align=center valign=top>
    <table width="100%" height="100%" cellspacing=0 border=2>

    <% for (int r = 1; r <= 2; r++) { %>

    <tr>
      <td height="50%" align=center valign=center>

        <%

          out.println(
            myCafeContent(
              response,
              getMyCookie(
                request,
                "c" + c + "r" + r
              ), c, r
            )
          )

        %>

      </td>
    </tr>

    <% } %>

    </table>
  </td>

  <% } %>

</tr>
</table>

</center>

</body>
</html>
```

As you can see, since we are using a simple table layout to format the page, we have used a couple of `for` loops to construct the table, build the cookie name and call the method that produces content.

The loops in the code dynamically builds the table as well as the strings for requesting the cookie values. This is a great way to save typing! If you ever find yourself writing tables that have a similar number of cells and columns, this is a great way to maintain uniformity.

You may have noticed the two include files at the beginning of this listing. The first, `cookieMonster.jsp`, is outlined below. To explain this file, let me first say that I have been programming my web sites in ASP with JavaScript for 3 years, and I have gotten very comfortable with setting and reading cookies by name. When I decided to teach myself JSP, one of the first challenges I faced was the way cookies are read in Java. There is no direct way to call a cookie by name. So, to get around that issue, I came up with this simple include file that I use whenever I need to work with cookies.

```
<% /* cookieMonster.jsp */ %>
<%!
public void createMyCookie (
  HttpServletResponse response,
  String name,
  String value,
  int expires
  ) {

  // Create a new cookie object to make our cookie with
  Cookie c = new Cookie(name, value);

  // Set the expires property of the cookie
  // This is expressed in seconds
  // i.e. 24 hrs = 60*60*24
  c.setMaxAge(expires);

  // Send the cookie to the header stream
  response.addCookie(c);
}

public String getMyCookie (
  HttpServletRequest request,
  String cookieName
  ) {

  // Let's get the cookie array
  Cookie c[] = request.getCookies();

  // Check to make sure we have cookies to search through
  if (c != null) {
    for (int i = 0; i < c.length; i ++) { // (1)
      if (c[i].getName().equals(cookieName)) { // (2, 3)
        return c[i].getValue(); // (4)
      }
    }
  }

  // If nothing is found, return nothing
  return "";
}
%>
```

These method for retrieving a cookie works by:

- searching through the cookies array
- retrieving the name of each cookie
- comparing it to what we are looking for, and once found
- returning the value of that cookie

The next include file in the listing is the `myCafeContent.jsp` file. This file contains the functions we call that will produce the content for each Content Zone. Remember earlier when we discussed the Content Objects? This is where those objects are located. Of course, you could easily make these into JavaBeans that you instantiate from the JSP page.

```
<% /* myCafeContent.jsp */ %>
<%!
String CONTENT_CODE_NEWS = "NEWS";
String CONTENT_CODE_ARTICLES = "ARTICLES";
String CONTENT_CODE_LINKS = "LINKS";
String CONTENT_CODE_SAMPLES = "SAMPLES";

public void myCafeContent(HttpServletResponse res, String cCode, int c,
                          int r) {

  // Determine which content area the
  // user defined for this spot

  out = res.getWriter();

  if (cCode.equals(CONTENT_CODE_NEWS))
    myCafeContentNews(res);
  else if (cCode.equals(CONTENT_CODE_ARTICLES))
    myCafeContentArticles(res);
  else if (cCode.equals(CONTENT_CODE_LINKS))
    myCafeContentLinks(res);
  else if (cCode.equals(CONTENT_CODE_SAMPLES))
    myCafeContentSamples(res);
  else {

    // These are the defaults
    // if the user has not customized
    // the site yet

    if (c == 1 && r == 1)
      myCafeContentNews(res);
    else if (c == 1 && r == 2)
      myCafeContentArticles(res);
    else if (c == 2 && r == 1)
      myCafeContentLinks(res);
    else if (c == 2 && r == 2)
      myCafeContentSamples(res);

  }

  out.println("This Works!\n");
  out.println("<BR>" + cCode);

  return;
}
%>
```

The first thing you should notice in this listing is the use of global variables. This isn't really necessary, but can be very helpful if we are going to compare those strings many times in a page.

The `myCafeContent()` function is the `public` function we call from the `myCafe.jsp` page all others are `private` and can only be called from within the include file. We pass to it the Content Code for the content we want to display, it compares it to it's list, calls the appropriate Content Object, which writes the content, then returns control back to the `myCafe.jsp` page.

If there are no values from the cookies we are requesting, that probably means one of several things:

- The user hasn't done any customization on the site
- The user is visiting from a machine other than the one the created their customization from.
- The user does not accept cookies.
- Or, the user has removed their cookies inadvertently.

To handle this case we have set some default parameters to call default Content Objects for each zone.

```
    if (c == 1 && r == 1)
      myCafeContentNews(res);
    else if (c == 1 && r == 2)
      myCafeContentArticles(res);
    else if (c == 2 && r == 1)
      myCafeContentLinks(res);
    else if (c == 2 && r == 2)
      myCafeContentSamples(res);
```

Each Content Object should look something like the next listing. This is very generic, and only here for conceptual purposes.

```
<%!
public void myCafeContentNews(HttpServletResponse response) {
  out = res.getWriter();

  /*
      ....
      connect to database or grab database object that alread
      exists and get news records
      ....
  */

  // iterate through the recordset
  while (rs.moveNext) {
    // print the html and content for each item
    out.println("<b>" + new String(rs("NEWS_HEADLINE")) + "</b>\n");
    out.println("<p>" + new String(rs("NEWS_EXCERPT")) + "</p>\n");
    out.println("<i>" + new String(rs("NEWS_DATE")) + "</i>\n");
  }

  // clean up your recordset object
  rs.Close();
  rs = null;

  return;
}
%>
```

We cycle through each content zone, produce the content, and serve the page. As you can see, this can be a very powerful way to allow users to customize their home page. With the right customization forms and the integration of content parameters, a user could arrange the content in a nearly infinite number of ways.

User Customization Form

To show you how to accomplish the task of allowing the user to customize their page, I have provided some source code for the customization form below. This customization form does not require any type of login process. It doesn't even need to recognize the user at all. It simply loads all of the cookies the user already has and pre-sets the form to reflect those values. If the user hasn't done any customization yet, the form is set to its defaults.

```
<%@ include file="cookieMonster.jsp" %>

<%!
String selected = new String();
int selected_news = 0;
int selected_articles = 0;
int selected_links = 0;
int selected_samples = 0;
%>

<html>
<head>
<title>
  myCafe Customizer Form
</title>
</head>

<table width="100%" height="100%" border=0>
<tr>
<td align=center valign=center>

  <p><b>
  Select an item from each zone to display
  the selected content for that zone.
  </b></p>

  <form action=myCafeCustomizerSubmit.jsp method=post>

  <table cellspacing=0 border=2 width="60%" height="60%">
  <tr>

    <% for (int c = 1; c <= 2; c++) { %>

    <td align=center valign=center width="50%">
      <table cellspacing=0 border=2 height="100%" width="100%">

      <% for (int r = 1; r <= 2; r++) { %>

      <tr>
        <td align=center valign=center height="50%">

          <%

          // Get the cookie value from the client

          selected = getMyCookie(request, "c" + c + "r" + r);

          // This is here to make sure
          // these values are fresh for
          // each trip through this loop
```

```
selected_news = 0;
selected_articles = 0;
selected_links = 0;
selected_samples = 0;

// Determine which content area the
// user defined for this spot

if (selected.equals("NEWS"))
  selected_news = 1;
else if (selected.equals("ARTICLES"))
  selected_articles = 1;
else if (selected.equals("LINKS"))
  selected_links = 1;
else if (selected.equals("SAMPLES"))
  selected_samples = 1;
else {

  // These are the defaults
  // if the user has not customized
  // the site yet

  if (c == 1 && r == 1)
    selected_news = 1;
  else if (c == 1 && r == 2)
    selected_articles = 1;
  else if (c == 2 && r == 1)
    selected_links = 1;
  else if (c == 2 && r == 2)
    selected_samples = 1;
}

// Start building the drop down box

out.println(
  "<select name=c" + c + "r" + r + ">\n"
);

// If this item is selected, make it so...

if (selected_news == 1) {
  out.println(
  "<option value=NEWS selected>Java News\n"
  );
} else {
  out.println(
  "<option value=NEWS>Java News\n"
  );
}

if (selected_articles == 1) {
  out.println(
  "<option value=ARTICLES selected>Latest Articles\n"
  );
} else {
  out.println(
  "<option value=ARTICLES>Latest Articles\n"
  );
}
```

```
          if (selected_links == 1) {
            out.println(
            "<option value=LINKS selected>Web Links\n"
            );
          } else {
            out.println(
            "<option value=LINKS>Web Links\n"
            );
          }

          if (selected_samples == 1) {
            out.println(
            "<option value=SAMPLES selected>Code Samples\n"
            );
          } else {
            out.println(
            "<option value=SAMPLES>Code Samples\n"
            );
          }

          out.println("</select>\n");

          %>

        </td>
      </tr>

      <% } %>

      </table>
    </td>

    <% } %>

  </tr>
  </table>

  <input type=reset value=Reset>
  <input type=submit value=Submit>

  </form>

</td>
</tr>
</table>

</body>
</html>
```

When the user submits the form, all of the needed cookies are set on the users machine for 30 days, or any other length of time that you can determine for your site. Every time the user returns to the web site, you will be able to read these cookies and serve them their own customized home page.

```
<%@ include file="cookieMonster.jsp" %>

<%
// Get form values
String c1r1 = new String(request.getParameter("c1r1"));
String c1r2 = new String(request.getParameter("c1r2"));
String c2r1 = new String(request.getParameter("c2r1"));
String c2r2 = new String(request.getParameter("c2r2"));

// Create cookies
createMyCookie(response, "c1r1", c1r1, 30*24*60*60);
createMyCookie(response, "c1r2", c1r2, 30*24*60*60);
createMyCookie(response, "c2r1", c2r1, 30*24*60*60);
createMyCookie(response, "c2r2", c2r2, 30*24*60*60);
%>

<html>
<head>
<title>
  myCafe Customizer Form Submit
</title>
</head>

<table width="100%" height="100%" border=0>
<tr>
  <td align=center valign=center>
    <p><b>Your layout has been saved.</b></p>
    <p><a href=myCafe.jsp>Click here</a> to continue</p>

  </td>
</tr>
</table>

</body>
</html>
```

The only limitation associated with using cookies is: if they visit the site from a machine other than the one from which they did their customization, their special content arrangements will not be available. The user would need to re-customize the page for every machine they plan on visiting the site from.

Summary

As you can see, with some careful planning and efficient layout of the information on your pages, you can make your site available for Co-Branding. Also, by applying the same ingenuity to how you present content on your site, you can also make your site available as a Portal site. For simplicity, the examples shown here have been kept very basic. If you want to see more complex examples of this co-branding system, visit the web site this was modeled after: http://www.jspcafe.com.

In the next chapter we will look at techniques for debugging your JSP code.

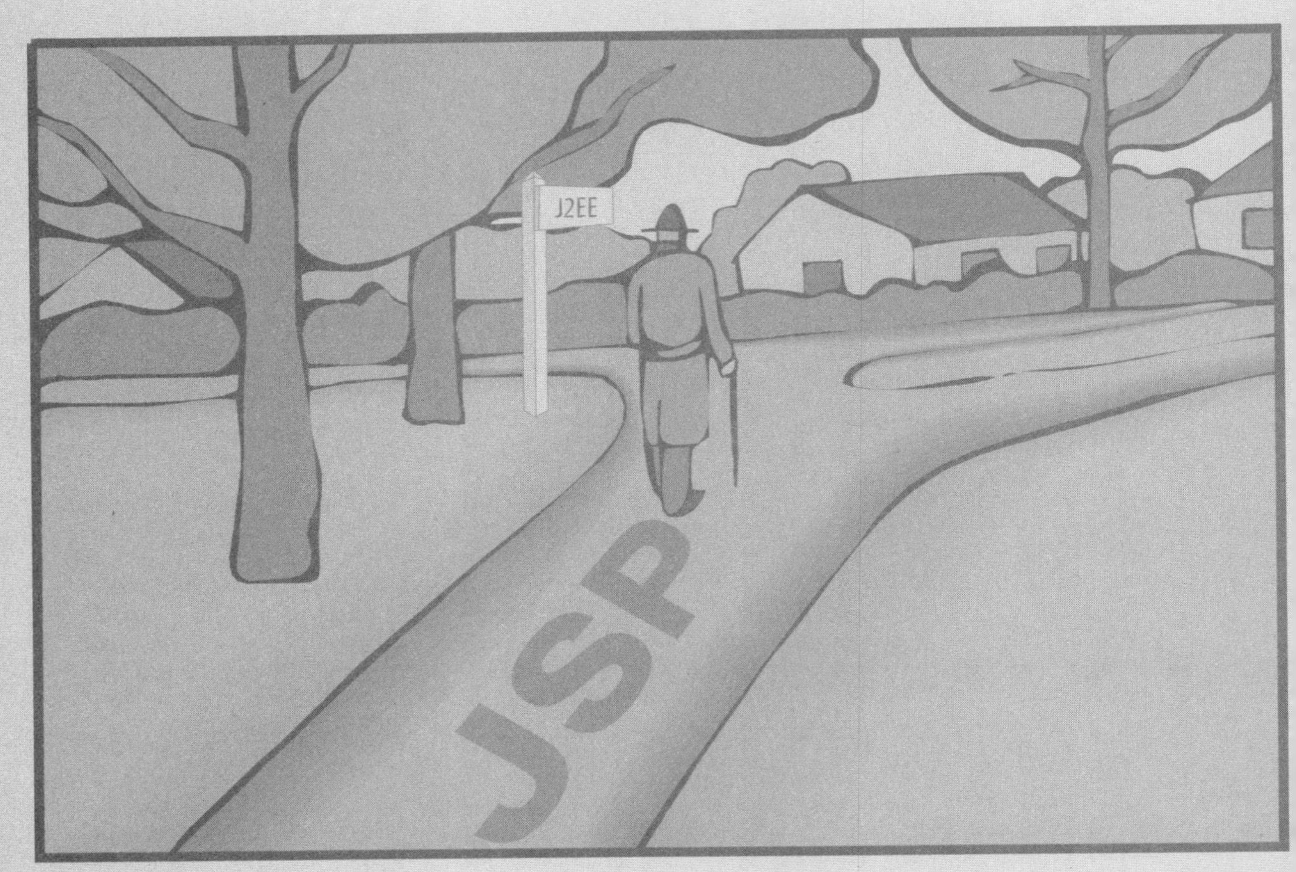
J2EE
JSP

10

Debugging JSP

Writing software in general isn't as linear and straightforward as we all would want it to be. When you finish a piece of code you have been working on for the last couple of hours, you know for sure that everything is correct and that it will do exactly what you planned. After trying to run it (or compile or whatever) you once again wake up from your dream, leave Utopia and come back to our real world where things do go wrong.

In the next phase you try to console yourself with the idea that these are just a few minor, trivial mistakes like missing closing brackets, missing semicolons or since we are using Java, using a lowercase character where it should be uppercase. With new courage you try again, just to find out that you're not quite finished yet. Most of the time you end up in a time consuming, frustrating spiral of testing, investigating, correcting, and testing again. And after a while you realize that they weren't all minor, trivial mistakes at all and that your initial wishes about 'having it right the first time' were more than naive.

It doesn't always have to go like that, but often the debugging and correcting takes far more time than the initial writing of a piece of code. It's a tedious job that most of us hate and in which you experience that, after all, computers are still very dumb machines.

There are lots of theories and methodologies about how we should do the initial writing, but for the debugging process it's really the experience and feeling of the developer that makes the difference. So let's look at it from the sunny side. It's because of the debugging phase that most programmers have total job security for the next couple of years and it's one of the main areas where you could really become a valuable expert.

In this chapter we use the term 'debugging' in its broadest sense. Debugging is more than just have some utility that allows you to step through your code while it executes. Printing out your code and just looking at it while sitting in the garden, can be also called 'debugging' in some cases. We will explore a few different techniques and tricks that can help you avoid, trace and correct errors in JSP.

Why Debugging JSP is so Hard

For a number of different reasons debugging JSP isn't easy. The most important issue is that you should understand what you're doing and get the feeling of what's happening underneath. JSP does a great job in hiding a lot of complexity when you write a page, but you still need a good insight in the layers below when it comes to debugging.

At least you should have some experience in writing Servlets. Without a good understanding of Servlets, what they are and how they work you won't be catching many JSP bugs. So if you haven't written a Servlet yourself, you should read a good book about it and try out a few examples. Of course, Servlet experience requires a good Java knowledge in the first place. The first seven chapters of *Professional Java Server Programming* from Wrox Press (ISBN1861002777) gives you excellent material on Servlets, also Jason Hunter's *Java Servlet Programming* from O'Reilly (ISBN 156592391X).

Maybe even more crucial is to know what HTML is. I assume most of you are familiar with this, but you should do the test and try to make a page in notepad without looking at a reference manual to find the correct usage of every tag. Unless you do this all day, it's amazing how many things you're still unsure about. (e.g. To select a radio button, should I use `<INPUT type="radio" CHECKED>` or `<INPUT type="radio" SELECTED>`?)

The mixing of all these different languages can make JSP code difficult to read. When you write Java code that dynamically generates a JavaScript function that writes HTML, you have some mental context switches that require a lot of concentration. And yes, you really find yourself doing these things in JSP. In fact it is what makes JSP so powerful. When you start debugging such code it becomes even more difficult, and you should understand all the possible things that can go wrong on all the different levels.

Even a relatively easy thing as putting quotes around a string can become code-from-hell if you have to consider more than three different languages in one line.

How about this example:

```
<INPUT="text" NAME="age" onBlur='javascript:checklevel( this.value,
<%=mybean.getValidation("age")%>,"he's too old")'>
```

Do I have to escape the single quote in "he's ..." and use "he\'s ..."?

If you try to avoid the problem by using double quotes for the whole `onBlur` value, then what about escaping the quotes around `"age"`? And this is still an easy one. Think about the problems if you don't use '`myBean`' and start coding `if` statements and other complex code between the `<%  %>` tags.

JSP saves you from typing all those `out.println()`'s in a servlet, but it also takes away the compilation phase, and the strong typing and syntax checking. Having the possibility to compile your class is an easy way of checking for errors. With JSP the compilation phase is just before runtime and that makes it more difficult to interpret errors, especially for programmers without good servlet experience.

IDE vs. Notepad/vi

The techniques you use to debug depends much on the way you develop. On one side of the spectrum we have fancy IDE's that allow you to create your code with drag and drop and by using wizards. The other extreme is the geek that despises you if you use anything other than notepad or vi (Of course, we all know that real geeks directly enter bytecode in HEX format).

The tools a programmer uses and his overall working habits and attitude can have a big impact on the debugging process. Both the type of errors that are encountered as the possibilities to locate and fix the bug are highly related to the tools used.

Both extremes have their own strengths and weaknesses As usual, most of us find themselves somewhere in the middle.

The IDE Approach

A good IDE can speed up the total development time drastically. You leave the boring repetitive stuff to the computer so you can take care of the real programming business. With features like drag and drop, templates, wizards, and so on amateurs can create some simple applications and after a while they learn to do the more complex things. An integrated debugger lets you step through the code and check or even change variables while the process is running.

The fact that JSP is still very new and rapidly evolving makes it hard for the IDE vendor to keep up with new specifications and implementations. The versions of JDK, JSDK, JSP, HTML you use, all have a big impact on your development possibilities. As a result most IDE's that support JSP don't always support the version you would like to use and are tightly bound to a specific implementation when it comes to debugging. When this IDE implementation differs from the deployment environment, you might get yourself in big trouble when you only find out at the end that some things don't work out as you planned.

An IDE can also hide too much, and make you end up with awkward or non-optimal code that may require specific workarounds. This is no problem at first, but it will be, when we come to the debugging phase. "The proof of the IDE is in the debugging."

I think that we're still a bit too early in the JSP evolution to have an environment that really hides the things you shouldn't care about and leave you with the essential part. We will see big evolutions here in the future, but in the meantime, I guess you do need to know the underlying basics.

Some IDE's that support JSP are VisualAge, Silverstream, DreamWeaver, Homesite and Forte for Java. BEA are also due to release WebGain very soon.

The Hardcore Camp

If you use a plain text editor like notepad and the command line, you really have full control over your programs and have the largest freedom. However, some tedious tasks, in which the computer is much better than us, are still to be done by hand. This certainly slows down the initial code-writing phase, but since the programmer is more tied to the code, he is likely to catch the bugs quicker afterwards. The main problem with this approach is that it is only for expert developers. But, being an expert developer, you will be able to find and correct bad code much easier anyway.

An important reason why some people refuse to use an IDE is that it creates a larger psychological distance between you and the application you're developing. It doesn't feel like you're in full control and it doesn't give you the aura of a 'real programmer'. Having said that, a JSP developer may not always be a Java developer and may have a web or graphic design background, so an IDE may sometimes provide a necessary distance between the user and code

The choice of development environment also depends on whether you are a programmer or a designer. A lot of effort is done to make JSP more suitable to be used by designers, while the programmers provide the necessary building blocks. Debugging JSP however, will remain the programmers' job for quite some time.

As we already pointed out, the best choice is somewhere in the middle. There are many editors available that still require typing the code, but offer some handy features notepad doesn't have. Compared to some of the full-fledged IDE's most of these tools cost almost nothing (Kawa, JpadPro, Visual SlickEdit, etc.).

If the HTML design is done by another person, using a heavy WYSIWYG editor could create HTML that's difficult to integrate with the JSP code. Again using an editor that doesn't hide the code and doesn't complain about the JSP tags is the best solution (Homesite, 1st Page).

Different Types of Errors

Since JSP is in fact a layer on top of Servlets and combines different languages, bugs can come from any one of these layers and in any language. The first step in debugging is to understand the error, get an idea where it comes from, and know where to look for it.

Compilation Errors

The first errors you typically encounter are compilation errors. When you request a page for the first time, the JSP is first transformed into a Servlet. That Servlet is compiled to a `.class` file and the Servlet engine uses that Servlet to create the page. In general, compiling the `.jsp` file into a Servlet doesn't often go wrong. When it does, the error message is quite easy to understand since it refers to the original `.jsp` file.

For example, if I type `<%@ page impot="java.sql.*" %>` instead of `import`, I get the error message:

```
Error compiling source file /test.jsp:
/test.jsp:1: Page directive: Invalid attribute, impot
```

The error reporting comes from the JSP engine and can be different for other implementations (in this example I used Apache/JServ with GNUJSP). As you can see, the compiler shows the file, line number, and some more info about the type of error.

Most compilation errors come from the second stage where the Java compiler transforms the `.java` file into a `.class` file. In this case the error report comes from the Java compiler. Since that compiler doesn't know anything about JSP, but is just using the automatically generated Servlet, interpreting this error report is much more difficult.

How do you know it's a compilation error?

- It doesn't work at all, you only get a bunch of errors in your browser.
- Probably there will be some information about what compile command was used by the JSP engine like:

```
Error compiling source file: file:f:/www/base/test2.jsp
```

  and probably some details about the internal compilation command.

- If you check the work directory the JSP engine uses to put its `.java` and `.class` files, you'll notice that it did generate a new `.java` file but no new `.class` file.
- Some servers allow you to compile the JSP off-line. This could also be used to trap compilation errors before putting the files on a server.

When a previous version of the JSP page was compiled successfully, but after some changes contains compile errors, some JSP engines only show this error the first time you request the page. With the second request the previous version is shown. I had this a few times with JServ/GNUJSP. This can really be surprising. Deleting the `.java` *and* `.class` *files in the work directory fixes this problem.*

The error reporting shows the type of error, line number, and a piece of code where the error is located; sometimes the line number refers to the line in the generated servlet so this isn't always very informative. More recent JSP engines do translate the javac error lines to the lines in your original JSP file, but this isn't always correct. The error type can help you a bit more but only if you know how to translate them. The best thing is to look at the bit of code the compiler complains about and see if you can locate this in your JSP code

The most common compilation errors are just small java syntax mistakes like missing '`;`', non-matching quotes, or typos in variable or class names, but sometimes it isn't easy to understand the messages. The following table gives you some examples of error messages I encountered with Apache/JServ and what they really mean. Again this isn't always the same for every setup and can vary depending on which JSP engine and java compiler you use. I found that the JServ error reporting is easier to read than Tomcat, for example:

Java Compile error	**Possible causes**
')' expected	when you put a '`;`' at the end of an expression like in `<%=getValue(i);%>` this is translated into `out.println(getvalue(i););` which is obviously an error

Table continued on following page

<table>
<tr><th>Java Compile error</th><th>Possible causes</th></tr>
<tr><td>try without catch, or catch without try with line numbers pointing to the end of the file</td><td>missing { or }.
The JSP engine puts all your code from the JSP page in one big<pre>try{
   ... your code ...
} catch(exception e){
   ...
}</pre>block. When the curly brackets in your code are not balanced this results in a 'catch without try' or a 'try without catch' error.</td></tr>
<tr><td>Funny error messages with HTML formatting like colors, hyperlinks, buttons, checkboxes, ...</td><td>If you forget the closing '%>' tag, the HTML code following is interpreted as Java code, is likely to give an error but and is shown in the error reporting. But, since that error report is shown in a browser these HTML tags are interpreted as HTML, which can give these funny results</td></tr>
</table>

If it really isn't clear what the error means, it can be good to look at the generated `.java` file. The directory where these files are stored depends on the JSP engine and is most likely specified as an init parameter for the JSP Servlet in the servlet configuration. Overall, system generated code is difficult to read, but most JSP engines produce code that's easy to understand. Normally you have a standard header that stays more or less the same for all generated servlets. In the middle you find your entire HTML code translated into strings that are printed to the `'out'` stream. Scriptlets are just copied. Some JSP engines (like the one from servletExec) don't copy the HTML code but use a function to extract the HTML portions from the original `.jsp` file. Luckily, they also add comments to specify the link between the generated servlet code and the position in the `.jsp` file like this:

```
// line:/test2.jsp:8
out.print ("test page\n\t\t");
```

This information is what an IDE debugger could use to let you step through the `.jsp` file itself, but since there's no standard way of providing these comments, IDE JSP debuggers often work with only a single JSP implementation. It is also these comment lines that are used to translate the javac error line numbers into JSP line numbers, when the engine shows you the compilation errors.

When you start using a newly installed JSP setup or when you use new packages, a 'class not found' compilation error is very likely a missing `import` statement or a `CLASSPATH` problem. These are easy to detect, but it's not always easy to solve them. The compilation command can help you find out what's missing. Every Servlet engine has it's own way you to have you specify the `CLASSPATH`. Again, a good understanding of how Servlets work can help you a lot.

Run Time Errors

When your code makes it through the compiler, the Servlet is run and, if you're unlucky, the run time errors start to appear. The first type of run time error is where an exception is thrown. Runtime errors aren't always 'all-or-nothing' like compilation errors. Whether there is an error might depend on the input parameters, the value of some variables, the user that's logged in ... If you specified an `errorpage`, the request is redirected to that page. Otherwise you get the JSP engine's default error. Normally this is a printout of the errortype (`NullPointerException` being one of my favorites), error message, and a stack trace.

> **If the stacktrace shows '(Compiled code)' instead of line numbers, you should try to start your servlet engine with JIT compilation disabled. You can do this by specifying `-Djava.compiler=NONE` as a start option for the engine.**

We said that for compilation errors the line number might not be that informative, but with run time errors it's about the only information shown. And in this case it almost always refers to the underlying servlet and not to the JSP source.

We already mentioned that your JSP code is put inside one big `try – catch` block in the Servlet. Since this block catches `Exception`, we never get the compilation error about not catching a particular type of exception. This `try – catch` block catches all the `RuntimeExceptions` and the `Exceptions` we should have caught in our code like `SQLException`. When an exception is thrown the output that was not yet flushed will be cleared; in most cases this means that we get an empty page with the error message but hardly any information about whether the first part of the code did work out fine:

- One way to achieve this is by inserting `out.flush();` after crucial places in your code: everything before the `flush()` is sent to the browser. This might very likely result in a bad HTML page, but it helps locating the error.
- Another possibility to achieve a similar result is by temporarily enclosing your entire `.jsp` file in a `try – catch` block yourself. Looking at the resulting HTML code gives you a very precise hint on where to look for the bug.

Another type of run time errors is where there are no exceptions thrown and, from a Java point of view, everything is working fine. But the resulting file is not what it should be. It can be wrong data that's being displayed or incorrect HTML formatting. It is particularly for these types of errors that the debugging techniques we'll explain later can be helpful.

HTML / JavaScript errors

When part of the HTML formatting or even JavaScript functions are dynamically generated, this can easily result in incorrect HTML pages. Some browsers are more susceptible than other for these errors, so that you might not immediately notice that there is a problem. In most cases the errors can be located by comparing the resulting output to a static HTML page that has correct formatting.

There are several utilities available that can check if your HTML syntax is correct. Some even allow you to have your page checked online like netmechanics (www.netmechanics.com). In general these problems are not really difficult but they might require some concentration for a more complex page. If you dynamically create JavaScript the complexity gets even bigger.

Other tools like SiteScope (www.freshwater.com) allow you to periodically request a specific URL and alert you if an error occurs or if something is missing on the page. Normally these tools are used to guarantee that a server is still running, but they could be just as well be used to find out if a certain JSP page is still displaying the correct content.

Debugging Techniques

In this section we will try to give an overview of the various techniques that might be used to catch the different types of errors we just discussed.

Eyeballing

It doesn't look very spectacular, but many bugs, especially the compilation errors, can still be found and fixed by simply looking at the code. This does require some concentration, but most code editors currently have several features that can help us.

Syntax coloring shows additional information about the code structure in a way that is easily perceived and interpreted. Unfortunately, most current syntax coloring cannot fully cope with the complexity of mixing 2 or 3 different languages or contexts. When we take the example about the string quotes again, we see that even Forte for Java doesn't color this consistently. Since it's just additional information, it doesn't always need to be 100% accurate as well. Even a very rough coloring scheme like highlighting some keywords, can help to keep an overview of the JSP page's structure.

Another useful feature is a 'find matching' utility. Finding the matching '{}' yourselves isn't easy in heavily nested structures, especially since it's not always clear how to maintain proper indentation in a JSP file.

Check out your editor's different features and learn how to use them. Not only with the mouse but also with the keyboard. Take your time to customize the settings, shortcut keys, coloring, and so on: it will save you a lot of time later on.

Comments

Comments in your code can help the debugging process in various ways. I'm not only talking about the obvious advantage of having your code well documented. Comments can be used in lots of other ways in the debugging process.

Since we're mixing different languages, we also have different types of comments.

Java Comments

The java single line (`//`) and multiple line (`/* */`) comments can be used to temporarily remove parts of the code. If the bug disappears, take a closer look at the code you just commented. The nice thing about the multi-line comment is that it can be used across HTML section in a JSP page so you can remove large parts very easily. The following code shows a part of a JSP file where we extract database data from a `ResultSet` object:

```
<TABLE>
<%while (rs.next()){%>
<TR><TD><%=rs.getString("first_name")%></TD>
<TD><%=rs.getString("last_name")%></TD>
<TD><%=rs.getString("order_date")%></TD></TR>
<%}%>
</TABLE>
```

To check whether the error occurs when filling the table you can remove the retrieval of the data from the `ResultSet` by using the multiline comments like this:

```
<TABLE>
<%/*while (rs.next()){%>
<TR><TD><%=rs.getString("first_name")%></TD>
<TD><%=rs.getString("last_name")%></TD>
<TD><%=rs.getString("order_date")%></TD></TR>
<%}*/%>
</TABLE>
```

The resulting HTML page will contain `<TABLE></TABLE>`, which will not ruin the normal HTML layout. Of course, you should pay attention as to where to put the comments, and to close the multi-line comment properly or you will get compilation errors again.

JSP Comments

JSP comments (<%-- --%>) can be used more or less like the Java multi-line comment but they should appear in the HTML portions of the JSP file. One important difference is that the code between the JSP comments isn't compiled into the servlet, so it can be used to remove code that would produce an error when the `.jsp` file is compiled into a `.java` file.

```
<TABLE>
<%-- <%while (rs.next()){%>
<TR><TD><%=rs.getString("first_name")%></TD>
<TD><%=rs.getString("last_name")%></TD>
<TD><%=rs.getString("order_date")%></TD></TR>
<%}%> --%>
</TABLE>
```

HTML Comments

HTML comments `<!--    -->` are fundamentally different from Java and JSP comments. HTML comments are processed like any other code in the JSP file and included in the output, and it's the user's browser that hides what's inside the comments. As a consequence, HTML comments cannot be used to temporarily remove incorrect code like the previous types.

These comments can be used to find out the value of a variable during processing without having this output interfere with the page layout. In our previous example, it might be good to know the internal ID number of the client:

```
<TABLE>
<%while (rs.next()){%>
<!--client ID: <%=rs.getString("client_id")%>-->
<TR><TD><%=rs.getString("first_name")%></TD>
<TD><%=rs.getString("last_name")%></TD>
<TD><%=rs.getString("order_date")%></TD></TR>
<%}%>
</TABLE>
```

The browser shows a page that's identical to the original one, but selecting View Source gives you the ID numbers right between the rest of the output. You should be careful about leaving too much debugging information like this in your final code. The HTML comment can be easily changed into JSP comment to hide the debugging information in a production environment.

Instead of just outputting values, HTML comments can be also used as process markers. In some cases it's more important to know whether a particular part of the code was executed, than to know the exact value of a variable. Small commented marks indicate whether a specific part of your code was processed (and how many times):

```
<TABLE>
<% int clientCounter = 0;
while (rs.next()){
clientcounter++;%>
<!--client row: <%=clientCounter%>-->
<TR><TD><%=rs.getString("first_name")%></TD>
<TD><%=rs.getString("last_name")%></TD>
<TD><%=rs.getString("order_date")%></TD></TR>
<%}%>
</TABLE>
```

This allows you to follow the code execution afterwards. Another use of these markers is to keep track of the HTML formatting. you should indent the Java code and the HTML code as best you can to make the code more readable. But a perfect solution isn't always possible. As a result, the produced HTML code will most likely not be properly indented and can be hard to read. Especially if you have nested tables, it can become very difficult to know to which `<TABLE>` a specific `<TD>` belongs to. Small HTML comments can help you with this. In this case you don't even have to use the comment tag but you could put your marker inside the `<TABLE>` and `<TD>` tag without having them displayed in the browser.

Consider the following basic example of a JSP page to create a nested table:

```
<HTML>
<HEAD></HEAD>
<BODY>
    <TABLE><TR>
        <% for (int i = 0;i<4;i++){ %>
            <TD>
            <TABLE>
            <% for (int j = 0;j<i+5;j++){ %>
                <TR><TD> line <%=j%> </TD></TR>
            <%}%>
            </TABLE></TD>
        <%}%>
    </TR></TABLE>
</body>
</HTML>
```

In this simple example the indentation can be done rather nicely and also the resulting HTML source is easy to follow:

```
<TABLE><TR>
    <TD>
    <TABLE>
        <TR><TD> line 0 </TD></TR>
        <TR><TD> line 1 </TD></TR>
        <TR><TD> line 2 </TD></TR>
        <TR><TD> line 3 </TD></TR>
        <TR><TD> line 4 </TD></TR>
</TABLE></TD>
```

```
    <TD>
    <TABLE>
       <TR><TD> line 0 </TD></TR>
```

However, when we add more code, the readability of the resulting HTML will suffer greatly. Line breaks are added everywhere and indentation is terrible.

Adding markers, like in the following example, can make it much easier to debug the HTML formatting if something goes wrong.

```
<HTML>
<HEAD></HEAD>
<BODY>
   <TABLE level="1"><TR>
      <% for (int i = 0;i<4;i++){ %>
         <TD level="1">
         <TABLE level="2">
         <% for (int j = 0;j<i+5;j++){ %>
            <TR level="2"><TD> line <%=j%> </TD></TR level="2">
         <%}%>
         </TABLE></TD level="1">
      <%}%>
   </TR></TABLE>
</body>
</HTML>
```

This page results in an HTML code like this:

```
<HTML>
<HEAD></HEAD>
<BODY>
   <TABLE level="1"><TR>
         <TD level="1">
         <TABLE level="2">
            <TR level="2"><TD> line 0 </TD></TR level="2">
            <TR level="2"><TD> line 1 </TD></TR level="2">
            <TR level="2"><TD> line 2 </TD></TR level="2">
            <TR level="2"><TD> line 3 </TD></TR level="2">
            <TR level="2"><TD> line 4 </TD></TR level="2">
         </TABLE> </TD level="1">
         <TD level="1">
         <TABLE level="2">
            <TR level="2"><TD> line 0 </TD></TR level="2">
```

Even when the page gets more complicated and more text and HTML formatting is added, it is still relatively easy to find out how the different tags relate to each other.

Some people might object that using these custom tag values is bad practice since it produces illegal HTML syntax, but the technique is so obvious that it will be used anyway. I didn't test this on all browsers but since some HTML editors use a similar technique to store additional information, I guess it will not give any problems

Another use of HTML comments is to insert timing information and profiling. This allows you to check how long it took to generate a specific part of your JSP file:

```
<%long startTime = System.currentTimeMillis();
ResultSet rs = pstmt.executeQuery()%>
<!--executeQuery: <%=(System.currentTimeMillis() - startTime)%>-->
<TABLE>
<%while (rs.next()){%>
<!—client ID: <%=rs.getString("client_id")%>-->
<TR><TD><%=rs.getString("first_name")%></TD>
<TD><%=rs.getString("last_name")%></TD>
<TD><%=rs.getString("order_date")%></TD></TR>
<%}%>
<!—get values: <%=(System.currentTimeMillis() - startTime)%>-->
</TABLE>
```

With this information it's possible to trace the execution time of the query and how much time was spend in getting the data and creating the table.

out.println(), log() and System.out.println()

The most obvious, and probably most used, debugging techniques are those where you insert small pieces of debugging code to output specific information like variable values.

As primitive as it might seem at first, a lot of bugs can be caught by these techniques. Let's briefly show the different possibilities.

log()

A simple way of outputting information is by using the `log()` function. `log()` is a function of `GenericServlet` so it can be used in JSP pages as well. The file to which the logging information is sent to depends on the Servlet engine you're using and on your Servlet configuration. While we can use this function to record debug information, strictly speaking the log isn't meant for this type of debugging purposes. Logging should really be used to keep an eye on what happens in a production environment. The log files do give an indication of new emerging bugs or the frequency of problems. For that reason it's good to use the `log()` function in the `catch` clause of exceptions which should normally not occur.

When you start debugging, making small changes and requesting the pages again and again, it's not very convenient to keep opening the log files and scrolling to the bottom every time to see what happened.

out.println()

Especially during the very early phase of testing and experimenting, writing debug information to the `out PrintWriter` is the easiest and most obvious choice.

Most of the possibilities of this technique are already covered when we talked about HTML comments. Remember to remove or comment the debug code from the final version of your code. It might be a good option to leave your debugging code in the JSP file but to let the output depend on the value of a request parameter. Requesting `yourfile.jsp?debug=true` switches the whole page in debug mode. Of course you should be careful because the debugging info is available for everybody, so you might think about some extra security when you use this.

```
<% boolean debug = false;
   if ("true".equals(request.getParameter("debug"))){
      debug = true;
   }%>
...
<%if (debug){out.println("your debugging info");}%>
```

A possible drawback of the previous two techniques is that they can only be used in a servlet or the JSP page itself. They cannot be used inside other classes, beans or EJB's like the following alternatives.

Singleton or static Debug object

To create your own `Debug` class like in Alan R. Williamson's *Java Servlets By Example* is probably the most flexible approach. A singleton class, or a class with only static functions, can be easily called from anywhere in your code. You can direct the output to whatever suits you best and there's the possibility to have a central switch to start and stop debugging mode.

The debug information can be rather easily directed to:

- A file
- A console-like window
- A network socket
- A buffer in memory
- The `out PrintWriter`

To do this you need to create your own `Debug` class that has the following outline:

```
public final class Debug{
   private Debug(){}
   public static void println(String logValue){
      // here you put the code to
      // output the logValue to whatever you like
      // (keep in mind that you can only use static class variables)
   }
```

The nice thing about the static `println()` method is that the effort to use this class is equal to using the `out PrintWriter`. Sending debug information is as easy as `Debug.println("my debug info");` and outputting information is not restricted to the servlet environment, but is also possible in other classes and JavaBeans you want to use in your JSP pages.

Since you create this class yourself, you can keep extending the possibilities as you need them, such as:

- Printing out the stack trace when needed
- Dump variables of a specific bean by using introspection
- Using a threshold level in order to use different debug levels
- Showing which class/method the debugging info came from...

A minor disadvantage of this technique is that it creates a tight coupling between all your code and the `Debug` class itself. This might limit the portability of your JavaBeans a bit.

System.out.println()

Printing to `System.out` is probably the oldest way to debug a program but it's still very useful. Although the possibilities are a bit more limited than using your own `Debug` class, the main advantage is that `System` is a core java object and is available everywhere. Just like we said about `log()`, you might object that `System.out` isn't meant for debugging info either and your debug output might interfere with the normal 'standard output'. However, in the context of Servlets/JSP it seems unlikely that `System.out` would be really used for something else.

It might be a problem that in most server setups you don't see the output at all. Most Servlet engines start a JVM without displaying a console window. In some cases it is possible to change the settings in order to display a console window anyway.

With Apache/JServ this can be achieved by using manual mode and starting the JServ JVM yourself. I created a list of batch files in order to stop and start the servlet engine in whatever mode I want. One file starts JServ in 'normal mode' by using `javaw.exe` like this:

```
SET CP="D:\java\jsdk2.0\lib\jsdk.jar";
SET CP=%CP%"F:\java\servlets\lib\servlet-2.0-plus.jar";
SET CP=%CP%"D:\Apache Group\Apache JServ\ApacheJserv.jar";
SET CP=%CP%"F:\java\classes";
SET CP=%CP%"D:\java\jdk1.2.2\lib\tools.jar";
SET CP=%CP%"F:\java\servlets\lib\jsp.jar";
SET CP=%CP%"F:\java\servlets\lib\gnujsp10.jar";
D:\java\jdk1.2.2\bin\javaw -classpath %CP% org.apache.jserv.JServ "D:\Apache
Group\Apache JServ\conf\jserv.properties"
```

When I want to see the `System.out`, I start JServ in visible mode. The only difference with the normal mode is that I use:

```
D:\java\jdk1.2.2\bin\java -Djava.compiler=NONE -classpath %CP%
org.apache.jserv.JServ "D:\Apache Group\Apache JServ\conf\jserv.properties"
```

in the last line. A similar solution is possible with Tomcat, for example. For other servers it might not be that easy to switch between these different modes.

By redirecting `System.out`, we can use this standard output technique, even if we cannot use a console window. In our example we use a custom-made `OutputStream` that keeps the information in an overflowing buffer in memory. By 'overflowing buffer' I mean that when the total size of the buffer becomes larger than a specified amount of bytes, the oldest information is deleted and we can have this mechanism running continuously without having the risk of using up all the available memory.

First, let's take a look at the `OverFlowBuffer`:

```
import java.io.*;
import java.util.*;
public class OverflowOutputStream extends OutputStream {
  StringBuffer buff;
  int size;

  public OverflowOutputStream(int size) {
    this.size = size;
    buff = new StringBuffer(size);
    buff.append(new Date().toString());
    buff.append("| ");
  }
```

```
  public OverflowOutputStream() {
    this(32 * 1024);
  }

  public String toString() {
    return buff.toString();
  }

  public void write(byte[] b) {
    if (buff.length() + b.length > size) {
      trunc();
    }
    if ((buff.length() > 1)
            && (buff.charAt(buff.length() - 1)) == '\n') {
      buff.append(new Date().toString());
      buff.append("| ");
    }
    buff.append(b);
  }

  public void write(byte[] b, int off, int len) {
    if (buff.length() + b.length > size) {
      trunc();
    }
    if ((buff.length() > 1)
            && (buff.charAt(buff.length() - 1)) == '\n') {
      buff.append(new Date().toString());
      buff.append("| ");
    }
    buff.append(new String(b, off, len));
  }

  public void write(int b) {
    if (buff.length() + 4 > size) {
      trunc();
    }
    if ((buff.length() > 1)
            && (buff.charAt(buff.length() - 1)) == '\n') {
      buff.append(new Date().toString());
      buff.append("| ");
    }
    buff.append(b);
  }

  public void reset() {
    buff = new StringBuffer(size);
    buff.append(new Date().toString());
    buff.append("| ");
  }

  void trunc() {
    buff.delete(0, buff.length() / 2);
  }
}
```

This class extends OutputStream in a very simple way and stores all the information in a StringBuffer. When the StringBuffer becomes too big, it is truncated. This is done very roughly, by just deleting the first half of the StringBuffer. The default buffer size is 32K so we will always keep at least the last 16K of information.

Now we can use this OverflowBuffer in a servlet that does the actual redirection and shows the contents of the buffer:

```
import java.io.*;
import javax.servlet.*;
import javax.servlet.http.*;
public class DebugServlet extends HttpServlet {
  OutputStream buff;
  public void doGet(HttpServletRequest req, HttpServletResponse res)
          throws ServletException, IOException {
    String option = req.getParameter("option");
    PrintWriter out = res.getWriter();
    if (buff == null) {

      // init. redirect System.out
      buff = new OverflowOutputStream();
      System.setOut(new PrintStream(buff));
    }
    out.println(buff.toString());
  }
}
```

The first time this Servlet is called, it redirects System.out to a new OverflowBuffer of 32K. On subsequent calls the contents of this buffer is shown. We could easily extend the servlet to allow commands for starting and stopping debug mode, clearing the buffer, or adjusting it's size, but even it its current form this Servlet can be quite useful

Debugging Concurrency

Server-side, non-visual components like Servlets and JSP are already difficult to debug, but the fact that the code might be run by (many) concurrent users on the same server makes things even worse. As you probably know a Servlet is instantiated once, and for each request a new thread is started that runs concurrently in this single instance. While this design results in very good performance, it also implies that your code must be thread-safe.

Concurrency bugs are difficult for a number of reasons:

- Unless you specifically tested your code for concurrency issues, the bugs will probably not be discovered early in the development phase, but maybe only when the final code is already deployed on a production server and the number of requests increases.
- The problems cannot be easily replicated, because millisecond-level timing of the concurrent requests is crucial. This is a typical example of a 'heisenbug' (named from Heisenberg's Uncertainty Principle), a bug that disappears when you try to isolate and find it.
- There are no easy tools to debug concurrency problems.

Java allows you to control concurrency by using the synchronized keyword. The drawback of using synchronized code is that performance can suffer greatly. Instead of synchronizing a large part of your JSP code, you could also use the SingleThreadModel by specifying <%@page isThreadSafe="false"%>.

The ability to write thread-safe code, and especially the ability to recognize and find potential concurrency problems, is more a matter of feeling and experience of the programmer than of following specific rules and procedures. Strict procedures would result in synchronizing too much code and slowing down the application. An experienced programmer will be able to make good decisions on where NOT to synchronize.

Where can we Expect Concurrency Problems in JSP

Although concurrency is a fairly complex issue, the possible sources of concurrency problems in JSP are quite limited.

Member Variables.

Avoid <%! %> variables as much as possible!

JSP differs from Servlets in this respect, since you are less inclined to use <%! %> tags in JSP. Most the code is put between <% %> and <%= %>, whereas in Servlets, creating member variables is much more obvious. In general, if you only use local variables you should not synchronize or set isThreadSafe to false in your JSP.

Static Methods and Singleton Classes

These types of classes are very vulnerable to concurrency. Since these are often used to provide general utilities like caching, connection pooling, system settings, and so on these components are probably used in many different contexts, not only in Servlets and JSP. Since you don't know in advance how these classes will be used, you should always use synchronized methods and blocks where needed.

ServletContext and Session

Objects that are put in the ServletContext or in the Session, like beans with 'application' or 'session' scope, can be accessed concurrently. The problem with objects in the ServletContext is similar to singleton classes.

Object instances stored in a session might seem less prone to concurrency errors at first, as these instances can only be used by a single person. In a normal situation it seems very unlikely that a person can make two concurrent requests, even when several browser windows are opened simultaneously. However, when you use frames in your HTML pages, it's not uncommon to receive two different requests from the same browser working on the same instance, so we should be careful here as well.

> **Using isThreadSafe="false" will only eliminate the first type of problems. By implementing the SingleThreadmodel, a Servlet can only be used for one request at a time, so this avoids concurrency within this Servlet. Since most Servlet engines create a pool of servlet instances it is still possible to have two different instances working on the same session or application object.**

How to Debug Concurrency Problems

The first thing we need is something to create several concurrent requests. You won't easily find the problem if you cannot replicate it. And even if you do think you found it, there's no way to check whether the code is really fixed. Utilities to stress-test your Servlets or web server like Apache's JMeter or Allaire's ServletKiller might help with this.

Use a lot of `System.out.println()` or `Debug.println()` calls to track the overlapping flow of the different concurrent requests.. Of course, since timing is so crucial, there's always the risk that logging this debugging information takes a little bit too much time and that the debugging process itself starts to interfere with the problem we try to investigate, so you should try to keep the debugging overhead as small as possible. Integrated debuggers that allow you to place breakpoints and step through the code won't really help you that much with concurrency problems. If you only step through one request, that thread is slowed down so much compared to the others that there would be hardly any concurrency left. On the other hand, if you use the breakpoints in all your threads, it will be very hard to mentally keep an overview of the complete situation. Often, single threaded step debugging already requires a lot of concentration. Following the flow of multiple threads becomes a nightmare. Even if you manage to follow the execution of multiple threads, you'll still need to make crucial but difficult decisions on which thread needs to do the next step, and which lines of code need to be processed consecutively.

> *According to the Weblogic technical support pages (http://www.weblogic.com/docs/techsupport/ejb.html),* `System.out.println()` *is also the best and least intrusive form of debugging EJB's when it comes to concurrency problems.*

Of course you should provide a way to distinguish the information coming from different threads in your debug output. This can be done by:

- Including the session ID:

```
System.out.println("info : "+session.getId());
```

- Including the thread name:

```
System.out.println("info : "+ Thread.currentThread().getName());
```

- Generating a local random number at the start of the page and including this with every debug call:

```
long debugRnd=Math.round( Math.random()* Integer.MAX_VALUE);
...
System.out.println("info : "+debugRnd);
```

- Including a counter to show how many concurrent requests you have at a specific moment:

```
<%! int threadCount = 0%>
<% threadCount ++ ;%>
...
System.out.println("threads : "+threadCount);
...
<% threadCount -- ;%>
```

Another approach is to synchronize as much as possible and use the `SingleThreadModel` until the error disappears. Then remove the synchronization gradually where it's not needed.

The best way to successfully debug concurrency problems is still to have enough experience and try to acquire a special feeling for it.

Separating your Code

In order to write quality software, you should never put real business logic in the GUI code. According to the discussions about the Model-View-Controller paradigm (MVC), JSP is not meant to contain lots of code. In JSP 1.1, custom actions will allow you to keep the Java code out of the JSP as much as possible. From the perspective of separating the work for the programmer and the web designer, this sounds great; it might also make the code more portable across several applications.

Separating your code into different classes, beans, EJB's, custom tags, etc. has a big impact on the debugging possibilities, because it allows you to run the same code in a different environment, for example as an application. In order to maintain this reusability and portability it's important not to link your beans to the Servlet context (I don't mean `ServletContext` here, but the servlet/JSP environment).

> **This means you shouldn't use code that relies on `ServletRequest`, `ServletResponse`, `HttpSession` and `ServletContext` in your beans because this would make it very difficult to use the beans in an application or another context.**

Passing the `out PrintWriter` to a bean is less a problem, but you should still try to avoid it.

When you create your own beans, you should always consider adding a `public static void main(String[] args)` method to them. This allows easy testing of each component separately and it's a useful way to store test cases and examples on how to use the component. For example, in my bean to send an email, I have the following `main()` method:

```
public static void main(String[] args){
  sendEmail instance = new sendEmail("mail.myserver.com");
  System.out.println(instance.send ("geert.vandamme@darling.be",
                     "geert.vandamme@darling.be", "testmail",
                     "hi, this is a mail to test the sendmail bean"));
}
```

The biggest advantage of using beans is that we can use introspection to check the bean's status and even manipulate it. The following code shows a simple example of a `BeanSnoop` Servlet that can be used to investigate objects that are stored in the session:

```
import java.io.*;
import java.util.*;
import java.lang.reflect.*;
import javax.servlet.*;
import javax.servlet.http.*;
```

```
public class BeanSnoop extends HttpServlet {

  public void doGet(HttpServletRequest req, HttpServletResponse res)
        throws ServletException, IOException {
    res.setContentType("text/html");
    PrintWriter out = res.getWriter();
    HttpSession session = req.getSession(true);
    out.println("<HTML><HEAD><TITLE>Bean Snoop</TITLE></HEAD>");
    out.println("<BODY><H1>Bean Snoop</H1>");

    /* the next section is only to let you add an object to the session so
       you can test this servlet. */
    out.println("This forms allows you to add new string values to the current
                 session to check out this servlet<BR>");
    out.println("<FORM>add string key <INPUT type=\"text\" name=\"key\"><BR>");
    out.println("add string value<INPUT type=\"text\" name=\"value\"><BR>");
    out.println("<INPUT type=\"submit\"></FORM><P>");

    String newKey = req.getParameter("key");
    String newValue = req.getParameter("value");
    if ((newKey != null) && (newValue != null)) {
      TestClass test = new TestClass();
      test.value1 = newValue;
      test.value2 = "fixed text";
      test.value3 = newKey + "-->" + newValue;
      session.putValue(newKey, test);
    }

    String URI = req.getRequestURI();
    String beanName = req.getParameter("name");
    if (beanName == null) {

      // show list of beans
      String[] names = session.getValueNames();
      for (int i = 0; i < names.length; i++) {
        out.print("<A HREF=");
        out.print(URI);
        out.print("?name=");
        out.print(names[i]);
        out.print(">");
        out.println(names[i]);
        out.print("</A><BR>");
      }
    } else {
      Object check = session.getValue(beanName);
      out.println("<H2> Checking object ");
      out.println(beanName);
      out.println("</H2><UL>");
      try {
        Class checkClass = check.getClass();
        Field[] fields = checkClass.getFields();
        for (int i = 0; i < fields.length; i++) {
          out.println("<LI>");
          out.println(fields[i].getName());
          out.println(" (");
          out.println(fields[i].getType().toString());
          out.println("): ");
          try {
            out.println(fields[i].get(check).toString());
          } catch (Exception e) {
            out.println(" ! Cannot be displayed !");
          }
```

```
}
        } catch (NullPointerException e) {
          out.println("null pointer Exception");
        }
      }
      out.println("</BODY></HTML>");
    }

    private class TestClass {
      public String value1;
      public String value2;
      public String value3;
    }

}
```

This Servlet shows you a list of all the objects stored in the session. If you click on any of the objects, you get a detailed view of all the fields in the object. To make things clear it also displays a form that lets you add a testobject to the session. This Servlet could be easily extended to allow:

- Checking objects that are inside another object. This example code can only show details for the objects directly stored in the session.
- Changing the values of the simple numeric and string fields.
- Calling functions.
- Using the Bean classes like `Introspector`, `PropertyDescriptor`, etc. would be more correct, but our example will work with any class, not just beans.
- Exploring objects stored in the `ServletContext` instead of the session.

Many web applications use the session object to store user information or e.g. the contents of a shopping basket. This Servlet gives you an easy way to check what's happening inside the session. Especially when using the "Model 2" approach, this Servlet can be very helpful. In this approach, a controller Servlet instantiates the specific beans and puts these in the session, and the request is forwarded to a JSP page that creates the layout. In this design it's possible to have the Servlet decide whether to add debug information by forwarding first to a Servlet like the `BeanSnoop` and only after that to the real output JSP page.

For checking the status and properties of beans with 'request scope', the possibilities are more limited. But you could use a similar approach to dump the detailed description at the bottom of your request within HTML comments.

Be careful if you install this kind of Servlet on a real server without using authorization, since it's a big security hole if someone finds the Servlet.

JDB Type Debugging

For some people, 'real' debugging is where you can set breakpoints, step through the code, dump variables and so on, like you use `jdb` with applets and applications. I discuss this technique at the end of the chapter because I only use this when everything else has failed. It is possible to do this type of detailed debugging with JSP, but it is not obvious. Again, using this technique requires a good understanding of the complete JSP process, because we're not actually debugging the JSP page itself, but the system-generated servlet underneath.

We already talked about the fact that every JSP engine has it's own way to create these Servlets. You'll have to get used to how your JSP engine works.

To set breakpoints and step through a JSP application, you need to start the layer around JSP in debug mode. Some Servlet engines (sometimes even the complete web server) are written in Java, such as JServ, JWS/Tomcat, Orion, and ServletRunner. In this case you could start this Java application by using `jdb.exe` instead of `java.exe`. If you start these applications through a script or batch file, you can easily create a copy of this script to start the server in debug mode.

Other, non-Java engines, probably have some Java utility that emulates the Servlet engine (and mostly also a web server) that allows starting in debug mode (for example, JRun and ServletExec both have a 'servletdebugger'). This way these engines can be used in the same way as a pure Java solution. The options you have for using this debugging technique are highly dependent on the Servlet engine you're using, and so I wouldn't recommend using a different engine for developing and debugging than the one you'll be using for deployment. You run the risk of spending hours looking for a bug really that comes from your development server. On the other hand, there is also the danger of not discovering a problem before the final code is deployed on the real server, which is even worse.

Starting the Debugger

If you use an IDE or an editor that has build-in debugging possibilities, you can have the editor itself start the web server or Servlet engine in debug mode. Since every Servlet engine and every editor has its own way to specify the specific settings, it's very difficult to give a detailed overview on how to start this type of debugging mode.

> *For example, if you use Kawa as an editor there's a tutorial about this type of debugging together with the JSDK webserver 2.1 on* http://penguin.tek-tools.com/kawa/docs/tutorial7.htm

This way you have the server started embedded in the editor itself.

Another, more flexible solution is to start the server manually and have the editor's debugger attached to that JVM.

Sounds difficult? Let's show you how I do this.

First of all I start the Servlet engine in debug mode. When we talked about printing to `System.out`, I showed the two different batch files I use to start JServ. In fact I also have a third file to start the debug mode. The last line of the file is now changed into:

```
D:\java\jdk1.2.2\bin\java -Xdebug -Djava.compiler=NONE -
Xbootclasspath:D:\java\jdk1.2.2\jre\lib\rt.jar;D:\java\jdk1.2.2\lib\tools.jar   -
classpath %CP% org.apache.jserv.JServ "D:\Apache Group\Apache
JServ\conf\jserv.properties"
```

This starts a console window and shows a password, for example:

```
Agent password=545xad
ApacheJServ/1.1b3
```

Using this password you can connect to this already running JVM. My current editor is JPadPro. When I select JDK/Debug Class a dialog window asks me to enter the class to debug. Instead of the class name however, I type in the password I got from the running JVM. In this case I enter:

```
password 545xad
```

There are two main reasons for using this second approach.

- You don't have to stop and start the Servlet engine with every new debug session.
- Remote debugging is possible by attaching to a JVM running on a different computer.

The hardcore freaks that are using Notepad or VI, can use this technique by typing `jdb.exe -password 545xad` on the command prompt and type `help` to get a full list of the commands they can use.

Setting Breakpoints

Since we're actually debugging the Servlet underneath the JSP, we should put a breakpoint there. This isn't always easy because you have to find this Servlet, and make a decision on where to put the breakpoint. Since, again, this is in the system-generated code, this might not be very obvious. The comment lines can help finding the corresponding lines in the original JSP file. Setting a breakpoint in the code that was put in a separate class is much easier. If you do need to put a breakpoint in the JSP code itself, a simple workaround is to create a special class for it:

```
public class DebugHelper {
  public static void breakpoint() {
    int dummy = 0;
  }
}
```

In this class we set a breakpoint on the third line. Adding a breakpoint to the JSP code can be done by including:

```
<%DebugHelper.breakpoint();%>
```

Stepping Through the Code

Your editor probably has menu items and buttons for stepping through the code, setting additional breakpoints, dump variables and so on. Make sure that your editor knows where to find the source files of the generated servlets and that you compiled your classes with the debug switch on (`-g`).

Future Directions

This is an area which is constantly changing and moving forward. We will see big improvements in this area soon. JSP IDE's will allow you to do what we described here in a point and click way, even in the original JSP file. Until then, I expect that this step debugging will remain a last option to find the most difficult bugs. The other techniques and tips we discussed will still remain important.

The Java Debug Interface (JDI) in Java 1.3 (see http://web2.java.sun.com/products/jpda/doc/index.html) is another important evolution, because it will allow us to create Servlets or other components that help us in debugging JSP files.

Summary

In this chapter we have looked at some of the techniques that we can use to make our code run as it should, whether it be spotting compilation errors or solving problems when the running code misbehaves.

We have looked at:

- Choice of tools both for code authoring but also for debugging.
- The different types of errors that you will encounter.
- Methods for working out what is going on.
- Debugging code running concurrently.

Although we may not be able to create perfect code every time, we can at least take steps to reduce the errors.

The next chapter describes an approach to providing global settings accessible from within your JSPs.

J2EE
JSP

11

Global Settings

This chapter shows a component that allows you to use settings on an application-wide scope. It allows you to set up a central repository for your web application where you can store information that's specific for your configuration or data.

This global settings component can be useful when:

- You want a connection to a database, without having the connection parameters (URL, userID, password) hard coded in a servlet or JSP.
- You have a bean to send emails, and you want to store the SMTP host and port in a central place.
- Creating your own user authentication system. The user information itself is in a database, but you want an easy way of getting and setting these parameters.
- You want to run multiple virtual servers on the same machine. In that case you want to be able to deploy your beans, servlets, and JSP pages on each of them and want them to work with the settings of that particular server.

Some servlet engines use a special file for this type of information (like JRun's `global.jsa`), but this is not (yet?) standard JSP. The solution we present here doesn't depend on such proprietary extensions so it can be used on different engines.

Design Decisions

So, what do we want from our global settings component?

Information from Different Sources

The architecture we use shouldn't make any restrictions on where the data comes from. Data can come from a number of various sources, from a file, a database, a directory server, a network socket, a servlet, RMI, etc. We also want to be able to mix several different sources in a single setup. For example, I want to store filenames and server parameters in a simple configuration file, but user settings come from the database. For each of these different sources we create a `SettingsSource` object.

String Values

For the moment we only need string values; numbers, dates, and text can all be represented by a string. The main disadvantage is of course performance. Converting an `int` to a `String` and back seems a waste of processing power. On the other hand, we typically don't use loads of setting values, only a few. By using the HTTP protocol, almost all our input and output are already strings. The main reason to use exclusively strings is that we want to make it as simple as possible.

Availability

We need a settings component that's available everywhere in our application. If possible, we want to create different applications, which have their own settings, on a single server. The opposite, a single application that spans several servers, would be nice as well. There are two main possibilities to achieve this.

ServletContext

The first solution is to store the settings in the `ServletContext`. This seems the most appropriate way. It allows us to set up multiple applications on a single server, in a single JVM that all use their own application settings. However there are some problems:

- The `ServletContext` can only be used to store objects if you're using JSDK 2.1.

- The code we need to get the settings out of the object that's stored in the `ServletContext` isn't just a simple line. We would have to use something like:

```
getServletContext().getAttribute("settings").getSetting("mail.server")
```

  It would be nice to have something shorter and easier to use. Every extra character is a reason for the developer to use a shortcut and hard code the values. But we all know that this type of temporary code often doesn't get cleaned up and leads to several problems. We don't want to give the JSP designer an excuse for not using this component.

The main problem, however, is that we can only access the `ServletContext` from within servlets or JSP. We cannot easily use it in a separate class.

Singleton Class / Static Methods

A singleton is a class that's created in such a way that there can never be more than one instantiation of that class. By using this singleton pattern, or a class with static methods in which even an instantiation of the class isn't necessary, we could use this settings object from any class by using only one line of code:

```
Settings.getInstance().getSetting("mail.server")
```

for a singleton, or

```
Settings.getSetting("mail.server")
```

for a class with static methods. If we use the singleton pattern, we could additionally provide some static methods for convenience.

We cannot define the scope of the settings component freely; it is defined by the JVM. Every object that is loaded by the same classloader shares the same settings.

So, each of the two approaches has its own advantages and problems.

> **We'll try to make a class so that both approaches still remain possible, but we will use it as a singleton throughout the rest of the chapter.**

Implementing the Settings Object

Now that we talked a bit about what we need and discussed some of the different design options, we will explain how we created the settings object used in our projects.

Architecture

The `Settings` class is the central object that handles all communication to the outside world. It doesn't do any real processing itself. It only routes each request to another object that knows where and how to get the required information. These objects that all implement the `SettingsSource` interface are dynamically created and kept in a list by the central `Settings` object.

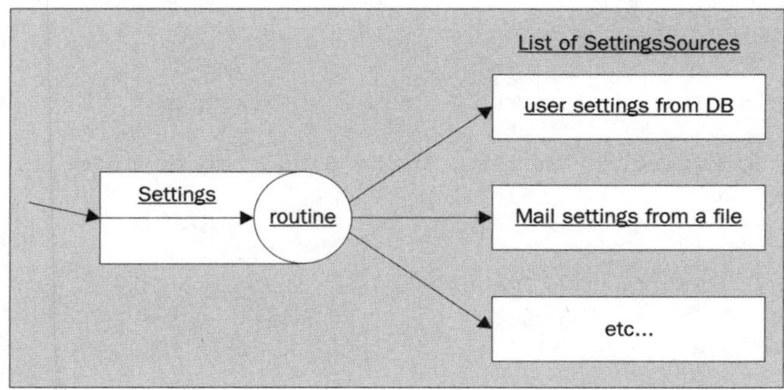

SettingsSource Interface

We create the basic interface of a `SettingsSource` as follows:

```
import java.io.*;
import java.util.*;
public interface SettingsSource{
   public void load(String param) throws IOException ;
   public void save() throws IOException;
   public String getSetting(String key);
   public void setSetting(String key,String value);
   public Enumeration getPropertyNames();
}
```

The main methods to be implemented are `getSetting()` and `setSetting()`. When created, a `SettingsSource` is initialized by using the `load()` method. This uses a `String` parameter that tells the specific object where or how to get its data. The parameter could be a URL, a file, and so on, depending on the specific implementation of the interface.

The `getPropertyNames()` method is less important. As we will see later, it allows us to loop through all the settings, which can be used to create servlets to administer the `Settings` object.

Settings

The `Settings` object itself is a bit more complicated. The basic skeleton of this singleton class is:

```
import java.io.*;
import java.util.*;

public class Settings {
  private static Settings instance;
  private Properties base = new Properties();
  private Hashtable settings = new Hashtable();
  private String baseFile;

  private Settings() {

    // private constructor
  }

  public Settings(String baseFile) throws IOException {

    // public constructor when not using Singleton approach
    load(baseFile);
  }

  public static Settings getInstance() {
    if (instance == null) {
      instance = new Settings();
    }
    return instance;
  }
```

The single instance is created the first time the getInstance() function is called. The second constructor allows us to use Settings as a normal class as well. The Properties object base keeps some general base settings, so that the Settings object knows when and how to create the specific SettingsSources as needed. These properties are stored in a configuration file that can be read (and saved) by the Properties object itself like this:

```
public synchronized void load (String file) throws IOException {
  // load or refresh base properties
  baseFile = file;
  File propFile=new File(file);
  base.load(new FileInputStream(propFile));
}

public synchronized void save () throws IOException {
  File propFile=new File(baseFile);
  base.store(new FileOutputStream(propFile),"");
}
```

This base configuration file has a simple 'key=value' structure with each setting on a new line. The Hashtable object settings contains a list of all the SettingsSource objects used together with the routing information. To fetch a value for a setting we use the name of the SettingsSource it comes from as a prefix (followed by a dot). Let's say we create a SettingsSource named db to store database connection parameters. If this SettingsSource contains testdatabase.password to store the password to a test database, we can use 'db.testdatabase.password' as the key to get this information from the general Settings object. The getSetting() method splits the prefix (db) from the real key, looks up the SettingsSource with this prefix, and delegates the remaining request (testdatabase.password) to that object.

```
public String getSetting(String key) {
  String index= "";
  int pos;
  String value = null;

  pos = key.indexOf(".");
  if (pos > -1){
    index = key.substring(0,pos);
  }
  if (index.equals("") || index.equals("include") ||
      index.equals("directory")) {
    //include and directory are reserved for basic functionality
    value = base.getProperty(key);
    return value;
  } else {
    key = key.substring(pos + 1);
  }
  SettingsSource temp = getSource(index);
  if (temp != null) {
    value = temp.getSetting(key);
  }
  return value;
}

public static String get(String key) {
  // convenience method as shortcut for:
  return getInstance().getSetting(key);
}
```

The crucial part here is where we look up the `SettingsSource` by its name (the prefix) and route the request to that object. The `getSource()` method uses a 'lazy instantiation' model. This means that a particular `SettingsSource` will only be created if and when it's needed and is stored in the hashtable for later use. The information that's needed to instantiate a specific `SettingsSource` uses the settings mechanism itself. All settings requests that use `include` as a prefix are handled by the base settings object itself.

```
private SettingsSource getSource(String index) {
  SettingsSource temp = (SettingsSource)settings.get(index);
  if (temp == null){
    String param = base.getProperty("include."+index+".param");
    String sourceType = base.getProperty("include."+index+".sourceType");
    if (sourceType == null){
      // use this as the default SettingsSource type
      sourceType = "FileSettings";
    }
    try{
      temp = (SettingsSource)Class.forName(sourceType).newInstance();
      temp.load(param);
      settings.put(index,temp);
    }
    catch (IOException e){
      System.out.println(e.getMessage());
    }
    catch (IllegalAccessException e){
      System.out.println(e.getMessage());
    }
    catch (InstantiationException e){
      System.out.println(e.getMessage());
    }
    catch (ClassNotFoundException e){
      System.out.println(e.getMessage());
    }
  }
  return temp;
}
```

`Class.forName().newInstance()` works as a factory that dynamically creates any implementation of a `SettingsSource`. The class names of the different sources are stored in the base properties of the `settings` object (the `Properties` file loaded in the `load()` function). The 2 parameters needed to instantiate a `SettingsSource` are the classname and optionally a parameter string. `include.sourcename.sourceType` defines the class name, and `include.sourcename.param` is used to initialize this specific `SettingsSource`.

For example, a `SettingsSource` implementation that uses a configuration file (we'll see the details for such a class later) to store some server specific information can be set up by specifying the following lines in the base configuration file.

```
# information from conf file D:/java/settings/server.conf
# using the prefix 'server'
include.server.sourceType=FileSettings
include.server.param=D:/java/settings/server.conf
```

Suppose that in this `server.conf` file there is a setting '`hostName`', we can retrieve this value by using:

```
Settings.get("server.hostName");
```

A First SettingsSource Implementation

Before we can show you how this works we need at least one type of SettingsSource. We will use the same principle we used in the Settings object itself to read a properties file. This means that this object will get its settings from a configuration file that has 'key=value' pairs stored in it. The code is similar to the load and save methods of the Settings object itself. The initialization parameter tells us the file to be read.

```
// default settings source, uses a properties file
import java.io.*;
import java.util.*;

public class FileSettings implements SettingsSource{
  private Properties prop = new Properties();
  private String fileName;



  public synchronized void load (String param) throws IOException {
  fileName = param;
  File propFile=new File(fileName);
  prop.load(new FileInputStream(propFile));
  }

  public synchronized void save () throws IOException {
      if (fileName != null){
         File propFile=new File(fileName);
        prop.store(new FileOutputStream(propFile),"");
      }
  }

  public String getSetting(String key) {
     return prop.getProperty(key);
  }

  public void setSetting(String key,String value) {
     prop.setProperty(key,value);
  }

  public Enumeration getPropertyNames(){
    return prop.propertyNames();
  }

}
```

The First Tests

In the first test we will only use the base Settings object and see if that works. The base settings are those that don't have a prefix or use 'include' or 'directory'. These are not routed to a SettingsSource but are handled by the main Settings object.

Let's first create a simple configuration file called init.conf file with this single line in it:

```
testvalue=yep, it's working
```

In the Settings object, we can add a main() method to easily test our setup:

```
public static void main(String[] args){
  // testing main
  try{
  getInstance().load(args[0]);
  }catch (IOException e){
    System.out.println(e.getMessage());
  }
  System.out.println("test value: " + getInstance().getSetting("testvalue"));
  // or with the shorter get() method:
  System.out.println("test 2: " +Settings.get("testvalue"));
}
```

If everything goes well, and you run the Settings class with the full path to init.conf as a first command line parameter you should get an output like this:

```
C:\>java Settings C:\java\settings\init.conf
test value: yep, it's working
test 2: yep, it's working
```

In the second test we will use the simple 'file' SettingsSource to store all mail-related settings. The configuration file we use for this settings is called mail.conf:

```
# mail server settings
SMTPHost=smtp.myserver.com
SMTPPort=25
# email adresses
webmaster=webmaster@darling.be
author=geert.vandamme@darling.be
```

To install this source in the Settings object, we need to specify the classname (FileSettings) and the path to mail.conf in the base configuration file init.conf by adding the following lines:

```
# information from conf file D:/java/settings/mail.conf
# using the prefix 'mail'
include.mail.sourceType=FileSettings
include.mail.param=D:/java/settings/mail.conf
```

Now, let's change the Settings' main method to test these new 'mail' parameters:

```
public static void main(String[] args) {
  // testing main
  try {
  getInstance().load(args[0]);
  } catch (IOException e) {
    System.out.println(e.getMessage());
  }
  System.out.print("We can use server ");
  System.out.print(Settings.get("mail.SMTPHost"));
  System.out.print(" on port ");
  System.out.println(Settings.get("mail.SMTPPort"));
  System.out.print("to send an email to ");
  System.out.println(Settings.get("mail.webmaster"));
}
```

Compile and run the Settings class again with init.conf as parameter and you will see how these values are filled in with the settings from the configuration file.

Another typical use of this `FileSettings` is to store database parameters. We're not really using a database here, but this gives us a central place to store the connection parameters. Since these parameters can easily change (new password, other location, etc.) keeping them in a central place can make your application much easier to maintain.

Another important issue here is that it doesn't always look safe to store things like database passwords in your JSP page. After all, these pages are located on a directory that's accessible from everywhere. In normal circumstances users don't have access to the JSP source, but a small bug or a simple mistake in your server configuration can make your source available for everyone. For example, many JSP engines that are developed on Unix platforms assume case-sensitive file names even when they are used on NT. In that case the JSP engine only compiles files with `.jsp` extension. If one requests `index.JSP` (uppercase) the web server shows the original JSP source file! (Hacker's tip;-)

A possible `db.conf` file that defines only one database might look something like this:

```
Mysqltest.driver=twz1.jdbc.mysql.jdbcMysqlDriver
Mysqltest.user=geert
Mysqltest.password=myverysecretpassword
Mysqltest.URL=jdbc:z1MySQL://localhost/test
```

As you can see, inside this file we use the name of the database as a prefix. We can retrieve the URL to the `Mysqltest` database by using `Settings.get("db.Mysqltest.URL");`

After installing this `db.conf` file in the base settings by adding:

```
include.db.sourceType=FileSettings
include.db.param=D:\\project\\settings\\data\\db.conf
```

to the `init.conf` file, we can use the `Settings` to get the different database connection parameters from anywhere in our application. Later on these parameters will be used by another type of `SettingsSource` that gets its information from a database.

The next figure describes our current setup:

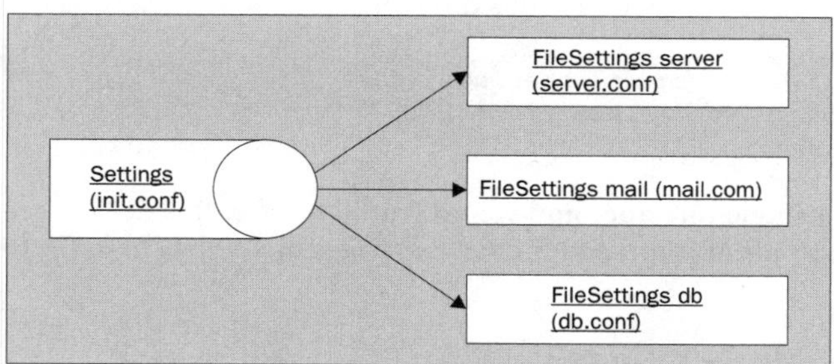

Virtual Directories

A first extension to this basic model is to use logical or virtual directories. Instead of using `D:\\project\\settings\\data\\init.conf`, it would be good if we could use something like `%conf%\\init.conf`. It might be possible to define this on an Operating System level as well, but I would like to use several different setups on a single server. When you create two versions of the same project (e.g. one for testing) it would be very handy if there is only one place to change the pathnames. Remember we reserved the `'directories'` prefix for the base settings? That's exactly what we'll use to store these virtual directories.

Add this method to the `Settings` object:

```
public String translateDirectory(String path) {
  int pos, oldpos;
  StringBuffer out = new StringBuffer();
  oldpos = 0;

  if (path != null) {
    pos = path.indexOf("%");
    while (pos > -1) {
      out.append(path.substring(oldpos,pos));
      oldpos = pos;
      pos = path.indexOf("%",pos + 1);
      if (pos == -1) {
        pos = path.length();
      }
      String dir = path.substring(oldpos + 1, pos);
      out.append(getSetting("directory."+dir));
      oldpos = pos+1;
      pos = path.indexOf("%",pos + 1);
    }
    out.append(path.substring(oldpos,path.length()));
  }
  return out.toString();
}
```

The translation from the virtual directory to a physical one is done by the `Settings` object itself. Change the `load()` method of the `FileSettings` (not the main `Settings` class!) object to:

```
public synchronized void load (String param) throws IOException {
  fileName = Settings.getInstance().translateDirectory(param);
  File propFile=new File(fileName);
  prop.load(new FileInputStream(propFile));
}
```

Now we can modify `init.conf` to use this directory:

```
directory.conf=D:\\project\\settings\\data
include.db.sourceType=FileSettings
include.db.param=%conf%\\db.conf
```

Since we have just a single directory and we only used it once, this doesn't seem to help us much yet. However, we can also use this function in our JSP pages or servlets to make them more portable, for example:

```
<% fileName = Settings.getInstance().translateDirectory
                 ("%data%\listing1.txt")%>
```

SettingsServlet

We've seen how to create the `Settings` object, and define a simple setup with one type of `SettingsSource`, but so far we only used it in the `Settings.main()` method.
To have the `Settings` object ready in our servlets or JSP, all we have to do is load the initial settings with a servlet that we 'load on startup'.

```
import java.io.*;
import javax.servlet.*;
import javax.servlet.http.*;
import java.util.*;

public class SettingsServlet extends HttpServlet {
  String rootFile;

  public void init(ServletConfig conf) throws ServletException {
    super.init(conf);
    rootFile= getInitParameter ("rootFile");
    try {
      Settings.load(rootFile);
    } catch (IOException e) {
      System.out.println(e.getMessage());
    }
  }
}
```

In JServ you can do this by adding the next few lines to your zones file:

```
servlet.settings.code=SettingsServlet
servlet.settings.initArgs=rootFile=D:\project\settings\data\init.conf
servlets.startup=settings
```

With Tomcat or Resin the setup looks like:

```
<servlet>
<servlet-name>Settings</servlet-name>
<servlet-class>SettingsServlet</servlet-class>
<init-param configFile='D:\java\settings\init.conf'/>
<load-on-startup>-2147483646</load-on-startup>
</servlet>
<servlet-mapping>
<servlet-name>Settings</servlet-name>
<url-pattern>/servlet/Settings</url-pattern>
</servlet-mapping>
```

Since this servlet's `init()` method is called when the servlet engine is started, the `Settings` object is initialized and available to every object that runs in the servlet engine.
At last we can start using the sessions in our JSP pages.
Try adding code like:

```
<A HREF=mailto:<%=Settings.get("mail.webmaster")%>>webmaster</A>
```

to one of your JSP pages.

In the `SettingsServlet` we only used the `init()` method, but we could use `doGet()` as well to check and manage our settings:

```
  public void doGet(HttpServletRequest req, HttpServletResponse res)
          throws ServletException, IOException {
    res.setContentType("text/html");
    PrintWriter out = res.getWriter();
    out
      .println("<HTML><HEAD><TITLE> SettingsTest </TITLE> </HEAD><BODY> ");
    if ("on".equals(req.getParameter("refresh"))) {
      try {
```

```
        Settings.load(configDir);
      } catch (IOException e) {
        out.println(e.getMessage());
      }
    }

    out.println("<A HREF=" + req.getRequestURI()
                + "?refresh=on>REFRESH</A><P>");
    out.println("<TABLE>");
    String sub = req.getParameter("sub");
    Enumeration temp;
    if ((sub == null) || ("".equals(sub))) {
      temp = Settings.getPropertyNames();
      sub = "";
    } else {
      temp = Settings.getPropertyNames(sub);
      sub = sub + ".";
    }
    while (temp.hasMoreElements()) {
      String name = (String) temp.nextElement();
      String value = Settings.getProperty(sub + name);
      out.println("<TR><TD>" + name + "</TD><TD>" + value
                  + "</TD></TR>");
    }
    out.println("</TABLE></BODY></HTML>");
  }
```

This servlet shows you a list of all the base properties in the `Settings` object. http://localhost/servlet/Settings?sub=mail shows you the settings specified in the 'mail' `SettingsSource`. Specifying ?refresh=on after the URL causes the servlet to reload all the settings (e.g. if you manually changed the configuration files).

> **Disable this function or use password protection if you use this servlet on a real internet server. If somebody knows the correct URL, they might find all your secret information like database passwords. You can disable this functionality for a specific `SettingsSource` by changing the `getPropertyNames()` function to return an empty `Enumeration`.**

The servlet could be easily expanded to:

- Enter, edit and save new settings.
- Add and configure `SettingsSource` objects.
- Track usage, performance, etc.

Settings from the Database

As a second example we'll show a `SettingsSource` implementation that gets its data from a database. To keep it simple we will only read the data, so it's a read-only `SettingsSource`.

The parameter used in the `load()` function consists of two parts, separated by a colon. The first parameter defines the database. This uses the `Settings` itself to get more detailed connection information like URL, driver, user ID and password from the `'db'` `SettingsSource` (as in the example we used previously).

The second part of the parameter is the `select` statement to get the `Settings`. It's a prepared statement that needs a single '?' as a placeholder for the key.

```
// DBSettings read settings from database
import java.io.*;
import java.util.*;
import java.sql.*;

public class DBSettings implements SettingsSource{
  private Connection conn;
  private PreparedStatement pstmt;
  private String query;

  public DBSettings() {
    // default constructor
  }

  public synchronized void load (String param) throws IOException {
    // parameter =  dbName:select statement
    int pos = param.indexOf(":");
    if (pos < 1){
      throw new IOException("no valid parameter");
    }
    String dbName = param.substring(0,pos).trim();
    String select = param.substring(pos+1).trim();
    try{
      String driver = Settings.get("db."+dbName+".driver");
      String URL = Settings.get("db."+dbName+".URL");
      String userId = Settings.get("db."+dbName+".user");
      String password = Settings.get("db."+dbName+".password");
      // maybe some other properties...
      Class.forName(driver);
      conn = DriverManager.getConnection(URL,userId,password);
      pstmt=conn.prepareStatement(select);
    }
    catch (SQLException e){
      System.out.println(e.getMessage());
      throw new IOException("no valid parameter");
    }
    catch (ClassNotFoundException e){
      System.out.println(e.getMessage());
      throw new IOException("no valid parameter");
    }
  }
public synchronized void save () throws IOException {
  // nothing, it's read only for the moment ;-)
  return;
}

  public String getSetting(String key) {
    String value = null;
    try{
      pstmt.clearParameters();
      pstmt.setString(1,key);
      ResultSet rs = pstmt.executeQuery();
      if (rs.next()){ // only first row
        value = rs.getString(1);
      }
      rs.close();
    }
      catch (SQLException e){
    System.out.println(e.getMessage());
```

```
      }
      return value;
    }

    public void setSetting(String key,String value) {
      return;
    }

    public Enumeration getPropertyNames(){
      Enumeration dummy = null;
      return dummy;
    }

    public void finalize(){
      try{
        pstmt.close();
        conn.close();
      }
      catch (SQLException e){}
      catch (NullPointerException e){}
    }
  }
```

Suppose we have the following table containing user information, in our `Mysqltest` database:

```
CREATE TABLE users (
  user_id int AUTO_INCREMENT PRIMARY KEY,
  user_name VARCHAR(100),
  userid VARCHAR(100),
  password VARCHAR(100) );
```

Setting up a `DBSettings` source like this:

```
include.userpasswords.sourceType = DBSettings
include.userpasswords.param = Mysqltest:select password from users where userid=?
```

allows us to create an authentication module that checks password information from the database with:

```
Settings.get("userpasswords."+userName);
```

How and Where to use These Settings

Now, all the components are created and configured so that we can start using the `Settings` object in our code. To get here we took the following steps:

- Created the main `Settings` object
- Created `init.conf` to install the different sources in our setup
- Created a 'file' implementation of `SettingsSource`
- Installed this `FileSettings` to read mail-related settings from `mail.conf`
- Installed this `FileSettings` a second time to read database parameters from `db.conf`
- Used the `SettingsServlet` to initialize the `Settings` object
- Optionally we also installed a component that retrieves its settings from a database. This component uses the already installed components to find out the parameters to connect to the database.

Using the settings in our JSP files is easy now, like in this `settingstest.jsp` example:

```
<HTML><HEAD><TITLE>Settings test</TITLE></HEAD>
<BODY>
If  everything is set up correctly, <BR>
let <A HREF="mailto:<%=Settings.get("mail.author")%>">me</A> know
</BODY></HTML>
```

Remember that the `Settings` object isn't just available in JSP code but can also be used in other classes. Some specific places I found this `Setting` object very useful are:

- **Connection pooling**. I have an object that manages the different database connection pools. The parameters to initialize these pools come from the `Settings`.
- **Global settings**. Parameters you often need but which depend on the specific server installation, such as where can I put temporary files, who to alert (for example by email) if something goes wrong, etc.
- **User preferences**. If I make a class that performs the user login and authentication, I can easily have this object look into the `Settings` to get and store user preferences:

```
    Settings.get("user."+userid+".profile")
```

Other Possible Implementations

We'll briefly mention some ideas for other possible implementations of the `SettingsSource` interface. Most of them are relatively easy to create but might provide some powerful possibilities. The first two and the last one don't really store settings on their own, but provide mechanisms to manage information from other sources.

Synonym/Proxy

A `SettingsSource` that does nothing more than delegate the `getSettings()` request to another `SettingsSource` so that we can use different prefixes to get the same data.

Cascading Proxy

This allows us to set up a single entry point to several `SettingsSources` that are checked one by one. As soon as a matching value is found, this setting value is returned.

XML

It would be nice to have an implementation that reads XML files instead of properties files.

RMI

Using RMI makes it possible to create a `Settings` setup that spans several physical machines (for load balancing or fail-over capabilities, for example).

Network Socket

Getting values from a network socket has about the same distributed possibilities as the RMI approach. The settings server could use its own `Settings` object itself.

Settings Object Itself

Another nice thing about this design is that the `Settings` object itself could implement `SettingsSource`! Using this option, we could easily set up some very complicated nested settings structures.

In the next chapter we will examine some of the possible approaches to designing JSP application architecture, and consider their advantages and disadvantages.

J2EE
JSP

12
JSP Architecture

This chapter will examine a variety of ways to architect a system with JavaServer Pages, Servlets, and JavaBeans. We will see a series of different architectures, each a development of the one before. The diagram below shows this process in outline; the individual parts of the diagram will be explained in turn later in the chapter.

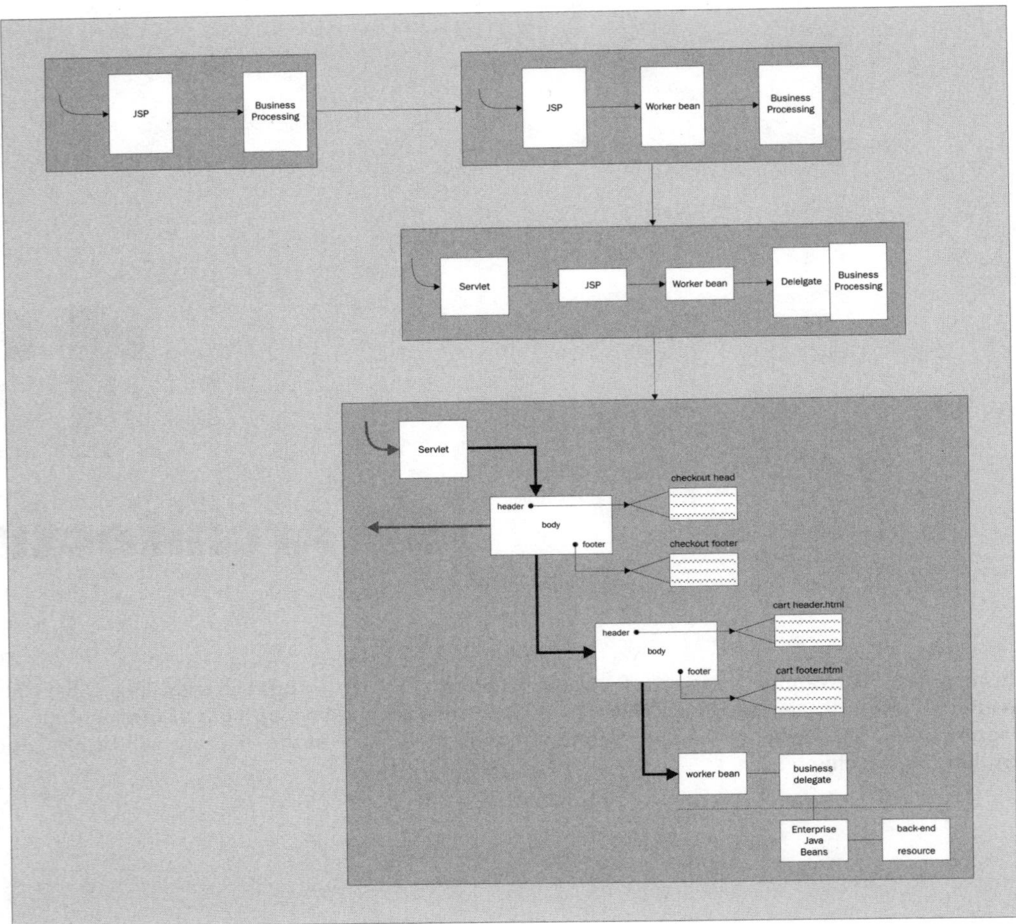

When Sun introduced Java ServerPages, some were quick to claim that Servlets had been replaced as the preferred request handling mechanism in web-enabled enterprise architectures. Although JSP is a key component of the Java 2 Platform Enterprise Edition (J2EE) specification, serving as the preferred request handler and response mechanism, we must investigate further to understand its relationship with Servlets. For all the latest information on J2EE, including documentation relating to some of the issues discussed in this chapter, please refer to http://java.sun.com/j2ee.

Other sections of this book explain the implementation details of JSP source translation and compilation into a Servlet. Understanding that JSP is built on top of the Servlet API, and utilizes Servlet semantics, raises some interesting questions. Should we no longer develop standalone Servlets in our web-enabled systems? Is there some way to combine Servlets and JSPs? If so, where do we place our Java code? Are there any other components involved in the request processing, such as JavaBeans? If so, where do they fit into the architecture and what type of role do they fulfill?

It is important to understand that, although JSP technology will be a powerful successor to basic Servlets, they have an evolutionary relationship and can be used in a cooperative and complementary manner.

Given this premise, we will investigate how these two technologies, each a Java Standard Extension, can be used co-operatively along with other components, such as JavaBeans, to create Java-based web-enabled systems. We will examine architectural issues as they relate to JSP and Servlets and discuss some effective designs while looking at the tradeoffs of each. Before jumping directly into a discussion of specific architectures, though, we will briefly examine the need to develop a variety of architectures.

Code Factoring and Role Separation

One of the main reasons why the Java Server Pages technology has evolved into what it is today (and it's still evolving) is the overwhelming technical need to simplify application design by separating dynamic content from static template display data. The foundation for JSP was laid down with the initial development of the Java Web Server from Sun, which utilized page compilation and focused on embedding HTML inside Java code. As applications came to be based more on business objects and n-tier architectures, the focus changed to separating HTML from Java code, while still maintaining the integrity and flexibility the technology provided.

In Chapter 5 we saw how beans and objects can be bound to different contexts just by defining a certain scope. Good application design builds on this idea and tries to separate the objects, the presentation and the manipulation of the objects into distinct, distinguishable layers.

Another benefit of utilizing JSP is that it allows us to more cleanly separate the roles of a web production/HTML designer individual from a software developer. Remember that a common development scenario with Servlets was to embed the HTML presentation markup within the Java code of the Servlet itself, which can be troublesome. In our discussion, we will consider the Servlet solely as a container for Java code, while our entire HTML presentation template is encapsulated within a JSP source page. The question then arises as to how much Java code should remain embedded within our JSP source pages, and if it is taken out of the JSP source page, where should it reside?

Let's investigate this further. On any web-based project, multiple roles and responsibilities will exist. For example, an individual who designs HTML pages fulfills a web production role while someone who writes software in the Java programming language fulfills a software development role.

On small-scale projects these roles might be filled by the same individual, or two individuals working closely together. On a larger project, they will likely be filled by multiple individuals, who might not have overlapping skill sets, and are less productive if made too dependent on the workflow of the other.

If code that could be factored out to a mediating Servlet is included instead within HTML markup, then the potential exists for individuals in the software development role and those in the web production role to become more dependent than necessary on the progress and workflow of the other. Such dependencies may create a more error-prone environment, where inadvertent changes to code by other team members become more common.

This gives us some insight into one reason why we continue to develop basic Servlets: they are an appropriate container for our common Java code that has been factored out of our JSP pages, giving our software development team an area of focus that is as loosely coupled to our JSP pages as possible. Certainly, there will be a need for these same individuals to work with the JSP source pages, but the dependency is reduced, and these pages become the focus of the web-production team instead. Of course, if the same individual fulfills both roles, as is typical on a smaller project, such dependencies are not a major concern.

So, we should try to minimize the Java code that we include within our JSP page, in order to uphold this cleaner separation of developer roles. As we have discussed, some of this Java code is appropriately factored to a mediating Servlet. Code that is common to multiple requests, such as authentication, is a good candidate for a mediating Servlet. Such code is included in one place, the Servlet, instead of potentially being cut and pasted into multiple JSPs.

We will also want to remove much of our business logic and data access code from our JSP page and encapsulate it within JavaBeans, called worker or helper beans. We start to see a pattern of code movement from our JSP into two areas: a Servlet (or JSP) that sits in front of the main JSP, and JavaBeans that sit in back. We refer to this common pattern as 'Factor Forward-Factor Back', as shown in the figure below:

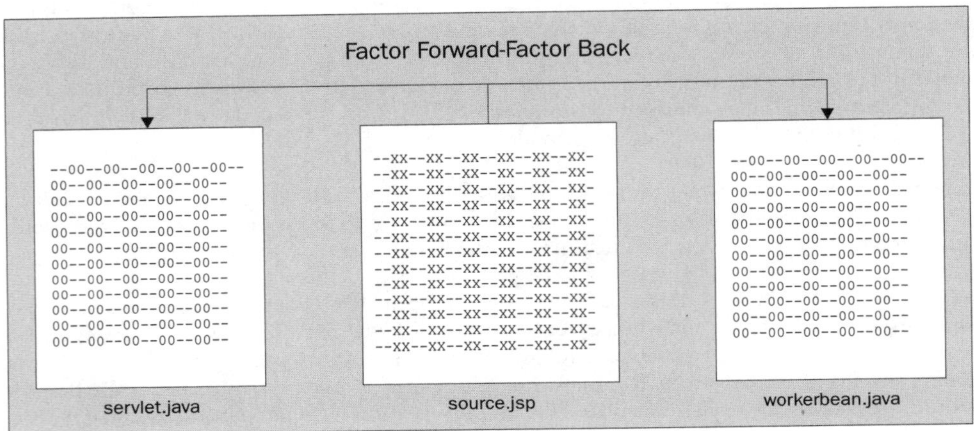

Another way to think about where code should be localized and encapsulated is that our JSP page should reveal as little as possible of our Java code implementation details.

Rather, the page should communicate our intent by revealing the delegating messages we send to worker beans, instructing them to get state from a model, or to complete some business processing.

Redirecting and Forwarding

Redirecting and forwarding requests in JSPs and Servlets takes place often, and it is important to understand the subtle difference between these two mechanisms even though they achieve the same goal (that is, a client asks for a resource on the server and a different resource is served to it):

- When a Servlet or JSP resource chooses to redirect the client (using a `response.sendRedirect(url)`) the request object does not reach the second resource directly since the underlying implementation is an HTTP redirect. The server sends an HTTP 302 message back to the client telling it that the resource has moved to another URL, and that the client should access it there.

  The bottom line is that the lifecycle of the initial request object that was accessed in the first JSP terminates with the end of the `service` method in the first JSP, or with the reply from the server.

- In a forward mechanism the request object is forwarded to the second resource, thus maintaining any object bindings to the request and its state, without a round trip to the client on the network.

  This allows the first JSP to do some work internally and then send information to the second JSP asking it to do its bit. (Servlets used a chaining mechanism to do this). See Chapter 5 to get a clearer picture of scope.

JSPs and Servlets can utilize the forwarding mechanism to delegate tasks amongst themselves, in the process of separating dynamic and static content.

Now, let's investigate how we build these systems.

Architectures

Before discussing specific architectures that we can use to build systems with Servlets and JSP, it is worth mentioning two basic ways of using the JSP technology. Each of the architectures discussed in this chapter will be based on one of these approaches:

- The first method is referred to here as the **page-centric** (or **Client-Server**) approach. This approach involves request invocations being made directly to JSP page.
- In the second method, the **dispatcher** (or **N-tier**) approach, a basic Servlet or JSP acts as a mediator or controller, delegating requests to JSP pages and JavaBeans.

We will examine these approaches in light of a simple example, which will evolve to satisfy the requirements of various scenarios. The initial scenario involves providing a web interface for guessing statistics about a soon-to-be-born baby. The guesses are stored, and can be reviewed later by the parents, to see who has guessed the closest. As the requirement scenarios become more sophisticated, such as adding the desire for a persistence mechanism, the solution scenarios will become more sophisticated, as well. Thus, our example will evolve and we will gain an understanding of how the various architectures that we discuss will help us build a system that satisfies these requirements in an elegant and effective manner.

Let's look at some examples of architectures that utilize these approaches and discuss the tradeoffs and usage.

The "Page-Centric" Approach

We start by looking at architectures based on the page-centric or client-server approach. We will look at the **page-view** and **page-view with bean** architectures.

Applications built using a client-server approach have been around for some time; they consist of one or more application programs running on client machines, and connecting to a server-based application to work. (A good example would be a PowerBuilder or Oracle Forms based system.) CGIs and pre-Servlet applications were generally based on this simple 2-tier model, and with the introduction of Servlets, 2-tier applications could also be created in Java.

This model allows JSPs or Servlets direct access to some resource like a database or legacy application to service a client's request: the early JSP specifications termed this a "Model 1" programming approach. The JSP page is where the incoming request is intercepted processed, and the response sent back to the client; JSPs only differed from Servlets in this scenario by providing cleaner code, and separating code from the content by placing data access in beans.

This is illustrated in the figure below.

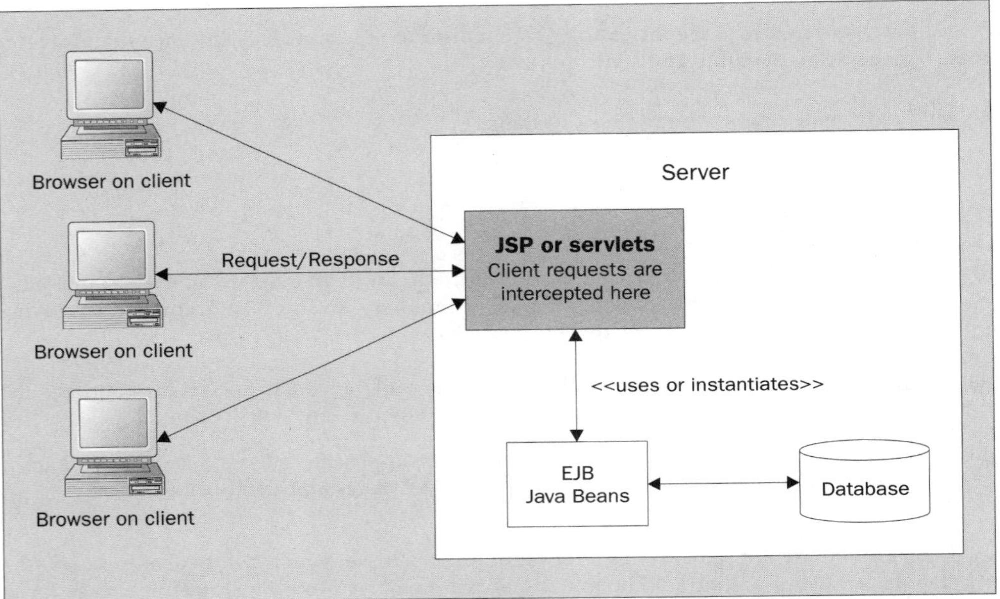

The advantage of such an approach is that it is simple to program, and allows the page author to generate dynamic content easily, based upon the request and the state of the resources.

However this architecture does not scale up well for a large number of simultaneous clients since there would be a significant amount of request processing to be performed, and each request must establish or share a potentially scarce/expensive connection to the resource in question. (A good example would be JDBC connections in servlets or JSPs and the need for connection pools.)

Indiscriminate usage of this architecture usually leads to a significant amount of Java code embedded within the JSP page. This may not seem to be much of a problem for Java developers but it is certainly an issue if the JSP pages are maintained by designers: the code tends to get in the designer's way, and you run the risk of your code becoming corrupted when others are tweaking the look and feel.

> *Of course, it is not necessary to use JSPs, to separate code and presentation in servlets: the use of templates is popular. There are a lot of toolkits that facilitate this, such as ATP (http://www.winwinsoft.com/atp/), MindTemplate (http://www.mindbright.se/english/technology/products/mindtemplate), or the more popular WebMacro (http://www.webmacro.org/), FreeMarker (http://freemarker.sourceforge.net), and PreparedHtml (http://www.its.washington.edu/~garth/prep.html)*

Page-View

This basic architecture involves direct request invocations to a server page with embedded Java code, and markup tags which dynamically generate output for substitution within the HTML.

This approach has many benefits. It is very easy to get started and is a low-overhead approach from a development standpoint. All of the Java code may be embedded within the HTML, so changes are confined to a limited area, reducing complexity. The figure below shows the architecture visually.

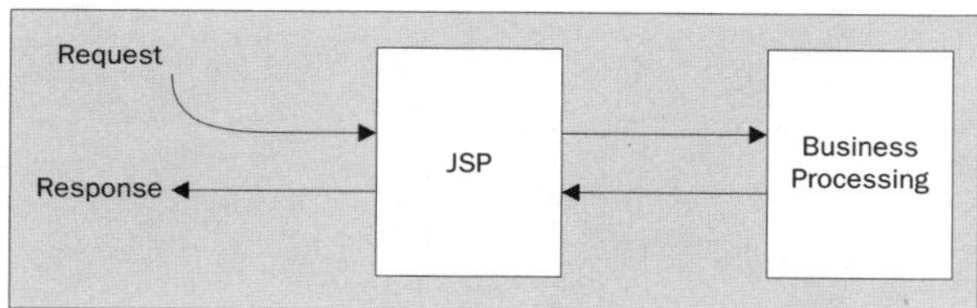

The big trade-off here is in the level of sophistication. As the scale of the system grows, some limitations of this approach surface, such as including too much business logic in the page instead of factoring forward to a mediating Servlet, or factoring back to a worker bean. As we discussed earlier, utilizing a Servlet and helper beans allow us to separate developer roles more cleanly, and improves the potential for code reuse. Let's start with a fairly simple example JSP page that follows this model, handling requests directly and including all the Java code within the JSP source page.

We begin with a basic description of the example application. All the examples in this chapter use the JSWDK version 1.0.1, using the default web application directory structure for simplicity. Thus, the JSP and HTML source are under the `<jswdk-root>/examples/jsp/` subdirectory and the Servlet (see later) is under `<jswdk-root>/examples/WEB-INF/servlets`.

The user interface is shown below:

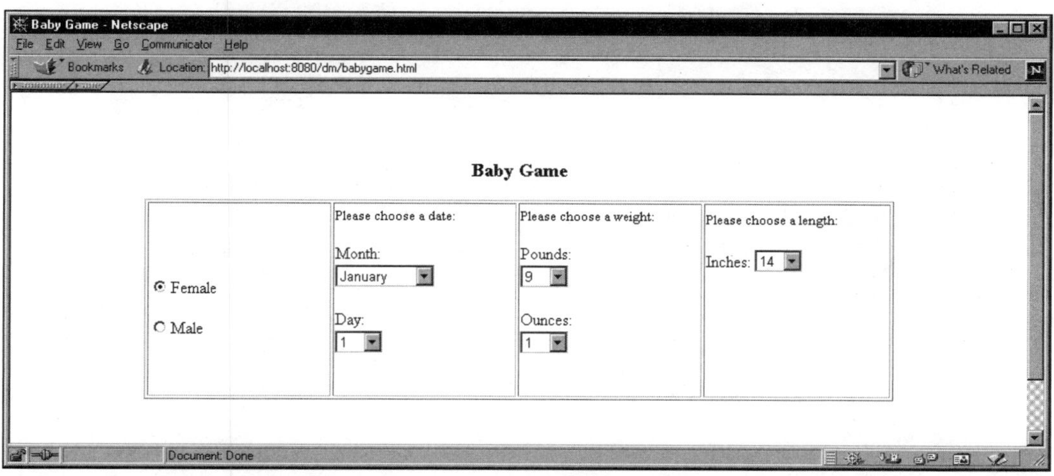

The HTML code for this page, `BabyGame1.html`, is stored in `<jswdk-root>/examples/jsp/pageview/` and includes a form that prompts a user for selections. The user is asked to make some guesses about the statistics of a baby to be born in the near future. The HTML code is as follows:

```
<html>
<head>
<title>Baby Game</title>
</head>
<body bgcolor="#FFFFFF">
<form method="post" action="BabyGame1.jsp" name="">
<center>
<h3>
Baby Game</h3></center>

<center>
<br>
<table BORDER COLS=5 WIDTH="75%" >
<caption>Please enter your own name:
<input type="text" name="guesser"></caption>

<tr>

<td>
<br><input type="radio" name="gender" value="Female" checked>Female
<p><input type="radio" name="gender" value="Male">Male
<p></td>

<td><font size=-1>Please choose a date:</font>
<p>Month: <select name="month">
<option value="January">January</option>
<option value="February">February</option>
...
<option value="December">December</option>
<br></select>
<p>Day: <select name="day">
<option value="1">1</option>
<option value="2">2</option>
...
<option value="31">31</option>

<br></select>
<p> </td>

<td><font size=-1>Please choose a weight:</font>
<p>Pounds: <select name="pounds">
<option value="5">5</option>
<option value="6">6</option>
...
<option value="12">12</option>
<br></select>
<p>Ounces: <select name="ounces">
<option value="1">1</option>
<option value="2">2</option>
...
<option value="15">15</option>

<br></select>
<p> </td>
```

```
<td><font size=-1>Please choose a length:</font>
<p>Inches: <select name="length">

<option value="14">14</option>
<option value="15">15</option>
...
<option value="25">25</option>

</select><p> <p> <p> </td>

</tr>
</table>
</center>

<br> 
<center>
<p><input type="submit" name="submit" value="Make Guess">
          
<input type="reset" name="reset" value="Reset">
</center>

<br></form>
</body>
</html>
```

This HTML form will POST the choices to our JSP, which is shown in source form below (`BabyGame1.jsp`, stored in directory `<jswdk-root>/examples/jsp/pageview/`). These choices are then stored and displayed by our simple JSP, which has handled the request directly.

The resulting display looks like this:

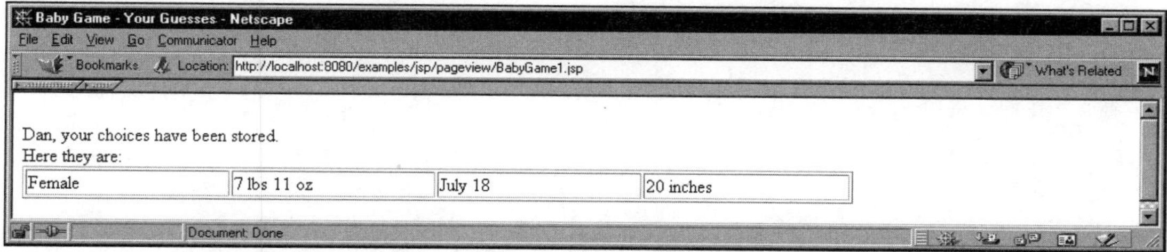

The first part of `BabyGame1.jsp` is responsible for extracting the values from each of the request parameters and populating the state of the JSP. The name of the individual making the guess is contained in a request parameter called `guesser`. Each of the statistics about the baby is stored in a request parameter with an intuitive name, such as `gender`, `length`, etc.

```
<HTML>
<HEAD><TITLE>Baby Game - Your Guesses</TITLE></HEAD>
<BODY bgcolor=FFFFFF>
<%@ page language="java" import="java.util.*,java.io.*" buffer="8k" %>

<%
   String guesser = request.getParameter("guesser");

   String gender = request.getParameter("gender");

   String pounds = request.getParameter("pounds");
   String ounces = request.getParameter("ounces");
```

```
    String month = request.getParameter("month");
    String day = request.getParameter("day");

    String length = request.getParameter("length");
```

After this task is complete, there is a validation check on the data. If the validation is unsuccessful, then the JSP completes its processing by sending the user an appropriate message:

```
    if(guesser == null || gender == null || pounds == null || ounces == null
        || month == null || day == null || length == null)
  { %>
  <br> There where some choices that were not selected.<br><br>
  Sorry, but you must complete all selections to play.<br>
  <font size=-1>(Please hit the browser 'back' button to continue)</font><br>
  <%}
```

Otherwise, upon successful validation of the request parameters, the data is stored to disk and a table is generated using the JSP state, which corresponds to the user's guesses. The guesses are stored within a `java.util.Properties` object, which, for example purposes, is flattened to a text file in the root directory of the JSP run time engine, in this case the JSWDK root directory. The name of the text file corresponds to the name of the guesser, which was provided in the HTML form. One could easily imagine an even more basic example where the data was merely displayed but not stored. Such an example would differ only in that the storage code in `BabyGame1.jsp` would be omitted:

```
  else
  {
  //Store guess info and display to user
  Properties p = new Properties();
  p.put("guesser", guesser);
  p.put("gender", gender);
  p.put("pounds", pounds);
  p.put("ounces", ounces);
  p.put("month", month);
  p.put("day", day);
  p.put("length", length);

  FileOutputStream outer = new FileOutputStream(guesser);
  p.save(outer, "Baby Game -- "+guesser+"'s guesses");
  outer.flush();
  outer.close();

  %>

  <br>
  <%= guesser %>, your choices have been stored.<br>  Here they are:<br>
  <table BORDER COLS=5 WIDTH="75%" >
  <caption></caption>

  <tr>

  <td> <%= gender %>
  </td>
  <td>
```

```
<%= pounds %> lbs <%= ounces %> oz
</td>
<td>
<%= month %> <%= day %>
</td>
<td>
<%= length %> inches
</td>

</tr>
</table>

<br>
<%}
%>
</BODY>
</HTML>
```

This JSP certainly was easy to build and is well suited to handling such simple needs. It is getting quite cluttered with Java code, though, and its processing requirements are extremely simplistic. More sophisticated business rules and data access code would require much more Java within the JSP and the source would become unwieldy quickly as it grows. Additionally, we are limited to mostly 'cut-and-paste' reuse, which means duplicate code and a more error-prone environment that is harder to maintain and debug.

In order to reduce the clutter of the current example and to provide a cleaner environment for future growth, we will look at another 'Page-Centric' architecture called 'Page-View with Bean' in the next section.

Page-View with Bean

This pattern is used when the Page-View architecture becomes too cluttered with business-related code and data access code. The Baby Game example now evolves into a more sophisticated design, as shown in the figure below.

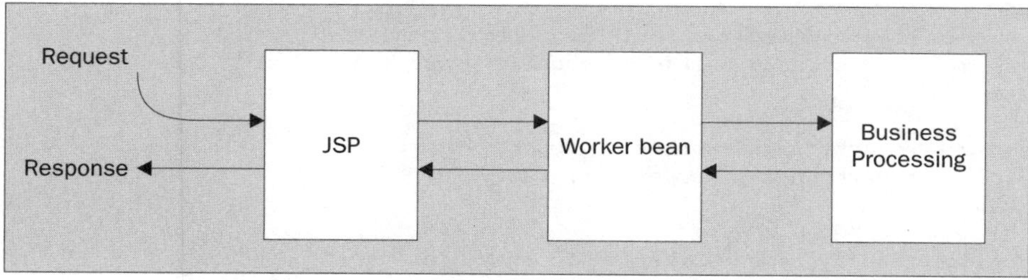

The modified JSP source page, `<jswdk-root>/examples/jsp/pageviewwithbean/BabyGame1.jsp`, is shown below, followed by the worker bean that works in tandem with the modified JSP in order to process the request. The HTML for the initial game interface remains unchanged. The resulting display to the user from the JSP is basically unchanged from that of the previous 'Page-View' example:

```
<HTML>
<HEAD><TITLE>Baby Game - Your Guesses</TITLE></HEAD>
<BODY bgcolor=FFFFFF>
<%@ page language="java" buffer="8k" %>
<jsp:useBean id="worker1" class="examples.pageviewwithbean.BabyGameWorker1"
 scope="request" />

<%-- Populate the JavaBean properties from the Request parameters. --%>
<%-- The semantics of the '*' wildcard is to copy all similarly-named --%>
<%-- Request parameters into worker1 properties. --%>
<jsp:setProperty name="worker1" property="*" />

<%
   if(worker1.getGuesser == null || worker1.getGender() == null ||
      worker1.getPounds() == null || worker1.getOunces() == null ||
      worker1.getMonth() == null || worker1.getDay() == null ||
      worker1.getLength() == null)
{ %>
<br> There where some choices that were not selected.<br><br>
Sorry, but you must complete all selections to play.<br>
<font size=-1>(Please hit the browser 'back' button to continue)</font><br>
<%}
else
{
worker1.store();
%>

<br>
<jsp:getProperty name="worker1" property="guesser" />, your choices have
been stored.<br>  Here they are:<br>
<table BORDER COLS=5 WIDTH="75%" >
<caption></caption>

<tr>

<td> <jsp:getProperty name="worker1" property="gender" />
</td>
<td>
<jsp:getProperty name="worker1" property="pounds" />  lbs
<jsp:getProperty name="worker1" property="ounces" />  oz
</td>
<td>
<jsp:getProperty name="worker1" property="month" />
<jsp:getProperty name="worker1" property="day" />
</td>
<td>
<jsp:getProperty name="worker1" property="length" />  inches
</td>

</tr>
</table>
```

```
<br>
<%}
%>
</BODY>
</HTML>
```

The source for the worker bean, `BabyGameWorker1`, is as follows:

```
package examples;

import java.io.*;
import java.util.Properties;

public class BabyGameWorker1
{
  private Properties p = new Properties();

  public String getGuesser() {
    return(String)p.get("guesser");
  }

  public void setGuesser(String aString) {
    p.put("guesser", aString);
  }

  // And similar "get" and "set" methods for Gender, Pounds, Ounces, Month,
  // Day, Length, and File.

  public Properties getProperties() {
    return p;
  }

  public void store() throws IOException {
    FileOutputStream outer = new FileOutputStream((String)p.get("guesser"));
    p.save(outer, "Baby Game -- "+p.get("guesser")+"'s guesses");
    outer.flush();
    outer.close();

  }
}
```

We see in these two listings that the Java code representing the business logic and simple data storage implementation has migrated from the JSP to the JavaBean worker. This refactoring leaves a much cleaner JSP with limited Java code, which can be comfortably owned by an individual in a web-production role, since it encapsulates mostly markup tags.

Additionally, a less technical individual could be provided with a property sheet for the JavaBean workers, providing a listing of properties that are made available to the JSP page by the particular worker bean, and the desired property may simply be plugged into the JSP `getProperty` action via the markup tag in order to obtain the attribute value. An example of a potential property sheet is shown below. Additionally, once a convention and format were agreed upon, an automated tool could be created to interrogate all JavaBeans of interest and generate property sheets automatically.

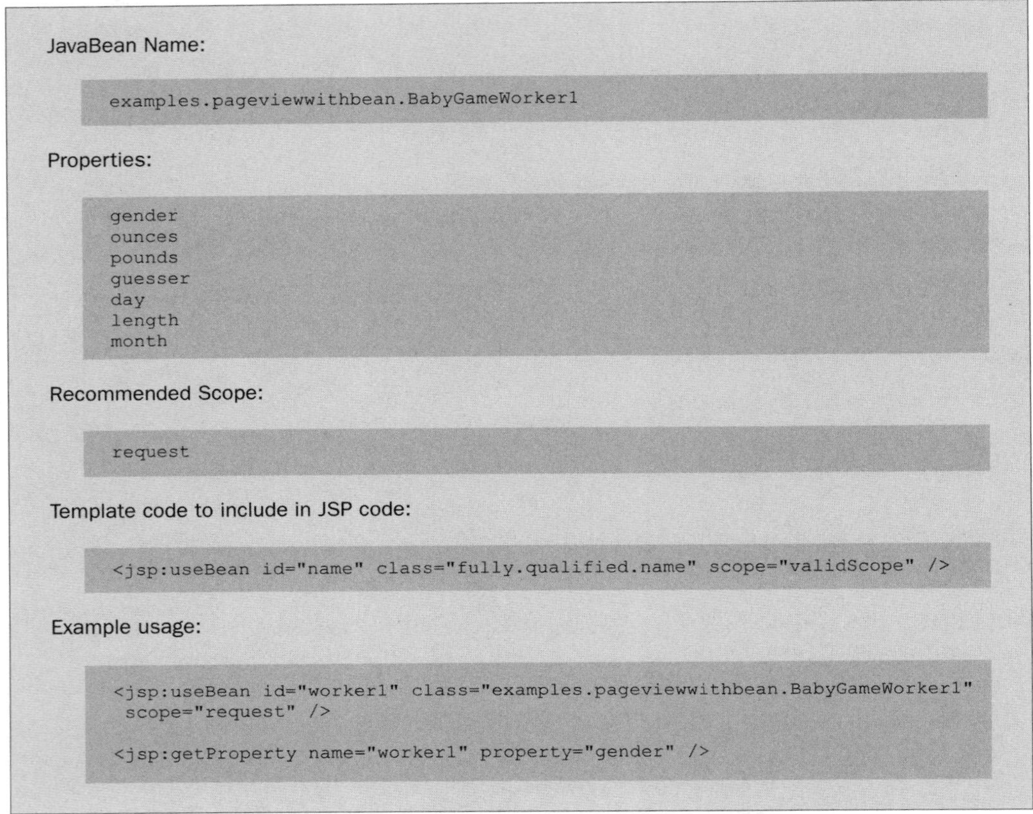

JavaBean Name:

```
examples.pageviewwithbean.BabyGameWorker1
```

Properties:

```
gender
ounces
pounds
guesser
day
length
month
```

Recommended Scope:

```
request
```

Template code to include in JSP code:

```
<jsp:useBean id="name" class="fully.qualified.name" scope="validScope" />
```

Example usage:

```
<jsp:useBean id="worker1" class="examples.pageviewwithbean.BabyGameWorker1"
 scope="request" />

<jsp:getProperty name="worker1" property="gender" />
```

Moreover, we now have created a bean that a software developer can own, such that functionality may be refined and modified without the need for changes to the HTML or markup within the JSP source page.

Another way to think about these changes is that we have created cleaner abstractions in our system by replacing implementation with intent. In other words, we have taken a bunch of code from our JSP source (the Java code that writes the guesses to a file on disk), encapsulated it within a bean, and replaced it with our intent, which is to store the data, `worker1.store()`.

Looping in JSP

So why might one choose to embed Java code in a JSP as opposed to using a predefined tag? An example would be in order to loop through some data and format HTML for output.

Earlier versions of the JSP specification included a tag syntax for looping through indexed properties of JavaBeans, so that no Java code was needed within the HTML for this purpose.

With the JSP software specification version 1.0, such tags were removed in favor of the creation of an extensible custom tag markup mechanism that could be used for this purpose and much more. Unfortunately, this custom tag functionality is first available in version 1.1 of the specification, and JSP engines supporting the custom tag libraries are only now becoming available.

Further Refinements

After deploying this solution, our expectant family decides to limit the group of people who are able to access the system, deciding to include only their family and friends. To this end, they decide to add an authentication mechanism to their system so that each individual will have to provide proof of identity before accessing the system.

If a simple authentication mechanism is added to the top of our JSP page and we want to ensure that each JSP page is protected by this device, then we will need to add some code to each and every JSP page to execute this authentication check. Whenever there is a duplication of code such as this, it is beneficial to explore options for migrating the duplicated code to a common area.

In the previous example we "factored back," as we moved business logic and data-access Java code from our JSP to our JavaBean, and in the next section we expand our example to "factor forward" into a Servlet, continuing our efforts to minimize the amount of inline Java code in our JSPs.

The "Dispatcher" Approach

We now move on to look at architectures based on the dispatcher or "N-tiered" approach, where a Servlet (or JSP) acts as a mediator or controller, delegating requests to JSP pages and JavaBeans. We will look at the **mediator-view**, **mediator-composite view**, and **service to workers** architectures.

In an N-tier application, the server side of the architecture is broken up into multiple tiers, as illustrated in the next figure:

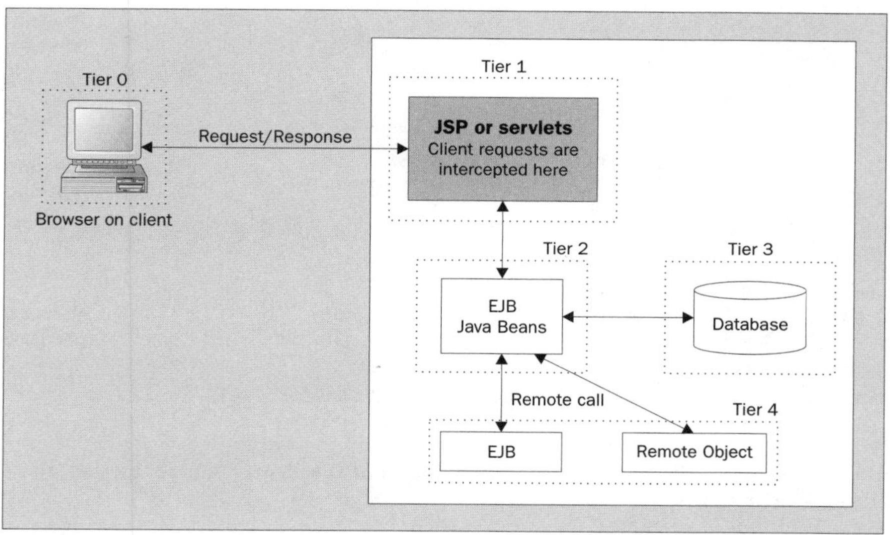

In this case, the application is composed of multiple tiers, where the middle tier, the JSP, interacts with the back end resources via another object or Enterprise JavaBeans component. The Enterprise JavaBeans server and the EJB provide managed access to resources, support transactions and access to underlying security mechanisms, thus addressing the resource sharing and performance issues of the 2-tier approach. This is the programming model supported by the Java 2 Enterprise Edition (J2EE) platform.

The first step in N-tiered application design should be identifying the correct objects and their interactions, in other words, object modeling. This is the part where class diagrams and tools like Rational Rose (http://www.rational.com) step in for architects. Quite often a line has to be drawn as to what objects need to be modeled: being over zealous can cause unnecessary complexity. If you get this part right, you're half way there!

The second part is identifying the JSPs or Servlets. As a rule of thumb, these should be divided into two categories, depending on the role they play, often called "web components" in the J2EE terminology

- Front end JSPs or Servlets that manage application flow and business logic evaluation. This is where a lot of method invocation on the objects, or usage of EJBs, can be coded. They are not responsible for any presentation, and act as a point to intercept the HTTP requests coming from the users. They provide a single entry point to an application, simplifying security management and making application state easier to maintain.
- Presentation JSPs that generate HTML (or even XML), with their main purpose in life being presentation of dynamic content. They contain only presentation and rendering logic.

The figure below shows the relationship between these two categories. The front-end component accepts a request, and then determines the appropriate presentation component to forward it to. The presentation component then processes the request and returns the response to another front component or directly back to the user:

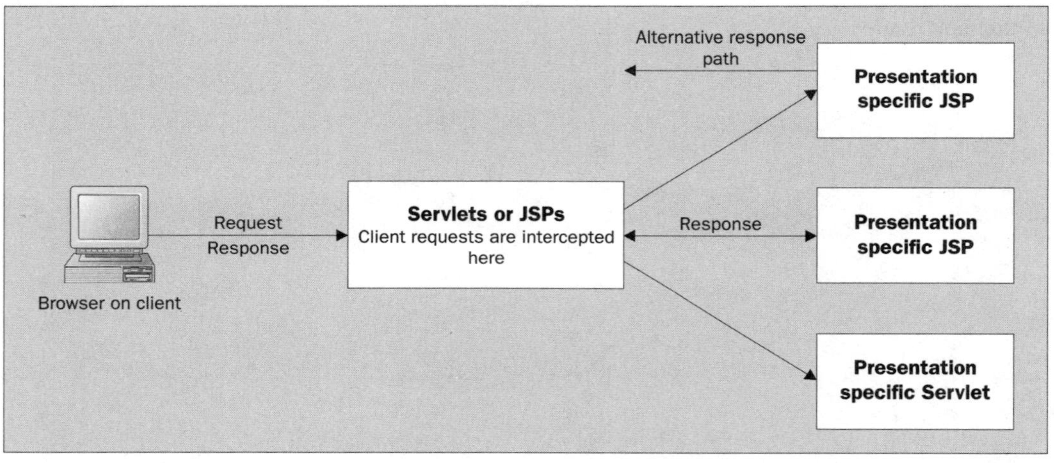

Sometimes this distinction is hard to maintain, but the clearer the distinction, the cleaner the design.

These categories are analogous to the Model-View design pattern, where the front-end component is the model and the presentation component the view. This approach was referred to as the 'Model 2' programming model in earlier releases of the JSP specifications. It differs from Model 1 essentially in the location at which the bulk of the request processing is performed. The figure below shows the Model 2 approach:

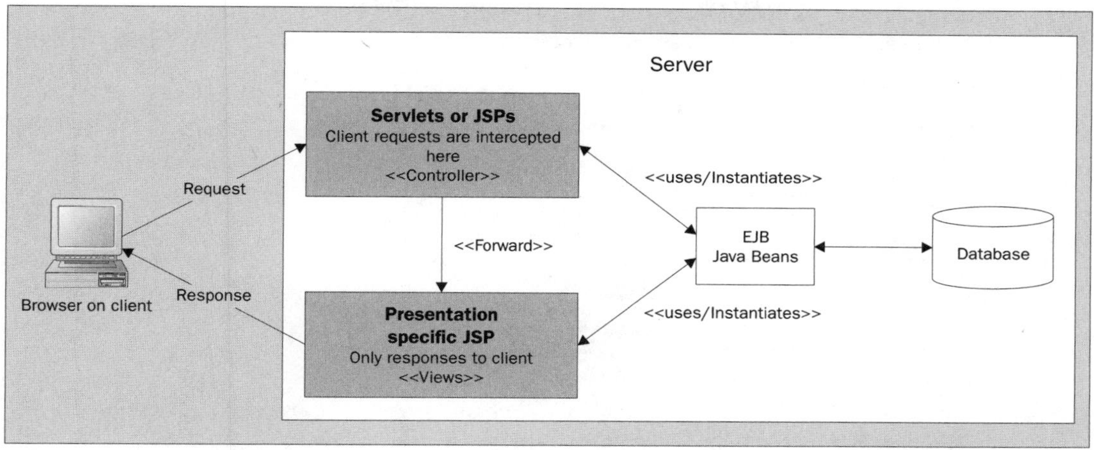

In this approach, JSPs are used to generate the presentation layer, and either JSPs or Servlets to perform process-intensive tasks. The front-end component acts as the controller and is in charge of the request processing and the creation of any beans or objects used by the presentation JSP, as well as deciding, depending on the user's actions, which JSP to forward the request to. There is no processing logic within the presentation JSP itself: it is simply responsible for retrieving any objects or beans that may have been previously created by the Servlet, and extracting the dynamic content for insertion within static templates.

Instead of writing Servlets for the front-end components you can choose, if you wish, to use a JSP that contains only code and doesn't have any presentation responsibilities. Whichever option is used (and in this chapter we only use Servlets in this role), this approach typically results in the cleanest separation of presentation from content, leading to delineation of the roles and responsibilities of the developers and page designers, especially in complex applications.

> *Beans that are used by JSPs are not the same as Enterprise JavaBeans (EJBs), but are usually simple classes that serve as data wrappers to encapsulate information. They have simple get and set methods for each bean property .The properties further correspond by name to the HTML variables on the screen. This allows the bean properties to be set dynamically by the* `jsp:usebean` *tag without doing an individual* `request.getParameter(parametername)` *on the* `request` *object. See Chapter 4 for bean usage.*

Mediator-View

Factoring common services, such as authentication out to a mediating Servlet allows us to remove potential duplication from our JSP pages. The code below is an example of a Servlet that provides us with central forwarding control for our game system, and includes a simple authentication check that will be reused across requests. A Bean could be used for this purpose, but you would have to add the same code to each page to perform the authentication checks. Instead, each request will be serviced by the Servlet, which now includes our authentication code.

The mediating Servlet, `BabyGameServlet.java`, is shown below. It is placed in the `<jswdk-root>/examples/WEB-INF/servlets/` directory:

```
import javax.servlet.*;
import javax.servlet.http.*;
import java.io.*;

public class BabyGameServlet extends HttpServlet {
  public void doGet(HttpServletRequest request,
                    HttpServletResponse response) {
    processRequest(request, response);
  }

  public void doPost(HttpServletRequest request,
                     HttpServletResponse response) {
    processRequest(request, response);
  }

  protected void processRequest(HttpServletRequest request,
                                 HttpServletResponse response) {

    try {

      // If we added actual authentication, this is where it would go
      // For example purposes, if the parameters exist, we consider the
      // auth successful.
      if ((request.getParameter("guesser") != null)
              && (request.getParameter("password") != null)) {

        // Note: Based on the successful authentication of this user we may
        // want to consider writing something into the session state that
        // signifies that this is the case.  For example, if we wanted to
        // limit direct access to certain JSP pages only to authenticated
        // users, then we could include code that would check for this
        // session state before allowing such access.

        // In order to reuse this Servlet for multiple examples, we pass as
        // a request parameter the resource name to which we dispatch our
        // request.
        getServletConfig().getServletContext()
          .getRequestDispatcher(request.getParameter("dispatchto"))
          .forward(request, response);
      } else {
        PrintWriter outy = response.getWriter();
        outy.println("Unable to authenticate, please try again.");
      }
    } catch (Exception ex) {
      ex.printStackTrace();
    }
  }
}
```

A new architectural pattern is emerging, with the mediating Servlet working with a JSP page and worker bean pair to fulfill a service request. This 'Mediator-View' architecture is shown below, and illustrating how each service is partitioned. The Servlet initially handles the request and delegates to a JSP software page/worker bean combination. The JSP populates bean properties from the request parameters and then uses the bean to prepare the data for presentation:

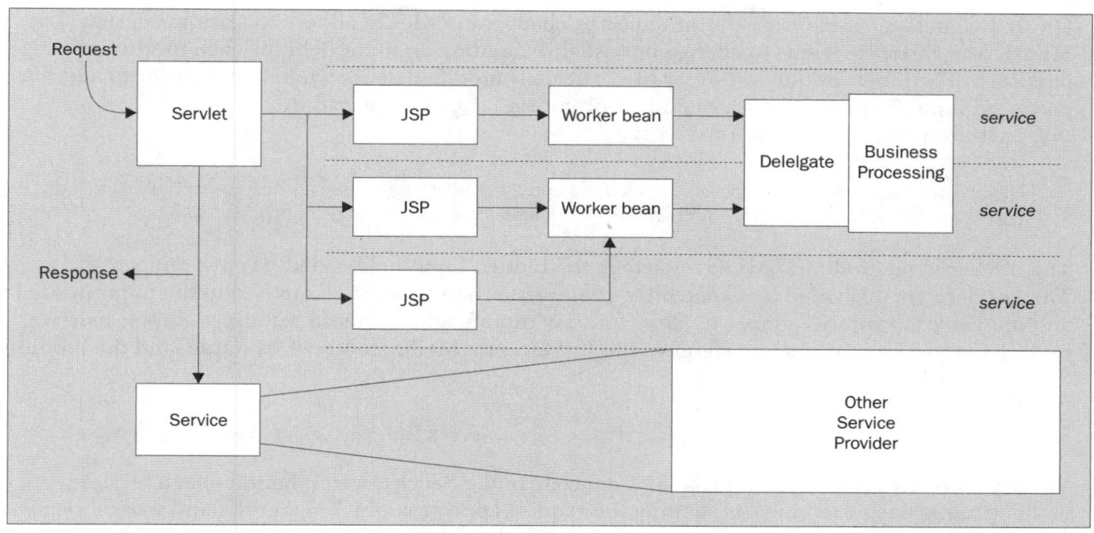

Continuing our attempts at creating the appropriate abstractions in our system, we shall consider how to better partition our business logic and data access code, attempting to reduce the coupling among the various parts of the system.

As we discussed, this request is handled first by a basic Servlet that dispatches to a JSP page for formatting and display. The JSP is responsible for delegating the processing of business functionality to a business delegate via a worker bean, which act as façades for the back-end resources. We call this component a **business delegate**, because it is a client-side business abstraction used to complete the basic business processing by abstracting out the code that deals with the back-end communication. The worker beans might communicate through the business delegate with the back-end via Enterprise JavaBeans components running in a scalable, load-balancing container.

In this case, we are able to decouple the EJB implementation from the JSP worker bean by moving the EJB-related code, such as the code relating to JNDI lookup, into the business delegate. If we include our EJB-related code in our worker beans, then we are closely coupling the bean to a specific underlying implementation, and if this implementation is modified or changed we must make modifications to our worker bean accordingly. So we have succeeded in creating abstractions that have reduced the coupling among the distinct pieces of our system. We can see how the worker bean and the business delegate reduce coupling between the client request and the ultimate back-end resource.

In other words, the public interfaces need not change even if the API to the underlying resource changes. The worker beans can be combined with different JSP pages in order to provide different views of the same underlying information. Also, the Servlet that initially handles each request, and is responsible for authenticating each user, may restrict direct access to our JSP pages, an added security mechanism. Once a user has been successfully authenticated, the Servlet might store certain information in that user's session, and access to certain JSP pages might only be allowed to users whose session state contained such that information. The mechanism could be made more fine grained by including authorization information within this session state that would directly relate to which pages a user may view.

Our baby guessing game example will need to change, in order to adhere to this new design. The HTML user interface needs to change only slightly, adding an input field for each user to enter a password. The table caption in `Babygame1.html` is modified as shown below in order to add the password input field, and the revised file, `babygame2.html`, is placed in `<jswdk-root>/examples/jsp/mediatorview/`:

```
<caption>Please enter your userID:<input type="text" name="guesser">Please enter
your Password:<input type="password" name="password"></caption> >
```

The other change to the HTML is to change the hidden input field called `dispatchto`. The Servlet uses this value to dispatch the request via the `forward()` method to the appropriate JSP, and the value is supplied simply to allow for easy modification of these examples. In this case we modify the `value` attribute to reference the JSP for our "Mediator-View" example, and the modified line looks like this:

```
<input type="hidden" name="dispatchto" value="/jsp/mediatorview/BabyGame2.jsp">
```

We have already seen the next piece of the puzzle in the Servlet, which handles each request, authenticating each user and dispatching the request appropriately. The Servlet and worker beans now contain Java code that is owned by an individual in the software development role, and the syntax and semantics of which may be modified without any changes to our JSP. The property sheets remain a simple contract between the web-production team and the software developers.

The benefit of a dispatcher approach is in the control the Servlet has on the request. Since the Servlet acts as the mediator, there is central forwarding control. As discussed, this also creates a nice role separation between the lower level coding in the Servlet and the JSP coding. A drawback of this architecture is that it involves more design work and more coding, since individual beans are created instead of code fragments. A very simple project might be overly burdened by this extra overhead, while more sophisticated efforts will benefit from the cleaner design.

Additionally, encapsulating as much Java code as possible into our Servlet and beans, and removing it from the JSP source, will also have the added benefit of encouraging more elegant and refined Java coding, because excessive Java code embedded within JSP source can quickly start to look like just another scripting language, and the cut-and-paste mentality tends to take over. Moreover, a software developer will be more inclined to refine code that they own, without potential dependencies and conflicts with a web-production person. Of course the irony is that such unwieldy pages that are filled with Java code are in more need than any of refactoring.

Updating our example to include improvements based on these very forces, we add to our worker bean a factory that vends multiple storage implementations based on a parameterized factory method. Our actual storage process may be modified easily and dynamically, simply by providing an implementation that adheres to the `Store` interface. We move our basic file storage code into an implementation called `SimpleStore` that implements the `Store` interface and is created by `StoreFactory`. We don't actually include data access code in this example, but it would reside in a worker bean and would reference the business delegate, which could then reference an EJB component. The `Store` interface also hides implementation details, in this case those of the storage mechanism behind it, exposing a well-defined interface instead.

The initial delegation point in this architecture is a JSP – we will see later another architecture in which the initial point of delegation is a worker bean (Service-to-Workers). The subtle difference between the two is worth discussing. In situations where there is on-going workflow that is necessary for the generation of the data model, requiring multiple business calls, one needs to decide where to encapsulate these business calls:

- In one case, the JSP may contain the business calls that are required to obtain the necessary state for the intermediate model, which will be stored in the associated worker bean(s). The JSP is not only responsible for the presentation of the data, but additionally has some responsibility for coordinating the business calls, and may interact with different beans in order to present multiple views of the same underlying models.

- On the other hand, if the Servlet delegates initially to a worker bean, then the Servlet will need to adopt the responsibility for controlling these business calls, utilizing the worker beans to make its requests. If the required data can be gathered with a single business call, then dispatching this call to the worker bean directly from the Servlet allows the bean to populate the entire intermediate model. The Servlet is then able to forward the request to the JSP for presentation.

As you may have noticed, in the former scenario the JSP's responsibilities are increased as it fulfills part of the role of the controller in addition to the view. One needs to decide what is right for the job and move code forward or back based on the workflow and presentation needs. One issue to consider is that adding business calls to a JSP page allows for reuse of this code conditionally across requests simply by nesting pages, as in Mediator-Composite View, which we will discuss shortly. Adding business invocations to the Servlet means either that these calls will be invoked for each request the Servlet handles, limiting its potential for reuse, or that the Servlet may become cluttered with conditional logic dictating which code to execute for a particular request.

The elements of the current "Mediator-View" example are:

- The HTML UI, which POSTs the request to the Servlet:
`<jswdk-root>/examples/jsp/mediatorview/babygame2.html`
- The Servlet, which dispatches to the JSP:
`<jswdk-root>/examples/WEB-INF/servlets/BabyGameServlet.java`
(source) and
`<jswdk-root>/examples/WEB-INF/servlets/BabyGameServlet.class`
(bytecode)
- The JSP:
`<jswdk-root>/examples/jsp/mediatorview/BabyGame2.jsp`
- The worker bean:
`examples.mediatorview.BabyGameWorker2.java`
- The supporting source code:
`examples.mediatorview.StoreFactory`, `examples.mediatorview.Store`, `examples.mediatorview.SimpleStore`, `examples.mediatorview.StoreException`, `examples.auth.AuthenticatoFactory`, `examples.auth.Authenticator`, `examples.auth.SimpleAuthenticator`, `examples.auth.AuthContext`, and `examples.auth.SimpleAuthContext`.

This supporting code must be included in the `CLASSPATH` that is used by the JSP engine.

The RequestDispatcher API

These architectures rely on a Servlet's dispatching a request to another resource. Prior to the Servlet API 2.1, dispatching of requests to another dynamic resource was cumbersome, and limited because it was not directly supported in the specification.

The Servlet API 2.1 introduces the RequestDispatcher. Accessible via the ServletContext, the RequestDispatcher implementation can dispatch a request to either a static resource, such as an HTML page, or another dynamic resource, such as a Servlet or JSP. A request can be either 'forwarded' or 'included', and state can be made available to the dispatched resource.

The include() method allows the programmatic equivalent of Server-Side Includes (SSI), while the forward() method transfers control to the designated dynamic resource. A Servlet that invokes RequestDispatcher.include() retains overall responsibility for the service request, handling the response to the client. In this case, the Servlet has the opportunity to do any sort of clean up after all the nested invocations have completed.

Once the Servlet dispatches to another dynamic resource with an invocation to RequestDispatcher.forward(), though, the Servlet has completed its work. An example of the latter type of forward dispatch is occurs in both the Mediator-View and Mediator-Composite View architectures.

The method signatures that a Servlet may use to dispatch a request to another resource, are:

```
public void forward(ServletRequest request, ServletResponse response)
  throws ServletException, java.io.IOException

public void include(ServletRequest request, ServletResponse response)
  throws ServletException, java.io.IOException
```

Here is an example from within a Servlet:

```
RequestDispatcher dispatcher =
  getServletContext().getRequestDispatcher("process.jsp");
request.setAttribute("user", user);
dispatcher.forward(request, response);
```

For a detailed description of the Servlet API, see Appendix C.

Mediator-Composite View

Sometimes we are building systems with dynamic template text as well as dynamic content. In other words, there is content being generated dynamically, and the template text that surrounds this data is also being constantly changed. Imagine that there are headers and footers in a page that are modified quite often, notifying individuals of status changes or information of special interest. It may not be desirable to recompile our JSP source each time this template text changes, since this involves a run time delay and resource load. If we simply type our header and footer text directly into our JSP source, then we will need to modify that source each time we want to change the template text, and our modified source will need to be re-translated in order to service another request, causing this run time latency, and this scenario will repeat itself each and every time the text undergoes even slight modification.

Moving the header and footer template text to external files provides us with a solution to this dependency on run time re-translation when our template changes. We move a portion of the template text from our JSP source to another file, replacing it with the JSP include action:

```
<jsp:include page="header.html" flush="true" />
```

Unlike its counterpart the `include` directive (signified with <%@), which includes text at translation time, the JSP `include` action substitutes the designated page into the JSP source *at run time.* Not only have we made our solution more modular, we have provided a way to change template text on the fly without the need for recompiling our JSP source. Of course, there is a run time cost for this processing, but it is far less expensive than a full source compile. Such flexibility is useful, especially since the JSP specification does not include much coverage of pre-compilation.

Not only can we dynamically include resources, such as static HTML template fragments within our JSP source, but we can also include other JSPs, creating a multiple-level nesting of pages. In this case, the presentation is built from numerous static and dynamic resources, which together make up the page presented to the user. Each of these resources is potentially composed of additional nested pages. Although the HTML template text is considered a static resource, meaning it is not generated dynamically at run time, these template fragments are potentially a dynamic piece of the interface, since each can be modified continually with immediate updates occurring in the containing presentation. This 'Mediator-Composite View' architecture is shown visually below:

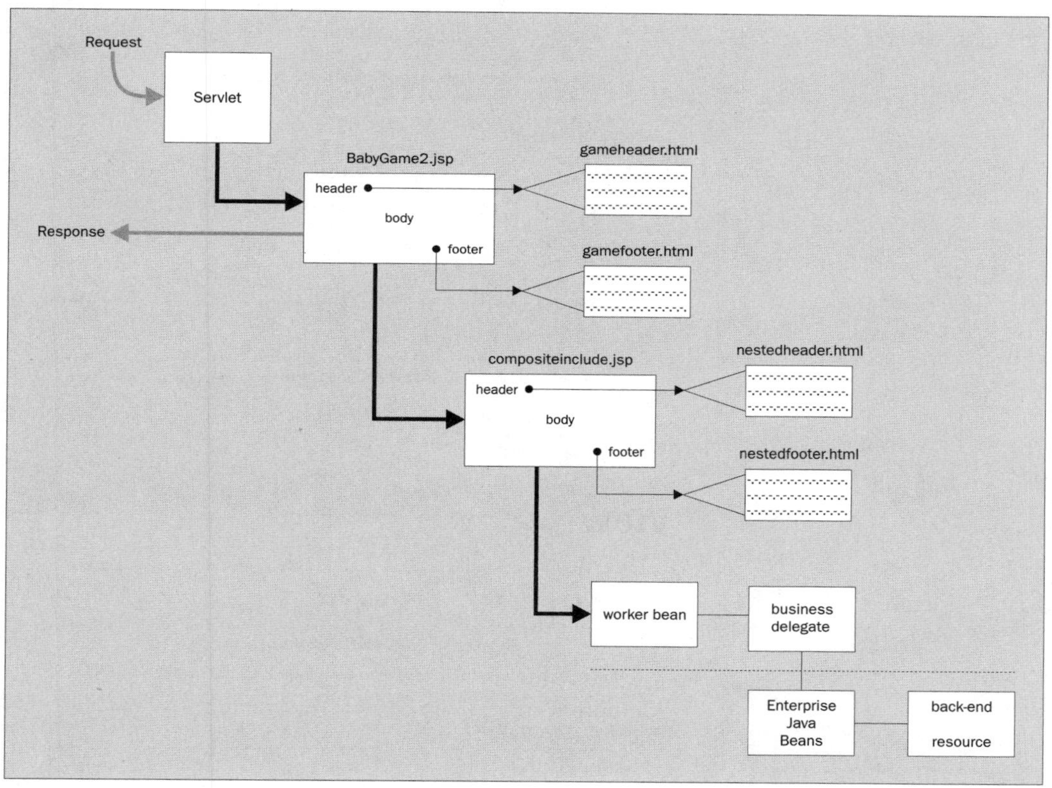

Each of these architectures builds on the previous ones in some way, and in this case we have modified the middle of the 'Mediator-View', while inheriting the front and back. As with the other dispatcher architectures, the Servlet mediator dispatches to a JSP, which imports the aforementioned static and dynamic resources. The figure above shows this nested server page including dynamic content generated via an invocation on a helper bean, which gets to the business processing through a delegate which once again acts as a façade to the back- end resource that may be "wrapped" in an Enterprise JavaBeans component.

As we have seen, the role of the delegate as a client-side business abstraction layer is to make business calls on the actual back-end resource, such as remote invocations on an Enterprise JavaBeans component. Once again, the role of the worker bean is to service the JSP page, preparing data for use and dynamic presentation by the page. The worker bean serves as an intermediate model for the JSP with which it is paired. Again, we are creating a more flexible architecture by abstracting out the worker bean and the business delegate, so that the model for the JSP is not actually responsible for remote invocations on business resources, and these two distinct parts of the system are more loosely coupled.

This architecture allows us to abstract out portions of our page, creating atomic pieces that can be plugged into a composite whole in different configurations. For example, a checkout page on a shopping site might present a user with the contents of a shopping cart. It is easy to imagine the shopping cart component as an atomic portion of the presentation that might be included by other pages, as well, such as a page that allows a user to survey, modify, or remove their current selections while still in "shopping" mode, as shown in the next two figures:

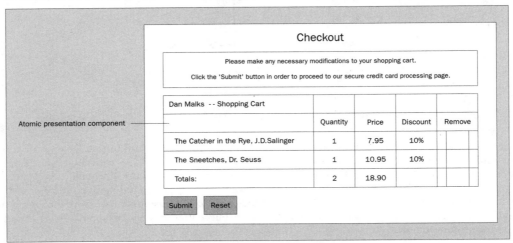

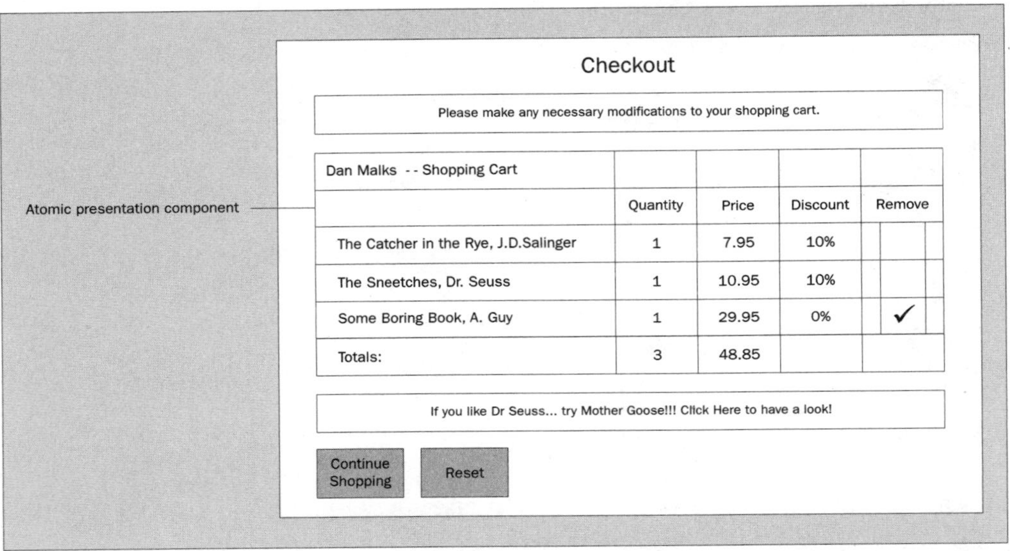

Checkout

Please make any necessary modifications to your shopping cart.

Click the 'Submit' button in order to proceed to our secure credit card processing page.

Atomic presentation component

Dan Malks -- Shopping Cart				
	Quantity	Price	Discount	Remove
The Catcher in the Rye, J.D.Salinger	1	7.95	10%	
The Sneetches, Dr. Seuss	1	10.95	10%	
Totals:	2	18.90		

Submit Reset

A presentation component that is nested within another page will often represent a fairly coarse-grained entity, such as the complete line-by-line inventory of the items in the aforementioned shopping cart, but may be decorated with different header and footer information based on the context of its usage within a page.

As an example, we will factor out the body of the presentation in our ongoing "Baby Game" example, and decorate it with some headers and footers. So how has our code changed to support this architecture?

Our HTML simply requires a change to the hidden input field `dispatchto`. Again, this value is used to dispatch to the appropriate JSP and is used simply to allow for easy modification of these examples. In this case we modify the value attribute to reference the JSP for our 'Mediator-Composite View' example. The modified line now looks like this:

```
<input type="hidden" name="dispatchto"
 value="/jsp/mediatorcompositeview/BabyGame2.jsp">
```

This modified user interface is now in
`<jswdk-root>/examples/jsp/mediatorcompositeview/babygame2.html`

Also, we have created some files containing the static header and footer template text to be included at runtime into our composite display. Here's an example of what one of these header files looks like:

```
<center>
<H3><B>Baby Game 2000! Fun for the whole family!</B></H3><BR>
<hr>
</center>

<br>
<br>
```

This file includes the header template for the presentation that results from our "Mediator-Composite View" example, as shown in the following screen shot:

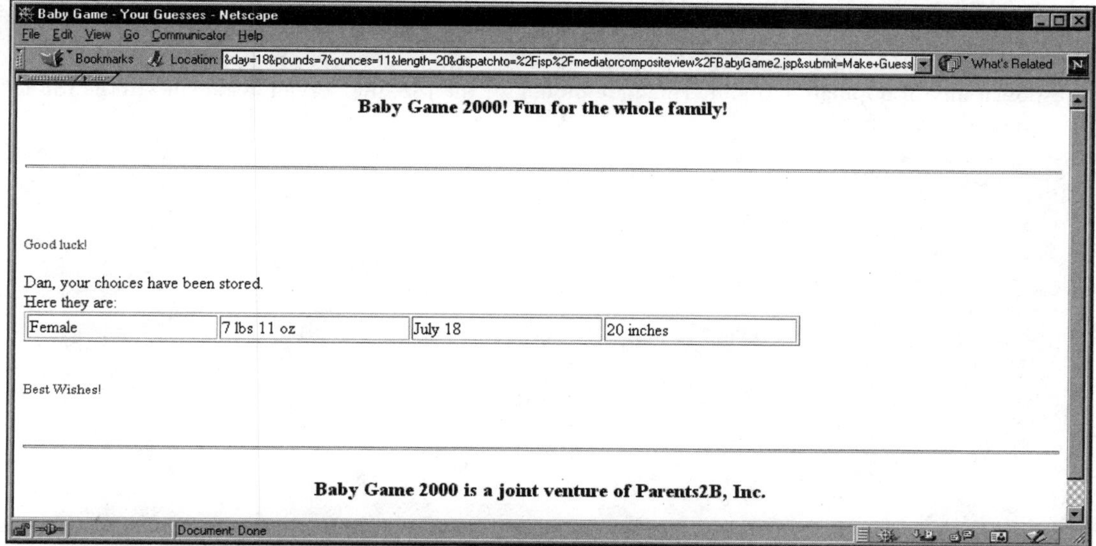

The elements of the current example are then:

- The HTML UI, which POSTs the request to the Servlet:
  `<jswdk-root>/examples/jsp/mediatorcompositeview/babygame2.html`
- The Servlet, which dispatches to the JSP:
  `<jswdk-root>/examples/WEB-INF/servlets/BabyGameServlet.java`
- The outermost JSP:
  `<jswdk-root>/examples/jsp/mediatorcompositeview/BabyGame2.jsp`
- The composite JSP, included within the outermost JSP:
  `<jswdk-root>/examples/jsp/mediatorcompositeview/compositeinclude.jsp`
- The worker bean:
  `examples.mediatorview.BabyGameWorker2`
- The supporting code, which is reused unchanged from the previous example:
  `examples.mediatorview.StoreFactory`, `examples.mediatorview.Store`, `examples.mediatorview.SimpleStore`, `examples.mediatorview.StoreException`, `examples.auth.AuthenticatorFactory`, `examples.auth.Authenticator`, `examples.auth.SimpleAuthenticator`, `examples.auth.AuthContext`, and `examples.auth.SimpleAuthContext`

  This supporting code must be included in the `CLASSPATH` that is used by the JSP engine.
- The static template text, which is included dynamically at runtime to create the composite display:
  `<jswdk-root>/examples/jsp/mediatorcompositeview/gameheader.html`,
  `<jswdk-root>/examples/jsp/mediatorcompositeview/gamefooter.html`,
  `<jswdk-root>/examples/jsp/mediatorcompositeview/nestedheader.html`,
  `<jswdk-root>/examples/jsp/mediatorcompositeview/nestedfooter.html`.

Service to Workers

The initial delegation point of the Service to Workers architecture, shown visually below, is a worker bean that processes our business and data access code, once again via a client-side business abstraction. As with each of the dispatcher architectures, the Servlet handles the request from the client, providing the opportunity for the processing of common services. After the worker bean has completed its responsibility of populating the intermediate model for the JSP, the Servlet dispatches to the JSP to generate the presentation:

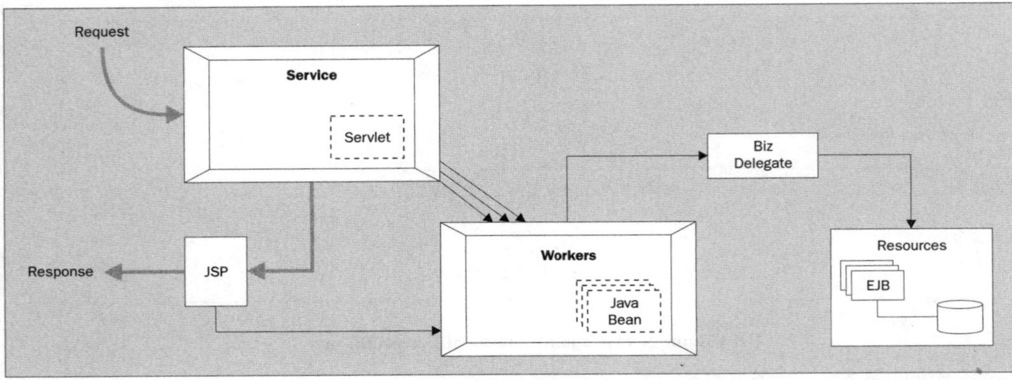

This architecture provides a cleaner separation between the view and the controller, since the JSP page is no longer making business calls, but simply accessing the state of the pre-populated worker bean. Depending on the workflow needs of the system, a decision will have to be made about the suitability of this architecture versus one where the initial delegation point is a JSP, such as the Mediator-View. The cleaner separation of view and controller is indeed an important factor in the decision as well, and often an overriding one. Certainly, if there is not a need for multiple business calls to generate the intermediate model, then this type of architecture is a good choice.

In some cases, though, we may only want portions of a model to be utilized in a display and we may not want to reuse this code across requests. If the granularity of the data access components necessitate multiple calls to retrieve the data, then the Mediator-View architecture may be better suited to handle this type of situation, since the server page will make business calls on the beans as necessary.

Our example will allow an authenticated user to examine his or her previously stored guesses. One could imagine this feature being expanded to allow modification of the previously stored data, as well.

The HTML for the user interface consists of a couple input fields for the user to enter their id and password for authentication purposes. The `dispatchto` hidden field has been modified appropriately, and another hidden field, a flag called `delegatetobean`, has been added, and signals to the Servlet that we want to use our worker bean as the initial dispatch point in this scenario. It allows us to reuse the Servlet that we have been utilizing throughout our discussion with minor modifications. The screen shot below shows this HTML page:

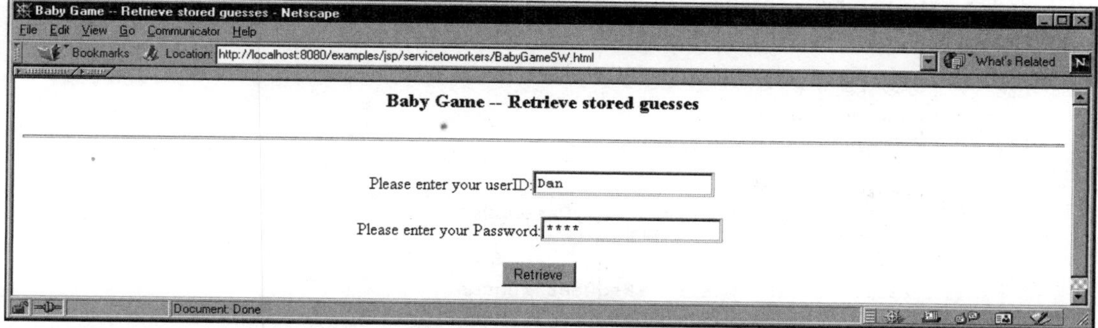

The HTML source for this page, `<jswdk-root>/examples/jsp/servicetoworkers/babygameSW.html`, is as follows:

```
<!-- babygameSW.html -->
<html>
<head>
<title>Baby Game -- Retrieve stored guesses</title>
</head>
<body bgcolor="#FFFFFF">
<form method="post" action="/examples/servlet/BabyGameServlet" name="">
<center>
<h3>
Baby Game -- Retrieve stored guesses</h3></center>

<center>
<hr>
<br>
```

```
Please enter your userID:<input type="text" name="guesser"><br><br>Please enter
your Password:<input type="password" name="password">
<br><br>
<input type=hidden name="dispatchto" value="/jsp/servicetoworkers/BabyGameSW.jsp">
<input type=hidden name="delegatetobean" value="true">

<input type=submit value="Retrieve">

</form>
</body>
</html>
```

The Servlet has been modified to include a conditional check for the `delegatetobean` flag. If it is set, then the Servlet uses the worker bean as the initial delegation point. In previous examples, the Servlet uses the JSP as the initial delegation point.

Adding this conditional, which will evaluate to `true` in this Service to Workers example only, allows us to reuse similar Servlet code throughout our discussion; the Servlet source is shown below. After successfully authenticating the user, the Servlet delegates to the worker bean (`BabyGameWorkerSW`), instructing it to load previously stored guesses based on the user's id. The worker bean is set as an attribute of the request object with the same bean id that is used in the presentation JSP (an id value of `"SWworker"`). This allows the JSP to share this previously instantiated and initialized bean, instead of creating a new one. In effect, we have passed the bean as an argument to the JSP.

The code for the Servlet is as follows, and is kept in `<jswdk-root>/examples/WEB-INF/servlets/BabyGameServlet.java`:

```
import javax.servlet.*;
import javax.servlet.http.*;
import java.io.*;

import examples.auth.*;
import examples.servicetoworker.BabyGameWorkerSW;

public class BabyGameServlet extends HttpServlet {
  public void doGet(HttpServletRequest request,
                    HttpServletResponse response) {
    processRequest(request, response);
  }

  public void doPost(HttpServletRequest request,
                     HttpServletResponse response) {
    processRequest(request, response);
  }

  protected void processRequest(HttpServletRequest request,
                                HttpServletResponse response) {
    try {
      String guesser = request.getParameter("guesser");
      String password = request.getParameter("password");

      // Authenticate each request
```

```
        Authenticator auth =
          AuthenticatorFactory.create(AuthenticatorFactory.SIMPLE);
        AuthContext authContext =
          AuthenticatorFactory
            .createContext(AuthenticatorFactory.SIMPLE);
        authContext.addValue("guesser", guesser);
        authContext.addValue("password", password);

        auth.init(authContext);

        if (auth.authenticate()) {
          String dispatchto = request.getParameter("dispatchto");
          String delegateToBean =
            request.getParameter("delegatetobean");

          // Delegate to worker bean
          if (delegateToBean != null) {
            BabyGameWorkerSW worker = new BabyGameWorkerSW();
            worker.load(guesser);
            request.setAttribute("SWworker", worker);
          }

          // In order to reuse this Servlet for multiple examples, we pass
          // as a request parameter the resource name to which we dispatch
          // our request
          getServletConfig().getServletContext()
            .getRequestDispatcher(dispatchto)
              .forward(request, response);
        } else {
          PrintWriter outy = response.getWriter();
          outy.println("Unable to authenticate, please try again.");
        }
      } catch (Exception ex) {
        ex.printStackTrace();
      }
    }
  }
```

In our earlier examples, we collected and stored a user's guesses to a text file. Now the example evolves such that the worker bean called `examples.servicetoworker.BabyGameWorkerSW` adds a method that loads our previously stored guesses from the store, based on an authenticated user's id. The method is defined as follows:

```
  public void load(String id) {
    try {
      Store storer = StoreFactory.createStore(StoreFactory.SIMPLE);
      Properties props = (Properties) storer.load(id);
      setProperties(props);
    } catch (StoreException e) {
      e.printStackTrace();
    }
  }
```

Additionally, the worker bean has a method that is included so that our example may make use of JSP error processing. The method is invoked as a guard clause from within the JSP in order to validate the accuracy of the data before it is presented to the user. The method throws an exception if the bean's state is incomplete, and is defined as follows:

```
public void validationGuard() throws Throwable {
  if (getGender() == null) {
    throw new Throwable("Error populating guess data.");
  }
}
```

The JSP, `<jswdk-root>/examples/jsp/servicetoworkers/BabyGameSW.jsp`, is shown below. Notice that it includes an explicit reference to an error page:

```
<HTML>
<HEAD><TITLE>Baby Game - Your Guesses</TITLE></HEAD>
<BODY bgcolor=FFFFFF>
<%@ page language="java" errorPage="errorPageSW.jsp" buffer="8k" %>
```

If an uncaught exception occurs within a JSP, the flow of control immediately transfers to the referenced error page, in this case `errorPageSW.jsp`. As mentioned, the JSP includes a guard clause at the beginning, which checks for valid data. If valid data does not exist, then the worker bean will throw an exception, which will present the error page to the user, notifying him or her of the problem. In our example, if the client enters an id and password for a valid user who has not previously stored any guesses, then the bean state will be invalid and the bean's `validationGuard()` method will indeed throw an exception. The error page display could easily be made as informative as necessary for the user:

```
<jsp:useBean id="SWworker" class="examples.servicetoworker.BabyGameWorkerSW"
scope="request" />
```

Notice also that the JSP has the same bean id that the Servlet previously included in its `setAttribute()` invocation. Thus, the JSP will reuse the existing bean, which was created in the Servlet:

```
<jsp:setProperty name="SWworker" property="*" />

<% SWworker.validationGuard(); %>

<br>
<jsp:getProperty name="SWworker" property="guesser" />, here are your previously
stored choices:<br>
<table BORDER COLS=5 WIDTH="75%" >
<caption></caption>
<tr>
<td> <jsp:getProperty name="SWworker" property="gender" />
</td>
<td>
<jsp:getProperty name="SWworker" property="pounds" />  lbs <jsp:getProperty
name="SWworker" property="ounces" />  oz
</td>
<td>
```

```
<jsp:getProperty name="SWworker" property="month" />  <jsp:getProperty
name="SWworker" property="day" />
</td>
<td>
<jsp:getProperty name="SWworker" property="length" />  inches
</td>
</tr>
</table>

<br>

</BODY>
</HTML>
```

The full elements of the 'Service To Workers' example are:

- The HTML UI, which POSTs the request to the Servlet: `<jswdk-root>/examples/jsp/servicetoworkers/babygameSW.html`
- The Servlet, which dispatches to the JSP: `<jswdk-root>/examples/WEB-INF/servlets/BabyGameServlet`
- The JSP: `<jswdk-root>/examples/jsp/servicetoworkers/BabyGameSW.jsp`
- The ErrorPage: `<jswdk-root>/examples/jsp/servicetoworkers/errorpageSW.jsp`
- The worker bean: `examples.servicetoworker.BabyGameWorkerSW`
- The supporting code, which is reused from a previous example: `examples.mediatorview.StoreFactory`, `examples.mediatorview.Store`, `examples.mediatorview.SimpleStore`, `examples.mediatorview.StoreException`, `examples.auth.AuthenticatorFactory`, `examples.auth.Authenticator`, `examples.auth.SimpleAuthenticator`, `examples.auth.AuthContext`, and `examples.auth.SimpleAuthContext`

Servlets versus JSPs

JSPs can be used for most purposes, but there are some scenarios where Servlets are more appropriate. As well as components such as the 'mediator' Servlets used earlier in this chapter, Servlets are well suited for handling binary data dynamically (for example, uploading files or creating dynamic images), since they need not contain any display logic.

Consider the following: a JSP needs to display a banner image based on who is referring the user to the site. This can be done by using the IMG tag like this:

```
<%@ page import="com.ibm.jspredbook.*;" errorPage="error.jsp" %>
<body bgcolor="#FFFFFF">
<!--the referer header is used to trap the url the user is coming from -->
<IMG SRC="/servlets/ImgServlet?from=<%=request.getHeader("Referer")%>">
</body>
</html>
```

The Servlet referenced in the `IMG` tag, `ImgServlet`, is coded as:

```
package com.ibm.projsp;

import javax.servlet.*;
import javax.servlet.http.*;
import java.util.*;
import java.io.*;

public class ImageServlet extends HttpServlet {
  private String docHome = ".";

  public void service(HttpServletRequest request,
                      HttpServletResponse response)
          throws ServletException, IOException {

    HttpSession session = request.getSession(true);
    ServletConfig config = getServletConfig();
    ServletContext application = config.getServletContext();
    File file = findFile(request, response);
    if (file == null) {
      return;
    } else {
      response.setContentType(application.getMimeType(file.getName()));
      response.setContentLength((int) file.length());
      sendFile(file, response);
    }

  }


  protected File findFile(HttpServletRequest request,
                          HttpServletResponse response) throws IOException {

    // We should store a flow-to-image mapping and return the appropriate
    // File, without any platform-specific paths. Right now we will just
    // return a GIF file.
    File file = new File("c://weblogic//images/myimage.gif");
    return file;
  }

  protected void sendFile(File file, HttpServletResponse response)
          throws IOException {
    int c = 0;
    FileInputStream fileinputstream = null;
    try {
      ServletOutputStream servletoutputstream =
        response.getOutputStream();
      fileinputstream = new FileInputStream(file);

      while ((c = fileinputstream.read()) != -1) {
        servletoutputstream.write(c);
      }
```

```
servletoutputstream.flush();
      }
      finally {
        if (fileinputstream != null) {
          fileinputstream.close();
        }
      }
    }

  }
```

This image can be cached in memory and updated every minute or so as needed. Keeping the data in memory and using a servlet can save time and improve performance by not requiring access to the file system every time a request is made.

Summary

We have examined how we architect systems using JSPs, Servlets, and JavaBeans, discussed benefits and limitations of various approaches and actually seen an example that evolves to satisfy the constraints of the various architectures.

We discussed a variety of architectural patterns, each of which we categorized as either a Page-Centric or Dispatcher type of architecture. Page-Centric architectures have a JSP handling the request directly, while Dispatcher architectures include a Servlet that handles the request and delegates to a JSP.

The architectural patterns we examined are:

- Page-View (Page-Centric)
- Page-View with Bean (Page-Centric)
- Mediator-View (Dispatcher)
- Mediator-Composite View (Dispatcher)
- Service-to-Workers (Dispatcher)

As we continue to investigate new ways to build our systems, we will continue to realize new architectural patterns. Additionally, the specifications for these technologies continue to be refined and improved in ways that will potentially demand modifications to current architectural patterns and the realization of additional ones. The ability (in the post-1.0 JSP specifications) to factor code and implementation details into a Custom Tag that might be used in place of a JavaBean is simply one example. The integration of these technologies more closely with XML and XSLT is another.

This is certainly an exciting and important area of technology that continues to change at a rapid pace. Hopefully, this information will help you better understand the current state of affairs with respect to JSP architectures, and thus feel better positioned to follow the evolution of these architectural issues in the future.

J2EE
JSP

13

Case Study: A Web Interface for "The Mutual Fund Company"

Introduction

The purpose of this case study is to look at the interaction of Java Server Pages Technology (JSP) with the Java Servlet API (Servlets). This chapter demonstrates how to use both JSPs and Servlets, using a fictional case study of how to take an existing legacy application and deploy it to the web using Java Server Pages and Java Servlets. The case study is based on the JSP 1.1 and Servlet 2.2 specifications.

Before JSPs, the Java Developer would typically prototype the User Interface using HTML then write the HTML out to the response object using a `PrintWriter` object. The User Interface would be created using a text editor or an HTML visual editor. An example is given below of `HelloWorldServlet.html`. This is the HTML file that would be created to prototype the User Interface.

```
<!DOCTYPE HTML PUBLIC "-//W3C//DTD HTML 4.0 Transitional//EN">
<html>
<head><title>HelloWorldServlet</title></head>
<body>
<table align="center" cellspacing="2" cellpadding="2" border="0">
<tr><td> </td></tr>
<tr><td><h1>Hello World Servlet</h1></td></tr>
</table>
</body>
</html>
```

Once the static web page was created, the developer would input the HTML code a Java Servlet class that would output the HTML to the browser. Below is an example of a servlet class, `HelloWorldServlet.java`, which would be used to generate the User Interface that was prototyped in the `HelloWorldServlet.html` page.

```
import javax.servlet.*;
import javax.servlet.http.*;
import java.io.*;

/**
 * Hello World Servlet
 */
public class HelloWorldServlet extends HttpServlet {

  public void service(HttpServletRequest req, HttpServletResponse res)
      throws IOException
  {
    // Must set the content type first
    res.setContentType("text/html");
    // Now we can obtain a PrintWriter
    PrintWriter out = res.getWriter();
    out.println("<!DOCTYPE HTML PUBLIC \"-//W3C//DTD HTML 4.0
Transitional//EN\">\n");
    out.println("<html>\n");
    out.println("<head><title>Hello World!</title></head>\n");
    out.println("<body>\n");
    out.println("<table align=\"center\" cellspacing=\"2\" cellpadding=\"2\"
border=\"0\">");
    out.println("<tr><td> </td></tr>\n");
    out.println("<tr><td><h1>Hello World Servlet</h1></td></tr>");
    out.println("</table>\n");
    out.println("</body>\n");
    out.println("</html>\n");
  }
}
```

The HTML, as in this example, would need to include escape characters ('\') around doubled quoted items in the HTML string. This method of transferring the HTML code into Java statements was and is a tedious task. If the HTML needed updating, the process of prototyping and inserting the new HTML into the Servlet would need to occur again. Servlet applications that consisted of several HTML pages increase the annoyance of the HTML to servlet transfer process. Developers, who had to do these tasks often, probably devised better ways. One common solution was to write a script to read the HTML file and generate the `println()` statements. Another method may have been to develop a Java Servlet that would read the HTML file in and perform some sort of tag substitution for the dynamic data. The tedious process of putting the HTML code into Servlet code raised the awareness of the need for a better way to separate the HTML code from the Java objects. Sun Microsystems responded by developing Java Server Pages. Java Server Pages provide an easier means of generating dynamic HTML pages with back-end data provided by server side solutions.

The concept of Java Server Pages is to isolate the presentation of data from the processing of the data on the server. This provides the opportunity to code the user interface in HTML with brief segments of embedded Java that will run on the server and access server-side data sources. Though this is simple in concept it does present a new problem. How do you choose where to use Java Server Pages and where to use Java Servlets? The following case study illustrates one way to develop a solution to a problem that is often encountered when developing HTML interfaces with Java Server Pages and Java Servlets.

Although Java Server Pages supports two "mark up" languages (HTML and XML) and provides the ability to create your own tag extensions to facilitate the generation of the user interface, this case study focuses only on HTML using JSP 1.1. The context of the case study is a company that would like to take an existing application and put it on the Internet. This case study will provide a solution to this frequently undertaken task. To make the case study flow, a fictional company "The Mutual Fund Company," abbreviated MFC, is used. (This is not to be confused with the Microsoft development library, Microsoft Foundation Classes.) The process will be broken down into component parts to create a better understanding of the issues involved in creating a web application using Servlets and JSPs. The case study will illustrate the process that MFC goes through in achieving its goal.

The topics covered in this chapter are as follows:

- Definition of Business Problem
- Description of Task
- Technology Selection
- Functional User Interface Design
- Package Definition
- Object Design
- Sequence Diagrams
- Implementation
- Setup of the Tomcat JSP/Servlet Engine for case study.
- Lessons Learned

Outline of Case Study

The case study is arranged in a way that will represent a typical development approach to creating a web application using Servlets and JSPs. The case study is used to present a common task, "moving a legacy application to the web", and illustrate where to use JSPs and where to use Servlets. The case study also presents examples using the JSP API and the Servlet API to create a web application.

Definition of the Business Problem

The Mutual Fund Company (MFC) has an existing infrastructure that manages customer accounts with the company. Its system uses a database for storing this information. MFC has received numerous requests from customers who want to view their account information over the Web. MFC sees this as an opportunity, not only to provide Internet access to customer accounts, but also as something that could grow into online trading and customer maintenance of their own accounts. MFC has a small web technology group that will be tasked with prototyping various Internet solutions to provide online access to customer information. MFC would like to use an iterative development approach to provide one feature for the online access and ask its customers for feedback. After the development of the first feature, MFC will ask the users of the feature for suggestions on other options they would like to see in future iterations.

The first feature that MFC has decided to demonstrate is "Viewing a Customer Account Summary". The requirements for viewing the account summary are as follows:

- Collect user information via a login process and compare that information with account data to ensure that online customers are who they say they are. MFC knows that there are other technologies that can provide user authentication, but it is not sure about the demand for an online account access product. The company has decided not to implement user certificates at this point. It wants to query the users of the online system to assist in determining how much effort the customer is willing to exert to use the new online system.
- Provide rapid access to customer account summaries.
- Utilize a technology that does not require the customer to download software. The online account access seems best suited to a browser approach. After polling its computer savvy customers MFC has decided to support the latest versions of popular browsers: Netscape 4.x and Internet Explorer 4.x and 5.x. The engineers will need to avoid using XML in the browser since browser support for XML is limited to Internet Explorer 5.x.

Description of the Task

The technology group has discovered that some customers have such large accounts that the backend processing can take up to 10 to 20 seconds to retrieve account information. Their suggestion to hide this delay from the customer is to use a "two-step user login/verification". The first step will be to collect the information needed to retrieve the account information and to launch an asynchronous request for the account information. The second step will be to collect customer data to be compared against the retrieved account information. This will provide extra time to retrieve the account information. This "two-step user login/verification" approach provides an additional layer of user authentication based on customer information that is only obtainable from a customer statement. The ability to obtain this information will be limited to the HTTP request from the customer and the HTTP response from the company's web server. The deployed application will implement an encrypted HTTP connection between the customer's browser and the web server. This will insure protection of the sensitive information passed between the customer's computer and the company's web server.

A social security number is needed to access the account summary for the customer. The social security number will be a US format social security number.

The requirement to enter this type of sensitive information is to illustrate unique information that the user will enter to retrieve the account record from server side data source. This is used only within the case study and is not recommended for web applications due to potential legal issues. There are better choices for unique id's into a system, but these are application dependent. The social security number is only used as an example and not recommended for a commercial web application.

The account summary includes customer information, company information, balance information, and investment summaries. The first step of the login/verification procedure will collect the social security number of the user. The second step will collect the password and other account information known to the user, thereby preventing anyone other than the customer who happens to know the customer's social security number. The technology group has decided to do the first iteration without any additional security. A secure sockets layer will be implemented later, to ensure secure access to the system.

MFC has decided to allow customers to choose a password to access the system. Realistically, MFC understands that Internet passwords are often easy to crack so it has insisted on the collection of additional information to verify the user. This information has been identified as the customer's account number, zip code, and email address.

Technology Selection

The technology group has decided to use the Java Server Pages technology combined with Java Servlets to create the web application. The choice of Java Server Pages and Java Servlets provides the greatest portability for the application. The Java technologies are built upon the Java Virtual Machine and they can be used in conjunction with most popular web servers that support the JSP and Servlet API or that support a "plug-in" that provides this support. The Java Developer Connection lists a number of products that support the JavaServer Pages technology and the Java Servlet API. The location of this list is http://java.sun.com/products/jsp/industry.html.

Given the portability of Java, the technology group can develop the prototype of the web application on the Microsoft Windows platform with minimal concern about the deployment platform. Once the prototype is complete the group will determine the hardware architecture and the operating system to ensure a robust application. The only restriction is that the operating system supports the latest production Java Virtual Machine.

The technology group has decided to use the Tomcat JSP/Servlet engine for development of the first internal iteration of the project. If this iteration is successful, they will purchase a commercial application server to host the JSP/Servlet application. The technology group understands that the leading web application servers support transaction processing and this will be needed later if the web application it is to perform 'online trading'.

Tomcat is part of the Jakarta Project by the Apache Software Foundation, http://jakarta.apache.org. The goal of Jakarta is to provide commercial-quality server solutions based on the Java Platform. The solutions are developed in an open and cooperative fashion. Sun Microsystems, on October 19, 1999 released their latest versions of JSP and Servlets source code to Apache to be developed and released under the Apache development process as the official JSP1.1/Servlets 2.2 reference implementation. This reference implementation, code-named Tomcat, will be the only reference implementation hereafter.

Functional User Interface Design

The technology group has contracted with a web interface design firm to build the web presence. The creative group will develop the interface templates for the application using conventional HTML pages. The technology group adds JSP tags to these pages and they will become the JavaServer Pages used in the web application.

While waiting on the interface design firm to deliver the "look and feel", the technology group has created two prototype screens that will be used in accessing the Web application. These screens will present the two-step login/verification process. The group has also produced an account summary page for displaying the customer account information.

loginStep1.html

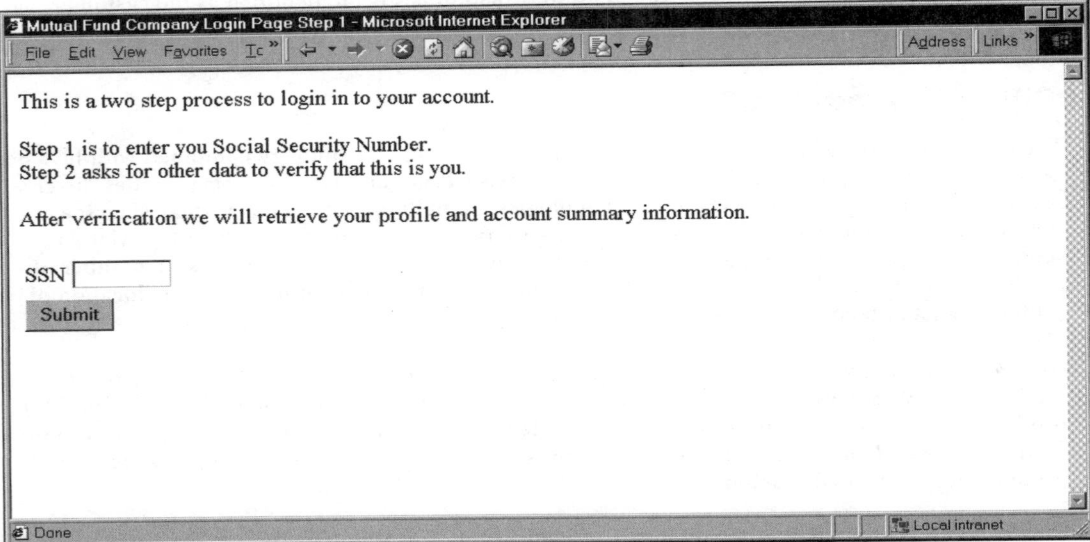

loginStep2.html

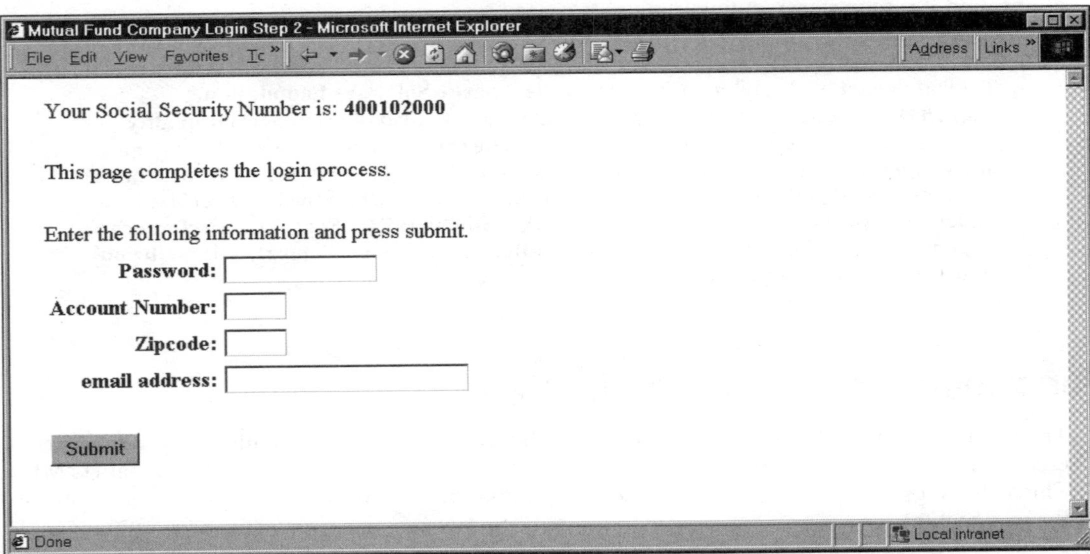

displayAccountSummary.html

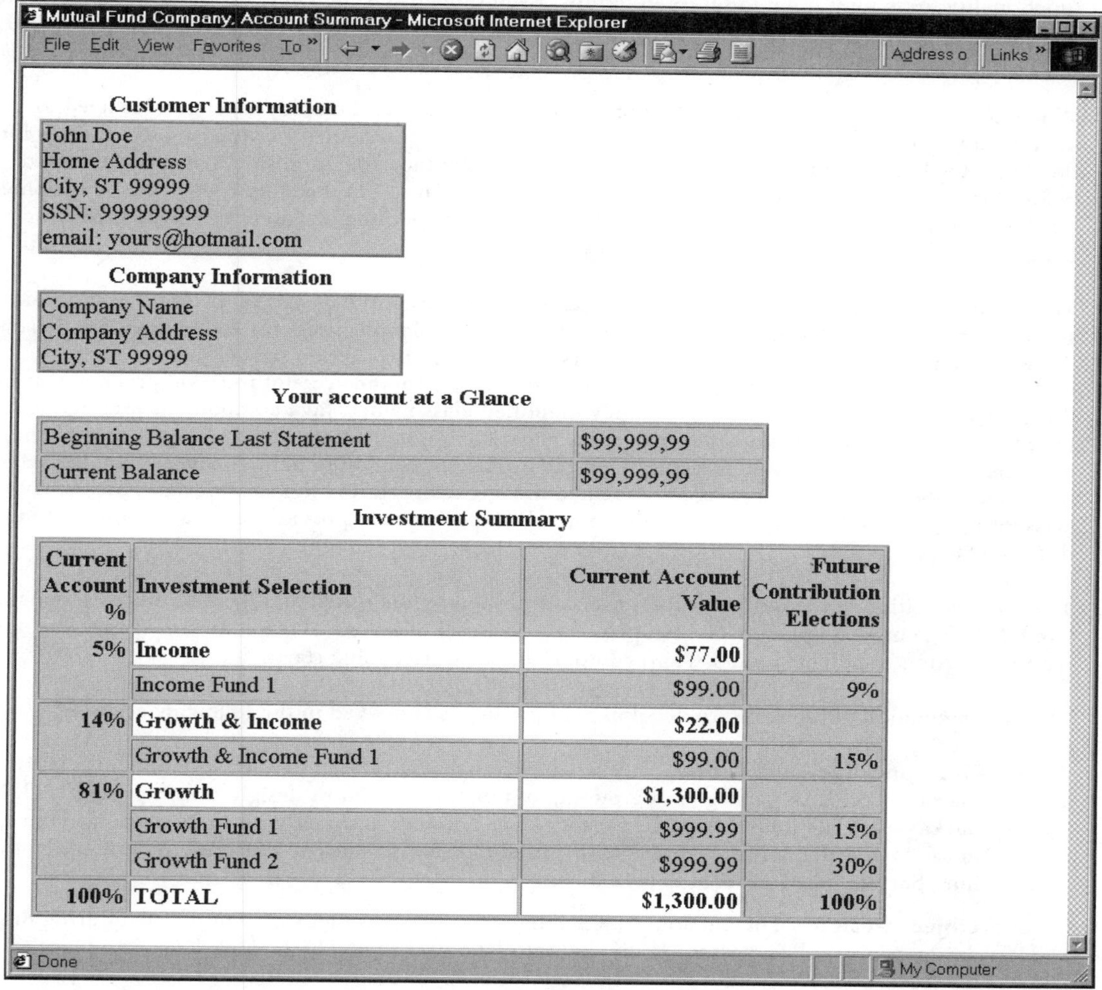

Though the screens are basic, they are functional and will provide the technology group with JSP tags and logic that will be the basis of the JSP files. They can be enhanced later to add a more creative touch, by adding background images, images for submit buttons, frames etc. The technology group will integrate the HTML templates from the web design interface firm prior to deploying the application.

The technology group, after the completion of the prototype interface screens, needs to think about the design of the web application. The engineers in the technology group want to use some of the latest techniques in designing the web application. They have decided that before they start writing code they will design the software architecture. Their development approach will use parts of the Unified Modeling Language as their Object Modeling language. This choice was based on the current trends in the software development community and the use of Java an object oriented programming language.

The engineers in the technology group have chosen to use an "iterative software development" model. In this model, features of the collective application will be developed as iterations. The first iteration will be the construction of the account retrieval process. This will establish categorization of functionality to be built upon in future iterations. Even though the engineers are using HTML prototype screens, their code will be near production quality. Their code will then be included with the HTML templates that represent the "look and feel of the application" and complete the first iteration.

When developing software, independent of the development model employed, engineers need to document the design. The documentation is an ongoing effort in the design process and provides for flexibility to change the design without changing code. The more of the design that is documented before the code is written the easier it is to change functionality. This actually speeds the development effort rather than slowing in down. It is a little slow in the beginning but saves time when the process is completed.

The following sections present the UML diagrams that represent the design of the first iteration of the software development cycle. The sequence of creating the following sections was actually a series of design sessions on a white board. The engineers in the technology group started with a written definition of the system, they constructed sequence diagrams of the account retrieval process. During the generation of the sequence diagrams they identified class names, Java components (Servlet, JSP, or Java Beans), and the interactions between these classes. After construction of the sequence diagrams, the engineers invited "Subject Matter Experts" on the legacy application to help uncover possible design flaws. Once the sequence diagrams were created the engineers started the class design process. After the class design process the design was grouped into UML packages to provide easy navigation within the documentation.

The documentation of the design process is accomplished by the use of an object modeling language like UML. The modeling language then presents a pictorial overview of the software without the need to read code. After the object model is agreed upon the software coding starts.

The documentation of the software development process is conveyed in the following sections:

- **UML package Definition** – This section arranges the prototype's functionality into UML packages. A UML package is a grouping of functionality; most design tools represent a UML package as a file folder. A UML package does not always correspond to the package concept in the Java programming language. It is used in the case study to illustrate the grouping of JSP files, Servlets, and server side Java Beans.
- **Object Design** – This section presents the class diagrams that were constructed during the design process. The classes are divided into Java packages. The Java packages are placed in the UML packages within the design tool for easy navigation. In the case study, the Java packages are related to the UML packages; however, this is not always the case.
- **Sequence Diagrams** – This section presents the interaction of the Objects and communicates data flow to the browser.

UML Package Definition

The project was broken up into distinct UML packages. These packages represent functionality and in our case study do not correspond to Java packages. The packages are shown below:

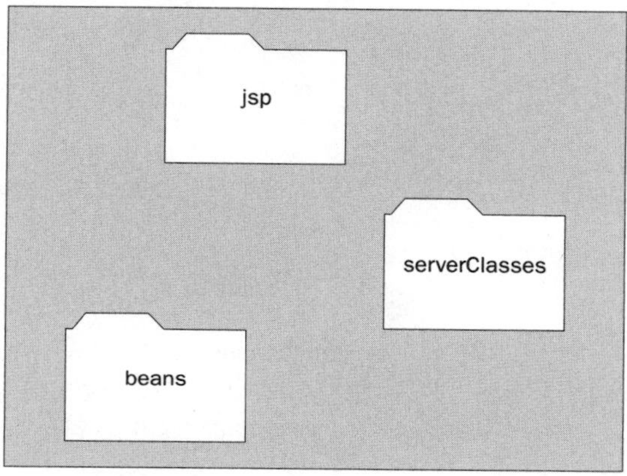

The `jsp` package will contain all the JSP files used in the application. The JSPs are grouped into three categories:

- display
- non-display intermediate processing
- errors

The display JSPs are `loginStep1.jsp`, `loginStep2.jsp`, `processingDelay.jsp`, and `displayAccountSummary.jsp`. The `processingDelay.jsp` screen is used to display something to the while the account information is being retrieved. This technique is useful when there is a noticeable delay in server side processing. This will be discussed later. The non-display intermediate processing JSPs are: `validateSSN.jsp` and `checkResponse.jsp`. The error JSPs are: `errorPage.jsp`, and `processingError.jsp`.

The `beans` package will contain the `CustomerInfoBean`. The bean is stored in the `HttpSession` and is used to pass data between the JSPs and the servlet. The use of the `HttpSession` object within the application requires that the client browser accept cookies. This is a relatively acceptable requirement in web application design. However, there are a small percentage of users that still will not accept cookies. This is an important design decision. If the web application cannot use cookies the bean can be redesigned to work in the application scope or the request scope. This will be discussed later when we look at the implementation of the bean in the JSP classes. For more information on the `HttpSession` and JSPs, see Chapter 5.

The serverClasses package above will contain two UML packages servlets and dataClasses. The data classes are used to transport information from the servlets to the JSP pages. These packages are shown below:

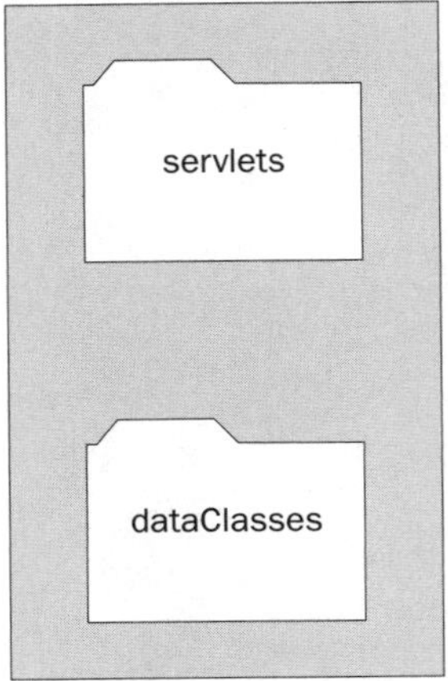

The servlets package will contain the servlets used in the application and the dataClasses package will contain the classes that are used to display data to the user through a JavaServer Page.

The UML packages separate out the servlets used to access the server side data source, the data transport classes, and the presentation JSP classes. The technology group set a lofty goal to limit Java code in the JSP pages to presentation of the HTML. The group has made another important design decision to use the HttpSession to pass data with both the CustomerInfoBean and the dataClasses will assist in this task by encapsulating the business rules and data manipulation. The implication to the users of the application is that they must accept cookies. There are other ways to design your web application without this requirement, but it does make implementation a little harder. Using the HttpSession will provide easier access to response data when presenting the customer profile information through the HTML interface. In their architecture, the technology group has chosen to encapsulate and aggregate the customer account information. (See the dataClasses object model ahead.)

Object Design

The technology group, through a series of meetings, designed the following classes for each of the packages. The following sections will show the class diagrams for each Java package. The location of the Java packages in Tomcat will be discussed in the Implementation section.

Beans package: "CustomerInfoBean" class.

The first step in the object design was to define the bean that will store the data from the loginStep1.jsp and the loginStep2.jsp. The loginStep1.html and the loginStep2.html files that produce the screens you saw previously are converted to the JSP pages by the addition of JSP tags. The class diagram for the CustomerInfoBean is shown below:

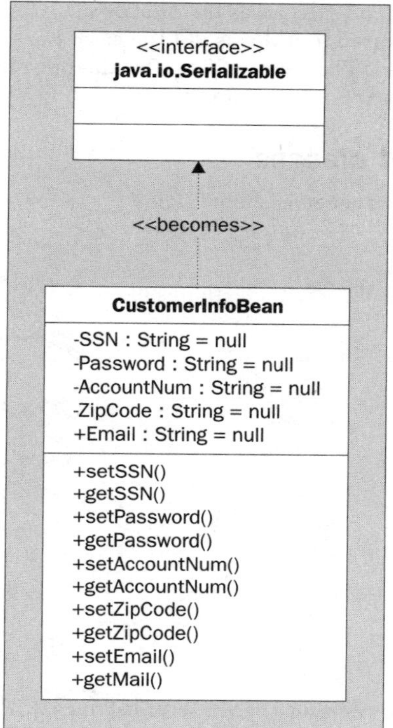

Since the `CustomerInfoBean` class is used as a JavaBean it must comply with the JavaBean specification. Complying with the JavaBean specification means the following:

- the Bean class must have a constructor that takes no arguments
- it must contain a `setAttributeName()` method for each attribute `attributeName` declared in the class
- it must contain a `getAttributeName()` method for each attribute `attributeName` declared in the class
- it must implement java.io.Serializable.

For example, see the example JavaBean `BeanClass.java` below:

```
public class BeanClass implments java.io.Serializable {

  private String myAttribute;

  public void setMyAttribute(String inAttribute) {
    myAttribute = inAttribute;
  }

  public String getMyAttribute() {
    return myAttribute;
  }

}
```

When you view the JSP source code that uses the CustomerInfoBean class you will find that some of the methods may appear to not be used, but this is not the case. For example, the getSsn() method in the loginStep1.jsp is used by the JSP to set the SSN after the page has been submitted. This is accomplished by the <jsp:setProperty> action tag.

JSP Package: JSP servlet classes

The class diagram for the jsp package is shown below:

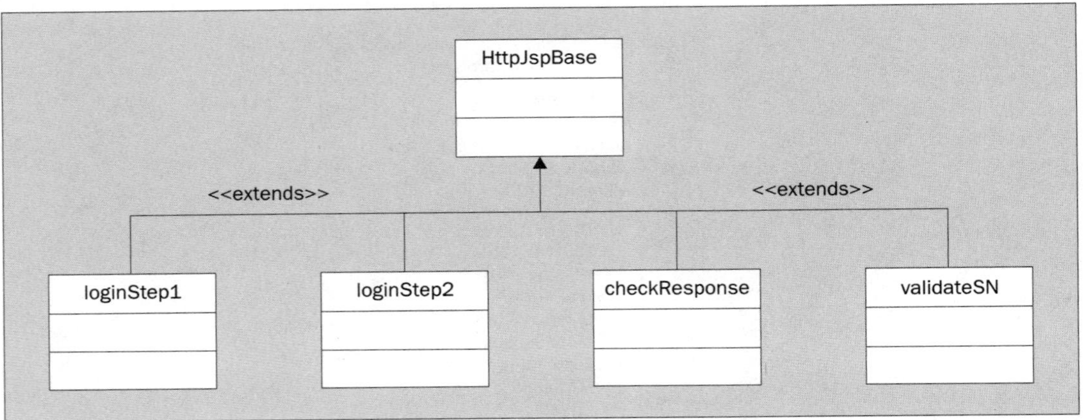

The jsp files are created by combining HTML with JSP tags, JSP scriptlets, and script expressions. The object diagram reflects inheritance in the code that is generated by the JSP compiler. Even though the developer deals with the classes as a file, Tomcat compiles them into servlets. The JSP compiler will read in and parse the JSP file and generate a servlet that extends the HttpJspBase class. The JSP tags and scriptlets will result in Java code that interacts with the traditional servlet classes HttpServletRequest and HttpServletResponse. In addition to these classes, the generated servlet will interact with the HttpJspBase class to obtain the needed information for processing the call to the _jspService() method. JSPs are not required to generate output to a browser as the checkResponse.jsp and validateSSN.jsp files illustrate. Please see chapters 2 and 3 for more information on the generated servlets from the JSP compiler.

Server Classes package

The serverClasses package contains the servlets in the application and a package for the dataClasses.

The first class diagram is for the servlets and is shown below:

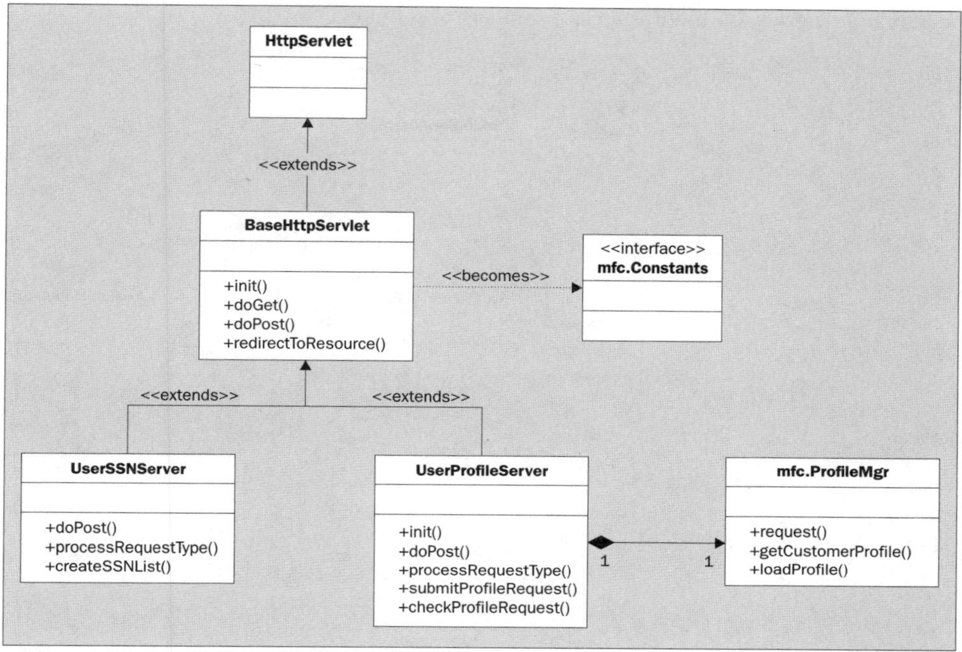

The `BaseHttpServlet` is an abstract class that encapsulates the functionality of the servlets in the application. The `doGet()` method is implemented to call the `doPost()` method of the derived servlet. The `redirectToResource()` method is a method common to the derived servlets. The `init()` method is a required implementation by derived servlets. The approach taken with the `BaseHttpServlet` is referred to as a "Template Method" design pattern, for more information on this, please refer to Design Patterns, Elements of reusable Object-Orientated Software from Addison Wesley. It describes a skeleton class that defines common abstract methods and common concrete method implementations some of which will probably overridden by subclasses, but defers implementation of other features to subclasses.

The `Constants` interface is used as a definition class for integers used throughout the application and the servlet classes implement it. The constants class is used to share the return values between the servlet and the JSPs. Thus, the JavaServer Pages will also import this class for making requests to the servlets.

The `ProfileMgr` is a class that encapsulates the profile access to the legacy system.

> **Note, in the case study, the `ProfileMgr` loads predefined customer profiles. In an actual implementation, this class would have database access to the customer profiles. The class would interface with the database to load the customer profiles and could potential store them if they were considered modifiable within the application. The actual implementation of this class will depend on the legacy application that stores the customer profiles.**

The next class diagram for the dataClasses is shown below:

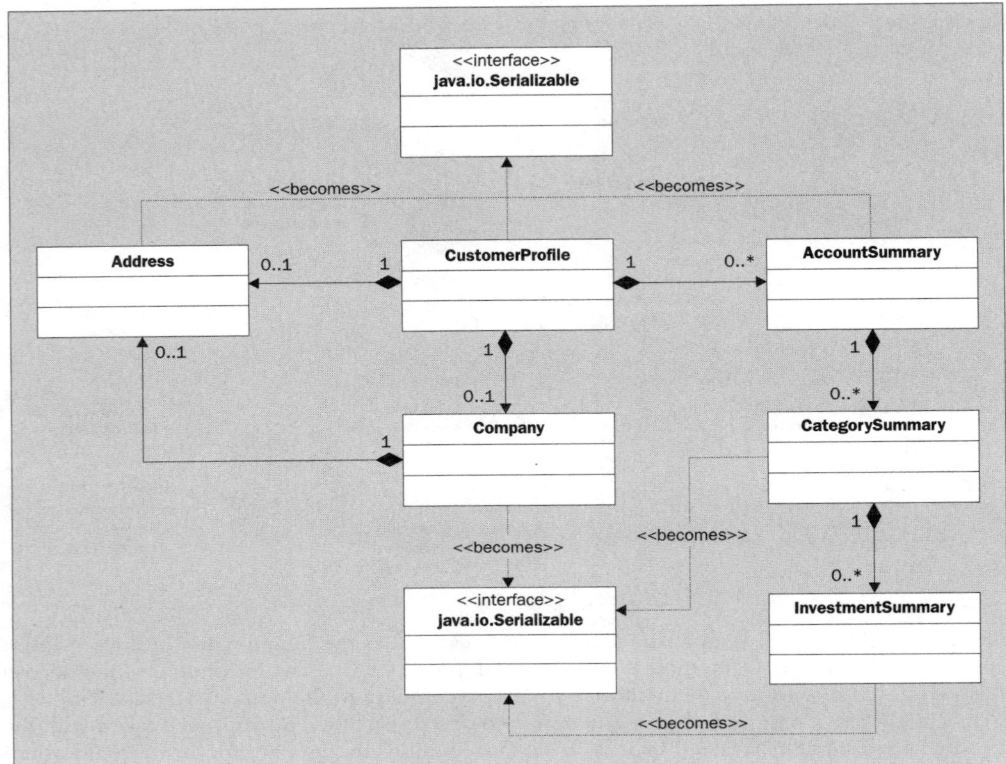

These objects illustrate the composition of the CustomerProfile that is returned by the ProfileMgr. They all implement Serializable, but this is not a requirement. This is done for two reasons.

1. It facilitates session persistence within an Application Server (e.g. BEA's WebLogic Application Server). Session persistence is needed if you deploy your application into a cluster. A cluster is a group of servers that work together to provide a more powerful and reliable application platform. It appears to its clients as a single server but is in fact a group of servers acting as one. Most commercial web applications (like the Mutual Fund Company's) use an application server that supports clustering. Clustering distributes the client requests among the cluster to provide scalability and high-availability of the web application.

2. It provides support for the use of distributed objects within the enterprise. Distributed objects are possible by using an object server and an object client. This can be implemented using RMI, CORBA, or Enterprise Java Beans. In an enterprise, there may be multiple systems that manage certain types of data. For example, if the customer accounts were managed by another application on a different operating system and implemented in another language we would need to communicate with this system to access and update the customer account information. Thus, the two systems would have to share the customer accounts. A nice choice of passing this information is to use distributed objects.

Sequence Diagrams

The sequence diagrams are broken into three sequences. The first two sequence diagrams illustrate the first step of the login process, and the last sequence diagram illustrates the second step of the login procedure.

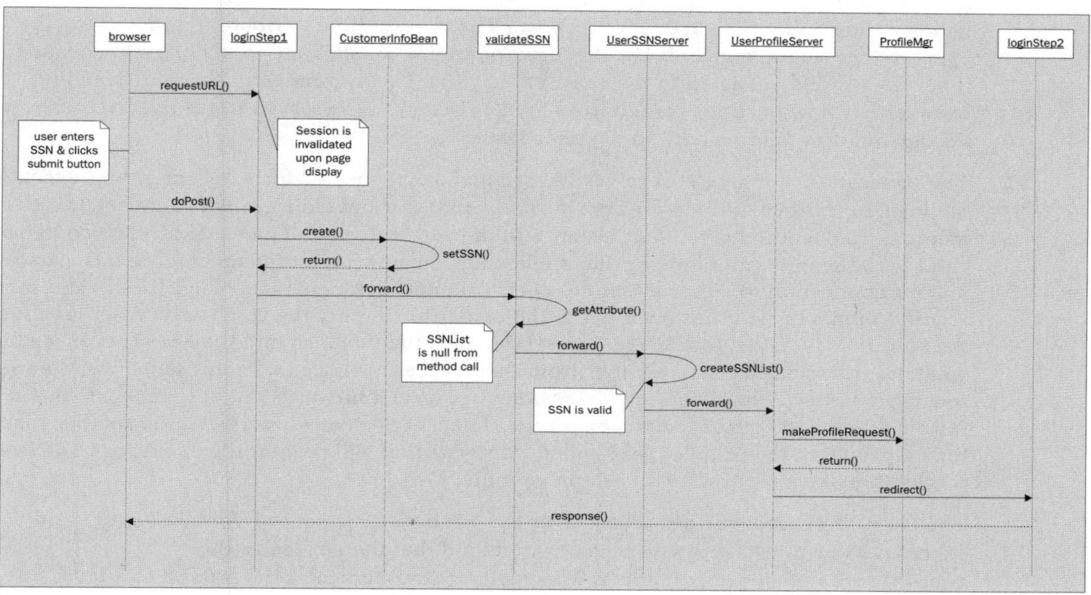

The explanation for the sequence diagram is as follows:

- The user enters the URL of `loginStep1.jsp` (http://localhost:8080/mutualFundCo/jsp/loginStep1.jsp) into the browser and presses enter. From this point forward, the JSP pages will be referred to as servlets since they are compiled into servlets before processing requests. In our context, the servlet for JSP page `loginStep1.jsp` will be called the `loginStep1.jsp` servlet. The non-descriptive name is used because a JSP/Servlet engines like Tomcat create generated names for the JSP servlets. For example, on the author's machine Tomcat created a servlet called: `_0002fjsp_0002floginStep_00031_0002ejsploginStep1_jsp_0.java` for the `loginStep1.jsp` page. These servlets will be located in the `work` directory under where you installed Tomcat.
- After entering the URL and pressing the **submit** button, the browser will send a `GET` request to the web server requesting the above URL.
- The `loginStep1.jsp` servlet creates an instance of the `CustomerInfoBean` class, invalidates any existing sessions that may be present in the request from the browser, and generates the `HttpServletResponse` message. The `HttpServletResponse` method generates the HTML page and sends it to the browser for display. (This, assuming the `loginStep1.jsp` has already been compiled into a servlet.)
- The user enters the SSN in the page and presses the **submit** button.
- The browser sends an `HttpRequest` to the web server to execute the `doPost()` method on the `loginStep1.jsp` servlet.

- The loginStep1.jsp servlet sets the social security number in the CustomerInfoBean and forwards the HttpRequest to the validateSSN.jsp servlet. The forward commands are only allowed if the servlet has not written anything to the client. If it has an IllegalStateException will be thrown.

- The validateSSN.jsp servlet adds a request-time attribute to the HttpRequest called reqType that will instruct the receiving servlet (UserSSNServer) to create an SSNList and validate the SSN in the CustomerInfoBean. The request-time attribute is added using the <jsp:param> action tag. This has the effect of adding an attribute to the original HttpRequest that is forwarded yet again to the UserSSNServer. The original HttpRequest from the browser has now been forwarded from the loginStep1.jsp servlet to the validateSSN.jsp servlet and now is forwarded to the UserSSNServer servlet.

- The UserSSNServer servlet receives the original HttpRequest for a doPost() and executes the logic to retrieve the request-time attribute reqType and calls its own createSSNList() method. This method creates an instance of the SSNList class. The SSNList class contains the valid social security numbers for the application. In an actual implementation, this class would make a connection to either a remote object or a data source and ask for a list of valid social security numbers. This has been left to the reader to simplify the case study. After creation of the SSNList class, the UserSSNServer servlet adds the SSNList into the ServletContext and validates the social security number from the CustomerInfoBean. In this sequence, the social security number is valid and the UserSSNServer servlet forwards the HttpRequest that it received to the UserProfileServer servlet. The UserSSNServer servlet adds another request-time attribute to the HttpRequest called reqType that will request the UserProfileServer servlet to make a request for a customer profile.

- The UserProfileServer servlet receives the original HttpRequest for a doPost() and executes its own makeProfileRequest() method that then executes the submitProfileRequest() method. This method communicates the request to a Java application that will make the asynchronous request. In our case, this is not truly an asynchronous request. After the request is made, the original HttpRequest is complete and the UserProfileServer servlet performs a redirect to the loginStep2.jsp servlet.

  The purpose of the asynchronous request is to allow time for the retrieval of the customer account information (called a profile in the application code). This implementation is beyond the scope of the case study. The purpose of the case study is to illustrate the use of JSPs and Servlets and exercise some of the more subtle functions of the JSP technology. Some possible implementations for the asynchronous request are as follows: Java Message Service, a threaded Java application, or a threaded remote request using RMI, CORBA, or EJB. There are no doubt other methods to launching the asynchronous request. The Java Message Service is interesting because it provides a non-proprietary message queue system for asynchronous messages.

The next sequence diagram is a special case of the previous one.

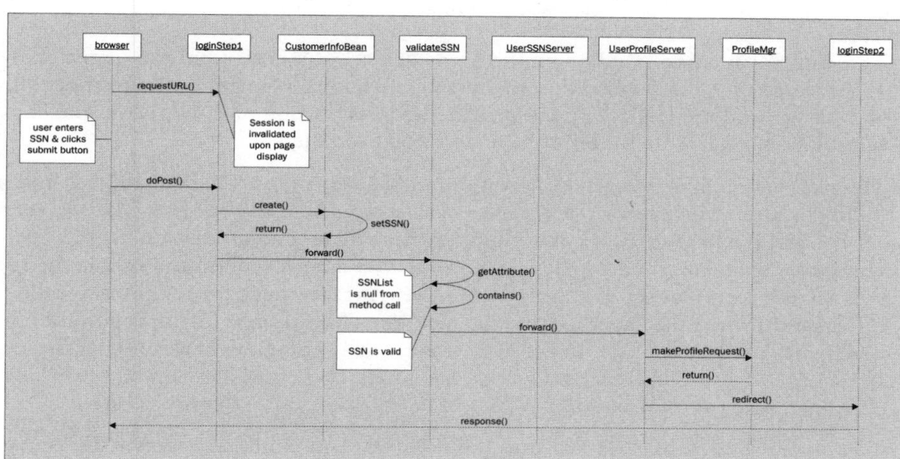

We will pick the explanation up from the point where the request is forwarded `validateSSN.jsp` servlet.

- The `loginStep1.jsp` servlet passes sets the social security number in the `CustomerInfoBean` and forwards the `HttpRequest` to the `validateSSN.jsp` servlet.
- The `validateSSN.jsp` servlet checks the `ServletContext` and finds the `SSNList` class. The servlet checks to see if the social security number is in the `SSNList`. In our sequence diagram, the social security number is valid and the original `HttpRequest`, is forwarded to the `UserProfileServer`. The rest of the sequence diagram is that same as the previous one.

This previous two sequence diagrams demonstrate how the JSP can obtain a reference to the global `ServletContext` and look for a class that is shared among all the servlets and JSPs within the web application. They demonstrated forwarding of the `HttpRequest` to other JSPs and servlets and finally they show the response using a `sendRedirect()`.

The next sequence diagram picks up with the `UserProfileServer` redirecting to the `loginStep2.jsp` servlet.

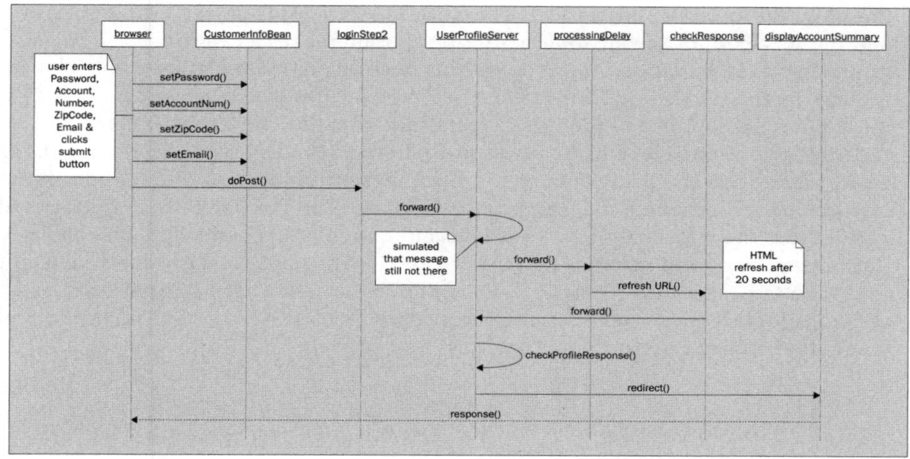

The next sequence diagram is a special case of the first sequence diagram. This is where the `SSNList` has already been created and is in the `ServletContext`.

- The `doGet()` method is called on the `loginStep2.jsp` servlet and the screen shown earlier for `loginStep2.html` is displayed in the browser. The browser has a new connection with the web server and the URL is updated in the address portion of the browser and shows: http://localhost:8080/mutualFundCo/jsp/LoginStep2.jsp.
- The user enters their password, account number, zipcode, and email address and presses the submit button. The browser sends a `doPost()` request to the `loginStep2.jsp` servlet. The servlet sets the password, account number, zipcode and email address on the `CustomerInfoBean`. The `loginStep2.jsp` servlet adds a request-time attribute `reqType` that will ask the recipient servlet, `UserProfileServlet`, to check for the profile (called account information when displayed). Then the new `HttpRequest` is forwarded to the `UserProfileServlet`. The `UserProfileServlet` is going to check to see if the `ProfileManager` has received a response to the asynchronous request to retrieve the customer account information.
- The `UserProfileServlet` executes the `doPost()` method, determines the `reqType`. At this point the `reqType` is a `CHECK_PROFILE_REQUEST`. If the `ProfileManager` interfaced with an asynchronous `ProfileManager` the profile would return a customer profile if it was available or would return a code that indicated it had not received a response yet. In our case study, the `UserProfileServlet` simply redirects the redirects to the `processingDealy.jsp` servlet.
- The `processingDelay.jsp` servlet displays an HTML message that says "Processing your response.". The request from the `loginStep2.jsp` servlet has completed. Now the `processingDealy.jsp` servlet needs to check to see if the asynchronous profile request has run to completion. We accomplish this by using an HTML Meta data directive to do a refresh. The Meta data entry in the JSP page is: `<META HTTP-EQUIV="Refresh" content="2; URL=checkResponse.jsp">`. The target of the refresh is the `checkResponse.jsp` servlet. The time for the refresh is 2 seconds, so the page waits two seconds and issues a refresh request. A refresh request is a client-pull request, so the `checkResponse.jsp` servlet will receive a `doGet()` request. The `checkResponse.jsp` servlet will add a request-time attribute before forwarding the request to the `UserProfileServlet`. The request-time attribute, `reqType` is for the `UserProfileServlet` serlvet to check the profile request again.
- The `UserProfileServlet` serlvet receives the `doGet()` request that was forwarded from the `checkResponse.jsp` servlet. The `doGet()` request is passed to the `doPost()` method and the servlet finds the attribute `reqType`. It then makes a call to the `checkProfileResponse()` method. This once again, is simulation code. This is the second request, so the `UserProfileServlet` serlvet executes the `getCustomerProfile()` method on the instance of the `ProfileManager` class. The `ProfileManager` class returns the `CustomerProfile` class that was introduced in the UML package `dataClasses`. The `CustomerProfile` class contains the Customer information and the `AccountSummary` instance. After retrieving the, `CustomerProfile` class the `UserProfileServlet` serlvet verifies that the information password, account number, zipcode, and email address is in the `CustomerInfoBean` matches that in the `CustomerProfile` class received from the `ProfileManager` class. When the validation is successful, the `UserProfileServlet` serlvet will place the received `CustomerProfile` class into the `HttpSession` and a redirect is sent to the `displayAccountSummary.jsp` servlet.

- The displayAccountSummary.jsp servlet receives a doGet() method call from the redirection of the UserProfileServlet serlvet. The displayAccountSummary.jsp servlet retrieves the CustomerProfile class from the HttpSession and interates over the collection of classes to display the previously shown displayAccountSummary.html page.

  This previous three sequence diagrams have explained the interactions involved in displaying a customer's account summary. The explanation under each sequence diagram was provided to help explain the sequence diagrams before viewing the source code. The next section will cover items in the implementation of the source code that are not covered in the previous discussions. Not all of the code will be presented in the next section, but it may be downloaded at the Wrox Press website: http://www.wrox.com

Implementation

This section presents the code described above in the UML packages, class diagrams, and sequence diagrams. It will be presented according to the flow in the first sequence diagram. On a general note, all of the code has developer type debug statements in it. The debug is left in the code for the benefit of the reader. The debug will appear on stdout and in any logs that capture stdout. In a production environment, you should use another technique. The log methods from the ServletContext are sufficient, but you may want to design something else that puts a time stamp, includes the name of the servlet or JSP, and has levels of debug.

The application consists of the following files:

- enterKeySubmit.js
- checkResonse.jsp
- displayAccountSummary.jsp
- errorPage.jsp
- getMethod.jsp
- loginStep1.jsp
- loginStep2.jsp
- processingDelay.jsp
- processingError.jsp
- sorry.jsp
- validateSSN.jsp
- BaseHttpServlet.java
- UserProfileServer.java
- UserSSNServer.java
- AccountSummary.java
- Address.java
- CategorySummary.java
- Company.java

- Constants.java
- CustomerInfoBean.java
- CustomerProfile.java
- InvestmentSummary.java
- ProfileMgr.java
- SSNList.java

The files will be covered in the order of the first sequence diagram.

loginStep1.jsp

The `loginStep1.jsp` file was created by adding JSP tags, scriptlets, and directives to the `loginStep1.html` page.

```
<!DOCTYPE HTML PUBLIC "-//W3C//DTD HTML 4.0 Transitional//EN">
<!-- loginStep1.jsp -->

<%@ page import = "mfc.CustomerInfoBean" errorPage = "errorPage.jsp" %>

<jsp:useBean id="customerInfo" class="mfc.CustomerInfoBean"
  scope="session"/>
```

The `page import` directive imports the class file for the `CustomerInfoBean` and establishes an `errorPage` that the JSP will forward to when any uncaught exceptions occur. The `<jsp:useBean>` action directive is used to establish a class instance variable for the bean. The instance variable is called `customerInfo` and the type of variable is an `mfc.CustomerInfoBean`. The action directive will create an instance of the bean for the defined scope if it has not already been constructed.

Next we see a deviation from the `loginStep1.html` file. It includes a JavaScript file that prevents the enter key from submitting the form. There is a feature in Internet Explorer that will allow a form to be submitted if the *Enter* key is pressed on a text input field. This feature exists in Netscape if there is only one text input field on the form. So, to make the application work better, I have included the JavaScript to prevent this. The JavaScript is located in a file `enterKeySubmit.js` and included the `loginStep1.jsp` page and the `loginStep2.jsp` page. The `onKeyPress` event handler is added to all text input fields in each form. When a key is pressed the function `checkWhich(evt)` sets a flag if key was the *Enter* key. When the `onSubmit` event is fired, the `checkForm` function is executed. If the `enterKeyPressed` variable is true, the `checkForm` function will return false and the form will not be submitted. It is a good idea to add client-side JavaScript to validate your forms. The author, has only included the JavaScript for the enter key as an example and to avoid confusion when executing the code. The other text fields should be validated using JavaScript before going to production.

```
<html>
<head>
  <title>Mutual Fund Company Login Page Step 1</title>
  <script language="JavaScript" src="enterKeySubmit.js">
  </script>
</head>
<body>
<p>
  This is a two step process to login in to your account.<BR><BR>
  Step 1 is to enter you Social Security Number. <BR>
  Step 2 asks for other data to verify that this is you.<BR><BR>
  After verification we will retrieve your profile and account summary
  information.
```

```
</p>
<form method="POST" onSubmit="return checkForm(this)">

<table cellspacing="2" cellpadding="2" border="0">
  <tr>
    <td>SSN</td>
    <td><input type="text" name="SSN" size="9" maxlength="9"
      onKeyPress="checkWhich(event)"></td>
  </tr>
</table>
<table cellspacing="2" cellpadding="2" border="0">
<tr>
    <td><input type="submit" name="submitStep1" value="Submit"></td>
</tr>
</table>
```

The next part of the `loginStep1.jsp` file declares an instance variable `jspName`. Then it uses an `include` directive to share common code between the JSPs.

```
<%! //Declaration
  static String jspName = "loginStep1.jsp: ";
%>
<%@ include file="getMethod.jsp" %>
```

The `include` is executed at translation-time (parsing of the JSP page by the compiler) and includes the code from the `getMethod.jsp` file. This file is listed after the `loginStep1.jsp` servlet.

The rest of the `loginStep1.jsp` listing is next.

```
<%
  if(method.equals("POST") == true) {
    System.out.println(jspName + "pressed submitStep1.");

    // Put the CustomerInfoBean in the session.
    session.putValue(session.getId(), customerInfo);
    System.out.println(jspName + "sessionId = " + session.getId());
%>
    <jsp:setProperty name="customerInfo" property="ssn" param="SSN"/>
    <jsp:forward page="validateSSN.jsp" />
<%
  } else {
    // Called upon page load

    // If the user has a session invalidate it.
    session.invalidate();
    System.out.println(jspName + "Invalidate current session.");

    // Get a new session for the user.
    session = request.getSession();
    System.out.println(jspName + "Session created, sessionId = " +
      session.getId());
  } //end if POST
%>
</form>
</body>
</html>
```

The CustomerInfoBean is stored in the session with the sessionId as a key. The sessionId is used as the key rather than a String name, so that if we later need to change the application to not use cookies, we could implement URL rewriting. URL rewriting is where you include the sessionId in the URL when calling a JSP or servlet. The sessionId is then used to retrieve an aggregate object what contains all of the classes you want stored in the session. If we were to do this we would create a wrapper class for all objects stored in the session and we would retrieve this wrapper class using the sessionId, which we would pass on every request. Note, the container managed URL re-writing in Tomcat breaks down after the processingDelay.jsp page is called.

Next in the loginStep1.jsp page, we skip down to the JSP action tag: <jsp:setProperty name="customerInfo" property="ssn" param="SSN"/> which will call the setSsn() method on the CustomerInfoBean and use the HTML field SSN as the argument to the set method. If the name of the method doesn't seem to follow the standard naming conventions, then you're right. However, the Tomcat JSP compiler cannot find the method setSSN() when the attribute is named ssn. Note, the author has experienced different naming problems with the WebLogic Application Server and attribute names. This will be something you will need to test on which ever JSP/Servlet engine you deploy your application. The 4.5.1 version of WebLogic, which only supports JSP1.0 and Servlets2.1, required that the attributes names match those of the accessors. The following class MyBean.java demonstrates this:

```
public class MyBean {
  private String SSN = null;
  private String Password = null;

  public String getSSN() {
    return SSN;
  }

  public void setSSN(String inSSN) {
    SSN = inSSN;
  }

  public String getPassword() {
    return Password;
  }

  public void setPassword(String inPassword) {
    Password = inPassword;
  }
}
```

If you will notice, in the loginStep1.jsp there is conditional logic for the POST method. This is an important point. Since the loginStep1.jsp is a servlet, it will process both the doGet() and the doPost() requests. Sometimes this requires conditional coding as is the case with loginStep1.jsp.

Proceeding to the <jsp:forward> action tag in the loginStep1.jsp, we see: <jsp:forward page="validateSSN.jsp" />. This action tag forwards the request to the relative URL validateSSN.jsp. When using a forward action, the servlet can't write to the client. If this has occurred an IllegalStateException will be thrown. When the forward action is executed all processing of the servlet is stopped. However, the servlet can add request-time attributes to before the forward as we will see in the validateSSN.jsp code below. The validateSSN.jsp listing follows the getMethod.jsp listing.

getMethod.jsp

Note, this JSP is not compiled into a servlet by itself. It is included into other JSP pages that in turn get compiled into servlets.

```
<!-- getMethod.jsp -->
<!--
  This jsp has not display component. It should be included in all
  jsp pages that desire to record the request method into standard out.
-->
<%! //Declaration
  String method = null;
%>
<%
  // This include file requires that the jsp files that include this
  //  must define jspName.
  String method = request.getMethod();
  System.out.println(jspName + "method = " + method);
%>
```

This JSP is used only for logging, but illustrates the `include` directive. This JSP file is also included in the following JSPs: `loginStep2.jsp`, `displayAccountSummary.jsp`, `validateSSN.jsp`, and `processingDelay.jsp`.

validateSSN.jsp

```
<!DOCTYPE HTML PUBLIC "-//W3C//DTD HTML 4.0 Transitional//EN">
<!-- validateSSN.jsp -->

<%@ page import = "mfc.CustomerInfoBean, mfc.Constants, java.util.*"
  errorPage="errorPage.jsp" %>
<jsp:useBean id="customerInfo" class="mfc.CustomerInfoBean" scope="session" />

<html>
<head>
  <title>Validate SSN</title>
</head>
<body>

<%! // declare variables.
  static String jspName = "validateSSN.jsp: ";
  CustomerInfoBean customerInfo;
  String ssn;
  StringBuffer errorMsgBuff;
%>
<%@ include file="getMethod.jsp" %>
<%
  // Initialize every page load.
  errorMsgBuff = null;

  String sessionId = session.getId();
  System.out.println(jspName + "sessionId = " + sessionId);
  ssn = customerInfo.getSsn();
  System.out.println(jspName + "SSN = " + ssn);
```

```
    ArrayList validSSNList =
      (ArrayList)getServletContext().getAttribute("ValidSSNList");
    if(validSSNList == null) {
      System.out.println(jspName + "got userinfo, " +
        "SSNList not constructed forward request to UserSSNServer " +
        "and ask for validation. ");
%>
```

In the previous section of code, the `validateSSN.jsp` servlet checks for the `ValidSSNList` in the global `ServletContext`. This demonstrates how servlets and JSPs can share global data. Since JSPs are servlets, they have full access to the Servlet API. The next group of action tags in the `validateSSN.jsp` is:

```
      <jsp:forward page="/servlet/UserSSNServer">
        <jsp:param name="reqType"
          value="<%= Integer.toString(Constants.CREATE_VALID_SSN_LIST) %>"/>
      </jsp:forward>
```

This action tag will forward the request to the `UserSSNServer` and will add a request-time attribute to pass to the servlet requesting that the servlet build the `ValidSSNList` and place it in the global `ServletContext`. The next section of scriptlet logic, is executed when the `ValidSSNList` is in the global `ServletContext`.

```
<%
   } else {
     if(validSSNList.contains(ssn)) {
       System.out.println(jspName + "got userinfo, " +
         "verify SSN and forward to UserProfileServer" +
         " with reqType=" +
         Integer.toString(Constants.MAKE_PROFILE_REQUEST) + ".");
       request.setAttribute("reqType",
         Integer.toString(Constants.MAKE_PROFILE_REQUEST));
     } else {
       errorMsgBuff = new StringBuffer("error message was: ");
       errorMsgBuff.append("The social security number you entered: '" +
         ssn + "' was not found in our system. Please try again if you have " +
         "entered the wrong number. If you have entered the correct number " +
         "and you would like to create an account call: 1-800-MFC-HELP.");
       session.setAttribute("errorMsg", errorMsgBuff.toString());
%>
       <jsp:forward page="sorry.jsp"/>
<%
     } // end if validSSNList.contains(ssn)
   } // end if validSSNList != null
%>

<jsp:forward page="/servlet/UserProfileServer"/>
  <jsp:param name="reqType"
    value="<%= Integer.toString(Constants.MAKE_PROFILE_REQUEST) %>"/>
</body>
</html>
```

In this case study, the `ValidSSNList` is an `ArrayList` collection that contains a list of valid social security numbers. This case study uses the global `ServletContext` to store the `ArrayList` to demonstrate that if validation data is too large or too sensitive to store on the client using JavaScript, you can use this technique. If you choose to implement something like this, you will want a servlet to execute on a timed basis to update the list with new Social Security numbers. However, putting a list of social security numbers in a global context is not the best choice for a secure web application.

CustomerInfoBean.java

Since the code for the `CustomerInfoBean` class is trivial, only a few of the methods will be included in the chapter listing.

```
package mfc;

import java.io.Serializable;

public class CustomerInfoBean implements Serializable {
  private String ssn;
  private String password;
  private String accountNum;
  private String zipCode;
  private String email;
  private static String cName = "CustomerInfoBean";

  public CustomerInfoBean() {
    System.out.println(cName + ": empty constructor.");
  }

  public void setSsn(String inSSN) {
    String mName = new String(cName + ".setSSN(): ");
    ssn = inSSN;
    System.out.println(mName + "set SSN = " + ssn);
  }

  public String getSsn() {
    return ssn;
  }

  public void setPassword(String inPassword) {
    String mName = new String(cName + ".setPassword(): ");
    password = inPassword;
    System.out.println(mName + "set Password = " + password);
  }

  public String getPassword() {
    return password;
  }

  public void setAccountNum(String inAccountNum) {
    String mName = new String(cName + ".setAccountNum(): ");
    accountNum = inAccountNum;
    System.out.println(mName + "set AccountNum = " +  accountNum);
  }
  //(similar code exists for the rest of the class attributes)
}
```

UserSSNServer.java

When the `ArrayList` is not in the `ServletContext`, the request that is forwarded to the `UserSSNServer` to create the `SSNList` and validate the user's SSN. The code for the `UserSSNServer.java` is below:

```
import java.io.*;
import java.util.*;
import javax.servlet.*;
import javax.servlet.http.*;
import mfc.SSNList;
```

```
import mfc.CustomerInfoBean;

public class UserSSNServer extends BaseHttpServlet {
  private static String cName = "UserSSNServer";
  private boolean debugFlag = true;

  public void init() throws ServletException {
    String mName = new String(cName + ".init(): ");
    System.out.println(mName + "start.");
    System.out.println(mName + "end.");
  } //end init

  public void doPost (HttpServletRequest request,
    HttpServletResponse response) throws ServletException, IOException {

    String mName = new String(cName + ".doPost(): ");

    System.out.println(mName + "start.");
    processRequestType(request, response);
    System.out.println(mName + "end.");
  } //end doPost
```

The `doPost()` method is called from when the `<jsp:forward>` action is called in the `validateSSN.jsp` servlet.

```
  public void processRequestType(HttpServletRequest request,
    HttpServletResponse response) throws ServletException, IOException {

    String mName = new String(cName + ".processRequestType(): ");
    System.out.println(mName + "start.");
    String reqTypeStr = (String)request.getParameter("reqType");
    System.out.println(mName + "reqTypeStr = " + reqTypeStr);

    int requestType = ERROR;
    // if did not find reqTypeStr in Parameter list throw exception.
    if(reqTypeStr == null) {
      throw new ServletException(mName + "reqTypeStr was null.");
    }
    requestType = Integer.parseInt(reqTypeStr);
    int rtn = ERROR;
    String target = null;
    switch(requestType) {

      case CREATE_VALID_SSN_LIST:
        createSSNList(request, response);
        break;

      default:
        System.out.println(mName + "default case.");
        throw new ServletException(mName + "default case reached.");
    }
    System.out.println(mName + "end.");
  } // end processRequestType
```

The `processRequestType()` method processes the attribute that was added to the request in the `validateSSN.jsp` servlet. The request-time attribute appears in the parameter list when forwarded to this servlet.

```
public void createSSNList(HttpServletRequest request,
  HttpServletResponse response) throws ServletException, IOException {

  String mName = new String(cName + ".createSSNList(): ");
  System.out.println(mName + "start.");
  ServletContext context = null;

  // construct the object that creates the SSN List.
  SSNList ssnList = new SSNList();
  ArrayList ssnArrayList = ssnList.getSSNList();
```

This list can be created with from an external data source. The data source may even be a remote data source. If this is the case you can encapsulate the details of accessing this data source within the `SSNList` class, however, you may need to handle any exceptions to inform the user of a system problem.

```
  // up the ArrayList into the Servlet Context so others may retrieve.
  context = getServletContext();
  context.setAttribute("ValidSSNList", ssnList.getSSNList());
  HttpSession session = request.getSession();
  CustomerInfoBean customerInfo =
    (CustomerInfoBean)session.getAttribute("customerInfo");

  StringBuffer errorMsgBuff = new StringBuffer("error message was: ");
  if(customerInfo == null) {
    errorMsgBuff.append("could not get UserInfo bean from the session.");
    session.setAttribute("errorMsg", errorMsgBuff.toString());
    redirectToResource(request, response, "/mutualFundCo/jsp/sorry.jsp");
  }
```

This portion of code demonstrates how to use a JSP page to display a dynamic error. The error text is added into the `HttpSession` and is retrieved by the `sorry.jsp` servlet when displayed to the user. The `redirectToResource()` method is contained in the `BaseHttpServlet` class to allow re-use for all servlets in the application.

```
  String ssn = customerInfo.getSsn();
  if(ssn == null) {
    System.out.println(mName + "SSN was not in the customerInfo bean.");
  } else {
    System.out.println(mName + "validate SSN");
    RequestDispatcher rd = null;
    if(ssnArrayList.contains(ssn) == true) {
      request.setAttribute("reqType", Integer.toString(MAKE_PROFILE_REQUEST));
      rd = getServletContext().getRequestDispatcher(
        "/servlet/UserProfileServer");
      rd.forward(request, response);
```

If the user entered a valid social security number, we need to forward the request to the `UserProfileServer` servlet to launch the asynchronous request for the customer profile. Also, note that the `reqType` is overridden with the `MAKE_PROFILE_REQUEST` for use in the `UserProfileServer` servlet.

```
    } else {
      errorMsgBuff.append("The social security number you entered: '" + ssn +
        "' was not found in our system. Please try again if you have" +
        "entered the wrong number. If you have entered the correct number "+
        "and you would like to create an account call: 1-800-MFC-HELP.");
      session.setAttribute("errorMsg", errorMsgBuff.toString());

      redirectToResource(request, response,
        "/mutualFundCo/jsp/sorry.jsp");        }
    }
    System.out.println(mName + "end.");
  } // end createSSNList

} //end UserSSNServer class
```

UserProfileServer.java

```
import java.io.*;
import java.util.*;
import javax.servlet.*;
import javax.servlet.http.*;
import mfc.Address;
import mfc.CustomerProfile;
import mfc.ProfileMgr;
import mfc.CustomerInfoBean;

public class UserProfileServer extends BaseHttpServlet {
  private static String cName = "UserProfileServer";

  public static final int REQUEST_MADE = 11;

  public static final int ERROR_ZIPCODE_MATCH = 20;
  public boolean debugFlag = true;
  private ProfileMgr profileMgr = null;

  public void init() throws ServletException {
    String mName = new String(cName + ".init(): ");
    System.out.println(mName + "start.");
    profileMgr = new ProfileMgr();
    System.out.println(mName + "end.");
  } //end init
```

The `ProfileMgr` class would normally access an external data source to obtain the customer profile. If this is the case, you should catch exceptions for the instantiation of the class.

```
  public void doPost (HttpServletRequest request,
    HttpServletResponse response) throws ServletException, IOException {

    String mName = new String(cName + ".doPost(): ");

    System.out.println(mName + "start.");
    processRequestType(request, response);
    System.out.println(mName + "end.");
  } //end doPost
```

```
public void processRequestType(HttpServletRequest request,
  HttpServletResponse response) throws ServletException, IOException {

  String mName = new String(cName + ".processRequestType(): ");
  System.out.println(mName + "start.");

  String reqTypeStr = (String)request.getAttribute("reqType");
  System.out.println(mName + "reqTypeStr = " + reqTypeStr);

  int requestType = ERROR;
  // if did not find reqType as an Attribute throw exception.
  if(reqTypeStr == null) {
    throw new ServletException(mName + "reqTypeStr was null.");
  }
  int rtn = ERROR;
  requestType = Integer.parseInt(reqTypeStr);
  String target = null;
  switch(requestType) {

    case MAKE_PROFILE_REQUEST:
      rtn = submitProfileRequest(request, response);
      target = "/mutualFundCo/jsp/loginStep2.jsp";
      redirectToResource(request, response, target);
      break;

    case CHECK_PROFILE_RESPONSE:
      // alreadyCheckedFlag = false
      rtn = checkProfileResponse(request, response, false);
      System.out.println(mName + "rtn = " + rtn);

      if(rtn == RESULTS_VALID) {
        target = "/mutualFundCo/jsp/displayAccountSummary.jsp";
      } else {
        target = "/mutualFundCo/jsp/processingDelay.jsp";
      }
      redirectToResource(request, response, target);
      break;
```

The first call to the servlet has been hard coded to not return the customer profile. If you implement this in a real application you may not include an `alreadyCheckedFlag`.

```
    case CHECK_PROFILE_RESPONSE_AGAIN:
      // alreadyCheckedFlag = true
      rtn = checkProfileResponse(request, response, true);

      System.out.println(mName + "rtn = " + rtn);

      if(rtn == RESULTS_VALID) {
        target = "/mutualFundCo/jsp/displayAccountSummary.jsp";
      } else if(rtn == ERROR || rtn == RESULTS_CHECK_FAILED) {
        target = "/mutualFundCo/jsp/processingError.jsp";
      } else {
        target = "/mutualFundCo/jsp/sorry.jsp";
      }
      redirectToResource(request, response, target);
      break;

    default:
      System.out.println(mName + "default case.");
      throw new ServletException(mName + "default case encountered.");
  }
```

```
    System.out.println(mName + "end.");
  } // end processRequestType

  public int submitProfileRequest(HttpServletRequest request,
    HttpServletResponse response) throws ServletException, IOException {

    String mName = new String(cName + ".submitProfileRequest(): ");
    System.out.println(mName + "start.");

    StringBuffer errorMsgBuff = new StringBuffer("error message was: ");
    HttpSession session = request.getSession();
    CustomerInfoBean customerInfo =
      (CustomerInfoBean)session.getAttribute("customerInfo");
    if(customerInfo == null) {
      errorMsgBuff.append("could not get UserInfo bean from the session.");
      session.setAttribute("errorMsg", errorMsgBuff.toString());
      redirectToResource(request, response, "/mutualFundCo/jsp/sorry.jsp");
    }
    // debug
    if(debugFlag == true) {
      System.out.println(mName + "sessionId = " + session.getId());
      System.out.println(mName + "SSN = " + customerInfo.getSsn());
    }
    profileMgr.request(customerInfo.getSsn());

    System.out.println(mName + "end.");
    return REQUEST_MADE;

  } // end submitProfileRequest

  public int checkProfileResponse(HttpServletRequest request,
    HttpServletResponse response, boolean alreadyCheckedFlag)
    throws ServletException, IOException {

    String mName = new String(cName + ".checkProfileResponse(): ");
    System.out.println(mName + "start.");

    StringBuffer errorMsgBuff = new StringBuffer("error message was: ");

    HttpSession session = request.getSession();
    CustomerInfoBean customerInfo =
      (CustomerInfoBean)session.getAttribute(session.getId());
```

In the code above, the servlet retrieves the `CustomerInfoBean` from the session using the same key that the JSP used.

```
    if(customerInfo == null) {
      errorMsgBuff.append("could not get UserInfo bean from the session.");
      session.setAttribute("errorMsg", errorMsgBuff.toString());
      redirectToResource(request, response, "/mutualFundCo/jsp/sorry.jsp");
    }

    // get values from the customerInfo bean
    String ssn = customerInfo.getSsn();
    String password = customerInfo.getPassword();
    String accountNum = customerInfo.getAccountNum();
    String zipCode = customerInfo.getZipCode();
    String email = customerInfo.getEmail();
```

```
// debug
if(debugFlag == true) {
  System.out.println(mName + "sessionId = " + session.getId());
  System.out.println(mName + "ssn = " +  ssn);
  System.out.println(mName + "password = " + password);
  System.out.println(mName + "accountNum = " + accountNum);
  System.out.println(mName + "zipCode = " + zipCode);
  System.out.println(mName + "email = " + email);
}

int rtn = ERROR;
CustomerProfile resp = null;
if(alreadyCheckedFlag == true) {
  resp = profileMgr.getCustomerProfile(ssn);
} else {
  // This is to simulate a delay in the backend system.
  System.out.println(mName + "first request.");
}

if(resp == null) {
  errorMsgBuff.append("no response received yet.");
  session.setAttribute("errorMsg", errorMsgBuff.toString());
  if(alreadyCheckedFlag == false) {
    rtn = STILL_PROCESSING;
    return rtn;
  } else {
    return TIMEOUT;
  }
} //end resp == null

// logic to compare returned CustomerProfile and data collected from
//  customer via JSP page.
Address custAddress = resp.getCustomerAddress();
String rtnZipCode = custAddress.getZipCode();
String rtnSSN = resp.getCustomerSSN();
String rtnAcctNum = resp.getAccountNumber();
String rtnEmail = resp.getEmailAddress();
String rtnPassword = resp.getPassword();
System.out.println("rtnZipCode = " + rtnZipCode);
System.out.println("rtnSSN = " + rtnSSN);
System.out.println("rtnAcctNum = " + rtnAcctNum);
System.out.println("rtnEmail = " + rtnEmail);
System.out.println("rtnPassword = " + rtnPassword);
boolean zipCodeCheckFlag = false;
boolean ssnCheckFlag = false;
boolean acctNumCheckFlag = false;
boolean emailCheckFlag = false;
boolean passwordCheckFlag = false;

if(rtnZipCode.equals(zipCode)) {
  System.out.println(mName + "ZipCode matched response.");
  zipCodeCheckFlag = true;
} else {
  errorMsgBuff.append("zipCode in response did not match " +
    "the zipCode in the retrieved CustomerProfile.");
  rtn = RESULTS_CHECK_FAILED;
} // end zipCode

// avoid string comparison if already failed
if(rtn != RESULTS_CHECK_FAILED) {
  if(rtnSSN.equals(ssn)) {
```

```
        ssnCheckFlag = true;
        System.out.println(mName + "SSN matched response.");
      } else {
        errorMsgBuff.append("SSN in response did not match " +
          "the SSN in the retrieved CustomerProfile.");
        rtn = RESULTS_CHECK_FAILED;
      } // end ssn
    } // end RESULTS_CHECK_FAILED

    // avoid string comparison if already failed
    if(rtn != RESULTS_CHECK_FAILED) {
      if(rtnAcctNum.equals(accountNum)) {
        System.out.println(mName + "Account Number matched response.");
        acctNumCheckFlag = true;
      } else {
        errorMsgBuff.append("Account Number in response did not match " +
          "the Account Number in the retrieved CustomerProfile.");
        rtn = RESULTS_CHECK_FAILED;
      } // end accountNum
    } // end RESULTS_CHECK_FAILED

    // avoid string comparison if already failed
    if(rtn != RESULTS_CHECK_FAILED) {
      if(rtnEmail.equals(email)) {
        emailCheckFlag = true;
        System.out.println(mName + "Email matched response.");
      } else {
        errorMsgBuff.append("Email Address in response did not match " +
          "the Email Address in the retrieved CustomerProfile.");
        rtn = RESULTS_CHECK_FAILED;
      } // end email
    } // end RESULTS_CHECK_FAILED

    // avoid string comparison if already failed
    if(rtn != RESULTS_CHECK_FAILED) {
      if(rtnPassword.equals(password)) {
        passwordCheckFlag = true;
        System.out.println(mName + "Password matched response.");
      } else {
        errorMsgBuff.append("Password in response did not match " +
          "the Password in the retrieved CustomerProfile.");
        rtn = RESULTS_CHECK_FAILED;
      } // end password
    } // end RESULTS_CHECK_FAILED

    if(zipCodeCheckFlag &&
        ssnCheckFlag &&
        acctNumCheckFlag &&
        emailCheckFlag &&
        passwordCheckFlag) {
      System.out.println(mName + "all checks matched response.");
      rtn = RESULTS_VALID;
    } // end CheckFlags

    if(rtn == RESULTS_VALID) {

      // This is on a per session basis, so won't step on other attributes.
      // add customerProfile to session.
      session.setAttribute("customerProfile", resp);
      System.out.println(mName + "added customerProfile to session.");
```

When the user input data has been verified against the retrieved data, the aggregate class is placed in the session before a `sendRedirect()` is made to the `displayAccountSummary.jsp` servlet.

```
      } else {
        // This is on a per session basis, so won't step on other attributes.
        session.setAttribute("errorMsg", errorMsgBuff.toString());
      } // end if RESULTS_VALID

      System.out.println(mName + "end.");
      return rtn;

    } // end checkProfileResponse

  } //end UserProfileServer class
```

This class is the workhorse of the application. The processing of the `MAKE_PROFILE_REQUEST` results in an asynchronous request to the `ProfileMgr` for the customer profile.

> **This is a simulated asynchronous request. It is being made because the back-end system can take 10 to 20 seconds to return the `CustomerProfile`. The second step of data collection is launched to provide time for the asynchronous request to return. The `ProfileMgr` simulates this asynchronous request.**

BaseHttpServlet.java

This servlet contains common code to all servlets. The `redirectToResource()` method is used extensively in the servlets.

```
import java.io.*;
import javax.servlet.*;
import javax.servlet.http.*;
import mfc.Constants;

abstract public class BaseHttpServlet extends HttpServlet
  implements mfc.Constants {

  private static String cName = "BaseHttpServlet";
  private boolean debugFlag = true;

  abstract public void init() throws ServletException;

  public void doGet(HttpServletRequest request,
    HttpServletResponse response) throws ServletException, IOException {
    String mName = new String(cName + ".doGet(): ");

    System.out.println(mName + "start.");
    System.out.println(mName + "*** send request to doPost.");
    doPost(request, response);
    System.out.println(mName + "end.");
  } // end doGet.
```

```
  abstract public void doPost(HttpServletRequest request,
    HttpServletResponse response) throws ServletException, IOException;

  abstract public void processRequestType(HttpServletRequest request,
    HttpServletResponse response) throws ServletException, IOException;

  public void redirectToResource(HttpServletRequest request,
    HttpServletResponse response, String resourceName)
    throws ServletException, IOException {

      String mName = new String(cName + ".redirectToResource(): ");
      System.out.println(mName + "start.");
      System.out.println(mName + "redirect to jsp=" + resourceName);
      int serverPort = request.getServerPort();
      String scheme = request.getScheme();
      String serverName = request.getServerName();
      StringBuffer urlBuffer = new StringBuffer(40);
      urlBuffer.append(scheme + "://" + serverName );
      urlBuffer.append(":" + serverPort);
      urlBuffer.append(resourceName);
      if(debugFlag == true) {
        System.out.println("urlBuffer = " + urlBuffer.toString());
        System.out.println(mName + "scheme = " + scheme);
        System.out.println(mName + "serverName = " + serverName);
        System.out.println(mName + "serverPort = " + serverPort);
        System.out.println(mName + "urlBuffer = " + urlBuffer.toString());
      }
      String location = response.encodeRedirectURL(urlBuffer.toString());
      response.sendRedirect(location);
      System.out.println(mName + "end.");
  } // end redirectToResource

} // end BaseHttpServlet class.
```

The `redirectToResource()` method is very important. It takes constructs the URL from the `HttpRequest` and builds a return path. If there is an error here you will not be able to retrieve data stored in the session. You may need to add some additional logic to ensure the cookie is the same across all requests. Note, this method still works when you configure your web server to listen to port 80 rather than port 8080 as in the default installation of Tomcat. If you use port 80, the port gets appended, but is not displayed in the browser.

loginStep2.jsp

```
<!DOCTYPE HTML PUBLIC "-//W3C//DTD HTML 4.0 Transitional//EN">
<!-- loginStep2.jsp -->

<%@ page import = "mfc.CustomerInfoBean, mfc.Constants"
  errorPage = "errorPage.jsp" %>

<jsp:useBean id="customerInfo" class="mfc.CustomerInfoBean"
  scope="session" />

<html>
<head>
  <title>Mutual Fund Company Login Step 2</title>
  <script language="JavaScript" src="enterKeySubmit.js">
  </script>
</head>

<body>
```

```
<%! // declare variables.
  static String jspName = "loginStep2.jsp: ";
%>
<%@ include file="getMethod.jsp" %>

<form method="POST" onSubmit="return checkForm(this)">
<table cellspacing="2" cellpadding="2" border="0" width="650">
  <tr>
    <td> </td>
    <td>
      Your Social Security Number is:
      <b><%=customerInfo.getSsn() %></b>
    </td>
    <td> </td>
  </tr>
  <tr>
    <td> </td>
    <td> </td>
    <td> </td>
  </tr>
  <tr>
    <td> </td>
    <td colspan="2"><p>This page completes the login process.</p></td>
  </tr>
  <tr>
    <td> </td>
    <td> </td>
    <td> </td>
  </tr>
</table>
<table cellspacing="2" cellpadding="2" border="0" width="650">
  <tr>
    <td> </td>
    <td>Enter the following information and press submit.</td>
  </tr>
  <tr>
    <td> </td>
    <td>
      <table cellspacing="2" cellpadding="2" border="0">
        <tr>
          <td align="right">
            <b>Password:</b>
          </td>
          <td>
            <b>
              <input type="password" name="Password" size="15"
                maxlength="15" onKeyPress="checkWhich(event)">
            </b>
          </td>
        </tr>
        <tr>
          <td align="right">
            <b>Account Number:</b>
          </td>
          <td>
            <b>
              <input type="text" name="AccountNum" size="5"
                maxlength="5" onKeyPress="checkWhich(event)">
            </b>
          </td>
        </tr>
        <tr>
```

```
          <td align="right">
            <b>Zipcode:</b>
          </td>
          <td>
            <b>
              <input type="text" name="ZipCode" size="5" maxlength="5"
                onKeyPress="checkWhich(event)">
            </b>
          </td>
        </tr>
        <tr>
          <td align="right">
            <b>email address:</b>
          </td>
          <td>
            <b><input type="text" name="Email" size="25" maxlength="46"
              onKeyPress="checkWhich(event)"></b>
          </td>
        </tr>
        <tr>
          <td> </td>
        </tr>
        <tr>
          <td>
            <input type="submit" name="submitStep2" value="Submit">
          </td>
        </tr>
      </table>
    </td>
  </tr>
</table>
</form>
<%
  System.out.println(jspName + "sessionId = " + session.getId());
  if(method.equals("POST") == true) {
%>
    <jsp:setProperty name="customerInfo" property="password"
      param="Password"/>
    <jsp:setProperty name="customerInfo" property="accountNum"
      param="AccountNum"/>
    <jsp:setProperty name="customerInfo" property="zipCode"
      param="ZipCode"/>
    <jsp:setProperty name="customerInfo" property="email"
      param="Email"/>
<%
    System.out.println(jspName + "ssn = " + customerInfo.getSsn());
    System.out.println(jspName + "email = " + customerInfo.getEmail());
    // Put the CustomerInfoBean in the session.
    session.setAttribute(session.getId(), customerInfo);
    System.out.println(jspName + "got customerInfo, " +
      "populate bean and forward to UserProfileServer with reqType=" +
      Constants.CHECK_PROFILE_RESPONSE);
    request.setAttribute("reqType",
      Integer.toString(Constants.CHECK_PROFILE_RESPONSE));
%>
<jsp:forward page="/servlet/UserProfileServer" />
<%
  } else {
    // Called upon page load.
    System.out.println(jspName + "sessionId = " + session.getId());
    if(customerInfo != null) {
```

```
        System.out.println(jspName + "ssn = " + customerInfo.getSsn());
      } else {
        System.out.println(jspName + "** Error: customerInfo is null.");
      }
    }
%>
</body>
</html>
```

This page collects more customer data, populates the `CustomerInfoBean`, sets the bean in the session, and puts the `reqType` variable in the request and forwards to the `UserProfileServer servlet`. The request made to the servlet is to `CHECK_PROFILE_RESPONSE`.

> **The `checkProfileRequest()` method in the `UserProfileServer` class simulates a lengthy transaction by returning the `STILL_PROCESSING` status.**

processingDelay.jsp

If the `CustomerProfile` is still not available the request is forwarded to `processingDelay.jsp`.

```
<!DOCTYPE HTML PUBLIC "-//W3C//DTD HTML 4.0 Transitional//EN">
<!-- processingDelay.jsp -->

<%@ page import = "mfc.Constants" %>
<html>
<head>
  <title>Processing your request</title>
  <META HTTP-EQUIV="Refresh" content="2; URL=checkResponse.jsp">
</head>

<body>
<h3>Processing your response.</h3>
<%! //Declarations
  static String jspName = "processingDelay.jsp: ";
%>
<%@ include file="getMethod.jsp" %>
<%
  System.out.println(jspName + " loaded page.");
  request.setAttribute("reqType",
    Integer.toString(Constants.CHECK_PROFILE_RESPONSE_AGAIN));
  System.out.println(jspName + "setAttribute for reqType = " +
    Constants.CHECK_PROFILE_RESPONSE_AGAIN);
  System.out.println(jspName + "will send request to UserProfileServer");
%>
</body>
</html>
```

This JSP will redirect the user to the `checkResponse.jsp` servlet after 2 seconds. It does this by using the an HTML `META` tag with the `Refresh` directive. The content includes the time and the target URL. The refresh executes a `GET` on the target URL.

> **The time used in the delay should be scaled with the account retrieval process. Two seconds was selected for the chapter code, however, the case study indicates 10 to 20 seconds for account retrieval. The lower value was chosen to minimize delay while executing the example. The `processingDelay.jsp` page can be used to present other information to the customer.**

The `processingDelay.jsp` servlet adds a request-time attribute before forwarding the request to the `UserProfileServer` that is used by the `checkResponse.jsp` servlet.

checkResponse.jsp

```
<!DOCTYPE HTML PUBLIC "-//W3C//DTD HTML 4.0 Transitional//EN">
<!-- checkResponse.jsp -->

<%@ page import = "mfc.CustomerInfoBean, mfc.Constants"
  errorPage = "errorPage.jsp" %>
<jsp:useBean id="customerInfo" class="mfc.CustomerInfoBean"
  scope="session"/>

<%
  System.out.println("ssn = " + customerInfo.getSsn() );
  request.setAttribute("reqType",
    Integer.toString(Constants.CHECK_PROFILE_RESPONSE_AGAIN));
  System.out.println("checkRequest.jsp setAttribute for reqType = " +
    Constants.CHECK_PROFILE_RESPONSE_AGAIN);
  System.out.println("forwarding request to UserProfileServer");
%>
<jsp:forward page="/servlet/UserProfileServer" />
```

The request is forwarded from the `checkRequest.jsp` to the `UserProfileServer`. Since the Refresh event is a client pull, the `doGet()` method is executed on the `UserProfileServer`. The `BaseHttpServlet` forwards the `doGet()` to the `doPost()` of the `UserProfileServer` and the request is processed. The `processRequestType()` method in the `UserProfileServer` can handle either Parameters or Attributes in the request object. The intermediate JSP uses the `setAttribute()` option to set the request type. Upon processing the request, the `checkProfileRequest()` method is executed again. This time the `CustomerProfile` is present from the `ProfileMgr` class.

processingError.jsp

The `processingError.jsp` servlet is used for displaying errors to the user. The text is dynamic and set in the `HttpSession` by the servlet before the redirection to this servlet. These dynamic errors are associated with user entered data that did not match retrieved data from the `CustomerProfile`.

```
<!DOCTYPE HTML PUBLIC "-//W3C//DTD HTML 4.0 Transitional//EN">
<!-- processingError.jsp -->

<html>
<head>
  <title>The Mutual Fund Company, Processing Error Page</title>
</head>
```

```
<body>
<h3>
  We have encountered a processing error while validating the data you
  provided against the Customer Account that we retrieved. <br><br>
  <%= session.getAttribute("errorMsg") %>
</h3>
<a href="loginStep1.jsp">Click here to try again.</a>
</body>
</html>
```

errorPage.jsp

The `errorPage.jsp` servlet is the default error page. Runtime exceptions that are encountered in the JSP files will go to this page. This servlet is declared almost all of the JSP pages. Notice, the important `page` directive declaring this as an error page.

```
<!DOCTYPE HTML PUBLIC "-//W3C//DTD HTML 4.0 Transitional//EN">
<!-- errorPage.jsp -->

<html>
<head>
  <title>Mutual Fund Company Error Page</title>
</head>
<body>
<%@ page isErrorPage="true" %>
<h1>Error encountered.<BR>
The exception was "<%= exception.getMessage() %> "<BR>
</h1>
<pre>
  <%
    PrintWriter pw = response.getWriter();
    exception.printStackTrace(pw);
  %>
</pre>

</body>
</html>
```

InvestmentSummary.java

The `InvestmentSummary` class is aggregated in the `CategorySummary` class.

```
package mfc;
import java.io.*;

public class InvestmentSummary implements Serializable {

  private float percentOfTotalFund = 0.0f;
  private String category = null;
  private String name = null;
  private float currentValue = 0.0f;
  private float futureContribution = 0.0f;
```

```
  public InvestmentSummary() {
  }

  /** set with a scaled Percentage e.g. 25.5 = 25.5% */
  public void setPercentageOfTotalFund(float inValue) {
    percentOfTotalFund = inValue;
  }

  public float getPercentageOfTotalFund() {
    return percentOfTotalFund;
  }

  //(similar code exists for the rest of the class attributes)
} // end InvestmentSummary class.
```

enterKeySubmit.js

This is the JavaScript file that is included in the `loginStep1.jsp` and the `loginStep2.jsp` pages. This JavaScript file prevents the form from submitting when an enter key is pressed on a text input field in a form. You need to follow the example in the two login pages when implementing it in the JSP page.

```
var nav4 = window.Event ? true : false;
var debugFlag = false;
var enterKeyCode = 13;
var targetObject;
var enterKeyPressed = false;

function checkWhich(evt) {
  var theKey
  if (nav4) {
    theKey = evt.which
  } else {
    if (evt.type == "keypress") {
      theKey = evt.keyCode
    }
    targetObject = evt.srcElement;
  } //end if nav4
  if(debugFlag) alert("theKey = " + theKey);
  if(theKey == enterKeyCode) {
    enterKeyPressed = true;
    if(debugFlag) {
      alert("targetObject.name = " + targetObject.name);
    }
  } //end if returnKey
  return true;
} //end checkWhich function.

function checkForm(formName) {
  if(debugFlag) {
    alert("checkForm called, must have been a submit. ");
  }
```

```
    if(enterKeyPressed == true) {
      enterKeyPressed = false;
      if(debugFlag) {
        alert("do not Submit, enter was pressed");
      }
      targetObject.focus();
      return false;
    } //end if enterKey
    return true;
  } //end checkForm function.
```

ProfileMgr.java

```
package mfc;
import java.util.*;

public class ProfileMgr implements Constants {
  private static String cName = "ProfileMgr";
  private Hashtable profileList = new Hashtable();

  public ProfileMgr() {
    System.out.println(cName + ": empty constructor.");
    // This is simulated with a manual load of the Profiles.
    loadProfiles();
  }

  public void request(String ssn) {
    String mName = new String(cName + ".request(): ");
    System.out.println(mName + "start.");
    System.out.println(mName + "initiate request for CustomerProfile for SSN = "
      + ssn);
    // This method would make a request from an external data source
    //  to add the Profile to the hashtable. In theory this is made
    //  as an asynchronous request since it may take a while to
    //  fetch the CustomerProfile.
    System.out.println(mName + "end.");
  } // end request.

  public CustomerProfile getCustomerProfile(String ssn) {
    CustomerProfile rtnProfile = null;
    if(profileList.containsKey(ssn) == true) {
      rtnProfile = (CustomerProfile)profileList.get(ssn);
    }
    return rtnProfile;
  } // end getCustomerProfile

  public void loadProfiles() {
    String mName = new String(cName + ".loadProfiles(): ");
    System.out.println(mName + "start.");
    // Creates a dummy profile. This normally would be created by
    //  database interaction.
    CustomerProfile profile = new CustomerProfile();
```

```
    Address custAddress = new Address();
    custAddress.setStreet("10 Main Street");
    custAddress.setCity("Denver");
    custAddress.setState("CO");
    custAddress.setZipCode("80201");
  profile.setCustomerAddress(custAddress);
    Company company = new Company();
    company.setCompanyName("Wacky WebWork, Inc.");
    Address compAddress = custAddress;
    company.setAddress(compAddress);
  profile.setCompany(company);
    AccountSummary acctSummary = new AccountSummary();
    acctSummary.setBeginBalanceLastStatement(41232.63f);
    acctSummary.setBalanceCurrent(50120.32f);
      CategorySummary[] categorySummaryList = new CategorySummary[3];

      InvestmentSummary[] investSummaryList = new InvestmentSummary[3];
        // First fund
        InvestmentSummary invest = new InvestmentSummary();
        invest.setPercentageOfTotalFund(12.15f);
        invest.setCategory("Growth");
        invest.setName("EuroPacific Growth Fund");
        invest.setCurrentValue(6089.62f);
        invest.setFutureContribution(5.0f);
      investSummaryList[0] = invest;

        // Second fund
        invest = new InvestmentSummary();
        invest.setPercentageOfTotalFund(36.45f);
        invest.setCategory("Growth");
        invest.setName("US Growth Fund");
        invest.setCurrentValue(18268.86f);
        invest.setFutureContribution(40.0f);
      investSummaryList[1] = invest;

        // Third fund
        invest = new InvestmentSummary();
        invest.setPercentageOfTotalFund(32.4f);
        invest.setCategory("Growth");
        invest.setName("Aggressive Growth Fund");
        invest.setCurrentValue(16238.98f);
        invest.setFutureContribution(40.0f);
      investSummaryList[2] = invest;

      CategorySummary catSummary = new CategorySummary();
      catSummary.setCategoryName("Growth");
      catSummary.setCategoryValue(40597.46f);
      catSummary.setPercentTotal(81.0f);
      catSummary.setInvestmentSummaryList(investSummaryList);
      categorySummaryList[0] = catSummary;

      investSummaryList = new InvestmentSummary[1];
        // Forth fund
        invest = new InvestmentSummary();
        invest.setPercentageOfTotalFund(40.0f);
        invest.setCategory("Growth & Income");
        invest.setName("Jefferson Mutual Growth & Income");
        invest.setCurrentValue(7016.84f);
        invest.setFutureContribution(15.0f);
      investSummaryList[0] = invest;
```

```
        catSummary = new CategorySummary();
        catSummary.setCategoryName("Growth & Income");
        catSummary.setCategoryValue(7016.84f);
        catSummary.setPercentTotal(14.0f);
        catSummary.setInvestmentSummaryList(investSummaryList);
        categorySummaryList[1] = catSummary;

        investSummaryList = new InvestmentSummary[1];
          // Fifth fund
          invest = new InvestmentSummary();
          invest.setPercentageOfTotalFund(5.0f);
          invest.setCategory("Income");
          invest.setName("US Income Fund");
          invest.setCurrentValue(2506.02f);
          invest.setFutureContribution(5.0f);
        investSummaryList[0] = invest;

        catSummary = new CategorySummary();
        catSummary.setCategoryName("Income");
        catSummary.setCategoryValue(2506.02f);
        catSummary.setPercentTotal(5.0f);
        catSummary.setInvestmentSummaryList(investSummaryList);
        categorySummaryList[2] = catSummary;

      acctSummary.setCategorySummary(categorySummaryList);
    profile.setAccountSummary(acctSummary);
    profile.setCustomerName("Joe Smith");
    profile.setCustomerSSN("400102000");
    profile.setAccountNumber("1234");
    profile.setEmailAddress("Joe.Smith@netscape.net");
    profile.setPassword("joe");

    // Add this profile to the profileList, key is the SSN
    profileList.put(profile.getCustomerSSN(), profile);

    CustomerProfile profile2 = new CustomerProfile();
      custAddress = new Address();
      custAddress.setStreet("1345 Logan Street");
      custAddress.setCity("Denver");
      custAddress.setState("CO");
      custAddress.setZipCode("80219");
    profile2.setCustomerAddress(custAddress);
    profile2.setAccountSummary(acctSummary);
    profile2.setCompany(company);
    profile2.setCustomerName("Jane Smith");
    profile2.setCustomerSSN("400102001");
    profile2.setAccountNumber("1235");
    profile2.setEmailAddress("jsmith@hotmail.com");
    profile2.setPassword("jsmith");
    profileList.put(profile2.getCustomerSSN(), profile2);
    System.out.println(mName + "end.");
  } // end loadProfiles.

} // end ProfileMgr class.
```

The `ProfileMgr` class is similar to the `SSNList` class. In a real project, it would have an external data store access and would be used to retrieve data from the back-end system.

CustomerProfile.java

The `ProfileMgr` class creates the `CustomerProfile` object. This object would normally be constructed in the back-end. This object represents the user's account information.

```
package mfc;
import java.io.*;

public class CustomerProfile implements Serializable {
  private static String cName = "CustomerProfile";
  private Address customerAddress = null;
  private Company company = null;
  private AccountSummary accountSummary = null;
  private String customerName = null;
  private String ssn = null;
  private String accountNumber = null;
  private String email = null;
  private String password = null;

  public CustomerProfile() {
    System.out.println(cName + ": empty constructor.");
  }

  public void setCustomerAddress(Address inAddress) {
    customerAddress = inAddress;
  }

  public Address getCustomerAddress() {
    return customerAddress;
  }

  public void setCompany(Company inCompany) {
    company = inCompany;
  }

  public Company getCompany() {
    return company;
  }
  //(similar code exists for the rest of the class attributes)
} // end CustomerProfile class.
```

SSNList.java

```
package mfc;

import java.util.*;

public class SSNList {
  private ArrayList validSSNList = null;

  public SSNList() {
    loadSSNValues();
  }

  public ArrayList getSSNList() {
    return validSSNList;
  }

  // Normally this would be loaded by an external data source.
```

```
    public void loadSSNValues() {
      validSSNList = new ArrayList();
      validSSNList.add("400102000");
      validSSNList.add("400102001");
      validSSNList.add("400102002");
      validSSNList.add("400102003");
      validSSNList.add("400102004");
      validSSNList.add("400102005");
      validSSNList.add("400102006");
      validSSNList.add("400102007");
      validSSNList.add("400102008");
      validSSNList.add("400102009");
      validSSNList.add("400102010");
      validSSNList.add("400102011");
      validSSNList.add("400102012");
      validSSNList.add("400102013");
      validSSNList.add("400102004");
    } // end loadSSNValues

  } // end SSNList
```

Address.java

The `Address` class is aggregated in the `CustomerProfile` class.

```
package mfc;
import java.io.*;

public class Address implements Serializable {
  private String street = null;
  private String city = null;
  private String state = null;
  private String zipCode = null;

  public Address() {
  }

  public void setStreet(String inStreet) {
    street = inStreet;
  }

  public String getStreet() {
    return street;
  }
  //(similar code exists for the rest of the class attributes)
} //end Address class.
```

Company.java

The `Company` class is aggregated in the `CustomerProfile` class.

```
package mfc;
import java.io.*;

public class Company implements Serializable {
  private String companyName = null;
  private Address companyAddress = null;
```

```
  public Company() {
  }

  public void setCompanyName(String inName) {
    companyName = inName;
  }

  public String getCompanyName() {
    return companyName;
  }

  public void setAddress(Address inAddress) {
    companyAddress = inAddress;
  }

  public Address getAddress() {
    return companyAddress;
  }

} // end Company class.
```

AccountSummary.java

The `AccountSummary` class is aggregated in the `CustomerProfile` class.

```
package mfc;
import java.io.*;

public class AccountSummary implements Serializable {

  private float beginBalanceLastStatement = 0.0f;
  private float balanceCurrent = 0.0f;
  private CategorySummary[] categorySummary = null;

  public AccountSummary() {
  }

  public void setBeginBalanceLastStatement(float inBegin) {
    beginBalanceLastStatement = inBegin;
  }

  public float getBeginBalanceLastStatement() {
    return beginBalanceLastStatement;
  }

  public void setBalanceCurrent(float inBalance) {
    balanceCurrent = inBalance;
  }

  public float getBalanceCurrent() {
    return balanceCurrent;
  }

  public void setCategorySummary(CategorySummary[] inCategorySummary) {
    categorySummary = inCategorySummary;
  }

  public CategorySummary[] getCategorySummary() {
    return categorySummary;
  }

} // end AccountSummary class.
```

Constants.java

```
package mfc;

public interface Constants {
  public static final int ERROR = -1;
  public static final int STILL_PROCESSING = 0;
  public static final int RESULTS_VALID = 1;
  public static final int RESULTS_CHECK_FAILED = 2;
  public static final int MAKE_PROFILE_REQUEST = 12;
  public static final int CHECK_PROFILE_RESPONSE = 13;
  public static final int CHECK_PROFILE_RESPONSE_AGAIN = 14;
  public static final int TIMEOUT = 15;
  public static final int CREATE_VALID_SSN_LIST = 20;
}
```

CustomerProfile.java

The `CustomerProfile` class aggregates the `Address` class and the `AccountSummary` class.

```
package mfc;
import java.io.*;

public class CustomerProfile implements Serializable {
  private static String cName = "CustomerProfile";
  private Address customerAddress = null;
  private Company company = null;
  private AccountSummary accountSummary = null;
  private String customerName = null;
  private String ssn = null;
  private String accountNumber = null;
  private String email = null;
  private String password = null;

  public CustomerProfile() {
    System.out.println(cName + ": empty constructor.");
  }

  public void setCustomerAddress(Address inAddress) {
    customerAddress = inAddress;
  }

  public Address getCustomerAddress() {
    return customerAddress;
  }

  public void setAccountSummary(AccountSummary inAccountSummary) {
    accountSummary = inAccountSummary;
  }

  public AccountSummary getAccountSummary() {
    return accountSummary;
  }

  //(similar code exists for the rest of the class attributes)
} // end CustomerProfile class.
```

CategorySummary.java

The `CategorySummary` class is aggregated in the `AccountSummary` class.

```
package mfc;
import java.io.*;

public class CategorySummary implements Serializable {
  private String categoryName = null;
  private float categoryValue = 0.0f;
  private float percentTotal = 0.0f;
  private InvestmentSummary[] investmentSummaryList = null;

  public CategorySummary() {
  }

  public void setCategoryName(String inCategoryName) {
    categoryName = inCategoryName;
  }

  public String getCategoryName() {
    return categoryName;
  }

  public void setCategoryValue(float inCategoryValue) {
    categoryValue = inCategoryValue;
  }

  public float getCategoryValue() {
    return categoryValue;
  }

  public void setPercentTotal(float inPercent) {
    percentTotal = inPercent;
  }

  public float getPercentTotal() {
    return percentTotal;
  }

  public void setInvestmentSummaryList(InvestmentSummary[] inList) {
    investmentSummaryList = inList;
  }

  public InvestmentSummary[] getInvestmentSummaryList() {
    return investmentSummaryList;
  }

} // end CategorySummary class.
```

The `ProfileMgr` in the case study creates two `CustomerProfile` objects for the following customers: "Joe Smith" and "Jane Smith".

The `getCustomerProfile()` request from the `UserProfileServer` will return a customer profile if the SSN matches. If the `CustomerProfile` is not `null`, verification is performed with the data provided in the `loginStep2.jsp`. This information is retrieved from the bean. The bean was stored in the session with the `sessionId` as the key. If the collected data matches the data in the `CustomerProfile`, the object is set in the session and the request is redirected to the `displayAccountSummary.jsp`.

displayAccountSummary.jsp

The `displayAccountSummary.jsp` servlet is used to display the `AccountSummary` information for the user.

```
<!DOCTYPE HTML PUBLIC "-//W3C//DTD HTML 4.0 Transitional//EN">
<!-- displayAccountSummary.jsp -->

<%@ page import = "mfc.AccountSummary, mfc.Address,
                   mfc.CategorySummary, mfc.Constants, mfc.Company,
                   mfc.CustomerProfile, mfc.InvestmentSummary,
                   java.text.*"
  errorPage = "errorPage.jsp" %>

<html>
<head>
  <title>The Mutual Fund Company Account Summary</title>
</head>

<body>
<h3>Here is your account summary information.</h3>
<%! // declare variables
  AccountSummary acct = null;
  Address add = null;
  Address cmpAdd = null;
  Company cmp = null;
  CustomerProfile cp = null;
  CategorySummary[] catList = null;
  InvestmentSummary[] investSummaryList = null;
  InvestmentSummary summaryLine = null;
  int numCats = 0;
  int icount = 0;
  float accountValue = 0.0f;
  NumberFormat nf = null;
  static String jspName = "displayAccountSummary.jsp: ";
%>
```

The declaration scriptlet is needed since the `jspName` variable is used in the included `getMethod.jsp` file. However, the other variable are simply instance variables and may be included in the scriptlet after the `include` directive.

```
<%@ include file="getMethod.jsp" %>
<%
  cp = (CustomerProfile)session.getAttribute("customerProfile");
  add = cp.getCustomerAddress();
  cmp = cp.getCompany();
  cmpAdd = cmp.getAddress();
  acct = cp.getAccountSummary();
  catList = acct.getCategorySummary();
  numCats = catList.length;
  nf = NumberFormat.getCurrencyInstance();
```

```
    nf.setMinimumFractionDigits(2);
    nf.setMaximumFractionDigits(2);
  %>
```

The `NumberFormat` class is used to format the floating point values in the `AccountSummary` class. When you need an internationalized application you will want to include the locale for on the `getCurrencyInstance()` method call.

```
  <table align="left" width="700" cellspacing="2" cellpadding="2"
    border="0">
  <tr>
      <td>
        <table align="left" bgcolor="#d6d6d6" width="300" cellspacing="0"
          cellpadding="0" border="2" frame="box" rules="none">
        <caption align="top"><b>Customer Information</b></caption>
        <tr>
          <td><%= cp.getCustomerName() %></td>
        </tr>
        <tr>
          <td><%= add.getStreet() %></td>
        </tr>
        <tr>
          <td><%= add.getCity() %>, <%= add.getState() %>
            <%= add.getZipCode() %>
          </td>
        </tr>
        <tr>
          <td>SSN: <%= cp.getCustomerSSN() %></td>
        </tr>
        <tr>
          <td>email: <%= cp.getEmailAddress() %></td>
        </tr>
        </table>
      </td>
  </tr>
  <tr>
      <td>
        <table align="left" bgcolor="#d6d6d6" width="300" cellspacing="0"
          cellpadding="0" border="2" frame="box" rules="none">
        <caption align="top"><b>Company Information</b></caption>
        <tr>
          <td><%= cmp.getCompanyName() %></td>
        </tr>
        <tr>
          <td><%= cmpAdd.getStreet() %></td>
        </tr>
        <tr>
          <td><%= cmpAdd.getCity() %>, <%= cmpAdd.getState() %>
            <%= cmpAdd.getZipCode() %>
          </td>
        </tr>
        </table>
      </td>
```

```
    </tr>
    <tr>
        <td>
          <table bgcolor="#d6d6d6" width="600" cellspacing="2"
            cellpadding="2" border="2" frame="box" rules="all">
          <caption align="top"><b>Your account at a Glance</b></caption>
          <tr>
            <td>Beginning Balance Last Statement</td>
            <td align="right">
              <%= nf.format(acct.getBeginBalanceLastStatement()) %>
            </td>
          </tr>
          <tr>
            <td>Current Balance</td>
            <td align="right">
              <%= nf.format(acct.getBalanceCurrent()) %>
            </td>
          </tr>
          </table>
        </td>
    </tr>
    <tr>
      <td>
        <table bgcolor="#d6d6d6" width="700" cellspacing="2" cellpadding="2"
          border="2">
        <caption align="top"><b>Investment Summary</b></caption>
        <tr>
          <th align="right" width="10%">Current Account %</th>
          <th align="left" width="50%">Investment Selection</th>
          <th align="right" width="30%">Current Account Value</th>
          <th align="right" width="10%">Future Contribution Elections</th>
        </tr>
        <!-- Category Header -->
```

The following scriptlet code is going to produce the `InvestmentSummary` table that was shown in the static html page, `displayAccountSummary.html`. The `InvestmentSummary` table has categories of investments. The number of categories is stored in the variable `numCats`. This value is designed into the aggregate classes and is simply the length of the `CategorySummary` array in `AccountSummary`. Each category has percentage that represents it percentage of the whole fund. Since the percentage spans all the rows in the category, it is printed along with the first row of the category. The first row of the category displays the category name and the total dollar amount. The following rows in this category are the individual funds within the current category. The `InvestmentSummary` is an array that contains the investments in the category. The length of the array (`icount`) is used to display each fund in the category. The colors are changed to make the display easier to read.

The ability for the JSP page to dynamically generate the page is based upon the design of the `AccountSummary` class. When presenting data from an external data source, don't be afraid to design the container classes so that it makes it easy to display the results. If you have an intermediate class that builds your display container you minimize the business logic in your JSPs and you may not have to change your JSP page every time you back-end data changes.

```
<%
for(int i=0; i<numCats; i++) {
  //get investSummaryList
  investSummaryList = catList[i].getInvestmentSummaryList();
  icount = investSummaryList.length;
  accountValue += catList[i].getCategoryValue();
%>
<tr>
  <td valign="top" align="right" rowspan="<%= (icount + 1) %>">
    <b><%= catList[i].getPercentTotal() %></b>
  </td>
  <td bgcolor="#ffffff">
    <b><%= catList[i].getCategoryName() %></b>
  </td>
  <td bgcolor="#ffffff" align="right">
    <b><%= nf.format(catList[i].getCategoryValue()) %></b>
  </td>
  <td> </td>
</tr>
<!-- Fund Entry -->
<%
  for(int j=0; j<icount; j++) {
%>
<tr>
  <td><%= investSummaryList[j].getName() %></td>
  <td align="right">
    <%= investSummaryList[j].getCurrentValue() %>
  </td>
  <td align="right">
    <%= investSummaryList[j].getFutureContribution() %>
  </td>
</tr>
<%
  } //end investmentSummaryList for category
} //end categoryList
%>
<tr>
<!-- Table End -->
  <td align="right"><b>100%</b></td>
  <td bgcolor="#ffffff"><b>TOTAL</b></td>
  <td bgcolor="#ffffff" align="right">
    <b><%= nf.format(accountValue) %></b>
  </td>
  <td align="right"><b>100%</b></td>
</tr>
</table>
</td>
</tr>
</table>
</body>
</html>
```

This Java Server Page demonstrates how a thoughtful design of you data classes can assist in displaying your data with minimum business logic in your JSP pages.

Setting up the Tomcat Servlet Engine

Go to the Apache web site, http://jakarta.apache.org. Select the latest release build link. For the Windows operating system, download jakarta-tomcat.zip and the jakarta-tools.zip. If you are using the UNIX or some derivative of UNIX, like Linux, download the tar versions of these files.

Install the both files on you computer. Set the following environment variables:

- JAVA_HOME to your version of the JDK.
- TOMCAT_HOME to where you installed Tomcat.
- CLASSPATH to include the servlet-2.2.0.jar jar file from the jakarta-tools file.

Locate the server.xml file under the conf directory. If your using a UNIX variant, its under the $TOMCAT_HOME/conf directory. In Windows it's under the %TOMCAT_HOME%\conf directory. Add the following to the server.xml file. The references to directories will be formatted in the UNIX style. If you are using Windows you will want to format these properly for the environment. You should remember that environment variables in UNIX are referenced as $VARIABLE_NAME and in Windows are referenced as %VARIABLE_NAME%.

```
<Context path="/mutualFundCo" docBase="webapps/mutualFundCo" debug="9"
   reloadable="true" >
</Context>
```

It should be within the <ContextManger></ContextManger> tags. The debug level can be set to any number from 0 to 9, where 0 is minimal logging. The reloadable flag should only be set to true for a development environment.

Create a directory under the $TOMCAT_HOME/webapps directory called mutualFundCo. Under that directory create two directories. One named jsp, the other named WEB-INF. Under the WEB-INF directory create a classes directory. Under the classes directory create an mfc directory.

Place the JSP files in the $TOMCAT_HOME/webapps/mutualFundCo/jsp directory. This directory should contain the following files:

- checkResponse.jsp
- displayAccountSummary.jsp
- errorPage.jsp
- getMethod.jsp
- loginStep1.jsp
- loginStep2.jsp
- processingDelay.jsp
- processingError.jsp
- sorry.jsp
- validateSSN.jsp

Place the servlet files in the $TOMCAT_HOME/webapps/mutualFundCo/WEB-INF/classes directory. This directory contain the following files:

- BaseHttpServlet.java
- UserProfileServer.java
- UserSSNServer.java

Place the `dataClasses` and the JavaBean in the `$TOMCAT_HOME/webapps/mutualFundCo/WEB-INF/classes/mfc` directory. This directory should contain the following files:

- `AccountSummary.java`
- `Address.java`
- `CategorySummary.java`
- `Company.java`
- `Constants.java`
- `CustomerInfoBean.java`
- `CustomerProfile.java`
- `InvestmentSummary.java`
- `ProfileMgr.java`
- `SSNList.java`
- `TestProfileMgr.java`

A `web.xml` file needs to be placed in the `WEB-INF` directory. For this example, you should put the following in this file.

```
<?xml version="1.0" encoding="ISO-8859-1"?>

<!DOCTYPE web-app
    PUBLIC "-//Sun Microsystems, Inc.//DTD Web Application 2.2//EN"
    "http://java.sun.com/j2ee/dtds/web-app_2.2.dtd">

<web-app>
</web-app>
```

> **If you desire some more advanced features of the servlet engine, like virtual naming or startup parameters, please reference the Servlet 2.2 specification from Sun Microsystems. The URL is http://java.sun.com/products/servlet/download.html.**

Compile the servlets, the `dataClasses`, and the JavaBean using the `javac` compiler.

Change to the `$TOMCAT_HOME/bin` directory and execute the startup script.

Then access the first page using the following URL: http://localhost:8080/mutualFundCo/jsp/loginStep1.jsp. Note, the Tomcat stand-alone JSP/servlet engine is configured to start on port 8080. This can be changed by altering the port in the `$TOMCAT_HOME/conf/server.xml` file to be port 80 as illustrated below:

```
<Connector className="org.apache.tomcat.service.SimpleTcpConnector">
<Parameter name="handler"
   value="org.apache.tomcat.service.http.HttpConnectionHandler"/>
     <Parameter name="port" value="80"/>
</Connector>
```

When the page appears enter the following social security number: 400102000 and press the Submit button.

After pressing the Submit button the following screen will appear:

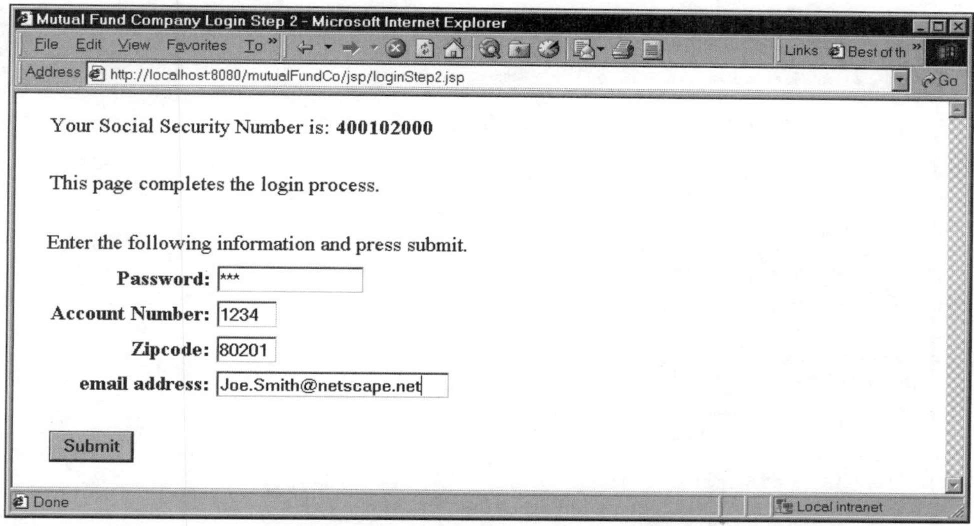

> **If you access your web server using its IP address rather than the hostname the session ID will be different between `loginStep1.jsp` and `loginStep2.jsp`. This is a limitation to using the `response.getServerName()` method within the `BaseHttpServlet` class. If you would like to construct a programmatic solution to this problem please consult the following methods: `HttpServletRequest.getRequestURI()` and `HttpUtils.getRequestURL()` to construct the proper URL.**

Enter joe for the Password, 1234 for the Account Number, 80201 for the Zipcode, Joe.Smith@netscape.net for the email address, and press the Submit button. You should see the following screen for two seconds:

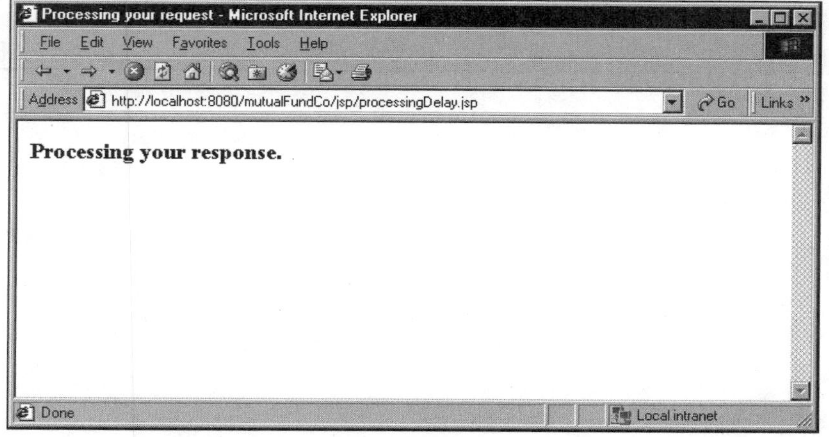

After 2 seconds the next screen you see should be the following:

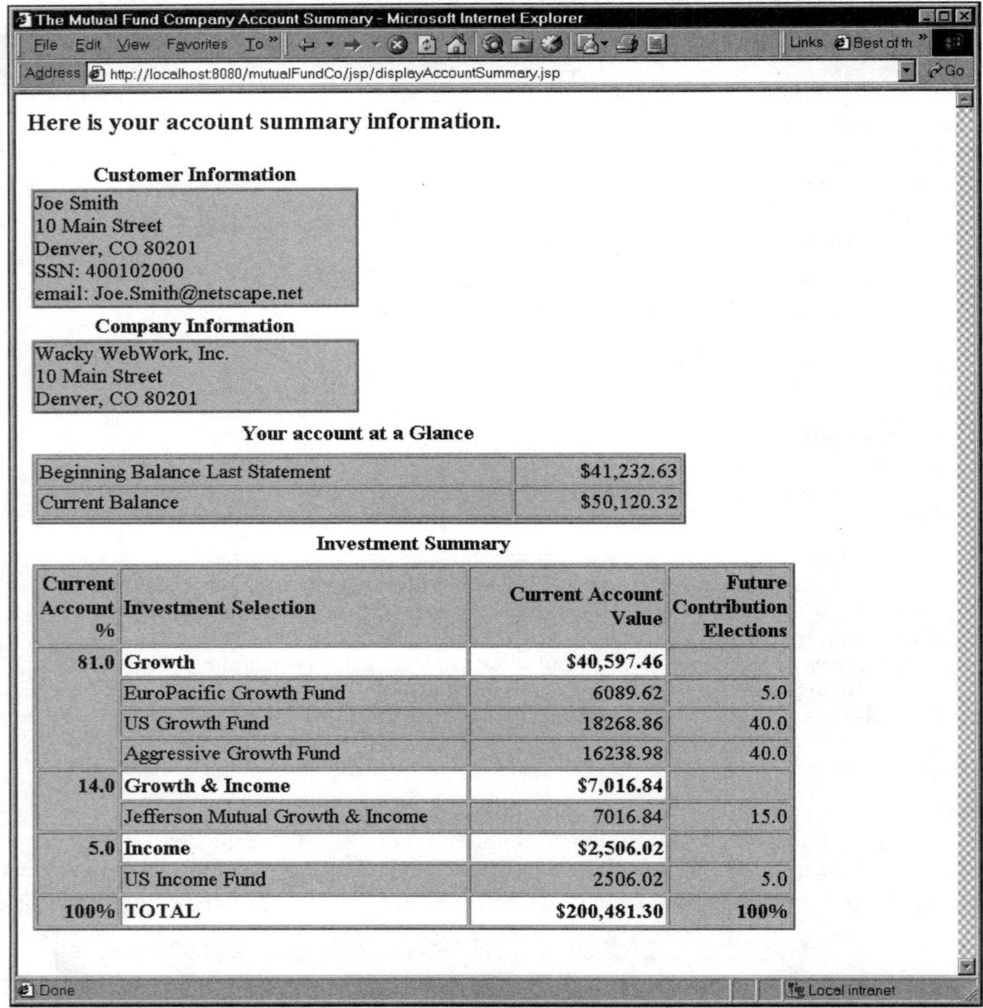

Summary

- The combination of Java Server Pages and Java Servlets provide an easier environment for developing a Web user interface than Java Servlets..
- How to use the `forward()` method and the `sendRedirect()` method that are on the `HttpServletRequest` instance.
- The `ServletContext` can be used to provide global access to data for early validation. This is not as quick as client side validation with JavaScript, but could be used to generate JavaScript on the fly for client validation.
- One method of displaying a large composite object to the client is to use the `HttpSession` as a transport to the display JSP page. This does require that the client accept cookies. You can add a session ID within the link itself as a name/value pair on each page. This can be added using the `request.encodeURL()` method or the `response.encodeRedirectURL()` method.
- Thought full design of data classes can simplify client display and provide good separation between business logic and presentation.

J2EE
JSP

14

Case Study: Publishing Data to the Web

This chapter describes my photography database, PhotoDB, which I use to organize and display images on my web site. I developed PhotoDB to complement my photography hobby and to enable me to efficiently publish many photographs on the web. You may find this chapter useful if you want a simple and practical introduction to publishing data on the web using a database and JSP.

You can access the latest version at http://www.magiccookie.com/photography/photodb/, and download the complete source code from http://www.magiccookie.com/software/.

Overview

The PhotoDB system consists of:

- A user interface rendered as HTML
- Some Java source code and JSP files.
- Meta data stored in a relational database
- Image files

The purpose of the Java and JSP source code is to map between the HTML interface and the data stored in the database and on disk. The basic architecture looks like the following:

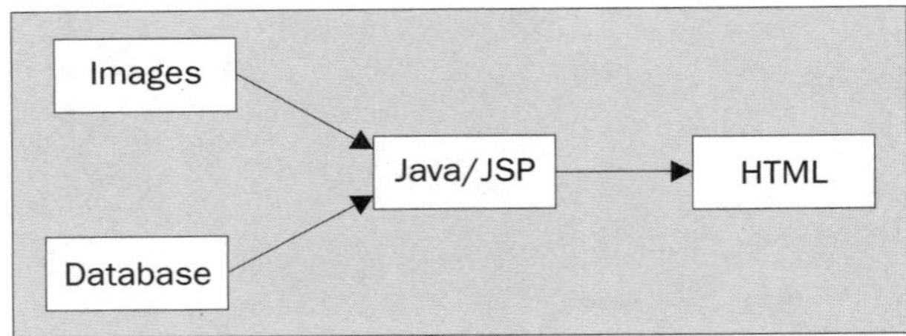

The PhotoDB application is divided into layers consisting of database access, application logic, and presentation:

The presentation layer of the software, which is responsible for creating the user interface, is implemented using JSP. The Java source files provide some application logic, utilities, and an interface to the data storage layer. The database access layer maps the underlying relational database to objects that are more readily manipulated in Java. In practice, the division between these layers is not perfect and there is some 'leakage' at their edges. For instance, some database access code is contained in the application logic classes and some application logic is contained in the JSP files.

Each time a user accesses a page in the PhotoDB application it generates a new request to the application. All requests have a somewhat generic flow that starts with a request for a JSP page. The JSP page then creates a `PhotoRequest` object (or a subclass thereof), and then the desired operation is performed and the resulting HTML rendered. For instance, to view a photograph, the user accesses the page `photo-view.jsp`. This page creates a `PhotoViewRequest` object. The `PhotoViewRequest` object extracts the name of the photograph to view and loads the data for the photograph from the database into a `Photo` object. The `photo-view.jsp` page then renders the HTML needed to display the image.

User Interface

Perhaps the best way to understand PhotoDB is to start by accessing some of the web pages that it generates. The full PhotoDB is accessible from my web site at http://www.magiccookie.com/photography/photodb.

> **I use the term *photograph* to refer to the original film slide or negative, and the term image to refer to an electronic replica of a photograph. Thus, there is only ever a single specific photograph, but there may be multiple *images* of the photograph. For instance, I make small and large scans of a photograph and store the scans as two different image files.**

PhotoDB provides two ways to organize photographs: by location and by category. Each photograph belongs to a single location, which corresponds to the physical place at which the original photograph was taken, for example, Yellowstone National Park. Every photograph must belong to one and only one location. In contrast, categories allow images to belong to a list of keyword-based categories. A photograph may belong to any number of categories. For example, a photograph might be of an insect and also of a flower, and therefore it would belong to both the insect and flower categories.

Viewing a Single Image

Clicking on a thumbnail of a photograph displays a larger version of the photograph. This detailed view also includes the photograph's description, notes, and links to the location and categories to which the photograph belongs.

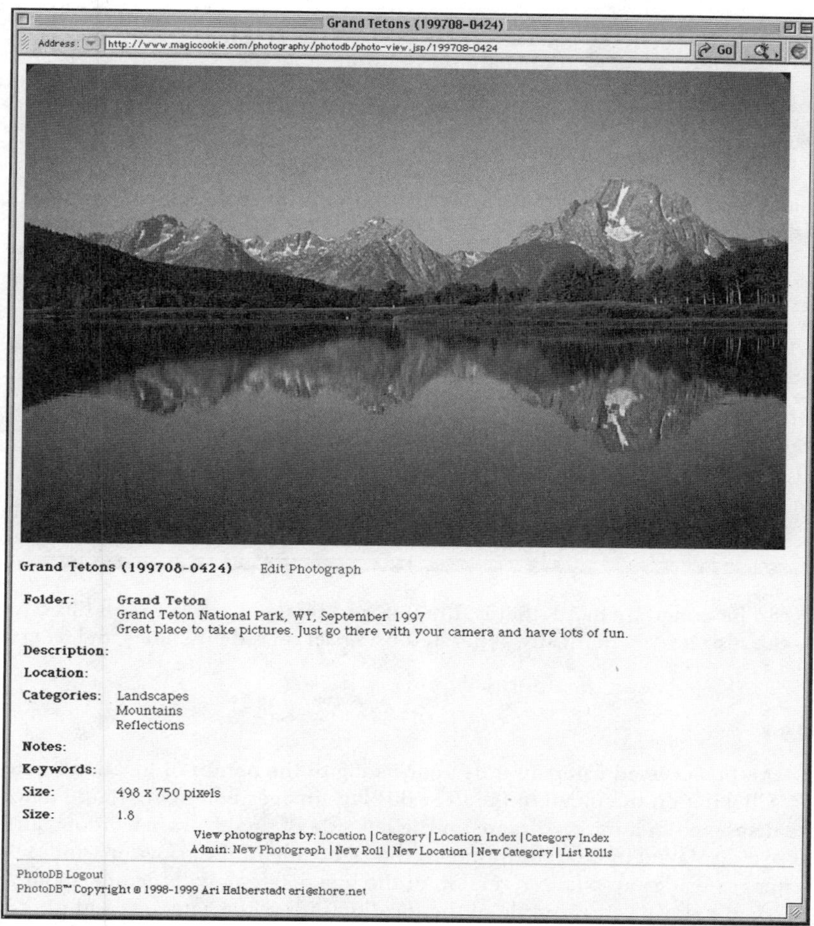

Embedded Images

There are images interspersed among my web pages. For example, my home page contains several images. Clicking on any thumbnail image displays a larger version of the photograph along with details about the photograph.

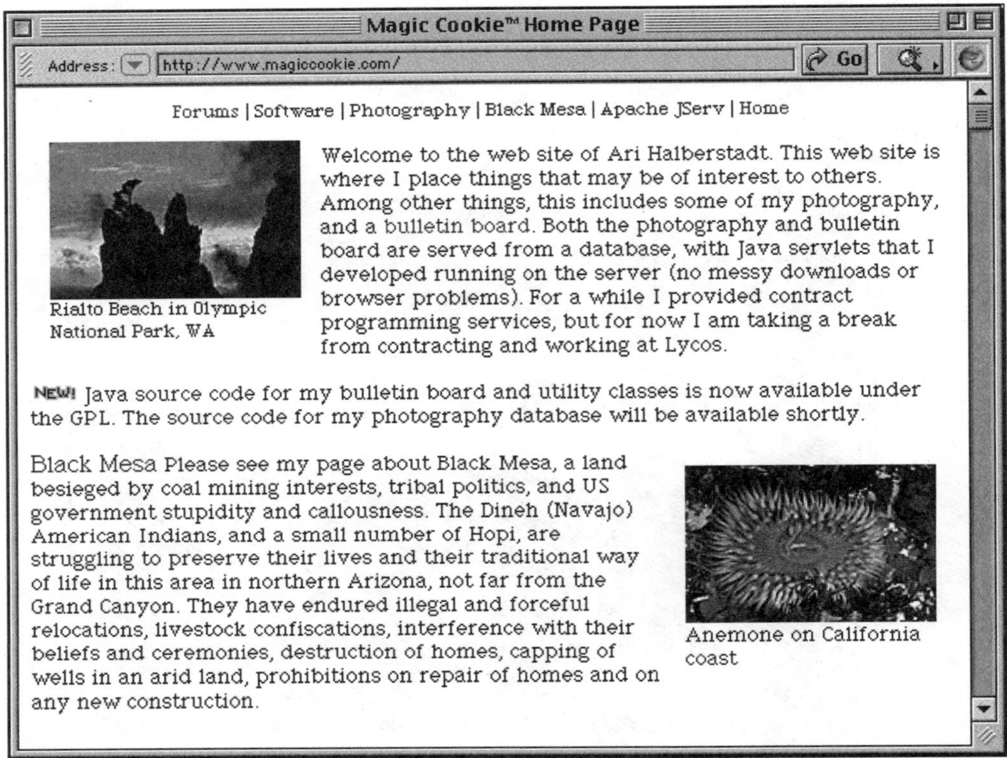

Thumbnails can be coded by hand, that is, the link and image tags are coded directly in the HTML. Thumbnails can also be automatically generated using server-side includes and a servlet included with PhotoDB.

Index Pages

Photographs can be accessed using an index consisting of the names of locations, categories, or photographs. Clicking on the name of the item displays images belonging to the item. The names of the items are displayed in a narrow frame on the left side of the browser window, and small 150x100 pixel images are displayed in a larger frame on the right side of the browser window. Clicking on one of the small images brings up a larger version of the image, along with details about the photograph and image. Shown below is an example of the location index; the category and photograph indexes are similar.

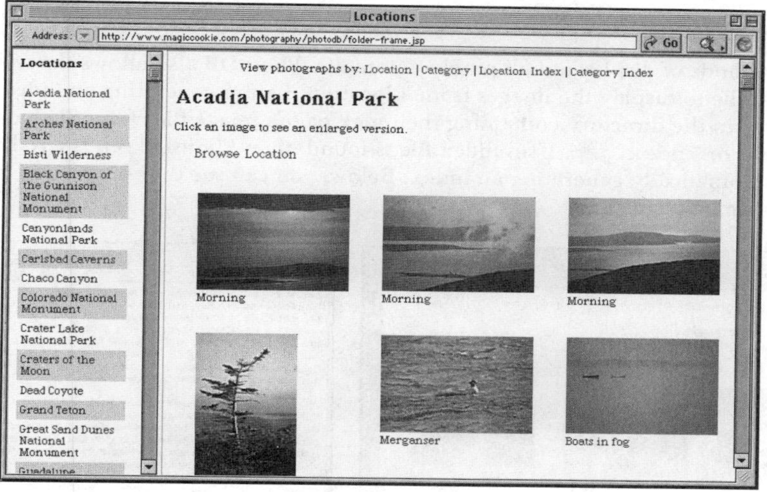

Gallery Pages

Another way to access the images is using what I call a gallery. A gallery of locations or categories shows one image from each location or category. Clicking on the image brings up a gallery of all the photographs belonging to the selected item. This provides a convenient way to showcase the best photographs from each location or category.

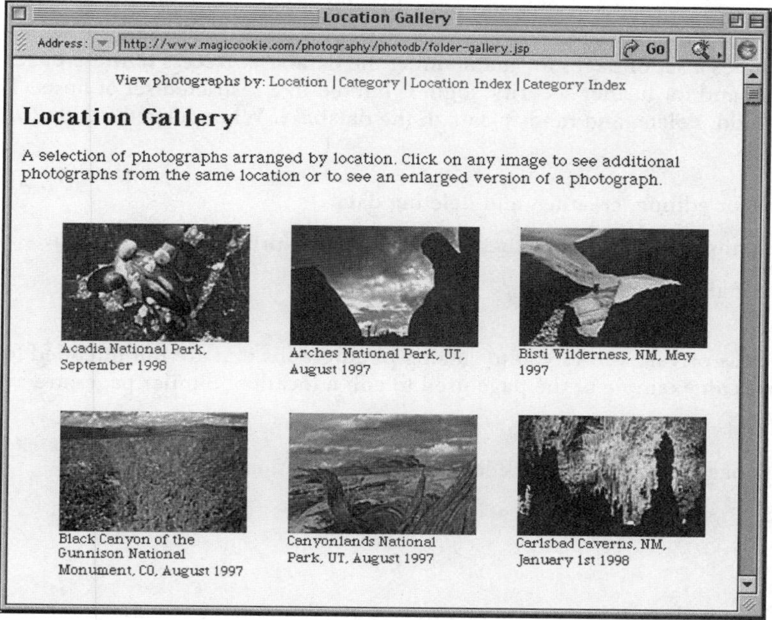

Custom Index Page

The above methods of display are all purely automatic. PhotoDB also allows the web site maintainer to use an HTML file to display the images from a location. Before generating an index page for a location, PhotoDB looks in the directory containing the index page's image files for a file named `index.html`, `index.jhtml`, or `index.jsp`. If an index file is found, then PhotoDB sends a redirect to the index file rather than automatically generating an index. Below, you can see the comparison between a standard and a custom index page.

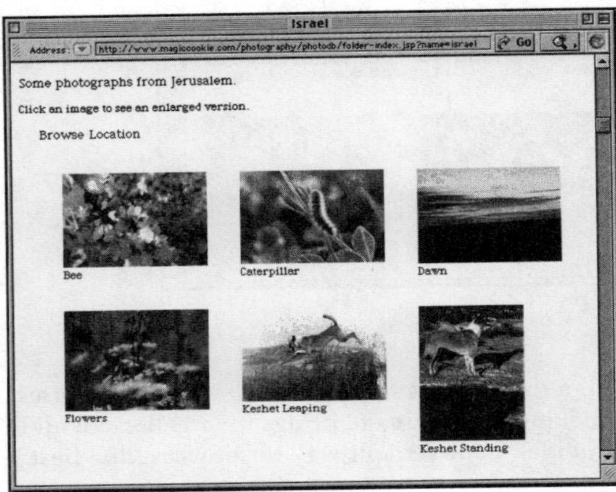

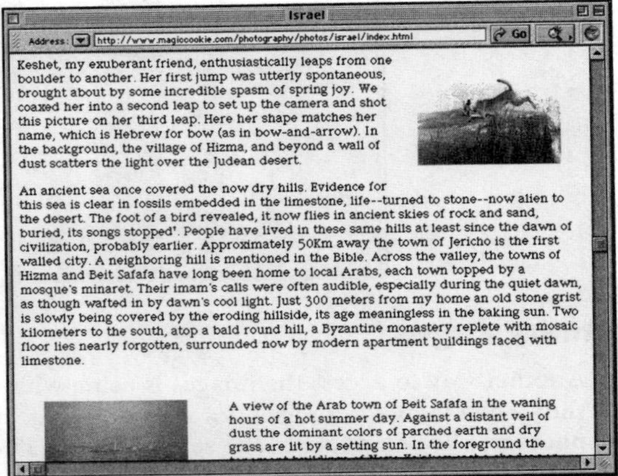

Editing Data

PhotoDB includes a set of pages for maintaining the database. Access to these pages requires a valid PhotoDB login and for further security, login is limited to a restricted set of hosts. These pages allow the webmaster to add, delete, and modify data in the database. When logged in, PhotoDB provides access to:

- pages for editing, creating, and deleting data
- photographs and locations that are designated as private
- a list of all the rolls of film

Marking items as private allows you to catalog photographs that are not intended for public access. Shown below is an example of the page used to edit a location. Similar pages are available for editing other data types.

The following page is used to edit the location Acadia National Park:

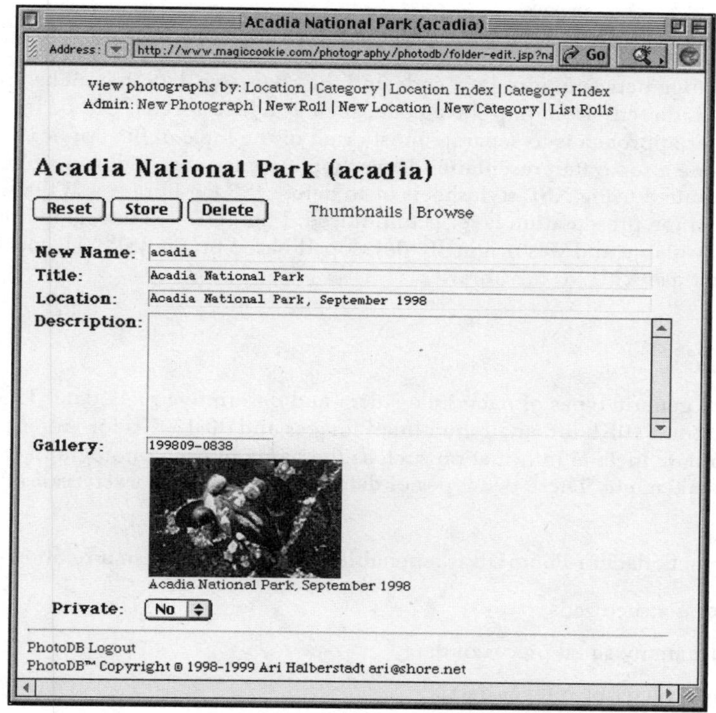

Selecting Technologies

This section discusses the technologies I selected to implement PhotoDB.

JDK Version

One decision that had to be made was which version of Java to support: the older JDK 1.1 or the latest Java 2 (JDK 1.2). Supporting the older JDK 1.1 has some advantages over requiring JDK 1.2. There are more runtime environments in which JDK 1.1 code can be executed. These include all JDK 1.1 runtime environments, and, since JDK 1.2 is backwards compatible with JDK 1.1, all JDK 1.2 environments as well. Linux was my primary development environment, yet at the time there was no version of JDK1.2 available for Linux, therefore I developed PhotoDB using JDK 1.1. Furthermore, to maintain compatibility with servlet containers like Apache and JServ, PhotoDB only requires JSDK v2.0, rather than the latest JSDK v2.2.

Presentation Layer

JSPs provide a bridge between pure Java code and the character data that make up a web page. Outputting HTML directly from pure Java code, such as a Java servlet, can be tedious and may be inflexible. A better approach is to separate most or all of the logic of the application into business objects and provide a separate presentation layer. Some approaches to this problem are to output XML data that are formatted using XSL stylesheets or to define JSP tag libraries so that the amount of Java code embedded in the presentation layer is minimized. PhotoDB was developed before XML/XSL became readily available and was originally developed based on the JSP v0.9 specification. Hence, PhotoDB does not use XML or tag libraries.

Data Storage

PhotoDB has two generic types of data: image data and descriptive meta data. The images are binary data, typically around 10Kb for small thumbnail images and 30-150Kb for larger images. The descriptive meta data include information such as the name of each photograph, where and when the photograph was taken, etc. These two types of data have different characteristics that affect their storage and retrieval.

The descriptive meta data in PhotoDB is amenable to representation in a relational database because:

- The data is structured.
- There are many small pieces of data.
- It is all character or integer data.
- The data need to be searched, retrieved, and recombined in various ways.

An object database could have provided an alternative to a relational database. Using an object database would simplify much of the database access code since there would have been no need for a separate data access layer. However, relational databases, including free databases such as PostgreSQL and mySQL, are more widely available and accessible, using SQL, is more standardized.

Image data, on the other hand, needs to be accessible to the web server. Web servers know how to get images off a disk. You can give a URL to a web server and it will read an image file and send it back to a web browser. While it is possible in most relational databases to store large binary data (such as image files), such support is not standardized and varies from one RDBMS to the next. Furthermore, by keeping images in plain files, the data are accessible for manipulation by other tools; for instance, I can use tools to automatically generate JPEG files of varying quality and size from an original scan.

Image Files

The standard and compact format for display of photographic color images on the Internet is JPEG. Hence, all the image files are stored as JPEGs on my web site. In principle, it should be possible to store images in any arbitrary format, though PhotoDB currently includes code to extract image attributes only from JPEG images.

Images must be stored digitally for access via PhotoDB. I do all my photography using film, either slide or negative. I then use a scanner to create digital files containing images of the photographs. I have written up a more detailed description of how I scan images and process them at http://www.magiccookie.com/photography.

JPEG is a poor storage format, it does not retain all the original information in an image. This makes JPEG a poor format for storage of original scans or digital images. A better image format for permanent storage would be TIFF or PNG, which retain image data and are highly portable. Automated tools can then be used to convert the high-quality images into lower-quality JPEG images.

Database

This section describes the database tables used in PhotoDB.

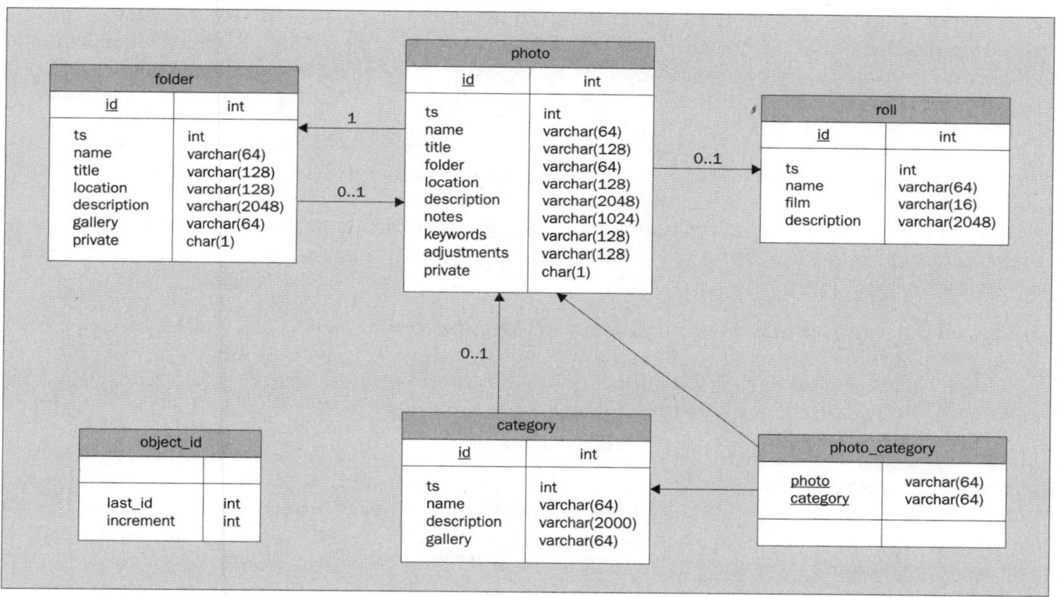

The objects manipulated by PhotoDB that must be stored in persistent storage correspond to photographs, folders, categories, and rolls of film. Each of these objects is mapped to a single database table and a corresponding Java class. Additional tables are used to provide many-to-many mappings between objects and to support generating unique object IDs.

Table	Description
`folder`	Represents folders.
`category`	Represents categories.
`photo`	Represents photographs.
`roll`	Represents a roll of film.
`photo_category`	Associates photographs with categories.
`object_id`	Keeps track of the last ID assigned to a row in the database. Used to generate unique object IDs.

The `folder`, `category`, `photo`, and `roll` tables correspond to persistent objects. These tables include the columns `id` and `ts`, which are used by the Java database mapping layer to identify individual objects and to support optimistic row locking (optimistic locking is explained in the section on data access).

Relationships Among Tables

Each photograph is associated with a `single` folder. By convention, this folder corresponds to the physical place at which the original photograph was taken, for example, Yellowstone National Park. Every photograph must belong to one and only one folder. This is a many-to-one relationship between photographs and folders, since each photograph may be associated with only one folder, while each folder may contain many photographs. This relationship is represented by storing a foreign key to the `folder` table in the `folder` column of the `photo` table.

Categories allow images to belong to any number of keyword-based categories. For instance, a photograph might be of an insect and also of a flower, and therefore it would belong to both the Insect and Flower categories. This is a many-to-many relationship: a category may contain any number of photographs and a photograph may belong to any number of categories. This relationship is represented in the `photo_category` table, which contains foreign keys to both the `photo` and `category` tables.

Folders and categories may have a particular photograph designated as a so-called gallery photograph. When the user views the gallery page of all folders or categories, the thumbnails displayed are those specified as gallery photographs. This relationship is represented as a foreign key from the `gallery` column of the `folder` and `category` tables to the name field of the `photo` table.

Photographs may be associated with rolls of film. There is a many-to-one relationship between photographs and rolls of film, since each photograph came from a single roll of film, while each roll of film may contain many photographs. This relationship is implicitly represented through a convention on the names of the photographs. The name of each photograph begins with the name of the roll of film, followed by the number of the photograph in the roll.

Notice that this is not a good way to maintain such a relationship: an explicit foreign key stored in a separate column is preferable, and a future version of PhotoDB should incorporate this change.

Foreign Keys

PhotoDB uses names of entries as foreign keys into other tables. For instance, the photo table contains a name field that is referenced by fields in several other tables. The folder table's gallery `field`, contains the name of a photograph from the `photo` table. This seemed like an adequate arrangement when I first created PhotoDB.

A drawback of using user-visible and modifiable data as a foreign key is that the data might change, requiring many rows in the database to be updated. The name of a photograph can be changed after the photograph has been created (consider the situation where one enters the wrong name). This means that code that is used to store a row to the `photo` table must update all the foreign key references to the updated row. For instance, the following code is found in the method store of the class `com.magiccookie.photodb.PhotoEditRequest`.

```
    // update dependent data
    if (! mCategory.getName().equals(mName) && ! mCategory.isNew()) {
      getDatabase().update("update " + Category.TABLE +
        " set name=" + getDatabase().quote(mCategory.getName()) +
        " where name=" + getDatabase().quote(mName));
      getDatabase().update("update " + Category.PHOTO_CATEGORY_TABLE +
        " set category=" + getDatabase().quote(mCategory.getName()) +
        " where category=" + getDatabase().quote(mName));
    }
```

The above method must therefore be aware of several unrelated database tables. If a new table is added that contains the name of a photograph as a foreign key, then this method will need to be revised so that the foreign key in the new table is updated. This introduces dependencies among modules that should not be present, leading to code that is harder to maintain than necessary.

Another drawback of text-based keys is that they are less efficient to index than numeric keys. After the initial version of PhotoDB, I added a numeric ID to tables in the database that correspond to Java objects. An ID is automatically assigned to new rows as they are inserted into the database. The ID is convenient for use from the classes that map objects to tables in the package `com.magiccookie.Database`. If I had to do PhotoDB over again, I would have used the numeric ID field as the sole foreign key, rather than replicating the names of photos, folders, and other items throughout the database.

Database Portability

SQL is supposed to be relatively standard. However, each vendor implements a slightly different version of SQL. Even things as simple as varchar and text types may differ between vendors. The solution I adopted in PhotoDB was two-fold:

- Code to the lowest-common denominator.
- Use a macro preprocessor to generate the SQL statements that create the initial database tables and objects.

The generic initialization scripts are in the directory `src/sql`. Two files are provided: `create-sql.m4` contains the data definition statements for constructing the database tables and indexes. The file `sample-sql.m4` contains statements that insert data for a small sample database and photographs included with PhotoDB. Scripts for a desired target RDBMS are automatically generated from these files using the `bin/mksql` script. This script uses Perl and GNU's m4 macro preprocessor to merge the macros defined in `src/sql/include.m4` with the SQL macro files to generate scripts for different RDBMSs. The resulting scripts are written to the sql directory.

Any text in `create-sql.m4` that is in all-caps is a macro defined either in the same file or in the `include.m4` file. Several of the macros map to an underlying data type supported by the database. For instance, the `TIMESTAMP` type maps to a numeric type at least 32 bits long, but uses a larger value, such as `bigint` or `int8`, if possible. The following table contains descriptions of some of the macros (some of the other macros are used only within the macro definition file).

Macro	Description
OID	Object ID, such as int4 or int8
OTS	Object timestamp, such as int4 or int8.
BOOLEAN	Boolean value, represented as the character 't' for true and 'f' for false.
VARCHAR	Same as SQL standard varchar.
TEXT	Arbitrary length text. A value in parenthesis indicates the minimum desired length.
TIMESTAMP	A timestamp represented as seconds since January 1, 1970, 00:00:00 GMT. Typically a 32 bit integer, though a larger type is used if supported by the RDBMS.
CHECK	A check constraint on a column.
GO	Statement terminator, such as a semicolon or the keyword GO.

For instance, the definition of the `object_id` table in the file `src/sql/create-sql.m4` is:

```
# Used to generate unique object IDs.
create table object_id (
  last_id     OID not null,
  increment   OID not null CHECK(increment > 0)
) GO
```

and the resulting table definition in `src/create-pgsql.sql` is:

```
create table object_id (
 last_id int8 not null,
 increment int8 not null check (increment > 0)
) ;
```

JSP Pages

The JSP pages implement the presentation layer and generate the HTML for displaying the pages. The pages in PhotoDB can be grouped by the type of objects that the pages access and by the type of functionality provided by the pages. The main objects in PhotoDB are photo, folder, category, and roll. Each object has a related set of JSP files. The other operations in PhotoDB can be grouped into security, error handling, header/footer, and testing. Security is handled with the files `login.jsp` and `logout.jsp`. Errors are reported using the file `error.jsp`. The shared header and footer used in each page are contained in the files `header.jsp` and `footer.jsp`. Finally, various tests are accessed via the file `test.jsp`.

The pages for accessing the folder and category objects provide similar functionality. These pages provide interfaces to:

Function	Page
Edit, create, or delete an item	folder-edit.jsp
	category-edit.jsp
List all items	folder-list.jsp
	category-list.jsp
View thumbnails of all images associated with an item	folder-index.jsp
	category-index.jsp
View thumbnails of selected images associated with an item	folder-gallery.jsp
	category-gallery.jsp
Load a frameset for listing and viewing items	folder-frame.jsp
	category-frame.jsp
	(folder-none.jsp and category-none.jsp are used as placeholders)

Three additional files provide a way to browse the photographs associated with a folder:

List photographs associated with a folder	photo-list.jsp
Load a frameset for browsing photographs belonging to a folder	photo-frame.jsp
	(photo-none.jsp is used as a placeholder)

The files for managing and viewing photographs are:

Editing, creating, or deleting a photograph	photo-edit.jsp
Viewing a photograph	photo-view.jsp

The pages for accessing the roll object are not publicly accessible and are provided simply to help the photographer organize the photographs and keep track of information such as the type of film used.

Editing, creating, and deleting a roll	roll-edit.jsp
Listing rolls	roll-list.jsp
Viewing photographs associated with a roll	roll-index.jsp

Simple JSP Page

A simple JSP page in PhotoDB is `category-none.jsp`, shown below in its entirety:

```
<%@ page errorPage="error.jsp" %>
<%@ page import="com.magiccookie.photodb.PhotoUtil" %>
<%@ page import="com.magiccookie.photodb.PhotoRequest" %>
```

```
<%
  PhotoRequest photoRequest = new PhotoRequest();
  try {
    photoRequest.init(request, response, out);
%>

<html>
<head>
<title>
No Category
</title>
</head>
<body>

<%@ include file="header.jsp" %>

<p>Select a category to view from the list to left. Most, but not all,
photographs have been categorized; to view all photographs you can
browse the
  <a href="<%=PhotoUtil.makeDocumentURL("folder-gallery.jsp")%>"
     target="_top">location gallery</a>
or
  <a href="<%=PhotoUtil.makeDocumentURL("folder-frame.jsp")%>"
     target="_top">location index</a>.
</p>

<%@ include file="footer.jsp" %>

</body>
</html>

<%
  } finally {
    photoRequest.destroy();
  }
%>
```

This page is displayed in the right frame when accessing the index of categories when no category has yet been selected by the user.

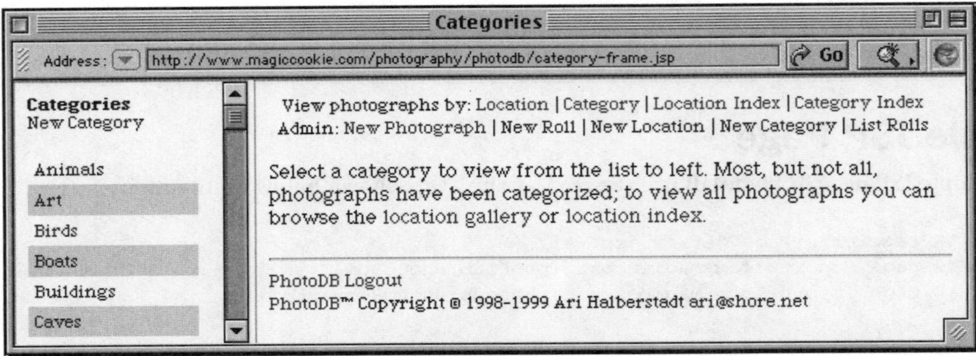

The page starts with several JSP directives enclosed in `<%@ ... %>`:

```
<%@ page errorPage="../error.jsp" %>
<%@ page import="com.magiccookie.photodb.PhotoUtil" %>
<%@ page import="com.magiccookie.photodb.PhotoRequest" %>
```

The first directive specifies an error page that will be loaded should the page throw an exception. All pages in PhotoDB use `error.jsp` to display error messages. The next two directives import Java classes for access from the page. The import directives are followed by a scriptlet, which is a section of Java code enclosed in `<% ... %>`:

```
<%
  PhotoRequest photoRequest = new PhotoRequest();
  try {
    photoRequest.init(request, response, out);
%>
```

Since this is a simple request, it just uses the plain `PhotoRequest` object. The request object is initialized with the predefined `request`, `response`, and `out` variables. Following the scriptlet is some plain HTML text:

```
<html>
<head>
<title>
No Category
</title>
</head>
<body>
```

This is followed by another JSP directive, again enclosed in `<%@ ... %>`:

```
<%@ include file="../header.jsp" %>
```

The include directive includes the specified JSP page. The file `header.jsp` is used in all the pages of PhotoDB to provide a common navigation menu. Following the include directive is some HTML text mixed in with Java expressions. The Java expressions are enclosed in `<%= ... %>`, which cause the result of the Java expressions to be written to the output stream as a string:

```
<p>Select a category to view from the list to left. Most, but not all,
photographs have been categorized; to view all photographs you can
browse the
  <a href="<%=PhotoUtil.makeDocumentURL("folder-gallery.jsp")%>"
     target="_top">location gallery</a>
or
  <a href="<%=PhotoUtil.makeDocumentURL("folder-frame.jsp")%>"
     target="_top">location index</a>.
</p>
```

The utility method `PhotoUtil.makeDocumentURL` returns a URL for another JSP page. This method comes in handy when dealing with different JSP runtime containers that may interpret URLs in slightly different ways. The utility function helps isolate the pages from any changes to the runtime environment or the location where the pages are installed. Using a utility method to specify a URL leads, unfortunately, to somewhat cumbersome expressions, but I find this preferable to dealing with idiosyncrasies of the runtime environment.

The bottom of the page is basically the same for all pages in PhotoDB:

```
<%@ include file="footer.jsp" %>

</body>
</html>

<%
  } finally {
    photoRequest.destroy();
  }
%>
```

A common footer, containing navigation, copyright, login/logout, and other shared links is output at the bottom of each page. This is followed by the closing `body` and `html` tags of a standard HTML page, and finally a call to the `destroy` method of the `photoRequest` object to ensure that any resources held by the object are released.

Header and Footer Pages

The header and footer are stored in the files `header.jsp` and `footer.jsp`. If adapting PhotoDB, you might want to customize these files to provide content and navigation links for the rest of your web site. The header and footer are included in other pages using the JSP `include` directive. Unlike the other pages in PhotoDB, the header and footer files output a fragment of an HTML page: they do not output the full HTML and body tags, so that the output of these files can be included in other HTML documents. The following listing shows the header file (`header.jsp`) provided with PhotoDB:

```
<%-- Header included at the start of every page. --%>

<%@ page import="com.magiccookie.photodb.PhotoUtil" %>

<small>
View photographs by:
<a href="<%=PhotoUtil.makeDocumentURL("folder-gallery.jsp")%>"
 target="_top">Location</a>
| <a href="<%=PhotoUtil.makeDocumentURL("category-gallery.jsp")%>"
 target="_top">Category</a>
| <a href="<%=PhotoUtil.makeDocumentURL("folder-frame.jsp")%>"
 target="_top">Location Index</a>
| <a href="<%=PhotoUtil.makeDocumentURL("category-frame.jsp")%>"
 target="_top">Category Index</a>
</small>

<% if (photoRequest.hasWriteAccess()) { %>
<br>
<small>
Admin:
<a href="<%=PhotoUtil.makeDocumentURL("photo-edit.jsp")%>"
 target="_top">New Photograph</a>
| <a href="<%=PhotoUtil.makeDocumentURL("roll-edit.jsp")%>"
 target="_top">New Roll</a>
| <a href="<%=PhotoUtil.makeDocumentURL("folder-edit.jsp")%>"
 target="_top">New Location</a>
| <a href="<%=PhotoUtil.makeDocumentURL("category-edit.jsp")%>"
 target="_top">New Category</a>
```

```
| <a href="<%=PhotoUtil.makeDocumentURL("roll-list.jsp")%>"
 target="_top">List Rolls</a>
</small>
<br>
<% } %>
```

The header includes links to the various files for accessing indexes of photographs. The static method `PhotoUtil.makeDocumentURL` is used to ensure that URLs are not hard coded into the JSP file. If the user is logged in, then links for creating new items and for accessing the list of rolls of film are included in the output.

The footer includes links for logging in and out of PhotoDB and a copyright message with a link to the magiccookie.com web site. The following listing shows the footer provided with PhotoDB:

```
<%-- Footer included at the end of every page. --%>
<%@ page import="com.magiccookie.photodb.PhotoUtil" %>
<hr>
<% if (photoRequest.isLoggedIn()) { %>
  <small><a href="<%=PhotoUtil.makeDocumentURL("logout.jsp")%>"
  target="_top">PhotoDB Logout</a></small><br>
<% } else if (photoRequest.canLogin()) { %>
  <small><a href="<%=PhotoUtil.makeDocumentURL("login.jsp")%>"
  target="_top">PhotoDB Login</a></small><br>
<% } %>
<small>
<a href="http://www.magiccookie.com/photography/photodb"
target="_top">PhotoDB</a>&#153; Copyright &copy; 1998-2000 Ari Halberstadt
<a href="mailto:ari@shore.net">ari@shore.net</a>
</small>
<br>
```

Category and Folder Pages

The category and folder groups of pages follow an identical pattern, as is evident from the file names:

Category Group	Folder Group
category-edit.jsp	folder-edit.jsp
category-frame.jsp	folder-frame.jsp
category-gallery.jsp	folder-gallery.jsp
category-index.jsp	folder-index.jsp
category-list.jsp	folder-list.jsp
category-none.jsp	folder-none.jsp

Since the files are similar it should be sufficient to describe only one set. The files used for accessing photographs are also quite similar. Since this chapter is not a comprehensive manual, I will skip the detailed descriptions of most of these files (the interested reader can download the complete files from the Internet).

category-frame.jsp

The file `category-frame.jsp` is used to display an index of all categories in a convenient frameset. This file loads a frameset consisting of two side-by-side frames, with the file `category-index.jsp` in the left frame and the file `category-none.jsp` in the right frame. The file `category-none.jsp` is a placeholder displayed before the user has selected a category. When the user selects a category to view, the file `category-index.jsp` is loaded into the right frame to display the photographs associated with the selected category. The file `category-frame.jsp` is shown below:

```
<%@ page errorPage="error.jsp" %>
<%@ page import="com.magiccookie.photodb.PhotoUtil" %>
<html>
<head>
<title>
  Categories
</title>
</head>
<frameset cols="150,*">
  <frame src="<%=PhotoUtil.makeDocumentURL("category-list.jsp")%>"
   name="category-list">
  <frame src="<%=PhotoUtil.makeDocumentURL("category-none.jsp")%>"
   name="category-view">
</frameset>
</html>
```

category-list.jsp

The file `category-list.jsp` displays a single-column list of all the categories in the database. When the user selects a category, the file `category-index.jsp` is loaded into the right frame to display the images belonging to the selected category.

The following screen-shot is of the category index, with a list of categories from `category-list.jsp` on the left and photographs belonging to the category, Rainbows, displayed using `category-index.jsp` in the right frame.

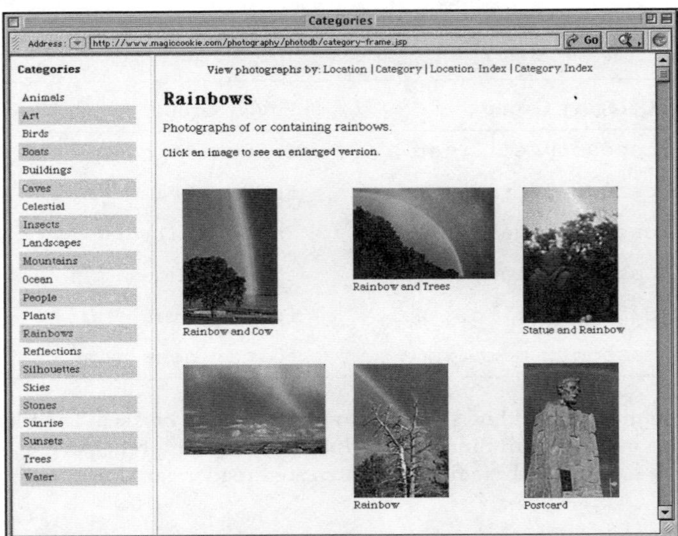

The file `category-list.jsp` is described below. The page starts with the usual page directives and boilerplate HTML (this is so similar among pages that it is not repeated here). A new `CategoryListRequest` object is created to process the request. This object derives from `QueryRequest` and encapsulates the code needed to query the database.

```
<%
  CategoryListRequest photoRequest = new CategoryListRequest();
  try {
    photoRequest.init(request, response, out);
%>
```

Since this is a frameset, the page's target is set, using the HTML code `<base target="category-view">`, to the name of the right-hand frame, so that clicking on the links will load the corresponding URL in the appropriate frame. Notice that this page does not include the header and footer pages, since they would not fit in the narrow frame and they will be displayed, instead, in the right-hand frame.

If the user has write access (is logged in), then a link to create a new category is displayed.

```
<% if (photoRequest.hasWriteAccess()) { %>
  <small><a href="<%=PhotoUtil.makeDocumentURL("category-edit.jsp")%>">New
Category</a></small><br>
<% } %>
```

Next, the `photoRequest` object, which is an instance of the class `CategoryListRequest`, is called to repeatedly retrieve a link to each category. An appropriate message is displayed if there are no categories in the database.

```
<table bgcolor="ffffff" width="100%" cellpadding="4" cellspacing="0" border="0">
  <% while (photoRequest.next()) { %>
    <tr bgcolor="<%=photoRequest.getColor()%>">
      <td><small><%=photoRequest.getIndexLink()%></small></td>
    </tr>
  <% } %>
</table>

<% if (photoRequest.getCount() == 0) { %>
  <p>There are no categories in the database.</p>
<% } %>
```

Finally, the usual page footer and HTML end tags are output and the request object is destroyed (again, this code is omitted since it is so similar among pages).

category-index.jsp

The file `category-index.jsp` displays the images associated with a category. The index appears in the frame to the right of the list of categories displayed by `category-list.jsp`. `category-index.jsp` starts with the usual boilerplate page directives and HTML code. Next, a `CategoryIndexRequest` object is created to handle the request.

```
<%
  CategoryIndexRequest photoRequest = new CategoryIndexRequest();
  try {
    photoRequest.init(request, response, out);
%>
```

This is followed by some typical HTML to render the standard top portion page. If the user has write access (is logged in) then a link to edit the category is displayed.

```
<% if (photoRequest.hasWriteAccess()) { %>
  <p><a href="<%=PhotoUtil.makeDocumentURL("category-
edit.jsp")%>?name=<%=HtmlUtil.encodeUrl(photoRequest.getCategory().getName())%>">E
dit Category</a></p>
<% } %>
```

Next, the `photoRequest` object, which is an instance of the class `CategoryIndexRequest`, is called to output table rows containing thumbnails of each of photographs associated with the category. An appropriate message is displayed if there are no categories in the database.

```
<center>
  <table border="0" cellpadding="10" cellspacing="10">
    <% photoRequest.printRows(); %>
  </table>
</center>

<% if (photoRequest.getThumbnailCount() == 0) { %>
  <p>There are no photographs in this category.</p>
<% } %>
```

Finally, the usual page footer and HTML end tags are output and the request object is destroyed.

category-gallery.jsp

The file `category-gallery.jsp` provides another way to access categories. Accessing this URL displays a single image from each category. The source code for `category-gallery.jsp` is very similar to `category-index.jsp`, except that a `CategoryGalleryRequest` object is used to process the request rather than a `CategoryIndexRequest` object. Since the two files are so similar there is little point in showing the full source code for `category-gallery.jsp`. The following screen-shot does show a Category gallery page being displayed using `category-gallery.jsp`.

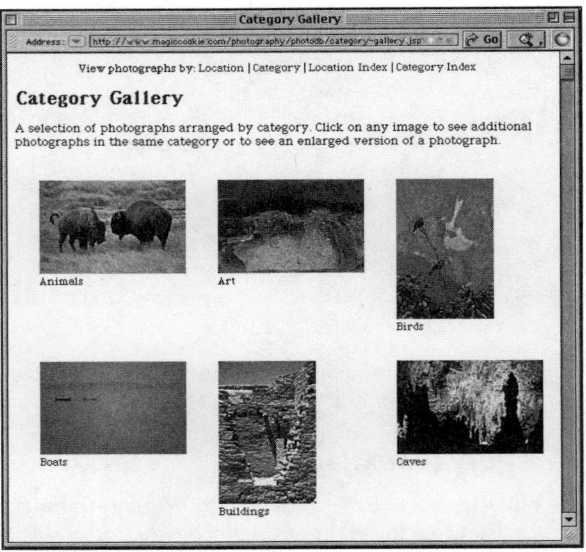

Clicking on any of the images in the category gallery displays all the images in the corresponding category using the file `category-index.jsp`. This is the same page used earlier in the two-frame example, except that this is a no-frames interface to the categories.

category-edit.jsp

If the user is logged in, then an Edit Category link is included in the thumbnails of photographs belonging to the category. Clicking this link displays a page for editing the category using the file `category-edit.jsp`. A New Category link is also available in the menus at the top of each page; this link displays the same `category-edit.jsp` page, though the form contains blank values so that a new category may be created.

The following screen-shot shows the Category Edit page with a list of categories from `category-list.jsp` in the left frame and information about the category displayed using `category-edit.jsp` in the right frame.

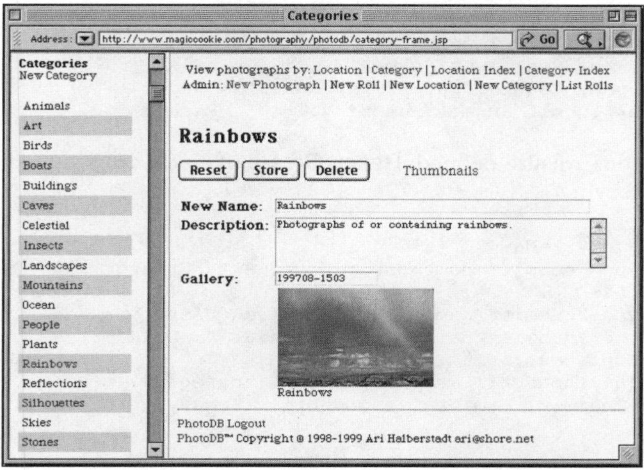

The file `category-edit.jsp` is shown below. The file starts with the usual boilerplate page directives and HTML code. Next, a `CategoryEditRequest` object is created to handle the request:

```
<%
  CategoryEditRequest photoRequest = new CategoryEditRequest();
  try {
    photoRequest.init(request, response, out);
    String message = photoRequest.handleRequest();
    Category category = photoRequest.getCategory();
    String title = category.isNew() ? "New Category" : category.getName();
%>
```

After the request object is created the usual HTML code is outputted. Since editing a category may alter its title, it is convenient to automatically refresh the left frame (containing the list of categories) when the title is changed. The page therefore outputs a bit of JavaScript to force a refresh of the list. (Using JavaScript to refresh a list frame is the only use of JavaScript in the entire PhotoDB application; the application will continue to work even if JavaScript is not supported in the browser.)

```
<input type="submit" name="reset" value="  Reset  ">
<% if (category.isNew()) { %>
    <input type="submit" name="store" value="  Create  ">
<% } else { %>
    <input type="submit" name="store" value="  Store  ">
    <input type="submit" name="delete" value="  Delete  ">
       
    <a href="<%=PhotoUtil.makeDocumentURL("category-
index.jsp")%>?name=<%=HtmlUtil.encodeUrl(category.getName())%>">Thumbnails</a>
<% } %>
```

This is followed by the title of the category and a message indicating the action taken by the page (e.g. update or delete):

```
<h2><%= title %></h2>

<p><%= HtmlUtil.encode(message) %></p>
```

The body of the edit form passes along the original name of the category in a hidden field, so that the `CategoryEditRequest` object can detect when the title is changed:

```
<form method="post" action="category-edit.jsp">
  <input type="hidden" name="name"
   value="<%=photoRequest.getInternalName()%>">
  <input type="submit" name="reset" value="  Reset  ">
```

Several submit buttons are also defined: **Reset**, **Create** (if a new category), and **Store** and **Delete** (if an existing category):

```
  <% if (category.isNew()) { %>
    <input type="submit" name="store" value="  Create  ">
  <% } else { %>
    <input type="submit" name="store" value="  Store  ">
    <input type="submit" name="delete" value="  Delete  ">
       
    <a href="<%=PhotoUtil.makeDocumentURL("category-
index.jsp")%>?name=<%=HtmlUtil.encodeUrl(category.getName())%>">Thumbnails</a>
  <% } %>
   <br>
```

An HTML table is displayed that contains editable values of the attributes of the category. If the category has a gallery image then a thumbnail of the gallery image is displayed:

```
<table border="0">
  <tr>
    <td><b>New Name:</b>
    <td><input type="text" name="newName" size="50"
         value="<%=HtmlUtil.encode(category.getName())%>">
  </tr>
  <tr valign="top">
    <td><b>Description:</b>
    <td><textarea name="description" rows="4" cols="50"
wrap="virtual"><%out.print(HtmlUtil.encode(category.getDescription()));%></textare
a>
  </tr>
  <tr valign="top">
    <td><b>Gallery:</b>
    <td><input type="text" name="gallery" size="16"
value="<%=HtmlUtil.encode(category.getGallery())%>">
      <%
        if (! category.getGallery().equals(Photo.NO_NAME))
        {
          Photo photo = new Photo(photoRequest.getDatabase(),
category.getGallery());
      %>
          <table border="0">
            <tr>
              <td width="150"><%=PhotoUtil.makeThumbnail(photo,
category.getName())%></td>
            </tr>
          </table>
      <% } %>
    </td>
  </tr>
</table>
```

Finally, the usual page footer and HTML end tags are output and the request object is destroyed.

Login and Logout Pages

PhotoDB requires that a user login before being allowed to edit data. The file `login.jsp` contains a simple login form allowing a user to login, while accessing the file `logout.jsp` logs the user out. Whether a user is logged is indicated by adding a `Boolean` value of `true` with the name defined by `PhotoUtil.LOGGED_IN` to the user's session. When the user is logged in, he or she is allowed to edit data and to view photographs and folders marked as private. The login page is as follows:

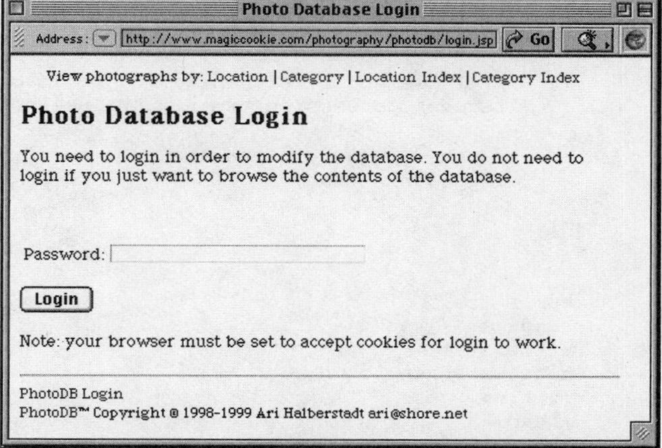

Following is the `login.jsp` file.

```
<%--
  Displays a login form and validates the data against an entry
  in a database table. Logging in is required to edit the photo
  database.
--%>

<%@ page errorPage="error.jsp" %>
<%@ page import="com.magiccookie.photodb.PhotoRequest" %>
<%@ page import="com.magiccookie.photodb.PhotoServlet" %>
<%@ page import="com.magiccookie.photodb.PhotoUtil" %>
<%@ page import="com.magiccookie.database.Query" %>
<%@ page import="com.magiccookie.database.Query" %>

<%
  // initialize request
  PhotoRequest photoRequest = new PhotoRequest();
  try {
    photoRequest.init(request, response, out);
%>

<%
  // will be set to true if the user entered the wrong password
  boolean failedLogin = false;

  // login is only allowed on certain machines
  if (! photoRequest.canLogin())
    throw new SecurityException("Cannot login from this host.");

  // get parameters
  String post = request.getParameter("post");
  String password = request.getParameter("password");

  // only try to login if the login button was clicked
  boolean loggedIn = false;
  if (post != null && post.equals("true")) {

    // check user name and password
    if (password == null)
      throw new IllegalArgumentException("Missing password");
    if (! PhotoServlet.getInstance().isLoginPassword(password))
      failedLogin = true;
    else {

      // if we got here then we logged in ok
      request.getSession(true).putValue(PhotoUtil.LOGGED_IN, Boolean.TRUE);

      // show logged-in message
      loggedIn = true;
    }
  }
%>

<html>
<head>
<title>
Photo Database Login
</title>
</head>
<body>
```

```
<%@ include file="header.jsp" %>

<h2>Photo Database Login</h2>

<% if (failedLogin) { %>

<p>Incorrect password.</p>

<% } if (loggedIn) { %>

<p>Successfully logged in. Select a link from the menu.</p>

<% } else { %>

<p>You need to login in order to modify the database. You do not need
to login if you just want to browse the contents of the database.</p>

<form method="post" action="<%=PhotoUtil.makeDocumentURL("login.jsp")%>">
  <input type="hidden" name="post" value="true">
  <table border="0">
    <tr>
      <td>Password:</td>
      <td><input type="password" size="32" name="password"></td>
    </tr>
  </table>
  <br>
  <input type="submit" name="login" value="  Login  ">
</form>

<br>

<p>Note: your browser must be set to accept cookies for login to work.</p>

<% } %>

<%@ include file="footer.jsp" %>

</body>
</html>

<%
  } finally {
    photoRequest.destroy();
  }
%>
photoRequestphotoRequestphotoRequestphotoRequestlogin.jsp
```

The login page uses a single JSP page to handle both GET and POST requests. When the page is first accessed it is loaded using a GET request. The page looks for a parameter called `post` to determine whether it is handling the initial GET request or a subsequent POST request. (The `getMethod` method of `HttpServletRequest` from the servlet API could also have been used to test this condition.) When loaded using a GET request there is no value for the `post` parameter, so the page skips the login test and just outputs the login form. When the user submits the form, the `login.jsp` page is against accessed, only this time the `post` parameter's value is set to `true`. The page then validates the password; if successful, it prints an appropriate message, otherwise it prints an error message and redisplays the login form.

Error Page

The page `error.jsp` is displayed when an exception is thrown from one of the JSP pages. Any error that prevents PhotoDB from successfully completing a request should display this page. Every JSP page (other than `error.jsp`) starts with a page directive that specifies that `error.jsp` is to be used to handle errors:

```
<%@ page errorPage="error.jsp" %>
```

The error page prints an error message followed by a link back to the default page for the application, which keeps the user from becoming stranded on the error page. The following is a sample error page displayed in response to a user error:

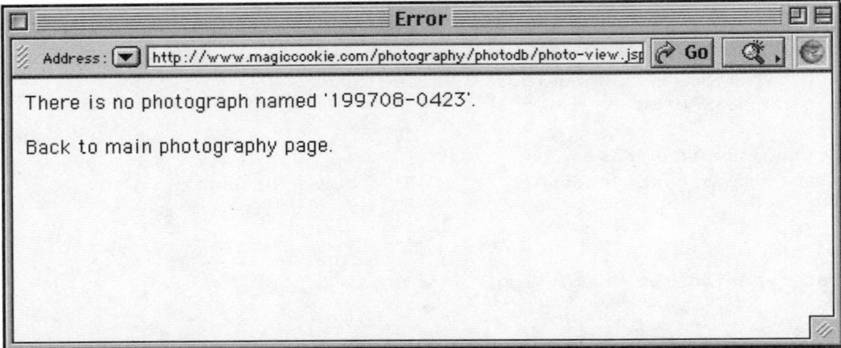

The error page is kept to a minimum of functionality, so that whatever error caused PhotoDB to fail is unlikely to also cause processing of the error page to fail. Unlike the other JSP pages in PhotoDB, the error page does not create a new `PhotoRequest` object.

The page starts with a JSP directive indicating that it is an error page. This makes the `exception` variable, which contains the exception object that caused the error page to be invoked, available to the page:

```
<%@ page isErrorPage="true" %>
```

This is followed by several `import` statements. Then, the error page decides how to handle the exception. If the page was invoked directly (indicated by a null exception object), then it creates a new dummy exception object with an appropriate error message. Next, it checks if the exception is a security exception, in which case it returns an `SC_UNAUTHORIZED` error to the caller. Using a standard HTTP error code enables client applications to possibly better interpret the cause of the error:

```
<%
  // exception could be null if page is invoked directly
  if (exception == null) {
    exception = new UnknownUserException("This error page is not meant to" +
      " be invoked directly, but only due to an internal error.");
  }

  // keep a log of the exception unless it's a user exception
  if (! (exception instanceof UserException))
    Log.println(Log.ERROR_CHANNEL, exception);
```

```
    // handle a security exception by returning an appropriate error code
    if (exception instanceof SecurityException) {
      try {
        response.sendError(HttpServletResponse.SC_UNAUTHORIZED,
                           exception.getMessage());
        return;
      } catch (IOException ignored) {
      }
    }
  %>
```

The page then outputs some plain HTML, which is followed by code to print the text of the exception object:

```
  <% if (exception instanceof UserException) { %>

    <p><%=exception.getMessage()%></p>

  <% } else { %>

    <p>There was an error while serving the page.</p>
    <pre><%exception.printStackTrace(new PrintWriter(out));%></pre>

  <% } %>
```

The code distinguishes between two types of exception, those caused by a user error and those caused by some other factor. A user error is any error caused by an action in the user interface; for example, entering an invalid value for a field, attempting to access a nonexistent photograph, or leaving out a required parameter from a request. Exceptions caused by a user's error do not need to be logged and do not require a full stack trace; a simple explanation in plain English should suffice. Other exceptions are caused either by errors in the software or problems in the environment, such as a misconfiguration or a problem accessing the database. These non-user errors require attention by the programmer or system administrator and therefore the error is logged and a full stack trace is printed.

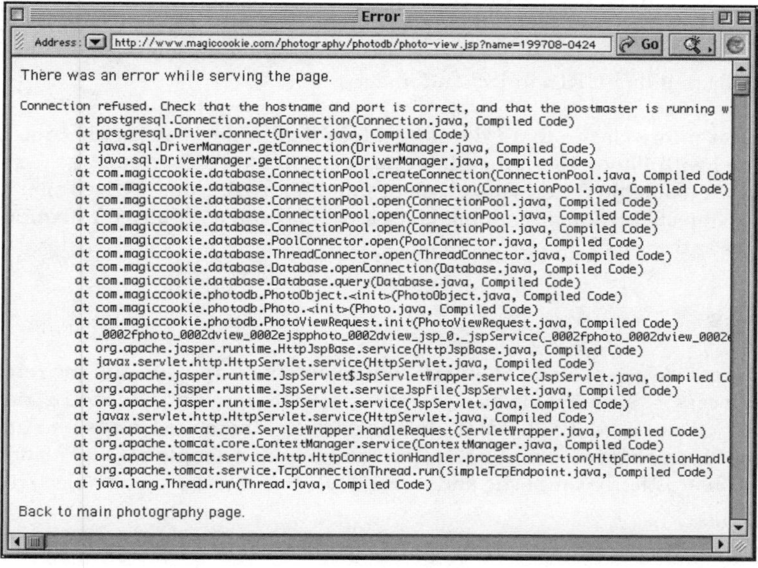

Index and Test Pages

The remaining pages in PhotoDB are the index and test pages, `index.jsp`. and `test.jsp`. The test page is used for testing some functionality and should not be accessed by regular users. The index page is the default page for PhotoDB. This is the page to which a link is provided from the error page, and to which PhotoServlet sends a redirect if it is invoked directly. The index provided with PhotoDB is very basic and provides a simple introduction to the program. You might want to customize the index page to provide information relevant to your own web site.

Java Source Code

The Java source code is contained in two packages: `com.magiccookie.photodb` and `com.magiccookie.image`.

Several classes form the data access layer. These classes map tables and rows in the database to Java objects. The data access layer includes the classes `Folder`, `Category`, `Photo`, and `Roll`. Instances of these objects are initialized from rows in the corresponding database tables. Not all data access is restricted to these classes, though, as some of the SQL statements for loading data are contained in the request classes.

Various classes handle the logic for the requests. The names of these classes, by convention, end with 'Request'. Generic requests that do not require specialized logic use the class `PhotoRequest`. Other requests with more specialized logic use subclasses of `PhotoRequest`. For instance, `PhotoEditRequest` implements the functionality needed to support the `photo-edit.jsp` page, which in turn provides a user interface for editing, creating and deleting photographs.

A special servlet, `PhotoServlet`, is used to handle shared state and configuration data used in the application. This servlet provides access to various initialization parameters and maintains the object that is used to connect to the database.

A utility class, `PhotoUtil`, provides various static utility methods, including methods for accessing image files and for building URLs to JSP and image files.

PhotoDB also uses utility classes that I developed for other projects. A jar file containing the utility classes is included with PhotoDB, in the file `webapp/WEB-INF/lib/mcutil.jar`. The source code for the utility classes is available for download, alongside PhotoDB, from my web site. The utility classes include a simple object/relational mapping layer as well as some utilities for manipulating HTML and logging messages and errors.

Data Access

The database access classes provide an interface between the Java code and the relational database. Basic database access is provided via classes in the package `com.magiccookie.database`, which is part of the utility classes used by PhotoDB. In this package, there are classes for database access, connection pooling, transaction handling, query handling, and simple object/relational mapping. This database access layer is fairly simplistic and is not a full commercial-grade object/relational mapping layer.

Object-Relational Mapping

When accessing a relational database from an object-oriented language one typically encounters what is known as the 'object/relational impedance mismatch'. This so-called impedance mismatch arises because a relational database accesses data as rows in tables. Data is accessed using a declarative query language which itself generates tables of data. To access data, you might ask an RDBMS for "all items whose date is October 15, 1999". However, Java is an object-oriented language, and represents data using a static inheritance graph of types combined with runtime instantiation of objects, a very different method of representing information than a RDBMS.

A programmer accessing a relational database using an object-oriented language may end up thinking and programming in two different paradigms. This can lead to code in which two essentially incompatible methods of representing information are interwoven. The programmer may, instead, use an object-relational mapping layer. Essentially, what the mapping layer does is convert data stored in a relational database into data stored in objects and vice versa. The mapping layer can also insulate the application from the database, so that the application logic and database schema can be modified somewhat independently.

The impedance mismatch is reduced or eliminated if you use an object-oriented database. These are databases that let an application store and manipulate objects instead of relations. Unfortunately, there is less industry standardization on how to access object databases than for relational databases. Each vendor may provide its own API and/or query language. The market for such databases is also currently much smaller than the market for relational databases and it may be harder to find a suitable object database.

Optimistic Locking

`DatabaseObject` uses optimistic locking when updating objects, which is both efficient and portable since it avoids the need for row-level locking in the DBMS. When a row is loaded into memory, the value of the row's `ts` column is kept with the data for the row. When updated data are written to the row, a check is made to ensure that the row's `ts` column has maintained its old value, and, in the same SQL update statement, the row's `ts` column is incremented. If the value of the `ts` column differed, then no data would be written and a `com.magiccookie.db.ConcurrentUpdateException` would be thrown. The entire compare/update/increment operation is contained in a single SQL update statement, and so is guaranteed to execute atomically.

Transactions

PhotoDB uses database transactions if they are supported by the RDBMS. PhotoDB uses objects of type `com.magiccookie.database.Transaction` (part of my utility classes mentioned earlier) to manage transactions. In the event that there is an error while storing data to the database PhotoDB will rollback the transaction.

```
Transaction trans = getDatabase().openTransaction();
try {
  trans.begin();
  ...
  trans.commit();
} finally {
  trans.end();
}
```

As shown in the above listing, a transaction is opened using the begin method of class Transaction. If the operation completes successfully then the commit method is called. The end method of the Transaction class is always called, both when the transaction was committed and when there is an error. If the end method is called and the transaction was not committed, then the transaction is rolled back, otherwise the method does nothing.

Persistent Objects

The class com.magiccookie.database.DatabaseObject provides an interface to a row in a database table. This class provides methods to automatically load column values from a row, to store an object in a row and to delete a row. Objects are identified using a unique object ID. A new object ID is automatically generated for each new row. The table object_id holds the value of the last reserved object ID. (A regular table is used to ensure portability across RDBMSs.)

The com.magiccookie.photodb.PhotoObject class extends the generic DatabaseObject class and adds a few methods that are used by all objects stored in the database. PhotoObject is not meant to be used directly, rather it is meant to be subclassed with representations of specific database tables. The classes Category, Folder, Photo, and Roll correspond to tables in the database and all extend PhotoObject. These classes are very similar and simple, they do not implement any logic, they just provide a convenient way to represent the data stored in the database. Since these classes are so similar, I will discuss only the PhotoObject and Photo classes.

PhotoObject provides several constructors. The default constructor is required by the database mapping layer to allow it to create a database object via a factory method. The other constructors are provided to construct a PhotoObject based on whether it represents: an entirely new object with no corresponding entry in the database, an existing row in the database (lookup can be done by name or by ID), data retrieved using a prior SQL query and converted into a Hashtable. Since the persistent objects have a name attribute, PhotoObject also provides name accessor functions using the methods getName and setName. PhotoObject also provides a couple of static methods, exists and lookupByName, for testing for and retrieving an object by its name.

```
package com.magiccookie.photodb;

import com.magiccookie.database.Database;
import com.magiccookie.database.DatabaseObject;
import com.magiccookie.database.OID;
import com.magiccookie.database.Query;
import com.magiccookie.database.Table;
import com.magiccookie.util.NullableHashtable;
import java.util.Vector;

/** An object in the photo database. This is the base class for
* the classes that map rows in the database to Java classes.
* Every object can be uniquely indexed within a table using
* either an object ID or the name of the object. (The reason
* both are unique has to do with the database mapping layer,
* which uses object IDs, and my photo database, which uses
* names of objects.)
*
* @author Copyright (c) 1998-2000 Ari Halberstadt
*/
public class PhotoObject extends DatabaseObject {

  /** An empty object name. */
  public static final String NO_NAME = "";
```

```
/** Construct a new empty object. */
public PhotoObject() {
}

/** Construct a new empty object for a row from the specified table. */
public PhotoObject(Database db, Table table) {
  init(db, table);
}

/** Construct an object for the row with the specified ID from
* the specified table. */
public PhotoObject(Database db, Table table, OID id) {
  init(db, table, id);
}

/** Construct an object for the row with the specified name from
* the specified table. */
public PhotoObject(Database db, Table table, String name) {
  Query query = db.query("select *" +
    " from " + table +
    " where name = " + db.quote(name));
  try {
    if (query.next())
      init(db, table, query.getMap());
    else {
      init(db, table);
      setName(name);
    }
  } finally {
    query.close();
  }
}

/** Construct an object using the specified values. The values
* are usually extracted from a complex query involving a join
* across multiple tables. */
public PhotoObject(Database db, Table table, NullableHashtable map) {
  init(db, table, map);
}

/** Return the name of the object. The format of the name
* depends on the type of object, e.g., a photograph might
* be named "199908-2304", while a folder might be named
* "yellowstone". */
public String getName() {
  return getString("name");
}

/** Set the name of the object. */
public void setName(String name) {
  setString("name", name);
}

/** Return true if a row with the specified name exists in the table.
* This is usually overloaded in derived classes so that the table
* parameter does not need to be passed in. */
public static boolean exists(Database db, Table table, String name) {
  return lookupByName(db, table, name) != null;
}
```

```
  /** Return the object corresponding to a row having the specified name in
   * the table, or null if there is no corresponding row. This is usually
   * overloaded in derived classes so that the table parameter does not
   * need to be passed in. */
  public static PhotoObject lookupByName(Database db, Table table, String name) {
    return (PhotoObject) lookup(db, table, "name = " + db.quote(name));
  }
}
```

The Photo class, shown below, is used to map rows in the photo table (the import statements and some of the getters and setters have been omitted to conserve space):

```
package com.magiccookie.photodb;

import com.magiccookie.database.Database;
import com.magiccookie.database.OID;
import com.magiccookie.database.Table;
import com.magiccookie.util.NullableHashtable;
import java.util.Vector;

/** Maps a row from the photo table.
 *
 * @author Copyright (c) 1998-2000 Ari Halberstadt
 */
public class Photo extends PhotoObject
{
  /** Name of table. */
  public static final String TABLE_NAME = "photo";

  /** Table description. */
  public static final Table TABLE = new PhotoTable();

  /** Construct a new photograph. */
  public Photo() {
  }

  /** Construct a new empty photograph belonging to the specified database. */
  public Photo(Database db) {
    super(db, TABLE);
  }

  /** Construct a photograph containing data from the row with the specified ID.
 */
  public Photo(Database db, OID id) {
    super(db, TABLE, id);
  }

  /** Construct a photograph containing data from the row with the specified name.
 */
  public Photo(Database db, String name) {
    super(db, TABLE, name);
  }

  /** Construct a photograph containing the specified values. */
  public Photo(Database db, NullableHashtable values) {
    super(db, TABLE, values);
  }

  /** Return the name of the folder to which the photograph belongs. */
  public String getFolder() {
    return getString("folder");
```

```
  }

    /** Set the name of the folder to which the photograph belongs. */
    public void setFolder(String folder) {
      setString("folder", folder);
    }

    /** Return the title of the photograph. */
    public String getTitle() {
      return getString("title");
    }

    /** Set the title of the photograph. */
    public void setTitle(String title) {
      setString("title", title);
    }

    // ... additional getters and setters for the various database columns ...

    /** Return true if there is a photograph with the specified name. */
    public static boolean exists(Database db, String name) {
      return PhotoObject.exists(db, TABLE, name);
    }

    /** Return the photograph with the specified name, or null if
    * there is no matching photograph. */
    public static Photo lookupByName(Database db, String name) {
      return (Photo) PhotoObject.lookupByName(db, TABLE, name);
    }

    /** An instance of this class describes the database table. */
    private static class PhotoTable extends Table {

      private static final Vector COLUMNS = new Vector();

      static {
        COLUMNS.addElement("id");
        COLUMNS.addElement("ts");
        COLUMNS.addElement("name");
        COLUMNS.addElement("folder");
        COLUMNS.addElement("title");
        COLUMNS.addElement("location");
        COLUMNS.addElement("description");
        COLUMNS.addElement("notes");
        COLUMNS.addElement("keywords");
        COLUMNS.addElement("adjustments");
        COLUMNS.addElement("private");
      }

      public PhotoTable() {
        super(Photo.class, TABLE_NAME, COLUMNS);
      }
    }
}
```

The `Photo` class provides constructors that parallel the constructors provided by the `PhotoObject` class. The only difference is that constructors in the `Photo` class do not require a `Table` object, rather, they pass the `Photo.TABLE` object up to the `PhotoObject` base class. Likewise, the static methods `exists` and `lookupByName` also pass along the `Photo.TABLE` object to the corresponding methods in `PhotoObject`. The remainder of the `Photo` class consists of simple accessors for each of the columns in the `photo` table.

The database mapping layer uses a special interface to describe a table and the rows contained therein. The Photo class includes a static inner class, PhotoTable, which extends the com.magiccookie.database.Table class. Only a single instance of this static inner class is ever instantiated in the Photo.TABLE static final class variable. The PhotoTable class specifies the name of the table in the database, lists the names of the columns mapped by the object, and specifies the class used to map rows from the specified table. This association between a table and a class allows the classes in com.magiccookie.database to construct an appropriate object when loading values from a table.

Querying for Multiple Objects

Often, more than one row needs to be retrieved from the database. The DatabaseObject class can load a row into memory if the row's ID is already known. One way to retrieve a set of rows would be to do a select query to retrieve the IDs of matching objects, then create instances of DatabaseObject for each ID that was retrieved. This is inefficient, because each DatabaseObject instance must then query the database to retrieve the contents of the row. When doing queries to retrieve many rows, it is therefore more efficient to retrieve all the desired data in a single query and then instantiate instances of DatabaseObject using the data that were retrieved. For example, the class CategoryGalleryRequest is used to retrieve the gallery photographs for all the categories in the database.

```
public class CategoryGalleryRequest extends ThumbnailRequest
{
  /** Return query to load all categories that have a gallery image. */
  protected String getQueryString() {
    StringBuffer query = new StringBuffer();
    query.append("select");
    query.append(" photo.*");
    query.append(", category.name as category_name");
    query.append(" from");
    query.append(" " + Photo.TABLE_NAME + " as photo");
    query.append(", " + Category.TABLE_NAME + " as category");
    query.append(" where photo.name = category.gallery");
    if (! hasPrivateAccess()) {
      query.append(" and photo.private <> " +
        getDatabase().quote(DatabaseObject.TRUE_STRING));
    }
    query.append(" order by category_name");
    return query.toString();
  }

  /** Return a thumbnail of the gallery image of the current category. */
  public String makeThumbnail() {
    NullableHashtable row = getQuery().getMap();
    String categoryName = (String) row.get("category_name");
    Photo photo = new Photo(getDatabase(), row);
    return PhotoUtil.makeThumbnail(photo, "category-index.jsp",
      categoryName, categoryName);
  }
}
```

The method getQueryString returns a SQL query string that is used to retrieve the desired data from the database. This query retrieves all of the columns from matching rows in the photo table as well as the name of the matching category. The matching category's name is placed in the column category_name of the query's results. The makeThumbnail method accesses the current row's data via the getMap method of the query object. The map contains name/value pairs for each of the columns retrieved by the query. The category name is then extracted directly from the results, while a new `Photo` object is created using the remainder of the results. The `Photo` class is a subclass of `DatabaseObject`. The `DatabaseObject` class ignores the `category_name` column because it does not belong to the `Photo` table. The net effect of this is that the database sees only a single query, rather than a large number of queries for each photograph.

Request Processing

Simple requests are handled using the basic `PhotoRequest` class, while more advanced requests use subclasses of `PhotoRequest`.

`PhotoRequest` provides methods to access the JSP page's `request` and `response`, and a `PrintWriter` that writes to the JSP page's `Writer` object. It also includes a method, `getDatabase` to access the database, this is a convenience method so that JSP pages do not need to explicitly access the `PhotoServlet` class. `PhotoRequest` also includes methods for checking for appropriate access, including whether login is allowed and whether the user has write access.

`PhotoRequest` includes an initialization method that must be called before any other method in the class.

```
<%
  PhotoRequest photoRequest = new PhotoRequest();
  try {
    photoRequest.init(request, response, out);
%>
```

The `init` method, which also sets shared HTTP header information, should be called before any other output is written to the stream. While I could have used a regular constructor instead of an initialization method, I was experimenting with approaches that required a default constructor and an initialization method. For example, combining an initialization method with a factory object would facilitate the use of an object pool to recycle `PhotoRequest` objects.

```
public void init(HttpServletRequest request,
  HttpServletResponse response,
  Writer output)
  throws SecurityException, DatabaseException
{
  response.setDateHeader("Expires",
    System.currentTimeMillis() + Time.SECOND *
PhotoServlet.getInstance().getResponseMaxAge());
  mRequest = request;
  mResponse = response;
  mOutput = new PrintWriter(output);
}
```

The `init` method writes an `Expires` HTTP header at the start of each request. The default value for this header is zero, indicating that the response expires immediately and should not be cached. The maximum age can be set to a larger value using the `response.maxAge` initialization parameter to the `PhotoServlet` servlet. Deciding on a value for the maximum age requires a reasonable compromise between cache efficiency and the rate at which data are updated in the database. The data are mostly static, so a relatively large maximum age would be reasonable.

After handling a request, the `destroy` method of the request object should be called. The `destroy` method releases database resources and may do other cleanup operations. A `finally` clause is used to ensure that the destroy method is always called.

```
<%
  } finally {
    photoRequest.destroy();
  }
%>
```

Query Requests

Several JSP pages execute a database query and then output the results in a HTML table. `QueryRequest` is an abstract class that provides a framework for these types of pages. The abstract method `getQueryString` – the only abstract method that must be provided by subclasses – returns an SQL query string, which is used by the base class to query the database.

The class `QueryRequest` is shown below.

```
public abstract class QueryRequest extends PhotoRequest {

  /** Query object. */
  private Query mQuery;

  /** Number of rows retrieved from query. */
  private int mCount;

  /** Return an SQL select statement used to run the
  * query. */
  protected abstract String getQueryString();

  /** Releases any resources held by the query. Should be called
  * when you are finished using the query object. */
  public void destroy() {
    if (mQuery != null)
      mQuery.close();
    super.destroy();
  }

  /** Return the query object that is used to query
  * and retrieve data from the database. */
  protected Query getQuery() {
    if (mQuery == null)
      mQuery = getDatabase().query(getQueryString());
    return mQuery;
  }

  /** Load next row from the result set. Return true if
  * the next row was loaded, or false if the entire result
  * set has been retrieved. The first time this is called
  * it actually executes the query, subsequent calls just
  * retrieve the data. */
  public boolean next() throws DatabaseException {
    boolean result = getQuery().next();
    if (result)
      ++mCount;
    else
      getQuery().close();
    return result;
  }
```

```
    /** Return the number of rows retrieved from the query. */
    public int getCount() {
      return mCount;
    }

    /** Return the color for a row. This is used to color rows using alternating
    * colors. This is a poor place to calculate this sort of thing, it should
    * be defined in a stylesheet. */
    public String getColor() {
      return PhotoUtil.ROW_COLORS[getCount() % 2];
    }
  }
```

To use a `QueryRequest` object, you would repeatedly call the `next` method to load each row returned by the query. The `getQuery` method returns a `Query` object, from which you can access the current row as a `Nullableashtable` using `getMap` or as a `DatabaseObject` using `getDatabaseObject`. The `getCount` method returns the number of rows retrieved.

`QueryRequest` also provides the `getColor` method to return the color in which the current row should be displayed. This assumes that an alternating color scheme is used to visually separate repeating elements. For instance, the lists of categories, folders, or photographs `category-gallery.jsp` draw each row in the list with an alternating background color.

Thumbnail Requests

Several pages display thumbnails of images. For example, `category-gallery.jsp` displays a thumbnail of the gallery image from each category. These pages all use classes that extend the class `ThumnailRequest`.

`ThumbnailRequest` is an abstract class that extends `QueryRequest`. `ThumbnailRequest` adds the abstract method `makeThumbnail` to the abstract methods declared by `QueryRequest`. The `makeThumbnail` method should return a string that contains HTML for displaying a thumbnail image of a photograph.

Once a concrete subclass of `ThumbnailRequest` has been provided, all a client JSP page must do is call the `printRows` method on the object. The `printRows` method prints a thumbnail for each row retrieved from the database (and for which there is a corresponding thumbnail). The method `getThumbnailCount` can be used to determine the number of thumbnails that were actually displayed. For instance, shown below is the manner in which the `CategoryIndexRequest` class is used in the `category-index.jsp` page.

```
<%
  CategoryIndexRequest photoRequest = new CategoryIndexRequest();
  try {
    photoRequest.init(request, response, out);
%>
...
<center>
  <table border="0" cellpadding="10" cellspacing="10">
    <% photoRequest.printRows(); %>
  </table>
</center>

<% if (photoRequest.getThumbnailCount() == 0) { %>
  <p>There are no photographs in this category.</p>
<% } %>
```

There is no database access code in the JSP page. All the SQL statements and data retrieval have been encapsulated into the `CategoryIndexRequest` class. This class provides a concrete implementation of the abstract class `ThumbnailRequest`. The `getQueryString` method returns a SQL statement to query the database for the photographs in the category. This method is executed by `ThumbnailRequest` when the `printRows` method is called by the JSP page.

```
/** Return query string to select photographs belonging to
* the specified category. */
protected String getQueryString() {
  String pt = Photo.TABLE.getName();
  String pct = Category.PHOTO_CATEGORY_TABLE;
  String query = "select " + pt + ".*" + ", " + pct + ".*" +
    " from " + pt + ", " + pct +
    " where " + pct + ".category=" +
getDatabase().quote(getCategory().getName()) +
    " and " + pct + ".photo=" + pt + ".name" +
    " and " + pt + ".private <> " +
getDatabase().quote(DatabaseObject.TRUE_STRING) +
    " order by " + pt + ".name";
  return query;
}
```

`ThumbnailRequest` then calls `makeThumbnail` for each row retrieved from the database. `MakeThumbnail` in turn instantiates a `Photo` object from the data in the row and constructs an HTML string containing the thumbnail. The base class `ThumbnailRequest` then writes the string to the output stream.

```
  /** Return a thumbnail for the current photograph. */
  public String makeThumbnail() {
    Photo photo = new Photo(getDatabase(), getQuery().getMap());
    return PhotoUtil.makeThumbnail(photo, photo.getTitle());
  }
}
```

Edit Requests

Requests that modify the database use classes that extend `EditRequest`.

The `EditRequest` class does not do much in itself. The `init` method of `EditRequest` throws a `SecurityException` if the user does not have write access. The subclasses `CategoryEditRequest`, `FolderEditRequest`, `PhotoEditRequest`, and `RollEditReqeust` each provide the logic needed to handle updating the corresponding data in the database. These three classes are similar, so a look at `CategoryEditRequest` should suffice.

`CategoryEditRequest` is used in the `category-edit.jsp` page. The `init` method of `CategoryEditRequest` loads a `Category` object based on the `name` parameter specified in a parameter to the JSP page. It then makes this object modifiable, and, if necessary, initializes it with default values. Then, the `init` method gets any new values that may have been passed in via a POST request to the `category-edit.jsp` page.

The `category-edit.jsp` page then calls the `handleRequest` method of `CategoryEditRequest`. This method dispatches–based on the value of parameters that specify the desired action – to a method that will handle the request. If the page was invoked using a plain GET request then the action parameters are not provided (indicating that the user has just loaded the page) and the `handleRequest` dispatcher method does nothing. After the `handleRequest` method returns, the `category-edit.jsp` page will display the values based on the category object contained in the `CategoryEditRequest` object.

The dispatcher can handle three different requests: reset, store, or delete. A reset request reloads the data from the database, discarding any changes made by the user. A store request writes the user's modifications to the database. Finally, a delete request deletes the row (and any dependent data) from the database. Shown below is the `store` method of `CategoryEditRequest`.

```
/** Store category to database. */
public String store() throws DatabaseException {
  // open transaction
  Transaction trans = getDatabase().openTransaction();
  try {
    trans.begin();

    // check for missing name
    if (mCategory.getName().equals(Category.NO_NAME))
      throw new DatabaseException("Missing category name.");

    // check for invalid name
    if (mCategory.getName().indexOf(',') != -1)
      throw new DatabaseException("Name cannot contain commas.");

    // check for duplicate name
    if (! mCategory.getName().equals(mName) &&
      Category.exists(getDatabase(), mCategory.getName()))
    {
      throw new DatabaseException("A category with name " +
        StringUtil.quote(mCategory.getName()) + " already exists.");
    }

    // update dependent data
    if (! mCategory.getName().equals(mName) && ! mCategory.isNew()) {
      getDatabase().update("update " + Category.TABLE +
        " set name=" + getDatabase().quote(mCategory.getName()) +
        " where name=" + getDatabase().quote(mName));
      getDatabase().update("update " + Category.PHOTO_CATEGORY_TABLE +
        " set category=" + getDatabase().quote(mCategory.getName()) +
        " where category=" + getDatabase().quote(mName));
    }

    // store category
    mCategory.store();

    // commit transaction
    trans.commit();

  } finally {
    trans.end();
  }

  return "Stored category";
}
```

The `store` method first opens a transaction. A transaction is required because storing a category involves several SQL query and update statements. The method then checks for missing or invalid data. The `photo_category` table contains foreign keys to the name column of category table, so any changes to a category's name must be updated in the `photo_category` table. After the `photo_category` table is updated, the `Category` object itself is written to the database.

The `delete` method of `EditCategoryRequest` is shown below.

```
/** Delete category from database. */
public String delete() throws DatabaseException {
  // open transaction
  Transaction trans = getDatabase().openTransaction();
  try {
    trans.begin();

    // check for missing name
    if (mCategory.getName().equals(Category.NO_NAME))
      throw new DatabaseException("Missing category name.");

    // delete dependent data
    getDatabase().update("delete from " + Category.PHOTO_CATEGORY_TABLE +
        " where category = " + getDatabase().quote(mName));

    // delete category
    mCategory.delete();

    // reinitialize with empty category
    mName = Category.NO_NAME;
    reset();

    // commit transaction
    trans.commit();

  } finally {
    trans.end();
  }

  return "Deleted category";
}
```

This method is similar to the `store` method. It opens a transaction, checks for invalid data, deletes dependent data from the `photo_category` table, then deletes the row from the `category` table. Finally, it reinitializes itself with a new `Category` object and commits the transaction.

Image File Attributes

To efficiently display images in HTML pages requires knowing the dimensions of the images, so that width and height attributes can be included in the HTML `img` tag. If the `img` tag's `height` and `width` attributes were omitted it would make layout of the page less efficient since the web browser would have to wait for the image file to be downloaded before it could properly position the elements of the page. The classes in the package `com.magiccookie.image` are used for extracting the dimensions of images from image files.

I found it necessary to write the classes in this package after trying to use the class `java.awt.Image`. The `java.awt.Image` class provides a generic standard method to access image files. Unfortunately, using this class in a server-side Java program presented some problems that depended on the runtime environment and the version of the JVM and libraries I was using. For example, I run my Linux machine without a monitor and therefore do not start up an X client on it. Both IBM's JDK 1.1.8 and the Blackdown port of Sun JDK 1.2 require access to the X11 libraries in order to process image files. This resulted in runtime error messages every time the PhotoDB software tried to access an image file.

The `java.awt.Image` class is cumbersome to use for simple access to an image's dimensions. I had written several wrapper classes to try and hide the complexity of using `java.awt.Image`. This was just a small amount of messy code, but it was messy code I would rather avoid, particularly when there were the other hidden runtime dependencies mentioned above. I did not want to deal with runtime issues, and certainly I did not want other people to have to deal with such issues. Since the image processing required in PhotoDB is so minimal, the obvious solution was simply to implement my own code to access an image's dimensions.

The interface `ImageAttributes` is a simple interface that defines two method signatures for accessing the width and height of an image.

```
public interface ImageAttributes
{
  public int getWidth();
  public int getHeight();
}
```

The `ImageAttributes` interface is implemented by the class `JPEGAttributes`.

The actual work of parsing a JPEG file is done in `JPEGCommentReader`, which is adapted from code available from the Independent JPEG Group's (IJG) archives at ftp://ftp.uu.net/graphics/.jpeg. `JPEGAttributes` includes a static private inner class, `JPEGReader`, which overrides the `processSOFMarker` method of `JPEGCommentReader` to get the width and height of the image from the first SOF marker in a JPEG file.

At the moment, all my photographs are stored as JPEG images, and to expedite matters I only implemented a class to extract image dimensions from JPEG files. Additional file types could easily be supported, for instance, using a `GIFAttributes` class to access attributes of GIF image files. Ideally, a factory object should be provided, with registration functions that provide a mapping between an image file's suffix and a class used to extract the image's attributes.

PhotoServlet

`PhotoServlet` is used by PhotoDB to interface with the runtime environment and to keep track of configuration data. Runtime environment issues that impact PhotoDB include database access, application startup and termination, paths to required files, URL paths to required pages, and initialization parameters. This servlet is not meant to be accessed by end users. Attempting to access it directly simply returns a redirect to the default URL for PhotoDB.

The servlet implements the singleton pattern, only one instance of the servlet may be created. The static `getInstance` method of `PhotoServlet` returns the single instance of the servlet. Various methods of the servlet provide access to the database and to data specified in the initialization parameters. For instance, the `getDatabase` method returns the `Database` object created in the `init` method. Other methods, such as `getDocumentPath` and `isLoginAllowed`, provide access to, or services that depend on, the servlet's initialization parameters.

Utilities

The `PhotoUtil` class contains static methods used throughout PhotoDB. This class has a private default constructor so that no instances of the class may be constructed. The utility methods are used for building URLs to image and JSP files and for building paths to the image files in the file system. Several methods are used for making thumbnail images and for locating an `Image` object for an image matching certain criteria.

The methods for building URLs and paths are needed so that the PhotoDB application can refer to its JSP pages and so that it can access image files. For instance, `category-frame.jsp` contains the following fragment:

```
<frameset cols="150,*">
  <frame src="<%=PhotoUtil.makeDocumentURL("category-list.jsp")%>" name="category-
list">
  <frame src="<%=PhotoUtil.makeDocumentURL("category-none.jsp")%>" name="category-
view">
</frameset>
```

The text `<%=PhotoUtil.makeDocumentURL("category-list.jsp")%>` evaluates to `path/category-list.jsp`, where `path` is the value of the `context.path` initialization parameter to the `PhotoServlet` servlet.

Another utility classes is `com.magiccookie.util.HtmlUtil`, which is used to encode URL and HTML text. Any data entered by a user could contain HTML tags and characters that cannot be included in URLs. To avoid problems caused by these characters, PhotoDB encodes all text entered by a user. For instance, the file `photo-view.jsp` includes the following fragment:

```
<tr valign="top">
  <td><b>Description:</b></td>
  <td><%=HtmlUtil.textToHtml(photo.getDescription())%></td>
</tr>
<tr valign="top">
  <td><b>Location:</b></td>
  <td><%=HtmlUtil.encode(photo.getLocation())%></td>
</tr>
```

The method `HtmlUtil.encode` encodes all ampersands and angle brackets into the corresponding HTML character entities. The method `HtmlUtil.textToHtml` strips out invalid HTML tags (such as body and head tags) and does basic formatting to insert line breaks into plain text so that paragraph breaks are preserved. The method `textToHtml` preserves most HTML tags allowing links and other HTML tags to be included in the text. The method `HtmlUtil.encodeUrl` encodes a string for inclusion in a URL.

The class `com.magiccookie.util.Log` writes messages to `System.err`. Messages are written to named channels, which allows messages for different functional components of the software to be individually enabled or disabled. For instance, all error messages are logged to the `error` channel, while SQL statements are logged to the '`sql`' channel and certain PhotoDB messages are logged to the channel '`photodb`'.

```
if (Log.ENABLED && Log.enabled(PhotoServlet.LOG_CHANNEL)) {
  Log.println(PhotoServlet.LOG_CHANNEL,
    "read image attributes from " + imagePath);
}
```

The log is controlled using several initialization parameters to the `PhotoServlet` servlet, which are specified in PhotoDB's deployment descriptor in the file `webapp/WEB-INF/web.xml`. The names of the relevant initialization parameters all start with '`log.`'

Security

Most of the pages in PhotoDB provide read-only access to data. Several pages, though, also provide an interface for adding, deleting, and modifying the data stored in the database. PhotoDB also supports private photographs and folders, which allow photographs to be cataloged without providing public access to the items. The editable pages and private items are accessable only if the user has logged in.

Access is authenticated using a simple password. The password is specified using the `login.password` initialization parameter to the `PhotoServlet` servlet; the default password is just '`password`'. PhotoDB can also restrict login access to a limited number of server machines. The list of servers on which login is allowed is specified using the `login.servers` initialization parameter to the `PhotoServlet` servlet. The default is to allow login from all servers. Restricting access to only some servers can be used to allow editing on a private web server whose data are then replicated to a public read-only server. This is not a comprehensive security model appropriate for a complex web site, but it is sufficient for a database of photographs maintained by a single individual.

Configuring PhotoDB requires providing the user account and password with which to access the database and the password with which to allow login to PhotoDB. These settings are provided in the deployment descriptor in `webapp/WEB-INF/web.xml`. If access to this file is compromised, then access to PhotoDB will also be compromised.

Installation

Installation of PhotoDB is a somewhat involved process due to the multiple components on which PhotoDB depends. This section lists the required components, provides recommendations for components as well as URLs from which each component may be downloaded, and provides instructions on installing and configuring PhotoDB.

> **These instructions are biased toward Unix systems. PhotoDB and the software it requires can, however, be installed on non-Unix systems.**

Requirements

PhotoDB requires the following components:

- JDK 1.1 or later
- a web server
- a servlet container that supports JSDK 2.0 or later
- a JavaServer Pages implementation that is compatible with version 1.0 of the JSP specification
- a relational database
- a JDBC driver for the database

For the purposes of these instructions, I will assume that you already have installed a working JDK, web server, and JSP container. I will also assume that you have selected an RDBMS for use with your system and have completed its installation procedure. Also, for the purposes of these instructions and unless otherwise noted, all partial paths are relative to the directory in which you installed PhotoDB.

PhotoDB should work with any JSP container that is compatible with version 1.0 of the JSP specification, such as Tomcat and Caucho Technologies' Resin. PhotoDB has been tested with Tomcat 3.1 and Resin 1.1.1. You can download Tomcat from http://jakarta.apache.org and Resin from http://www.caucho.com. Notice that Tomcat and Resin are each a combination web server, servlet container and JSP container, so you would not need to install these additional components. Both Tomcat and Resin can also be invoked from a web server such as Apache.

PhotoDB has been tested with two database systems, mySQL 3.22.32 on Linux Intel using Terrence W. Zellers' twz1jdbcForMysql 1.0.4-GA JDBC driver and PostgreSQL 6.5.2. You can download mySQL from http://www.tcx.se and PostgreSQL from http://www.postgresql.org.

Installation Steps

The steps to install PhotoDB are:

- Install the PhotoDB files on your system. The files are all contained in a single directory and can be stored anywhere on your system, such as `/usr/local/photodb`
- Create a database, and (optionally) the sample database
- Configure the application to access the database
- Point your servlet container and web server to the PhotoDB files

Create a Database

Using your RDBMS' tools, you need to create an account with which PhotoDB can access the database. Then, you need to create a database for PhotoDB. SQL script files, in the directory `sql`, are provided for creating the database tables. Versions of the scripts are provided for each supported RDBMS: `create-pgsql.sql` for PostgreSQL and `create-mysql.sql` for mySQL. You can also populate the database with sample data using the `sample-pgsql.sql` or `sample-mysql.sql` scripts.

PostgreSQL

Create a user and database for PostgreSQL and then create the tables in the database, as shown below.

```
$ createuser photodb
Enter user's postgres ID -> 10000
Is user "photodb" allowed to create databases (y/n) n
Is user "photodb" a superuser? (y/n) n
createuser: photodb was successfully added
Shall I create a database for "photodb" (y/n) y
$ psql -u -f sql/create-pgsql.sql -d photodb
Username: photodb
Password: xxxxxx
```

If you want to use the sample database, load the sample data:

```
$ psql -u -f sql/sample.sql -d photodb
Username: photodb
Password: xxxxxx
```

mySQL

First, create a user account for photodb.

```
$ mysql --user=root --password mysql
Enter password: xxxxxx
mysql> insert into user values('localhost','photodb',password('xxxxxx'),
    -> 'Y','Y','Y','Y','Y','Y','N','N','N','N','N','N','Y','Y');
```

Next, create the database and then create the tables in the database, as shown below.

```
$ mysqladmin --user=photodb --password create photodb
Enter password: xxxxxx
$ mysql --user=photodb --password photodb < sql/create-mysql.sql
Enter password: xxxxxx
```

If you want to use the sample database, load the sample data:

```
$ mysql --user=photodb --password photodb < sql/sample-mysql.sql
Enter password: xxxxxx
```

Configure Servlet

The deployment descriptor is contained in the file `webapp/WEB-INF/web.xml`. You will need to edit the initialization parameters for the `PhotoServlet` servlet in this file in order to access your database. Set the `db.driver`, `db.url`, `db.user`, and `db.password` initialization parameters to the values appropriate for your database.

The deployment descriptor also contains additional initialization parameters that you may want to edit. For instance, you could change the location in which the image files are stored or the URLs used to access PhotoDB. You can also enable logging of various information, such as SQL statements generated by PhotoDB, which can be helpful when trying to fix problems in the installation. If you want to access PhotoDB from a URL other than one starting with `/photodb`, then you should edit the `context.path` initialization parameter so that PhotoDB will be able to locate its files (this parameter is needed to maintain compatability with JSDK 2.0).

Point servlet container to PhotoDB files

This step is very dependent on the servlet container. For instance, you can configure Tomcat by adding the following lines to Tomcat's `conf/server.xml` file:

```
<Context path="/photodb" docBase="/usr/local/photodb/webapp">
</Context>
```

Similarly, you can configure Resin by adding the following lines to Resin's `conf/resin.conf` file:

```
<web-app id='photodb'>
  <app-dir>/usr/local/photodb/webapp</app-dir>
</web-app>
```

You will also need to ensure that the classes for your database's JDBC driver are in the servlet container's or PhotoDB application's classpath.

If you are using a separate web server, such as Apache, then you will also need to ensure that the web server can access the directory containing the image files, e.g., /usr/local/photodb/webapp/photos. For instance, you can add Alias and Directory configuration directives to Apache's httpd.conf file to allow access to the directory.

Test PhotoDB

If you successfully completed the preceding steps, then you should be able to access PhotoDB using a URL such as http://localhost:8080/photodb (adjust the host and port values as required for your configuration). This should display the default introductory page for PhotoDB. To view the sample photographs, access http://localhost:8080/photodb/folder-gallery.jsp.

Search Engines

Some search engines do not index pages with URLs containing CGI parameters. For instance, a URL of the form http://www.magiccookie.com/photodb/photo-view.jsp?name=199709-0336 would not be indexed by these search engines. This means that most of the descriptive text available via PhotoDB would be hidden from search engines. A simple solution is to generate and accept URLs in a format that search engines will index. The above URL would be indexed by search engines if it were rewritten as the following URL:

```
http://www.magiccookie.com/photodb/photo-view.jsp/199709-0336
```

The pathinfo.enable initialization parameter for the PhotoServlet servlet controls how PhotoDB generates links. If pathinfo.enable is true, then PhotoDB will include extra path information in the dynamically generated links to its own pages. This parameter is, by default, set to false to ensure compatability with all servlet containers. You can set this parameter's value by editing the deployment descriptor in the file webapp/WEB-INF/web.xml.

Using the extra path information approach, the JSP container and/or web server might interpret a relative URL as being relative to the full URL including the extra path information. For instance, trying to access the menu.jsp file could now result in an attempt to access http://www.magiccookie.com/photodb/photo-view.jsp/199709-0336/menu.jsp rather than the expected http://www.magiccookie.com/photodb/menu.jsp.

Using extra path information works with Resin but not with Tomcat. You can still use the extra path information approach with servlet containers like Tomcat if you access the servlet container via a web server that can do URL rewriting. In this approach, the URL received in the HTTP request is rewritten before being passed to the servlet container. For instance, the URL http://www.magiccookie.com/photodb/photo-view.jsp/199709-0336 is rewritten internally into the URL http://www.magiccookie.com/photodb/photo-view.jsp?name=199709-0336.

In the Apache web server, I used mod_rewrite by adding the following rewrite rule to the httpd.conf configuration file:

```
<IfModule mod_rewrite.c>
  RewriteEngine on
  RewriteRule ^/photodb/(.*)\.jsp/(.*) /photodb/$1.jsp?name=$2
</IfModule>
```

This rule rewrites any URL to a JSP file in PhotoDB that is followed by a slash into the same URL, except that the slash is replaced with `?name=`. (Other web servers may provide similar means for rewriting or matching URLs.)

Using PhotoDB

Using PhotoDB should be apparent from the links provided on the various pages. (If it is not immediately apparent to people how to use PhotoDB then the interface is probably deficient and could be improved.) To edit data and to view private folders and photographs the user must login. The default password is simply `password`. Each page on PhotoDB includes a link that allows logging in. This link is displayed, although only on servers from which login is allowed (see the `login.servers` initialization parameter to the `PhotoServlet` servlet). Once logged in, various pages will include links to edit and to create new items.

Naming Items

PhotoDB allows folders and photographs to have both a name and a title. The name is used for internal purposes while the title is used for display purposes. The names of photographs and folders are used to construct URLs and for names of files and directories containing images. For instance, `acadia` or `yosemite` are typical folder names. In contrast, the title of a folder could be much longer and would give the full title of the location, such as *Acadia National Park* or *Yosemite National Park*.

The name of a photograph is intended to correspond to a cataloging system that the photographer uses to match photographs with original slides or negatives. The name must be suitable for use in URLs, as well as the name of a file in the file system. A photograph's name must also be unique. For instance, I number all my photographs with a 10-digit (11 character) code consisting of a four digit year, a two digit month, a dash, a two digit roll number for that month, and a two digit shot number for the roll. For instance, `199709-0336` is a valid photograph number. (This numbering system will need an extra digit should I ever shoot more than 99 rolls in a single month.) The title of this photograph, on the other hand, is the slightly more descriptive *Pair* (this photograph shows a pair of birds in front of a mountain at Grand Teton National Park; you can view the photograph using the URL http://www.magiccode.com/photography/photodb/photo-view?name=199709-0336).

Image Files

Images are stored in regular files in the file system. Storing the image files outside of the database is efficient and provides access via the web server as well as access via image–processing applications. Each photograph has two matching image files. One file is used for small thumbnail images and the other is used for large detailed views of the image. Currently, PhotoDB only knows how to parse JPEG image files, though additional formats could be supported.

PhotoDB locates an image file for a particular photograph by building a path to the image file. All image files must be kept under a single root directory, which is specified using the `image.directory` initialization parameter to the `PhotoServlet` servlet. Within this root directory, each folder in PhotoDB must have a corresponding directory. The image files are, in turn, stored within the directories to which their corresponding photographs belong. Each photograph must have a unique name.

The name of the image file is then composed of the name of the photograph, followed by a string corresponding to the desired image size (`-lg` or `-sm`), followed by a suffix corresponding to the type of the image file.

For instance, assume that the root directory containing the image files is `/usr/local/photodb/webapp/photos` and that the photograph named `199708-0424` is in the folder `grand-teton`. To display a small version of this image, PhotoDB constructs the path `/usr/local/photodb/webapp/photos/grand-teton/199708-0424-sm.jpg`, while to display a large version of the photograph it constructs the path `/usr/local/photodb/webapp/photos/grand-teton/199708-0424-lg.jpg`.

Image files must also be accessible to the web server via a URL. When building a URL to an image file, PhotoDB follows similar rules as for image files. For instance, if the images are accessed via the URL /photodb/photos, then the URLs for the above images would be /photodb/photos/grand-teton/199708-0424-sm.jpg and /photodb/photos/grand-teton/199708-0424-lg.jpg.

Using Thumbnails in HTML Pages

You can use the thumbnail servlet included with PhotoDB to automatically generate HTML code to include a thumbnail image in a page. In this context, a thumbnail consists of a small version of an image from PhotoDB, along with caption text and a link to view details of the image. The thumbnail servlet is useful since it will automatically use the correct image size attributes and will load the caption for the thumbnail from the database, ensuring that the thumbnail is consistent with the database.

The thumbnail servlet accepts a name parameter containing the name of a photograph. For instance, you can include a thumbnail in a JSP page using the following code:

```
<jsp:include page="thumbnail" flush="true"/>
        <jsp:param name="name" value="199708-0424"/>
</jsp:include>
```

The thumbnail servlet can also select a random image. If you provide more than one name parameter, then an image is selected at random from the list of photographs. For instance, the following example will select one of the four named photographs at random each time it is invoked.

```
<jsp:include page="thumbnail" flush="true">
        <jsp:param name="name" value="199708-0424"/>
        <jsp:param name="name" value="199708-2016"/>
        <jsp:param name="name" value="199705-1232"/>
        <jsp:param name="name" value="199708-1303"/>
</jsp:include>
```

Summary

PhotoDB is a useful application and I enjoy being able to share my photographs on my web site, particularly using my own software.

JavaServer Pages are a reasonable way to create the presentation layer for a web site, though there are drawbacks and limitations to the approach of using plain JSP pages to render HTML. Better tool integration, including debuggers for JSP pages, as well as automatic recompilation of `.java` files (not only the `.jsp` files) would be helpful.

Database access and application logic should be abstracted as much as possible from JSP pages. Creating some kind of request handling object or bean is nearly inevitable to ensure that the logic of an application is separated from its presentation and to keep the presentation layer simple.

J2EE
JSP

15

Security and Personalization with JNDI

In this chapter we're going to cover two topics that at first glance don't seem to have anything to do with each other. By the end of this chapter you'll see that you can tie the two together so that they can both improve how you feel about the security of your site and improve how your users feel about using your Web site.

In this chapter we're going to cover:

- Defining security
- Servlet/JSP security
- Encryption and Public Key Infrastructure
- Directory Services and JNDI
- Providing Website Personalization through Authentication

We'll also be using the following software:

- Apache Web Server
- Tomcat Servlet Engine
- Sun's JNDI
- iPlanet Directory Server

While we'll specifically look at Apache, Tomcat and iPlanet, in practice you can use whatever Web or LDAP server you want. The same is true if you want to use a different servlet engine.

Security

Security is a subject we don't like to think about. Often we take it for granted and don't even tackle the issue until it's too late (e.g. someone has broken in and stolen a bunch of credit card numbers). Security requires us to think evil thoughts about our friends and co-workers, or even our customers. Most people don't like to think thoughts like that about people they have to deal with on a daily basis.

However, this is the wrong way to focus on the subject.

Security is designed to make our systems safe for our users and ourselves because accidents and crime will happen. I strongly believe that good security design makes for more reliable systems, which makes for happier friends, colleagues, and users. While companies that sell security products focus on all of the horrible things that can happen if you don't use their product, often security simply protects us from doing stupid things. For example, most of us have at one time or another pressed the *Delete* key accidentally and erased essential files.

What is Security?

Security is the process (or effort) that protects your valuables. It's a process because you cannot just purchase a security widget and expect your systems to be secure. To be secure they must be protected from physical attack, poorly written software that can be exploited, poor passwords or users who grant access to unauthorized people. The best way to make security work is to make security a part of your everyday life so that you don't even think twice about it. Remember, if any area of security is weak, then your entire security is weak.

When talking about computers, security can have different meanings, including:

- Security boundaries
- Physical security
- System security
- Application security
- Access control
- Message verification
- Message ownership

We'll soon cover what each of these topics mean, but I do want to point out that encryption is not one of the bullets in our list. That's because encryption is not the same thing as security. Encryption is simply the act of encoding a message. The practice of encryption dates back to the ancient world, while computer security has really only become known in the last 20 years. Encryption can play a role in computer security, but the terms are distinct.

Another important concept is that security is like a chain. All chains are only as strong as their weakest link. So remember for a system, application, or site to be truly secure all of the parts have to be secure.

Finally you must determine how much security you are going to put in place. While you don't want to make it easy to get access to your most prized possessions, you also don't want to spend enormous amounts of time, money, or energy protecting trivial items. The optimal point is to set your security up so that it requires more effort to break than what the assets that are protected are worth. You will also need to know who your primary enemies are. For example, the resources you put in place to defeat a single user are different than what you'll do if your primary enemy is a large military unit.

Security Boundaries

Security boundaries describe the different areas or policies that define how you will implement your security. For example if you're a company who does business over a public Internet site you might decide that you can't trust anything coming from your users. This sounds harsh, but in reality you don't have any control over their systems or their user authentication mechanisms. A malicious person could take over their system and use that access to attack your network.

Thus you could choose to not connect your Web servers to your internal network. Instead you only allow your Web servers to communicate with your internal databases that the Web servers use to build your Web applications and separate the Web servers from the databases via a firewall.

Next you know that your databases are the primary product of your Website (e.g. you provide an Internet auction service). Because users don't have direct access to the databases (they only have access via your Web applications) you can trust your database machines more than you can your Web servers. However, you cannot fully trust them because they do talk to your Web servers. While the Web server firewall does offer some protection for the databases, if the databases are compromised you don't want to let the attackers have full access to your network, so you setup another firewall, between the databases and your internal network but it has fewer restrictions on it than the Web server firewall.

Finally, you decide that your company is small enough that you trust any authenticated user that is inside the company firewall.

Physical Security

The first step is to make sure that your machine(s) are physically secure. What this means is to physically protect the hardware and personnel that contain or run your machines. This can range from locks on your doors, to armed guards or to James Bond-like biometric locks.

This step is critical. All of the other security layers depend upon this layer being secure. Nearly every security precaution you can take on your system can be negated if the physical system can be attacked. Keep in mind the source of an attack can range from a malicious employee, to fire, to an armed terrorist group.

When you think about physical security don't forget about laptops and palmtops. These machines are often the hardest to secure, and yet can contain some of the most sensitive data about your organization. Passwords, social engineering information (such as information someone can use to fake their way past secretaries, etc), or confidential plans may all be stored on those hard-drives. A nefarious person or organization might use this data to break into your organization, to hatch their own plans based on your designs, improve their own product so they are much better than your weak points, or may just use this information as a tool for bribery.

System Security

By system security I mean the ability to secure the underlying operating system, including the OS kernel and the essential utilities that make up the rest of the operating system. Limit the number of user accounts that you give out and only allow them access to your systems via secure authentication mechanisms like SSH or Kerberos. Use firewalls and routers to limit what types of data are allowed to go over your network. Finally if you must allow file transfers, use the new WebDAV protocol instead of FTP. WebDAV, which extends the HTTP protocol, can easily be protected with SSL and doesn't usually require local accounts, which further limits the damage a compromised user account can do. Because of the way FTP has been defined it is difficult to secure and almost always requires a local account to grant writing privileges. Compromised local accounts are in my experience the number one problem faced by a network manager because the amount of damage that is possible with local accounts is much greater.

Application Security

By application security I mean that you should do defensive programming. Make sure that you take care of your memory (something Java does pretty well already for you). This means freeing all of your pointers (either when using JNI or when developing in a language besides Java), and preventing buffer overflows (something the JVM should take care of for you, but you'd better check your JVM). Many security holes exist because you can overflow the buffer of a program and in turn that allows you to execute commands in the stack space of the program. If that program happens to have super-user privileges, the amount of damage that is possible is quite large.

You must be very careful when developing applications, such as Web applications, that run on behalf of other users. These applications must take extra care when making system calls to external programs. This is because a user over the Web might try to pass commands that do evil things to your system (like delete all of the files on your hard drive) if you don't do the proper checks.

Also, remember that on the Web the need for security doesn't stop once you have the data from the browser. For example I know of several companies, which go to great lengths to protect a Web catalog ordering system using Secure Sockets Layer (SSL) but the application that processes the order simply emails it to someone inside the company for processing. Sure, it's secure from the browser to the server, but after that, it is resent in the open, totally invalidating the security of SSL. You might as well have the person send the purchasing agent an email with all of the information. That's usually easier than writing a lot of complicated database code to process the order.

Access Control

Access control is the process you perform to determine if a particular connection belongs to a particular user (user authentication), and then to determine if they have the right to perform the requested action (user authorization).

User Authentication

User authentication is the process we perform to verify that a user is who they say they are. This is accomplished through the use of a shared secret. The shared secret can be in the form of something both of us know (e.g. a password), something you own (e.g. a smart-card) or something intrinsic to your person (e.g. your fingerprint).

User Authorization

User authorization is the process we perform that determines whether someone has access to a particular system, application or data.

Authorization may or may not require user authentication. For example, many public Web sites allow you to browse through their Web pages without even prompting your for a username or password. Their access controls authorize all users to browse their content.

However, they probably only allow particular users (e.g. the Web developers group) to update the site's content. Whether or not a user plays a particular role (e.g. they are a member of the Web developers group) is determined by their user authentication.

We'll talk more about access control later in this chapter.

Message Verification

Message verification means a process you perform to verify that the message Party B has is the same one Party A sent. Verification is an extremely common process in a networked environment (parity checks are a form of message verification). It is also a very important process. For example, if you're running a Web site that allows people to trade stocks, your users will want to make sure that when they said "buy at $20" it doesn't get translated to "buy at $200".

We'll talk more later about message verification.

Message Ownership

The concept of message ownership means the ability to perform non-repudiation checks on a sent message. Or, to put it more bluntly, 'digital signatures'. We need a mechanism that allows us to prove that someone sent a particular message, so that the message can't be easily faked or disowned. For example, if someone signs a contract on the Web for a million widgets, it shouldn't be easy for the person who signed the order to say "that's not my signature". Likewise, it shouldn't be easy for someone to forge a signature on a contract as well.

Tying this together

As you can see, these various layers are intricately tied together. For example, if a person orders 1000 widgets, it doesn't matter if their digital signature is valid if we can't verify that the message we received is the one that was sent.

It also doesn't matter how much security we put into our user authentication system if someone can walk into our computer room and gain physical access to the machine. Once physical access is acquired, it's usually fairly simple to get past other security measures we've put in place for network access.

Finally when you start to put a security policy/plan in place, remember don't spend a whole lot more on the security system than the object(s) it's designed to protect. It's rather ludicrous to spend a million dollars on an advanced biometric recognition system to protect a five-dollar children's toy. And also don't make the security system so hard to use that people don't use it because it's such a hassle. If it takes a user 15 minutes to open up a system to perform a 15 second task that they must do once an hour, users are not likely to relock the system when they are done with it.

Thus you must make compromises, just make sure that you know what those compromises are, and that you can live with them.

Personalization

Personalization doesn't seem to fit into security. I'll also admit that in computing ages of the past, the two concepts have not meshed well, or we often forego one for the other.

However, we now live in the age of the Web. And in the age of the Web, we are in the era of the 'portal' and customization. A portal is simply a Website that attempts to provide you with everything you need about a particular topic. It's increasingly common for portals to enable you to tailor the site to fit your needs. They allow you to select what links to show on the portal, to change the background colors, decide what stock prices to show, etc.

Now, again you're asking yourself, "what does this have to do with security?".

The answer to this question is trickery. Often we put good security in place but it is not used. This is because security is the broccoli of the computing world. What I mean is that I don't like broccoli, much to my parents' dismay when I was growing up. So to get me to eat it, they would try different things to make me ignore the fact that it was broccoli in my food (I hope that when we're done in this chapter my suggestions work a whole lot better than my parents' attempts with a certain picky eater).

If you provide a user with a positive experience while using the security, and you don't make the security so obtrusive that they always know that it's there, people will use it. After all the Secure Socket Layers (SSL) protocol has made public key cryptography nearly ubiquitous, even though public key cryptography is one of the most difficult security implementations to promote.

In the rest of this chapter, we will use personalization as a demonstration application of JSP security.

A Brief Introduction to Cryptography

Because of limitations in the early computing infrastructure (e.g. CPU power wasn't anywhere near what it is today) and the fact that the early Internet was primarily an academic research network, protecting the basic protocols wasn't a high priority.

Now that we're dealing with billions of dollars of e-commerce on the public Internet, we need a way to protect that data. The best way to ensure that data sent over an unsecured network is read only by the parties who the data is intended for is to encrypt that data.

Encryption literally means to encode data. We encode data all of the time. For example, we encode binary information as Base 64 (which replaces all non-printable characters with something that is ASCII printable text) so that we can transmit it over SMTP, because SMTP handles only ASCII text. However, it's trivial to decode Base 64 encoded data, so we normally don't call it encryption.

When we talk about encrypting data we usually mean encoding data in a way that uses complex mathematical formulas that are extremely hard to decode without knowing a secret key. I'm not a math whiz and I don't expect most of you reading this book are either, so I'm going to spare you the math behind this. After all we're application programmers, all we want are APIs to use, and we'll leave the devilish details to the math geeks.

Symmetric vs Asymmetric Encryption

However, we should know a little bit about the types of cryptography. There are two basic types of cryptography: symmetric and asymmetric.

Symmetric Encryption

Symmetric encryption is when you use the same key for encrypting the data as you do for decrypting it. It can also be called symmetric cryptography and is the type of cryptography most people are familiar with. Popular examples of this type of cryptography are DES and Blowfish.

One of the problems of symmetric cryptography is in the sharing of the key, in particular when you must share the key over an insecure network with someone whom you've never physically met.

The problem is not in actually transmitting the key to someone, but rather is who else has access to the key while it's in transit. Remember that if someone has the key they can encrypt and decrypt anything that uses this key for its encryption.

Asymetric Encryption

Under asymmetric encryption we move away from a single key for encrypting and decrypting, to two separate keys for these operations.

One key is the private key, and the second key is the public key. Data that is encrypted with the private key can only be decrypted with the public key, and data that is encrypted with the public key can only be decrypted with the private key.

The private key should be protected rigorously. If the private key is ever stolen or lost, the whole security of a public-key based system is destroyed.

The public key, as its name implies, can be shared with anyone. In general you should perform some tests to make sure that the public key actually belongs to the person or organization you think it does.

These tests could mean calling up the holder of the private key and verifying that their public key fingerprint matches your copy, or you could have the key 'signed' by the private key of someone else you trust. The term "digitally signed", that means that the data was encrypted by somebody's private key.

Popular examples of public key encryption are PGP, El-Gamal, and RSA. The RSA algorithm (named after the initials for its inventors) is the most famous asymmetric encryption algorithm. However, it's patented in the United States and thus US citizens must pay licensing fees to use this algorithm. El-Gamal (also named after its inventor) is not as widely known, but is popular in cryptographic circles because it is unencumbered by any patents.

Message Digests

When we send data across the wire, we need a way to verify that the data arrived intact and that it wasn't changed en route. While we could do a byte-by-byte check of the data, that can take up a lot of computing time. There is another technique we can use to perform this: Message Authentication Check (MAC). We use a hashing algorithm on the data we wish to verify.

The way this process works is that the person who creates the data creates the original hash of the data and sends a copy of this hash along with the data. When we receive the data, we create our own hash and compare it to the hash that the original person sent to us. If the hashes match, we assume the data has not been corrupted in transit.

Two popular hashing algorithms used in cryptography are MD5 and the Secure Hashing Algorithm (SHA). These algorithms generate a hash of the data that is unique to that particular piece of data. If a single byte is changed in the message, and the hash is recomputed, the resulting hash will be different.

As far I know there are still no known hash collisions (two different pieces of data that hash out to the same values), and no known way of recreating the original data by simply using what is found in the hash value. Because it's accepted that there is only one possible unique hash for any given data, the MD5 and SHA-1 hashing algorithms are considered to be the preferred algorithms for use in an cryptographic system.

Since these algorithms are suitable for use as message digests in a cryptographic system, these digest algorithms are now used for 'encrypting' passwords. The reason we use a hashing algorithm for storing passwords is that we don't want anyone (including ourselves) to be able to decrypt the stored password. We do this for two reasons. One is simply to improve performance: it takes a lot of work to encrypt/decrypt data. We can avoid this by simply hashing the password and storing that in our password database. When a user enters their password, we can hash that value, and then compare it to our stored password. If they match, then the user is considered authenticated. If they don't, the user is told their authentication failed. Another reason to use hashes is that you can't decrypt the data. If it was encrypted and someone got a hold of the key, they could decrypt all of the user's passwords.

One final property of these hashing algorithms is that they will produce a hash of uniform size, regardless of the amount of data they are given. A MD5 hash will always be 16 bytes long and a SHA hash will always be 20 bytes long. For example if you give an MD5 hash a million bytes of data you will get a 16 byte hash value. Or, if you give it 5 bytes of data, you still get a 16 byte hash.

This is one reason why we often use hashes in digital signatures: the data we want to sign is much bigger than the values either one of the hash algorithms produces.

Digital Signatures

In the physical world we assign special meaning to a persons signature. We use them to sign contracts, letters, timecards, etc. For a legal document to become valid it requires a person's signature. We find signatures so valuable that many people even collect the signatures of famous people.

The reason why we consider signatures so valuable is that they provide a cheap non-repudiation service with very little effort. What we mean by this is that if I later claim that you owe me money because of a contract you signed, and you deny you signed the contract, we can visit a handwriting specialist who can verify your signature.

In the digital world, it's not so easy. Computers are very good at repeating the same thing over and over without losing any of the original's quality. Thus, if we had a way to get you to enter your physical signature into the computer, it would be trivial to make a thousand or million copies of your signature without anyone being able to tell the difference from the original.

Thus we've had to come up with a different mechanism for providing digital signatures, through the use of cryptography.

A digital signature is a data file that has been encrypted, usually using public key cryptography. The reason why we use public key cryptography for digital signatures is because it uses two keys, the private key and the public key. A user signs a document by encrypting the document with their private key, and the signature can then be verified by using the user's public key.

However, encrypting/decrypting a large document (for example a several page contract) uses a lot of computing resources. So, to minimize the amount of resources you need and the time required for encrypting/decrypting the data, we can produce a digital signature by using a cryptographically secure hashing algorithm like MD5 or SHA, and then encrypting the resulting hash with our private key.

The person who receives the document can then decrypt the digest using your public key. They can further verify that the message was received unchanged by re-computing the message digest and checking to see if the message digests matches.

User Authentication

Whenever we want to control access to our applications, we must determine whether the current connection should have access or not. The process of associating a given connection with a particular user is called authentication. We assume the connection belongs to a user if the user can provide us with the shared secret.

There are three basic ways of sharing a secret between a user and an application.

- Something the user knows
- Something the user has
- Something Inherent to the user

Something the User Knows

This method is the most common mechanism, the password. If the user knows the same password we have stored in our password database then we consider them authenticated.

Something the User Has

This method requires the user to provide some element to the application. Usually this is in the form of some type of digital certificate, though we can require that the digital certificate be provided from a smart-card.

Something Inherent to the User

This method, typically called biometrics, requires the user to provide some element of their body, like a fingerprint, voice print, or retinal scan. This subject is beyond the scope of this book.

Variations

In practice we usually use a combination of the above, to improve security. For example, we don't like to simply rely on passwords, because most people use easy to guess passwords, or they write them down or even share them with anyone who asks. Digital certificates are better because they don't require the user to remember anything. However, digital certificates are simply electronic files so they can be shared.

A better approach would be to require a user to type in a password and present a digital certificate. In this case for someone to impersonate another user, they would need to know the password and have a copy of the digital certificate. While it's still possible to do, it's harder than either simply having the password or the digital certificate.

What is a Digital Certificate?

I've already mentioned digital certificates a couple of times. A digital certificate is a public key with extra information contained in it that helps verify who the public key belongs to. The most common standard for digital certificates is X.509.

In the X.509 standard, the digital certificate contains an unique Distinguished Name, so that you can easily separate one certificate from another. It can also contain a serial number, the algorithm the public key uses, the size of the key, an expiration date, and other data that can be used to verify the owner of the public key (we'll cover X.509 certificates in more detail later in the chapter). The most important part of the verification data is the signature of the Certificate Authority (CA). A CA is an entity that issues digital certificates.

When using digital certificates, the CA plays the role of a trusted intermediary. This is an important role because, in a public network with millions of people and systems that need to interact with each other, it's impossible for you to individually verify every certificate that you come in contact with.

However, you can build a web of trust. For example, you can say that you trust me and that anyone that I say I trust, you can trust as well because you trust me. This is the role a CA plays in the world of digital certificates.

A CA is trusted to verify that the owners of the digital certificates it issues are in fact who they say they are. We can tell our applications to trust particular CAs, and any certificates they issue. Besides issuing certificates, a CA must also play a role in letting you know when you can no longer trust a certificate. This is called certificate revocation.

An example of a popular public CA is Verisign at http://www.verisign.com.

Public Key Infrastructure

The infrastructure necessary to issue, verify, and revoke digital certificates is called Public Key Infrastructure or PKI.

In PKI you must have a system where you can easily issue new digital certificates, verify that the certificates are owned by a particular user or entity and perhaps most importantly know when you can no longer trust a particular digital certificate.

A PKI will consist of one or more Certificate Authorities and a verification database (often in the form of a directory service like LDAP).

We'll talk later in this chapter about how you can use a PKI from JSP.

Introducing the Secure Sockets Layer

As we've discussed before, data that travels over the network using the Internet protocols is sent in the clear and anyone can read it if they want to. This means your credit card numbers, which stocks you want to trade, or what team you picked in this week's fantasy sports pool.

The easiest way to protect the data that goes between a client and a server over TCP/IP is to use the Secure Sockets Layer protocol.

The Secure Sockets Layer (SSL) protocol was created by Netscape to secure traffic over the World Wide Web. SSL has become a de facto standard for encrypting all manner of Internet traffic. While it began life as a proprietary protocol, Netscape always intended to make it an open standard, and that is what it has become through the IETF. The new standard is called Transport Security Layer, though it is still popularly referred to as the Secure Sockets Layer.

The SSL specification allows us to encrypt data so that only the client and server have access to that data. It also allows us to verify the identity of the client and the server.

How SSL Works

SSL can be used to encrypt traffic over any open network. All SSL transactions occur in six steps:

1. The client sends the server its SSL protocol version (e.g. SSLv2 or SSLv3), some random data, its maximum bit size (e.g. 40-bit or 128-bit), plus some other information needed for doing an SSL transaction. We use random data to make it harder for someone to forge the client connection. The bit size is important because the more number of bits, the harder it is to decrypt a message with brute force. However, because of the laws of certain countries governing the exportation of cryptographic products, you may be forced to use a lower bit size like 40 instead of the more secure 128 bits.

2. The server sends back a similar set of data to the client, except that it also sends the client a copy of the server's certificate and its public key. The server's certificate contains information that 'vouches' for the server's identity.

3. The client decides whether the server can be trusted. (See the next section, 'How a Client Determines a Server's Trustworthiness.')

4. If the client doesn't trust the server, it disconnects from it. If, however, the client does trust the server, then it sends back an initial secret key that is signed with the server's public key.

5. The server decrypts the message and can also ask for client SSL authentication (this latter part is optional). The server then sends back some information that the client and server will use to encode their messages, including measures to reduce the likelihood of any data tampering in between the client and server.

6. The client and server carry on their normal transaction except that it is now encrypted with SSL.

How a Client Determines a Server's Trustworthiness

As part of the negotiation process of setting up an SSL connection (a process called the "SSL handshake"), the server will send the client a certificate.

A certificate is a record of some key information that the client can use to determine whether or not the server can be considered trustworthy. This record must meet four criteria to be considered OK:

1. The certificate's expiration date must be on or after today's date.

2. The Certificate Authority that issued the certificate must be trusted.

3. The public key of the Certificate Authority that issued the certificate must validate the digital signature of the Certificate Authority that is on the certificate.

4. The domain name that is listed on the certificate must match the server's domain name.

Here is an example of a server certificate as presented in Netscape Communicator:

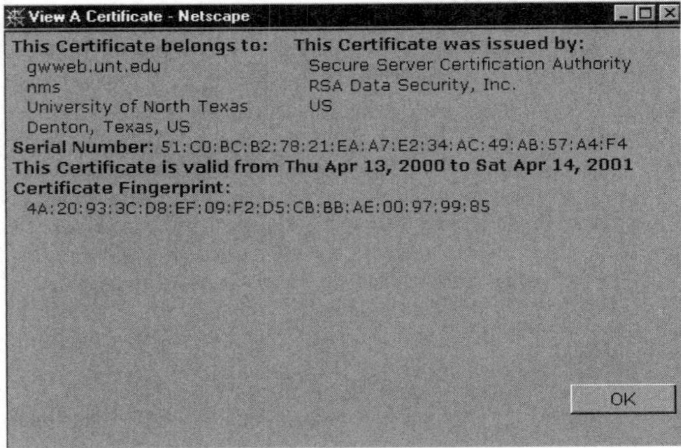

You can retrieve a server's certificate by clicking on the 'closed lock' in the lower left-hand corner of the Navigator browser window.

Client Authentication with SSL

As part of an SSL session, a server has the ability to require that the client verifies its identity using the same process that the client uses to verify a server's identity, except the roles are reversed.

The application that is running behind the SSL transaction (e.g. a Web server) has the ability to register itself with the SSL session to tell it that it wants to perform extra checks on the certificate. For example, the initial SSL verification will check that the certificate has not expired and has been signed by one of the recognized certificate authorities. The Web server could do further verification by determining if the presented certificate matched a certificate belonging to a particular user in a directory server. Later, an application can use the certificate to determine the role of the user for determining access to the application.

Using certificates for authentication is generally agreed to be high assurance, because both the server and the client must verify their identities to each other.

Using SSL with JSPs

In the current specification the use of SSL is encouraged, in particular to protect sensitive data like passwords; however, there's no current recommendation on how to accomplish this. The best solution at the moment is to use a Web server that supports SSL and use that to encrypt your connection. Hopefully in the future Tomcat, the reference implementation for servlets/JSP (and an open-source project from Apache), will support this in its stand-alone Web server.

None of the JSP engines currently support SSL authentication either, unless the Web server you are running supports it. Even if your Web server supports SSL encryption, this does not necessarily mean that you can get access to the SSL certificate to do any extra authentication or authorization based on this information. This will change in the future, but as I write this chapter, exactly how this will be done is still up in the air.

Authentication and Authorization

When you talk about securing your applications, it is important to separate authentication from authorization. Authentication is the process by which you determine a client's identity; authorization is the process by which you determine what actions a particular client can perform.

For example, take an application I worked on at the university where I am employed. The project was to Web-enable our mainframe applications, which could be divided into two types. One was general student applications (registering for class, paying tuition, etc.); the second was student administration applications (applications that university staff used to maintain student data).

Because the applications actually operated against the mainframe, we had a two-step authorization process that coincided with our authentication mechanism. After our application authenticated a person, we were able to determine whether they were a student or a staff member.

If the client was authenticated as a student, the user was only allowed access to his or her own records. The user was only allowed to update items specific to the application (for example, which classes they wanted to take).

If the client was authenticated as an administrative staff member, then they were allowed to update any record under their jurisdiction. For example the registrar's office could update a student's biographical and academic record, the financial aid office was allowed to update a student's financial aid status, and the office of student accounting could update a student's tuition payment status.

Authentication

With JSPs there are three ways you can authenticate a client to your application, either with your Web server, your Servlet engine or in the application itself.

Web Server Authentication

First is you can let the Web server handle it. All of the popular Web servers that can run servlets/JSPs today have some mechanism to limit access to the content the Web server handles, including JSPs. Exactly how to configure this information is dependent upon the server you are running.

In Apache, for example, if you wanted to limit access to any files under the `/opt/apache/stuff` directory you could use a directive like this in your `httpd.conf` file:

```
<Directory "/opt/apache/stuff">
AuthType Basic
AuthName "Restricted Directory"
AuthUserFile /web/users
AuthGroupFile /web/groups
require group admin
</Directory>
```

Whenever a user requests a file from this directory they would be prompted to enter a username and password by their browser. If they successfully entered their information correctly, the server would then check to see what group they were in as dictated by the `require group admin` line. If their username was found to be in the group named `admin` then they would be allowed to retrieve the file, otherwise they would be rejected.

This method or its equivalent is the most popular, because most of the time JSPs will be deployed with a working Web server like Apache or IIS.

Servlet Engine Authentication

As part of the JSP 2.2 specification, the servlet engine is required to provide you with four basic methods of authentication that you can use to control access to your servlets and JSPs. We'll briefly talk about them here and then actually show how to do this with the Tomcat engine.

The four methods of authentication are:

- Basic authentication
- Digest authentication
- HTTPS Client authentication
- Form Based authentication

Basic Authentication

This method is one of the two specified standards for use in authenticating users via HTTP. This is the authentication method used whenever your browser pops open a box like this:

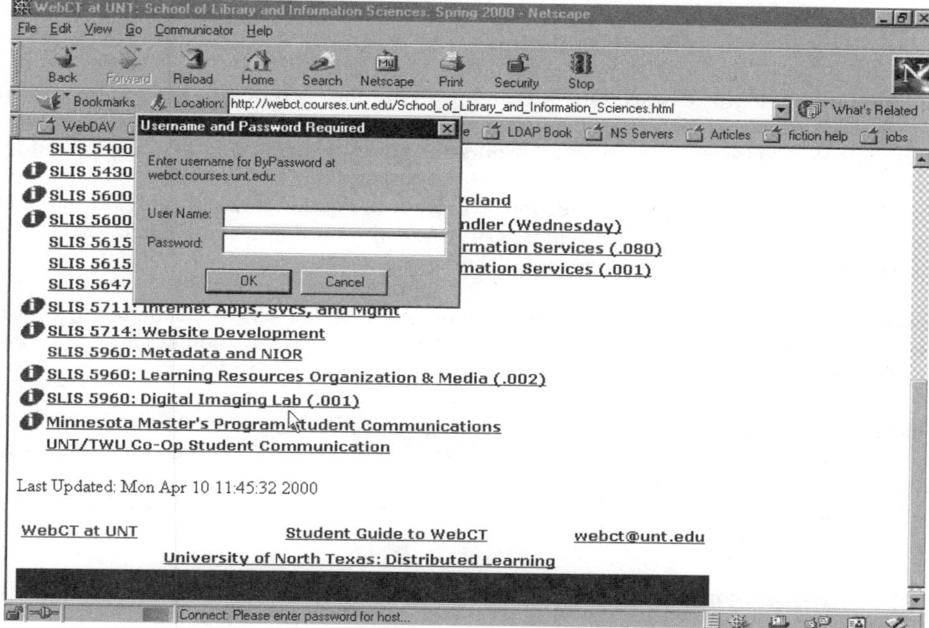

The data is encoded in the AUTHORIZATION header in the HTTP request. Except for the fact that the data is encoded in Base64 for transport, it is otherwise not encrypted in any form or fashion. Thus if you are going to use basic authentication in your applications, make sure that you do so over an SSL encrypted network connection to prevent people from sniffing the username and password as it goes over the wire.

Digest Authentication

This is the same as basic authentication except that the password is MD5 encrypted first by the browser before sending it over the wire. None of the current browsers support Digest Authentication, thus this portion of the HTTP protocol is of little use to you in practice.

Also, it is still possible to capture the digested password and reuse it later, so you should also encrypt any communications when using Digest Authentication.

HTTPS Client Authentication

You can also request that the client authenticate itself to you via a digital certificate following the SSL protocol. I imagine that you'll be able to either hook in a directory server or similar PKI setup to further verify a client, but nobody supports this yet in their server engine.

All of the major browsers and Web servers support the ability to authenticate to a server via a digital certificate.

Form Based Authentication

One of the nice things that appeared in the current servlet specification was the recognition of an authentication method outside the scope of traditional HTTP.

It's very common to require users to authenticate themselves to an application via a form instead of using Basic Authentication or digital certificates.

We often use forms for two reasons. One is that you want to use a different authentication database than what the web server uses as its default. For example you might wish to do this if you have an LDAP server but your Web server only supports a proprietary internal database. While you could write a plugin for the server's API, this is often a very serious undertaking and usually requires more time than what you have for a particular project. Second, you want to enable the user to logout of the system. This is not easily done with either Basic or digital certificates without doing some serious low-level code writing on the server. It's fairly easily accomplished using cookies.

The servlet specification writers know about this, and realized that servlets (remember, JSPs are simply a derivative of servlets) would often end up having their own authentication system via forms if one was not provided for them. So form authentication was written into the standard.

Now what does this mean to you the servlet/JSP programmer? This means that you now don't have worry about adding your own authentication mechanism to your application. Instead you can concentrate on providing the business logic and use the authorization information the servlet engine gives you (e.g. this user has a name of Bob and he has been identified as belonging to the engineering group).

Individual Applications

Individual applications may also wish to implement their own authentication mechanism, generally through the use of forms. The most common reason to use this type of authentication mechanism is when you don't have direct control over the Web server you're application is hosted on (e.g. your putting your JSPs on a third-party hosting service).

Authorization

Authorization can be controlled in several ways. You can go from letting anyone access your application, to limiting it by IP addresses, to a particular digital certificate.

You'll be likely to be performing authorization based around the results of a user's authentication. After a user has been authenticated you can further determine whether they should have access to your system based on their username (e.g. anyone with the username of 'bob' is allowed in), their principal name, or what roles they are assigned.

A Principal is an object that represents a user in a Java security context. This could be simply a username or it could be data that represents a digital certificate or it could be a digital representation of fingerprint from a biometric authentication system. It's just a generic interface that allows us to interact with any authentication system. Under JSP most often the Principal object will simply correspond to the username of the client that was given when prompted for a username and password.

A user can also be assigned one or more roles. A role is a group of users that you can use in your application to determine what type of access a particular user might have. For example a user might have a role of employee, engineer and manager. Thus, you might have a set of applications that allow employees to do one thing, another set of applications that are limited only to members of the engineering roles, and finally you could have certain applications (e.g. human resources) that are limited to users who fulfill a managerial role.

Data Integrity and Privacy

When building networked applications like JSPs, you often want to verify that your server received the data sent from the client intact. And because there are some people out there who you wouldn't want to have access to the data that goes across the wire, you need to encrypt the data to prevent it from being seen.

To guard against these dangers, the servlet specification allows you to require data sent from the client be sent via a guaranteed transport like SSL. While you can certainly do this in an application today, this is often available to you only if your Web server supports SSL. This marks the first time that someone has given you the ability to specify such a request without having to code it yourself into your applications.

Securing JSPs

Well we certainly have talked a lot; now it's time to actually get our hands a bit dirty. We will be building a series of applications that ultimately will enable us to build a personalized 'Web Portal' using JSPs and the security features of the Servlet 2.2 specification.

Our tools of choice are going to be:

- The Tomcat Servlet engine
- The Apache Web server
- The iPlanet Directory server
- JSPs
- JDK 1.2 or later, with JNDI

Standard JSP Security

As we have learned, the Servlet specification does spell out some criteria on security that implementers must follow.

The first is the ability for the developer who deploys their JSPs to be able to declare a security policy in their deployment description file (e.g. the `web.xml` file) that is included in each context's `WEB-INF` directory.

Here is an example security policy – in fact this is the default security policy used by Tomcat, which is the Servlet/JSP reference implementation. While I'm talking about Tomcat in this chapter, this particular implementation is based upon the Servlet specification. Thus all of the Servlet engine vendors that support the Java Servlet specification must support this configuration model.

First you must declare that you'll be describing a security policy using the `security-constraint` tag:

```
<security-constraint>
```

Next you need to describe the resources (e.g. files, directories, servlets) that you'll be protecting with the `url-pattern` tag.

```
<web-resource-collection>
<url-pattern>/jsp/security/protected/*</url-pattern>
```

This pattern restricts all files under the `/jsp/security/protected/` directory.

You'll also be describing the HTTP methods that you'll be restricting access to. For example you might allow anonymous access for fetching files via a `GET`, but you might require anyone who wants to `POST` data to the server be authenticated.

This is done with the `http-method` tag.

```
<http-method>DELETE</http-method>
<http-method>GET</http-method>
<http-method>POST</http-method>
<http-method>PUT</http-method>
</web-resource-collection>
```

Next, you specify which roles a user must be in before they are allowed access. You do this with the `auth-constraint` and `role-name` tags:

```
<auth-constraint>
<!-- Anyone with one of the listed roles may access this area -->
<role-name>Accounting Managers</role-name>
<role-name>tomcat</role-name>
<role-name>role1</role-name>
</auth-constraint>
</security-constraint>
```

The Servlet specification allows us to change how we perform the authentication as long as the authentication code of the Servlet engine provides the necessary data to fulfill the tags we have talked about so far.

We can specify how we wish the Servlet engine to authenticate users by changing the data we give in the `login-config` tag.

Here is an example that shows how to configure the Servlet engine for using HTTP BASIC authentication.

```
<login-config>
<auth-method>BASIC</auth-method>
<realm-name>Example Basic Authentication Area</realm-name>
</login-config>
```

Here is an example that shows how you could configure the Servlet engine for using a form based authentication.

```
<login-config>
<auth-method>EXPERIMENTAL_FORM</auth-method>
<realm-name>Example Form-Based Authentication Area</realm-name>
<form-login-config>
<form-login-page>/jsp/security/login/login.jsp</form-login-page>
<form-error-page>/jsp/security/login/error.jsp</form-error-page>
</form-login-config>
</login-config>
```

The Servlet specification defines how form authentication must be set up for the Servlet engine to handle it. Your first step is that you must define a form for users to login with, using the `form-login-page` tag. The next step is you must define a page for the user to be sent to if the authentication attempt fails via the `form-error-page` tag.

The HTML form that the login page generates must also meet a certain criteria.

```
<form method="POST" action="j_security_check">
<input type="text" name="j_username">
<input type="password" name="j_password">
</form>
```

The method must be POST, the action must be `j_security_check`, the username must be provided by the field `j_username` and the password must be provided by the field `j_password`.

The rest of the HTML can be whatever the developer wants it to be. For example, you can add extra information to the user about how get an id and password, or apply a standard style to the page.

It is up to the Servlet engine to perform the actual authentication. This could mean that the Servlet engine looks up the username and password from a local text file, in a remote user database or an existing directory service like LDAP.

Later on in this chapter we'll see how Tomcat, the Servlet reference implementation handles these tasks.

A Note On Realms

You'll notice in the login configuration elements that there is a `realm-name` tag. This tag denotes an HTTP realm, which essentially is how the browser and server can determine what parts of the web site they are authenticated for.

The term realm can also mean a security realm, which may or may not apply to the same realm as your HTTP realm. For example you can have an HTTP realm called 'My Site' but under your Java security code you could dictate that only people who are a member of the 'Mark's Friends' security realm are allowed to access 'My Site'.

Now it's time to do some actual coding.

Default Tomcat Authentication

The example JSP and servlets directory contains a protected directory to demonstrate the `auth-config` setup as indicated by the Servlet specification. If you open the `web.xml` file located in the `TOMCAT_HOME/webapps/examples/WEB-INF` directory you'll see the login configuration.

Most of this you've already seen above, but I present it here in full text so that you can get a better idea of how it fits together.

```
<security-constraint>
<web-resource-collection>
   <web-resource-name>Protected Area</web-resource-name>
   <!-- Define the context-relative URL(s) to be protected -->
   <url-pattern>/jsp/security/protected/*</url-pattern>
   <!-- If you list http methods, only those methods are protected -->
   <http-method>DELETE</http-method>
      <http-method>GET</http-method>
      <http-method>POST</http-method>
      <http-method>PUT</http-method>
</web-resource-collection>

<auth-constraint>
   <!-- Anyone with one of the listed roles may access this area -->
   <!-- mark wilcox test role -->
      <role-name>Accounting Managers</role-name>
      <role-name>tomcat</role-name>
      <role-name>role1</role-name>
</auth-constraint>
</security-constraint>

<!-- Default login configuration uses BASIC authentication -->
<login-config>
   <auth-method>BASIC</auth-method>
   <realm-name>Example Basic Authentication Area</realm-name>
</login-config>

<!-- If you want to experiment with form-based logins, comment
     out the <login-config> element above and replace it with
     this one.  Note that we are currently using a nonstandard
     authentication method, because the code to support form
     based login is incomplete and only lightly tested.  -->
<!--
<login-config>
   <auth-method>EXPERIMENTAL_FORM</auth-method>
   <realm-name>Example Form-Based Authentication Area</realm-name>
```

```
        <form-login-config>
            <form-login-page>/jsp/security/login/login.jsp</form-login-page>
            <form-error-page>/jsp/security/login/error.jsp</form-error-page>
        </form-login-config>
    </login-config>
    -->
```

This sets up the ability to restrict access to all files under the `/jsp/security/protected/` directory for the HTTP methods `GET`, `POST`, `PUT` or `DELETE` using basic authentication. Only people who are authenticated and associated with the roles `Tomcat` or `Role1` will be allowed access to the site.

By default, Tomcat comes with a security provider that keeps its usernames, passwords and roles stored in XML file called `tomcat-users.xml` in the `TOMCAT_HOME/conf` directory:

```
<tomcat-users>
    <user name="tomcat" password="tomcat" roles="tomcat" />
    <user name="role1"  password="tomcat" roles="role1"  />
    <user name="both"   password="tomcat" roles="tomcat,role1" />
</tomcat-users>
```

You shouldn't use this as your production authentication database for Tomcat because anyone who can read this file can see all of the passwords without having to do any type of work to decrypt them. Instead you should write your own security interceptor that encrypts the passwords. We will soon see how you can develop your own replacement for this default system.

If you enter the URL http://localhost:8080/examples/jsp/security/protected/ you'll be prompted for a username and password, as our next figure shows.

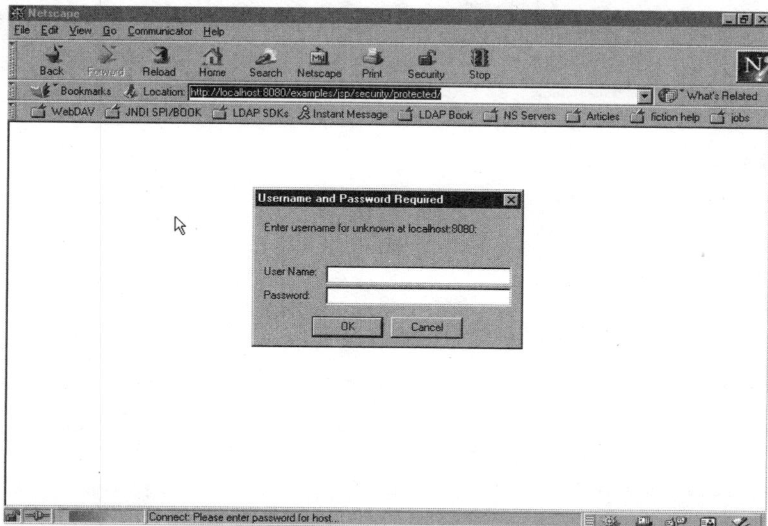

Enter the username as tomcat and the password as tomcat.

The next screen shows that you entered your password correctly. It displays your current username and principal name (they are the same for the current example, but this is not necessarily the case for all authentication databases).

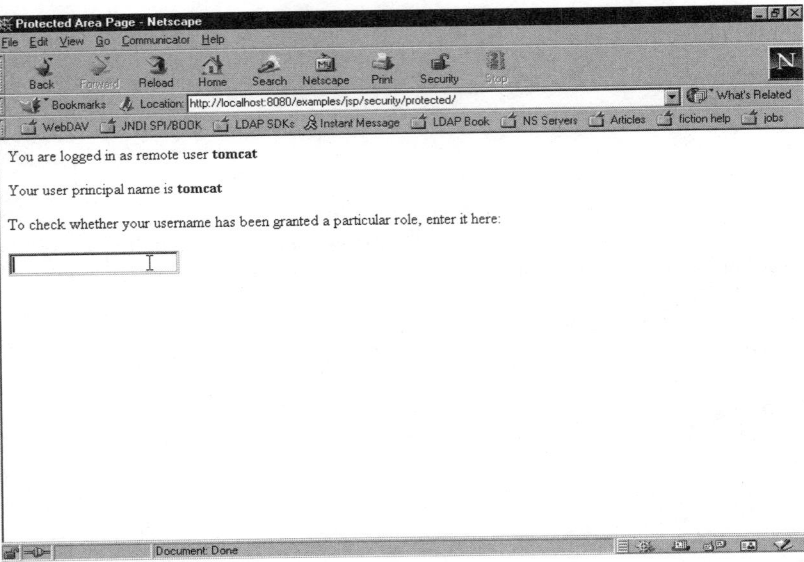

If you enter the name of a role in the box, for example tomcat, and press *Enter*, the JSP will tell you whether or not you are authorized for that role.

Our next screen shows the result of this operation.

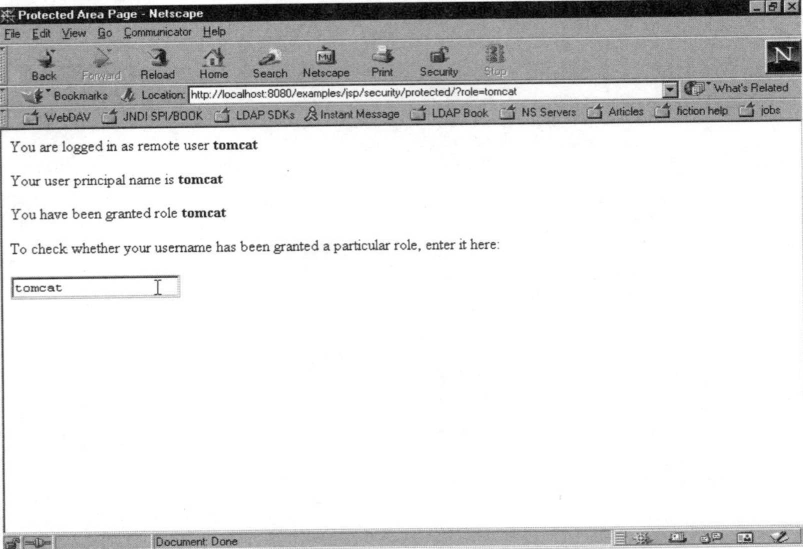

The default authentication engine in Tomcat is nice for testing purposes, but it's probably not one we would like to use for production purposes.

There are a few reasons why we wouldn't want to use the default `tomcat-users.xml` implementation. One reason is that the passwords are stored in plain text. Second, it's difficult to manage, in particular if you have a large number of users. Third, it doesn't easily integrate with any existing authentication system you may have. Fourth, it doesn't easily scale across a Web farm.

However, we can get around all of these problems by writing our own authorization plugin for Tomcat. Our next project will be to write an authorization plugin that allows us to use LDAP for our user database. The reason I call it an authorization instead of just an authentication plugin is because the plugin must not only authenticate a user to the server but also determine what roles that user is in.

This project will require the JNDI SDK with an LDAP service provider and a LDAP server. I used the iPlanet Directory server, but you should be able to use the LDAP server of your choice.

Naming and Directory Services

Since you are an Internet programmer you realize that for the Internet to be usable we must be able to tell different services apart from each other and we must be able to find services that might be useful to us. A naming service helps determine names for a collection of like objects. For example on the Internet we have DNS to help ensure that each host on the Internet has an unique name so that we can tell the Web server at Wrox from the Web server at Yahoo!. A directory service is a specialized database that enables us to quickly find things. For a directory service to be useful it needs a naming service, but a naming service doesn't always need to have a directory service.

In this section we're going to discuss how the Java Naming Directory Interfaces (JNDI) API enables you to add these types of capabilities to your network applications.

Naming Services

A naming service is a service that provides for the creation of a standard name for a given set of data. For example, on the Internet, each host (each web server with a live Internet connection) has what is called a Fully Qualified Domain Name (FQDN).

The hostname and the sub-domain names are managed by the organization that owns the domain name (e.g. `unt.edu` which is owned by the University of North Texas). The domain name is provided to an organization by the InterNIC, which ensures that each domain name is unique. Through the use of sub-domains and domain names we can have systems that share the same hostname (e.g. www) yet are considered entirely separate entities. For example `www.cs.wrox.com` is different from `www.wrox.com`. In this case the sub-domain `cs.wrox.com` is actually "below" the root domain of `wrox.com`, providing for its own unique namespace.

Directory Services

A directory service is aspecial type of database that is designed to be read from very quickly through various indexing, caching and disk access techniques. They are also typically described using a hierarchical information model. Directory services also presume a specialized set of search services as opposed to a RDBMS system like Oracle or Microsoft SQL Server, which allow you a more generalized set of querying services.

A directory service will always have a naming service (but a naming service doesn't necessarily have to have a directory service). An example of a directory service in the physical world is a telephone book. A telephone book allows us to lookup the telephone number of a person or business quickly, if we know the name of the person whose number we want.

There is a plethora of directory (and pseudo-directory) services in use on our networks today. One directory service we use every day on the Internet is the Domain Naming Service (DNS), which takes a FQDN and returns that FQDN's IP address. All Internet communication uses the Internet Protocol suite (consisting of TCP, UDP and IP). For successful communication between two computers, each system must know the IP address of the other.

IP addresses consist of 32 bit numbers, such as `198.137.240.92`, while hostnames take the form of something like `www.yahoo.com`. Computers are better at dealing with numbers, but humans (most humans anyway), are better at remembering names. Every time you try to connect to an Internet server using its name, your computer must first get the server's IP address via DNS.

Most likely your organization also uses one of the following directory services:

- Novell Directory Services (NDS)
- Network Information Services (NIS/NIS+)
- Windows NT Domains
- Active Directory Services (ADS)

Each of these directory services (although the NT Domains service isn't a true directory service, many people try to use it as one) provides more information than the simple name to IP mapping we get from DNS. Each one also allows us to store information about users (e.g. userid, passwords, names, etc.), user groups (e.g. for access control) and computers (e.g. their Ethernet and IP addresses). NDS and ADS allow more functions (such as the location of network printers, software, and so on) than either NIS or NT Domains.

Because there are so many directory services, and we have so many systems on our networks, some larger problems have arisen. Essentially, it boils down to three issues, keeping track of users, keeping track of network resources such as computers and printers and making sure that you have consistent data in all of your data stores.

For example in many organizations you'll find that your users will need access to a Novell system (which uses NDS) for file and print sharing, an account on a Windows NT box for running Microsoft based applications (which may also include many of the services that NDS or UNIX provides) and finally an account on a UNIX box (using NIS) for email and web page publication.

Unfortunately for network managers (in particular in a decentralized environment), none of these directory services interact with each other. As a result, users often end up with different ids and passwords on each system (which in turn leads to insecure passwords, because users have trouble remembering multiple passwords). As a further security risk, if a user leaves the organization, it's very difficult to make sure that all of the former user's accounts are removed.

Each directory service also has its own particular protocol, which makes it very difficult for the traditional application developer to interact with several different directory services.

Why LDAP?

For the Java developer, one solution is to use JNDI, which provides a standard API to a variety of directory services.

The Lightweight Directory Access Protocol (LDAP) was developed in the early 1990s as a standard directory protocol. Since LDAP is now the most popular directory protocol, and JNDI can access LDAP, we'll be spending most of our time talking about how to harness LDAP to improve your Java applications with JNDI.

LDAP can trace its roots back to the X.500 protocol (aka. the "Heavy" Directory Access Protocol), which was originally based on the OSI networking protocols (an early "competitor" to the Internet protocols).

LDAP defines how clients should access data on the server. It does not specify how the data should be stored on the server. Most often you'll interact with a server that's been specifically built for LDAP such as the openLDAP or Netscape Directory server. However, LDAP can become a front-end to any type of data store. Because of this, most popular directory services now have an LDAP front-end of some type including NIS, NDS, Active Directory, and even Windows NT Domains.

LDAP Data

The data in LDAP is organized in a tree, called a Directory Information Tree (DIT). Each "leaf" in the DIT is called an entry. The first entry in a DIT is called the root entry.

An entry is comprised of a unique Distinguished Name (DN) and any number of attribute/value pairs. The DN is the name of an entry. The DN is like the primary key of a relational database. A DN also shows the relation of the entry to the rest of the DIT, in a manner similar to the way the full path name of a file shows the relation of a particular file on your hard-drive to the rest of the files on your system. A path to a file on your system reads left to right when reading from root to file. A DN reads right to left when reading from root to entry.

LDAP attributes are in the form of mnemonics such as cn meaning common name, o for organization and ou for organizational unit. Often you'll see the root of a DIT to be the DN of the organization and then branches out via different organizational units.
Here is an example of a DN:

```
uid=scarter, ou=People, o=airius.com
```

The leftmost part of a DN is called a Relative Distinguished Name (RDN) and is made up of an attribute/value that is in the entry. The RDN in the example above would be `uid=scarter`.

LDAP attributes often use mnemonics as their names. Overleaf are some of the more common LDAP attributes and what they define.

LDAP Attribute	Definition
cn	common name
sn	surname
givenname	first name
uid	userid
dn	Distinguished Name
mail	email address

Any attribute can have one or more values, if defined by the schema. For example, a user can have more than one email address so they could have more than on value for their `mail` attribute. Attribute values can be either text or binary data. Attributes are referred to in name/value pairs.

There is also a special attribute called `objectclass`. The `objectclass` attribute of an entry specifies what attributes are required and what attributes are allowed in a particular entry. Like objects in Java, object classes in LDAP can be extended. When an object class is extended, it keeps the existing attributes, but you can specify new attributes for a particular entry.

Here is an example LDAP entry represented in the LDAP Data Interchange Format (LDIF), which is the most common way to show LDAP data in human readable format:

```
dn: uid=scarter, ou=People, o=fedup.com
cn: Sam Carter
sn: Carter
givenname: Sam
```

The `objectclass` attribute is a special attribute. This tells the LDAP server which attributes are required to be in the entry and which other attributes are simply allowed. An `objectclass` is like a RDBMS table. They are also hierarchical in nature and the attributes of one `objectclass` can be inherited by another.

```
objectclass: top
objectclass: person
objectclass: organizationalPerson
objectclass: inetOrgPerson
ou: Accounting
ou: People
l: Sunnyvale
uid: scarter
mail: scarter@fedup.com
telephonenumber: +1 408 555 4798
facsimiletelephonenumber: +1 408 555 9751
roomnumber: 4612
```

Attributes also have matching rules. These rules tell the server how it should consider whether a particular entry is a "match" or not for a given query.

The possible matching rules are:

Matching Rule	Meaning
DN	Attribute is in the form of a Distinguished Name
Case Insensitive String (CIS)	Attribute can match if values of the query equals the attribute's value, regardless of case.
Case Sensitive String (CSS)	Attribute can match if values of the query equals the attributes' value including the case.
Telephone	Is the same as CIS except that things like "-" and "()" are ignored when determining the match, but + and "" aren't.
Integer	Attribute match is determined using only numbers.
Binary	Attribute matches if the value of the query and the value of the attributes are the same binary values (e.g. searching a LDAP database for a particular photo).

The definition of attributes, attribute matching rules, and the relationship between object classes and attributes are defined in the server's schema. "Out of the box" the server already contains a pre-defined schema, but you can extend the schema (as long as the server supports the LDAP v3 protocol as defined in RFC 2251) to include your own attributes and object classes.

LDAP servers also support referrals (e.g. pointers to other LDAP directories where data resides), so a single LDAP server could search millions of entries from one client request. You can replicate LDAP data to improve reliability and speed. Finally LDAP has a very strong security model using ACLS to protect data inside the server and supporting the Secure Sockets Layer (SSL)/Transport Layer Security (TLS) and Simple Authentication & Security Layer (SASL) protocols.

LDAP has growing momentum both as the standard protocol for electronic address books and as the central directory service for network services. For more information about LDAP see the book, *Implementing LDAP*, ISBN 1-86100-21-1, from Wrox Press.

Introducing JNDI

While LDAP is growing in popularity and in usage, it's still a long way from being ubiquitous. Other directory services such as NIS (primarily developed by Sun) and Novell's NDS (though the latest versions of NDS are LDAP aware) are still in widespread use. Another issue for the developers of Java was that for Java to succeed as an enterprise development language, it needed to support existing distributed computing standards such as the Common Object Request Broker Architecture (CORBA), which is heavily used in large organizations that have many different types of applications interacting with each other. CORBA is a language and platform independent architecture for enabling distributed application programming (where an application on one machine can access a function of a different application located on a different machine as if it was calling an internal function). CORBA uses a naming service for defining the location of the available objects. You can find out more about CORBA at http://www.corba.org.

So, to make it easier on Java application developers a standard API was created for interacting with naming and directory services, similar to what Java application developers have for databases in JDBC. This API is very important for the long-term development of Java, particularly the Enterprise JavaBeans (EJB) initiative. A key component of the EJB initiative is the ability to store and retrieve Java objects on the network. A directory service (most likely LDAP), is going to be the primary data store for Java objects. This is because when loading objects from the network, you want to be able to locate them quickly, and a directory service enables very fast lookup and retrieval of data, which can be a person's record or binary data like a serialized Java object.

It would probably help to understand the relationships of directory services, JNDI and LDAP by looking at some diagrams.

Our first diagram shows the relationship between a client and a variety of directory services. Each directory service requires its own API, which adds complexity and code bloat to our client application:

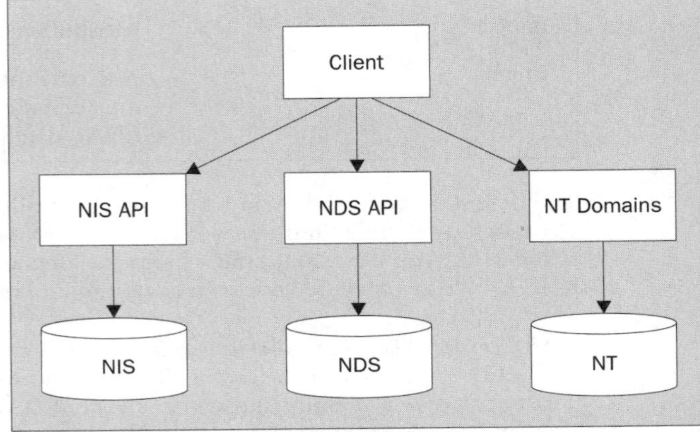

Our next example shows how we could simplify this with JNDI. With JNDI, we still have multiple servers and multiple APIs underneath, but to the application developer, it is effectively a single API.

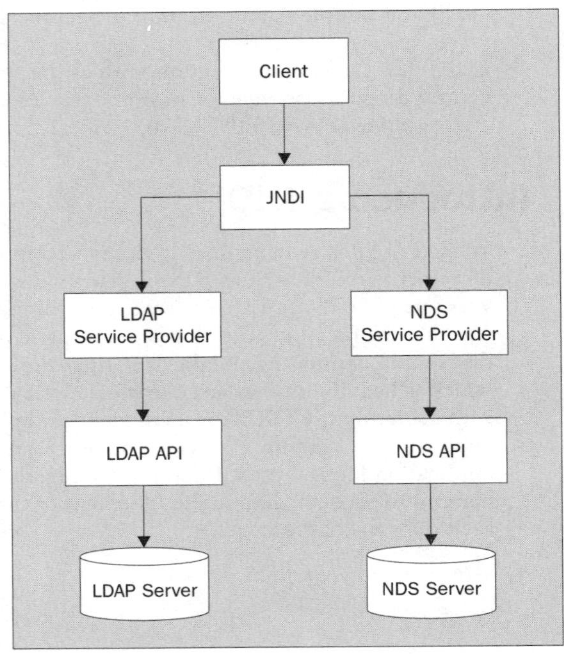

While the application developer now has an easier time developing network applications because they can concentrate on a single API, the developer still faces potential problems because not all JNDI service providers (JNDI terminology for the "drivers" that allow you to interact with different directory services) are created equal. Also, each directory service is still a bit different (they name their entries differently, have different capabilities, and so on).

Under JNDI, most of the specifics of the protocol are hidden from you. For example there's not a way to get direct access to the specific LDAP connection and you can't send any LDAP command that is not provided by the API and/or your specific service provider. Also under LDAP the connection and the authentication step are two separate processes that JNDI treats as one.

Finally we show how JNDI and LDAP can work together, for a much more elegant solution:

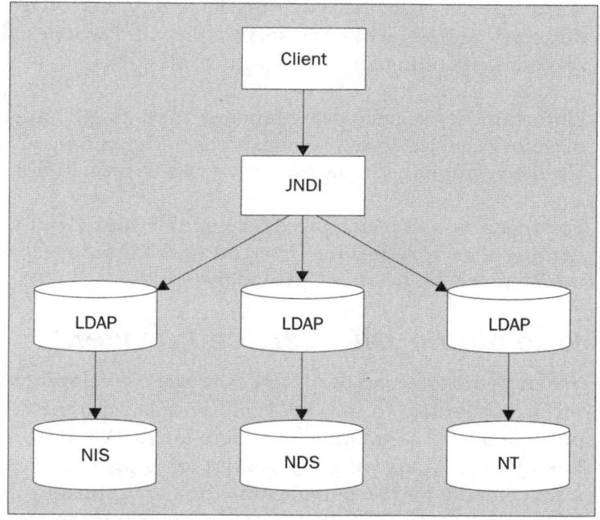

In this final example, we use JNDI to communicate with an LDAP server (s). To the developer, they are only having to worry about one particular protocol (LDAP) and API(JNDI).In this example we are relying on the availability of vendors providing LDAP interfaces to their respective protocols. And this is not such a far-fetched idea. For each of these popular directory services, there are products that allow you to communicate with them via LDAP.

While there are advantages of using LDAP and JNDI such as reducing the complexity of learning multiple protocols and APIs there are disadvantages as well. For example by adding more objects that must be created and managed to implement JNDI, can negatively affect your application's performance. Because you don't have direct access to an LDAP connection, it's difficult to check to see if the connection is still alive without performing an LDAP operation. Another disadvantage is that under JNDI you cannot perform a true LDAP compare. The LDAP compare operation allows you to determine if an entry in the server has an attribute matching a given value. While this sounds like a LDAP search, the difference is that under a compare, the LDAP server will only return a result code representing TRUE or FALSE instead of returning a complete search result set. Returning only a result code is much quicker and less intensive than returning a complete search result set.

Luckily if you need direct access to a real LDAP API you can use the Netscape Directory SDK for Java, which you can find at http://www.mozilla.org/directory/.

JNDI Service Providers, AKA JNDI Drivers

You can't use JNDI without using a service provider, so it's helpful to understand what they are.

A service provider is a set of Java classes that enable you to communicate with a directory service similar to the way a JDBC driver enables you to communicate with a database. For a service provider to be available for use in JNDI it must implement the `Context` interface (actually most of the service providers you will use will likely implement the `DirectoryContext` interface which extends the `Context` interface to enable directory services).

What this means is that you only have to learn JNDI to know the API calls to connect to a naming or directory service, while the service provider worries about the ugly details (e.g. the actual network protocol, encoding/decoding values, etc).

Unfortunately service providers are not a magic bullet. You must know something about the underlying directory service so that you can correctly name your entries and build the correct search queries. Unlike relational databases, directory services do not share a common query language such as SQL.

So to sum up, a service provider enables your JNDI applications to communicate with a naming/directory service. The rest of the interfaces, classes, and exceptions all revolve around your interaction with a service provider.

How to obtain JNDI Service Providers

When you download the JNDI Software Development Kit (SDK), it will come with a number of existing service providers from Sun (a SDK comes with the API plus documentation and extras such as service providers). These include providers for LDAP, NIS, COS (CORBA Object Service), RMI Registry, and File System. Many different vendors also provide service providers for other directory services, or as replacements for the default providers that Sun ships. For example Novell has a service provider for NDS, while both IBM and Netscape have written alternative service providers for LDAP.

It is easy to switch between service providers. For example to use the default Sun LDAP service provider you would make a call like this:

```
//Specify which class to use for our JNDI provider
env.put(Context.INITIAL_CONTEXT_FACTORY,
        "com.sun.jndi.ldap.LdapCtxFactory");
```

Now to switch to using IBM's LDAP service provider you would simply replace the `com.sun.jndi.ldap.LdapCtxFactory` with the full package name of the IBM LDAP service provider like this:

```
//Specify which class to use for our JNDI provider
env.put(Context.INITIAL_CONTEXT_FACTORY, "com.ibm.jndi.LDAPCtxFactory");
```

The IBM service provider can be found at the IBM AlphaWorks site http://alphaworks.ibm.com.

There is a list of existing service providers at http://java.sun.com/products/jndi/serviceproviders.html.

Developing your own service provider

You may also need to implement your own service provider in particular if you need to use a directory service (such as Windows NT domains).

In the JNDI SDK Sun provides an example of how to write a service provider. The JNDI tutorial contains information on how to write a service provider, and it's available at: http://java.sun.com/products/jndi/tutorial/index.html.

Sun also provides a PDF document that describes the process of writing a service provider at ftp://ftp.javasoft.com/docs/jndi/jndispi.pdf.

And Netscape's LDAP service provider is available as an open-source project at http://www.mozilla.org/directory/.

Basic LDAP Operations

Before you can perform any type of operation on an LDAP sever, you must first obtain a reference and a network connection to the LDAP server. You must also specify how you wish to be bound to the server – either anonymously or as an authenticated user. Many LDAP servers allow some type of anonymous access (generally read-only abilities for attributes like e-mail addresses & telephone numbers), but LDAP also supports security features via ACLs that are dependent upon who the connection is authenticated as.

For example, an LDAP server may have several layers of rights for any given entry:

- Anonymous users can see an employee's e-mail address and telephone number
- The employee can see their entire entry, but can modify only certain attributes such as telephone number, password and office room number
- A user's manager can update an employee's telephone number and office room number, but nothing else. They can also see the employee's entire record
- A small group, the Directory Administrators, have full rights to the entire server including the ability to add or remove any entry

Standard LDAP Operations

There are a few standard operations in LDAP. They are:

- Connect to the LDAP server
- Bind to the LDAP server (you can think of this step as authenticating)
- Perform a series of LDAP operations: search the server, add a new entry, modify an entry, delete an entry
- Disconnect from the LDAP server

Since we only need to know enough LDAP for this chapter to authenticate and lookup user data we will only cover how to search an LDAP server. If you want more information on LDAP or JNDI, see the resources at the end of this chapter.

Security Interceptors

In Tomcat, authentication is managed through the use of a Security Interceptor. An interceptor is a request handler for Tomcat that processes each request so that the server can do such things as prepare headers, change the working directory, etc. A Security Interceptor determines if the requesting client should have access to a particular file or JSP/servlet.

In this section we'll learn how to develop a Security Interceptor and to configure Tomcat to use it.

Writing the Code

The name of our interceptor is going to be `com.mjwilcox.ldapAuthCheck`.

You need to create a path called `com/mjwilcox/ldapAuthCheck.java`. You can root this anywhere you normally put your Java development files. We'll copy the compiled class to its proper location when we're finished.

Our `ldapAuthCheck` class will extend the `org.apache.tomcat.request.SecurityCheck` class. This class takes care of a lot of overhead. This overhead includes parsing the userid and password regardless of which method the client uses to send us the information (e.g. basic or form). All we must do is override two methods, `checkPassword()` and `isUserInRole()`. For our LDAP based interceptor, we'll also override the `authenticate()` method so that we can configure our class.

Our first few lines are simply a package declaration and importing necessary classes.

```
package com.mjwilcox;

import java.util.Hashtable;
import java.util.Enumeration;

import javax.naming.*;
import javax.naming.directory.*;
import javax.naming.event.*;
import javax.naming.ldap.*;

import org.apache.tomcat.core.*;
import org.apache.tomcat.util.*;
import org.apache.tomcat.util.xml.*;
import java.io.*;
import java.net.*;
import java.util.*;
import javax.servlet.http.*;
import org.xml.sax.*;
```

Next we define the name of our class.

```
public class ldapAuthCheck extends org.apache.tomcat.request.SecurityCheck {
```

Here we declare some variables we will use in our class.

```
  // user variables
  private String ldapHost = "";   // name of LDAP server
  private int ldapPort = 389;     // port the server runs on
  private String searchBase = ""; // search base for the DIT
  private String managerDN = "";  // entry to bind as for initial search DN
  private String managerPW = "";  // entry to bind as for initial search pwd

  // application variables

  // initial context implementation
  private static String INITCTX = "com.sun.jndi.ldap.LdapCtxFactory";

  // for now users can't change the scope of the search
  private static int scope =
    SearchControls.SUBTREE_SCOPE;   // search scope

  private Hashtable userCache = new Hashtable();
                                    // cache of names and DNs
  private org.apache.tomcat.core.Context ourCTX = null;

  // use for debugging/logging
  private Hashtable userRoles = new Hashtable();

  // keep track of the roles a user plays
  private Hashtable env = null;    // store LDAP configuration information
```

Here we define a default constructor.

```
  /** default constructor */
  public void ldapAuthCheck() {}
```

Next we extend the `contextInit()` method so that we can grab our default `org.apache.tomcat.core.Context` object. The reason we must give the full package name is that JNDI also defines a `Context` object and Java will prevent us from using two different classes named `Context` unless they are in separate packages. The default `Context` is used by our class primarily for logging.

```
  public void contextInit(org.apache.tomcat.core.Context ctx)
          throws TomcatException {
    ourCTX = ctx;
    super.contextInit(ctx);
  }
```

The next several methods are getter and setter methods allowing us to get and set the LDAP configuration variables.

```
    /** set the host name of the LDAP server */
    public void setHost(String host) {
      ldapHost = host;
    }

    /** get the host name of the LDAP server */
    public String getHost() {
      return ldapHost;
    }

    /** set the port of the LDAP server */
    public void setPort(int port) {
      ldapPort = port;
    }

    /** get the port of the LDAP server */
    public int getPort() {
      return ldapPort;
    }

    /** set the LDAP search base */
    public void setSearchbase(String base) {
      searchBase = base;
    }

    /** get the LDAP search base */
    public String getSearchbase() {
      return searchBase;
    }

    /** set the connection 'manager' DN */
    public void setManagerDN(String dn) {
      managerDN = dn;
    }

    /** get the connection 'manager' DN */
    public String getManagerDN() {
      return managerDN;
    }

    /** set the connection 'manager' password */
    public void setManagerPW (String password) {
      managerPW = password;
    }

    /** get the connection 'manager' password */
    public String getManagerPW() {
      return managerPW;
    }
```

The checkPassword() method is inherited from the SecurityCheck class and is the method that performs the actual user authentication. It takes two strings, one that represents the user's name and another that represents the user's password. It then returns a boolean value that represents whether the given password matched the password stored for the given user in the authentication database.

The actual LDAP authentication part is done in another method, LDAPAuthenticate().

```
/** inherited from SecurityCheck*/
protected boolean checkPassword(String user, String pass) {
  ourCTX.log("checkPassword true/false is a "
             + LDAPauthenticate(user, pass));
  return LDAPauthenticate(user, pass);
}
```

The userInRole() method also overrides a method in SecurityCheck. This method determines whether or not a user is in a particular role. In LDAP this means that the code checks to see if the user is a member of a particular LDAP group.

Just like checkPassword(), the bulk of the LDAP work is done in another method called LDAPuserInRole().

Also there is a known bug in this class. While it will successfully determine if a user is in a role or not, it does not set this information in the Request object like SecurityCheck does. This is because the actual API for Security Interceptors is not well defined and thus I wasn't actually able to implement it at this time.

```
protected boolean userInRole(String user, String role) {
  ourCTX.log("role is " + LDAPuserInRole(user,role));
  return LDAPuserInRole(user,role);
}
```

Our next method also extends SecurityCheck. We use it simply to get some configuration information for our own use and then let SecurityCheck itself handle the rest of it.

```
//we use this to simply populate our environment
public int authenticate(Request req, Response response) {
  org.apache.tomcat.core.Context ctx=req.getContext();
  env = getEnv(ctx);
  return super.authenticate(req,response);
}
```

The getEnv() method populates our configuration information from the web.xml in a context's WEB-INF directory. We'll see exactly how to do that later on in this section.

```
/** set up LDAP configuration */
private Hashtable getEnv(org.apache.tomcat.core.Context ctx) {
  //get data from XML file
  try {
    ldapHost = ctx.getInitParameter("com.mjwilcox.ldapAuthCheck.ldaphost");
    Integer tempPort = new Integer(ctx.getInitParameter
```

```
                              ("com.mjwilcox.ldapAuthCheck.ldapport"));
      ldapPort = tempPort.intValue();
      searchBase = ctx.getInitParameter
                  ("com.mjwilcox.ldapAuthCheck.searchbase");
      managerDN = ctx.getInitParameter
                  ("com.mjwilcox.ldapAuthCheck.managerdn");
      managerPW = ctx.getInitParameter
                  ("com.mjwilcox.ldapAuthCheck.managerpw");
      // if null, set to anonymous connection
      if ((managerDN == null) || (managerPW == null)) {
        managerDN = "";
        managerPW = "";
      }

      Hashtable env = new Hashtable();
      //Specify which class to use for our JNDI provider
```

One step we must perform is to populate some hash table entries with particular named keys and values for JNDI.

The first one of these is the `javax.naming.Context.INITIAL_CONTEXT_FACTORY`, which will tell JNDI which service provider to use.

```
      env.put(javax.naming.Context.INITIAL_CONTEXT_FACTORY, INITCTX);
```

Next we must specify which protocol, host and port to connect to. For LDAP this is in the form of `ldap://host_name:port`.

We use a `StringBuffer` object to build this data because it's more efficient than to use a series of `String` concatenations.

```
      //specify which host and port
      StringBuffer jndiHost = new StringBuffer (); //hold JNDI host url
      jndiHost.append("ldap://");
      jndiHost.append(ldapHost);
      jndiHost.append(":");
      jndiHost.append(ldapPort);
      env.put(javax.naming.Context.PROVIDER_URL,jndiHost.toString());
```

Next we set the initial authentication methods and binding names and password. Under JNDI the 'simple' authentication method means that the user will provide a clear text password. We'll talk more about LDAP authentication later in this section.

```
      //Security Information
      env.put(javax.naming.Context.SECURITY_AUTHENTICATION,"simple");
      env.put(javax.naming.Context.SECURITY_PRINCIPAL,managerDN);
      env.put(javax.naming.Context.SECURITY_CREDENTIALS,managerPW);
      return env;
    } catch (NullPointerException ne) {
      ctx.log("getEnv had a null pointer exception "+ne.toString());
    } catch (NumberFormatException nfe) {
      ctx.log("getEnv had a number format exception "+nfe.toString());
    }
```

```
      return null;
    }
```

Our next piece of code performs the actual LDAP authentication.

We use a traditional LDAP authentication methodology here. What I mean is that we first take the provider username and attempt to retrieve a Distinguished Name (DN) for an entry that contains a `uid` value that matches the username.

Then we attempt to rebind to the server using the found DN and password. If the rebind succeeds we return `true`, otherwise we return `false`.

We must remember to check to see that our environment has been setup, otherwise we'll just end up throwing an exception.

In LDAP it is possible for a user to connect to the server anonymously. For example you might allow users to search your directory server anonymously when looking up user's email addresses from a public 'white pages' server. While this is a nice feature for providing address book type of services, it' s a potential hazard when it comes to an authentication service. This is because under LDAP, any connection that doesn't provide a password is assumed to be connecting anonymously.

Thus we need to check for empty or null passwords because an LDAP v3 server might give us a false positive because the server will assume the connection wants to bind anonymously and report that the authentication succeeded.

```
  /** performs simple LDAP authentication */
  private boolean LDAPauthenticate (String username, String password) {
    if ((env == null) || (password == null) || (password.equals(""))) {
      return false;
    }
```

First we connect to the LDAP server by initiating a `DirContext` object.

```
    try {
      //Get a reference to a directory context
      DirContext ctx = new InitialDirContext(env);
```

Next we will attempt to search the LDAP server looking for an entry that matches the LDAP search filter, "`uid=username`". An LDAP filter is like a SQL query. To speed up the search and limit the overhead for both the LDAP server and our JSP engine we'll limit the number of attributes we have returned to us from the server.

```
      /*
      retrieve the user's entry
      assume their userid is stored in the uid attribute
      we also limit the returned attributes to just their uid
      because we don't really need anything retrieved from the LDAP server so
      we spare the extra overhead
     */
```

```
StringBuffer filterBuffer = new StringBuffer ("uid=");
filterBuffer.append(username);

String[] attrIDs = {"uid"};
SearchControls ctls = new SearchControls();
ctls.setReturningAttributes(attrIDs);        // return no attrs
ctls.setSearchScope(scope);

// Search for objects with those matching attributes
NamingEnumeration results = ctx.search(searchBase,
                                   filterBuffer.toString(),ctls);
```

If we have any results then we need to step through them and get the user's DN using the `getName()` method of the `SearchResult` JNDI class.

```
StringBuffer dnBuffer = new StringBuffer (); //hold DN of results

while (results != null && results.hasMore()) {
  SearchResult sr = (SearchResult) results.next();
  dnBuffer.append(sr.getName());
```

The `getName()` method only returns the first part of the name, it doesn't include our search base. So we must add that to our name to get the user's full DN, which is required for authentication.

```
  dnBuffer.append(",");
  dnBuffer.append(searchBase);
```

Next we put the DN into a cache for lookup later.

```
  userCache.put(username,dnBuffer.toString());
```

Now we change our authentication credentials from the DN and password we set during initialization to the user's DN and password.

```
  //now attempt to rebind to the server as the user
  ctx.removeFromEnvironment(javax.naming.Context.SECURITY_PRINCIPAL);
  ctx.removeFromEnvironment(javax.naming.Context.SECURITY_CREDENTIALS);
  ctx.addToEnvironment(javax.naming.Context.SECURITY_PRINCIPAL,
                       dnBuffer.toString());
  ctx.addToEnvironment(javax.naming.Context.SECURITY_CREDENTIALS,
                       password);
```

Finally we build a very simple search that will look only at the user's LDAP entry to minimize the amount of time needed to perform the operation. If we don't throw an exception, authentication succeeds.

```
  //attempt an operation to see if we are still authenticated
  // Set up search controls
  ctls = new SearchControls();
  ctls.setReturningAttributes(new String[0]);       // return no attrs
  ctls.setSearchScope(SearchControls.OBJECT_SCOPE);// search object only
```

```
      //JNDI compare, least resource intensive operation
      //only testing if our authentication succeeds or fails
      NamingEnumeration authResults = ctx.search(dnBuffer.toString(),
                                                  "(uid=mark)",ctls);

      return true;
    }
```

If any errors are thrown we log them and return `false`.

```
    } catch (NamingException ne) {
      ourCTX.log( "naming exception error: " + ne.toString());
      return false;
    }

    return false;
  }
```

Our next method, `LDAPuserInRole()`, takes two strings, a username and a groupname, which we use to manage user's roles in LDAP.

We check for group membership using the two most common group objects in LDAP, `groupOfUniqueNames` and `groufOfNames`. There is a third type of group, dynamic groups, which is supported only by the iPlanet directory server, so I didn't add that code here.

```
  /** check to see if user is in proper role which in our case is an LDAP group.
  Right now this is very simple. The string name must match the CN attribute of a
  group. We only handle members of groupOfMembers and groupOfUniquemembers. No
  inherited groups or dynamic groups at this time. */
  private boolean LDAPuserInRole (String username, String groupname) {
```

The first item on our list is to retrieve the user's DN from our cache. If there is not a DN then we assume the user has not been authenticated and we return false.

```
    String userDN = (String) userCache.get(username);
    if (userDN == null) return false;
```

Next we setup our LDAP connection.

```
    try {
      //Get a reference to a directory context
      DirContext ctx = new InitialDirContext(env);
```

Now we build our LDAP filter. This filter is much more complex than our authentication example. What this filter translates to is "are there any `groupOfUniqueNames` or `groupofNames` with a common name matching the `groupname` we were given AND a member matching the user we were given".

`GroupofUniqueNames` objects store their membership in the `uniquemember` attribute and the GroupOfNames objects store their membership in the member attribute. Both have a common name attribute (`cn`) and the values for their respective membership are stored as DNs.

```
    //look for group and member at the same time
    StringBuffer filterBuffer = new StringBuffer ("(&(cn=");
    filterBuffer.append(groupname);
    filterBuffer.append(")(|(uniquemember=");
    filterBuffer.append(userDN);
    filterBuffer.append(")(member=");
    filterBuffer.append(userDN);
    filterBuffer.append(")))");
```

An example search filter might look like this:

```
(&(cn=accounting managers)(|(uniquemember= uid=mewilcox, ou=people, dc=acme,
dc=com)(member= uid=mewilcox,ou=people,dc=acme, dc=com)))
```

We don't really need any values, but to please JNDI, we'll ask for a single value, "`uniquemember`".

```
    String[] attrIDs = {"uniquemember"};
    SearchControls ctls = new SearchControls();
    ctls.setReturningAttributes(attrIDs);
    ctls.setSearchScope(scope);

    // Search for objects with those matching attributes
    NamingEnumeration results = ctx.search(searchBase,
                                          filterBuffer.toString(),ctls);
```

If we have any results then we have a winner and we can return a positive match.

```
    StringBuffer dnBuffer = new StringBuffer (); //hold DN of results

    if (results != null && results.hasMore()) {
      return true;
    }
```

Otherwise we must return `false`. If an error is thrown we also log the error and return `false`.

```
  } catch (NamingException ne) {
    ourCTX.log( "inRole naming exception error: " + ne.toString());
  }

  return false;
}
```

Finally we have a main method we can use to test-drive the class outside of Tomcat.

```
  // test-drive function
  public static void main (String args[]) {
    ldapAuthCheck la = new ldapAuthCheck();
    la.setHost("ldap.acme.com");
    la.setPort(389);
    la.setSearchbase("ou=people,dc=acme,dc=com");
```

```
        System.out.println("authentication is " +
                           la.LDAPauthenticate("user","password") );
    }
  }
```

Remember you can find the code for this chapter and the rest of the book at http://www.wrox.com.

Our next step is to save and compile the code. You need to make sure that all of the JAR files that are in the `lib` directory of your Tomcat distribution are in your `CLASSPATH`.

Configuring Tomcat

The first step is to copy the folder `com` and its children (e.g. `mjwilcox` and the `ldapAuthCheck.class` file) into the directory `$TOMCAT_HOME/classes`. This way, the class will be found by Tomcat on startup without having to mess with the Java `CLASSPATH`.

The next step is to tell Tomcat that we want to use our own interceptor. To do this we must edit the `server.xml` file in the `$TOMCAT_HOME/conf` directory.

We need to comment out the old interceptor and replace it with our own interceptor.

```
<!-- <RequestInterceptor className="org.apache.tomcat.request.SecurityCheck" /> -->
<RequestInterceptor className= "com.mjwilcox.ldapAuthCheck" />
```

Finally we must configure our interceptor in each context that it will be used.

For example, we can edit the `web.xml` file in the `$TOMCAT_HOME/webapps/examples/WEB-INF` directory to set up our LDAP server for authenticating users to access the default protected site.

We can pass configuration information using the `context-param` element, which must be located outside of any servlet configuration element(s).

Here is an example configuration that I used on my server.

```
<!-- configure our LDAP server -->
  <context-param>
    <param-name>
      com.mjwilcox.ldapAuthCheck.ldaphost
    </param-name>
    <param-value>
     localhost
    </param-value>
  </context-param>

  <context-param>
    <param-name>
      com.mjwilcox.ldapAuthCheck.ldapport
    </param-name>
    <param-value>
      389
```

```
      </param-value>
    </context-param>

  <context-param>
     <param-name>
       com.mjwilcox.ldapAuthCheck.searchbase
     </param-name>
     <param-value>
       o=airius.com
     </param-value>
    </context-param>
  <context-param>
  <!-- configuring managerdn and managerpw are optional -->
      <param-name>
        com.mjwilcox.ldapAuthCheck.managerdn
      </param-name>
      <param-value>
        cn=Directory Manager
      </param-value>
    </context-param>

    <context-param>
      <param-name>
        com.mjwilcox.ldapAuthCheck.managerpw
      </param-name>
      <param-value>
        password
      </param-value>
    </context-param>
```

We use names like `com.mjwilcox.ldapAuthCheck.managerpw` to prevent naming collisions in our `web.xml` file since there is not a way to separate configuration information out in the `context-param` element.

Next we can specify additional allowed roles. For example, I am logging in as Sam Carter (one of the default users in the iPlanet `Airius.ldif` file) who is a member of the Accounting Managers group. To enable him to get access to the site, I need to add the Accounting Managers to the roles element like this.

```
  <auth-constraint>
  <!-- Anyone with one of the listed roles may access this area -->
    <role-name>Accounting Managers</role-name>
    <role-name>tomcat</role-name>
    <role-name>role1</role-name>
  </auth-constraint>
```

After we have done this we need to restart Tomcat and then you can go back to http://localhost:8080/examples/jsp/security/protected/. This time you should be able to enter a userid and password for an LDAP user to get access.

More SSL

If you use a networked authentication system like LDAP, you should also protect the connection between your Web server and the LDAP server via SSL or similar encryption devices, even if you have your Web server SSL enabled.

The Web server's SSL connection will only protect the connection between the browser and the Web server, not between the servlet/JSP and the systems it connects to.

Putting it Together

OK, now we will put the authentication engine together with personalization. Our final project will authenticate users to our LDAP server, and then we will build a personalized 'portal' site that integrates information from their LDAP entry to build a simple, customized Web site.

This application will also show you how you can put your own authentication mechanism into your own JSPs instead of relying on the Web server or Servlet engine. The number one reason why you would want to do this is because you want to let people logout of the application, something that is not easily accomplished by any other method.

First lets take a look at what the application will look like and then we'll look at the code.

Our first screen shot shows the traditional form login page.

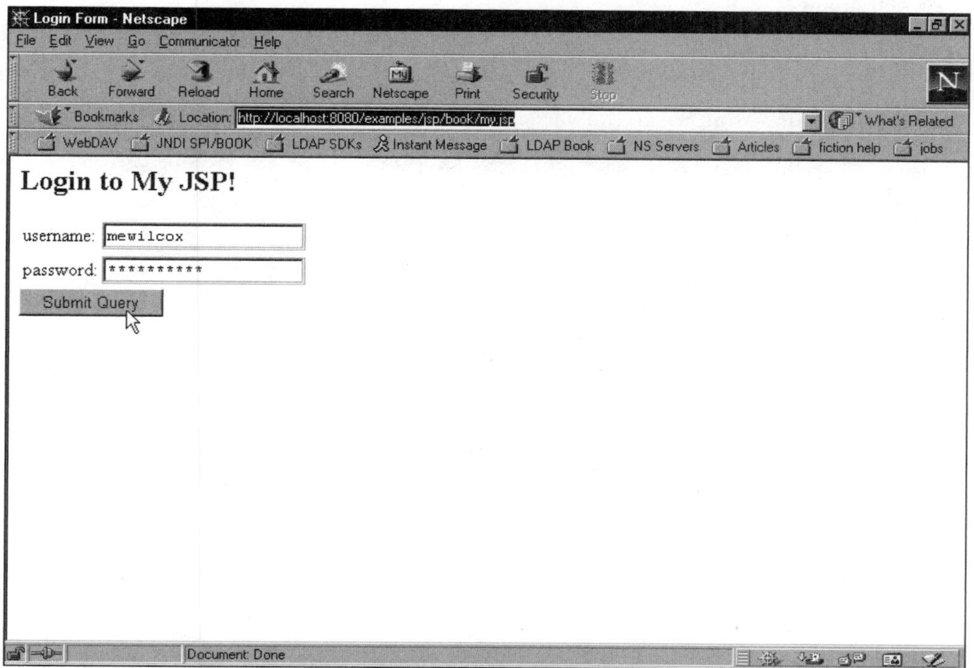

If we authenticate to the server it will welcome us with our name and then show us a list of links that we have stored in the LDAP server.

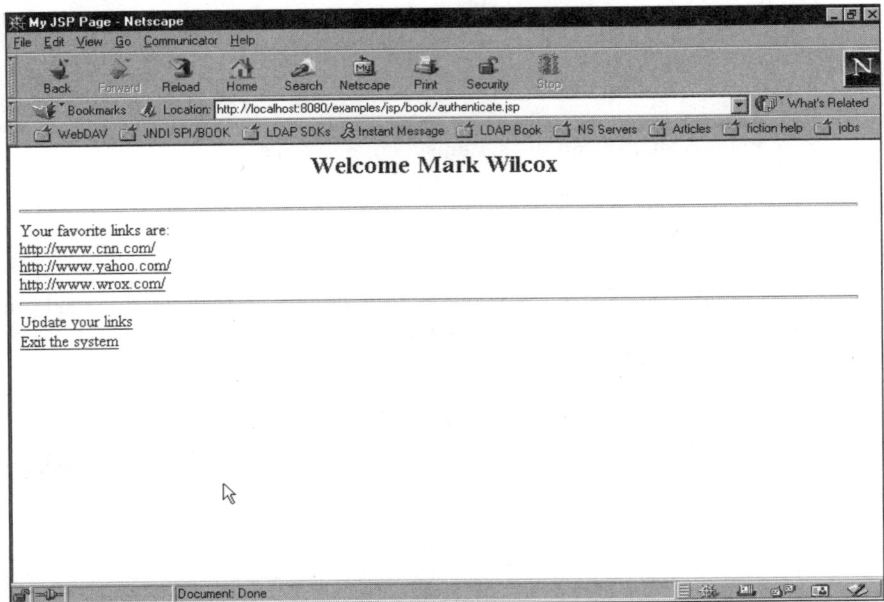

Finally we can update our list of links.

If we choose one of the radio buttons it removes that link. If we enter data into the text boxes it adds it our list of links.

If the submission is successful, we are forwarded to an updated version of the second screen.

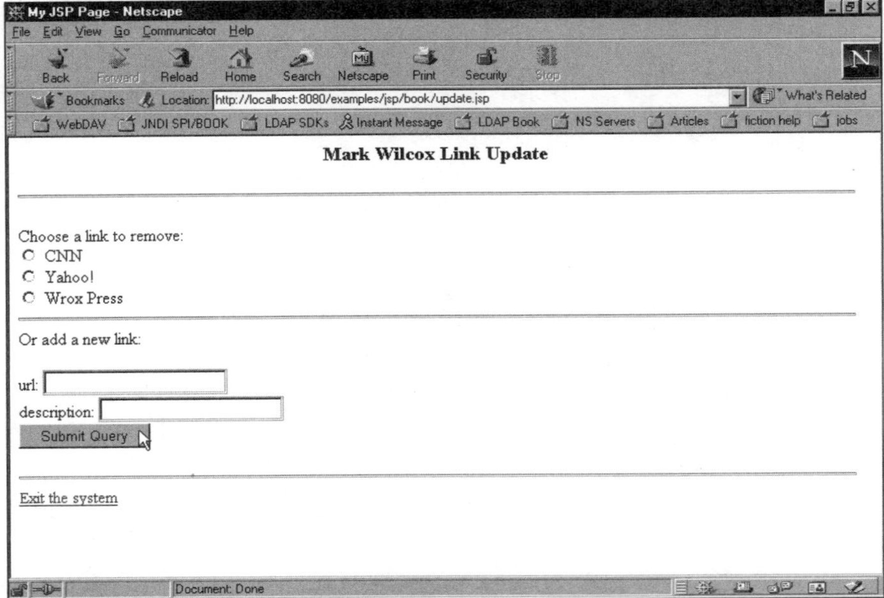

The Code

The code that makes this work is made up of JSPs, and some traditional JavaBeans that do the bulk of the LDAP work.

First we need an LDAP entry to work with. Here is an example LDIF file (LDIF is the current standard for displaying LDAP data in a human-readable format) named `mewilcox.ldif`, which you can load into your LDAP server. Or you can provide one of your own if you like. Just make sure that the `objectclass` you choose can accept the `labeleduri` attribute (this is a standard attribute for the `inetorgperson objectclass`).

```
dn:uid=mewilcox,ou=people,o=airius.com
objectclass:top
objectclass:person
objectclass:organizationalperson
objectclass:inetorgperson
sn:Wilcox
givenname:Mark
cn:Mark Wilcox
uid:mewilcox
userpassword:opensesame
mail:mewilcox@airius.com
labeleduri:http://www.wrox.com/ "Wrox Press"
labeleduri:http://www.yahoo.com/ "Yahoo!"
labeleduri:http://www.cnn.com/ "CNN"
postalcode:75068
```

Our first step is to create a package directory for all of the Java classes our JSPs will use. I named my package `jsp.book` so I created a directory called `jsp` and a directory called `book` inside the `jsp` directory. These directories should be in the `classes` directory of your `WEB-INF` directory where you keep your Web applications. For example in Tomcat this would be `$TOMCAT_HOME/webapps/examples/WEB-INF/classes`.

Now we are ready to begin coding. I'm going to discuss the Java classes with the JSPs that use them.

First we need a login page. This is a simple HTML page like this:

```
<!DOCTYPE HTML PUBLIC "-//W3C//DTD HTML 4.0 Transitional//EN">

<html>
<head>
  <title>Login Form</title>
</head>
<h2>Login to My JSP!</h2>
<body bgcolor="#ffffff">
<form name="myjsp" action="authenticate.jsp" method="POST">
<table border="0">
<tr><td>username:</td><td><input type="text" name="uid"></td></tr>
<tr><td>password:</td><td><input type="password" name="password"></td></tr>
</table>
<input type="submit">
</form>

</body>
</html>
```

Next we need to create our Java class and JSP to perform our authentication.

The Java class we use called `jsp.book.doAuth`. This class is very similar to the LDAP authentication class we wrote earlier for Tomcat. I'm only going show the changed parts here.

```
//getData.java
//a bean to retrieve user data for our personalization project

package jsp.book;
...
//this is private in our Tomcat interceptor
public boolean LDAPauthenticate (String username, String password)
...
```

We also remove all of the Tomcat libraries and methods because we don't need them in our class. You can consult the full source code to see all of the changes.

Our first JSP, `authenticate.jsp`, retrieves the parameters and calls our authenticate bean.

```
<!DOCTYPE HTML PUBLIC "-//W3C//DTD HTML 4.0 Transitional//EN">

<html>
<head>
  <title>Authenticate Engine</title>
</head>

<body bgcolor="#ffffff">
<%@ page session="true" import="java.util.*"
%>

<%
String uid =  request.getParameter("uid");
String password = request.getParameter("password");
```

If we are missing our userid or password, we send the user back to the login form.

```
//if uid or password are null or empty redirect to login form
 if ( (uid == null) || (uid.equals("")) || (password == null) ||
(password.equals("")))
    {
        %>
<jsp:forward page="login.htm" />
```

Next we initialize our authentication bean.

```
//now we can do authentication
  String host = "localhost";
  int port = 389;
  String base = "ou=people,o=airius.com";
```

```
    jsp.book.doAuth la = new jsp.book.doAuth();
    la.setHost(host);
    la.setPort(port);
    la.setSearchbase(base);

    boolean isAuthenticated = la.LDAPauthenticate(uid,password);
```

Next we create a `Hashtable` to store information that the rest of our application needs such as whether the user is authenticated or not and their username. We will store the `Hashtable` in the Servlet's `Session` object. This allows the Servlet engine to keep track of the object in memory and we don't have to worry about implementing cookies. We simply grab the `Hashtable` from the `Session` object when we need it.

```
   //hashtable to store authentication information
    Hashtable mytable = new Hashtable();

    mytable.put("AUTHENTICATED",new Boolean(isAuthenticated));
    mytable.put("USER",uid);
    session.putValue("hashtable", mytable);
```

If we authenticate successfully we forward the user to the page that lists their links. If their authentication fails we send them back to the login page.

```
   if ( isAuthenticated == false)
     {
      %>
       <jsp:forward page="login.htm" />
      <% }
     else
     {    %>
     <jsp:forward page="my.jsp" />
         <%

     }
    %>

   </body>
   </html>
```

Next we need to look at our code that retrieves the user's personalization information. This requires two classes, `jsp.book.portalPerson` and `jsp.book.getUser`.

We'll look at the `portalPerson` class first. This class is a utility class designed to make it easier for us to get information about a person in our JSP application. It is actually a very simple bean that provides get and set methods for a string representing the user name and a `Hashtable` that keeps track of a user's URLs.

```
   package jsp.book;

   import java.util.*;

   /** class for storing portal information on a person in LDAP */
```

```
public class portalPerson {
  private String name = "";
  private Hashtable urlTable = new Hashtable();

  public portalPerson() {}
  public void setName(String data) {
    name = data;
  }

  public String getName() {
    return name;
  }

  public void addUrl(String name, String url) {
    urlTable.put(name, url);
  }

  public Hashtable getUrlTable() {
    return urlTable;
  }
}
```

Next is our `getUser` class, which retrieves the user's information from the LDAP server and puts it into a `portalPerson` object, which can then be returned to the JSP application.

It also is the same application as our `doAuth` class except that it replaces the `ldapAuthenticate()` method with a `getPerson()` method that returns the `portalPerson` object. This is very similar to the search code we saw earlier for our LDAP authentication classes, except that it puts its results into a new `portalPerson` object.

```
  /** return a portalPerson object with data populated from the
      LDAP server */
  public portalPerson getPerson(String username) {
    portalPerson person = new portalPerson();
    try {
      Hashtable env = new Hashtable();

      // Specify which class to use for our JNDI provider
      env.put(javax.naming.Context.INITIAL_CONTEXT_FACTORY, INITCTX);

      // specify which host and port
      StringBuffer jndiHost = new StringBuffer();   // hold JNDI host url
      jndiHost.append("ldap://");
      jndiHost.append(ldapHost);
      jndiHost.append(":");
      jndiHost.append(ldapPort);
      env.put(javax.naming.Context.PROVIDER_URL, jndiHost.toString());

      // Security Information
      env.put(javax.naming.Context.SECURITY_AUTHENTICATION, "simple");
      env.put(javax.naming.Context.SECURITY_PRINCIPAL, managerDN);
      env.put(javax.naming.Context.SECURITY_CREDENTIALS, managerPW);
```

```
      // Get a reference to a directory context
      DirContext ctx = new InitialDirContext(env);
      StringBuffer dnBuffer = new StringBuffer();
      dnBuffer.append("uid=");
      dnBuffer.append(username);
      dnBuffer.append(",");
      dnBuffer.append(searchBase);

      // attributes to retrieve
      String[] attrs = {
        "uid", "labeleduri", "postalcode", "cn", "mail"
      };
      Attributes result = ctx.getAttributes(dnBuffer.toString(),
                                            attrs);

      if (result == null) {
        return null;
      } else {
        Attribute attr = result.get("cn");
        if (attr != null) {
          NamingEnumeration vals = attr.getAll();
          while (vals.hasMoreElements()) {
            String s = (String) vals.nextElement();
            person.setName(s);
            break;
          }
        } else {
          return null;
        }
        attr = result.get("labeleduri");
        if (attr != null) {
          NamingEnumeration vals = attr.getAll();
          while (vals.hasMoreElements()) {
            String uri = (String) vals.nextElement();
            int first = uri.indexOf("\"");
            int last = uri.lastIndexOf("\"");

            // break the labeleduri value into its components
            String url = uri.substring(0, first - 1);
            String link = uri.substring(first + 1, last);

            person.addUrl(url, link);
          }
        }
      }
    } catch (NamingException ne) {
      System.err.println(ne.toString());
      return null;
    }
    return person;
  }
```

Here is the JSP we use, `my.jsp`.

First we check to make sure that all that the username is valid and still authenticated. If they are not we send the user to the login page, otherwise we continue on.

```
<!DOCTYPE HTML PUBLIC "-//W3C//DTD HTML 4.0 Transitional//EN">

<html>
<head>
  <title>My JSP Page</title>
</head>

<body bgcolor="#ffffff">
<%@ page session="true" import="java.util.*" %>

<jsp:useBean id="hashtable" class="java.util.Hashtable"    scope="session"/>

<%
   try
   {
    Boolean authtest = (Boolean) hashtable.get("AUTHENTICATED");

    String user = (String) hashtable.get("USER");

    if (authtest.booleanValue() == false ) {
%>
<jsp:forward page="login.htm" />
<%
    }
```

Next we initialize our LDAP values and retrieve the `portalPerson` object corresponding to our given username.

```
//now we can do authentication
  String host = "localhost";
  int port = 389;
  String base = "ou=people,o=airius.com";

  jsp.book.getUser gu = new jsp.book.getUser();
  gu.setHost(host);
  gu.setPort(port);
  gu.setSearchbase(base);

  jsp.book.portalPerson person = gu.getPerson(user);
%>
```

Next we print out their name.

```
<center><h2>Welcome <%= person.getName() %> </h2></center>
```

Now we print out a list of their favorite hyperlinks.

```
<hr>
Your favorite links are:<br>
<%
   Hashtable urls = person.getUrlTable();

   Enumeration keys = urls.keys();

   while (keys.hasMoreElements())
   {
      String link = (String) keys.nextElement();
      String url = (String) urls.get(link);

%>
   <a href=" <%= url %> "><%= link %></a><br>
  <%
     }

   } catch(NullPointerException e) {
   %>
     <jsp:forward page="login.htm" />
  <%
   }
   %>

<hr>
<a href="update.jsp">Update your links</a> <br>
<a href="exit.jsp">Exit the system</a>
</body>
</html>
```

The next application we need is allow a user to update their list of links. This is accomplished with the `jsp.book.updateUser` class.

Again it reuses most of our code, differing only in the method it provides, `updateUser()`. Most of the code in this method also duplicates earlier efforts so we will concentrate on what's different.

The method signature looks like this.

```
public void updateUser(String username, String url, boolean replace)
```

What we need to concentrate on is updating an LDAP entry. Modifying an LDAP server is usually restricted to only properly authenticated users (e.g. anonymous users normally can't change the values in an LDAP server). Second LDAP updates take the form of an ADD, which means you add a new entry to the server, a `MODIFY` which changes the attribute/values of an existing entry and `DELETE` which removes an existing entry from the server.

We will be performing a `MODIFY` in our example. An LDAP `MODIFY` can also take one of three forms. One form is an ADD, which adds a new value to the attribute. `REPLACE` is another form, which replaces all of the values in an existing attribute with a the value passed to it, and `DELETE` which removes the matching value passed to it from the attribute. If a `DELETE` is handed only an attribute name it will remove all of the values from that attribute.

In our application we say that if the user wants to remove an URL, we will delete that value from the LDAP server. We accomplish this by using an LDAP `MODIFY DELETE`.

LDAP modifications in JNDI are accomplished via the `ModificationItem` and `BasicAttribute` classes and the `modifyAttributes()` method of the `DirContext` class. A `ModificationItem` is an array that stores the type of modification to be performed and the attribute/values to be used in the modification.

Here is an example of an LDAP `MODIFY DELETE`.

```
ModificationItem[] mods = new ModificationItem[1];
if ( replace == true)
{
  Attribute mod0 = new BasicAttribute("labeleduri", url);

  //as long as we give it a value, this will only remove this value
  mods[0] = new ModificationItem(DirContext.REMOVE_ATTRIBUTE, mod0);
}
```

If the user fills in the text boxes we add a new entry to their `labeleduri` attribute.

Here is an example of an LDAP `MODIFY ADD`.

```
else
{
  Attribute mod0 = new BasicAttribute("labeleduri", url);
  mods[0] = new ModificationItem(DirContext.ADD_ATTRIBUTE, mod0);
}
```

Finally we update the entry by giving the `modifyAttributes()` method the DN of the entry to be modified and the `ModificationItems` marked for update.

```
/* make the change */
ctx.modifyAttributes(dnBuffer.toString(), mods);
```

Now, on to our JSPs.

First we have `update.jsp` which simply prints out the form for update. It's exactly the same code as `my.jsp`, except that it prints out a form instead of hyperlinks.

```
<form name="profile" method="post" action="doupdate.jsp">
Choose a link to remove:<br>
<%
   Hashtable urls = person.getUrlTable();

   Enumeration keys = urls.keys();

   while (keys.hasMoreElements())
  {

    String link = (String) keys.nextElement();
    String url = (String) urls.get(link);
```

```
        StringBuffer dataBuffer = new StringBuffer(link);
        dataBuffer.append(" \"");
        dataBuffer.append(url);
        dataBuffer.append("\"");
    %>
    <input type="radio" name="link" value='<%=dataBuffer.toString()%>'> <%= url %>
    <br>
    <%
      }
    %>
    <hr>
    Or add a new link:<p>
    url: <input type="text" name="url"><br>
    description: <input type="text" name="description"><br>
     <%

     }
     catch(NullPointerException e)
     {
     %>
     <jsp:forward page="login.htm" />
     <%
     }
     %>
    <input type="submit">
    </form>
```

Next is our JSP that calls `updateUser()` which we name `doupdate.jsp`. It is also similar to our other JSPs except it adds a couple of configuration parameters and it parses the update form.

```
    //must be authenticated to update
    String mgr = "cn=Directory Manager";
    String pwd = "password";


    String url, description = null;
    String value = request.getParameter("link");
    jsp.book.updateUser uu = new jsp.book.updateUser();
    uu.setHost(host);
    uu.setPort(port);
    uu.setSearchbase(base);
    uu.setManagerDN(mgr);
    uu.setManagerPW(pwd);

    boolean replace = false;

    if (value == null)
    {
       url = request.getParameter("url");
       description = request.getParameter("description");

       StringBuffer urlBuffer = new StringBuffer(url);
       urlBuffer.append(" \"");
       urlBuffer.append(description);
       urlBuffer.append("\"");
```

```
    value = urlBuffer.toString();
}
else
{
    replace = true;
}

uu.updateUser(user,value,replace);

%>
```

After we've successfully updated the user's account we send them back to `my.jsp`, otherwise we send them to the login page.

Finally we have a JSP that allows the user to exit the application. All we do is set the `AUTHENTICATE` key in the `Hashtable` to `false`, and then redirect the user to the login page.

```
<jsp:useBean id="hashtable" class="java.util.Hashtable"    scope="session"/>

<%

      hashtable.put("AUTHENTICATED",new Boolean(false));


%>
<jsp:forward page="login.htm" />
...
```

Summary

Security is such an important topic that a single chapter cannot do it proper justice. However, by realizing that security is made up of many different parts that must work together, you can reduce your risk without sacrificing usability or performance.

The Java platform provides many different means of applying security including adding specifications to the Servlet specification that JSP inherits from.

Directory services like LDAP allow you to more easily manage security by centralizing users in a centrally network-accessible database. It also enables you provide personalization to your Web applications by leveraging your existing security infrastructure.

Finally, security with Servlets and JSPs is still an evolving subject. However, the basics are there and it is possible to build a secure platform today with existing tools.

Other Resources

- Implementing LDAP, Mark Wilcox, Wrox Press, 1861002211
- Java Secure Coding Guidelines, http://java.sun.com/security/seccodeguide.html
- Java Security Web, http://java.sun.com/security/
- Applied Cryptography, Bruce Schneier, John Wiley & Sons, 0-471-11709-9

J2EE
JSP

16

Case Study: Implementing a Membership Based E-Commerce Application

Now that we have learned about all the powerful features offered by the combination of Java Server Pages and Servlets, we are going to put this knowledge in to practice and look at how these technologies can help us resolve some problems from the real world.

In the fast growing world of e-commerce and web application development, some of the big challenges faced by Internet developers have been not only to provide a security layer to interface with the large amount of data residing on back-end storage (protecting the system from the street user), but also to efficiently collect information from users in order to establish a bank of data that is critical to the success of a business (taking advantage of the user's interest). In this chapter, we will see how a JSP/Servlet based membership system can not only help us solve some of these business problems, but also provides a clean and easy-to-extend platform that seamlessly integrates into the rest of the enterprise architecture.

Birth of the 'E-Commerce' Concept

You probably have heard about the term 'e-commerce'. If you haven't, maybe it might be time for you to turn on your tv or get out of your room. Over the last few years, most of the corporations seem to have come to an agreement that a requirement for their survival was to "get on the web". Once past this understanding, their next challenge has been to redefine their strategies and adapt them to the technology offered by the Internet network. One of the big differences between the web-based e-commerce world and the old Electronic Data Interchange network is that this new system gives everybody (consumer and businesses) the opportunity to be part of the game. The disintermediation (direct contact between buyer and manufacturer) of commercial transactions has not only reshuffled the cards between the actors of the trading game, but has also given new players the opportunity to join the new market. The emergence of a modern form of commercial exchange (that some call the **Net Economy**) has given birth to a new type of business, where companies offering simple price brokerage services can turn into multi-million dollar corporations.

Definition of our Business Problem

In order to succeed in this new trading environment, one has to redefine his business logic and then start to think about system design. In our Case Study, we will focus on the concepts of membership and registration of users as it applies to the selling of goods on the Internet.

Why is Membership Important?

The greatest thing about the Internet is that it is a wide-open network where anyone can connect anywhere at anytime to get all kinds of information. But this easiness carries its own problem: you just can't put all your business critical data up there on your server for anybody to browse. Moreover, in lots of business cases there are requirements to identify users of specific resources in order to apply specific business rules. If you are a doing online banking, you don't want anybody to connect to your bank web site and play with your account. As internet sites are progressively reflecting the complexity of real business environments, the online applications have to be able to perform operations in which users are known (authenticated) by the system. The security layers that applied to the old mainframe world had to be carried over to the net, in order to create the same type of safe environment. Once the user is known, a higher level of granularity can be applied to content through access control of data resources, and all user actions can be logged for security reasons. In the same token, authentication brings personalization of the content. The online application can learn about you and establish for you a specific user profile and tailor the site to an individual (see myYahoo). Creating a database of members can also be a strategic part of your business model, as it enables you to identify a population of users that is specifically interested by the services you provide or the goods you sell.

Designing a Membership Based Web Application

The easiest way to jump into the design phase is by starting to think about the way people are going to use the system. Once you have gathered enough information about the tasks that are performed by the users, it will be easier to lay out the application architecture, the object model and the data architecture.

Before starting to dig into technical details or even thinking about the technologies that we might want to use, it is important to keep the big picture in mind and never forget it during the development process: we want to build a system that is based on these three following strengths:

- Ease of use
- Ease of management
- Ease of upgrade
- All of the above while keeping the system scalable.

These principles will help us keep a high level of perspective when confronted with technical issues. They also help us to understand that the users of the system are not only what we call the end users but also the ones that define its content or the ones that extend its capabilities. This implies that we want to create an interface that is convivial while ensuring that our application architecture will be easy to build upon, as well as focusing on the way our system can be updated without major pain. With all these objectives in mind we can start digging into the application design.

The Business Logic

In order to be able to define our application architecture, we must first clearly state what our objectives are and determine the business logic that will drive the system behavior. We want to build a system that will help people ordering their groceries through the web by creating an online store based on ease of use and continuous availability. At the same time, one of our objectives is to create an online experience which is not only unique to the user, but that also makes him feel that he has a loyal attachment to the system and will want to be back again (the concept of "stickiness"). By giving our users the opportunity to become members of our virtual grocery store, we grant them some privileges that will make their online experience better. We can create for them a customer profile including their personal information, their preferences in terms of payment options or billing addresses, even preferences in term of product price ranges and product types. By providing our online customer with this sense of easiness and customization, we hope to have them change their habits (shopping in the "real world" only) by making online grocery shopping part of their everyday life.

Business Processes

The processes that make up our global business logic are:

- **Registration process**: new users are given the opportunity to become members of our store by filling out one of our online form and selecting their preferences
- **Login process**: registered users are given the possibility to login and retrieve their online profile
- **Catalog Browsing process**: users can go through our product listing and prices
- **Selection process**: users can choose to put products in their online shopping cart
- **Checkout process**: users can choose to buy their selection and get their order processed

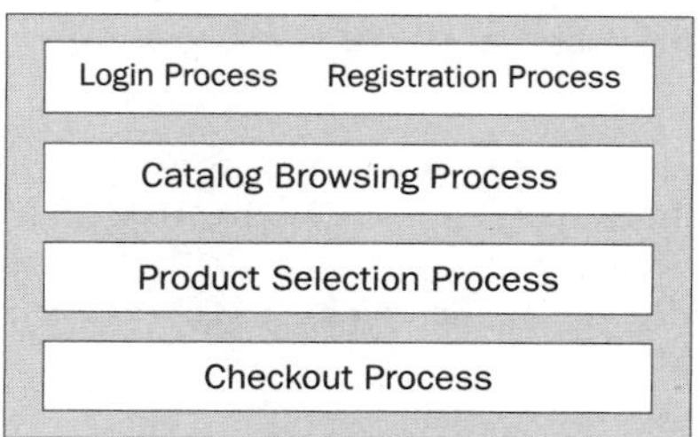

In this chapter we will primarily focus on describing the Registration and Login processes.

The Registration Process

This it the part of the web application that enables the new user to register with the system. It can be seen as a contract binding the user and the online shopping entity. This implicit contract would basically state: "If you give us information about yourself, we will grant you access to our shopping mall".

The user is then presented with a form to fill out. The information entered will serve several purposes:

- First the user is asked to create a unique user ID which will uniquely identify him on the system. At this point the system should make sure that the chosen ID does not already exist in the repository system. If so, the user should be notified about it and be prompted to select a new one.
- The user can choose a password of his choice to protect his membership and prevent somebody else from using his account without his consent.
- Some contact information (phone number, email address) can be used by the system administrator to contact the user when necessary.
- Billing and shipping addresses can also be provided, and will be used when the user places an order from the online grocery store.
- Other customization information can be provided. This could be a choice of colors for the menus or choice of browsing with frames or without frames.

Once the user has entered the information and once the data has been validated by the system, the user can be given the option to review/modify it. When this last verification has been performed, we can create the user profile and save the data in the repository for later retrieval.

The Login process allows the user to identify himself to the system. Here are the main functions of the login subsystem:

- Checking for authorization credential: the user must provide an existing user ID to be allowed to enter the system. This step basically serves the purpose of putting a name on the user. It carries the idea of identification of the user.
- Authentication mechanism: this is one step beyond authorization. Authentication is a security measure that protects the system against impersonation. Most system implement password checking as the main authentication mechanism, but other (more secure) mechanisms can be implemented, such as digital certificate checking, voice checking or even fingerprint verification mechanisms.
- Information and preferences. This is more of a convenience for the online user, who likes to see that his personal information was securely saved and retrieved by the system. It also enables us to bring some kind of customization to the user's online experience, and helps giving a feel of dynamism to the content of the application.

The Login/RegistrationFlow

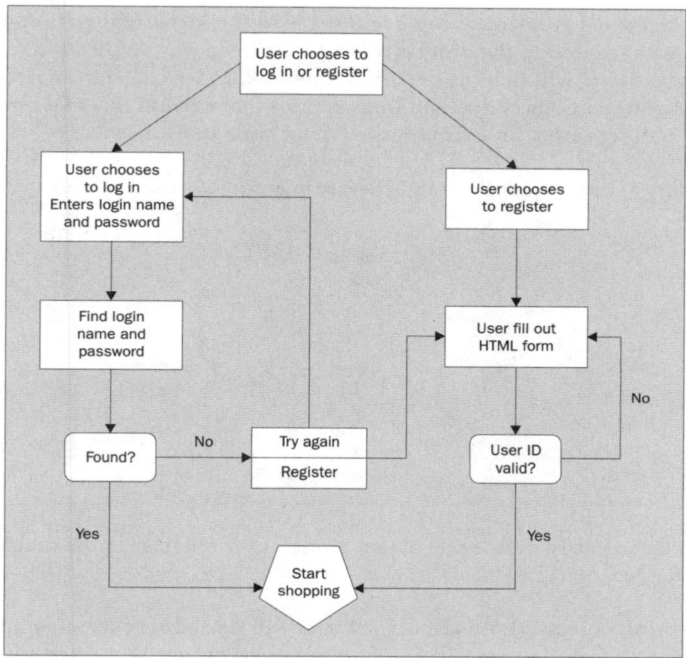

The entry page of our application gives to the user a choice between logging in (1) or registering (2).

For **logging in**, the application expects the user to provide a valid combination of login name and password. The application performs then the validation process of the name and password information against some data repository where these values are stored. If the user is authenticated, they can proceed to the online grocery store and start shopping. If the authentication fails, the user is forwarded to an error page informing him of the failure of the operation. The error page gives him another choice of either trying to log in again or going to the registration page in order to obtain a new membership.

The **registration** process enables our user to obtain a new membership. The user fills out a HTML form and submits information to the server. Here our application can perform some checking on the information provided. The most important validation is to enforce uniqueness on the user ID chosen by the user, since this user ID will be used as the key element to identify this user (our repository will also enforce uniqueness of this attribute) and for retrieval of the information at login time.

Most systems today also invite the user to enter his password twice, given that the password fields have the ability to mask the characters entered. This option diminishes the probability that the user will maybe mistype their password. Some systems also provide a "Hint" text field where the user can enter a few words that will be saved along with his information and will help him remembering his password if he forgets it.

Defining our Object Model

Now that we have looked at our business logic and detailed the login/registration process, let's start to think about how we want to design the objects that will make up our application. The way Java supports object-oriented programming will help us greatly in this task, as we can start to define a solution to our problem by defining abstract objects that will map entities that exist in our real business world. A User object, for example, will represent an existing user of our web application.

We basically now that we have the following processes centered around a user:

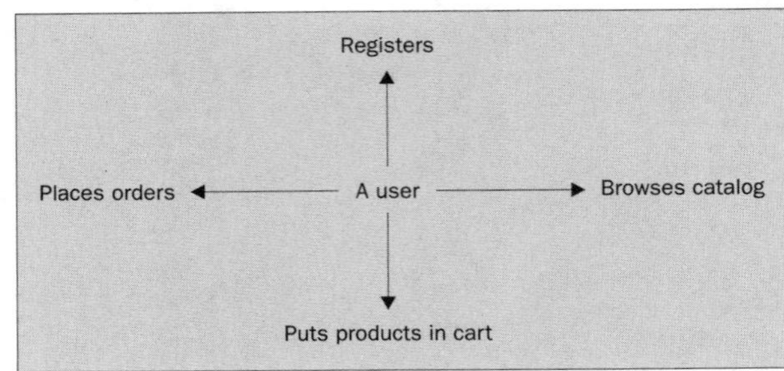

From this schema, we can easily define our object model. Our objects can be divided into two categories:

- Logic Processing objects: those are objects that will do some processing and will most likely take the shape of a servlet (we will see later why servlets are best fitted for handling the processing of our application logic).

- Business objects: these guys are real Java objects and can be abstracted out into some JavaBeans-like classes, meaning reusable objects whose properties follow the JavaBean naming patterns Their task is not only to encapsulate the business logic of the application but also to contain the data that is processed by the system. These can become **persistent objects** by being stored in the repository.

So far, we can draw the following model:

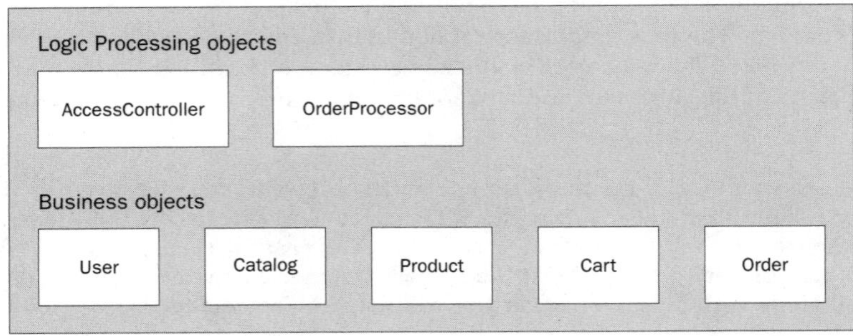

You can see on the scheme that we defined the following objects:

- The `AccessControler` object, that will be responsible for granting or denying access to our application resources.
- The `OrderProcessor` object will process orders made by our customers.
- The `User` object will represent one of our web site members.
- The `Catalog` objet will contain information about the products we sell.
- The `Product` object will represent a single product from our catalog.
- The `Cart` object will be responsible for keeping track of products selected by the user.
- The `Order` object will represent an order passed by a customer.

Now that we have defined our objects, let's look at our data structure.

Defining the Data Structure of our Business Objects

The definition of the data structure will give us the opportunity to define the way information should flow in our application. Since we adopted an object oriented approach, we just have to logically deduct the data items from the object we designed. For each object, we can list the properties in which data will be stored and the type of data that we will set for each field. Then, we will implement the methods that will help us set and get the properties for these objects.

Properties of the User Object

The choice of the properties assigned to the `User` object is driven by the type of information that will be required by our application regarding a particular user. As most web applications, we will need to identify our member using a uniquely defined user ID. Our user will protect his/her account access with a password that will be stored and automatically encrypted by our LDAP server. The other properties correspond to contact information for a user (address fields, phone number and email address), and can be used by our application for defining a member's Billing and Shipping locations, or for sending orders confirmation once a transaction has been performed through the site:

Property	Data Type
`User ID`	`String`
`Password`	`String`
`Given name`	`String`
`Surname`	`String`
`Street`	`String`
`City`	`String`
`Postal code`	`String`
`Telephone number`	`String`
`Email address`	`String`

Properties of the Catalog Object

Our `Catalog` object will be mapping a real catalog structure: it will be made of a list of Pages containing a list of `Products`. A `Page` will simply be an array of Products (objects of type `Product`). An `ArrayList` containing all these pages will then make up our Catalog. The number of products per page will be defined by the next property, `Products per page`. The last property will hold the current page number. This will help us manage the pagination of our data once we start working on the user interface:

Property	Data Type
`Catalog content`	`ArrayList` of `Pages`
`Pages`	`ArrayList` of `Products`
`Products per page`	`Integer`
`Page number`	`Integer`

Properties of the Product Object

The `Product` object will properties that define its `Name`, `Picture`, `Price` and `Reference number`:

Property	Data Type
`Name`	`String`
`Picture`	`String`
`Price`	`String`
`Reference number`	`Integer`

Properties of the Cart Object

The `Cart` object is one of the most important entity in any ecommerce application. This one will remain pretty basic and will inform the application of the type of objects selected by the `User`. It will conveniently calculate the Total Price for these objects and will give a count of the number of objects that it contains.

Property	Data Type
`Cart content`	`ArrayList` of `Products`
`Total price`	`Float`
`Count of products`	`Integer`

Properties of the ProductReferencer Object

We will use an object called `ProductReferencer` that will keep an indexed list of the products. This small class is just a convenient way for the cart to get a copy of the product object selected by the user from the catalog.

Property	Data Type
`Product list`	`ArrayList` of `Products`

Choosing the Right Technology

Within the last few sections, we have been going through the steps of defining the core components of our e-commerce application. Now that we have defined our objects and attributed to each of them the responsibility of holding some data, we need to complete the puzzle by choosing a database system that will store our information for later retrieval.

Selection of a Back-End Repository

There are two main sources of data that we need to take into account: the data that refers to the user and the data that makes up our catalog. As this case study is related to the design of a membership-based system, we will focus here on the user-related data and will just load the catalog-related data from a flat file instead of digging into the complexity of relational databases.

LDAP Server: A Great Choice for Storing our User Information

Although there is a wide number of standard databases out there that can be used for storing our data, choosing an LDAP server is actually a wise choice when the information you manipulate is related to users and organizations. Being the 'son' of the OSI DAP protocol, Lightweight Directory Access Protocol specializes as well in Directory Services but is a reengineered and simplified version of its predecessor. Running over standard TCP/IP, LDAP servers are becoming increasingly popular among IS departments that want to standardize their directory services across an entire organization.

LDAP servers are similar to databases but are optimized for read access and their data structure nicely maps the hierarchical structure of an organization. By defining user/organization/location objects, they make it easy for a programmer to store object models into this type of data architecture. More over, LDAP gives you the opportunity to store user passwords and perform user authentication, so it will perfectly fit the needs of our case study.

Why JSP, Servlets, and LDAP are Great Together

Among the headaches that application architects have to face, one of them is to identify the technologies that will provide the maximum of benefits to the organization for the minimum cost. In the web standpoint, the task has been made easy to them because of the emergence of de facto standards for the Internet communication. With the adoption of common standards such as the HTTP protocol for transferring information, HTML for formatting content and the web browser as the universal interface to the flows of data, all your work is already done in choosing the technologies that will make up your web application.

As you've already read in previous chapters, the combination of Java Server Pages and Servlets is quickly becoming a standard for building clean portable and scalable web applications. In your quest for **separation of content, logic, and presentation**, LDAP brings to the table an easy to program set of API's that will speed up your development process and bring the content that will make your application dynamic. The Netscape Directory SDK for Java is the programming kit that will make your Java web application interface easily with a Directory Server.

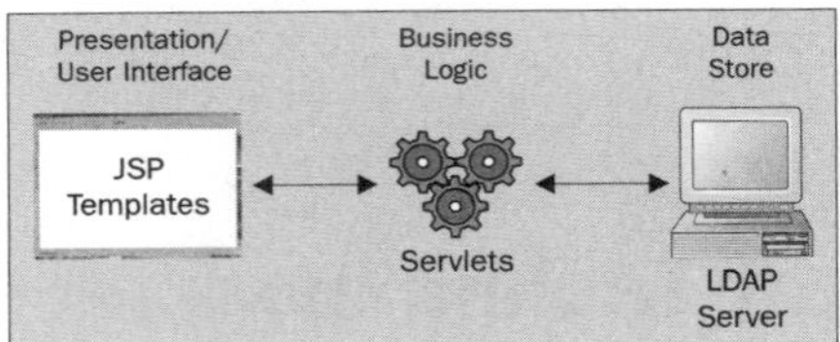

> **The Netscape Directory SDK for Java 4.0 is available for free download at http://www.iplanet.com/downloads/developer/detail_43_183.html**
>
> **At the time of writing, the Netscape Directory Server version 4.11 could be downloaded and test driven from http://www.iplanet.com/downloads/testdrive/index.html**

Installing and Running the Netscape Directory Server

Here we are going to step though the installation process of the LDAP server 4.1 under Windows NT without getting into too many detail. Please refer to the server documentation or to dedicated LDAP book for a deeper step by step installation.

Run the file `d411diu.exe` to start the installation of Netscape Directory Server 4.11. Once you accept the license agreement, select the following options:

- Choose Netscape Servers
- Select Custom.

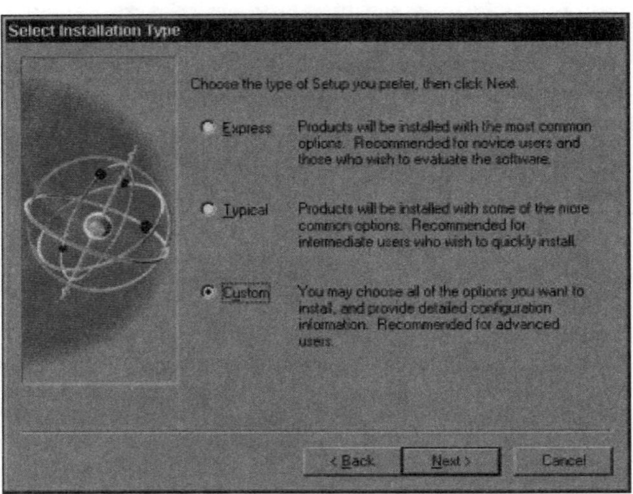

- Then enter the path to the directory in which you want to install the server.
- In the **Select Products** window, accept the defaults.
- Accept the default for **Configuration Directory Server** and **General Settings**, as well as for the **Administration domain** windows.
- In the Directory Server 4.1 **Populate Database** window, check the box called **Install Sample Organizational Structure** and choose the option **Populate with sample Database**. This will install the sample LDAP data that comes with the directory server, which we will use to run our sample case study.
- Once you reached the **Configuration summary** window, you are ready to install. Click on **Next** and the installation program will start copying the files in the directory you selected.
- When install is done, reboot your machine and Windows should start the LDAP server for you. You can make sure the server is started by right-clicking on the taskbar, and selecting **Task manager**. Then on the **Process** tab you should see two processes called `ns-slapd.exe` and `slapd.exe`. If by any chance, the server was not started, look in the directory in which you installed the server and find a subdirectory called `slapd/<machine_name>/`, where `<machine_name>` is the name you gave to your machine under this instance of Windows NT. From there, execute the file named `start-slapd.bat` to start the server.

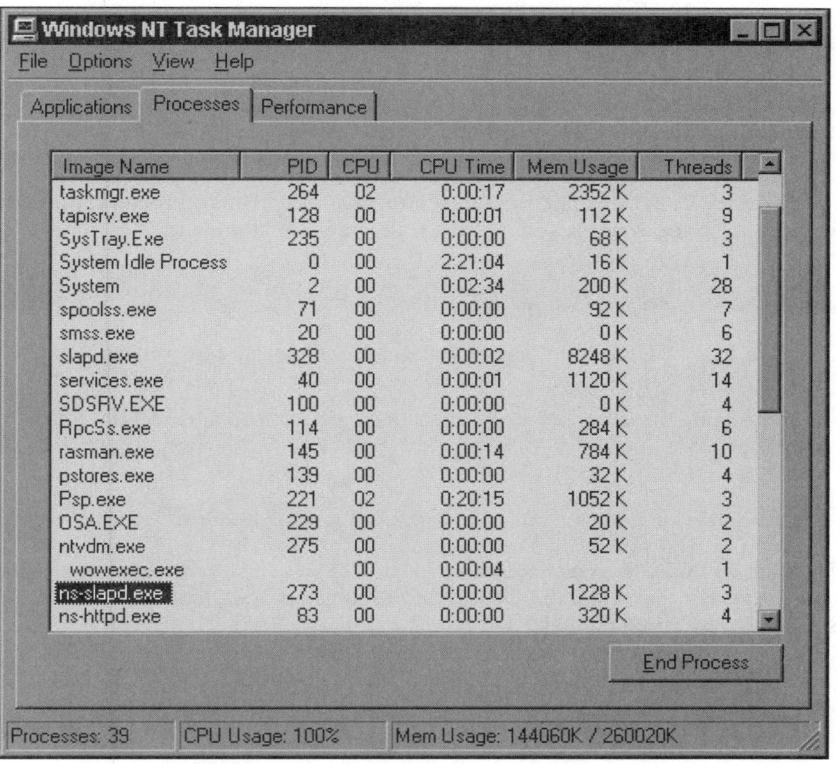

Setting up a Servlet-JSP Compliant Web Server

Now that we have setup our LDAP server, let's start to worry about the web server. We are using Java Server Pages version 1.1/Servlets version 2.2, so we will run our case study with both the light and flexible JavaServer Web Development Kit 1.0 from Sun and with the more industrial strength web server iPlanet Web Server 4.1 from the Sun-Netscape Alliance.

Running our Case Study on the JavaServer Web Development Kit 1.0

> **You can download a free copy of the JavaServer Web Development Kit 1.0 (JSWDK) at http://java.sun.com/products/jsp/download.html**
>
> **The file `README.html` located in the server root directory will instruct you how to setup the server.**

- In the directory in which you installed the JSWDK, you will find a file called `webserver.xml`, which lets you adjust server and application settings, including default port and web application attributes such as document base location and URI request mapping. Open up this file and add the line that we highlighted in the following section:

```
<WebServer id="webServer">
  <Service id="service0">
    <WebApplication id="examples" mapping="/examples" docBase="examples"/>
    <WebApplication id="wroxdemo" mapping="/wroxdemo" docBase="examples"/>
  </Service>
</WebServer>
```

- In the `examples/Web-inf` directory under the server root directory, open the file `mappings.properties` and add the following line at the end:

```
/wroxdemo/AccessController=AccessController
```

  This line maps a URI to the name of a resource (a servlet) in your application.

- From the same directory, open `servlets.properties` and add the following line at the end of the file:

```
AccessController.code=com.wrox.projsp.membership.AccessControllerServlet
```

  This line will map the resource name to the explicit class name of your servlet. Basically, it tells the server that when the URL http://<your_server>/wroxdemo/AccessController is accessed, the servlet named `com.wrox.projsp.membership.AccessControllerServlet` should be invoked and return some content to the client.

- Add the file `projsp.jar` to your classpath

The JSWDK is now ready to run our code. You can start the web server by executing the file `startserver.bat` from the JSWDK root directory:

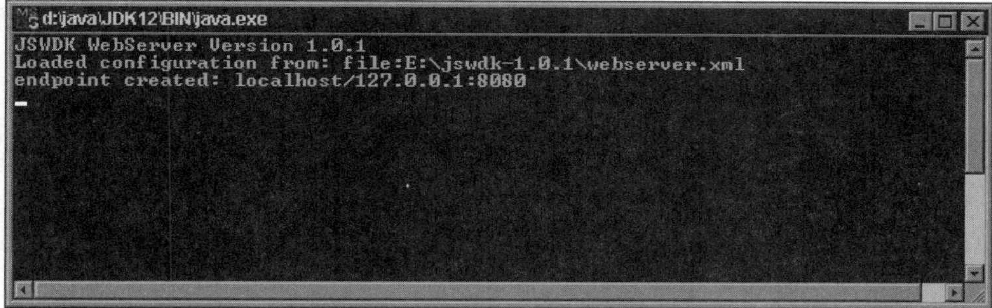

Now test the server by connecting to the port to which the server is set to run on:

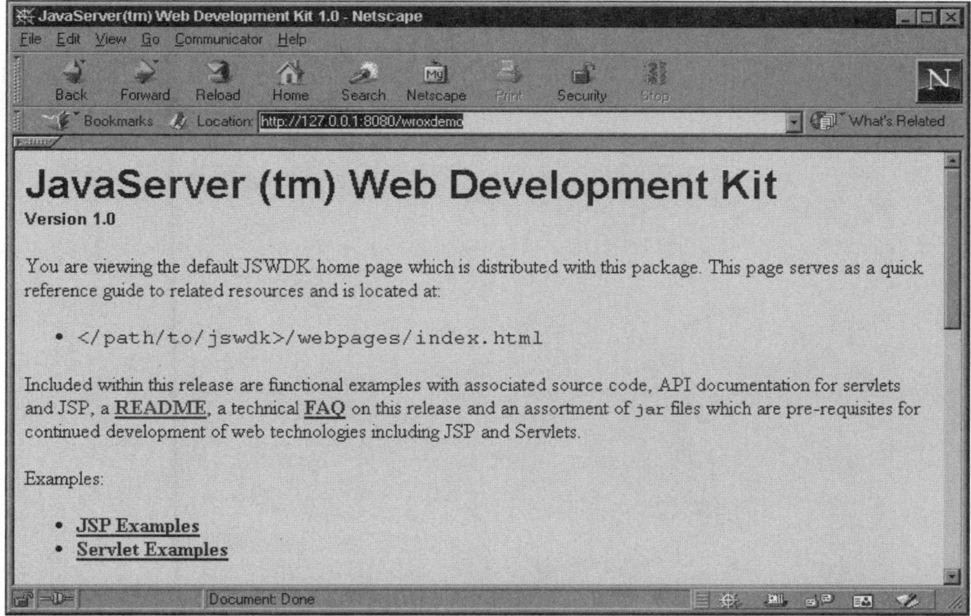

Note that you can run the JSWDK samples JSP and Servlets from this page by following the appropriate links.

Running our Case Study on the iPlanet Web Server 4.1

> **At the time of writing, you can download a trial copy of the iPlanet Web Server 4.1from http://www.iplanet.com/downloads/testdrive/index.html**

Go through the following steps to install iPlanet Web Server 4.1 under Windows NT 4.0:

- Execute the file `f41diu.exe`
- Accept the license agreement and choose a Typical install.
- Next choose the destination directory for the server files.
- In the Components to install window, you can select change and remove the components that you don't want. Our case study requires the Server Core, Java Runtime Environment, and Java and Servlets components; the other components can be removed.
- Choose a password for the admin server
- Choose a port for your admin web server
- IPlanet WS will install a default web server instance for you. The Default Webserver window lets you configure this server instance.
- The next window that needs our attention is the JDK Configuration window. For JSP to run with the server, installing the JRE (Java Runtime Environment) is not enough. The server needs a Java compiler in order to compile our Java Server Pages into Servlets at runtime. This is the reason why we need to point our server to an install of Java 2 (or later version) on our machine.

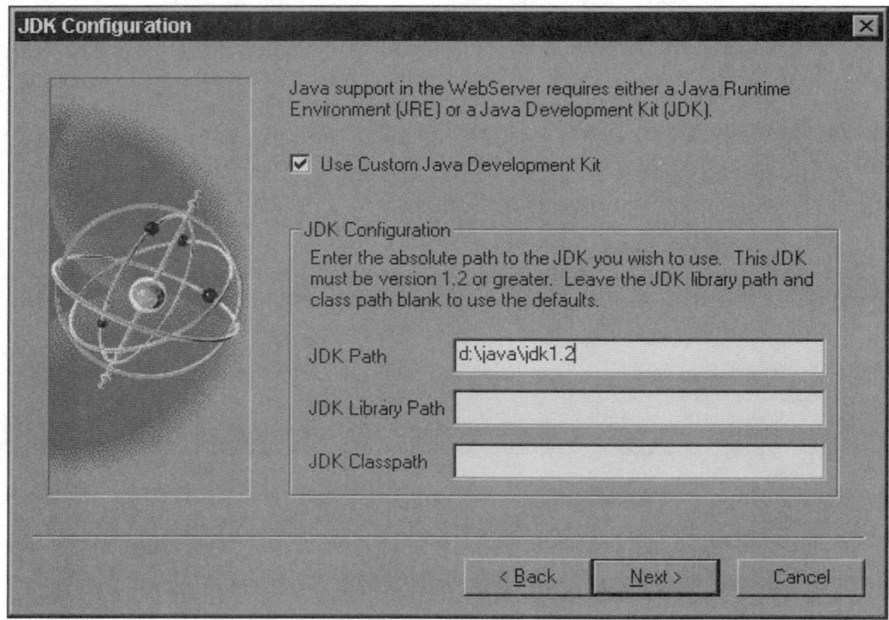

- The installation program will then install the files on your machine. Once the install is over, reboot your machine and connect to your admin server port and enter your admin password.

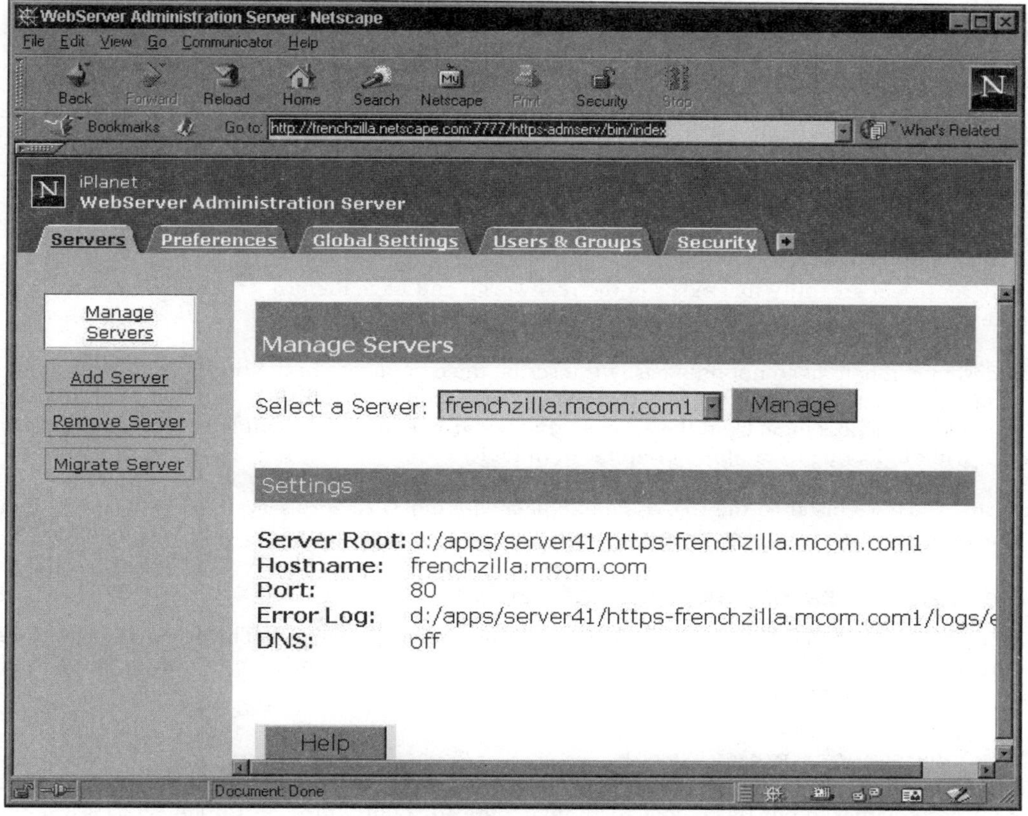

Now let's install our web application using the iPlanet Admin Server:

- Select your server instance and click on Manage.
- Once in the Server Manager for your server instance, click on the Servlets tab.
- Make sure that the Servlet engine and JSP are activated.
- Click on the link named Configure Servlet Attributes (left panel) and enter `AccessController` in the Servlet Name field and `com.wrox.projsp.membership.AccessControllerServlet` in the Servlet Code field. Then press OK and Save and Apply.
- Now click on Configure Servlet Virtual Path Translation and enter `/wroxdemo/AccessController` in the Virtual Path field and `AccessController` in the Servlet Name field. Then press OK and Save and Apply.
- Finally, select Configure JVM Attributes and add the path to our `projsp.jar` file to the Classpath field, then OK and Save and Apply.

The iPlanet server is now ready to run our application.

Putting It All Together

Now that we have defined our object model and our data structure, we can proceed to the implementation of our business objects.

Implementing our Business Objects

The business objects will be represented as **JavaBeans**, meaning that they will be implemented as reusable components that have the responsibility of encapsulating the business logic. These objects usually represent an entity that exists in the real world, and have the properties of their real counterparts as well. For example, a user object will have a name property, an address property etc…

This design can help us to not only easily transcribe the complexity of the real world in our system, by matching an instance of an object to a real object (an instance of User for one of our members), but also to isolate the business logic from the application logic. By doing so, we can later modify our business objects without having to modify our application logic.

Note that since we installed the LDAP sample data with our Directory server, we will use this fictional organization database to store our information. The sample organization installed is name `airius.com`.

Our Main Business Object: The User Bean

The first business object that we will be implementing is the `User` object. This class is responsible for storing information about our grocery shopping site members. All our business objects will be part of the `com.wrox.projsp.busobj` package.

```
package com.wrox.projsp.busobj;
```

The property names of our `User` object will match the attributes of the person object as it is defined in the LDAP repository. The attributes that we will be using to define our member are the following:

LDAP Person Attributes	Meaning
`Uid`	The user ID
`Password`	The password
`Givenname`	The user's given name
`Sn`	The user's surname
`Street`	The user's street name
`L`	The user's location
`St`	The state name
`PostalCode`	The postal code
`Telephonenumber`	The user's telephone number
`Mail`	The user's email address

To give you a more concrete idea of what this represents, let's look at what a person's node represented in the LDAP tree:

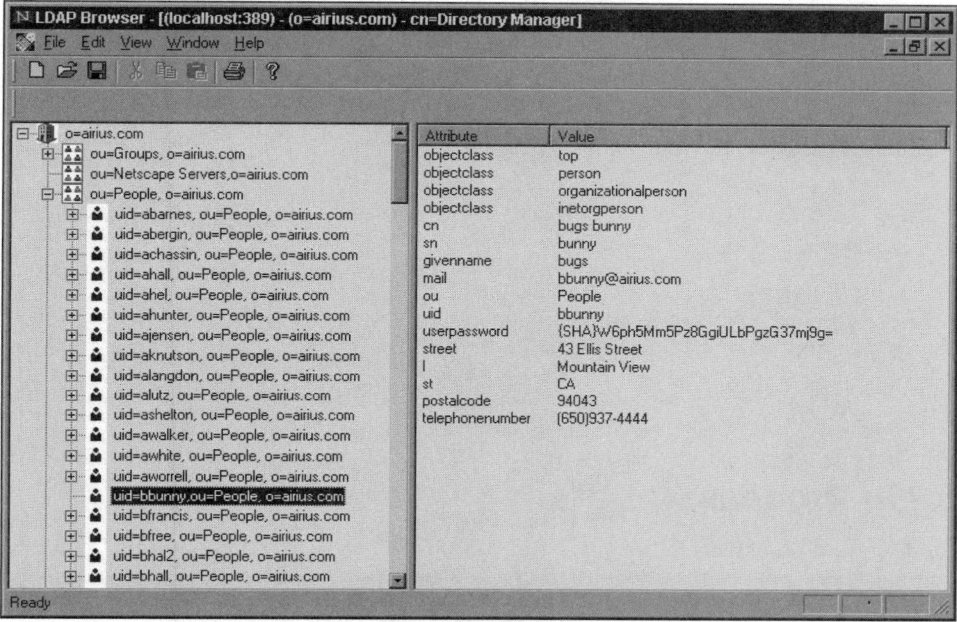

You can see in the left pane the attributes that describe the user Bugs Bunny, who is part of the `airius.com` organization, in the Organizational Unit ("ou" attribute) called People.

In order to match these attributes, let's define the properties for our `User` object using the same name. This will enable us to easily retrieve the same properties when looking for a member at login time:

```
public class User implements com.wrox.projsp.membership.ProJSPConstants {
  String uid             = "";
  String password        = "";
  String givenname       = "";
  String sn              = "";
  String street          = "";
  String l               = "";
  String st              = "";
  String postalCode      = "";
  String telephonenumber = "";
  String mail            = "";
```

Like a JavaBean, the `User` class will implement methods used to get and set the properties of the object, as follows:

```
  // setter methods //
  public void setUid(String name) {
    uid = name;
  }
  public void setPassword(String name) {
```

```
    password = name;
  }

  // etc.


  // getter methods //
  public boolean getUidIsSet() {
    return uidIsSet;
  }

  public String getUid() {
    return uid;
  }

  public String getPassword() {
    return password;
  }

  // etc.
```

The Login Process in Detail

We will now focus on exploring the process of controlling access to our application. This process can be decomposed in two phases: the registration of a new user and the authentication of existing members.

This is where our LDAP server is going to help us accomplishing these two tasks. In the case of registration, it will let us bind as a Directory administrator and add a new user to our list of registered members. For the authentication process, we will bind using the userID/password provided by the member and the LDAP server will try to authenticate this user for us.

Here is a snapshot of our application entry page:

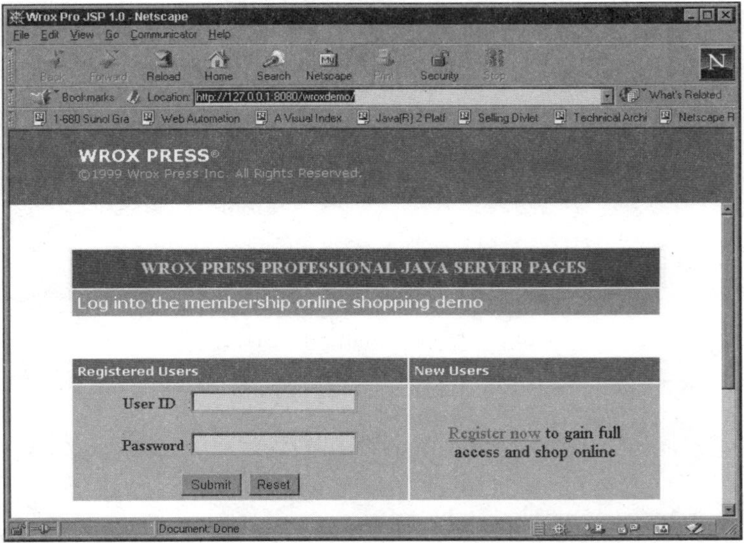

You can see that our user is offered two options: either logging in or registering his profile in order to get a membership to our online application.

Creating a New User: Writing to the LDAP Repository

We will here cover the case where the user that connects to our web application is not a registered member of our online grocery shopping mall, meaning that we have no record of his profile in our repository. Thus, this person can not login using a user ID and password, but will have to register his profile using our membership online application form.

This form is a standard HTML form. It is intended to collect all the necessary information from the new member. All this data is then posted to a template called `newcomer.jsp`. Note that you would typically use a secure server (using the Secure Socket Layer protocol) to send this sensitive information from the client to the web server.

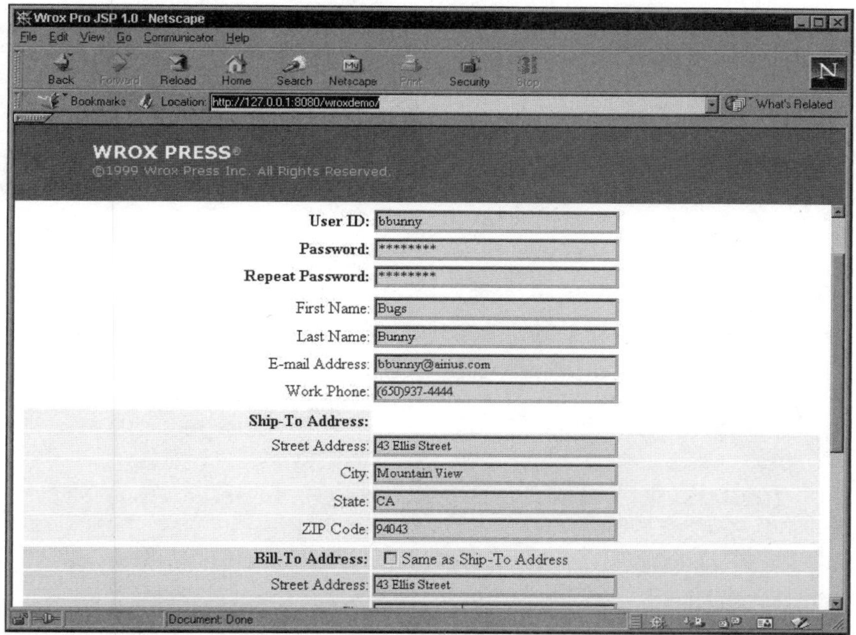

Once the user has entered the requested information, we can proceed to the next step and create our user object.

This is going to be our first JSP template. We now want to give this user a chance to review his information before writing his profile to the repository. This is the time to create an instance of the user object with the information we collected on the `information.jsp` registration form.
Note that here, some logic could be added to enforce uniqueness of the `userID` in our LDAP repository.

First, we inform our JSP engine that we want to import the class necessary to create our `User` object:

```
<%@ page import = "com.wrox.projsp.busobj.User" %>
```

We then instantiate our `User` class and populate it with the collected information by using the following syntax:

```
<jsp:useBean id="newUser" class="com.wrox.projsp.busobj.User"
  scope="session"/>
<jsp:setProperty name="newUser" property="*"/>
```

We here create an instance of the class `com.wrox.projsp.busobj.User`, and we give this instance the name `newUser`. This instance of `User` will have a session scope, and its properties will be populated with all the matching attributes that were posted from the `information.html` form.

Now that our bean has been instantiated and its properties set, we can use it to create dynamic content on our page, wherever we need to display information about this `User` instance. Since we want to give our user a chance to review the information he entered, we create a table listing all the properties previously entered (except for the password):

```
<table BORDER="1" CELLSPACING="1" WIDTH="424">
  <tr>
    <td WIDTH="36%" VALIGN="MIDDLE" BGCOLOR="#666699"><strong>
      <font color="#ffffff" SIZE="-1"><p align="right">User ID</font>
      </strong></td>
    <td WIDTH="64%" VALIGN="MIDDLE"><strong><font COLOR="#666699">
      <p ALIGN="LEFT"> <%= newUser.getUid() %>
      </font></strong> </td>
  </tr>
  <tr>
    <td WIDTH="36%" VALIGN="MIDDLE" BGCOLOR="#666699"><p ALIGN="RIGHT">
      <strong><font COLOR="#ffffff" SIZE="-1">First Name:</font>
      </strong></td>
    <td WIDTH="64%" VALIGN="MIDDLE"><strong><font COLOR="#666699">
      <p ALIGN="LEFT"> <%= newUser.getGivenname() %>
      </font></strong> </td>
  </tr>
  <tr>
    <td WIDTH="36%" VALIGN="MIDDLE" BGCOLOR="#666699"><strong>
      <font COLOR="#ffffff" SIZE="-1"><p ALIGN="RIGHT">Last Name:</font>
      </strong></td>
    <td WIDTH="64%" VALIGN="MIDDLE"><strong><font COLOR="#666699">
      <p ALIGN="LEFT"><strong><font COLOR="#666699">
      <p ALIGN="LEFT"> <%= newUser.getSn() %></font>
      </strong> </td>
  </tr>
  <tr>
    <td WIDTH="36%" VALIGN="MIDDLE" BGCOLOR="#666699"><strong>
      <font color="#ffffff" SIZE="-1"><p align="right">E-mail
      Address:</font></strong></td>
    <td WIDTH="64%" VALIGN="MIDDLE"><strong><font COLOR="#666699">
      <p ALIGN="LEFT"> <%= newUser.getMail() %></font>
      </strong> </td>
  </tr>
```

At this point, we still haven't written anything to the repository. And the reason for this is that we want to give our user a chance to modify his information before making an expensive call to our LDAP database.

If our user chooses to modify his information, we use some simple client side JavaScript to send him back to the previous page:

```
<input TYPE="button" VALUE="&lt; Modify" onClick="history.go(-1)">
```

If the user chooses to create a new profile, we invoke the method `SaveNewUserProfile()` for this instance of the `User` class. We do this by giving a name and value to our Submit button in our `newcomer.jsp` template:

```
<form method="POST" action=" shoppingMall.jsp ">
<input TYPE="submit" NAME="choice" VALUE="Create my profile and start
   shopping !">
```

Our target JSP file (`shoppingMall.jsp`) will take charge of setting the `choice` property (through the `setChoice()` method) for our `User` class, and this will trigger the `SaveNewUserProfile()` in this instance of the `User` object. This is what happens in our `User` class:

When our `shoppingMall.jsp` is loaded, it invokes the following method on our `User` object:

```
public void setChoice(String s) {
  choice = s;
  if (choice != null && choice.startsWith("Create")) {
    SaveNewUserProfile();
  }
  reset();
}
```

Our `choice` property gets initialized with the value `"Create my profile and start shopping !"`.

We then use this property setter method to trigger our `SaveNewUserProfile()`, after checking that our `choice` string has the value we expect it to have. If it does, we proceed and save this user's profile to the repository.

The SaveNewUserProfile() Method

This method performs a standard insert to the LDAP Server. We will here add an entry for our user under the 'people' organizational unit in the `airius.com` tree (`airius.com` is the root node of the company defined in our sample data). This entry will encapsulate all the attributes describing our new member. Here is what the code looks like:

```
private void SaveNewUserProfile() {
  String new_dn = "uid=" + uid + ",ou=People, o=airius.com";
  String objectclass_values [] = {"top", "person", "organizationalperson",
                                  "inetorgperson"};
  String cn_values [] = {givenname + " " +  sn};
  String sn_values [] = {sn};
  String givenname_values [] = {givenname};
```

```
String uid_values [] = {uid};
String mail_values[] = {mail};
String street_values[] = {street};
LDAPAttributeSet attrib_set = null;
LDAPAttribute attribute = null;
LDAPEntry entry = null;

LDAPConnection ld = null;

try {
  ld = new LDAPConnection();

  /* let's bind as directory manager , so we have */
  /* rights to write to the server */
  ld.connect(HOST_NAME, LDAP_PORT, ADMIN_DN, ADMIN_PWD);
  attrib_set = new LDAPAttributeSet();

  attribute = new LDAPAttribute("objectclass",objectclass_values);
  attrib_set.add(attribute);

  attribute = new LDAPAttribute("cn", cn_values);
  attrib_set.add(attribute);

  attribute = new LDAPAttribute("sn", sn_values);
  attrib_set.add(attribute);

  attribute = new LDAPAttribute("givenname",givenname_values);
  attrib_set.add(attribute);

  attribute = new LDAPAttribute("mail", mail_values);
  attrib_set.add(attribute);

  attribute = new LDAPAttribute("ou", "People");
  attrib_set.add(attribute);

  attribute = new LDAPAttribute("uid",uid_values);
  attrib_set.add(attribute);

  attribute = new LDAPAttribute("userpassword", password);
  attrib_set.add(attribute);

  attribute = new LDAPAttribute("street", street_values);
  attrib_set.add(attribute);

  attribute = new LDAPAttribute("l", l);
  attrib_set.add(attribute);

  attribute = new LDAPAttribute("st", st);
  attrib_set.add(attribute);

  attribute = new LDAPAttribute("postalCode", postalCode);
  attrib_set.add(attribute);
```

```
        attribute = new LDAPAttribute("telephonenumber", telephonenumber);
        attrib_set.add(attribute);

        /* create the entry object */
        entry = new LDAPEntry(new_dn,attrib_set);

        /* add the object */
        ld.add(entry);

        if (ld != null) {
          ld.disconnect();
        }
      } catch(LDAPException e) {
        e.printStackTrace();
      }
    }
```

As you can see here, we bind to our Directory server as the directory manager (note though, that it is usually safer to create a user with rights to accomplish this task than using the Directory Manager account. The issues are identical to using the `root` account in UNIX).

```
ld.connect(HOST_NAME, LDAP_PORT, ADMIN_DN, ADMIN_PWD);
```

Note that the parameters used with the `connect()` method are defined in the interface named `ProJSPConstants.java`, that our `User` class implements. This interface is just a convenient way to locate all our environment variables for our application. Classes that need to access these variables could just implement this interface.

Here, we first create individual attributes for each piece of information, and then package all our attributes in a `LDAPAttributeSet` class. We finally add this `LDAPAttributeSet` to an `LDAPEntry` object and write the `LDAPEntry` to our `LDAPConnection` object. And that's it, the magic has happened and our user has been added to our LDAP database.

Now, before we get into the authentication part of our LDAP communication process, let's look how we can make our JSP page a more reusable component for our application.

Making our Information Page a Reusable Template

Here, the idea is to reuse the `information.jsp` to give our member a chance to update his information. There could be some reasons why at some point during the course of his browsing of our application, our member would be willing to modify some of the information that define his membership. For example, when checking out his cart, our user might want to change their e-mail address or any account information.

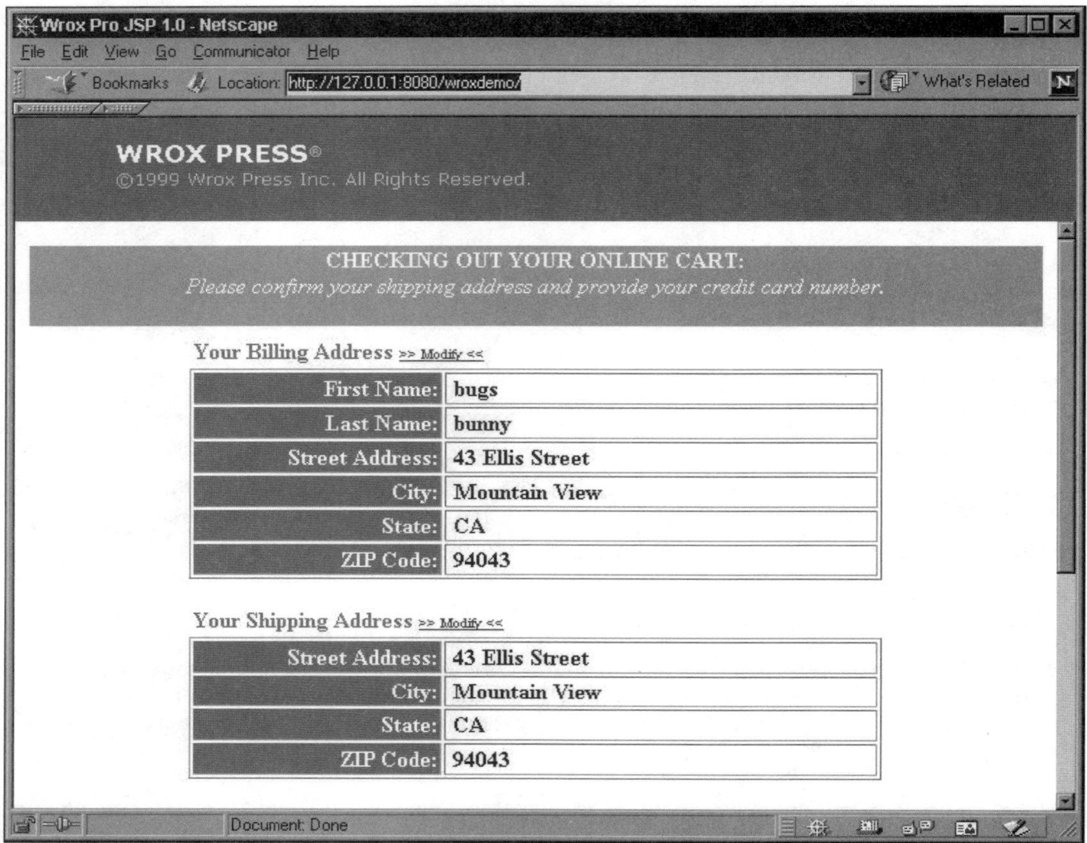

Here, by clicking on the Modify link, our member can be given a chance to modify his data.

We could then simply redisplay our information form for him to update the necessary fields. The problem is that we do not want him to modify some specific fields, such as the user ID or password fields. We will then use the power of JSP to add some logic to our page:

What we know is that when the user sees this form for the first time, their user ID has not been set yet. We can then just add simple method to our `User` object to inform us of the status of the user ID.

```
public boolean isUIDSet() {
  if(uid.equals("") || uid == null) {
    return false;
  } else {
    return true;
  }
}
```

We will then set this property in our `User` class when the user ID is set for the first time, which could happen at one of two times:

- When the user creates their new profile
- When the user logs in and his profile is retrieved from the LDAP server

```
public void setUid(String name) {
  uid = name;
}
```

We can then easily choose to hide or display the password fields depending on whether the user ID field has been yet set:

```
<% if(!newUser.isUIDSet ())
{ %>
  <tr>
    <td width="44%" align="right"><font face="Times New Roman"><b>User
      ID:</b></font></td>
    <td width="56%"><font face="Times New Roman"><input type="text"
       name="uid" size="20" value="<%= newUser.getUid() %>" ></font></td>
  </tr>
  <tr>
    <td width="44%" align="right"><font face="Times New Roman">
      <b>Password:</b></font></td>
    <td width="56%"><font face="Times New Roman"><input type="password"
      name="password" size="20"> </font></td>
  </tr>
  <tr>
    <td width="44%" align="right"><font face="Times New Roman"><b>Repeat
      Password:</b></font></td>
    <td width="56%"><font face="Times New Roman"><input type="password"
      size="20"> </font></td>
  </tr>
<% } %>
```

If the user ID has not been set yet, the user ID and password fields will be correctly displayed:

User ID: bbunny
Password: ********
Repeat Password: ********
First Name: Bugs
Last Name: Bunny
E-mail Address: bbunny@airius.com
Work Phone: (650)937-4444

If the user ID has been set, we will hide the password fields and only display the user ID (versus displaying it in an editable text field):

```
<% if(newUser.isUIDSet ())
{ %>
  <tr>
    <td width="44%" align="right"><font face="Times New Roman"><b>User
      ID:</b></font></td>
    <td width="56%"><font face="Times New Roman"><%= newUser.getUid() %>
      </font></td>
  </tr>
<% } %>
```

We should get something like this:

User ID: bbunny
First Name: bugs
Last Name: bunny
E-mail Address: bbunny@airius.com
Work Phone: (650)937-4444

The fields are populated with the existing information, but we hide the password fields and make the user ID field non-editable.

> **This type of construct replaces the `<INCLUDEIF>` and `<EXCLUDEIF>` tags that were used in Java Server Pages version 0.92.**

The Login Process: Authenticating a Member using the LDAP Server

Our LDAP server is now full of information about our users. Our members will be happy to connect to our site and retrieve their profile by just entering their user ID and password. On our side, the process of authentication enables us to provide more granular access rights to our resources. Here's a general picture of the way the LDAP authentication process works:

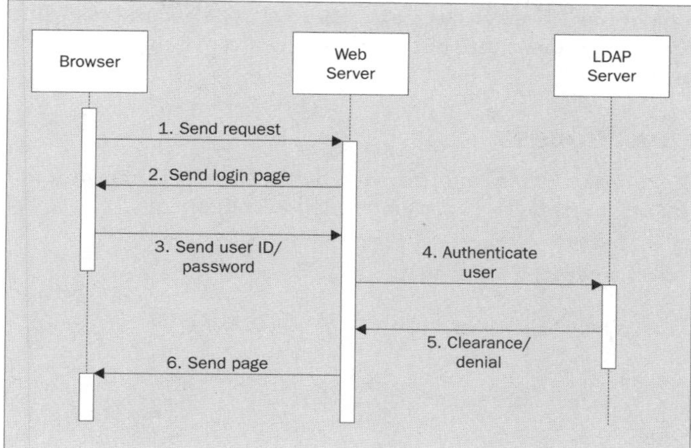

Note that the use of an LDAP Directory server is particularly suited to our needs. It not only gives us the possibility to store our data using an interface easy to deal with, but also gives us the authentication functionality that we are looking for. This authentication mechanism is implemented in our `AccessControllerServlet`, which is invoked when the user clicks on the Submit button from our login page:

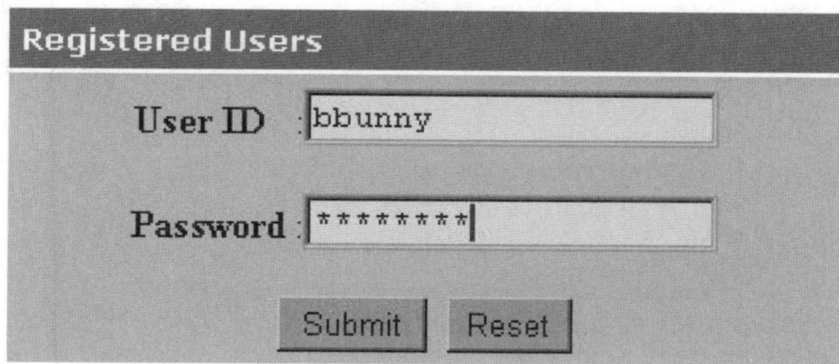

Here is how we invoke our servlet from our HTML file (`launch.html`):

```
<form method="POST" action="/wroxdemo/servlet/AccessController">
<div align="center"><center><p><strong>
  User ID</strong>   :<input type="text" name="ID" size="20">
</p></center></div>
<div align="center"><center><p><strong>
  Password</strong> :<input type="password" name="password" size="20">
</p></center></div><div align="center"><center><p>
  <input type="submit" value="Submit" name="B1"> 
  <input type="reset" value="Reset" name="B2">
</p></center></div>
</form>
```

The file `launch.html` file contains some client side JavaScript code that will show you how to have the cursor automatically displayed in the User ID text field when the user loads the page.

Let's now have a look at our AccessControllerServlet. This process will be split in two distinct sections: we initially try to authenticate our user, and then move on to the retrieval of his information if the first section was successful.

The Authentication Process

First, we will use the doPost() method provided by the Servlet framework to collect the user ID and password entered by our user. Here's what our code looks like:

```
package com.wrox.projsp.membership;

import netscape.ldap.*;

import java.io.*;
import java.util.*;
import javax.servlet.*;
import javax.servlet.http.*;

public class AccessControllerServlet extends HttpServlet
  implements ProJSPConstants {
  private LDAPConnection ld;

  public void doPost(HttpServletRequest req, HttpServletResponse res)
         throws ServletException, IOException {

    // store value of userID
    String userID = req.getParameter("ID");

    // store password value
    String password = req.getParameter("password");

    if (!allowedUser(userID, password)) {

      // User not allowd. Inform the user..
      res.sendRedirect("/wroxdemo/notfound.html");
    } else {

      // User has been authenticated,
      // let's search his/her attributes
      String userAttrb = RetrieveUserAttributes(userID);

      res.sendRedirect("/wroxdemo/shoppingMall.jsp?" + userAttrb);
    }
  }
```

So far, everything is pretty straightforward. We extract user ID and password from the HttpServletRequest object and pass them as arguments to the allowedUser() method, which is responsible for telling us if this user has been authenticated. Depending on the result returned by this method, we will either send the user to an error page or will grant access to our online grocery shopping mall.

Let's now explore the allowedUser() function. The first thing we do is make sure that neither of the two fields was as left blank. If so, we return false (note that this can be easily done with some client side JavaScript, given that you wish to use some in your web application):

```
private boolean allowedUser(String uid,
                            String pwd) throws IOException {
  if (uid.equals("") || pwd.equals("")) {
    return false;
```

We then define and initialize our variables for this function: a new LDAPConnection object, an LDAPEntry and a String that will hold the Distinguished Name for our User object.

```
  ld = new LDAPConnection();
  LDAPEntry findEntry = null;
  String dn = null;
  boolean status = false;
```

Now we create a filter based on our user ID, open our connection, initialize a LDAPSearchResults object and start our search based on our filter and our search base defined in the ProJSPConstants interface. Since the LDAPSearchResults class extends the Enumeration class, we just iterate through this object's instance to get our LDAPEntry object. We then use the getDN() method of the LDAPEntry class to retrieve the DN for this entry, and try to authenticate our member to the LDAP server using the dn and password attributes:

```
  try {
     String MY_FILTER = "uid=" + uid;
     ld.connect(HOST_NAME, LDAP_PORT);

     LDAPSearchResults res = null;
     res = ld.search(LDAP_SEARCHBASE, LDAPConnection.SCOPE_SUB,
                     MY_FILTER, null, false);
     while (res.hasMoreElements()) {
       findEntry = res.next();
       dn = findEntry.getDN();

       // now let's bind to the server
       ld.authenticate(dn, pwd);

       // if no exception is thrown
       // the process is successful
       status = true;
     }
  } catch (LDAPException e) {
    System.out.println(e.toString());
  } catch (Exception x) {
    x.printStackTrace();
  }

  return status;
}
```

If ld.authenticate() doesn't throw an exception, we passed and our function will return true, false otherwise. We are now getting back to our initial doPost() block: if the user could not be authenticated, we redirect him to our error page. Otherwise, we go ahead to step 2 and try to retrieve his information.

In order to prevent a user from accessing our catalog directly without registering, we add a few lines of code to our JSP files, checking if our `User` object has been instantiated and the user ID property set:

```
<% if (newUser.getUid().equals("")) { %>
<jsp:forward page="unauthorized.html"/>
<% } %>
```

If the `getUid()` method evaluate to an empty string, we forward our user to an error page.

The Information Retrieval Process

Since the process of opening a new connection over TCP/IP is pretty expensive, we want to make sure that we recycle the `LDAPConnection` object that we used for authentication for retrieving our member data. We then first make sure our connection is still alive (otherwise we create a new one), and create a `String` array containing all the attributes that we want to get back for this user object:

```
private String RetrieveUserAttributes(String uid) {
  if (ld == null) {
    ld = new LDAPConnection();
  }

  String attrs [] = {"uid", "givenname", "sn", "mail", "telephonenumber",
                     "street", "l", "st", "postalCode"};
  String SEARCH_FILTER = "uid=" + uid;
  LDAPSearchResults res = null;
  StringBuffer sb = new StringBuffer();
```

We then pass this array of attributes to the `search()` method of the `LDAPConnection` object in order to retrieve them from the LDAP Server:

```
  try {
    res = ld.search(LDAP_SEARCHBASE,
                    LDAPConnection.SCOPE_SUB,
                    SEARCH_FILTER,
                    attrs,
                    false );
```

We now know that we are going to get back an `Enumeration`-like object back (an `LDAPEntry`), containing (hopefully) our data. From this `LDAPEntry` we will extract a `LDAPAttributeSet` object that should contain our list of attributes All we need to do then is find a way to pass directly this data to our JSP page (`shoppingMall.jsp`) so that our `User` bean gets instantiated with these attributes.

One easy way to accomplish this task could be to iterate through the `LDAPAttributeSet` in order to get pairs of the style `attributeName=value`, and then append these pairs to a query string that we will add to our URL when we redirect our user to the `shoppingMall.jsp` file. Note though, that the length of URLs being limited, you might want to prefer using a POST method if you suspect that your query string is going to be very long.

For these to work, let's just add our data to the `StringBuffer` object that we created above:

```
/* Get the individiual results */
while (res.hasMoreElements()) {
  LDAPEntry findEntry = null;
  findEntry = (LDAPEntry) res.next();

  LDAPAttributeSet attributeSet = findEntry.getAttributeSet();

  for (int i=0; i < attributeSet.size(); i++) {
    LDAPAttribute attribute =   (LDAPAttribute)attributeSet.elementAt(i);
    String attrName = attribute.getName();
    sb.append("&");
    sb.append(java.net.URLEncoder.encode(attrName));
    sb.append("=");

    Enumeration enumVals = attribute.getStringValues();

    if (enumVals != null) {
      while ( enumVals.hasMoreElements() ) {
        String nextValue = ( String )enumVals.nextElement();
        sb.append(java.net.URLEncoder.encode( nextValue ));
      }
    }
  }
}
```

Our `StringBuffer` should then contain a string that looks like this:

```
uid=bbunny&givenname=bugs&sn=bunny&mail=bbunny%40airius.com&telephonenumber=%28650
%299374444&street=43+Ellis+Street&l=Mountain+View&st=CA&postalCode=94043
```

Note that we had to 'URLEncode' our pairs `attributeName=value` in order for our query string to be understood by the web server. The `encode()` static method of class `java.net.URLEncoder` performs this job for you. It basically converts all special characters (like space or "@" sign for example) into a MIME format called **x-www-form-urlencoded** format.

As we saw earlier in the `doPost()` method, when login is successful, we redirect our member to the `shoppingMall.jsp` and append this query string to the URI in order for our template to process the data:

```
res.sendRedirect ("/wroxdemo/shoppingMall.jsp?" + userAttrb);
```

Finally, we make sure to close our LDAP connection by enclosing our `disconnect()` call into a `finally` block:

```
finally {
  try {
    if (ld != null) ld.disconnect();
  } catch (LDAPException e) {}
}
```

Instantiating the User Bean for our Existing Member

Our shoppingMall.jsp template does not care how the data is passed to it. It can be done though a GET method (as we just did with our query string) or POST method (as we do it in newcomer.jsp) and the bean still gets instantiated and populated with the data coming from either the LDAP server or the registration page:

```
<%@ page import = "com.wrox.projsp.busobj.User" %>

<jsp:useBean id="newUser" class="com.wrox.projsp.busobj.User"
  scope="session"/>
<jsp:setProperty name="newUser" property="*"/>
```

The Dynamic Online Grocery Store

We have accomplished our task. We now have a web based application that is membership-enabled. Registered users can easily login through our application front end and start selecting products from our catalog. So let's now take a quick look at the way our online grocery store works.

As you can see in the following screenshot, most of the content of our Shopping Mall is generated dynamically:

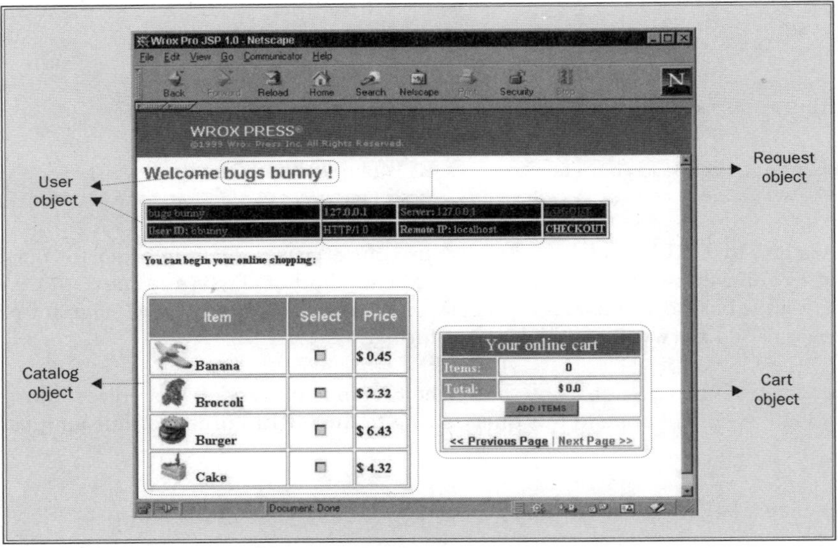

At the top of the page, we display information related to our member using the instance of the User object that we described previously. The topmost table also displays some of the environment variables located in the always available Request object.

The bottom left table displays one of our catalog pages. Each row is made of a product name, picture and price, along with a check box enabling the user to select the product. The bottom right table dynamically informs the user of the current status of his selection, and gives him the opportunity to modify the content of the shopping cart. So let's now take a look at how we manage our catalog of products and electronic cart.

The Online Catalog

Following the concept of separation of content/logic/presentation, we have designed our catalog in a way that isolates the data from the display mechanism as well as the business logic. This enables us to make sure that our application (and our catalog module) will be easy to update and easy to extend:

- Easy to update because when we want to modify the content, we only have to deal with the content and not the business logic and presentation.
- Easy to extend for the same reason: when we want to modify our business logic and extend the capabilities of our catalog, the content won't get in the way.

In our example, we load the data from a flat file, as we don't want to spend too much time dealing with an extra data source but rather focus on the overall design of our web application. This will fit the purpose of demonstrating the advantages of separating content from presentation In the real world, you would probably get your catalog content from some standard relational database.

We get our catalog content from a file called `catalog.dat`. The `loadCatalog()` method of the `Catalog` object is responsible from extracting the data from the file and create our online catalog. For each line in the file we create a `Product` object, and then create a page of products every time we reach the value defined by the `NUMBER_OF_PRODUCTS_PER_PAGE` variable. We finally put each page in the catalog:

```
package com.wrox.projsp.busobj;

import java.util.ArrayList;
import java.io.*;

public class Catalog
  implements com.wrox.projsp.membership.ProJSPConstants {
  static int NUMBER_OF_PRODUCTS_PER_PAGE = 4;

  static ArrayList ourCatalog = new ArrayList();
  int currentPageIndex = 0;

  public Catalog() {
    loadCatalog();
  }


  private void loadCatalog() {
    FileInputStream fis = null;
    StreamTokenizer in;
    String name, picture, price;
    Product product;
    ArrayList catalogPage = new ArrayList();

    try {

      fis = new FileInputStream(CATALOG_DATASOURCE);
      Reader r = new BufferedReader(new InputStreamReader(fis));
      in = new StreamTokenizer(r);
      int c = 0;
```

```
        int refNumber = 0;

        in.nextToken();
        while (in.ttype != in.TT_EOF) {
          name = new String(in.sval);
          in.nextToken();

          picture = new String(in.sval);
          in.nextToken();

          price = new String(in.sval);
          in.nextToken();

          product = new Product(name, picture, price, refNumber);
          catalogPage.add(product);
          ProductReferencer.addProduct(product);

          c = c + 1;

          // let's put 4 products per page //
          if (c == NUMBER_OF_PRODUCTS_PER_PAGE) {
            ourCatalog.add(catalogPage);
            catalogPage = new ArrayList();
            c = 0;
          }
          refNumber = refNumber + 1;
        }
      }

      // etc.
```

Our product object is a simple class containing properties such as `Price`, `Name`, `referenceNumber` and `Picture`, and the related setter and getter methods:

```
package com.wrox.projsp.busobj;

public class Product {

  private String name    = null;
  private String picture = null;
  private String price   = null;
  private int referenceNumber;

  // etc.
```

Now that we detailed content and logic, let's look at the presentation. Our multipurpose `shoppingMall.jsp` instantiates a `Catalog` object and displays a catalog page based on the value of our `currentPageIndex` variable (default value of `0` refers to the first page in our array of pages):

```
<%@ page import = "com.wrox.projsp.busobj.Catalog" %>

<jsp:useBean id="Catalog" class="com.wrox.projsp.busobj.Catalog"
  scope="session"/>
<jsp:setProperty name="Catalog" property="currentPageIndex"/>
```

Here's how our catalog table is created: we basically create an `Arraylist` object that we populate with the `Products` that make up this page. The `getCatalogPage()` method from the `Catalog` object is responsible for passing to us the page (`Arraylist` of `Product` objects) based on the current value of our `currentPageIndex` variable. We then iterate through the page array and create the `Products` that we display in the table:

```
<form method="POST" action="shoppingMall.jsp">

<table border="0" width="100%" height="250">
      <tr>
      <td width="50%" height="270"><table border="1" width="100%"></td>
      </tr>
      <tr>
      <td width="53%" height="46" bgcolor="#9999CC">
         <center><strong><big><font color="#FFFFFF"
         face="Roman">Item</font></big></strong></center></td>
      <td width="27%" height="46" bgcolor="#9999CC">
         <center><strong><big><font color="#FFFFFF"
         face="Roman">Select</font></big></strong></center></td>
      <td width="30%" height="46" bgcolor="#9999CC">
         <center><strong><big><font color="#FFFFFF"
         face="Roman">Price</font></big></strong></center></td>
      </tr>

<% ArrayList thisPage = Catalog.getCatalogPage();
   for( int i=0 ; i < thisPage.size() ; i++ ) {
     Product p = (Product)thisPage.get(i); %>

      <tr>
      <td width="53%" height="19"><big><strong>
         <img src="<%= p.getPicture() %>" width="50" height="35">
         <%= p.getName() %></strong></big></td>
      <td width="27%" height="19" align="center">
      <input type="checkbox" name="item"
         value="<%= p.getReferenceNumber() %>"></td>
      <td width="30%" height="19"><strong><big>$
       <%= p.getPrice() %></big></strong></td>
      </tr>

<% } %>

</table>
```

Our `ProductReferencer` business object keeps an indexed list of all our products. In order to easily retrieve the products selected by our user, we assign the product index value as the value of our checkboxes:

```
<input type="checkbox" name="item" value="<%= p.getReferenceNumber() %>
```

Then when the user add products to the cart, our online cart will get these reference numbers and ask the `ProductReferencer` to send back an array of products corresponding to the list of references.

The Pagination Mechanism

The `Catalog` pagination mechanism is simple. When our user clicks on either of the Previous Page or Next Page Link, we set the value of the `currentPageIndex` variable to either increase or decrease and pass it to the `setCurrentPageIndex()` method of the `Catalog` object via a query string:

```
<strong>
<a href="shoppingMall.jsp?currentPageIndex=decrease"">&lt;&lt;
Previous Page</a> | <a href="shoppingMall.jsp?currentPageIndex=increase">
<font face="Roman" color="#666699"><strong>
Next Page &gt;&gt;
</strong>
```

The `setCurrentPageIndex()` method is actually triggered by this line at the beginning of our JSP template:

```
<jsp:setProperty name="Catalog" property="currentPageIndex"/>
```

`setCurrentPageIndex()` then calculates the value of the new page index based on the `Catalog.CurrentPageIndex` value and the value of the `selection` string passed from the link that was selected:

```
public void setCurrentPageIndex(String selection) {
  if (selection.equals("increase")
          && currentPageIndex != (ourCatalog.size() - 1)) {
    currentPageIndex = currentPageIndex + 1;
  } else if (selection.equals("decrease")
             && currentPageIndex != 0) {
    currentPageIndex = currentPageIndex - 1;
  } else if (selection.equals("increase")
             && currentPageIndex == (ourCatalog.size() - 1)) {
    currentPageIndex = 0;
  } else if (selection.equals("decrease")
             && currentPageIndex == 0) {
    currentPageIndex = (ourCatalog.size() - 1);
  }
}
```

The Online Cart

Our online `Cart` is basically a business object represented by an `ArrayList` of `Product` objects, to which we can add and remove products.

```
package com.wrox.projsp.busobj;

import java.util.ArrayList;

public class Cart {
  ArrayList ourCart = new ArrayList();
  float totalPrice = (float) 0;

  private void addProduct(Product p) {
    ourCart.add(p);
```

```
    }

    private void removeItem(int n) {
      ourCart.remove(n);
    }
```

When our `Cart` object gets its array of Product Reference numbers (when the user selects products and clicks **Add items**), it iterates through this array, asks the `ProductReferencer` to pass back the products corresponding to this index numbers, and adds them to the `Cart`:

```
  public void setItem(String [] b) {
    for(int i = 0; i < b.length; i++) {
      Product p = ProductReferencer.getProduct(Integer.parseInt(b[i]));
      addProduct(p);
    }
    calculateNewPrice();
  }
```

The process is identical for removing products. When a user wants to remove products from the cart, he selects the items to remove and clicks on **Remove items** on the right panel. (The template file handling the removal process is `remove.jsp`.)

Please select the items you want to remove from your cart:

Remove Items	Select
Cantaloupe	☐
Corn	☐
Donut	☐
Fries	☐
Grapes	☐

We then remove the products contained in the cart by getting their index value in the cart `ArrayList`:

```
  public void setRemoval(String [] b) {
    int itemIndex;

    for(int i = 0; i < b.length; i++) {
      itemIndex = Integer.parseInt(b[i]);
      removeItem(itemIndex);
    }
    calculateNewPrice();
  }
```

The Checkout Process

We complement our web application by adding a **product review process** and simplified **checkout process**. The product review process gives our user a chance to review the content of the cart one more time before checking out. The page basically displays the detailed content of the cart and gives the user a chance to proceed with checking out or go back and modify the cart content:

CHECKING OUT YOUR ONLINE CART
Please review your selection

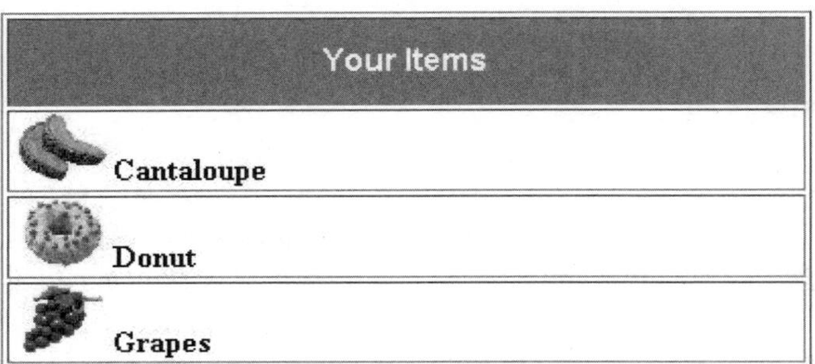

The `proceed.jsp` template sums up the entire process, prepares the final checkout and initiates the order creation process. It first presents the user with the Ship-To and Bill-To address that will be used for shipment and billing, and gives the user a chance to modify them by providing a Modify link.

We then prompt the user for his specific payment information, which is their credit card information.

Most e-commerce sites now provide users with a choice of direct online payment or payment by phone for people that are reluctant to give their credit card information online. They also provide complex systems of order management and an order tracking mechanism that enables members to check on the status of their orders:

ORDER PROCESSED

bugs, your order has been processed.

Your order tracking number is: #7837-390-33.

Thanks for shopping online !

Enhancing our Membership Based Application

We now have a membership based web application that is functional. Our members can login or register, browse our catalog of products, add and remove items from the electronic cart and checkout their purchased goods. Of course an real web application would have to deal with a much higher level of complexity, but the basic object model and data flow would be similar.

Once you start to feel comfortable with the combination of JSP 1.1, Servlets 2.2, and LDAP server, you can go ahead and try to improve our web application in several ways. You can:

- Modify the LDAP server schema to add attributes that would match more closely the requirements of your application (for example, Ship-to Address and Bill-to Address for customer)
- Try to save the user's GUI preferences to enhance your members' online experience
- Save the cart for users that wish to checkout at a later time
- Add a order tracking system enabling customer to check the status of the orders
- Add database support for storing products
- Add some logic to make sure that strings entered in both password fields match
- Add middle-tier application server support to get more robust, scalable and high-performance web application

Summary

Over this chapter, we have shown how an e-commerce corporation can take advantage of using a membership-based system using Java Server Pages and Servlets technologies combined with a LDAP server in the backend. Specifically, we developed the following topics:

- What is a membership-based application and how it can be used to enhance online customer's browsing experience.
- The use and advantages of LDAP server for access to data models mapping organizational structures.
- How to set up Netscape Directory Server 4.1 to run our Case Study.
- How to take advantage of Java Server Pages and Servlets to build a web application that cleanly separate content and presentation from business logic.
- How to setup JavaServer Web Development Kit 1.0.1 and the iPlanet Web Server 4.1 to run our JSP based web application.
- How to design and implement a component based business object model that will make our application easy to extend.

J2EE
JSP

17

Case Study: J2EE, EJBs, and Tag Libraries

The JavaServer Pages technology is a part of a bigger platform: the **Java2 Enterprise Edition** (J2EE). In this chapter I will try to give a short introduction to what the Java2 Enterprise Edition is about, and show a simple case study where I design a J2EE application (a simple online bookstore) from scratch. I am a part of the team behind the Orion Application Server, a Java application server supporting the full J2EE standard (http://www.orionserver.com).

Introduction to J2EE

Until recently, companies wishing to develop a serious enterprise system have had to build their own framework to handle complex issues like persistence (often including a lot of SQL code), transactions, security, and making sure the system is scalable.

This is hard work, and it is a natural step to develop servers that handle all this "plumbing" for the application to speed up development and ensure scalability and maximum performance. These servers are called application servers.

The Java 2 Enterprise Edition is a specification that aims to provide a standard for Java application servers. This is a good thing for several reasons:

- No investment in a single proprietary platform.
- Best-of-breed implementation. You can select the implementation that best suits your needs and provides your application with the best scalability and performance.
- Price competition between different vendors ensures good pricing.
- The broad knowledge base that comes with an established standard makes it easier to find good developers, good education, and everything that comes with it.

How about the disadvantages, like bad compatibility? Some people might argue that an open specification and different implementations inevitably leads to bad compatibility problems, and this has been the case with several earlier specifications. To avoid this, many measures have been taken: whether this will be enough remains to be seen. The most important things that could make the difference are:

- A Compatibility Test Suite (CTS). All J2EE compliant application servers have to pass a number of tests to guarantee that they indeed work as the specification mandates.
- A Reference Implementation, the J2EE RI, is available, with sources, to vendors that are in the process of building J2EE compliant application servers.
- Binary compatibility for applications. Binary formats like WAR and EAR files can be directly moved between application servers, ensuring that not even recompilation is required when moving an application from one server to another.

Overview

The Java 2 Enterprise Edition is a specification consisting of many parts. J2EE is made up of a lot of different technologies, and a specification for how these work together. The main parts of the J2EE runtime environment are:

- **Application components**. There are four mandatory types of application components that a J2EE compliant product must support:
  - Application clients. These are fat clients written as normal Java applications. They normally access the application server using Remote Method Invocation (RMI).
  - Applets. These are graphical clients that normally execute within a web browser.
  - Servlets and JavaServer Pages.
  - Enterprise JavaBeans. These are components that execute in a container in the application server that manages them and handles much of the "plumbing" for them. These are more thoroughly discussed in a later section.
- **Containers**. Every kind of component lives inside a container that provides the component with runtime services. There is one type of container for every type of component. The most interesting containers for us are the web container that the servlets and JavaServer Pages live in, and the EJB container that manages the Enterprise Java Beans.

- **Resource manager drivers**. A resource manager driver is a driver that provides some kind of connectivity to an external component. The only type that is supported today is a driver that implements any of the J2EE standard services, like Java Messaging Service (JMS), Java DataBase Connectivity (JDBC), or JavaMail. In future versions of the specification something called connectors will be supported, and they will provide support for easily making drivers for connecting to external applications, for example Enterprise Resource Planning (ERP) systems.
- **Database**. Databases are accessible via JDBC, and need to be accessible from all component types except for applets.

The J2EE platform also includes some standard services that must be provided by a J2EE compliant product. They include the following mandatory services:

- HTTP. The J2EE server must make its services available via the HTTP protocol through support for servlets and JSP pages.
- HTTPS. A J2EE server must also be able to layer HTTP over SSL to make connections secure.
- Java Transaction API (JTA). A J2EE server must implement transaction support.
- JavaIDL. J2EE clients are required to be able to connect to CORBA objects using the JavaIDL ORB.
- JDBC
- Java Naming and Directory Interface (JNDI). Naming and directory services are used server wide and have to be present.
- JavaMail and JavaBeans Activation Framework. The J2EE platform includes services for sending email over the Internet. To support this the JavaBeans Activation Framework is also needed.

The following services, however, are optional:

- **RMI-IIOP**. RMI-IIOP support is not yet required by a J2EE implementation, but it will become so in future versions. However, a J2EE application is already required to use the RMI-IIOP APIs when accessing Enterprise Java Beans via RMI.
- **Java Message Service** (JMS) allows enterprise messaging. A J2EE server does not yet have to implement this service, but it will be required in later versions.

Web applications

The servlet 2.2 specification adds the concept of web applications, which are collections of web resources, such as servlets, JSPs, HTML pages, etc. A web application is rooted at a specific path in a web server, and can be conveniently distributed as a Java Archive (JAR) file with a `.war` filename extension. Later in this chapter we will build a web application for the webshop example.

Enterprise applications

The J2EE specification introduces the concept of Enterprise applications. An Enterprise application contains J2EE modules, which could be web applications, EJBs, application clients (normal Java applications talking to a J2EE server), and applets. A J2EE Enterprise archive is packaged as a Java Archive file with a `.ear` filename extension. For a more complete explanation of enterprise applications, read chapter 8 of the J2EE specification, available at http://java.sun.com/j2ee/docs.html.

Sun J2EE Blueprints

The Sun J2EE Blueprints, available online at http://java.sun.com/j2ee/blueprints/, describe how to build J2EE applications. They describe best practices, and contain a real example of a full J2EE application, the Java Pet Store.

Platform roles

One of the important concepts in J2EE is platform roles. The J2EE standard provides separation between different roles, so that different players in the market can specialize on their role. Increased specialization will hopefully increase productivity as individuals and organizations focus on building competence in one area.

The roles that are discussed in the J2EE specification are:

- J2EE Product Provider. This is the application server vendor.
- Application Component Provider. Companies like The Theory Center specialize in building components that take care of certain common tasks: these could be components for e-commerce, or for some other common application.
- Application Assembler. The application assembler uses a set of components and builds an application from them, which is then delivered as an Enterprise Archive (`.ear` file).
- Deployer. The deployer is the one who deploys the applications into production environments. This usually means that the deployer installs, configures, and executes the application.
- System Administrator. The system administrator monitors the application's well-being and administers the application after it has been deployed.
- Tool Provider. Finally, a tool provider makes tools for development and packaging of the application components.

Obviously, one player can have many of these roles, and that is probably the situation we will see until the market has fully matured. We see today that certain companies span across many roles, like BEA Systems (http://www.bea.com), which is a J2EE product provider, an application component provider, and a tool provider.

Platform Contracts

The J2EE platform communicates with the outside world in a few different ways. These ways, known as contracts, are well defined, and separated into:

- APIs. The J2EE Application Programming Interfaces defines the interface between the application components and the platform.
- Network protocols. For access by outside applications, specific network protocols have to be implemented by the J2EE product. These are normally HTTP (and HTTPS) and RMI.
- Deployment descriptors. The deployer specifies the behavior and configuration of a J2EE application using deployment descriptors. These are a standard way to specify the configurations of all the application components using XML.

Scalability and Fault tolerance

In a modern environment, a large enterprise application has to be able to survive large numbers of users, high loads, and even server failures without collapsing. The J2EE platform makes sure this is possible, but does not mandate how it is to be done (for example, how to build clusters of J2EE servers): this is left to the J2EE product provider. Normally these implement transparent failure handling and load balancing across a cluster of servers.

Future directions

Of course, development doesn't stop with the current specification of the J2EE platform. All the covered technologies will develop over time and more problems will be solved. Examples of things that will make an impact shortly are:

- With CORBA 3, the CORBA Component Model provides a superset of the EJB specification for building server side components. There is also a process of standardizing how fault tolerance is handled in CORBA. This might eventually give us the possibility of deploying applications in a cluster across not only multiple machines, but also multiple application server implementations, giving another level of fault tolerance as software failures in one application server can be masked.
- J2EE 1.3 is currently under development, and is likely to include better JMS support and integration of EJB with JMS. It also introduces the Connectors API for access to legacy systems. It will also contain the new versions of the contained standards, like EJB 2.0, JSP 1.2, and Servlet 2.3. These specifications are currently being developed.
- The platform roles will become clearer. As companies specialize in one platform role we might see a new industry. New business opportunities will appear for people who are ready to take on a niche.

Enterprise Java Beans

Enterprise Java Beans (EJB) is a technology specification from Sun, which standardizes how to build server side components for distributed applications.

Overview of EJB

To gain a better understanding of what EJB is all about, let us start with breaking the architecture apart and look at the different parts.

The Components

The components, the actual beans, are large-grained objects representing either some functionality (like a shopping cart) or some data (like a customer bean that holds information about a customer). There is a big difference between these kinds of components, and because of this EJBs exist in two basic types: Session beans, and Entity beans. The main differences are outlined in this table:

Type of bean	Purpose	Client access	Persistence	Transactions
Session bean	Perform work	One client	Normally transient	Usually initiates transactions
Entity bean	Represent persistent object	May have many clients	Persistent	Can take part in transactions

Session Beans

A Session bean is a collection of functionality. It can be seen as an extension to the client, since a session bean is connected to a specific client and when the client disconnects the session bean is destroyed. In other words, a session bean is transient. In the normal case, a session bean does all the work and talks to entity beans for access to persistent data.

Entity Beans

An entity bean represents a persistent object. Often, the content of the bean is stored in a relational database, but the contents could also be stored directly to disk, in an object database, or some other storage. The persistence of the entity beans can either be declarative (the administrator simply defines in what data source and table the bean data is stored) or manual (the component developer explicitly writes code that handles the persistence). These two modes are called **Container Managed Persistence** (CMP) and **Bean Managed Persistence** (BMP).

The advantage of Container Managed Persistence is simplicity, separation, and room for optimization by the application server. Since you don't write any code for the persistence, a layer of complexity is removed. This also means that you don't tie yourself to a certain data store, and it means that the application server can optimize access to the data source since it controls all access to it. Bean Managed Persistence has the advantage of giving the bean developer full control to store data in more customizable or advanced ways. Contrary to what some people believe, CMP usually is much faster than BMP, due to the optimizations the application server can do to the more abstract description. With a BMP bean the bean developer has written actual code for persistence, so there is no room for the application server to use any smart tricks. So, for many reasons, CMP is what should be used in most cases. Only use BMP when you need absolutely full control of the persistence.

To summarize,

Use CMP if you need:	Use BMP if you need:
Performance	Full control
Simplicity	
Database portability	

EJB container

Enterprise Java Beans run within a container, which controls the beans and provides them with system services. The services a container offers are:

- Transactions. The EJB specification provides transactional semantics for components, allowing the component developer to specify transactional properties of components.
- Security
- Remote access (RMI)
- Life cycle management
- Database connection pooling. To provide efficient access to databases it is better to make clients share database connections – this means a new database connection doesn't have to be opened for every client request. Instead there is a pool of a number of connections, and when a client wants a database connection it gets an already opened connection to use so there is no start-up time. When the client doesn't need the connection any more, it's returned to the pool so that it can be reused. The EJB server handles this pooling.

Limitations when writing EJBs

When writing portable components in which resources are handled by an application server, certain things have to be done to make sure that the application server can really take control of resource management. If the EJBs try to access certain resources themselves, it will be impossible for the server to optimize their use. Because of, this some restrictions apply to writing EJBs, and you cannot do any of the following things:

- Manage threads
- Access files directly
- Use graphics
- Listen to a socket or use multicast sockets
- Load a native library
- Change the `SocketFactory` for `ServerSocket` and `Socket`
- Change the `StreamHandlerFactory` for the `URL` class

Stateful and Stateless Operation

There are two kinds of Session EJBs: stateful and stateless. A stateful Session bean is a bean that contains state for the client of the Session bean. Keeping state in a Session bean can be very usable and simple, for example when implementing the shopping cart for the webshop we are building. What does this mean for scalability, though? There needs to be one instance of the stateful session bean for each client, and every instance will contain some state. This could mean that memory usage gets high when there are many concurrent users, and it could also make clustering more difficult since state would have to be replicated to the cluster if a client is to access the bean through another server.

JMS

The Java Message Service (JMS) is a standardized interface that enables Java programs to create, send, receive, and read messages using any enterprise messaging system that supports JMS. Just as JDBC provides an abstraction for database access so that your code will not be database dependent, JMS gives you the possibility to write code that will not be dependent on the underlying messaging system, be it IBM MQSeries, Java Message Queue, BEA Weblogic, Orion, or any JMS compliant messaging system.

JMS Capabilites

JMS supports both **publish/subscribe messaging** and **point-to-point messaging**.

- In publish-subscribe messaging, clients publish messages to, and subscribe to messages from, so-called topics. A topic can be seen as a chat room for messaging clients: everyone can join, and will then receive all messages sent to the topic. It can also send messages with that topic and everyone that is subscribed will receive the message. The topic is fully dynamic and automatically adjusts as publishers and subscribers enter and leave.
- In point-to-point messaging, a client sends a message directly to another client.

The JMS API definitions must be included in a J2EE compliant application server, but the server is not required to actually implement the JMS services. A future version of the J2EE specification will, however, require J2EE-compliant application servers to provide support for JMS messaging, and make those services available to the application developer.

Servlets/JSP

Servlets and JavaServer pages are an important part of J2EE, and are described extensively in this book.

The Java Transaction API and the Java Transaction Service (JTA/JTS)

Transactions enable developers to guarantee that a batch of operations execute atomically. The classic example is that when doing a bank transfer between two accounts the withdrawal from one account and the deposit to another account must *both* succeed, or the changes should be undone to both accounts. Transactions can also be used to guarantee consistency, isolation (if two customers are doing transfers between the same accounts at the same time they must not interfere with one another), and durability (the data is not lost if a failure occurs). A transaction that fulfils these requirements is called an ACID transaction, for Atomicity, Consistency, Isolation, and Durability.

A **distributed transaction** is a transaction that spans multiple data sources, and must be handled with protocols that make sure that the ACID properties are kept between the different databases.

The J2EE platform gives the developer two main options for handling transaction demarcation. The server can automatically handle the boundaries for a transaction, by committing when a method completes without throwing an exception, or you can specify that transaction demarcation is handled manually. In the latter case, a session bean or a servlet uses the `javax.jta.UserTransaction` interface to initiate and commit (or rollback) a transaction. There is also support for application code to register as an event listener for a transaction, and thus for finding out about the progress of a transaction.

Transactions and Enterprise Java Beans

In EJBs, you can let the transactions be controlled automatically by the server (declaratively), you can handle transactions programmatically in an EJB, or they can be handled in client code. Declarative transactions can be specified at the method-level, which means that each method in an enterprise bean class can perform transactions differently. For even finer-grained transaction control, the developer can control transactions programmatically via the Java Transaction API (JTA), which can also be used for client-controlled transactions. Application code can register as a transaction participant by implementing an optional `Synchronization` interface.

The underlying transaction service in a J2EE product is vendor-specific, and does not affect application code. Not all J2EE product vendors support distributed transactions.

Transaction support for an EJB is set to one of the following:

- `NotSupported`: Never participate in a transaction
- `Supports`: If invoked from inside a transaction, take part in it; If not, do not start a new transaction.
- `RequiresNew`: Every method invocation on the component starts a new transaction
- `Required`: If invoked inside a transaction, take part in it; otherwise start a new transaction.
- `Mandatory`: If invoked with an active transaction, participate in it, if not, throw `javax.transaction.TransactionRequiredException`.
- `Never`: If invoked with an active transaction, throw `java.rmi.RemoteException`.

These conditions are summarized in the following table:

EJB's Transaction attribute	Caller's transaction context	EJB's transaction context
`NotSupported`	None	None
`NotSupported`	Transaction	None
`Supports`	None	None
`Supports`	Transaction	Transaction
`RequiresNew`	None	Transaction
`RequiresNew`	Transaction	New transaction
`Required`	None	Transaction
`Required`	Transaction	Transaction
`Mandatory`	None	Exception
`Mandatory`	Transaction	Transaction
`Never`	None	None
`Never`	Transaction	Exception

JDBC

The Java DataBase Connectivity API gives J2EE applications access through a common interface to datasources for which there exist JDBC drivers. Normally this will mean a relational database, and JDBC drivers are available for all popular relational Database Management Systems.

JNDI

The Java Naming and Directory Interface provides a common interface for accessing naming and directory services. Just like with JDBC, JNDI drivers can be made for different naming and directory services, such as Domain Name Service (DNS), COSNaming, LDAP directory servers, and proprietary naming systems. A J2EE server provides a JNDI tree where developers can bind their EJBs, JDBC datasources, JavaMail sessions, and other values.

JavaMail

JavaMail gives a J2EE application the possibility to send and receive emails.

Like many other J2EE technologies, JavaMail is based on pluggable service providers that do the actual work for a specific mail protocol. This means that many different mail protocols can be supported, and implementations for the most common protocols are available.

XML and XSL

In the current J2EE version (1.2) XML support is not mandated, but it will become mandated in the future. We will not mention XML further at present, but restrict ourselves to a brief note about XSL (Extensible Stylesheet Language). XSL is two things:

- A language for transforming XML documents
- An XML vocabulary for specifying formatting semantics.

The first part is referred to as XSLT (XSL Transformations, http://www.w3.org/TR/xslt). It can be used to transform XML documents into HTML, and will be used in this way later in this chapter. The second part is similar to Cascading Style Sheets (CSS), and is used for providing formatting.

For more info about XSL, see http://www.w3.org/Style/XSL/

Introduction to the Case Study

The Java 2 Enterprise Edition is a very broad platform, and simplifies development of many types of applications. To choose one application as an example for this book can therefore be a matter of finding a familiar application that is well understood and well known. For this reason I chose to develop a very simple web store.

Our example is not a supposed to be a complete webstore, but an example of J2EE technologies working together to build an application. If you want to look at a more complete webstore implementation using J2EE that exemplifies many features in a great way, Sun has made a sample webstore (the Java Pet Store) available at http://java.sun.com/blueprints/.

In the example, I show how different approaches can be used for the system: how to achieve a strict separation between different layers in the webstore, and also a more pragmatic approach. This chapter does not contain all the sources, since they are fairly large. Instead, I will just provide parts of the source code in this chapter but of course you can find complete sources online at http://www.wrox.com, along with the `.ear` file for this project. You can also find the webshop live on http://www.orionserver.com/wroxshop/.

Requirements for the Webstore Application

Our requirements for the webstore application can be summarized as follows:

Interface Requirements

The webstore is to be based on the very common shopping cart model. The requirements are that a customer can add items to his shopping cart, change the number of items of a specific product, remove items, and all the time have a clear view of what is in the cart. He should not have to create an account or log in before selecting products to buy.

Feature Requirements

- Customer management: the webstore must include customer management, but does not have to handle personalization in any way. The customers have to reside in a database.
- Product management: the products are found in a database.

Design Requirements

Separation of presentation, logic and data is a well-known mantra of modern software engineering. It is certainly important to encapsulate certain parts of a system to make it easier to understand and to develop and maintain. The common rules of separation claim that you should separate between presentation, logic, and data. In the design section the solution adopted for this is discussed more thoroughly. The application should:

- Exemplify these models and explain the good and bad things with the models (to be explained further):
- Show both XML and HTML JSPs.
- Show both direct access to entity beans, and going via a session bean for all EJB access.
- Show how to use both custom tag extension libraries and third party tag extension libraries.

Limitations

This example is not supposed to demonstrate how to build and deploy a real life production webstore. The purpose is to show how to use different J2EE technologies together. For that reason, many issues are not handled in this example, including:

- Security. No regard is taken to security in this simple example. Deploying the webstore using the HTTPS protocol is very simple and basically an administration issue that is server-dependent.
- Order processing.
- Payment. Obviously, in this example no real purchases are made and none of the issues with payment are handled.
- Product categories. Normally we would like to present a hierarchical view of products with different product categories. In this example we skip that part but we keep this in mind when we design things and discuss how it can be easily added.

Webstore Design

So, with the requirements in place, we can start to design the application.

Basic Architectural Design

One of the requirements was that we separate different parts of the implementation from each other. The MVC model was discussed, and this is the fundamental division for a normal computer program, but it is a pretty non-granular division and for a specific system there are usually aspects that should be separated from each other. For the webstore, I have chosen to divide the application into four different main layers, some of which contain sub-layers. Normally only three layers are described, but I chose to introduce an information structure layer which, in my opinion, does not quite fall into the presentation layer. This information structure layer contains information about the structure and contents of the presented information. Later, I will start by designing this layer.

Layers

The layers of our application are then:

- Presentation layer, consisting of the presentation details (colors, fonts, etc.) using CSS, and the presentation structure, using XSLT.
- Information structure layer, using JSPs to generate XML.
- Logic layer, using tag extension libraries to interface the logic to the information structure layer, and session beans.
- Data layer, comprising entity beans (data interface) and the database.

It might seem like overkill to use XML/XSL instead of plain HTML with this structure, since the use of tag extension libraries will almost fully separate the logic from the HTML pages. For this reason, I chose to demonstrate both techniques: some JSPs will use XML and some pages will use HTML. This example is not a recommendation on how to make the best web store and, in many cases, if you use JSP 1.1 and tag extension libraries, you can get nice separation without XML. The reason for using XML here is to demonstrate how it can be done and, even though I've mostly spoken about separation, there are some other advantages of using XML that might be applicable in some cases. Some of these are:

- XML will be (and already is in some cases) handled directly by clients in the future. This means that the XSL can live client-side and the presentation can be changed without a round trip to the server.
- XSLT provides advanced transformation rules that can be performed without writing any code. Standard tag extension libraries will later make this possible in pure HTML JSPs.

The structure now looks like this:

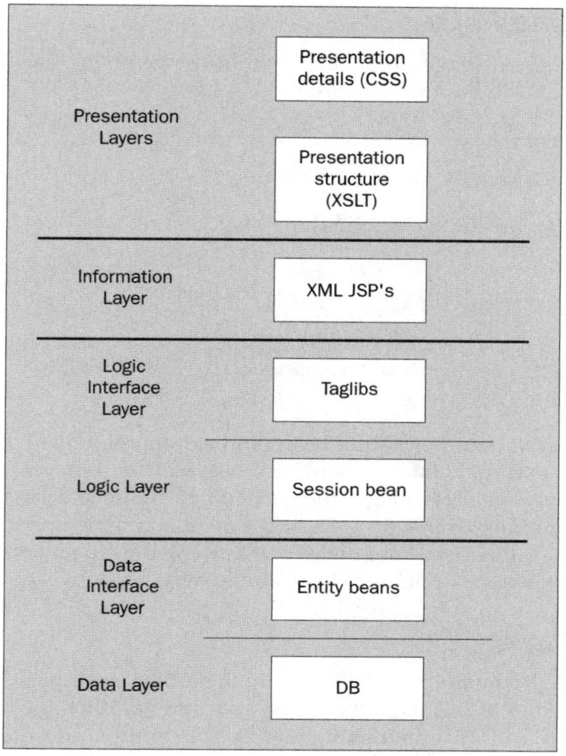

Designing the JSPs

To start with, we design the information structure of the webstore. I chose to start at this end because this is something that is easy to imagine without knowing the other parts of the system. If we start with the actual structure of our site, we will get to know what will be required for the other parts. In this section, all the JSPs will be designed in XML. However, because we are aiming to show different ways of doing things, not all JSPs will be implemented in XML. Hopefully you will see the advantages and disadvantages of different approaches.

The Welcome Page

The first page a user will see is what we call the welcome page. In this case, we will let the welcome page simply contain a product browsing facility, and a control bar where you can see what is in your shopping cart, and also log in, proceed to checkout, etc. We choose to separate this into two HTML frames, one for the product browsing, and one for the control bar.

The Product Browsing Page

The top frame will contain the page from which you browse and buy the actual products. The structure of this is simple; the page will basically consist of:

- A title and welcome text
- A structure containing the items in the store

If we model this in XML, we could get something like:

```
<title>
  Welcome to the Professional JavaServer Pages sample store
</title>
<items>
  <item name="foo" price="$200" image="foo.gif"/>
</items>
```

The welcome text is part of the information layer, and can therefore be coded into the actual JSP. The items, however, should exist in a database and be retrieved from it in real time, so that up to date product information is always presented to the user. When we need access to data in a database, we use an Entity bean as the interface to this data. Exactly how this is done is decided later in the implementation section, but we make a note now that we will need an entity EJB for the products. We will need to know this when we design our beans in the next section.

The Toolbar/Cart Page

The bottom frame of the welcome page will contain the toolbar/cart page. From now on I will just call it the cart page. The structure of this page should be very simple. We basically want to present the contents of the cart (and be able to modify it), and be able to proceed to checkout and log in or out. For this, we need the cart contents and the user needs to be logged in. We model this as XML and it looks something like:

```
<cart>
  <item name="foo" price="$200" count="2">
  <item name="bar" price="$300" count="1">
</cart>
<user name="baz"/>
```

Of course, the items and user will not be hard-coded into the page but extracted from EJBs through the use of tag extensions for cart and user management.

The Checkout Page

The checkout page is the page the customer goes to when he is done browsing the product. This page will look a lot like the cart page: it will present the items in the cart, allow a customer to log in and log out, but it also needs to be able to present the customer information. This means we will have a structure that looks something like this (in XML):

```
<cart>
  <item name="foo" price="$200" count="2">
  <item name="bar" price="$300" count="1">
</cart>
<user name="foo" email="foo@bar.com" address="baz" postalcode="12345"/>
```

As in the cart page, the user information and the cart information will be got using tag extensions.

Pages for functions

Beside our normal viewable pages, we will need a few JSPs that simply do something and don't present anything.

- Login page
- Logout page

Since these do not present anything they will basically just be calls to tag extensions using EJBs, and will therefore not need any information structure design.

Designing the EJBs

We have already concluded that we need a few Enterprise Java Beans for our design. We start by designing our cart bean, which is connected to a certain client for which it holds conversational state. Thus, it is a part of a stateful business process and can be nicely modeled by a stateful session bean. We will keep this Session bean in the JSP Session for easy access.

CartBean

The cart bean should, as we concluded, be a stateful session bean, storing the contents of a customer's shopping cart. A decision we must make is whether to expose our internal storage structure to the outside world. Normally this should be encapsulated and `getProducts()` should just return a collection of items. In this case, however, I chose to return a `HashMap` hashed on the product id and containing the number of that item in the cart, because that is a very simple way to keep track of the items. That means the cart must support these operations:

- `addProduct(String isbn)`
- `HashMap getProducts()`
- `updateProduct(String isbn, int count)`
- `getTotalCost()`
- `login(String name, String password)`
- `logout()`
- `getCustomer()`

ProductBean

The product bean represents a product in a database, and is a typical entity bean. To simplify development we will use Container Managed Persistence. The bean will contain a few attributes:

- ISBN. This will be the primary key (it is a good primary key since it is unique for every product).
- Title (of the product)
- Price
- Author

The product-browsing page needs to be able to get all the products. This can be done using a custom finder, which we call `findAll()`. How this is implemented is discussed in the implementation section.

CustomerBean

The customer bean also represents a persistent entity and is therefore modeled as another CMP entity bean. The attributes for this bean are:

- Name
- Password
- Address
- Postal code
- E-mail

Designing the Tag Extension Libraries

Our design requires two tag extension libraries, for the User library and the Cart.

User Tag Extension Library

The User tag extension library has to be able to let a user log in and out, and needs to allow JSPs to find out who the currently logged in user is. We also want a tag that can be used to find out if there is no user logged in, to be able to present a login form in that case. The only function that needs to take any arguments is `login`, which needs a username and a password. These arguments should not, however, be hard coded in the page, since this will be input from the actual user, so the arguments to the `login` tag should be the parameter names that will contain the username and password. With this design, the tags look something like this:

The login tag:

```
<user:login name="username" password="password"/>
```

(attributes are params, not hardcoded names)

The `logout` tag:

```
<user:logout/>
```

The `getUser` tag:

```
<user:getUser id="user">
  Contents to only exist if someone is logged in.
  The logged in user is made available as the user variable.
</user:getUser>
```

The `noUser` tag:

```
<user:noUser>
  Contents to exist only if no-one is logged in.
</user:noUser>
```

Cart Tag Extension Library

The Cart tag extension library is used to add items to the Cart EJB, and to update the products that have already been put there. For this, one tag is enough – the case of removing a product is covered by updating a product's count to `0`. The attribute `count` is optional. If it is not set, the product count will be set to `1`: this is used for adding a product.

```
<cart:updateProduct product="productname" count="1"/>
```

For the cart page, and for the checkout and order, we also need to be able to iterate through all products in the `Cart` bean, so we need a tag that iterates through the cart:

```
<cart:iterate id="product" countid="count">
  Contents to iterate
</cart:iterate>
```

Finally, we also need to get the total cost of all products in the cart:

```
<cart:totalCost/>
```

That concludes our basic design of our components. This design does not include design of our XSLTs or CSSs, because these parts are not central to the concepts I am trying to demonstrate. The CSS part will be skipped totally for the rest of this chapter.

Implementing Webstore

We can now go through the implementations of our different parts step by step. We have designed all the important parts, so where we start implementing can simply be a choice of what can be tested without implementing the rest. We start implementing the EJBs, since they can function without any of the other components. But before doing this, we need to decide on the package naming. The following packages are used:

- `com.wrox.webshop.ejb.cart`
- `com.wrox.webshop.ejb.customer`
- `com.wrox.webshop.ejb.product`
- `com.wrox.webshop.tags`

Implementing the EJBs

We want to keep all our EJBs in one package, that we will turn into a `.jar` file for easy distribution and for inclusion into a `.ear` Enterprise Archive.

For this we use the following directory structure:

```
META-INF/
  ejb-jar.xml
com/wrox/webshop/ejb/
  cart/
    Classes for the Cart EJB
  customer/
    Classes for the Customer EJB
  product/
    Classes for the Product EJB
```

The file ejb-jar.xml is the deployment descriptor for the EJBs, and is discussed later in this section.

Let us implement the EJBs in the same order as we designed them, starting with the cart bean.

CartBean

You need to create 3 files for your bean: an interface for the bean, a home for the bean and the bean itself: Cart.java, CartHome.java and CartBean.java.

Cart.java defines the interface for your bean. It is an interface and must extend EJBObject, and is placed in the com.wrox.webshop.ejb.cart package .To be able to use the RMI and java.util classes, as well as the EJB and our own packages, we add a few imports. To the top of the file, add the following:

```
package com.wrox.webshop.ejb.cart;

import java.util.*;
import java.rmi.*;
import javax.ejb.*;

import com.wrox.webshop.ejb.customer.*;
```

After these imports we put the definition of the interface. It should look like:

```
public interface Cart extends EJBObject
```

Now we will define the methods of the interface. According to the design, this bean will have seven methods. They must all throw RemoteException and be public. Some of the methods must be able to throw other exception. A failed login must result in an exception, and the calculation of the total cost could possibly go wrong. I added a generic CartException for this case. These definitions should look like:

```
  public void addProduct(String isbn) throws RemoteException;

  public HashMap getProducts() throws RemoteException;

  public void updateProduct(String isbn, int count) throws RemoteException;

  public int getTotalCost() throws CartException, RemoteException;

  public void login(String name, String password)
    throws RemoteException, LoginException;

  public void logout() throws RemoteException;

  public Customer getCustomer() throws RemoteException;
```

Now the definition of the Cart interface is done. Now let us create the CartHome interface. Again, we start by specifying the package and importing a few classes:

```
package com.wrox.webshop.ejb.cart;

import java.rmi.*;
import javax.ejb.*;
```

The CartHome interface must extend the EJBHome interface:

```
public interface CartHome extends EJBHome
```

and will only contain one method, create(), which must throw CreateException and RemoteException:

```
   public Cart create() throws CreateException, RemoteException;
```

Now the CartHome interface is done, and we can begin to write the code for the actual bean implementation. This is done in the class CartBean. As usual, we start with package definition and imports. The class itself must implement SessionBean.

```
package com.wrox.webshop.ejb.cart;

import java.rmi.*;
import java.util.*;

import javax.ejb.*;
import javax.naming.*;

import com.wrox.webshop.ejb.product.*;
import com.wrox.webshop.ejb.customer.*;

public class CartBean implements SessionBean
```

The contents of the cart is kept as a HashMap. We also need to keep the logged in Customer and we reserve a field for the SessionContext:

```
   private SessionContext context;
   private HashMap items;
   private Customer customer;
```

The SessionBean interface contains a few methods we must implement, which gives the bean access to its context/environment. These are:

- public void ejbCreate()
- public void ejbActivate()
- public void ejbPassivate()
- public void ejbRemove()
- public void setSessionContext(SessionContext context)

In this bean we don't need to implement these, but just give them empty bodies, except for the setSessionContext() method which we simply implement by storing the context in a private variable in case we need it later.

Now we implement the actual functionality of the bean, by implementing the methods we earlier defined to be in the interface Cart. These were addProduct(String isbn), getProducts(), updateProduct(), getTotalCost(), login(String username, String password), logout(), and getCustomer().

The method addProduct() should just add a product to the cart. If the product already exists in the cart, we increase the count by 1:

```
public void addProduct(String isbn) {
  if (isbn != null && !(isbn.equals("null"))) {
    Integer count = (Integer) items.get(isbn);
    if (count == null) count = new Integer(0);
    items.put(isbn, new Integer(count.intValue()+1));
  }
}
```

The method getProducts() should just return the Hashtable:

```
public Hashtable getProducts() {
  return items;
}
```

The method updateProduct(String isbn, int count) should update the count of a specific product to the count specified; if the count is 0, it will be removed.

```
public void updateProduct(String isbn, int count) {
  if (isbn != null) {
    if (count==0) {
      items.remove(isbn);
    } else {
      items.put(isbn, new Integer(count));
    }
  }
}
```

The method for calculating the total cost looks like this:

```
public int getTotalCost() throws RemoteException, CartException {
  int totalCost = 0;
  Iterator iterator = items.keySet().iterator();

  try {
    InitialContext context = new InitialContext();
    ProductHome productHome =
      (ProductHome) javax.rmi.PortableRemoteObject
        .narrow(context.lookup("Product"), ProductHome.class);

    while (iterator.hasNext()) {
      try {
        String productID = (String) iterator.next();
        Product product = productHome.findByPrimaryKey(productID);
        totalCost += product.getPrice()
                     * ((Integer) items.get(productID)).intValue();
      } catch (FinderException e) {
        throw new CartException(e.getMessage());
      }
    }
  } catch (NamingException e) {
    throw new CartException(e.getMessage());
  }
  return totalCost;
}
```

The `login()`, `logout()`, and `getCustomer()` methods are implemented as:

```
  public void login(String username, String password)
          throws LoginException, RemoteException {
    try {
      InitialContext context = new InitialContext();
      CustomerHome customerHome =
        (CustomerHome) javax.rmi.PortableRemoteObject
          .narrow(context.lookup("Customer"), CustomerHome.class);
      Customer customer = customerHome.findByPrimaryKey(username);
      if (customer.authenticate(password)) {
        this.customer = customer;
      } else {
        throw new LoginException();
      }
    } catch (FinderException e) {
      throw new LoginException();
    } catch (NamingException e) {
      throw new LoginException();
    }
  }

  public void logout() {
    customer = null;
  }

  public Customer getCustomer() {
    return customer;
  }
```

Now the `CartBean` class is all done, and we finish off by defining the two exceptions we use:

```
package com.wrox.webshop.ejb.cart;

public class CartException extends Exception {
  public CartException() {}

  public CartException(String message) {
    super(message);
  }
}
```

```
package com.wrox.webshop.ejb.cart;

public class LoginException extends Exception {
  public LoginException() {}

  public LoginException(String message) {
    super(message);
  }
}
```

Now all classes for the bean are done, and we proceed to the next bean before writing the bean deployment descriptor.

ProductBean

The product bean was designed to be a CMP (Container Managed Persistence) Entity bean with a few attributes:

- isbn, (the primary key)
- Title of the product
- author
- price

It also was designed to implement one custom finder method, `findAll()`, that would return all existing products.

This means the bean should basically just contain these fields and their get-methods, and set-methods for those fields that are not read-only. We make all but the isbn attribute (which we call `ID`) both writeable and readable, giving us a remote interface that looks like this:

```
package com.wrox.webshop.ejb.product;

import java.rmi.*;
import javax.ejb.*;

public interface Product extends EJBObject {
  public String getID() throws RemoteException;
  public String getName() throws RemoteException;
  public String getAuthor() throws RemoteException;
  public double getPrice() throws RemoteException;

  public void setName(String name) throws RemoteException;
  public void setAuthor(String author) throws RemoteException;
  public void setPrice(double price) throws RemoteException;
}
```

The home interface will also be pretty simple. An entity bean normally contains at least a `create()` method and a `findByPrimaryKey()` method: the first gets called when an Entity bean is created using the home, and the `findByPrimaryKey()` method finds an object based on its primary key. We also want to be able to find books based on the title (name). We call this one `findByName(String name)`. Besides these methods, we only need the `findAll()` method:

```
package com.wrox.webshop.ejb.product;

import javax.ejb.*;
import java.rmi.*;
import java.util.*;

public interface ProductHome extends EJBHome {
  public Product create(String id)
          throws CreateException, RemoteException;

  public Product findByPrimaryKey(String key)
          throws RemoteException, FinderException;

  public Collection findAll() throws RemoteException, FinderException;

  public Collection findByName(String name)
          throws RemoteException, FinderException;
}
```

Now it is time to make the actual bean class, which will simply be an implementation of our remote interface with the additional methods that needs to be defined when implementing the interface `javax.ejb.EntityBean`. Note that we do not actually define the `ProductBean` class to implement the `Product` interface in the class declaration; this is possible since the `ProductBean` will never be used directly. Rather, the application server will handle these invocations and generate classes that do implement the interface. For space reasons, the full source is not listed here, but you can find it online.

CustomerBean

I choose to implement the `CustomerBean` as an extension of the `EJBUser` implementation that comes with the Orion Application Server. It can easily be built from scratch without using this `EJBUser` bean if you are using another application server. In the design we concluded that the `CustomerBean` would be another CMP entity bean and that we would need these attributes:

- Name
- Password
- Address
- Postal code
- E-mail

The `EJBUser` bean already contains a name and a password.

As usual we start with the remote interface – we do not show the code again. The home interface will not contain anything special this time, just the `create()` and `findByPrimaryKey()` methods. The primary key is the username, which must be unique. The `create()` method will this time require a username and a password. Again, the source can be found online.

Having created the remote and home interfaces, we make the actual bean class. This one is basically the same as for the `Product` bean, but without the methods that are inherited from the `EJBUserBean`.

Deployment Descriptors

J2EE uses deployment descriptors, which contain meta-information about components. The descriptors are written in XML format, but different component types uses different tags. In the deployment descriptor for EJBs you define such things as

- Bean properties, like name, type (Session or Entity), classes, fields (for entity beans), etc.
- Transaction settings
- Security settings

The deployment descriptor for our EJB jar is called `ejb-jar.xml`, and looks like this:

```
<?xml version="1.0"?>
<!DOCTYPE ejb-jar SYSTEM "ejb-jar.dtd">
<ejb-jar>
  <description>Wrox webshop beans</description>
  <enterprise-beans>
    <entity>
      <description>Product in the webshop</description>
      <ejb-name>Product</ejb-name>
      <home>com.wrox.webshop.ejb.product.ProductHome</home>
      <remote>com.wrox.webshop.ejb.product.Product</remote>
```

```
    <ejb-class>com.wrox.webshop.ejb.product.ProductBean</ejb-class>
    <prim-key-class>java.lang.String</prim-key-class>
    <reentrant>True</reentrant>
    <persistence-type>Container</persistence-type>
    <cmp-field><field-name>id</field-name></cmp-field>
    <cmp-field><field-name>name</field-name></cmp-field>
    <cmp-field><field-name>author</field-name></cmp-field>
    <cmp-field><field-name>price</field-name></cmp-field>
    <primkey-field>id</primkey-field>
  </entity>
  <entity>
    <display-name>com.wrox.webshop.ejb.customer.Customer</display-name>
    <description>Customer in the webshop</description>
    <ejb-name>Customer</ejb-name>
    <home>com.wrox.webshop.ejb.customer.CustomerHome</home>
    <remote>com.wrox.webshop.ejb.customer.Customer</remote>
    <ejb-class>com.wrox.webshop.ejb.customer.CustomerBean</ejb-class>
    <persistence-type>Container</persistence-type>
    <primkey-class>java.lang.String</primkey-class>
    <reentrant>False</reentrant>
    <cmp-field>
      <field-name>username</field-name>
    </cmp-field>
    <cmp-field>
      <field-name>password</field-name>
    </cmp-field>
    <cmp-field>
      <field-name>locale</field-name>
    </cmp-field>
    <cmp-field>
      <field-name>postalCode</field-name>
    </cmp-field>
    <cmp-field>
      <field-name>address</field-name>
    </cmp-field>
    <cmp-field>
      <field-name>email</field-name>
    </cmp-field>
    <primkey-field>username</primkey-field>
  </entity>

  <session>
    <description>Webshop cart</description>
    <ejb-name>Cart</ejb-name>
    <home>com.wrox.webshop.ejb.cart.CartHome</home>
    <remote>com.wrox.webshop.ejb.cart.Cart</remote>
    <ejb-class>com.wrox.webshop.ejb.cart.CartBean</ejb-class>
    <session-type>Stateful</session-type>
    <transaction-type>Container</transaction-type>
  </session>
</enterprise-beans>
<assembly-descriptor>
  <container-transaction>
    <method>
      <ejb-name>Customer</ejb-name>
      <method-name>*</method-name>
    </method>
    <method>
      <ejb-name>Product</ejb-name>
      <method-name>*</method-name>
    </method>
```

```
        <method>
          <ejb-name>Cart</ejb-name>
          <method-name>*</method-name>
        </method>
        <trans-attribute>NotSupported</trans-attribute>
      </container-transaction>
    </assembly-descriptor>
  </ejb-jar>
```

After having finished the deployment descriptor, our EJBs are all done. We compile our java files and package it all up into a file called `webshop-ejb.jar`, which contains the bean classes and the deployment descriptor `ejb-jar.xml` in the `META-INF` directory, as described earlier in this section.

Implementing the Tag Extension Libraries

For the sake of not going through the same process twice, I chose to combine the two tag extension libraries I designed into one. This was purely done to make the example more accessible, in book form and not something I am would recommend in a normal project.

In the design section, we decided that the user tag extension library needs four tags and that the cart tag extension library also needs four tags. These eight tags are:

the `login` tag:

```
<user:login name="username" password="password"/>
```

the `logout` tag:

```
<user:logout/>
```

the `getUser` tag:

```
<user:getUser id="user">
  Contents to exist only if someone is logged in.
  The logged in user is made available as the user variable.
</user:getUser>
```

the `noUser` tag:

```
<user:noUser>
  Contents to exist only if no-one is logged in.
</user:noUser>
```

the `updateProduct` tag:

```
<cart:updateProduct product="productname" count="1"/>
```

the `iterate` tag:

```
<cart:iterate id="product" countid="count">
  Contents to iterate
</cart:iterate>
```

and finally, the totalcost tag:

```
<cart:totalCost/>
```

The login and logout tag need only to call the login() and logout() methods on the Cart session bean. The getUser() tag should use the Cart bean to get the logged in user/customer and add an implicit variable to the JSP, and the noUser tag should just use the Cart to see if anyone is logged in and execute the contained code if nobody is. The updateProduct() tag will be an invocation to the Cart bean, the iterate tag will iterate over the results of a call to the Cart bean, and finally the totalCost tag will simply call the corresponding method on the Cart. As you might have noticed, all these tags contain very little actual logic, but they rather make up an interface between the JSPs and the EJBs. I still see them as a part of the logic layer, but they make up the logic layer's interface towards the information structure layer.

Tag extension libraries are covered in Chapter 8, and we will not cover them in detail here. We will look in only at the getUser tag here.

The getUser tag needs to get a reference to the Cart. This reference will be kept as a JSP session variable, and can easily be retrieved by the tag by accessing the pageContext. The contents of the tag should be evaluated only if someone is logged on, in which case a variable should also be set so that the contents of the tag can access the user.

```
package com.wrox.webshop.tags;

import java.rmi.*;
import javax.servlet.jsp.*;
import javax.servlet.jsp.tagext.*;

import com.wrox.webshop.ejb.customer.*;
import com.wrox.webshop.ejb.cart.*;

public class GetUserTag extends TagSupport {

  /**
   * Method called at start of Tag
   * @return either a EVAL_BODY_INCLUDE or a SKIP_BODY
   */
  public int doStartTag() throws javax.servlet.jsp.JspException {

    // if no cart is available or noone logged in, don't evaluate body
    int returnCode = SKIP_BODY;

    // get cart.
    Cart cart = (Cart) pageContext.getSession().getAttribute("cart");

    if (cart != null) {
      try {
        Customer customer = cart.getCustomer();
        if (customer != null) {
          pageContext.setAttribute(getId(), customer);
          returnCode = EVAL_BODY_INCLUDE;
        }
      } catch (RemoteException e) {
        throw new JspException(e.getMessage());
      }
    }
```

```
      return returnCode;
    }
  }
```

A mentioned, this tag will need to introduce a new variable for access by the JSP content of the tag. Because of this we also need a `TagExtraInfo` class that will tell the JSP compiler about this variable:

```
package com.wrox.webshop.tags;

import javax.servlet.jsp.tagext.*;

public class UserExtraInfo extends TagExtraInfo {
  public UserExtraInfo() {}

  public VariableInfo[] getVariableInfo(TagData data) {
    return new VariableInfo[] {
      new VariableInfo(data.getId(),
                       "com.wrox.webshop.ejb.customer.Customer",
                       true, VariableInfo.AT_BEGIN)
    };
  }
}
```

Finally, the tag descriptor has to be written. The descriptor for this tag needs to contain a reference not only to the `Tag` class, but also to the `TagExtraInfo` class for the tag. We also want to specify that the content of the body of the tag is JSP, and that we have one attribute, called `id`, which is required. Based on this specification, the tag descriptor looks like this:

```
  <tag>
    <name>getUser</name>
    <tagclass>com.wrox.webshop.tags.GetUserTag</tagclass>
    <teiclass>com.wrox.webshop.tags.UserExtraInfo</teiclass>
    <bodycontent>JSP</bodycontent>
    <info>getUser</info>
    <attribute>
      <name>id</name>
      <required>true</required>
    </attribute>
  </tag>
```

We merge the individual tag descriptors into a tag library descriptor (`.tld`) file, which becomes the deployment descriptor for our tag extension library.

We will also want to package the tags into one `carttags.jar` file for easy distribution and use in other projects. For this we need this file structure:

```
META-INF/
  Taglib.tld
com/wrox/webshop/tags/
  Tag classes
```

When we have this structure, we can easily create the `carttags.jar` using the `jar` tool included in the Java 2 SDK.

Now we have implemented the tag library, we have everything that is needed for the JSPs to function, so let's get on to those.

Implementing the JSPs

We implement the JSPs in the same order as we designed them. I chose to describe three JSPs in detail here: the product browsing page, the toolbar/cart page, and the logout page. The rest can be found online at http://www.wrox.com.

The Product Browsing Page

When we designed this page, we decided to use this structure for the page:

```
<title>
  Welcome to the Professional JavaServer Pages Book Store
</title>
<items>
  <item name="foo" price="$200" image="foo.gif"/>
</items>
```

The items were to be fetched from the database via the entity bean `Product`, and we want to use the `Product` EJB to generate a list of `<item>` tags. To do this we can use a tag extension library for using EJBs that is supplied with the Orion Application Server, and is available for free so that it can be used with any J2EE application server. You can download it at http://www.orionserver.com/tags/. This tag library contains tags that allow us to easily get hold of the home interface of beans, and to iterate through the existing beans. In this case this is done in the following way:

```
<ejb:useHome id="productHome"
    type="com.wrox.webshop.ejb.product.ProductHome"
    location="Product" />
<ejb:iterate id="product" type="com.wrox.webshop.ejb.product.Product"
    collection="<%=productHome.findAll()%>" max="-1">
  <item isbn="<jsp:getProperty name="product" property="ID"/>"
      name="<jsp:getProperty name="product" property="name"/>"
      price="<jsp:getProperty name="product" property="price"/>"/>
</ejb:iterate>
```

Together, this gives us the JSP:

```
<?xml version="1.0"?>
<?xml-stylesheet href="/items.xsl"?>
<%@ taglib uri="ejbtags.jar" prefix="ejb" %>
<doc>
  <title>
    Welcome to the Professional JavaServer Pages Book Store
  </title>
  <items>
    <ejb:useHome id="productHome"
        type="com.wrox.webshop.ejb.product.ProductHome"
        location="Product" />
    <ejb:iterate id="product" type="com.wrox.webshop.ejb.product.Product"
        collection="<%=productHome.findAll()%>" max="-1">
      <item isbn="<jsp:getProperty name="product" property="ID"/>"
```

```
            name="<jsp:getProperty name="product" property="name"/>"
            price="<jsp:getProperty name="product" property="price"/>"/>
      </ejb:iterate>
    </items>
  </doc>
```

The result of this page will look something like this (assuming the database has been populated with books and assuming that an XSL file has been written.):

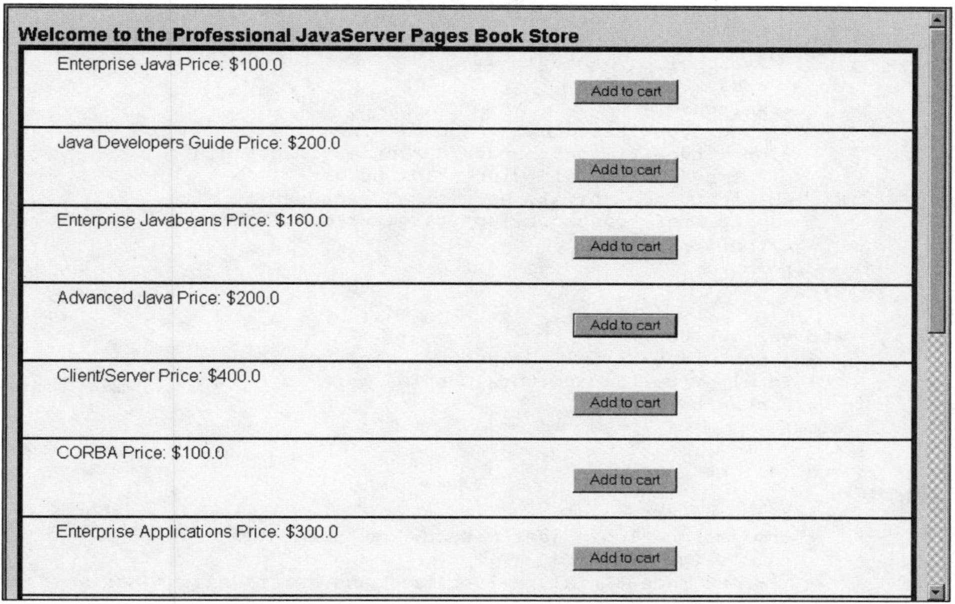

The Toolbar/Cart Page

This page was designed to have an information structure that looks like:

```
<cart>
  <item name="foo" price="$200" count="2">
  <item name="bar" price="$300" count="1">
</cart>
<user name="baz"/>
```

We want to implement this as a HTML JSP, to show how this looks compared to an XML JSP. This means that the JSP gets a fair bit larger, but we can still keep nearly all logic out of it by using tag libraries.

```
<%@ taglib uri="carttags.jar" prefix="cart" %>
<%@ taglib uri="ejbtags.jar" prefix="ejb" %>
<%@ page import="com.wrox.webshop.ejb.cart.*"%>
<%@ page import="com.wrox.webshop.ejb.customer.*"%>

<html>
  <body bgcolor="#ffee77">
    <cart:updateProduct product="<%= request.getParameter("product") %>"/>
```

```
<table width="100%" border="0" cellspacing="0" cellpadding="0">
  <tr>
    <td valign="top">
      <form action="cart.jsp" method="get" name="">
        <select name="product">
          <cart:iterate id="product" countid="count">
            <jsp:useBean id="product" scope="page"
                type="com.wrox.webshop.ejb.product.Product"/>
            <jsp:useBean id="count" scope="page"
                type="java.lang.Integer"/>
            <option value="<%= product.getID() %>" selected>
              <%= count %> of <%= product.getName() %>
            </option>
          </cart:iterate>
        </select>
        <input type="text" name="count" size="1">
        <input type="image" border="0" name="imageField"
            src="update.gif" width="10" height="10">
        <b><font face="Arial, Helvetica, sans-serif" size="-2">
            <a href="checkout.jsp" target="_top">(Checkout)</a>
        </font></b>
      </form>
    </td>

    <td valign="top">
      <b><font face="Arial, Helvetica, sans-serif" size="-2">
        Total price: $<cart:totalCost/>
      </font></b>
    </td>

    <td valign="top">

    <cart:noUser>
      <form action="login.jsp" method="get" name="">
        <div align="right">
          <font face="Arial, Helvetica, sans-serif" size="--">
            Name
          </font>
          <b><font face="Arial, Helvetica, sans-serif" size="-2">
            <input type="text" name="Name" size="10">
          </font></b>
          <font face="Arial, Helvetica, sans-serif" size="-1">
            Password
          </font>
          <b><font face="Arial, Helvetica, sans-serif" size="-2">
            <input type="password" name="Password" size="10">
            <input type="submit" value="Log in">
          </font></b>
        </div>
      </form>
    </cart:noUser>

    <cart:getUser id="user">
        <font face="Arial, Helvetica, sans-serif" size="-1">
          User <%= user.getName() %> logged in
        </font>
      <a href="logout.jsp?page=cart.jsp">(Log out)</a>
    </cart:getUser>
  </tr>
</table>
</body>
</html>
```

The result of this page looks something like this, with the product browsing page in the top frame and the cart in the lower frame:

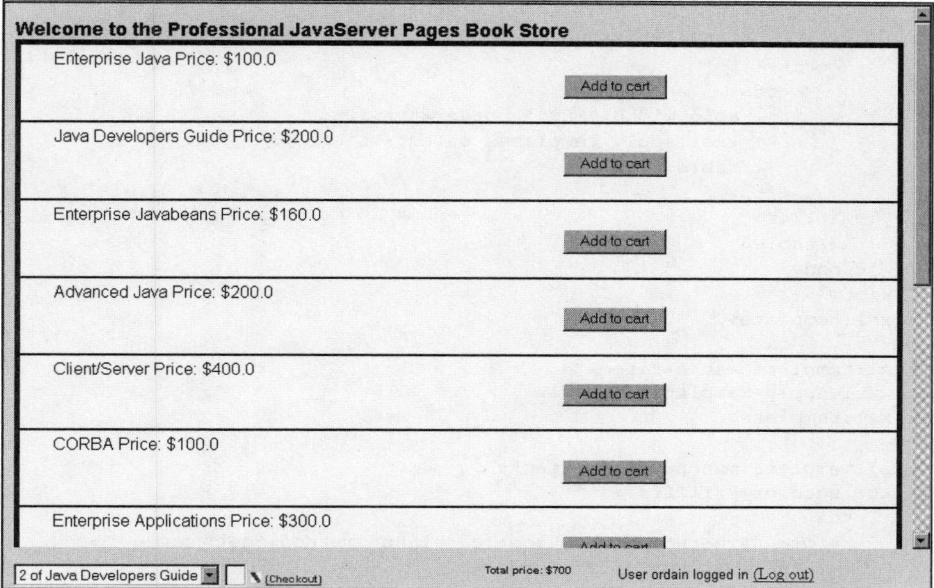

The Logout Page

The third kind of JSP we use is a pure functional JSP without any presentation, and some people might say that this should be a Servlet and not a JSP. This being a book about JSP, I still want to show how this could be made using a JSP in a nice, clean way. Since this logout function might be used from many places, I include the possibility to supply a page parameter that specifies what file to load after the logout has been performed.

```
<%@ taglib uri="carttags.jar" prefix="user" %>

<user:logout/>
<jsp:forward page=" <%= request.getParameter("page") %>"/>
```

With all our JSPs implemented, we finally need to implement the XSL file we use for the product browsing page.

Implementing the XSL

The XSL transformation file for the product page mainly contains HTML. The key statements that get the information from the JSP and insert them into the HTML output are highlighted:

```
<xsl:stylesheet xmlns:xsl="http://www.w3.org/XSL/Transform/1.0"
                xmlns="http://www.w3.org/TR/xhtml1">

  <xsl:output method="xml" indent="yes"/>

  <xsl:template match="doc">
    <html>
```

```
      <body bgcolor="#ffee77">
        <font face="Arial, Helvetica, sans-serif" size="+1"><b>
          <xsl:value-of select="title"/>
        </b></font>
        <table width="100%" border="0" cellpadding="1" bgcolor="#000000">
          <tr>
            <td>
              <table width="100%" border="0">
                <xsl:apply-templates select="items"/>
              </table>
            </td>
          </tr>
        </table>
      </body>
    </html>
  </xsl:template>

  <xsl:template match="items">
    <xsl:apply-templates/>
  </xsl:template>

  <xsl:template match="items/item">
    <tr bgcolor="#ffffff">
      <td>
        <form target="cart" action="cart.jsp" method="get" name="">
          <table width="100%" border="0">
            <tr>
              <td width="3%"></td>
              <td width="71%">
                <font face="Arial, Helvetica, sans-serif">
                  <xsl:value-of select="@name"/>
                  Price: $<xsl:value-of select="@price"/>
                </font>
              </td>
              <td width="26%"></td>
            </tr>
            <tr>
              <td width="3%"></td>
              <td width="71%">
                <div align="right">
                  <input type="Submit" name="action" value="Add to cart"/>
                  <input type="Hidden" name="product" value="{@isbn}"/>
                </div>
              </td>
              <td width="26%"></td>
            </tr>
          </table>
        </form>
      </td>
    </tr>
  </xsl:template>
</xsl:stylesheet>
```

Packaging the Web Application

As well packaging the EJBs into webshop-ejb.jar and the tag library into carttags.jar, we want to package our entire web application as an archive. To do this we prepare a file structure for the web application:

```
WEB-INF/
web.xml
  lib/
    carttags.jar
    ejbtags.jar
    utiltags.jar

cart.jsp
checkout.jsp
index.html
items.jsp
items.xsl
login.jsp
logout.jsp
purchase.jsp
```

The directory WEB-INF will contain one file, called web.xml, which is the deployment descriptor for the web application.

When we have this file structure, all we have to do to create a web-application archive is to package it up as webshop-web.war using the jar tool.

Packaging the Enterprise Application

We now have two files, a file for the EJBs, webshop-ejb.jar and a file for the web application, webshop-web.war. We want to make this into one single distributable Enterprise application archive file, webshop.ear. To do this we need an application deployment descriptor, a file is called application.xml which must be located in the META-INF directory in the root of the webshop.ear file. This means we have a structure with three files:

```
META-INF/
  application.xml
webshop-ejb.jar
webshop-web.war
```

The application.xml deployment descriptor will basically just contain a name and links to contained modules; it looks like this:

```
<?xml version="1.0"?>
<!DOCTYPE application PUBLIC "-//Sun Microsystems, Inc.//DTD J2EE
Application 1.2//EN" "http://java.sun.com/j2ee/dtds/application_1_2.dtd">

<application>
  <display-name>Wrox webshop</display-name>
  <module>
    <ejb>webshop-ejb.jar</ejb>
```

```
    </module>
    <module>
      <web>
        <web-uri>webshop-web.jar</web-uri>
        <context-root>/</context-root>
      </web>
    </module>
  </application>
```

Summary

J2EE is a far too large a subject to be fully described in one chapter. Please see this chapter as a short introduction, and go on to read up on J2EE elsewhere. J2EE is becoming a very big thing in the industry, and has the possibility of bringing standard reusable components to the server and revolutionizing the whole industry. Only the future can tell whether this will happen or not.

Further Reading

For more detailed descriptions of how to use J2EE technologies to construct enterprise applications, refer to the J2EE home at Sun Microsystems at http://java.sun.com/j2ee/.

J2EE
JSP

18

Case Study: Streaming Data with JSP

This chapter examines the use of streaming data, and describes:

- an Applet for receiving and playing streaming media
- a class for transmitting a media stream
- a custom JSP tag for deploying the transmitter and receiver
- a simple example of JSP code using the custom tag
- a trick to stream individual Web pages

Assuming that at this stage in the book you already have a JSP container installed on a machine, the only preparation required for this chapter is to install the Java Media Framework (JMF) API (available from http://java.sun.com/products/java-media/jmf), collect some multimedia files, and acquire a faster machine.

Multimedia and the Web

There is a wide range of pre-packaged software products available with multimedia content, from games to encyclopedias. A good encyclopedia CD will allow the user to move seamlessly from text and charts describing the economy of a country, to a video of the local market place, perhaps allowing the capture of a still image, and from there jump to other market places of the world. It is now common to find Web sites that look and act like these programs, presenting hypertext and still images, with perhaps a little audio and video footage to promote the site to multimedia status. The most significant difference between off-the-shelf packages and Web sites is probably to be found in the level of interactivity.

The approach by Webmasters to multimedia is restrained in large part due to current bandwidth limitations of the Internet, but lack of imagination and technical ingenuity can also be factors. With increasing bandwidth, not to mention increasing raw power at both client and server ends it is a good time to take a look at the way multimedia is presented over the Web compared to other channels such as CD and DVD distributions, and consider the possibilities for improvement.

Streaming in Brief

Streaming can fairly well be defined as the movement of a continuous flow of data between two points (in much of Sun's documentation, they refer to streams in this very general sense). If we are playing an audio CD, the data will be continually transferred from the CD's laser to a converter which will transform the data into the material we wish to hear. There is a stream of data although it doesn't have to travel far, only between the source CD and the destination converter. To ensure the audio is delivered at the correct rate, it is certain that the data from the CD will be buffered to some extent. In terms of the Web, the source of a stream will usually be a media file on a server, and the destination a converter or player which may well be integrated with a user's browser.

There is a distinction between streaming and other forms of file transfer which is clear by example - if we have an audio file of Beethoven's 6th on a Web site, we can spend 30 minutes downloading a copy before we can listen to it from our hard drive. On the other hand, if the symphony was streamed to us, we only need wait a couple of seconds for the first few bytes to arrive before we can start to listen. Thus streaming offers a great improvement in terms of interactivity.

Unfortunately, the path from a Web server to our browser is considerably longer and narrower than that between a CD and our sound system, and bandwidth is a issue. Consider for a moment that standard CD audio contains 2 x16-bit data sent 44,100 times a second, that is 1.4 Mbps, and a typical Web user might be connected through a 33.6 kbps modem – bandwidth is a *major* issue. Here we are only talking of audio; video is even more demanding. Fortunately the problem has been eased considerably by designers of real-time codecs (compressors-decompressors, sometimes coders-decoders). In a similar manner to the way in which files may be compressed, flowing data may have redundant information removed prior to transmission, with the information being reconstructed after reception. Such a system is processor-intensive (the coding and decoding is taking place in real time), but the demands on bandwidth are significantly reduced. Trade-offs are also available due to the fact that media data doesn't have to be perfect – e.g. poorly recorded speech can still be intelligible. Streaming technology for Java is relatively straightforward, and is readily available (free to download).

HTTP Streaming

As well as using streams for shifting media, it is possible to stream all kinds of data. As an example, consider the following JSP code, `stream.jsp`:

```
<html>
<head><title>Stream</title></head>
<body>
<%
int i = 0;
boolean temp = true;
while(temp) {
```

```
    try {
        out.println("<br>" + i++);
      } catch (Exception e) {}
  }
  %>
```

The code includes a simple 'scriptlet' that contains an infinite loop. The temp variable is necessary to get the code through the JSP compiler. Using `while(true)` directly gives a Statement not reached error for a statement generated internally by the JSP container.

The Web page generated by this code is slightly unconventional, in that it doesn't really have an end. When loaded by a browser it will stream a list of numbers, which will grow until the browser decides to call it a day (Netscape is out of memory). There are only a few circumstances where such a stream could be of use - a stress test of browsers springs to mind.

The previous code uses the HTTP protocol for its stream, which is perfectly acceptable and it is possible to write a player that will use this protocol for media files on the Web. More commonly a protocol specifically designed for media will be used, which can include an appropriate codec. A suitable protocol and associated tools are freely available for Java programmers, and are to be found within the Java Media Framework, in the form of RTP (Real-Time Transport Protocol).

Streaming and JSP

Current Web media streaming solutions generally rely on proprietary server-side streaming engines together with browser plug-ins (see links at the end of the chapter). The results lack much of the interactivity that is found in traditional multimedia applications, and this is also in contrast with the comparative responsiveness of hypertext. A possible solution for the discrepancy may be found by using JSP to control Java-based streaming systems. The code presented here is a minor exploration of some of the options presented by such a combination

Java Media Framework

The JMF is a standard Java extension, designed to allow the developer to create applications with sound and video elements. The specification and implementations are available from http://www.java.sun.com. It is an API with many of the 'nuts and bolts' already assembled, with high-level classes that cover most aspects of multimedia that a programmer would wish for. The JMF is currently on version 2, and this version added support for media capture (recording) to the presentation (playback) facilities of JMF 1.0. Most commonly encountered media formats are catered to, and provision is now made for arbitrary plug-ins and proprietary interfaces. A significant part of the JMF provides support for the Real-Time Transport Protocol (RTP), which is rather convenient for the case in hand. This provision makes it relatively straightforward to send and receive real-time media streams across a network. That is, virtually *any* network, and potentially *any* media (digital media at least – watercolors can get a bit messy).

It is not appropriate to cover the operation of JMF in any depth here. Documentation for the JMF API is still rather thin on the ground, though the key references are the JMF v2.0 Specification (HTML API doc) and the JMF API Guide (in HTML and PDF formats), which are available to download, as is the API source code – see the links at the end of this chapter.

Interactive JSP Streaming Media System

The system described here will have the arrangement as follows:

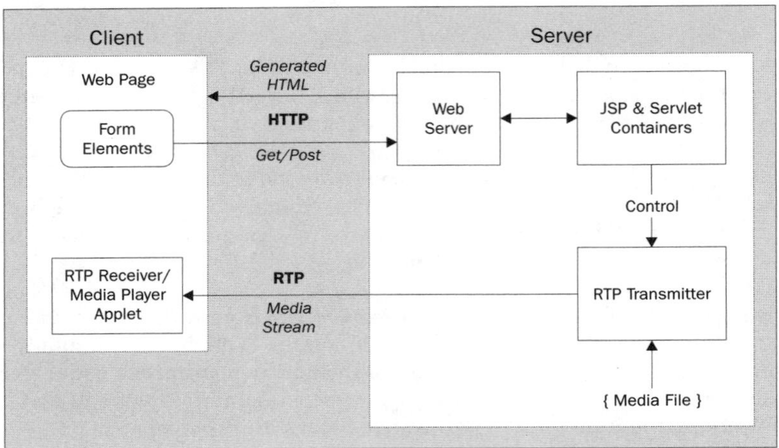

The setup is a relatively standard use of JSP to provide interaction with the user by dynamically generating Web pages in response to the user's actions - clicking on form buttons etc. Here the user also can have a media player on their browser, which will present media transmitted from the source server. This in itself is nothing fresh, but with JSP controlling the transmitter the `GET` and `POST` messages from the clients browser may be used to control any aspect of the media show.

There now follows the code of the Receiver, Transmitter and the controlling JSP for a minimal version of this system. This code should only be considered experimental, at best, 'proof of concept' - there are important issues that are not resolved here, and no cure is offered for the problem of speed.

Media Receiver

To be able to use media from the Web some form of receiver/viewer is required, and a standalone application would do the trick. To keep things portable the following receiver is an Applet, to be used in a standard browser with appropriate Java plugins.

The following diagram shows the key objects in an RTP receiver:

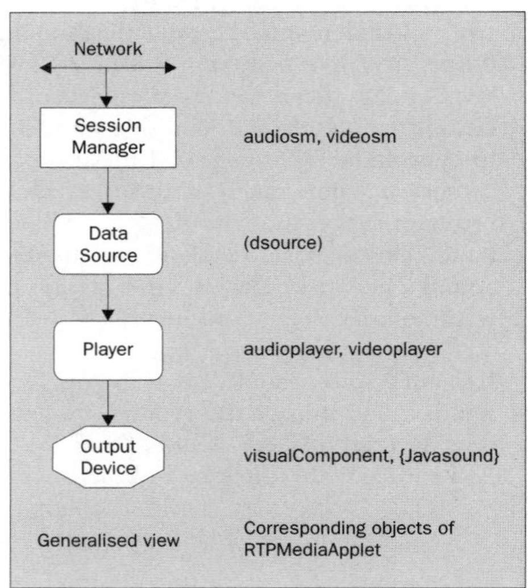

The SessionManager coordinates an RTP session, and can have various listeners added to allow a program to respond to RTP events. The elements that need co-coordinating include the data streams and participants. The participants include the local participant, whether a sender or receiver of data and any other remote senders or receivers. Within JMF there is flexibility for configuring a system for broadcast (one transmitter to many receivers), unicast (one transmitter to one receiver) and various shades in between.

The streams that the SessionManager looks after can be one of two types : ReceiveStream or SendStream. In our receiver we listen out for NewReceiveStream event, and when one occurs we obtain the DataSource associated with the stream. The DataSource is essentially a point of connection with the stream, and it is this that allows us to create one of the central JMF objects, the Player. The Player is one of two types of Controller (the other being Processor), and takes data from its DataSource and presents this as sound or video. A Player is quite complex internally, but only a couple of characteristics concern us here. The Player is a control mechanism for our media, and can be any one of six states. 'Started' is the state the Player is in when our media is playing, but the other primary state, 'Stopped' has five sub-states, each of which represents another stage in the preparation of the Player.

The methods available to use on a Player depend on its current state, so it is important to be able to determine this. There are two alternatives here - directly polling the Player using the getState() method, or using a ControllerListener to notify us of the state transitions. In our Applet we only need to watch one of the Player's state change sequences, that from Unrealized through Realizing to Realized. In the Realized state we can ask the Player for its VisualComponent (if it has one), an AWT Component that will be the screen of our video player. When a Player is first created i.e. instantiated, it will be in the Unrealized state. Here it exists, but knows nothing about the media it will be expected to play. When Realized, the player has all information about resources it needs to begin playing. Not surprisingly, this transition is usually initiated by calling the realize() method. In the next phases, Prefetching and Prefetched, the Player is obtaining, then has obtained the resources it needs. This all sounds very complicated, but fortunately the transitions will occur automatically when the start() method is called, we just need to pounce and retrieve the visual component when the Player generates a RealizeCompleteEvent.

A media file may contain video data, audio data or both. In this Applet, the assumption is made that the most one would want to receive at any given time is one video and one audio stream. This corresponds well with common media file formats. To see how we want the Applet to operate, take a look at the HTML used to launch it:

```
<HTML>
<HEAD><TITLE>RTP Media Player</TITLE></HEAD>
<BODY BGCOLOR="6060FF">
<APPLET CODE=RTPMediaApplet.class width=320 height=240>
<param NAME=video VALUE="On">
<param NAME=videosession VALUE="224.1.1.50">
<param NAME=videoport VALUE="3336">
<param NAME=audio VALUE="On">
<param NAME=audiosession VALUE="224.1.1.50">
<param NAME=audioport VALUE="3338">
</APPLET>
</BODY>
</HTML>
```

We have On/Off options for each media type, which must be specified, and we also have to specify an IP address and port for each. It is convenient to use the same IP address for both streams, but this means we must use different ports. The values used for the IP addresses and ports will depend on the network environment, and here arbitrary addresses that will work on a local network are used. Note that for each data stream port (here 3336, 3338) a control port is also used (3337, 3339).

Essentially our Applet waits for a stream to come along, creates a `SessionManager` to control the reception and a passes the data on to a `Player`, which handles the presentation.

The code as usual, begins with imports:

```
// Start of RTPMediaApplet.java
import java.applet.Applet;
import java.io.*;
import java.awt.*;
import java.util.Vector;
import java.net.*;
import javax.media.*;
import javax.media.protocol.*;
import javax.media.rtp.*;
import javax.media.rtp.rtcp.*;
import javax.media.rtp.event.*;
import com.sun.media.rtp.RTPSessionMgr;
```

The first half of the imported packages are familiar core Java. These are followed by the general JMF packages and the Real-Time Transport Protocol specific packages. The final package is a proprietary session manager that is not contained in the JMF spec, but coming from Sun there is a chance that it will remain available and compatible.

Predictably our Applet extends `Applet`, but it also implements two crucial interfaces. `ReceiveStreamListener` monitors incoming streams and `ControllerListener` responds to changes in the state of a `Player`.

```
public class RTPMediaApplet extends Applet
  implements ControllerListener, ReceiveStreamListener {
  InetAddress destaddr;
  String address;
  String portstr;
  String medium;
  Player videoplayer = null;
  Player audioplayer = null;
  SessionManager videosm = null;
  SessionManager audiosm = null;
  Component visualComponent = null;
  int width = 160;
  int height = 120;
```

RTP is network and transport protocol independent, but here we are using Sun's `SessionManager`, which works over IP, but details are not available. To be able to communicate over IP we need to define an IP address and port number – initially as strings `address` and `portstr`. These will later take on their 'true' forms (`InetAddress` and `int` respectively). We then have a `Player` and a `SessionManager` for each of our possible media types. The video presented by JMF appears as an AWT `Component`, `visualComponent` and it is to this that `width` and `height` refer.

Our `init()` method (automatically called by the Applet) retrieves the arguments from the HTML and creates RTP Session Managers as necessary:

```
public void init() {
  int port;
  medium = getParameter("video");
  if (medium.equals("On")) {
    address = getParameter("videosession");
    portstr = getParameter("videoport");
    port = (new Integer(portstr)).intValue();
    videosm = createSessionManager(address, port);
    if (videosm == null) {
      return;
    }
  }
  medium = getParameter("audio");
  if (medium.equals("On")) {
    address = getParameter("audiosession");
    portstr = getParameter("audioport");
    port = (new Integer(portstr)).intValue();
    audiosm = createSessionManager(address, port);
    if (audiosm == null) {
      return;
    }
  }
}
```

Note that in case of no session managers being available, the method simply returns. This would lead to the user being presented with an unexplained Applet error - not good practice. There are many places throughout where correct procedure should have us throwing an exception and handling that exception in a useful fashion. For the sake of brevity good practice is strayed from, with the caveat that this code as it stands should be used for development only.

The `start()` method does just that to any existing players:

```
public void start() {
  if (videoplayer != null) {
    videoplayer.start();
  }
  if (audioplayer != null) {
    audioplayer.start();
  }
}
```

An `update()` method is required by the `ReceiveStreamListener` interface. Here it responds to new incoming streams (signaled by a `NewReceiveStreamEvent` from a `SessionManager`, all other events may be safely ignored) by creating players using `Manager`, a JMF class that provides access to system resources. The players have a listener (on the state of the player) added, and are then started:

```
public void update(ReceiveStreamEvent event) {
  SessionManager source = (SessionManager) event.getSource();
  Player newplayer = null;
```

```
    if (event instanceof NewReceiveStreamEvent) {
      try {
        ReceiveStream stream =
          ((NewReceiveStreamEvent) event).getReceiveStream();
        DataSource dsource = stream.getDataSource();
        newplayer = Manager.createPlayer(dsource);
      } catch (Exception e) {}

      if (newplayer == null) {
        return;
      }

      if (source == videosm) {
        if (videoplayer == null) {
          videoplayer = newplayer;
          newplayer.addControllerListener(this);
          newplayer.start();
        }
      }

      if (source == audiosm) {
        if (audioplayer == null) {
          audioplayer = newplayer;
          newplayer.addControllerListener(this);
          newplayer.start();
        }
      }
    }
  }
```

The listeners on the players will respond to a `ControllerEvent`, and the only one we are interested in, `RealizeCompleteEvent`, is handled in the next block of code:

```
  public synchronized void controllerUpdate(ControllerEvent event) {
    Player player = null;
    Controller controller = (Controller) event.getSource();
    if (controller instanceof Player) {
      player = (Player) event.getSource();
    }
    if (player == null) {
      return;

    }
    if (event instanceof RealizeCompleteEvent) {
      if ((visualComponent = player.getVisualComponent()) != null) {
        width = visualComponent.getPreferredSize().width;
        height = visualComponent.getPreferredSize().height;
      }
      add(visualComponent);
    }
  }
```

The `RealizeCompleteEvent` announces that the media is ready for showing (curtains part at the cinema). If there is a video stream, this will have caused a suitable player to be created (in `update()` above) which should now have a visual component ready for displaying. This will be added to the Applet's window (projector on).

The next block of code takes the local address details and creates an RTP `SessionManager`. Here information about participants in the session are provided, i.e. the sender and receiver. It is possible to retrieve session reports from RTP streams, and basic information is supplied for the initialization of the session. There isn't space here to go into the rather opaque details of this method, so please just treat this as a black box for now, and refer to the JMF Guide (see links) for further information.

```
public SessionManager createSessionManager(String destaddrstr,
                                           int port) {
  SessionManager sessionmgr = new RTPSessionMgr();
  if (sessionmgr == null) {
    return null;
  }
  sessionmgr.addReceiveStreamListener(this);
  String cname = sessionmgr.generateCNAME();
  String username = "jmf-wrox";
  SessionAddress localaddr = new SessionAddress();
  try {
    destaddr = InetAddress.getByName(destaddrstr);
  } catch (Exception e) {}
  SessionAddress sessaddr = new SessionAddress(destaddr, port,
          destaddr, port + 1);

  SourceDescription[] userdesclist = new SourceDescription[2];

  userdesclist[0] =
    new SourceDescription(SourceDescription.SOURCE_DESC_NAME,
                          username, 1, false);
  userdesclist[1] =
    new SourceDescription(SourceDescription.SOURCE_DESC_CNAME,
                          cname, 1, false);
  try {
    sessionmgr.initSession(localaddr, sessionmgr.generateSSRC(),
                           userdesclist, 0.05, 0.25);
    sessionmgr.startSession(sessaddr, 1, null);
  } catch (Exception e) {
    return null;
  }
  return sessionmgr;
}
```

The operation of the next piece of code is a little clearer:

```
public void stop() {
  if (videoplayer != null) {
    videoplayer.close();
  }
  if (audioplayer != null) {
```

```
        audioplayer.close();
      }
    }
```

If they are non-null, the players are stopped and their resources released. We can then release any other resources, including those used by the session managers:

```
    public void destroy() {
      String reason = "Finished.";
      if (videosm != null) {
        videosm.closeSession(reason);
        videoplayer = null;
        videosm = null;
      }

      if (audiosm != null) {
        audiosm.closeSession(reason);
        audioplayer = null;
        audiosm = null;
      }
      super.destroy();
    }
  }
  // End of RTPMediaApplet.java
```

This Applet is relatively general purpose, and can be used in conjunction and tested with the JMStudio application bundled with the JMF API.

Media Transmitter

A significant part of the following code is devoted to discovering the contents of a file and transforming it into a transmission format, but in other respects the code is very similar to the Applet above. One notable difference is that rather than having separate objects (`audiosm`, `videosm` etc.) to handle video and audio data, the `SessionManagers` and so on are held in arrays. This is possible because from a transmitting point of view, the content of the stream is irrelevant.

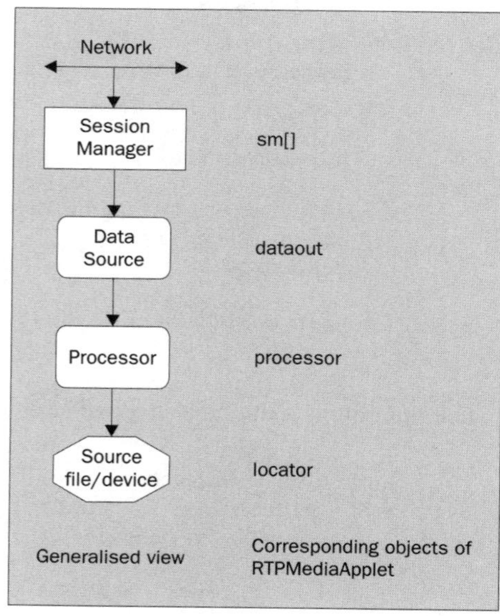

In the system described here the transmitter is essentially set up for simple broadcast.

For the transmitter, the media data is extracted from the files by means of a `Processor`, another JMF `Controller` like the `Player`. The `Processor` has considerably more facilities than the `Player`, and is used here for its ability to analyze a media file and allow us to operate on the contents of the file programmatically. The `Processor` has all the states of a `Player`, and two extra: *Configuring* and *Configured*. These refer to the `Processor` getting the details of a file (or device) and having them ready for us to program. Once we have made the data available it is then passed to an RTP `SessionManager`, which will handle the transmission stream.

The same packages are required as before (except for `Applet`):

```
// Start of RTPTransmit.java
import java.awt.Dimension;
import javax.media.*;
import javax.media.rtp.*;
import javax.media.rtp.event.*;
import javax.media.protocol.*;
import javax.media.format.*;
import javax.media.control.TrackControl;
import java.io.*;
import java.awt.*;
import javax.media.rtp.rtcp.SourceDescription;
import java.net.InetAddress;
import com.sun.media.rtp.RTPSessionMgr;
```

Whereas the receiver needed a `ReceiveStreamListener`, here we need a `SendStreamListener` interface to monitor events on the outgoing stream. The states of the `Processor` are handled in a different way to those of the `Player` above, polling the `Processor`'s state rather than implementing a `ControllerListener`. The choice was fairly arbitrary and is provided for example only - the listener approach could lead to clearer code. The `MediaLocator` will tell us the source of our media data – here it is only used to get data from files, but the same code could be used to transmit from a capture data source such as a video camera.

```
public class RTPTransmit implements SendStreamListener {
  MediaLocator locator;
  String ipAddress;
  InetAddress ip;
  int port;
  Processor processor = null;
  DataSink rtptransmitter = null;
  DataSource dataout = null;
  int ntracks = 0;
  int timeout = 1000;
  InetAddress destaddr;
  String address;
  String[] medium;
  SessionManager[] sm;
  SendStream[] ss;
```

Next the constructor, and some self-explanatory methods:

```
public RTPTransmit() {}

public void setLocator(String loc) {
  locator = new MediaLocator(loc);
}

public void setIPAddress(String addr) {
  address = addr;
}

public void setPort(int prt) {
  port = prt;
}

public int getWidth() {
  return width;
}

public int getHeight() {
  return height;
}
```

The use of a public constructor with no arguments and a string of `setXXX()` and `getXXX()` methods might give a clue as to how this class is going to be used – this is a book about JSP after all. For consistency each `setXXX()` should really be matched with a `getXXX()` (and vice versa), but some of these methods aren't needed here and so are left out for brevity.

The `init` method is used as an entry point to sequentially call internal methods. A shortcut has been used with these methods (also used by Sun, incidentally) that many programmers might find objectionable - if the methods are successful, they return `null`, otherwise they return an error string. A more standard approach would be for them to return the object created (if successful) or throw exceptions (if unsuccessful).

```
public synchronized String init() {
  String result;
  result = createProcessor();
  if (result != null) {
    return result;
  }
  result = createTransmitter();
  if (result != null) {
    processor.close();
    processor = null;
    return result;
  }
  return null;
}
```

Mention was made earlier of processors having states. The next block of code deals with one of the transitions – the configuring of the `Processor`. It is here that the processor sees for the first time the data source (file or captured) and tries to figure out what it will have to do with it. When the `Processor` is configured it will send a `ConfigureCompleteEvent`, but unlike in the Applet code, here we have no listener. Instead the state of the processor is polled until the required state is achieved. While the processor is away configuring itself, we have a timing loop that releases the system while we wait.

```
public String createProcessor() {
  if (locator == null) {
    return "Nothing located.";
  }
  try {
    processor = Manager.createProcessor(locator);
  } catch (Exception e) {
    return e.getMessage();
  }
  processor.configure();
  int t;
  for (t = 0; t < timeout; t++) {
    if (processor.getState() == Processor.Configured) {
      break;
    }
    try {
      Thread.currentThread().sleep(100);
    } catch (Exception e) {}
  }
  if (t == timeout) {
    System.out.println("Error configuring");
  }
  System.out.println("Configuring = " + t);
```

To avoid an infinite loop lockup, the variable `t` is compared to the `timeout`. This variable is output at the end of this code block, to give an idea of how long was actually required. Throughout this code a lot of non-essential `System.out.println(...)` calls have been left in, as troubleshooting can be a grind with JMF, due to its dependence on system resources such as sound devices.

The media as stored in files and handled by the processor can be viewed in terms of tracks. For example, a `.avi` file might contain one audio and one video track. The next block examines these tracks and attempts to convert them into a format that the RTP transmission section can understand.

```
TrackControl[] tracks = processor.getTrackControls();

if (tracks == null || tracks.length < 1) {
  return "Couldn't find tracks in processor";
}

Format[] format = new Format[tracks.length];
medium = new String[tracks.length];

for (int i = 0; i < tracks.length; i++) {
  format[i] = tracks[i].getFormat();
  System.out.println(tracks[i].getFormat());
```

```
      if (tracks[i].isEnabled()) {
        if (format[i] instanceof VideoFormat) {
          medium[i] = "video";
          Dimension size = ((VideoFormat) format[i]).getSize();
          width = (int) size.getWidth();
          height = (int) size.getHeight();
          float frameRate = ((VideoFormat) format[i]).getFrameRate();
          VideoFormat jpegFormat =
            new VideoFormat(VideoFormat.JPEG_RTP, size,
                            Format.NOT_SPECIFIED, Format.byteArray,
                            frameRate);
          if (tracks[i].setFormat(jpegFormat) != null) {
            ntracks++;
          }
        } else if (format[i] instanceof AudioFormat) {
          medium[i] = "audio";
          AudioFormat af = (AudioFormat) format[i];
          AudioFormat mpegFormat =
            new AudioFormat(AudioFormat.MPEG_RTP);
          if (tracks[i].setFormat(mpegFormat) != null) {
            ntracks++;
          }
        }
      }
    }
    System.out.println("Number of tracks = " + ntracks);
```

Though versatile, JMF is limited to the formats it can deal with and the number of tracks it has successfully transformed is counted by `ntracks`.

The `ContentDescriptor` below makes another step towards getting the data ready for transmission by identifying the media data container. Here we have another processor state change, and this is handled in the manner as `processor.configure()` above:

```
    ContentDescriptor cd =
      new ContentDescriptor(ContentDescriptor.RAW);
    processor.setContentDescriptor(cd);
    processor.realize();

    for (t = 0; t < timeout; t++) {
      if (processor.getState() == Controller.Realized) {
        break;
      }
      try {
        Thread.currentThread().sleep(100);
      } catch (InterruptedException ie) {}
    }
    System.out.println("Realizing = " + t);
    if (t == timeout) {
      System.out.println("Error realizing");
    }
    dataout = processor.getDataOutput();
    return null;
  }
```

The `realize()` process can take a significant amount of time while resources are analyzed, and may be a bottleneck in some systems.

The `dataout` object is the connection through which the processed streams are supplied, and to which the send streams will shortly be attached.

The next method simply returns the duration (playing time in milliseconds) of the media:

```
public long getDuration() {
  if (processor != null) {
    Time time = processor.getDuration();
    if (time == Duration.DURATION_UNKNOWN) {
      return 0;
    }
    return time.getNanoseconds() / 1000000;
  } else {
    return -1;
  }
}
```

We can now create a session manager and a send stream for each usable track:

```
public String createTransmitter() {
  sm = new SessionManager[ntracks];
  ss = new SendStream[ntracks];

  for (int i = 0; i < ntracks; i++) {
    sm[i] = createSessionManager(address, port + 2 * i);

    System.out.println("SM " + i + "  Medium = " + medium[i]);
    System.out.println("Address = " + address + "  Port = " + port
                       + 2 * i);
    try {
      ss[i] = sm[i].createSendStream(dataout, i);
    } catch (Exception e) {
      return "createSendStream error=" + e.getMessage();
    }
  }
  return null;
}
```

To give an idea of what is going on, there is a bit more data output to the console (wherever that may be).

At last we can start transmitting, by starting the `processor` (to provide the `dataout`) and the send streams (to provide a conduit for the data):

```
public String transmit() {
  System.out.println("Processor started");
  processor.start();
  for (int i = 0; i < ntracks; i++) {
    try {
```

```
          ss[i].start();
          System.out.println("ss[" + i + "] start");
        } catch (Exception e) {
          return e.getMessage();
        }
      }
      return null;
    }
```

As we have implemented SendStreamListener, we need an update() method (in this case it could be useful point for debugging information to be sent to the console):

```
    public void update(SendStreamEvent event) {
      SessionManager source = (SessionManager) event.getSource();
    }
```

Fortunately the description of the next method doesn't need repeating:

```
    public SessionManager createSessionManager(String destaddrstr,
                                               int port) {

      // ... as in RTPMediaApplet.java ...
    }
```

The last two methods are self-explanatory:

```
    public synchronized void stop() {
      if (processor != null) {
        System.out.println("Processor stopped");
        processor.stop();
        processor.close();
        processor = null;
        destroy();
      }
    }

    public void destroy() {
      for (int i = 0; i < ntracks; i++) {
        if (sm[i] != null) {
          sm[i].closeSession("Finished.");
          sm[i] = null;
        }
      }
    }
  }   // End of RTPTransmit.java
```

As with the receiver Applet, the transmitter class is pretty general purpose. It is possible to set the media locator of the transmitter to a captured audio source, and offer live streaming audio.

For testing, a simple command line program could be written containing the lines:

```
RTPTransmit rt = new RTPTransmit();
rt.setLocator("file:///f:/clip2.avi");
rt.setIPAddress("224.1.1.50");
rt.setPort(3336);
String result = rt.init();
rt.transmit();
```

A delay or loop should come after this code, to stop the code exiting prematurely, and ideally the `rt.stop()` method should be called. Once running correctly the transmit class can be used in conjunction with the receiver Applet or JMStudio. As an interesting alternative, the classes can be used with the code that follow.

JSP Control

Having a transmitter and receiver ready, we can now return to JSP. To allow full interaction, we need to allow the user to be able to control the media from the browser. This may be achieved using server-side Java as follows:

Based on user input, we should have our system dynamically generate client side code to launch the receiver Applet. At the same time, the transmitter on the server side should be prompted to start sending the media stream.

Bear in mind that the page layout and presentation will be put together by Joe HTML-Hacker; it is important to use simple JSP calls to get the streaming going. One way of achieving this would be to call the transmitter as a JavaBean – it already has the characteristics. An alternative, as described below, is to create a custom tag. This is easier for Joe to use, allows greater separation of the JSP code and has the added advantage of providing a convenient place to put the code that will launch the Applet. A simple way of using the code, as demonstrated here, is as a multimedia 'slideshow', where a slide could be text and images (included as HTML in the JSP, or as `<%@ include file="x.html"%>` directives) with a soundtrack (using our streaming system), or the favorite, a video with sound.

We start with an attempt to organize the project files, by putting the tag into a package, and then including the standard packages needed for custom tags:

```
// Start of SlideTag.java
package media;

import javax.servlet.jsp.*;
import javax.servlet.jsp.JspException;
import javax.servlet.jsp.tagext.TagSupport;
import RTPTransmit;
```

The class members should be familiar from the transmitter and receiver, the `hasvideo` and `hasaudio` strings being used to help provide the `<param name=video value="On">` tags needed in the Applet. The constructor calls the superclass `TagSupport` as required:

```
public class SlideTag extends TagSupport {
  private String IPAddress = new String();
  private int port;
  private String type=new String();
  private String locator=new String();
```

```
    private long duration = 0;
    private String hasvideo = new String();
    private String hasaudio = new String();
    public String code = new String();

    public SlideTag() {
      super();
    }
```

The following set of methods allow JSP to send details of the media:

```
    public void setIPAddress(String addr) {
      this.IPAddress = addr;
    }

    public void setPort(String portstr) {
      this.port = (new Integer(portstr)).intValue();
    }

    public void setLocator(String value) {
      this.locator = value;
    }
```

To simplify the tag arguments, a value `type` is used, which can have one three values: "`video`", "`audio`" and "`mixed`". The "`mixed`" alternative would be used where a source file contains both audio and video. Here we change these arguments into the form required by the Applet:

```
    public void setType(String t) {
      this.type = t;
      hasvideo = "Off";
      if (t.equals("video") || t.equals("mixed")) {
        hasvideo = "On";
      }
      hasaudio = "Off";
      if (t.equals("audio") || t.equals("mixed")) {
        hasaudio = "On";
      }
    }
```

The next block of code sets up the transmitter by setting the TCP/IP details and the source file location. The duration of the media is retrieved here - although it isn't actually used in this application, it may be useful in other applications:

```
    public int doStartTag() throws JspException {
      RTPTransmit rt = new RTPTransmit();
      rt.setIPAddress(IPAddress);
      rt.setPort(port);
      rt.setLocator(locator);
      rt.init();
      duration = rt.getDuration();
      duration = duration < 1 ? 1000 : duration;
```

Turning to the client side, we create a string containing the HTML needed to launch the Applet. Although this may seem an abuse of the facilities – JSP being a move away from hard coding HTML in servlets – it is justifiable here as this code block is unlikely to change.

```
        code = "<applet code=RTPMediaApplet.class" + " width="
                + rt.getWidth() + " height=" + rt.getHeight() + ">"
                + "<param name=video value=\"" + hasvideo + "\">"
                + "<param name=videosession value=\"" + IPAddress + "\">"
                + "<param name=videoport value=\"" + port + "\">"
                + "<param name=audio value=\"" + hasaudio + "\">"
                + "<param name=audiosession value=\"" + IPAddress + "\">"
                + "<param name=audioport value=\"" + (port + 2) + "\">"
                + "</applet>";
```

Now we can push out the generated code in the prescribed fashion:

```
        JspWriter out = pageContext.getOut();
        try {
          out.println(code);
          out.println("<BR>IPAddress = " + IPAddress);
          out.println("<BR>port = " + port);
          out.println("<BR>locator = " + locator);
          out.println("<BR>Duration = " + duration);
        } catch (Exception e) {
          System.out.println(e);
        }
```

By now our RTP transmitter should be ready, so we can set that going, before returning to the calling JSP page:

```
        rt.transmit();
        return EVAL_BODY_INCLUDE;
    }
  }// End of SlideTag.java
```

Once we have compiled the tag class, we have to make some minor additions to our environment to be able to use it.

First we have to add the tag to our tag libraries. This will let the system know what attributes can be used with the tag, in other words which methods are exposed. The required property is set to `false` throughout – it may be desirable to change this once the application is finalized. The easiest way to add the tag to the libraries is to make a copy of an existing tag library file (e.g. `example-taglib.tld`) and insert the following block in line with the existing tags:

```
  <tag>
    <name>slides</name>
    <tagclass>media.SlideTag</tagclass>
    <bodycontent>JSP</bodycontent>
    <info>
      Creates multimedia 'slides' for JSP playback
    </info>
```

```
    <attribute>
      <name>IPAddress</name>
      <required>false</required>
    </attribute>
    <attribute>
      <name>port</name>
      <required>false</required>
    </attribute>
    <attribute>
      <name>type</name>
      <required>false</required>
    </attribute>
    <attribute>
      <name>locator</name>
      <required>false</required>
    </attribute>
    <attribute>
      <name>delay</name>
      <required>false</required>
    </attribute>
    <attribute>
      <name>code</name>
      <required>false</required>
    </attribute>
  </tag>
```

The next step is to make the system aware of the new tag library. This we achieve by inserting the following lines into `web.xml`:

```
    <taglib>
        <taglib-uri>
           http://coyote/taglibs
        </taglib-uri>
        <taglib-location>
           /WEB-INF/jsp/wroxmedia-taglib.tld
        </taglib-location>
    </taglib>
```

The tag is now ready for use, and so we can take a look at the kind of JSP file we can use. Assuming we have a series of media files on the root of drive `F:`, for example `F:\clip1.avi`, `F:\clip2.avi` etc. we can then create a series of JSP files, each one playing an individual media clip. The first of these would be along the lines of:

```
<%@ taglib uri="http://coyote/taglibs" prefix="m" %>
<HTML>
<HEAD>
<TITLE>Media Slides</TITLE>
</HEAD>
<BODY BGCOLOR="blue" TEXT="white">
<H2>Multimedia Presentation</H2>

<m:slides IPAddress="224.1.1.50" port="3336" type="mixed"
locator="file:///f:/clip2.avi">
```

```
<FORM METHOD=GET ACTION=slides2.jsp>
<INPUT TYPE=SUBMIT NAME=ACTION VALUE="Next">
</FORM>
</BODY>
</HTML>
```

As you can see, it couldn't be much simpler. All the media transmission, reception, and presentation is handled by that one line of code. The form method is included as a simple way of moving to the next media page – clicking on the **Next** button will move on to the next page, `slides2.jsp`.

To look at this in operation, pointing a browser at `slides1.jsp` will (rather slowly) produce a log along the lines of:

```
Starting tomcat. Check logs/tomcat.log for error messages
Open log file: F:\tomcat\bin\jmf.log
Configuring = 4
IV32, 216x192, FrameRate=10.0, Length=9772 0 extra bytes
LINEAR, 22050.0 Hz, 8-bit, Mono, Unsigned, FrameSize=8 bits
Number of tracks = 2
Realizing = 46
SM 0  Medium = video
Address = 224.1.1.50  Port = 33360
SM 1  Medium = audio
Address = 224.1.1.50  Port = 33362
Processor started
ss[0] start
ss[1] start
```

Here we have pointed the system at a file that contains both audio and video streams. Once the transmitter has configured the processor, it gives us the details of the encoding of the media streams. Once the processor has been realized, we are given the details of two RTP session managers before the processor is started. Finally the send streams are started.

At the browser end, nothing will happen until the tag has well and truly started, whereupon the user will be bombarded with a stream of security messages, the most choice of which is Netscape:

Granting the following is high risk:

Contacting and connecting with other computers over a network.

Once you have granted the very soul of your computer, the result in the browser window will look something like this:

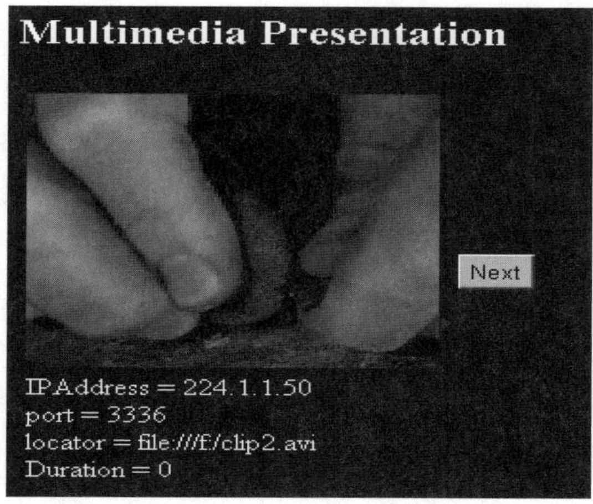

The Bad News

Now might be a good time to mention some of the drawbacks of this system. First and foremost, the video player and transmitter take a painfully long time to start (of the order of a minute for a 200x200 pixel screen size, with audio on an average machine). Using a Java media player in isolation (e.g. JMStudio) will slowly demonstrate that a large part of the latency is due to JMF, which we can only hope will be reduced in subsequent releases.

Having said that, the delay could be significantly reduced by optimizing the code – for example ensuring that the loading of the Applet and the preparation of the transmitter take place simultaneously. A side effect of this lack of synch is that the start of the video can be missed if the Applet isn't ready in time. In addition, the end of the transmission is not currently stopped gracefully – a Stop (form) button and a timed stop message based on the duration parameter could be the answer here.

Another vital issue that has not been covered is the allocation of transmission-reception ports, as currently every visitor will be placed on the same address and port. This could result in reception of unwanted 'signals', or more likely crash the system (the JSP server anyway – the Applet is relatively robust). A check for the next available port shouldn't be too difficult.

Moving away from streaming media, and back to the mechanics of http streaming, we have a little novelty application that has a great deal of serious potential.

A JavaScript Tier

So far we have an operating system, a Web server, JSP and servlet containers, a browser, a couple of JVMs (and the rest), let's now add JavaScript. This may be an anathema to some Java purists, but a very large proportion of browsers provide some form of support, and it can do things that would be unwieldy by other means.

Recalling the servlet at the start of this chapter, a continuous stream of data was pumped out to the browser, and appeared as one continuous page. Wouldn't it be nice to be able to pump out individual, discrete, pages in the same fashion? With a pinch of JavaScript together with JSP this is possible (the credit for this technique goes to Just van den Broeke – http://www.justobjects.nl).

Three files are needed, the first of which is a frames index (`index.html`), which contains a JavaScript function called `push()`:

```
<HTML><HEAD>
<TITLE>Title</TITLE>
<SCRIPT LANGUAGE="JavaScript">
function push(pushpage)
{
window.frames['pushFrame'].document.
                    writeln("<HTML><HEAD></HEAD><BODY>");

window.frames['pushFrame'].document.
                    writeln(pushpage);

window.frames['pushFrame'].document.
                    writeln(</BODY></HTML>);
```

```
window.frames['pushFrame'].document.close();
}
</SCRIPT>
</HEAD>
<FRAMESET BORDER=0 COLS="*,0">
     <FRAME SRC="display.html"
             NAME="pushFrame" BORDER=0 SCROLLING=no>
     <FRAME SRC="streamer.jsp"
             NAME="jspFrame" BORDER=0 SCROLLING=no>
</FRAMESET>
```

This page we want to load into our browser, but it will remain hidden, loading in the other two files `display.html` and `streamer.jsp`.

The page that will be visible is `display.html`:

```
<HTML><HEAD>
<TITLE>Please wait...</TITLE>
</HEAD><BODY>
  Please wait...
</BODY></HTML>
```

Not very interesting in itself, but in the meantime, in the undergrowth, `streamer.jsp` is loading:

```
<HTML><HEAD>
<TITLE>Stream</TITLE>
</HEAD><BODY>
<%
int i = 0;
while(true) {
  try {
    out.print("<script language=JavaScript>parent.push('");
    out.println(i);
    out.println("')</script> ");
    out.flush();
  }
}
%>
</BODY>
</HTML>
```

Stripping away the JSP code, we have the output:

```
<SCRIPT LANGUAGE=JavaScript>
  parent.push( i_as_a_string )
</SCRIPT>
```

This calls the method `push()` in the parent frame (`index.html`) with the string representation of i as an argument. The `push` method is a series of commands along the lines of:

```
window.frames['pushFrame'].document.writeln(...)
```

This will write the contents of the `writeln(...)` to window frame `pushFrame`, that is to say `display.html`. What we write just so happens to be an HTML page header, plus some content sent by the JSP page (in this case `i`) and an HTML page footer.

Voila! Streaming pages.

Troubleshooting

The first step in resolving problems with a system such as the media streaming Web application is to confirm that all the individual components are functioning correctly. The search for a failing component can be narrowed by checking log files, which can be time consuming but patience occasionally pays off. In this case, the system components include:

- Java compiler – try compiling a 'Hello World' type command-line program.
- JVM – try running the 'Hello World' program (current releases of the Hotspot engine can suffer crash-like trauma with JMF, try the `javac -classic` option).
- Web server & browser with JRE - try browsing a simple HTML page, then a 'Hello World' applet.
- JMF extensions – try compiling and running some of Sun's example programs (e.g. JMStudio).
- Servlet and JSP containers – try the supplied examples, starting with 'Hello World'.

Once the general area of a problem has been identified, try to fix this in isolation before returning to the whole system. It may be necessary to go back to the READMEs, FAQs and HOWTOs (RTFM!), then there are always Internet resources such as newsgroups and mailing lists. Chances are that if you're having a particular problem, someone else has had it before. Once in a blue moon the answer can be found in a 'known bugs' list.

Common problems with a Java Web application are:

- Environment variable omissions – check `PATH`, `CLASSPATH` (and `JAVA_HOME`, `TOMCAT_HOME`, etc, as appropriate), these settings may be hidden in startup scripts/batch files.
- Module omissions/version inadequacies – make sure everything needed is installed and of a recent enough version.
- Server not configured correctly – check the Web server, servlet and JSP settings (e.g. `httpd.conf` in Apache).
- Communication problems – check the underlying network setup on server and client (TCP/IP settings etc.) and if a firewall is installed check its configuration.

When looking for bugs in your Java code, simple techniques can help: include lots of:

```
System.out.println("Value of myvariable = "+myvariable);
```

or the Servlet equivalent:

```
out.println("Value of myvariable = "+myvariable);
```

Such debugging aids can easily be included as code fragments in JSP pages.

File locations

With a clean install of Tomcat 3.x on Apache 1.3.x (Linux i386 / Windows, others not tested), the application has a fair chance of running if the application files are placed in the following locations (all below `tomcat/webapps/examples/`):

- `WEB-INF/classes/RTPTransmit.class`
- `WEB-INF/classes/media/SlideTag.class`
- `jsp/RTPTransmit.class`
- `jsp/media/RTPMediaApplet.class`
- `jsp/media/index.html`
- `jsp/media/display.html`
- `jsp/media/slides1.jsp`
- `WEB-INF/web.xml`
- `WEB-INF/jsp/wroxmedia-taglib.tld`

> **Remember to include `jmf.jar` and `servlet.jar` in your `CLASSPATH`.**

Other resources

- RTP - Internet Engineering Task Force: `http://www.ietf.org`
- Java Media Framework (inc. RTP): `http://java.sun.com/products/java-media/jmf`
- Codecs: `http://www.terran-int.com/CodecCentral/`
- JSP Javascript: `http://www.caucho.com/index.html`
- 'Pushlets': `http://www.justobjects.nl`
- Apache, Tomcat etc: `http://www.apache.org`

J2EE
JSP

19

Case Study: Weather with JSP, XSLT, and WAP

Introduction

This chapter is about WAP applications, and how JSPs can be used in creating such applications. WAP stands for **Wireless Application Protocol**. WAP applications are very much like Web applications, except they are designed for 'microbrowsers' that are embedded in small wireless devices, such as cell phones and PDAs. The content for WAP applications usually comes from a Web server, through an intermediate WAP gateway. This chapter will focus on how to generate both Web pages and WAP pages from the same content on a Web server, and what role JSPs can play in the process.

> *We should make it clear that although this chapter does not assume any previous knowledge of WAP, it is not going to be a detailed tutorial. There are books written on the subject, including Wrox's* Professional WAP Programming. *Our goal is to develop a framework within which different ways of generating Web and WAP content can be developed and compared. JSPs will form an important part of that framework.*

The specific application of this chapter is small – a weather report – but it goes much further than generating WAP content from an XML file. It is a complete 3–tier application, in the sense that it has a dedicated component that retrieves data from a database and makes it available in a generic format, for either Web or WAP output. The database component is quite robust, (it provides for security and connection pooling) so the application can be scaled up easily.

The chapter will proceed as follows:

- Try it out: a WAP application (see installation instructions below if you don't have a WAP viewer)
- An architecture for a Web JSP application
- An example: Weather application
- A background section: Wireless Application Environment and Wireless Markup Language
- The weather application adapted for WAP
- A background section: XML parsing and XSLT
- A different approach to the Web-WAP problem, using XSLT
- Comparative analysis and conclusions

A WAP Application

WAP phones are still far from universal, especially in the US, compared to Europe and Japan. Fortunately, a number of WAP simulators are freely available on the Web. We use the one from Phone.com, http://updev.phone.com/ (you have to register and log in to download it).

Installation Instructions

To install the WAP simulator, simply download and unpack the installer. (If the installer somehow gets corrupted during download, make sure you empty the cache of your browser before downloading again.) The Web site has fairly complete installation instructions.

In addition to the simulator, you will need jdk1.2.2 or later and a Web server that supports servlets and JSPs. We have done our programs within the `examples` folder of Apache Tomcat, version 3.1. Tomcat has its own Web server and the servlet/JSP engine.

Configuring Tomcat to work with our JSP WML examples (as opposed to XSLT examples) is fairly easy: you only need to make one addition to the `jakarta-tomcat\conf\web.xml` file. Later in the chapter, when you get to the XSLT sections, you will also need `xt.jar`, part of the xt release from `www.jclark.com/xml`. This is an XSLT processor that needs an XML parser to do its job. You can use James Clark's parser `xp.jar` or any other parser, as James Clark's readme file in turn explains. The section 'Running the example with XSLServlet' later in the chapter goes through this part of installations in more detail. At that time, you will need to make two more additions to the `web.xml` file of Tomcat.

The web.xml File

We have placed the Tomcat 3.1 distribution into `C:\jakarta-tomcat`, which means that the `web.xml` file for MIME types (and servlet information, later) is within `C:\jakarta-tomcat\conf`. Rather than making you set up a new 'webapp', we use the existing webapp, `C:\jakarta-tomcat\webapps\examples`. We have made a `weather` subdirectory of that directory and place our JSP files there.

The addition to `web.xml` that you need right now has to do with MIME types for WML, WMLScript and WBMP. (These are all parts of the Wireless Application Protocol that we will be discussing at length later in the chapter.) You can review our `web.xml` file and compare it with the original distribution file to see where the additions should go. The text of the addition is as follows:

```
<mime-mapping>
  <extension>
    wml
  </extension>
  <mime-type>
    text/vnd.wap.wml
  </mime-type>
</mime-mapping>
<mime-mapping>
  <extension>
    wmls
  </extension>
  <mime-type>
    vnd.wap.wmlscript
  </mime-type>
</mime-mapping>
<mime-mapping>
  <extension>
    bmp
  </extension>
  <mime-type>
    image/bmp
  </mime-type>
</mime-mapping>
<mime-mapping>
  <extension>
    wbmp
  </extension>
  <mime-type>
    image/vnd.wap.wbmp
  </mime-type>
</mime-mapping>
```

Once you have `web.xml` fixed, download and unzip our book code (`MyNajsp.zip`), move `MyNajsp.jar` somewhere in the classpath, and you should be all set to try out the examples for this chapter.

Web and Wap examples

To view the Web examples, point your browser at:

http://localhost:8080/examples/jsp/weather/weather.htm

and to view the WAP examples, point the phone.com simulator at:

http://localhost:8080/examples/jsp/weather/weather.wml

Both of them use `weather.jsp` in the same directory, which includes `configure.jsp` in the same directory. We will go through these files in great detail shortly; for now, just be aware that `configure.jsp` can be set to redirect output either to JSP output files or to XSLT stylesheets

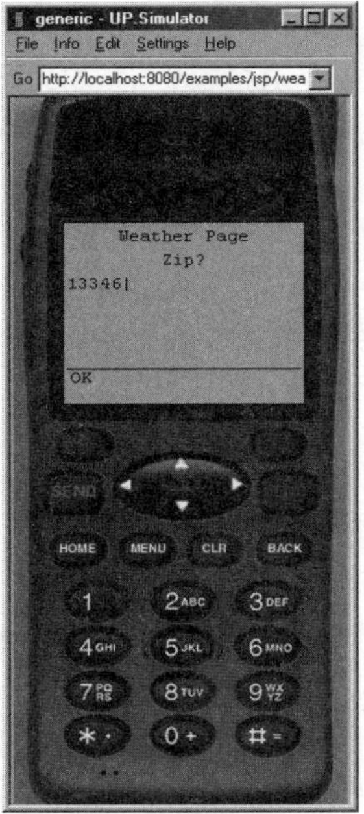

For this first tryout, point the simulator's microbrowser at `weather.wml`, and if all is well, you will see the screen here:

Select a query, click on Go! and enjoy your first simulated wireless experience, before taking a look inside at how it all works. If something goes wrong, try `weather.htm` in your Web browser, and the error messages, if any, will be clearer.

An Architecture For a Web JSP Application

There are many ways to structure a Web application using JSPs, and they are all good as long as they keep procedural logic separate from output templates. Our design allows for a compact and elegant conversation between the client, the main JSP page, the main bean, and output JSP pages (see diagram below). The idea is that a JSP page functioning as an output template contains a form whose `ACTION` attribute is the URL of the main JSP page functioning as a servlet. The main JSP page interacts with the main bean using two string variables: `beanCmd` and `jspCmd`. The `beanCmd` variable determines the kind of action the bean executes; the `jspCmd` variable determines the output template that the main JSP page selects for sending back the response. Most of those output template JSP pages include a `continue.jsp` page that contains the form with an XHTML form for input. The `ACTION` attribute of the form is the URL of the main JSP page:

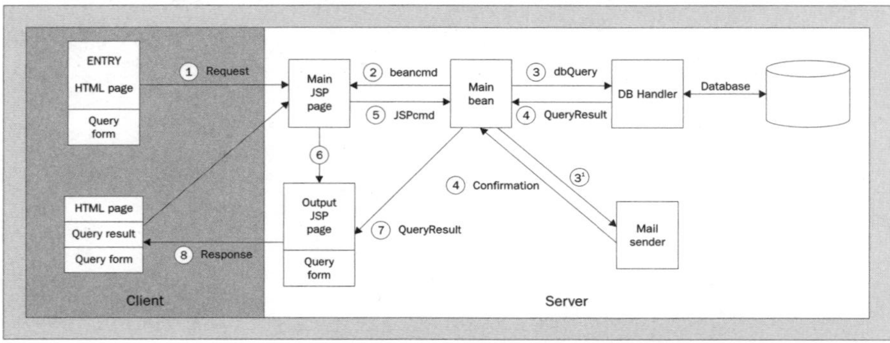

An Example: Database Lookup and Email

For instance, suppose we have a database of peoples' names, emails and their birthdays. Our application can do two things: retrieve data from the database and send an email to a person, presumably with a birthday message. The client, after logging in and establishing a session, selects and submits a command. The form for doing it, looks like this:

```
<form name="theForm" action="birthday.jsp"
   method="post" onsubmit="return onsub()">
   <!-- onsub() is a JavaScript function that checks user input -->

Select a BirthdayBean Command:
<select name="beanCmd" size=1>
 <option value="dodb" selected>do a Database Operation</option>
 <option value="send">send message</option>
 <option value="logout">logout</option>
</select><br>

Select a Database Operation:
<!-- material having to do with specifying a database query,
   presented and explained in the DBHandler section below -->

To send mail, fill in the fields below: <br>
 Send to: <input type=text name=toaddr value="" size=20><br>
 Subject: <input type=text name=subject value="" size=20><br>
 <textarea name=msgtext rows=10 cols=50>Enter your message here.</textarea>
</form>
```

Some elements of this form will be presented and explained in a section on database queries below. When submitted, the form goes to the main page of the application, `Birthday.jsp`.

The Main Page and the Bean

The main page uses a bean, `BirthdayBean`, whose properties include `beanCmd` and `jspCmd`:

```
 String bbcmd=null; //BirthdayBeanCommand from JSP specifies action:
     // login; dodb; send; logout;
 String jspcmd=null; // JSPCommand from BirthdayBean specifies display:
    // birthdaylist; list; change; msgsent; error; logout
```

`Birthday.jsp`, at some point, calls the `doCommand()` method of the bean, whose operation depends on the value of `beanCmd`. The `doCommand()` method sets the `jspCmd` property. That property determines which of several supporting JSP files gets included in the response page. The main JSP page looks like this:

```
<html>
<head><title>Birthday JSP/Birthday Bean/Database/Mail</title></head>
<body>
<%@ page import="java.util.*, MyNa.utils.*" errorPage="errorpage.jsp" %>
<jsp:useBean id="bbean" scope="session" class="birthday.BirthdayBean" />
<jsp:setProperty name="bbean" property="*" />
```

```
<% bbean.processRequest(request); %>
<%
 bbean.doCommand(); // usually, this is all we need after setting properties
 String msgtext=""; // accumulate messages here, if needed.
 String select=bbean.getJspcmd();

 if("logout".equals(select)){ %>
   Goodbye, come again soon.
<% }else if("error".equals(select)){ %>
  Something went wrong: <%= bbean.getErrorString() %>
  Click your back button and try again, or tell us.

<!-- the remaining options all include the file continue.jsp,
   either directly or from another file -->

<% }else if("change".equals(select)){ %>
  We changed <%= bbean.getNumberAffected() %> rows.
  <%@ include file="continue.jsp" %>
<% }else if("msgsent".equals(select)){ %>
  Congratulations, you sent a message.
  <%@ include file="continue.jsp" %>
<% }else if("list".equals(select)){ %>
   <%@ include file="listall.jsp" %>
<% }else if("birthdaylist".equals(select)){ %>
   <%@ include file="birthdaylist.jsp" %>

<% }else { %>
 Unimplemented command [<%= select %>]; how did this happen?
<% } %>
</body></html>
```

Output Files

Output files, other than logout and error outputs, combine the data coming from the bean with the `continue.jsp` page that sets up the next round of conversation. Consider the file `birthdaylist.jsp`:

```
<h2>Here are the birthdays you requested </h2>
<%
 String[][]rows=bbean.getResultTable();
 if(rows.length==0){
%>
 Sorry, nobody has a birthday coinciding with <%= bbean.getWhen() %>.
<%
 }else{
%>
  <table border="1">
<%
  for(int i=0;i<rows.length;i++){
%>
   <tr>
<%
   String[] row=rows[i];
   for(int j=0;j<row.length;j++){
    msgtext+=row[j]+"\t";
%>
```

```
          <td><%= row[j] %></td>
        <% } %>
      </tr>
      <% msgtext+="\n"; } %>
    </table>
  <% } %>

    <%@ include file="continue.jsp" %>
```

The file `continue.jsp` contains the form you have just seen, preceded by some JavaScript functions that are used to verify the form input:

```
  <!-- This is continue.jsp, included by several jsp files.
  -->
  <script>
  ...
  </script>

  <form name="theForm" action="birthday.jsp"
     method="post" onsubmit="return onsub()">
     <!-- onsub() is a JavaScript function that checks user input -->
  ...
  <textarea name=msgtext rows=10 cols=50>Enter your message here.</textarea>
  </form>
```

For the example application in this chapter, we are going to modify this design so we can process queries both from the wired and the wireless Web. The main modification is that instead of *including* output JSP files, we will *forward* the request to different files, depending on the nature of the query and on whether it comes from Web or WAP. This will necessitate some changes in how the JSP pages interact with the main bean.

The revised design is shown in the diagram below. Its details will become clear as we discuss the JSP pages and the main bean:

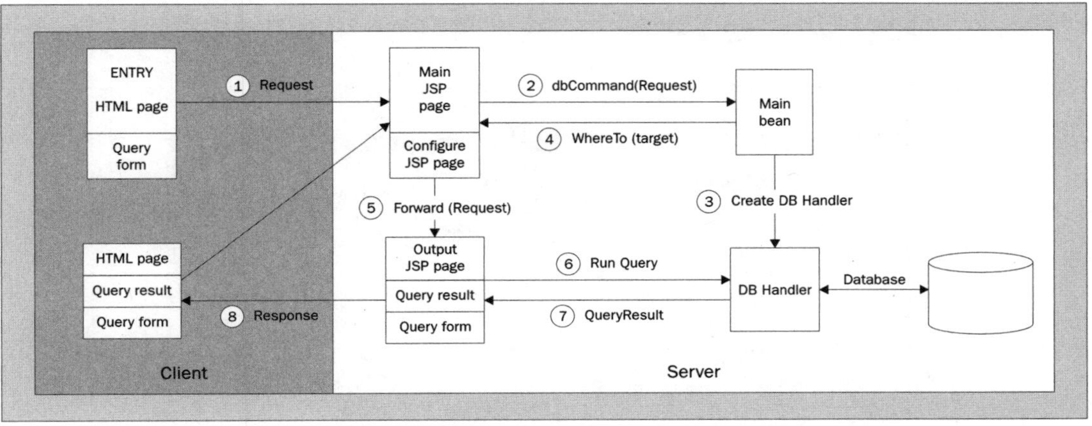

The subject matter of our application is weather reports, something we thought a WAP user might find useful.

Weather Reports

We assume that we have a database called `WEATHER`, with a table called `FORECAST`. The table, we assume, is regularly updated by some other application. Each row in the table has the following fields:

- Zip code (the primary key), date and time
- Current temperature, as of last update
- Day's low and high temperatures
- Probability of precipitation, expressed as percentage points
- Warnings, if any
- Tomorrow's forecast
- Day after tomorrow's forecast

If you point your browser at `weather.htm` you will see the following screen (with the dropdown list dropped down):

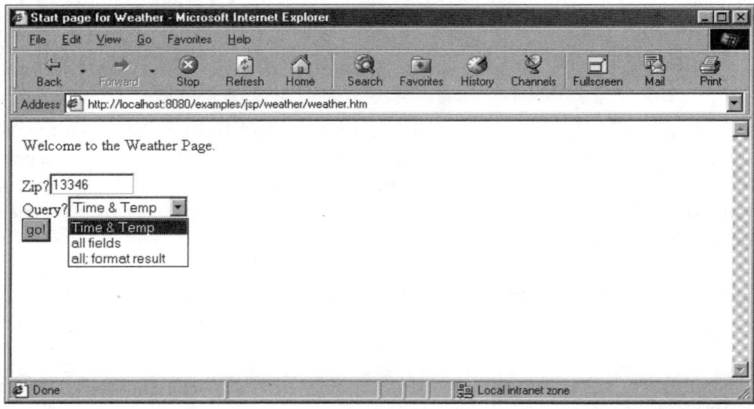

Run the 'AllTable' query, and you will get a screen that looks like this:

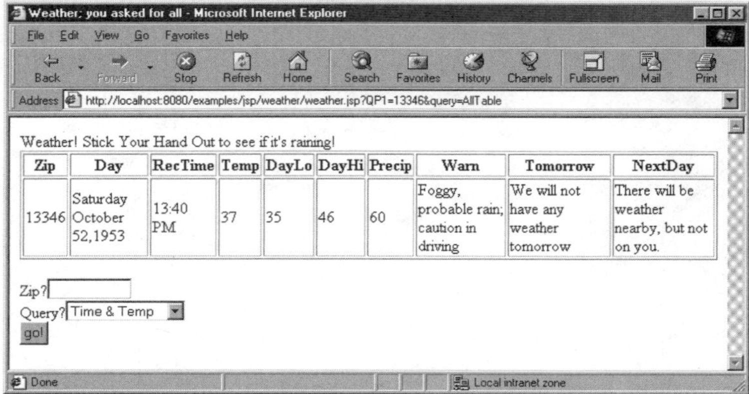

We will present the weather application in the following order:

- The entry page
- The main JSP page (Java code only)
- The configuration page and two back-end utility classes
- The main bean
- The output JSP pages.

The Entry Page

The application's entry page has been kept deliberately simple:

```
<html>
<head><title> Start page for Weather </title></head>
<body>

<!-- database fields are as follows:
 Zip,Day,RecTime,Temp,DayLo,DayHi,Precip%,Warn,Tomorrow,NextDay
 -->

Welcome to the Weather Page. <br />

<form method="POST" action="weather.jsp" >
Enter your Zip code:
 <input name="QP1" type="TEXT" size="10" ><br />
Select a query:
<select name="query" size="1">
 <option selected value="TimeTemp">Time &amp; Temperatures </option>
 <option value="AllTable">all fields, formatted as table </option>
 <option value="AllText">all fields, formatted as text</option>
</select><br />

<input type="submit" value="go!">

</form>
</body>
</html>
```

The nature of the queries and the process of specifying a query will be discussed shortly. For now, just note two details:

- Each query has a name ("TimeTemp" etc.)
- Query parameters are the values of input fields with names like `QP1`, `QP2`, and so on. (In this example, there is only one query parameter.)

When submitted, the form goes to the main JSP page, `weather.jsp`.

The Main JSP Page

This page has no output elements, only Java code. It carries out the following tasks:

- Instantiate the main bean, qBean
- Configure the bean using the configure.jsp file that gets included in weather.jsp
- Call the bean's doCommand() method with the Request object as argument
- Forward the request to the output file determined by the bean's whereTo() method

In the next example, the destination is the output file corresponding to the submitted query. In the next section, the number of destinations will double, to include JSP pages that produce output for WAP microbrowsers:

```
<html>
<head><title> Fwd page for Weather </title></head>
<body>

<!-- database fields are as follows:
 Zip,Day,RecTime,Temp,DayLo,DayHi,Precip%,Warn,Tomorrow,NextDay
 -->

<%@ page errorPage="errorpage.jsp" %>
<jsp:useBean id="qBean" class="weather.QBean" scope="session"/>

<%@ include file="configure.jsp" %>
<%
  qBean.doCommand(request);
  if(true){
   out.clear();
   pageContext.forward(qBean.whereTo());
   return;
  }
%>
</body>
</html>
```

Two items in this page require an explanation: the configuration page and the bean.

The Configuration Page

The configuration page includes the call to qBean.configure(). The task of configure() is to set up an object of our DBHandler class, presented in the next section. Although configure() is called once per request, it will have no effect after the session is set up and a DBHandler object is stored in it. (The method starts with an if statement that checks to see whether the DBHandler is null or not.)

This is not the ideal way to handle configuration, and in our own practice we do it differently: we instantiate and configure the main bean, including a DBHandler, from an XML configuration file. However this would have required considerably more background explanation. The method used in this chapter does allow a system administrator to configure the database access and alter the target files without introducing too many new concepts.

Here is `configure.jsp`; it contains nothing but Java code:

```
<%
 // information for connecting to database
String[]dbParams=new String[]{
 "sun.jdbc.odbc.JdbcOdbcDriver",
 "jdbc:odbc:WEATHER",
 "userName",
 "defaultPassword"
};

 // queries available to the client
String[][]dbQueries=new String[][]{

 {"AllTable", // all fields formatted as a table
  "SELECT * FROM FORECAST WHERE zip=?"},

 {"AllText",  // all fields formatted as a paragraph of text
  "SELECT * FROM FORECAST WHERE zip=?"},

 {"TimeTemp", // Date and temperature only
  "SELECT RecTime,Temp,DayLo,DayHi FROM FORECAST WHERE Zip=?"}
};

 // associate each query with an output JSP file
String[][]responseTargets=new String[][]{
 {"AllTable ","/jsp/weather/xhtml/AllTable.jsp"},
 {"AllText ","/jsp/weather/xhtml/AllText.jsp"},
 {"TimeTemp","/jsp/weather/xhtml/TimeTemp.jsp"}
};
 // this code is actually run once per session
 qBean.doConfigure(dbParams,dbQueries,responseTargets);
%>
```

As you can see, there are three sections in the file. The first section has to do with information that is needed to connect to a database using a JDBC driver; in effect, information needed to create a `Connection` object.

The second section has to do with running queries. It consists of name–value pairs, where each value is a string you would use to create a `PreparedStatement` object. These values are stored in a `Dictionary`-like object, indexed by the corresponding names. In order to run a query, the user only has to specify its name (in a select element of the form) and provide the values for the parameters of the `PreparedStatement`. Since these parameters are ordered, the form elements for entering query parameters must have such names as `Parameter1`, `Parameter2`, and so on, or, to shorten them for the Wireless Web where every byte counts, `QP1`, `QP2`, and so on. This is the convention we follow; it is further elaborated in the next section on `DBHandler`.

Finally, the third section selects an output template depending on the name of the query. It also consists of name–value pairs where the names are the names of queries and values are the names of JSP files to forward the request to.

A Look at the Back-End

The centerpiece of the back end processing is the main bean, `QBean.java`, that dispatches queries from the main JSP page to an appropriate handler and forwards the result to the appropriate page for output. It uses two custom classes to do its job: `DBHandler` and `Dict`. While the details are a bit involved, the main ideas behind these two classes can be summarized compactly. We do it here, to take the mystery out of it and also to explain how the application gets initialized from the request data.

The DBHandler Class

Our main tool for database processing is the `DBHandler` class. There is a `DBHandler` object for each database that is used by the application within a user session. This means that a `DBHandler` object needs three kinds of information:

- Information about the database: the JDBC driver and the database URL
- Information about the user: username and password
- Information about the applications: what queries does the application make available to the user?

The first two items on this list are just `Strings`, and you have seen them specified in the configuration file. How does one represent queries? `DBHandler` contains an inner class called `Query` that implements the "named query" abstraction: a `Query` object is, in effect, a query string for a `PreparedStatement` (in the JDBC sense) with a name given to it. `DBHandler` contains a `Hashtable` of such `Query` objects, indexed by their names. The configuration file you have just seen results in a `DBHandler` object whose queries `Hashtable` contains three `Query` objects, named `AllTable`, `AllText` and `TimeTemp`.

A `DBHandler` is created once per session. Once it is created, it connects to the database (through a connection pool) and creates its `PreparedStatement` objects. After that, the program is ready to accept queries from the query entry page. This page, for our weather application, contains the following form (repeated from before):

```
<form method="POST" action="weather.jsp" >
Enter your Zip code:<input name="QP1" type="TEXT" size="10" ><br />
Select a query:
<select name="query" size="1">
 <option selected value="TimeTemp">Time &amp; Temperatures </option>
 <option value="AllTable">all fields, formatted as table </option>
 <option value="AllText">all fields, formatted as text</option>
</select><br />
<input type="submit" value="go!">

</form></body></html>
```

To run a query, the user selects that query by name (from a select element, typically) and fills in the entry fields for query parameters (named `QP1`, `QP2`, and so on). This information gets to the `DBHandler` via the `Request` object and the main bean. The `DBHandler` retrieves the `PreparedStatement` using the name given, replaces its question marks with the values of `QP`s, and runs the query.

This is an outline. It will be fleshed out to a certain extent as we go through the code of the main bean. For complete detail, including the connection pooling mechanism that is built into the `DBHandler`, consult the code.

The Dict Class

The `Dict` class is a convenience class for storing and retrieving `Strings`. It is derived from `Properties` (itself derived from `Hashtable`). The reason we extend `Properties` rather than use the class directly is because we want a few additional features, as follows:

- Since `Dict` is used for configuration by sysadmins, we make the keys case-insensitive: `"Key"`, `"key"` and `"KEY"` all map to the same value.
- We make it possible to place a limit on the total length of the output, set by the `outLimit` variable. This is useful for HTML, crucial for WML.
- We define a `setDef()` method, overloaded so that it can take either a single name-value pair, or an array of such pairs (a 2-dimensional array of `Strings`), or two parallel arrays of names and values, or, indeed, a `Request` object arriving from a servlet or a JSP page.
- Finally, we define a `getDef()` method that is like the `getProperty()` method of `Properties`, except it makes the retrieval case-insensitive and it keeps track of `outLimit`.

The entire class is 50 lines, all shown here:

```
package MyNa.jspUtil;
import java.util.Properties;
import javax.servlet.http.HttpServletRequest;

public class Dict extends Properties {
int outLimit;

public Dict(int outLimit){this.outLimit=outLimit;}
public Dict(){this(-1);}// default for outLimit is -1, no limit

public void setOutLimit(int outLimit){
 this.outLimit=outLimit;
}
public int getOutLimit(){
 return outLimit;
}

public void setDef(String name,String val){
 setProperty(name.toUpperCase(),val);
}
public void setDef(String[][]pairs){
 for(int i=0;i<pairs.length;i++)
  setDef(pairs[i][0],pairs[i][1]);
}
public void setDef(String[]names,String[]vals){
 int len=names.length; if(len>vals.length)len=vals.length;
 for(int i=0;i<len;i++)
  setDef(names[i],vals[i]);
}
public void setDef(HttpServletRequest req){
 java.util.Enumeration enum=req.getParameterNames();
 while(enum.hasMoreElements()){
```

```
    String name=(String)enum.nextElement();
    String val=req.getParameter(name);
    setDef(name,val);
   }
  }
  public String getDef(String name){
   return getDef(name,"");
  }
  public String getDef(String name,String dflt){
   String val=getProperty(name.toUpperCase(),dflt);

   if(outLimit<0)// negative limit means everything goes
    return val;
   int len=val.length();
   if(len>outLimit){
    val=val.substring(0,outLimit);
    outLimit=0;
   } else outLimit-=len;
   return val;
  }
  } // end of Dict class
```

Most of this code is relatively straightforward, except perhaps the second version of `getDef()`. Remember that `outLimit` sets the allowed length of output, so every time we output a string, we subtract its length from `outLimit`. If the length of the string is greater than the remaining quota of characters, we output as much as we can and set `outLimit` to `0`.

With the supporting classes cleared, time to look inside the main bean.

The Main Bean

The primary tasks of the main bean are to set up a `DBHandler` and to forward the request to the right target. All the pertinent information has to be extracted from the request object. It follows that the bean needs three variables: a `DBHandler`, a `Dict` to hold the request object information, and a `Dict` to hold the targets after they are extracted from request. Here is the beginning of the bean's code:

```
package MyNa.jspUtil;
import java.sql.SQLException;
import javax.servlet.http.HttpServletRequest;

public class QBean {

DBHandler dbH=null;
Dict targets=null;
Dict requestDict=null;

public QBean(){}

public Dict getTargets(){return targets;}
public Dict getRequestDict(){return requestDict;}
```

configure()

The first thing that the bean does is `configure()`, called from `configure.jsp`. The call, as you may remember, looks like this:

```
qBean.doConfigure(dbParams,dbQueries,responseTargets);
```

Here, `dbParams` is an array of strings that contains database connection information, and the other two arguments are two-dimensional arrays of strings in which each row is a name-value pair. (You may want to review the composition of `configure.jsp` at this point.) Not surprisingly, they end up as `Dict` objects:

```
public void doConfigure(
 String[]dbParams,      // dbName,jdbc driver name,username and password
 String[][]dbQueries,    // query name,sql string for PreparedStatement
 String[][]responseTargets)// query name,output JSP page
  throws SQLException{
 if(dbH!=null)return;    // we only do this once per session
 targets=new Dict();
 targets.setDef(responseTargets);// store response targets in the Dict
 dbH=makeDBHandler(dbParams,dbQueries);
}
```

Now, how do you make a `DBHandler`? Actually, it's quite easy:

```
private DBHandler makeDBHandler(
 String[]dbParams,
 String[][]dbQueries)
   throws SQLException{
 String dbDriver=dbParams[0];
 String dbName=dbParams[1];

 //set dbUser, dbPwd or leave as null if not provided
 String dbUser, dbPwd;
 if(dbParams.length<3)dbUser=null; else dbUser=dbParams[2];
 if(dbParams.length<4)dbPwd=null; else dbPwd=dbParams[3];

 String []qNames=Misc.column(0,dbQueries);
 String []qSqlStrings=Misc.column(1,dbQueries);
 return new DBHandler(dbDriver,dbName,
           dbUser,dbPwd,
           qNames,qSqlStrings);
}// DBHandler is created, ready to run queries
```

This concludes the `configure()` part, executed from `configure.jsp` that is included in the main JSP page, `weather.jsp`. As you can see, although `configure()` is called on every request, its code gets executed only once, when the session is first created.

doCommand() and whereTo()

The main JSP page calls `doCommand()` and `whereTo()` which get executed on every request. `doCommand()` does not do much at all; it just wraps the `Request` object into a `Dict` and calls `setupRequestDict()`, a placeholder method that can be used, as needed, to validate the request information; we leave it empty:

```
public void doCommand(HttpServletRequest request){
 requestDict=new Dict();
 requestDict.setDef(request);
 setupRequestDict(); // check through parameter name assumptions
}
private void setupRequestDict(){
 // here we can check the request and complain if we don't like it
}
```

The business of identifying which page to forward the request to is carried out by `whereTo()`. By now, all request information is in the `requestDict`, and all targets are in the `targets Dict`, so we use `getDef()` a lot.

```
public String whereTo(){
 String targetType=requestDict.getDef("target","");
 if(0==targetType.length())targetType=requestDict.getDef("query","");
 if(0==targetType.length())targetType="error";
 return targets.getDef(targetType,"");
}
```

To give an example, if the query is `"AllTable"`, then `requestDict.getDef("query")` will return `"AllTable"`, and `targets.getDef("AllTable")` will return `"xhtml/AllTable.jsp"`, the name of the JSP page to forward the request to.

What About the Query?

The main bean does include a method for executing the query, `queryResult()`, but it is not called from any of the JSP pages that you have seen: it is called from the target page to which the request is forwarded. The `queryResult()` method, in turn, calls an output method of the `DBHandler`. The `DBHandler` has several such methods that differ in how the result set is packaged: it can be a two-dimensional array of `Strings`, or a lazily evaluated sequence whose elements are not computed until they are used. Whatever the format, the result of the query is returned as a variable within an object that implements our `QueryResult` interface. `QueryResult` extends the `XmlDoc` interface, both within the `MyNa.jspUtil` package:

```
public interface XmlOb {
 public String toXmlString();
}

public interface QueryResult extends XmlOb {
 public String[] getColumnHeaders();
 public String[] getColumnTypes();
 public String[][]getRows();
}
```

As you can see, an object that implements `XmlOb` knows how to write itself out to an XML string. An object that implements `QueryResult`, in addition, can provide two `String` arrays of equal size that specify the names and data types of record fields. The fields themselves are returned, as a `String` matrix, by the `getRows()` method.

Here is the `queryResult()` method that calls the `DBHandler`'s `getQueryResult()`. Note that the argument to `getQueryResult()` is a `Dict`, not a `Request` object. There is no dependence on the specific servlet/JSP context: `DBHandler` doesn't know or care where the `Dict` object comes from. It can, for instance, come from an XML file or from a socket stream.

```
public QueryResult queryResult()throws SQLException{
 // called from receiving page, not forwarding page.
 return dbH.getQueryResult(requestDict);
}
```

And that's all there is to the main bean; time to move on downstream to the output pages.

JSP Pages for Output

There are three output pages corresponding to three queries: `TimeTemp`, `AllTable` and `AllText`. The first two are identical except for the title: both show the query result formatted as a table, followed by an entry form whose action is the main JSP page. Here is `AllTable.jsp`:

```
<?xml version="1.0" encoding="UTF-8"?>
<!DOCTYPE html
   PUBLIC "-//W3C//DTD XHTML 1.0 Strict//EN"
  "DTD/xhtml1-strict.dtd">
<html xmlns=" http://www.w3.org/1999/xhtml" xml:lang="en" lang="en">

<head><title>Weather; you asked for all </title></head>
<body>
<%@ page errorPage="../errorpage.jsp" %>
<jsp:useBean id="qBean" scope="session" class="MyNa.jspUtil.QBean" />

<%
 String[][]rows=qBean.queryResult().getRows();
 if(rows.length<2){ // title row should be always there
%>
 Sorry, no weather is happening in your zip-code.

<% }else{                          %>

  Weather! Stick Your Hand Out to see if it's raining!<br />
  <table border="1">
<%  for(int i=0;i<rows.length;i++){            %>
   <tr>
<%
   String[] row=rows[i];
   for(int j=0;j<row.length;j++){
%>
       <td><%= row[j] %></td>
<%   }                           %>
   </tr>
<% }                              %>
```

```
    </table>
  <% } %>
  <form method="POST" action="weather.jsp" >
  Zip?<input name="QP1" type="TEXT" size="10" ><br />
  Query?<select name="query" size="1">
   <option selected value="TimeTemp">Time &amp; Temperatures </option>
   <option value="AllTable">all fields, formatted as table </option>
   <option value="AllText">all fields, formatted as text</option>
  </select><br />
  <input type="submit" value="go!">
  </form>

  </body>
  </html>
```

Note how this page gets the result set from the DBHandler as a String matrix and dumps it directly to output, without any regard for its size. This is acceptable for a Web application, but a risky thing to do in a WAP application. It is for this reason that we provide an "AllText" query in which the output is crafted by hand and so can be controlled more precisely. A different output page for the "AllText" query will be one of several changes in the application as we adapt it for WAP. Before we move on to that, let us quickly consider the question of how this application can be used to update weather reports, in addition to displaying them.

Updating the Database and Adding Queries

In order to be able to update the FORECAST table, you don't need any new Java code: you simply use an UPDATE SQL query instead of a SELECT one. Here are the additions that need to be made:

First, we add a query to the end of the query list in configure.jsp:

```
    {"TimeTemp",
     "SELECT RecTime,Temp,DayLo,DayHi FROM FORECAST WHERE Zip=?"},
    {"addOne",
     "INSERT INTO FORECAST VALUES(?,?,Now,?,?,?,?,?,?,?)"}
  };
```

Here, the "?" is, as before, a place holder for a field value, and "Now" is a (MS Access–specific) way of referring to the current date.

Second, we add a new response target to the target list in the same file:

```
    {"AllText","/jsp/weather/xhtml/AllText.jsp"},
    {"addOne","/jsp/weather/xhtml/TimeTemp.jsp"}
```

We can use the same TimeTemp.jsp because (like AllTable.jsp) it just loops through whatever is in the String matrix. In this case, it will be a single column, with the second row showing an integer, the number of rows affected.

Third, we add eight more input elements (text boxes) to the form in weather.htm. The new elements are for query parameters and therefore named QP2, QP3, and so on. (There are ten fields altogether, and one of them is the current date.)

Finally, we add another option to the select element in `weather.htm`:

```
<option value="addOne">addOne </option>
```

If you enter data in the text boxes and select **addOne** from the list of available queries, this is the response you will see (the HTML source):

```
Weather! Stick Your Hand Out to see if it's raining!<br />
  <table border="1">
   <tr>
       <td>NumberOfRowsAffected</td>
   </tr>
   <tr>
       <td>1</td>
   </tr>
  </table>
```

The weather report for the zip code that you had entered has been updated, as you can verify by running a `TimeTemp` query. Of course, in real life it is unlikely that the updates will be entered manually from an HTML form (although one can think of a junior high school project to keep the school's WeatherPage up to date). More likely, they will come from another application. This is easy to integrate into our framework, especially if the application sends them over packaged as a `Dict` object.

Adding Queries

The update query we have just discussed is an example of what you need to do to add queries in our framework. Here is the summary: in order to add a new query:

- Write the query in SQL, with question marks for parameters to be entered by the user.
- Give the query a name.
- Modify the entry HTML form, in two ways:
  - Add the new query to the select element.
  - Add entry elements if the new query has more parameters than previously provided for.
- Modify `configure.jsp`, in two ways:
  - Add a new item to the query list (a pair of `query-name` and `query-sql-string`).
  - Add a new item to the list of output JSP pages.
- Create an output JSP page for the new query.

A new query is ready for use. As we said, in the "real" framework, instead of modifying `configure.jsp` you would edit an XML configuration file, but editing `configure.jsp` works fine.

From a Wired to a Wireless Environment

We are finally ready to move on to WAP. First, we will go through two brief background sections, one to overview the entire **Wireless Application Environment**, the other to cover **WML**, the **Wireless Markup Language**. Then we will modify our framework so that it can produce WML as well as XHTML output. The changes are quite similar to (in fact, simpler than) those you need to add a query, because the queries will remain the same.

This is what we will need to do:

- Add material to `configure.jsp` to show more targets.
- Add output pages that produce WML rather than XHTML. This may involve changes in the JSP Java code sections, to adapt the output to WAP display conditions.
- Add a WML initial entry page, `weather.wml`.

We tried to make the section that describes these changes self-contained: it includes enough explanatory comments to make its WML parts understandable. If you want a WAP conceptual framework before you start it, read through the overview sections first. If you already know it, or want to piece it together as you go along, you can proceed directly to WAP Weather.

Wireless Application Environment (WAE)

The first thing you need to know in order to write Wireless-Web applications is WML, with **WMLScript** a close second. These are the equivalents of HTML and JavaScript on the "fiber-and-copper" Web. Both WML and WMLScript are components of the WAE, Wireless Application Environment, which also includes specifications for the microbrowser, binary encodings for WML and WMLScript text, specifications for telephony applications and so on. In this section, we briefly explain how it all fits together in the WAE application model.

Internet Applications and the Protocol Stack

WAE is best understood in comparison with the Web because that's how it was designed, with the Web constantly in mind. As you may know, the Web and other internet applications (ftp, telnet, and so on) use protocols built on top of more basic protocols that handle the more basic task of getting bits from one place to another quickly, reliably and securely. These include IP, TCP, and TLS (Transport Level Security, formerly SSL, Secure Socket Layer). They form the foundation of the "protocol stack" on top of which sit application–level protocols such as HTTP 1.1, the protocol of the Web.

The designers of WAP have created a parallel protocol stack of similar functionality. They are shown in the diagram below, adapted from *Wireless Application Protocol Architecture Specification*, WAPForum 1998, p.15. The main differences between the two stacks have to do with the nature of the wireless world: WAP protocols are lightweight, and frequently use compact binary encodings of data. They also support push: notifications sent from the server without a request from the client. (For instance, notifying your pager that your flight has been cancelled.):

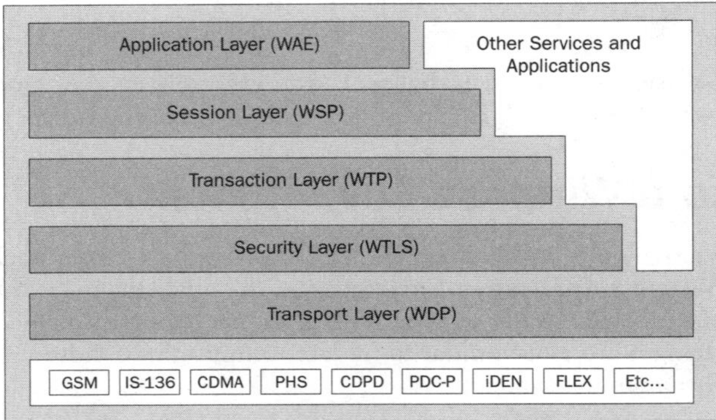

In summary, the bottom protocol, WDP sits on top of a variety of signal bearers, some of them carrying IP packets, others not. There is a list of supported bearers that is growing rapidly. The next layer is Security which provides the same services as TLS. Just as on the Web, you activate this layer by using `https` instead of `http` in your URLs. The next layer is Transaction, not to be confused with transaction processing in applications: it simply has to do with packet transactions between the client and the server. Depending on application requirements, it supports unreliable one-way requests, reliable one-way requests, and reliable two-way request-response transactions, which is the same as what Web browsers do. This sets the stage for the Session Layer, which is a binary version of HTTP 1.1, with an additional capability to suspend and resume a session quickly. (You have a call waiting!)

HTTP Reminders

HTTP is a stateless request-response protocol. The client sends in a request, the server processes it and sends a response. After that, the session is over and the connection is reset. To maintain the identity of a client across sessions, you need session-tracking tools, such as cookies.

The Request

Requests are in three parts: the request line, a header section and the body of the request. The format of the request line is:

```
Method    Request-URI   Protocol
GET       /index.html   HTTP/1.0
```

The first item is a command to carry out. By far the most common one is `GET`, that fetches a page. The `POST` command is frequently used to submit form data. WebDAV, the protocol for authoring over the Web, uses the `PUT` command. The remaining commands are rarely used.

After the request line come the headers. They are name–value pairs, in the following format:

```
Keyword:          Value
User-Agent:       Generic
Accept:           image/gif, image/x-xbitmap, image/jpeg, */*
Connection:       Keep-Alive
```

The `User-Agent` keyword tells the server what browser is being used, so the server can send files optimized for the particular browser type. The `Accept` keyword informs the server what kinds of data the user-agent can handle. The header lines are terminated by a blank line, i.e. a carriage return/linefeed (`\r\n`) sequence.

After sending the request and headers the client may send additional data. This data usually comes from a form that is submitted using the `POST` method. This additional information is called request entity. Finally, a blank line (`\r\n\r\n`) terminates the request.

The Response

The response is also in three parts: the status line, the headers and the body. The status line contains three fields: the HTTP version, status code, and a description of status code in the following format:

```
Protocol    Status-code        Description
```

For example, the status line:

```
HTTP/1.1  200  OK
```

says that the server uses version 1.1 of HTTP in its response, and that the client request was successful. You don't usually see the 200 code because the requested page is displayed instead, but you frequently see the 404 code that indicates that the requested page has not been found.

The headers are again name-value pairs, for instance:

```
Date: Wed, 19 May 1999 18:20:56 GMT
Server: Apache/1.3.6 (Unix) PHP/3.0.7
Last-Modified: Mon, 17 May 1999 15:46:21 GMT
Accept-Ranges: bytes
Content-Length: 10352
Connection: close
Content-Type: text/html; charset=iso-8859-1
```

These are mostly self-explanatory. The server sends a blank line to end the headers.

Setting Response Headers

Without any action on your part, the server will send back a number of headers based on its settings and the information it has received from the user agent. If the page it is sending back is generated by a servlet, you can specify the headers you want and their values by the `setHeader()` method of the response object:

```
res.setHeader("Content-length",byteArray.length);
```

If the page is static, or if you are using some other method for generating Web pages (but why would you?), then you can set response headers from inside the page using the `meta` element and its attributes:

```
<meta http-equiv="Cache-Control" content="no-cache" />
```

This is equivalent to sending a response header:

```
Cache-Control: no-cache
```

Using meta elements instead of response headers puts more burden on the scarce resources of a WAP browser. Whenever possible, use response headers instead.

The WAP Programming Model

HTTP requests and responses are rather verbose character sequences that would severely strain the resources of wireless devices. WAP uses compact binary encodings instead, known as the WAP Binary **XML Content Format** or **WBXML**. Developed by WAPForum, it was submitted (24 June 1999) as a Note to W3C for consideration, because a standard binary encoding for the HTTP protocol is something that the Web at large might well want to use.

In order to translate back and forth between the Web content and its binary encoding for WAP clients, we need a layer of software that would sit between the Web server and the wireless Web. That layer of software is called a **WAP Gateway**. In addition to translating content, WAP Gateways also translate between the Web and WAP protocols. Several WAP Gateway products are available, from Ericsson, Nokia, Phone.com, IBM, and others. There is also an open-source project, www.kannel.org.

WAP user agents talk exclusively to WAP Gateways that encapsulate all the encoding and decoding work that needs to be done. This is shown in the diagram below, adapted from *Wireless Application Protocol Architecture Specification*, WAPForum 1998, p.12.

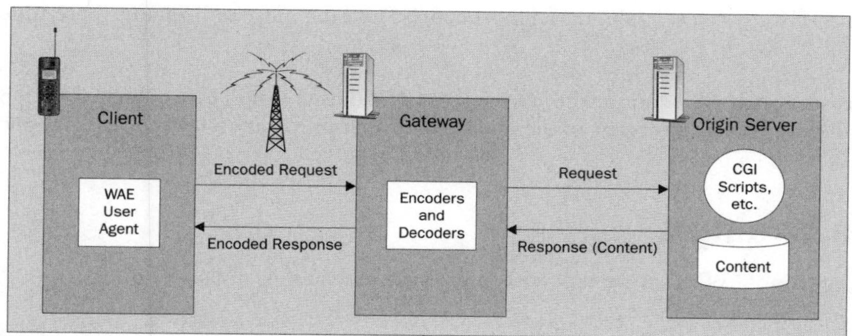

A WAP request–response exchange goes through these stages:

- User enters a URL on a WAP device and submits it as a request.
- The device translates the URL (and additional information, if any) into the binary format and sends it to the URL's Web server.
- The encoded request travels to the WAP Gateway associated with the URL's Web server.
- The WAP Gateway translates the request back into HTTP and submits it to the server.
- The server produces its response and returns it to the WAP Gateway.
- The Gateway translates the request into the binary format and sends to the WAP device that originated the request.
- The WAP device renders the page on its display, running embedded scripts, if there are any.

Apart from binary encodings, the operation of a WAP microbrowser is very similar to the familiar HTML and JavaScript response processing in a Web client, except the microbrowser uses WML and WMLScript. We're not going to use WMLScript in this example, but an overview of WML will help navigate the rest of the chapter.

WML

WML is an XML language, just like XHTML or MathML or SVG. This means that WML has a fixed set of tags and associated attributes that are defined in the WML Document Type Definition (DTD). The DTD specifies the rules of WML, such as: what elements can a given element contain and in what order, or which attributes have default values and what those default values are. You don't have to know how to read the DTD in order to learn those rules, but you have to learn the rules in order to create WML documents. In the subsections that follow, we sometimes introduce a DTD rule, immediately followed by an explanation and an example. We recommend that you learn how to read the complete DTD, because it is both the most concise and the most authoritative description of WML's syntax.

In this short section, it is not our goal to cover all of WML: that would be a subject for a long chapter or two. We will only give an overview of the main features, in preparation for the larger application in the next section.

A Simple Example

Here is a very simple WML document, just so we have an example at hand:

```
<?xml version="1.0"?>
<!DOCTYPE wml PUBLIC "-//WAPFORUM//DTD WML 1.1//EN"
 "http://www.wapforum.org/DTD/wml_1.1.xml">
<wml>
 <card id="start">
  <p align="center" >
   <big><strong>
   <br/>Hello, Wireless World!
   <br/>Now what?
   </strong></big>
  </p>
  <do type="accept" label="Go!">
   <go href="http://www.wapforum.com" />
   <!-- NB: wapforum.com and wapforum.org point to the same site -->
  </do>
  <do type="accept" label="help" >
   <go href="#help" />
  </do>
 </card>
 <card id="help">
  <p align="center">
   <big>How can I help you?</big>
  </p>
 </card>
</wml>
```

Click on the button below Go! and it tries to connect to wapforum; click on the button under help and get:

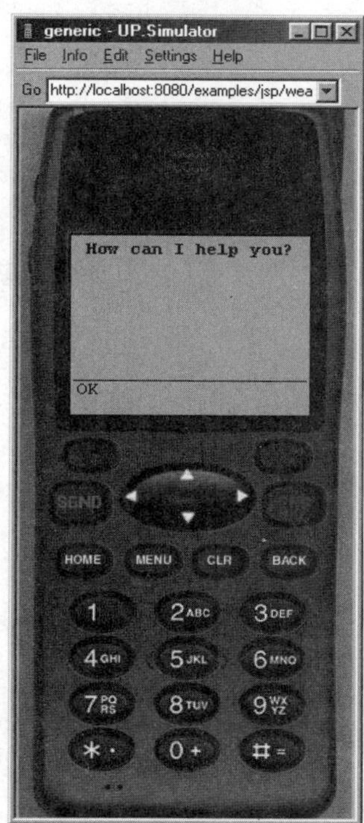

The first line of this example is the standard XML declaration. Such a declaration is found in the beginning of any XML document, be it WML, XHTML, JSP (in its XML form) or any other XML language. The second and third lines identify the document type and give its public identifier and the place where it can be found (a URL or a directory path). These are also standard XML features. Since the document type is identified as `wml`, this is also the tag of the root element of the page.

The Composition of the <wml> Element

The `<wml>` element can have an optional `<head>` and an optional `<template>` before the actual content. The content is not packaged into a single `<body>`, but rather into a sequence of elements of type `<card>`. This is intended to remind WML authors that their content must come in small chunks that can "fit on a card". To reinforce it further, WML documents are not called pages but **decks**, as in "a deck of cards". A WML deck can have one or more **cards**. This is concisely summed up by the DTD rule below. As usual, a question mark indicates an optional element, and + means "one or more". The rule reads: "a wml element consists of an optional head, followed by an optional template, followed by one or more cards".

```
<!ELEMENT wml ( head?, template?, card+ )>
```

The <head> and <template> Elements

A `<head>`, if present, can contain any number of `<access>` and `<meta>` elements, in any order. Empty heads are not allowed: if you create a `<head>` you have to put something into it:

```
<!ELEMENT head ( access | meta )+>
```

The `<access>` element allows you to restrict access to certain domains or directory paths. The `<meta>` element is similar to the `<meta>` element of XHTML; one of its common uses, as you saw in the weather example, is cache control.

A `<template>`, if present, contains material that is common to all cards. For instance, if all cards perform the same task in response to a timer event, then the event handler (a `<do>` element with an `ontimer` attribute) can go into the `<template>` element. In general, `<template>` can contain any number of "navigation elements" (`<do>` and `<onevent>`) in any order:

```
<!ENTITY % navelmts "do | onevent">
<!ELEMENT template (%navelmts;)*>
```

What's in the Cards? Text and Action

The composition of a card is defined by this rule:

```
<!ELEMENT card (onevent*, timer?, (do | p | pre)*)>
```

This says: a card can start with 0 or more `<onevent>` elements, followed by an optional `<timer>` element followed by 0 or more `<do>`, `<p>` and `<pre>` elements, in any order. `<p>` and `<pre>` elements contain the visible content of the card, while the rest of them have to do with tasks and events.

This rule points to two major differences between WML and HTML. One is that in HTML all event handling involves a scripting language, typically JavaScript: while event handling attributes, such as `onclick`, are declared in the HTML DTD, the ***values*** of those attributes take you outside HTML. In WML, you can perform some basic tasks without leaving the language.

The second major difference between HTML and WML is that in WML all visible elements appear within a `<p>` or a `<pre>`. In addition to formatted text, images and anchors, this includes tables and input elements that in HTML would appear in a form. (There is no `<form>` element in WML; its functions are divided between the input elements of `<p>` or `<pre>` and the `<postfield>` elements of `<do>`, see below.)

The <p> and <pre> Elements

The `<p>` elements contains formatted text (including tables), images, anchors and input elements.

Text, Images and Anchors

This is where WML vocabulary is the most similar to HTML. Text formatting and layout elements are:

- `<em>`: indicates emphasis; frequently rendered as italics
- `<strong>`: strong emphasis; frequently rendered as bold face
- `<big> <small>`: font sizes
- `<i> <b> <u>`: italics, bold face and underlined
- `<br/>`: the line break
- `<table>, <tr>, <td>`: table formatting

Text alignment is controlled by the `align` attribute with possible values `left`, `right` and `center`. The `mode` attribute has the values `wrap` and `nowrap`. The main tool for text layout is `<br/>`. (If you haven't done much XML yet, note how empty elements have to show both their beginning and their end.)

Images are introduced by an `<img>` element with an `href` attribute. There are two anchor elements, `<a>` and `<anchor>`. `<a>`, with its `href` attribute, works the same as in HTML. The `<anchor>` element can include different tasks, not necessarily forward navigation to a URL. The rule for `<anchor>` is:

```
<!ELEMENT anchor ( #PCDATA | br | img | go | prev | refresh )*>
```

In other words, in addition to text, line breaks and images, an `<anchor>` can include any number of "task elements", `<go>`, `<prev>` and `<refresh>`. A subsection on task elements is coming up soon.

Input Elements

Input elements appear inside a `<p>` or a `<pre>`, as in this example:

```
<card>
 <p>Select where you want to go:
  <select>
   <option onpick="http://bigcityhelp.com/movies.wml">
    Movies close by
   </option>
```

```
    <option onpick="http://bigcityhelp.com/pubs.wml">
     Pubs close by
    </option>
   </select>
  </p>
</card>
```

The following input elements are available: <input> and <select>. A <select> element, just as in HTML, contains any number of <option> elements. In WML, <option> elements can be grouped into an <optgroup>. This compensates for the absence of radio buttons and check boxes. <optgroup>s can be nested, as the following DTD rule shows:

```
<!ELEMENT optgroup (optgroup|option)+ >
```

Flow, Fields and <fieldset> Elements

The cover term for text elements, images and anchors, is flow elements. The cover term for flow and input elements together is fields. Fields can be grouped together using a <fieldset> element that can also contain the "action element" <do>. Fieldsets can be nested; in fact, a <fieldset> is itself included in fields:

```
<!ENTITY % flow "%text; | %layout; | img | anchor |a |table">
<!ENTITY % fields "%flow; | input | select | fieldset">
<!ELEMENT fieldset (%fields; | do)* >
<!ELEMENT p (%fields; | do)*>
<!ELEMENT pre (#PCDATA |a |br |i |b |em |strong | input | select )*>
```

As you can see, the action element <do> pops up all over the place: at the card level, inside a <p> and inside a fieldset within a <p>. Since we have completed our discussion of <p> and <pre>, it's time to see some action.

Tasks and Events

In WML, you can specify tasks to be carried out in response to events. Let's talk about tasks first.

What Tasks are There?

There are four task elements altogether: go, prev, refresh and noop. This looks like a very modest collection of tasks but there's more to it than immediately meets the eye. For instance, each task element can have side effects: it can contain <setvar> elements that set the values of variables as a side effect of the task. In addition, the <go> element can function like an HTML form.

The <go> and <prev> Elements

The difference between these two elements is in how they use the history stack of the microbrowser. If the user navigates using a <go> element, then its href attribute must be given a URL value, and that value is added to the top of the history stack. If the user navigates using a <prev> element then there are no attributes, and the browser switches to the previous element on the history stack.

The <go> element can also function as a form: it has a method attribute ("post" or "get"), it has an href element whose value can be a JSP page, and it can contain <postfield> elements that are sent as request data.

```
<!ELEMENT go (postfield | setvar)*>
```

This says: a <go> element can contain zero or more <postfield> and <setvar> elements, in any order.

The <postfield> Element and Variables

As you know, input elements are in <p> but <postfield> elements are in <go>, which does not contain input fields. How does the data get from inputs to postfields? The answer is, via **variables**, another WML feature that distinguishes it from HTML. Here is an example:

```
<go href="http://www.wapserv.com:8080/emerg.jsp" method="post">
 <postfield name="un" value="$uname"/>
 <postfield name="em" value="$email"/>
</go>
```

Here, $uname is a variable reference. The value of the variable comes from an input element: somewhere in the deck there is a <p> that looks like this:

```
<fieldset title="PersonalInfo" >
 Username:
 <input name="uname" maxlength="15" emptyok="false" /> <br/>
 Email address:
 <input name="email" maxlength="15" emptyok="false" /> <br/>
</fieldset>
```

The <refresh> Element

In addition to input fields, variable values can be set in <setvar> elements. If all you want to do is reset some variables without changing location or submitting a form, use the <refresh> task:

```
<refresh>
 <setvar name="v1" value="new" />
 <setvar name="v2" value="new" />
</refresh>
```

The <noop> Element and Event Shadowing

The <noop> task is primarily used to block, on the card level, an event handler that is defined in the <template>. An event handler defined in the <template> applies to all cards; what if you wanted it to apply to all except one? You would define the same event handler for that one card and give it the <noop> task. The card–level definition overrides (or "shadows") the deck–level definition.

This completes our discussion of tasks; on to events and event handlers.

What Kinds of Events are There?

There are two kinds of events: those that require a user interaction with some sort of a widget and those that are attached to WML elements. The first kind are called **user events**. User events are specified in <do> elements. The second kind are called **intrinsic events**. Intrinsic events are processed by event handlers.

Event handlers for intrinsic events are:

- onpick: user selects an option, as in the example above
- oneventforward: user navigates to a card using a <go> element or equivalent
- oneventbackward: user navigates to a card using a <prev> element or equivalent
- ontimer: a <timer> element expires

onpick is an attribute of <option>; the rest are attributes of <card>. The card–level event handlers can also be specified as values of the type attribute of the <onevent> element within a card, as in:

```
<onevent type="oneventforward" >
 <refresh><!-- you've seen this refresh task a moment ago -->
  <setvar name="v1" value="new" />
  <setvar name="v2" value="new" />
 </refresh>
</onevent>
```

The oneventforward and oneventbackward Event Handlers

What kind of task would you want to carry out in response to forward navigation? A <go> task would make it simply a redirection, which is a wasteful thing to do: if you know where you want to go, why not go there directly. A <prev> task would simply send you back without anything gained. The task that does make sense is <refresh> because you may want to reset all your variables when a new visitor to the card appears. oneventbackward is also likely to be used for cleanup.

The ontimer Event Handler

If you want the user to move on quickly, you would use the <timer> element. A timer sets of an event after a period of time, specified in tenth of seconds:

```
<!-- Question in a timed quiz -->
 <card id="Q1">
  <onevent type="ontimer" >
   <setvar name="A1" value="overtime" />
   <go href="#Q2"/>
  </onevent>
  <timer value="20"/><!-- two seconds -->
  <p >
   Q1: The capital of Cooninga is:
   <select id="A1">
    ...
   </select>
  </p>
  <do>
   <go href="#Q2" label="Next Question"/>
  </do>
 </card>
```

If the task for an ontimer event is a single <go> element then you can use a shorter version, with ontimer as a card attribute:

```
<!-- Overview of choices -->
 <card id="Overview" ontimer="#MainDish"/>
  <timer value="20"/>
  <p >
   Main courses are fish, chicken and vegetarian.<br/>
   Desserts are chocolate mousse and ice cream. <br/>
   Get ready to make your selections.
  </p>
 </card>
 <card id="MainDish" ontimer="#Dessert">
  <p>
   Select a dish:
   <select id="main">
    <option>...
```

User Events and the <do> Element

You have seen user events in the first example of this section. We repeat it here for convenience:

```
<do type="accept" label="Go!">
 <go href="http://www.wapforum.com" />
</do>
<do type="accept" label="Help">
 <go href="#help" />
</do>
```

All user events appear in <do> elements. The type of event is indicated by the required type attribute of <do>. The most common type is accept; it means that the deck will wait to accept input from the user before proceeding with the action. The label attribute defines the "widget" to use; the default is "ok". Other types have their own widgets. The widgets don't have to be visual; they may indicate a spoken command, or whatever the device can handle.

Other possible values of the type attribute are:

- help: Some sort of help. A Help widget is somehow made available; in our simulator, a Help option appears on the Menu button. In the example above we use type="accept" label="help".
- prev: Go to the top item on the history stack. The only type that is pre–defined.
- reset: Reset the context to default values.
- options: A context–sensitive request to show additional options.
- delete: Delete the current item or selected option.
- unknown: Equivalent to empty string. Substituted for any unrecognized type.

This is about as much WML as we need for the rest of the chapter. If you want to find out more, take a look at *Professional WAP Programming* also from Wrox Press.

Summary of WML Tags

In conclusion, here is a listing of all WML 1.1 tags, grouped by category. The numbers in parentheses show the number of tags in each category.

wml, head, meta, access, template (5)

<wml> is the root element. <head> is the first child of <wml>, optional. <head> contains <meta> and <access> elements.

<template> is the second child of <wml>, also optional. It contains descriptions of tasks that are common to all card elements.

card, onevent, timer, do, p, pre (6)

<head> and <template> are optional but there has to be at least one card in the deck, and there can be any number of them.

A <card> consists of: any number (including 0) of <onevent> elements, followed by at most one <timer>, followed by any number of <do>, <p> and <pre> elements, in any order.

<pre> is for pre–formatted text. <p> is for all formatted text, including <table>. <p> can also contain images, anchors, and input elements that in HTML would appear in a form.

p Content (19)

<p> can contain text elements, tables, images, anchors, and input elements.

Text Elements and Images (12)

Text formatting elements are mostly familiar from HTML, except that in WML they all appear inside a <p> element:

- em: indicates emphasis; frequently rendered as italics
- strong: strong emphasis; frequently rendered as bold face
- big, small: font sizes
- i, b, u: italics, bold face and underline
- table, tr, td: table formatting
- br: line break
- img: image

anchor, a (2)

<a> is strictly for forward navigation; <anchor> can contain any number of task elements.

Input Elements and Grouping Elements (5)

Input elements are also similar to their HTML counterparts, with minor differences. One additional element is <optgroup>, for grouping together several options within a <select> element. This compensates for the absence of radio buttons and checkboxes. So does <fieldset> that allows you to group together several text and input elements:

- input: much like a text box in HTML
- select, option: much like the same elements in HTML
- optgroup: for grouping several sub-options together within a <select>
- fieldset: to group several text and input elements together

Task Elements (4)

The task elements are <go>, <prev>, <refresh> and <noop>. See the preceding section for a detailed description and the section below for examples of use.

Event Related (3)

- <onevent> is a generic element for handling intrinsic events.
- <do> is a generic element for handling user events.
- <timer> is an element that generates an event after a specific delay.

Event-Handling Attributes

If the task to be performed by the event handler is <go> then we simply give the URL as a value to the appropriate attribute. For instance, instead of saying:

```
<card...>
 <onevent type="ontimer">
  <go href="some URL or another">
 </onevent>
 ...
</card>
```

you would say simply:

```
<card ... ontimer="some URL or another">
```

There are four event-handling attributes, three for <card> (ontimer, onenterforward, onenterbackward) and one for <select> (onpick).

Variable Related (2)

The <setvar> element lets you set variable values, e.g., within a <refresh> task. <postfield> (used within a <go> element when it functions as a form) receives its values as variables that are set by input elements.

This concludes our overview of WML; now let us continue with the weather application.

The WAP Weather Application

As we noted earlier, in order to incorporate WAP capability, we don't need any revisions to the framework or any new Java code. Let us recapitulate the changes that we do need to make:

- Add material to `configure.jsp` to show more targets.
- Add output pages that produce WML rather than XHTML. This may involve changes in the JSP Java code sections, to adapt the output to WAP display conditions.
- Add a WML initial entry page, `weather.wml`.

The overall framework is summarized by the same diagram as before:

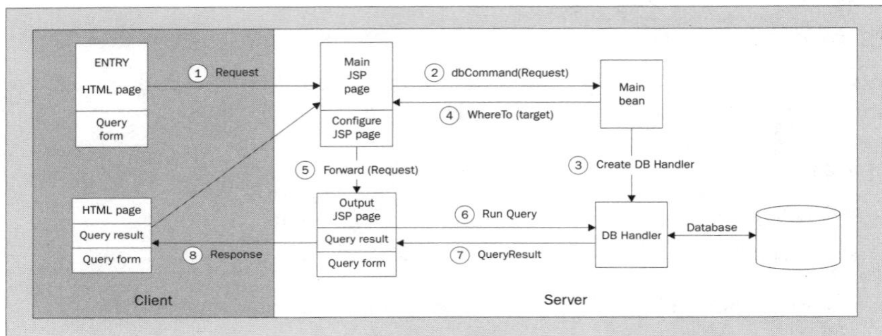

More Targets

The revised `configure.jsp` is very much the same; only the targets section is changed:

```
<%
 String[]dbParams=new String[]{
  ...
  // the rest of the database access section, unchanged
 };
 String[][]dbQueries=new String[][]{
  ...
  // the rest of the queries section, unchanged
 };

String[][]responseTargets=new String[][]{
 {"error","/jsp/weather/errorpage.jsp"},

 {"all","/jsp/weather/xhtml/AllTable.jsp"},
 {"allForm","/jsp/weather/xhtml/AllText.jsp"},
 {"TimeTemp","/jsp/weather/xhtml/TimeTemp.jsp"},

 {"wml-all","/jsp/weather/wml/ AllTable.jsp"},
 {"wml-allForm","/jsp/weather/wml/ AllText.jsp"},
 {"wml-TimeTemp","/jsp/weather/wml/TimeTemp.jsp"}
};
 qBean.configure(dbParams,dbQueries,responseTargets);
%>
```

As you can see, three JSP pages have been added for WML output. Since they mix JSP elements with WML elements, they are not very suitable as the first example of WML. We will show the WML entry page first, followed by the WML output pages. Much of it will be familiar from the preceding section, but we have made this section deliberately self-contained, so if you have read the preceding section you can skip the comments and just read the code.

The WML Entry Page

WML is an XML language, so the page begins with an XML declaration. The rest of it is a WML deck consisting of a single card:

```
<?xml version="1.0"?>
<!DOCTYPE wml PUBLIC "-//PHONE.COM//DTD WML 1.1//EN"
                  "http://www.phone.com/dtd/wml11.dtd">
<wml>
 <card id="start" title="Weather">

 <do type="accept" label="Go!" >
  <go href="weather.jsp"><!-- submitted to a JSP page -->
    <postfield name="query" value="$query" />
    <postfield name="QP1" value="$QP1" />
    <postfield name="target" value="wml-$(query)" />
  </go>
 </do>
 <p align="center">Weather Page</p>

 <p>
  Zip?
  <input name="QP1" format="*N" maxlength="10" value="" /><br />
  Query?
  <select name="query">
      <option value="TimeTemp" > time &amp; temp </option>
      <option value="AllTable" > all fields as a table </option>
      <option value="AllText" > all fields as text </option>
     </select>
 </p>
 </card>
</wml>
```

As you can see, the root element is `<wml>`. It contains an element called `<card>`. In this case, there is only one card, but in general, instead of a single monolithic <body> a WML page consists of any number of cards. In addition, WML pages are not called pages but decks.

A WML card consists of any number of `<p>` and `<do>` elements, in any order. `<p>` elements are for text, `<do>` elements are for action. Text elements of WML are very similar to XHTML but, as you can see, they can contain user input elements, `<input>` and `<select>`. An important feature of WML is variables: if an input element's name is `QP1`, then the value of that element is stored in a variable named `$QP1`.

The single `<do>` element of our page has two attributes, `type` and `label`. The `accept` type means that the element will wait to accept user action before it proceeds with its task. How the user action will manifest itself depends on the device: it may be a button click, or a voice command, or a sequence of phone keys pressed. In any event, the label for this action is specified as `Go!`.

If the label attribute is not specified, the default is OK. Here is what this deck looks like in the Phone.com emulator. Note that the single card is broken into two screens because there are two input elements in it: WAP devices frequently do that whether they are asked to or not. (You have already seen the first screen at the very beginning of the chapter.)

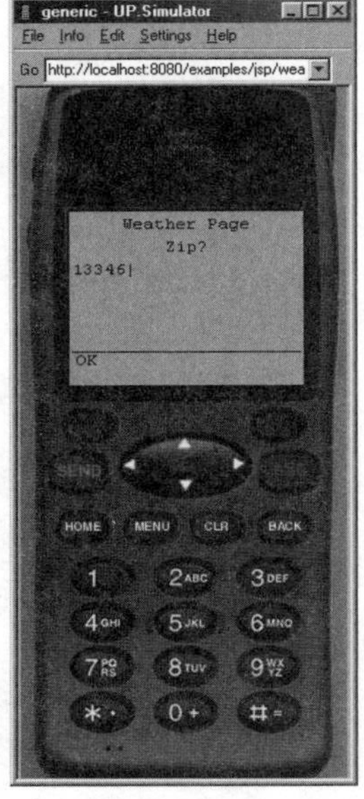

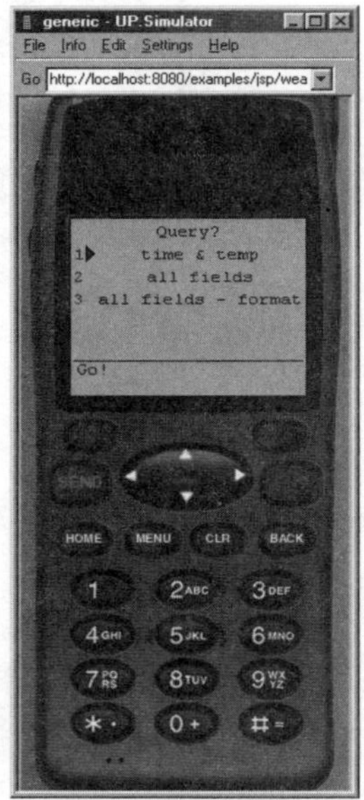

The <do> element of our page consists of a single "task" element, <go>. We repeat it here for convenience:

```
<do type="accept" label="Go!" >
 <go href="weather.jsp">
   <postfield name="query" value="$query" />
   <postfield name="QP1" value="$QP1" />
```

```
        <postfield name="target" value="wml-$(query)" />
      </go>
    </do>
```

The <go> element can be used simply to jump to another URL, but it can also function as a form. The destination is specified as an `href` attribute in either case. (There is no special <form> tag in WML.) Entry fields are called "postfields" because the default method is "post". Notice how postfields get their values from input elements via WML variables. The values can also be calculated; in the last postfield, the value is the result of concatenating "`wml-`" and `$query`.

So, this was our first real WML page; it wasn't too bad, was it? Let's look at our first JSP page that outputs WML.

JSP Pages for WML Output: TimeTemp.jsp

Since the `TimeTemp` query does not produce a lot of output, we will keep the same structure as before, formatting the output as a table and making no checks for the size of the output. However, we will rotate the table 90 degrees, showing each record in a column. This will not make much difference for the `TimeTemp` query, but in `AllTable` query, using the old format, we would end up with ten columns. Ten columns cannot possibly all fit in a WAP display, and the user would have to do horizontal scrolling in order to see them all. Horizontal scrolling is extremely awkward in WAP devices and should be avoided. This is how the output of `TimeTemp` looks in the simulator:

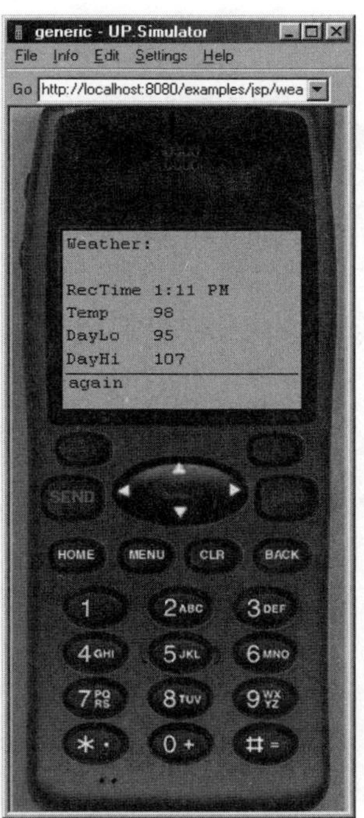

Declarations and the <head>

We will present `TimeTemp.jsp` in small chunks, interrupting for discussion. The first chunk begins with declarations and goes through the <head> element:

```
<%@ page contentType="text/vnd.wap.wml;charset=ISO-8859-1" %>
<?xml version="1.0"?>
<!DOCTYPE wml PUBLIC "-//PHONE.COM//DTD WML 1.1//EN"
                "http://www.phone.com/dtd/wml11.dtd">
<wml>
```

```
<%@ page errorPage="../wmlerrorpage.jsp" %>
<jsp:useBean id="qBean" scope="session" class="MyNa.jspUtil.QBean" />

<head>
 <meta http-equiv="Cache-Control" content="no-cache" forua="true"/>
</head>
```

As you can see, the <wml> element can contain a <head> before the cards. A common use for a <head> is to contain <meta> elements with `http-equiv` attributes. As we explained above in our brief summary of HTTP, a <meta> element in that says:

```
<meta http-equiv="Cache-Control" content="no-cache" />
```

is equivalent to including a "static" HTTP header:

```
Cache-Control: no-cache
```

and both have the effect of disabling caching in the browser. This is no difference in WML from XHTML, but that it is used in WML more often. By default, WAP devices cache very aggressively, to minimize network traffic, but in an application that tries to monitor rapidly evolving events, caching becomes a liability. So we set cache control to "`no-cache`", and set the `forua` (FOR User–Agent) attribute to "`true`", because the default value is "`false`" and <meta> elements whose `forua` is "`false`" do not get sent to the client.

The rest of the deck consists of two cards. The first card shows the query output as a table. Since all the table elements are the same in WML as in XHTML, that card is going to look familiar. The second card contains the "form" (a <do> element) to submit another query. This will also look familiar: it is the same card as the entry WML deck that we have just discussed.

The Table and the Form

The first card starts with a <do> element that sends you to the next card; the label is "Again", as in "submit your query Again". The rest of the card is very similar to the JSP page for XHTML output, except that the table is contained in a <p>, according to the rules of WML syntax, and the table is rotated:

```
<card id="output" title="TimeTemp">
 <do type="accept" label="Again" >
  <go href="#askCard" />
 </do>
<%
 MyNa.jspUtil.QueryResult qR=qBean.queryResult();
 String[][]rows=(null==qR)?null:qR.getRows();
 if(null==rows || rows.length<1){
%>

 <p>Sorry, no weather in zip-code.</p>

<% }else{ String[]headers=qR.getColumnHeaders(); %>

  <p>Weather:</p>
   <p>
```

```
  <table columns="2">
<% // we use only rows[0] to generate a 2-column table of fields
   for(int j=0;j<headers.length;j++){
%>
   <tr>
     <td><%= headers[j] %></td><td><%= rows[0][j] %></td>
   </tr>

<% } %>

  </table>
  </p>

<% } %>

</card>
```

The rest of the page contains no JSP–specific elements, only the second and final card of the output WML deck that is the same as the start card of the entry deck:

```
<card id="askCard" title="Weather">
<do type="accept" label="Go!" >
 <go href="weather.jsp">
   <postfield name="query" value="$query" />
   <postfield name="QP1" value="$QP1" />
   <postfield name="target" value="wml-$(query)" />
 </go>
 </do>
<p align="center">Weather Page</p>
<p>
 Zip?<input name="QP1" format="*N" maxlength="10" value="" /><br />
Query?      <select name="query">
      <option value="TimeTemp" > time &amp; temp </option>
      <option value="all" > all fields </option>
      <option value="allForm" > all fields-format </option>
     </select>
</p>
</card></wml>
```

JSP Pages for WML Output: AllTable.jsp

The code for `AllTable.jsp` is identical to `TimeTemp.jsp`, so we can simply show the output:

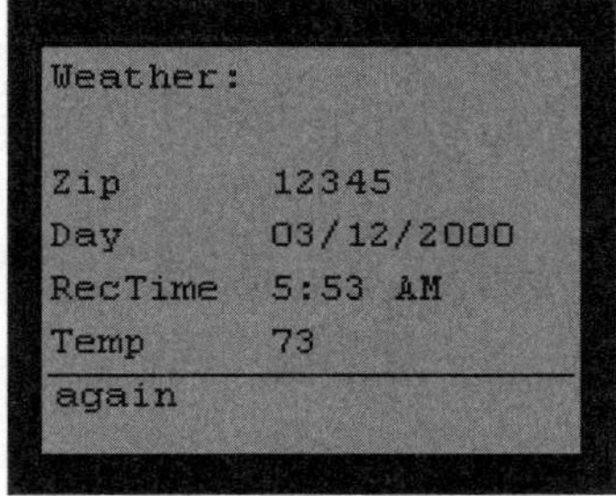

This screen shows only part of the output; the user can scroll through the rest line–by–line, using the down arrow on the simulator, or whatever other widget is available. With AllText, the deck is organized into cards that become individual screens of the output.

JSP Pages for WML Output: AllText.jsp

While `TimeTemp.jsp` and `AllTable.jsp` make an accommodation for the WAP environment by reformatting the table, they still make no provisions for controlling the size of the output. In this version, we abandon the format of a table produced by a loop and go to the AllText format that allows more flexible control.

The beginning of this page, up to and including the `<head>` element, is exactly the same, so we skip it and go directly to where it starts outputting the first card. As this point we introduce a change: after the `DBHandler` delivers the result set as a string matrix, we package the string matrix into a `Dict` and release output via the `getDef()` method of the `Dict` class, that controls for output size. (You may want to review the `Dict` section above, within the larger section on the back-end classes.) Here's how it works:

```
 <card id="output" title="AllText">
  <do type="accept" label="again" > <go href="#ask" /> </do>
  <do type="accept" label="details" > <go href="#details" /> </do>
 <% // Zip,Day,RecTime,Temp,DayLo,DayHi,Precip%,Warn,Tomorrow,NextDay

  MyNa.jspUtil.QueryResult qR=qBean.queryResult();
  String[][]rows=(null==qR)?null:qR.getRows();
  if(rows==null || rows.length<1){ // title row should be always there
 %>
  <p>Sorry, no weather in your zip </p>
 </card>
 <% }else{ Dict D=new Dict(); D.setDef(qR.getColumnHeaders(),rows[0]);
 D.setOutLimit(300);
  %>
 <p>
 zip: <%=D.getDef("zip")%> <br/>
 temp: <%=D.getDef("temp")%><br/>
 at <%= D.getDef("RECTIME") %> <br/>
 day's lo: <%= D.getDef("daylo") %> <br/>
 day's hi: <%= D.getDef("dayhi") %>
 </p>
 </card>
```

This method of output size control is rather primitive: it will break off output in the middle of a word or a number if the limit on the number of characters is reached. A more sophisticated approach would accumulate output in a `StringBuffer` and release it by meaningful units – but we are going to leave this as an exercise for the reader:

```
zip: 12345
temp: 73
at 5:53 AM
day's lo: 65
day's hi: 85

again          details
```

There are three more cards in the deck to be generated: the already familiar "ask" card which we skip, a "details" card, and a "moreDetails" card. Note that the card above does not display all the fields: potentially lengthy warnings and tomorrow's forecasts are left out until the user asks for them. (They are, however, downloaded with the deck.):

```
<card id="details" title="TimeTemp">
 <do type="accept" label="again" > <go href="#ask" /> </do>
 <do type="accept" label="more" > <go href="#moreDetails" /> </do>
<p>
day: <%=D.getDef("day") %><br/>
precip: <%=D.getDef("precip") %>
</p>
</card>
```

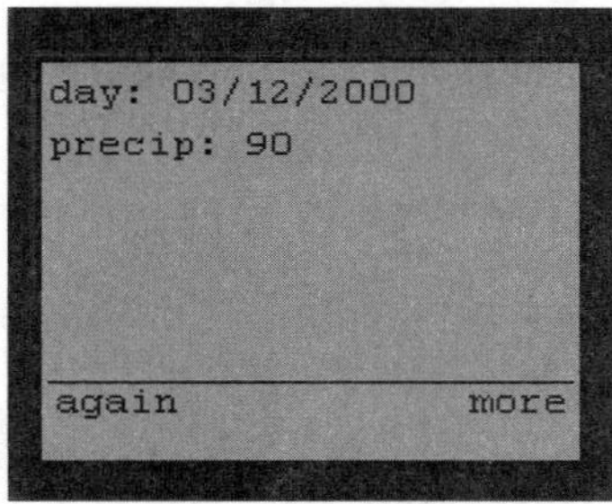


```
<card id="moreDetails" title="TimeTemp">
 <do type="accept" label="again" > <go href="#ask" /> </do>
 <do type="accept" label="basics" > <go href="#output" /> </do>
<p>
<% String W=D.getDef("warn"); if (W.length()>0){ %>
Warning: <%= W %> <br/>
<% } %>
Tomorrow: <%= D.getDef("tomorrow") %> <br/>
NextDay: <%= D.getDef("nextday") %>
</p>
</card>
<% } %>
```

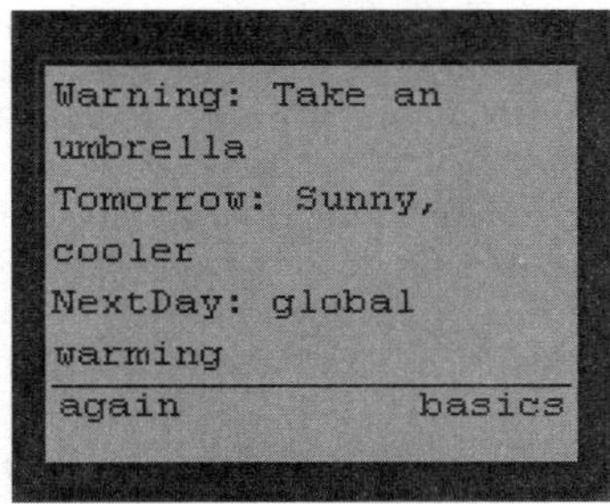

This completes the output JSP pages and our first WAP application. We are now going to show a different approach to the problem of generating both XHTML and WML from the same information source. We will stay with weather reports and with a relational database as the source of information, but our infrastructure will remain general: we can talk about other things, the information may come from a variety of sources, and the size of the application can be substantially increased.

A Different Approach: XSL

In summary, the role of output JSP pages in our weather application is to act as a transformer between the output of a database query and the response sent to the user agent. Whether the user agent is Web or WAP, the input to JSP pages is the same, a two–dimensional array of strings, itself generated from a query resultset. The output is, at some level of generality, also the same: an XML document of a specific document type (XHTML or WML). The task of the JSP pages in the middle is to generate an XML document from a two–dimensional array of strings. JSPs, as you can see, can carry out the task easily but, as often with JSPs, there is a concern that a sysadmin who is not a programmer will find it hard to maintain a JSP page that mixes Java code with XML tags. And in any event, at this early stage in the development of XML technologies, it is important to explore the alternatives.

One alternative is to use another general-purpose tool for generating XML documents. It is called **XSL(T): eXtensible Stylesheet Language for Transformations**. In this section, we will re-implement the weather application using XSLT. Except for the output component, only a few lines will need to be added to the main bean; the rest of the application will remain unchanged. A major implementation effort has gone into the background task of converting a two-dimensional array of strings into something that an XSL processor can handle, but this task and the new component that implements it are not specific to this application, or even to the entire WAP–Web problem. The new component, consisting of the `XmlStringDoc` and `XmlQueryStringDoc` classes, will be of use every time an XML document needs to be generated from a non–XML object in memory.

This section will have to build on some background in XML parsing and XSL. The next two subsections, "XML parsing" and "XSLT" will introduce all the concepts that are necessary for understanding the XSL-based WAP applications (but not the "virtual document" component).

XML Parsing

An XML parser, most generally, is a program that takes an XML document on input and makes its components available for processing by other programs. A Java XML parser usually makes those components available to a Java program. The components that most programs are interested in are elements and attributes, but processing instructions and comments are also made available, at least by some parsers. External entities and DTD's are more problematic.

There are two standard ways in which a parser makes XML components available to another application: one lays out the document in time, the other in space. **SAX**, the **Simple API for XML**, associates an event with each tag (opening or closing) and with each block of text. You just write the event handlers and sit back to watch the document pass by. **DOM**, the **Document Object Model**, describes the document as a tree. You can traverse it, edit it, do what you please with it, as long as you can store it all at once. We will not be using DOM in this chapter, but we will have much more to say on SAX in a moment.

There are many XML parsers to choose from, most of them Java parsers. Sun, IBM, Microsoft, Oracle and a number of smaller companies have on-going XML parser projects, with stable releases and regular upgrades. The reason there are so many parsers is because XML is increasingly viewed as the best format for data interchange between applications and components of applications (including, as one particular case, data interchange between a Web server and a Web browser). In order to use XML that way, you need a parser.

The Parser and the Application

The relationship between the parser and the application is specified in two places. First, the XML 1.0 recommendation has various things to say about how a "conformant processor" must or may or should respond to various aspects of the document. Second, SAX and DOM spell out the interfaces that an application can expect from the parser. These are just interfaces that have to be implemented, and they cover many, but not all, aspects of converting a document into events or data structures that an application can use.

The rest of the picture comes from the parser. The relationship of the parser to XML 1.0 is in terms of conformance, from "very conformant" to "terribly non-conformant". There is a good conformance study of different parsers at http://www.xml.com/pub/1999/09/conformance/summary.html.

The relationship of the parser to SAX and DOM is two-fold. First, it implements SAX and DOM interfaces. In the process, new classes are defined, and the interfaces may be extended. Second, the parser fills in the gaps that SAX and DOM are silent about. In particular, SAX and DOM say nothing about how an application obtains an instance of the parser class, and how that instance gets access to the document that it is called upon to parse. For Java, this gap has been recently (March 2000) filled by Sun's "Java API for XML Parsing (JAXP)", available from http://java.sun.com/xml; the API is implemented as the `javax.xml` package. The package includes Java interfaces from SAX and DOM, and the basic interfaces and classes that a Java XML parser must implement.

More on SAX

To elaborate on SAX first, we usually don't know or care how the parsing process unfolds and in what order lexical analysis and production rules are applied. However, we can visualize that process as a steady progression through the text that sends notifications of certain important events: the document has started, an element has started, an element has ended, a character sequence between two elements has been found, and so on. **SAX provides standard names for callback functions that are triggered by these events.** Writing a SAX application mostly consists of implementing those callbacks. Here are some of their declarations, from the `org.xml.sax.DocumentHandler` interface:

```
void characters(char[] ch, int start, int length)
   Receive notification of character data.
 void endDocument()
   Receive notification of the end of a document.
 void endElement(java.lang.String name)
   Receive notification of the end of an element.
 void processingInstruction(java.lang.String target, java.lang.String data)
   Receive notification of a processing instruction.
void startElement(java.lang.String name, AttributeList atts)
   Receive notification of the beginning of an element.
void startDocument()
   Receive notification of the beginning of a document.
```

Some of the best parsers, including Sun's parser and James Clark's xp, are constructed by implementing SAX interfaces. In other words, SAX event handlers can be used to construct a DOM tree. They don't have to be so used: if you can structure your document processing as a single sweep through the document, without too many references back to already processed elements, then all you need is SAX event handlers.

In addition to programming–language–independent interfaces, SAX specification provides a Java class, `HandlerBase`, which contains a default implementation of those interfaces. Instead of implementing all the interfaces directly, a Java class that wants to use a SAX parser can extend `HandlerBase` and override only those methods that are needed for the application.

A Simple Example

Here is a simple example of using a SAX parser to echo an XML file. It is adapted from the first example in Sun's Java XML tutorial, http://java.sun.com/xml/docs/tutorial/TOC.html. We will only show the `main()` method and a couple of event handlers.

Imports and the main() Method

```
import java.io.*;
import org.xml.sax.*;
import org.xml.sax.helpers.ParserFactory;
import com.sun.xml.parser.Resolver;

public class Echo01 extends HandlerBase
{
 public static void main (String argv [])
 throws IOException
 {
 InputSource input;
 if (argv.length != 1) {
  System.err.println ("Usage: command filename");
  System.exit (1);
 }

 try {
  // Set up output stream
  out = new OutputStreamWriter (System.out, "UTF-8");

  // Turn the XML input file into an XML "input source" object
  input = Resolver.createInputSource (new File (argv [0]));

  // Get an instance of the non-validating parser.
  Parser parser;
  parser = ParserFactory.makeParser ("com.sun.xml.parser.Parser");
  parser.setDocumentHandler ( new Echo01() );
   // Parse the input source
  parser.parse (input);

  } catch (Throwable t) {
   t.printStackTrace ();
  }
  System.exit (0);
 }
 static private Writer out;
```

Examples of Callbacks

In the code below, `emit()` and `nl()` are helper methods that output character content in a safe and system-independent way:

```
//===========================================================
// SAX DocumentHandler methods
//===========================================================

public void startDocument ()
throws SAXException
{
 emit ("<?xml version='1.0' encoding='UTF-8'?>");
 nl();
}

public void endDocument ()
throws SAXException
{
 try {
  nl();
  out.flush ();
 } catch (IOException e) {
  throw new SAXException ("I/O error", e);
 }
}

public void startElement (String name, AttributeList attrs)
throws SAXException
{
 emit ("<"+name);
 if (attrs != null) {
  for (int i = 0; i < attrs.getLength (); i++) {
   emit (" ");
   emit (attrs.getName(i)+"=\""+attrs.getValue (i)+"\"");
  }
 }
 emit (">");
}
```

This short sample should give you an idea of how you work with document handler methods of SAX. Now, suppose that instead of slavishly echoing a document, we want to transform it in some ways. The transformations can range from extremely simple (keep only elements with a specific tag, skip the rest), to extremely hard (create a summary in French by extracting the first sentence of the first child of each `<section>` element and translating that sentence into French using a machine translation program). All programmable transformations can be done using a Java parser and other Java programs; however, some of them should be made available to people who are not Java programmers. In other words, there should be a simpler language in which people can express such ideas as:

- Extract all and only `<desk>` elements from the `<furniture-inventory>` document; order them by the value of their price attribute.
- Count the number of `<error>` elements in the `<student-composition>` document.

- Find all <stage-direction> elements that contain the word "Enter" or "Enters"; find all the <speech> elements that are immediate right siblings of such <stage-direction> elements; find the <speaker> child element of such <speech> elements; count the percentage of such <speech> elements whose <speaker> is one of those who are named in the <stage-direction>; compare such ratios for different plays by different authors.

Expressions in such a language would be given to a processor that contains an XML parser. Given an expression, the processor would call the parser to parse the document, then carry out the transformations described in the expression and output the result. As you know or might have guessed, XSLT is exactly such a language.

XSLT, XPath and Document Transformations

Why is a language for document transformation called a stylesheet language? The answer is found in the history of XSL that forms a useful background for its understanding.

How XSLT Came About

The history of **XSL** (**eXtensible Stylesheet Language**) has been brief but eventful. Work on XSL started in 1997, with the goal of producing a stylesheet language for specifying how an XML document is to be displayed in the browser. That goal has not yet been reached. In the meantime, two other specifications, both having to do with *transforming* rather than *formatting* XML, became recommendations in November 1999, even though they did not exist as independent projects until fairly late in that year. As the XSL project unfolded, different parts of it grew at different speeds, and their relative importance and state of preparedness were changing. Eventually, XSLT and XPath got carved out into separate products and completed, while the document formatting part is still in working draft.

That a style sheet language was needed for XML to function was obvious from the beginning: if users can define their own elements, they have to be able to specify how those elements will look when displayed in the browser window or other media. Also from the beginning, the intent was to make the style sheet language more powerful than **Cascading Style Sheets (CSS)**. CSS has a good deal of control over *how* different elements are displayed, but very little control over *what* gets displayed and in what order. XSL was intended to be able to add, remove and reorder the elements of the document tree, so, for instance, the style sheet could handle multiple reports from a database table, showing different fields and sorting records in different ways.

Initially, the tree–transformation part of XSL was meant to be an aid to the formatting part, but several factors conspired to bring it to greater prominence. One of the factors was that it was easier to deal with and build a consensus about. Another one was a changing understanding of the role of XML. As XML's role was evolving from a tool for document markup to (also being) a tool for data interchange between applications and components of applications, the transformation "module" was developing an independent significance, totally unrelated to formatting and display. At some point, these forces brought about a split between XSL for Formatting and XSL for Transformation (XSLT). The XSLT part was taken over by James Clark who brought it to a swift completion while at the same time producing xt, a fully compliant reference implementation of the XSLT processor. (See below on how it is used in our application.)

What's XPath?

An essential feature of a tree transformation language is the ability to refer to tree paths, both in absolute terms (starting from the root) and relative to the current position in the tree. In order to achieve its goals, XSLT needed a "sub-language" whose expressions could specify paths and, more importantly, sets of paths that satisfy a certain condition, or match a certain pattern. As work on XSLT unfolded, this "sub-language" was naturally growing in size and sophistication: it was becoming more and more like a "regular expression language for tree paths". At some point, it was realized that exactly the same sub-language is needed for XLink/XPointer, a specification for hypertext links between XML documents and parts of documents. Here again, the idea was to make the linking facility more powerful and flexible than HTML's `<A>` or `<LINK>` tags, so that both the source and the target(s) of a link can be specified in structural terms. The result was that the sub–language for tree path description became separated from both XSLT and XLink/XPointer and assumed independent existence under the name of **XPath**. XPath was also brought to a swift completion, on the same date as XSLT, by James Clark and Steve DeRose, representing the XSL and the XML–Linking Working Groups, respectively.

Where Does XSLT Happen?

There are basically two scenarios. The first is for a browser to come equipped with both an XML parser and an XSLT processor working together. Such a parser would display an XML document directly, using an XSL stylesheet attached to the document. At the time of writing (March 2000), only Internet Explorer 5 can do this, but it uses an obsolete version of XSLT.

In the second scenario, an XML parser and an XSLT processor, working together somewhere in the background, produce a transformed XML document (or any kind of document) and send it to another piece of software to do something with it. The output can be an XHTML or HTML file and the receiving application may well be a Web browser. Or, the output may be a WML file and the receiving application will then be a WAP microbrowser (with a WAP Gateway in between, of course). This is what we're going to do, as an alternative to using JSP pages for output.

In both of these scenarios, it is the XSLT processor that drives the process: it invokes the parser, and receives and transforms the parser output. A parser, as you saw, expects an "input source", a data flow that comes from a local file, or a URL, or a stream, or even a string, as long as those sources have XML markup. In our case, we have plain strings without markup, and, as we said in the introduction to this section, an additional software component is needed to convert that data into a "virtual document" that a parser will be willing to consider. We will deal with this complication in a moment, after we present a simple example of XSLT (with a little bit of XPath).

What is Needed to Try XSLT?

To try XSLT you need an XSLT processor and an XML parser. For the XSLT processor, we use James Clark's xt. (James Clark is the editor of the XSLT Recommendation and a co–editor of the XPath Recommendation.) For the parser, we use Sun's Technical Release 2, recently superceded by the Java API for XML Parsing (JAXP) package. You will also need the Java Development Kit, version 1.2 or later. To download, go to:

- The Java 1.2 SDK, from http://java.sun.com/products/jdk/1.2/
- JAXP, from http://java.sun.com/products/xml/
- James Clark's xt, from http://www.jclark.com/xml/

To install, just make sure that xml.jar from Sun and xt.jar from James Clark are in the classpath. To run, give this command (wrapped here for readability):

```
java -Dcom.jclark.xsl.sax.parser=com.sun.xml.parser.Parser
   com.jclark.xsl.sax.Driver <xml-file> <xsl-stylesheet> <output-file>
```

The -D option tells the "Driver" which xml parser to use. For more detail, see xt.htm in the xt distribution.

xt can also be run as a servlet, XSLServlet. We explain how to configure the servlet/jsp engine for that after we go through our first XSLT example.

The XSLT Processing Model

An XSLT stylesheet resembles a JSP page in that it has some constant material that the processor just passes through to output, and some material that gets transformed and recombined before being sent to output.

Since an XSLT stylesheet is an XML document, it starts with a standard XML declaration that includes namespace declarations. Following the declarations, there may be some top–level elements that set up the general framework for output, perhaps declare some variables or import some parameters from the command line.

Once processing begins, it proceeds as follows. At any given time, there is a *current list* of nodes from the source document, usually found by *matching a pattern.* (The pattern is specified as an XPath expression.) Output corresponding to the current node list is created by processing that list; "processing" usually means *instantiating a template* associated with the pattern. Typically, the code looks like this:

```
<xsl:template match="[a match expression specifying which nodes to process]">
 [template material; may contain more XSLT markup]
</xsl:template>
```

In the course of processing the current node list, new source nodes can be added to that list, usually by the <xsl:apply-templates/> element.

The entire transformation process begins by processing a list containing just the root node. The transformation process ends when the source node list is empty. This picture is a bit over-simplified, but adequate for now.

A Simple Example

For a simple example of using XSLT, consider an XML file, rows.xml, that describes the contents of a database table:

```
<table>
 <row>
  <field name='Zip'>13346</field>
  <field name='Day'>Saturday October 22,1953</field>
  <field name='RecTime'>13:40 PM </field>
  <field name='Temp'>37</field>
```

```
    <field name='DayLo'>35 </field>
    <field name='DayHi'>46 </field>
    <field name='Precip'>60</field>
    <field name='Warn'>Foggy, probable rain; caution in driving</field>
    <field name='Tomorrow'>We will not have any weather tomorrow</field>
    <field name='NextDay'>There will be weather nearby, but not on you.</field>
  </row>
  <row>
    <field name='Zip'>11111</field>
    <field name='Day'>Saturday October 12,1913</field>
    <field name='RecTime'>12:11 PM </field>
    <field name='Temp'>98</field>
    <field name='DayLo'>95 </field>
    <field name='DayHi'>107 </field>
    <field name='Precip'>0</field>
    <field name='Warn'>do not go outside if you can help it</field>
    <field name='Tomorrow'>Flood planned for early afternoon</field>
    <field name='NextDay'>More of the same</field>
  </row>
</table>
```

The corresponding database table would have two rows of data. In response to the "all" query addressed to that table, our weather application would return a string matrix with three rows: a row of labels, and two rows of data strings. The JSP page `all.jsp` would use the string matrix to construct an HTML page with a table in it. We want to use XSL to convert our XML file into an HTML file that is identical to the output constructed by the `AllTable.jsp` page.

Here is the stylesheet, broken into pieces for ease of discussion. After the piecemeal presentation we'll bring it all together.

The Declaration

An XSL stylesheet is an XML document whose root element is `<xsl:stylesheet>`. The `xsl:` namespace that it uses is defined in the beginning of the stylesheet. (Warning: IE5 XSL also uses the `xsl:` prefix but defines it differently.) In this particular stylesheet, we also have a default namespace, defined to be the namespace of XHTML. In other words, all tags that are not qualified by a namespace prefix are assumed to come from the XHTML strict DTD:

```
<xsl:stylesheet version="1.0"
 xmlns:xsl="http://www.w3.org/1999/XSL/Transform"
 xmlns="http://www.w3.org/TR/xhtml1/strict"
>
```

Top-level Elements

There is a single top-level element in this stylesheet, `<xsl:output>`. Its `method` attribute specifies that html output will be produced. Its `indent` attribute says that the processor can add whitespace to give output a little formatting:

```
<xsl:output method="html" indent="yes" />
```

If we wanted a top–level parameter, e.g. `tablesize`, we would declare it thus:

```
<xsl:param name="tablesize" select="4" />
```

This would set the default value of the parameter to 4; the default can be overridden from the command line or from an HTML form, depending on how the XSLT processor is invoked. (See below on running the example.)

The Rest in Outline

In this particular stylesheet, there is a single `<xsl:template>` element whose match attribute matches the root node. All processing takes place inside that element; more precisely, inside an `<xsl:choose>` element within the `<xsl:template>` element. In outline, the rest of the stylesheet looks like this:

```
<xsl:template match="/"><!-- matches the root of the XML document tree -->

<!-- first block of HTML material to pass through to output -->

 <xsl:variable ... /><!-- declares and initializes a variable -->

 <xsl:choose>
 <!--
  checks to see if there is output;
  if not, outputs a message; otherwise outputs a table
 -->
</xsl:choose>

<!-- second block of HTML material for output -->

 </xsl:template>
</xsl:stylesheet>
```

Fixed HTML Material

The first block of HTML material is the beginning of an HTML document:

```
<html>
<head><title>Weather; you asked for all </title></head>
<body>
```

The second block of HTML material is the form (the same form that was in the `continue.jsp` page) and the closing tags:

```
<form method="POST" action="weather.jsp" >
 Zip?<input name="QP1" type="TEXT" size="10" /><br />
  Query?<select name="query" size="1">
  <option selected="yes" value="TimeTemp">Time andTemp </option>
  <option value="all">all fields </option>
  <option value="allForm">all with format result </option>
 </select><br />
 <input type="submit" value="go!" />
</form>
</body></html>
```

In between is the interesting part.

A Little XSLT: Declare a Variable

First we declare a variable that would refer to all the `<row>` elements. A detail to note is that the root of the document tree that XSLT is working on is not the root element but its parent. If the XML document had, for instance, processing instructions as siblings to the root element, they would also be children of the root of the tree.

Since our `<xsl:template>` element selected the root, we want to refer to its child by the name `<table>` and select all the children of `<table>` who are `<row>` elements:

```
<xsl:variable name="rows" select="table/row" />
```

Since `<table>` in our simple example of this section only has `<row>` children, we would achieve the same result by saying "select all children of `<table>`":

```
<xsl:variable name="rows" select="table/*" />
```

A Little XPath

The expressions that appear in quotes as values of match or select attributes are XPath expressions. You have seen several: "`/`" refers to the root; "`table`" refers to those children of the current element whose name is "table"; "`table/*`" refers to all children of `<table>`. As you will see in a moment, XPath also has functional expressions.

As an exercise in XPath (which will prove useful in the next section) we will rewrite the select attribute of the line above in two more ways. As it stands, it means, "select all grandchildren of the current node such that their tag name is 'row'". In our document, we would get the same set of nodes if we said, "select all descendants of the current node such that ...". There is a compact way in XPath to say, "all descendants": you simply put "`//`". So, the select attribute for "all descendants such that the tag name of the descendant is '`row`'" becomes: "`//row`".

This expression is very compact because the condition, "such that the tag name of the descendant is '`row`'" is not spelled out, it is an implicit convention designed to minimize keystrokes and bytes to send over the network. We can spell this condition out explicitly using the "additional predicate" convention: after specifying a set of nodes in XPath, you can add an additional boolean expression in square brackets that will further filter the resulting set. Here is an example:

```
<xsl:variable name="rows" select="//*[name(.)='row']" />
```

Here "`//*`" stands for "all descendants", and the additional condition in square brackets says, "such that the name of the descendant equals to 'row'. The '`.`' in the expression refers to the "currently considered node".

While more verbose, the syntax is not hard to understand. In the actual application, we will use the more verbose version.

More XSLT: Output a Table

Here is the rest of the stylesheet, mostly self–explanatory and quite readable:

```
<xsl:choose>
<xsl:when test="count($rows)=0">
Sorry, no weather is happening in your zip-code.
</xsl:when>
<xsl:otherwise>
 <table border="1">
  <tr>
   <xsl:for-each select="$rows[1]/field">
     <th> <xsl:value-of select="@name" /> </th>
   </xsl:for-each>
  </tr>
  <xsl:for-each select="$rows">
  <tr>
   <xsl:for-each select="*" >
    <td> <xsl:value-of select="." /> </td>
   </xsl:for-each>
  </tr>
  </xsl:for-each>
</table>
</xsl:otherwise>
</xsl:choose>
```

The XPath expression that is the value of `test` contains both a variable reference (`$rows`) and a function call. The variable refers to an array, and we can refer to its first element as `$rows[1]`. (XSLT arrays are NOT 0–based because XSLT is primarily addressed to people who do not know C or Java.) The XPath expression `@name` refers to the `name` attribute.

There are several `<xsl:value-of>` elements in this stylesheet. The value of an attribute is its "normalized" value, after all the entities have been replaced and white space normalized. The value of an XML element is the concatenation of the text values of all its children. So, for instance, if you say:

```
<xsl:template match="/">
  <xsl:value-of select="."/>
</xsl:template>
```

you will get the entire text of the document run together, without any markup. As you may have guessed, the XPath expression "." refers to the currently selected node. Here is the text of our first stylesheet all together (this is file `xslWmlAllTable.xsl` within the `examples/xslrules` directory):

```
<xsl:stylesheet version="1.0"
 xmlns:xsl="http://www.w3.org/1999/XSL/Transform"
 xmlns="http://www.w3.org/TR/xhtml1/strict"
>
<xsl:output method="html" indent="yes"  />
<xsl:template match="/">
<html>
<head><title>Weather; you asked for all </title></head>
<body>
```

```
  <xsl:variable name="rows" select="table/row" />
  <xsl:choose>
  <xsl:when test="count($rows)=0">
  Sorry, no weather is happening in your zip-code.
  </xsl:when>
  <xsl:otherwise>
   <table border="1">
    <tr>
     <xsl:for-each select="$rows[1]/field">
       <th> <xsl:value-of select="@name" /> </th>
     </xsl:for-each>
    </tr>
    <xsl:for-each select="$rows">
    <tr>
     <xsl:for-each select="*" >
      <td> <xsl:value-of select="." /> </td>
     </xsl:for-each>
    </tr>
    </xsl:for-each>
  </table>
  </xsl:otherwise>
 </xsl:choose>

  <form method="POST" action="weather.jsp" >
  Zip?<input name="QP1" type="TEXT" size="10" /><br />
   Query?<select name="query" size="1">
   <option selected value="TimeTemp">Time &amp; Temperatures </option>
   <option value="AllTable">all fields, formatted as table </option>
   <option value="AllText">all fields, formatted as text</option>

  </select><br />
  <input type="submit" value="go!" />
  </form>
  </body>
 </html>
  </xsl:template>
 </xsl:stylesheet>
```

Running the Example with XSLServlet

Clark's xt can be run from the command line or as a servlet, XSLServlet. We have already shown the command line; what we haven't said is that, following the arguments you can have any number of parameter settings, in the form `param-name=param-value`:

```
java -Dcom.jclark.xsl.sax.parser=com.sun.xml.parser.Parser
   com.jclark.xsl.sax.Driver rows.xml xslAllTable.xsl rows.htm
   table-rows=10 table-cols=17
```

It is common to have a `.bat` file (or an equivalent Unix shell script) that looks like this:

```
java -Dcom.jclark.xsl.sax.parser=com.sun.xml.parser.Parser
   com.jclark.xsl.sax.Driver %1 %2 %3
```

In this section we will show how to configure Tomcat 3.1 to run XSLT stylesheets using XSLServlet. This section is, in effect, configuration instructions for the rest of the chapter.

Configuring Tomcat and XSLServlet

There are two issues involved in configuring the XSLServlet:

- How to specify the parser, and
- How to make the servlet known to the server.

For the parser, go into `tomcat.bat` (or the equivalent Unix file) in the Tomcat root directory. The classpath is specified in that file, and the Java processor is called explicitly. Put the same `-D` option in that file that you use on command line.

Regarding the servlet–server connection, the "Servlet Usage" section of `xt.htm` that comes with the xt distribution, describes it so:

Servlet Usage

"XT can be used as a servlet. This requires a servlet engine that implements at least version 2.1 of the Java Servlet API. The servlet class is `com.jclark.xsl.sax.XSLServlet`. The servlet requires an init parameter stylesheet; the value is the path of the stylesheet in a form suitable to be passed to `ServletContext.getResource`. The translated path gives the XML document to be transformed. An extension of `.xml` will be automatically added to the translated path if necessary. (Some browsers assume that a URL ending in `.xml` is an XML document.) Parameters from the query part of the URL are passed in as parameters to the stylesheet. The stylesheet is cached on initialization."

This is how it works out in the case of Tomcat. We have an xml file `rows.xml` and a stylesheet to go with it, `xslAllTable.xsl`. You want to be able to invoke the stylesheet on the file from a browser by saying:

```
http://localhost:8080/xslAllTable/xslrules/rows
```

Here, `xslAllTable` is a virtual path, `xslrules` is a real directory, and `rows.xml` is a file in that directory. (Note that you don't want to put `.xml` in the end because (quoting from the quote above) "some browsers" will then assume that you just want the xml file with the browser's default stylesheet rather than the result of the servlet running your stylesheet on it.) In order to have this usage available, you follow these steps:

- Create an `xslrules` subdirectory of the default directory for Web pages, such as `C:/Tomcat/webpages`; put the xml file and the stylesheet into that directory.
- Modify Tomcat's `web.xml` file to add servlet–mapping and servlet elements, one for each stylesheet. The two addtions are as follows:

Within `<servlet-mapping>` elements:

```
<servlet-mapping>
    <servlet-name>
      xslAllTable
    </servlet-name>
    <url-pattern>
      /xslAllTable/*
    </url-pattern>
```

```
  </servlet-mapping>
  <servlet-mapping>
    <servlet-name>
      xslAllText
    </servlet-name>
    <url-pattern>
      /xslAllText/*
    </url-pattern>
  </servlet-mapping>
  <servlet-mapping>
    <servlet-name>
      xslTimeTemp
    </servlet-name>
    <url-pattern>
      /xslTimeTemp/*
    </url-pattern>
  </servlet-mapping>
  <servlet-mapping>
    <servlet-name>
      xslWmlAllTable
    </servlet-name>
    <url-pattern>
      /xslWmlAllTable/*
    </url-pattern>
  </servlet-mapping>
  <servlet-mapping>
    <servlet-name>
      xslWmlAllText
    </servlet-name>
    <url-pattern>
      /xslWmlAllText/*
    </url-pattern>
  </servlet-mapping>
  <servlet-mapping>
    <servlet-name>
      xslWmlTimeTemp
    </servlet-name>
    <url-pattern>
      /xslWmlTimeTemp/*
    </url-pattern>
  </servlet-mapping>
```

Within <servlet> elements:

```
<servlet>
    <servlet-name>
      xslAllTable
    </servlet-name>
    <servlet-class>
      MyNa.jspUtil.XSLSessionServlet
    </servlet-class>
    <init-param>
      <param-name>stylesheet</param-name>
      <param-value>/xslrules/xslAllTable.xsl</param-value>
    </init-param>
  </servlet>
  <servlet>
    <servlet-name>
      xslAllText
    </servlet-name>
    <servlet-class>
```

```
      MyNa.jspUtil.XSLSessionServlet
    </servlet-class>
    <init-param>
      <param-name>stylesheet</param-name>
      <param-value>/xslrules/xslAllText.xsl</param-value>
    </init-param>
  </servlet>
  <servlet>
    <servlet-name>
      xslTimeTemp
    </servlet-name>
    <servlet-class>
      MyNa.jspUtil.XSLSessionServlet
    </servlet-class>
    <init-param>
      <param-name>stylesheet</param-name>
      <param-value>/xslrules/xslTimeTemp.xsl</param-value>
    </init-param>
  </servlet>
  <servlet>
    <servlet-name>
      xslWmlAllTable
    </servlet-name>
    <servlet-class>
      MyNa.jspUtil.XSLSessionServlet
    </servlet-class>
    <init-param>
      <param-name>stylesheet</param-name>
      <param-value>/xslrules/xslWmlAllTable.xsl</param-value>
    </init-param>
  </servlet>
  <servlet>
    <servlet-name>
      xslWmlAllText
    </servlet-name>
    <servlet-class>
      MyNa.jspUtil.XSLSessionServlet
    </servlet-class>
    <init-param>
      <param-name>stylesheet</param-name>
      <param-value>/xslrules/xslWmlAllText.xsl</param-value>
    </init-param>
  </servlet>
  <servlet>
    <servlet-name>
      xslWmlTimeTemp
    </servlet-name>
    <servlet-class>
      MyNa.jspUtil.XSLSessionServlet
    </servlet-class>
    <init-param>
      <param-name>stylesheet</param-name>
      <param-value>/xslrules/xslWmlTimeTemp.xsl</param-value>
    </init-param>
  </servlet>
```

With these additions in place, you should be all set. To use a different stylesheet, say `innerloop.xsl`, on the same XML file, you would add another `<servlet-mapping>` element and another `<servlet>` element. Furthermore, if `innerloop.xsl` has a top–level parameter called `tablesize` then you can set this parameter to 8 from the browser by typing in the location window:

```
http://localhost:8080/xslnest/xslrules/rows.xml?tablesize=8
```

Or you can use an HTML form. This is really quite convenient. The only problem is that, as `xt.htm` tells us, "the stylesheet is cached on initialization", and so this setup is not good for debugging.

Same for WML?

Adapting this stylesheet for WAP so that it produces WML from the same XML document would be a fairly simple affair. The structure of the stylesheet would be exactly the same, and the WML filler material would come from the JSP implementation of the preceding section. So, we will skip this stage and move on to the real thing, integrating the stylesheet with query output within an application. We want to be able to run the stylesheet on an object in memory (such as a two-dimensional array of strings) that is not an XML stream at all. Once we learn how to do that, we can produce a complete XSL solution to the Web-WAP problem. It will still be using JSPs, but not for output templates. Instead of forwarding the request to an output JSP file, we will be forwarding it to XSLServlet, to run an XSL stylesheet on the result of the query. Some people will argue that this has major advantages because XSLT is a more congenial tool for non-programmers. It is probably too early to make such assertions with any certainty, especially since both XSLT and JSP are rapidly moving targets. Our goal is to provide a framework within which both can be used and compared to each other.

Web–WAP with XSLT

The revised XSLT–based system for Web–WAP generation is described by the following diagram:

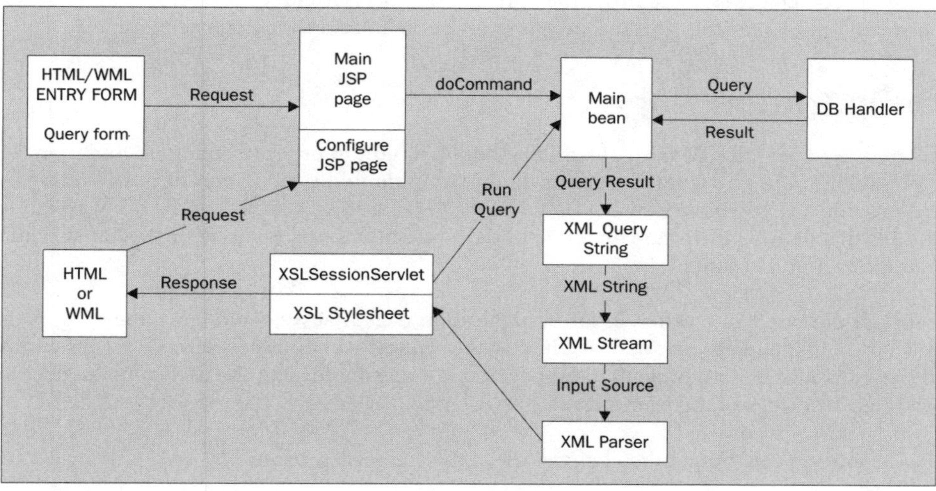

The main addition to the previous design is the "conversion module" in the middle that converts the result of the query into something that an XML parser can parse and deliver to the XSLT processor.

Apart from that, the changes that need to be made are as follows:

- The entry pages (`.xhtml` or `.wml`) will remain the same (but see below on `configure.jsp` changes).
- The main JSP page will remain the same.
- The configuration page, `configure.jsp`, will show more targets.
- The main bean will have four more lines added to its `doCommand()` method. Three of them take care of making the session and session ID available to the stylesheet; the last one is a call on a new mechanism for controlling the size of the output. (The `getDef()` method is no longer helpful because the stylesheet will be getting its information from parsed XML nodes rather than from a `Dict`.)
- The new mechanism itself is the XSLPrune that prunes the size of the stylesheet's output.
- We provide two classes that are minor revisions of classes provided within xt. In both cases our classes contain small but crucial additions. One class is `XSLSessionServlet`, a modified copy of `XSLServlet` that passes the session ID to the stylesheet as a stylesheet parameter. The other is `XMLOutputHandler`, a copy of the xt class of the same name, with a few lines added to provide an XSLT "mode" for any content-type specified by the application. In our case here, the mode is wml, of course.
- Within the stylesheet, a major addition is the mechanism for running Java methods from within XSLT. (It is the stylesheet, not a JSP page, that calls `qBean.queryResult()` in this version of the framework.)

We will present the changes in the order they are listed here, saving the "conversion module" till the end. If you just want to see the XSLT code, jump to the `xslTimeTemp.xsl` section.

The Configuration Page

The configuration page, as you recall, is for a sysadmin to edit in order to configure and maintain the system. We thought the task would be easier if, instead of doubling the names of possible targets again, we would provide a single binary switch between the JSP-based system and an XSLT–based one. The assumption is that at any given time only one of the two systems will be in use, and that switching between them will be infrequent.

It is because of the `boolean` switch in the configuration page that we could leave the entry pages (both `.htm` and `.wml`) unchanged, ignorant of whether the request will be processed using JSPs and XSLT. The alternative would be to double the number of targets again, forcing the user to make decisions about the inner workings of the framework.

We show the entire page, but all the changes are in the "targets" section:

```
<% // configure.jsp
String[]dbParams=new String[]{ // database and user information
 "sun.jdbc.odbc.JdbcOdbcDriver",
 "jdbc:odbc:WEATHER",
 "userName",
 "defaultPassword"
};
```

```
String[][]dbQueries=new String[][]{ // queries allowed from client
 {"AllTable",
  "SELECT * FROM FORECAST WHERE zip=?"},
 {"AllText",
  "SELECT * FROM FORECAST WHERE zip=?"},
 {"TimeTemp",
  "SELECT RecTime,Temp,DayLo,DayHi FROM FORECAST WHERE Zip=?"}
};
```

```
boolean sendToXSLNotJSP=false; // the switch, initially set to do JSP

String[][]responseTargets;
if(!sendToXSLNotJSP)
 responseTargets=new String[][]{ // default targets for a JSP system
  {"error","/jsp/weather/errorpage.jsp"},
  {"AllTable","/jsp/weather/xhtml/AllTable.jsp"},
  {"AllText","/jsp/weather/xhtml/AllText.jsp"},
  {"TimeTemp","/jsp/weather/xhtml/TimeTemp.jsp"},
  {"wml-AllTable","/jsp/weather/wml/AllTable.jsp"},
  {"wml-AllText","/jsp/weather/wml/AllText.jsp"},
  {"wml-TimeTemp","/jsp/weather/wml/TimeTemp.jsp"}
};
else responseTargets=new String[][]{ // targets for an XSLT system
  {"error","/jsp/weather/errorpage.jsp"},
  {"AllTable","/xslAllTable/xslrules/weather.xml"},
  {"TimeTemp","/xslTimeTemp/xslrules/weather.xml"},
  {"AllText","/xslAllText/xslrules/weather.xml"},
  {"wml-AllTable","/xslWmlAllTable/xslrules/weather.xml"},
  {"wml-AllText","/xslWmlAllText/xslrules/weather.xml"},
  {"wml-TimeTemp","/xslWmlTimeTemp/xslrules/weather.xml"}
};
```

```
 qBean.configure(dbParams,dbQueries,responseTargets); // once per session
%>
```

The new targets mean that there are six stylesheets, from `xslAllTable.xsl` to `xslWmlTimeTemp.xsl`, in the directory `xslrules`. Also in that directory is an XML file, `weather.xml`. In a framework that uses XML more (either for configuration or data interchange or both), this file could contain useful information. In our toy example, it is simply ignored, as the stylesheet synthesizes its output from the result of the query.

doCommand() in the Main Bean

The expanded `doCommand()` looks like this:

```
public void doCommand(HttpServletRequest request){
 requestDict=new Dict();
 requestDict.setDef(request);
 setupRequestDict(); // check through parameter name assumptions

// the following lines are for use with XSLSessionServlet;
// they are irrelevant but harmless for jsp output

 javax.servlet.http.HttpSession session=request.getSession(true);
```

```
  String sessionId=session.getId();

  SessionCache.getInstance().put(sessionId,session);
  XSLPrune.reset(sessionId);
}
```

The first two lines of the addition extract the session object and its session ID out of Request. Line 3 stores it in SessionCache, indexed by its ID. This is needed for the task of constructing a NodeIterator object that xt can work on. This is described in the last subsection of this section. The SessionCache is a subclass of our Cache class that is also used in connection pooling.

The final addition is a call on XSLPrune.reset(). XSLPrune is the Java class that keeps track of the amount of output per request. Since the tracking has to restart with each new request, a call to reset() is needed.

XSLPrune.java

The XSLPrune class maintains a private static Hashtable of "pruners", one for each session. Its only instance variable is outLimit, an integer, settable by setOutLimit(), gettable by getOutLimit(). The only constructor receives an integer argument and makes it the outLimit. The constructor is private so that the only way to create a pruner is from the prune() method (see below). That method makes sure that there is a single pruner per session:

```
package MyNa.jspUtil;

public class XSLPrune { // a utility for pruning XSL output

private static java.util.Hashtable pruners=null;
private int outLimit;

public int getOutLimit(){return outLimit;}
public void setOutLimit(int outLimit){this.outLimit=outLimit;}

private XSLPrune(int outLimit){setOutLimit(outLimit);}
```

The reset() method that you've seen in QBean a moment ago removes the pruner corresponding to a given session ID. This resets the quota of characters for the next request to the outLimit for that request:

```
public synchronized static void reset(String label){
 if(null==pruners)return;
 pruners.remove(label);
}
```

Finally, the prune() method, the reason why this class exists. It is static and synchronized, just as reset() is. It takes three arguments: String label, which is a session ID; String out, the string to output; and Double maxOut, the limit on the number of characters that can be sent to output. Why Double? you may ask. The reason is that this method will be called from a stylesheet, and XSLT has only one numeric type, a double. In the code below, there is an expected conversion to intValue.

Writing Java code that is to be called from XSLT has another, more subtle restriction. XSLT does not guarantee any specific order in which its elements, including template elements and calls on extension functions, will be evaluated. This restriction determines the way in which `prune()` and the entire `XSLPrune` class are written. As you read through the code below, watch how the current value of `outLimit` becomes the `maxOut` argument of the next call on `prune()` which, in turn, becomes the current value of `outLimit`. In this way, if there are several calls on `prune()` within the same stylesheet, they will work properly no matter in what order they are evaluated, or even if they are evaluated in parallel (`prune()` is synchronized):

```
public synchronized static String prune(
     String label,  // a session ID
     String out,    // string to output
     Double maxOut){ // maximum output; an integer deep down inside
  if(null==pruners)
   pruners=new java.util.Hashtable();
  int outLim=maxOut.intValue();
  XSLPrune pruner=(XSLPrune)(pruners.get(label));
  if(null==pruner) // no pruner, create a new one for this session,
          // with session-specific limit provided by maxOut
   pruners.put(label,pruner=new XSLPrune(outLim));
  outLim=pruner.getOutLimit(); // has no effect if a new pruner
  if(outLim<0)return out; // no limit
  int len=out.length();
  if(outLim>len){
   pruner.setOutLimit(outLim-len);
   return out;
  }
  out=out.substring(0,outLim); // len > outLim
  pruner.setOutLimit(0);
  return out;
}
} // end of XSLPrune class
```

XSLSessionServlet and XMLOutputHandler

We'll start with more extensive changes to `XMLOutputHandler`. The class has an `init()` method, declared as:

```
public DocumentHandler init(Destination dest, AttributeList atts)
    throws IOException {
```

The task of the method is to produce a `DocumentHandler` for output with all its properties set up on the basis of attributes in the `AttributeList` argument. One of the main things to configure is the output stream, `this.out`. The original xt code sets the stream's content type to `"application/xml"`:

```
this.out = dest.getOutputStream("application/xml", null);
```

Even though WML is an XML language, WAP expects a special content–type, `text/vnd.wap.wml`. We pass it to `init()` as a media–type attribute. Here is the modified code:

```
public DocumentHandler init(Destination dest, AttributeList atts)
    throws IOException {
```

```
// start modifications
 String mediaType = atts.getValue("media-type");
 if (mediaType == null)
   mediaType = "application/xml";
 encoding = atts.getValue("encoding");
 if (encoding == null) {
   // not all Java implementations support ASCII
   writer = dest.getWriter(mediaType, "iso-8859-1");
   // use character references for non-ASCII characters
   maxRepresentableChar = '\u007F';
 }
 else {
   writer = dest.getWriter(mediaType, encoding);
  this.out = dest.getWriter(mediaType, null);
// end modifications; the rest is James Clark's original code
  this.keepOpen = dest.keepOpen();
  if ("yes".equals(atts.getValue("omit-xml-declaration")))
   omitXmlDeclaration = true;
  this.standalone = atts.getValue("standalone");
  this.doctypeSystem = atts.getValue("doctype-system");
  this.doctypePublic = atts.getValue("doctype-public");
  if (this.doctypeSystem != null || this.doctypePublic != null)
   outputDoctype = true;
  if ("yes".equals(atts.getValue("indent")))
   return new Indenter(this, this);
  return this;
 }
```

XSLSessionServlet

The `MyNa.jspUtil.XSLSessionServlet` class is a copy of James Clark's `XSLSessionServlet` as distributed with xt, except for two changes. First, there is a "new" one–line `doPost()` function, consisting of a call on `doGet()`. Second, the two lines below have been added to `doGet()`:

```
String sessionID=request.getSession(true).getId();
xsl.setParameter("theSessionID",sessionID);
```

This is how our stylesheets get the session ID. Recall that our `QBean` has an additional line that stores the session itself in the `SessionCache`, indexed by its ID. Since the stylesheet is now in possession of the ID, it can pass it to a Java method that can use it to retrieve the session object itself. Since the session has the main bean (`qBean`) stored in it, the stylesheet can, indirectly, call `qBean`'s `queryResult()` method, just as our output JSP pages did. We just have to make sure that the stylesheet gets a top–level parameter called "`theSessionID`":

```
<xsl:param name="theSessionID" select="NoHttpSessionIDProvided"/>
```

It is time to open up a stylesheet. We will start with one of those that output HTML.

xslTimeTemp.xsl

We will again present the stylesheet in small chunks, with comments, before displaying it all together.

Declarations and top-level elements

Much of this is familiar from the earlier simple example, but watch for how a special namespace is declared to correspond to a Java class:

```
<xsl:stylesheet version="1.0"
 xmlns:xsl="http://www.w3.org/1999/XSL/Transform"
 xmlns="http://www.w3.org/TR/xhtml1/strict"
 xmlns:xqd="http://www.jclark.com/xt/java/MyNa.jspUtil.XmlQueryStringDoc"
 exclude-result-prefixes="xqd #default"
>
<xsl:output method="html" indent="yes"  />

<xsl:param name="theSessionID" select="NoHttpSessionIDProvided"/>
```

The `xqd` namespace is declared to be associated with the `XmlQueryStringDoc` class in the `MyNa.jspUtil` package. This is the class that runs the query, converts its `QueryResult` to an XML string and passes it on to an XML parser. This is all done by a static `queryResult()` method that returns a `NodeIterator` object, which is the kind of object that xt expects from its parser.

We are going to use the `queryResult()` method within the stylesheet. Java methods are one particular kind of what are called "extension functions" in the XSLT recommendation. The recommendation says about them, that although the 1.0 version of the XSLT does not define a standard mechanism for implementing such extensions, the "XSL Working Group intends to define such a mechanism in a future version of this specification or in a separate specification." (Introduction). Since James Clark is the editor of the current version and is likely to be involved in producing the next one, it makes sense to see how extension functions are implemented in xt.

The first step, as you can see, is to associate a namespace prefix with a Java class. The class must be identified by its fully-qualified name appended to http://www.jclark.com/xt/java/. Since you don't want extension namespace prefixes to appear on output, you list them within the value of the `exclude-result-prefixes` attribute of `xsl:stylesheet`. (There is also an `extension-element-prefixes` attribute that has the same effect.) Listing the default namespace as excluded is a minor optimization.

Overview of the Rest

The rest of the stylesheet is structured exactly as the stylesheet of the preceding section. We repeat the outline:

```
<xsl:template match="/"><!-- matches the root of the XML document tree -->

<!-- first block of HTML material to pass through to output -->

 <xsl:variable ... /><!-- declares and initializes a variable -->

 <xsl:choose>
 <!--
  checks to see if there is output;
  if not, outputs a message; otherwise outputs a table
 -->
</xsl:choose>

<!-- second block of HTML material for output -->
```

```
  </xsl:template>
</xsl:stylesheet>
```

An Extension-Function Call

The first block of HTML material is exactly the same as before, but the variable is initialized differently:

```
<xsl:variable name="rows"
       select="xqd:query-result($theSessionID)//*[name(.)='row']" />
```

This packs a lot of material into the select attribute. The first thing to notice is the convention for calling static Java methods. If the name of the class is associated with the "xqd" prefix then a call on the `queryResult()` method becomes "`xqd:query-result(...)`". Second, notice that the session ID, stored as a parameter of the stylesheet, is passed to the method as a stylesheet variable, `$theSessionID`.

The method, as we said, returns a `NodeIterator` object that points to the root of the tree that the stylesheet is going to process. We use the verbose syntax, "`//*[name(.)='row']`", to refer to "all descendants of the root such that the name of the descendant is 'row'". For reasons we have not been able to clarify, when xt receives its `NodeIterator` from an outside function call (rather than from its own call on the XML parser) it only allows verbose syntax in XPath expressions.

The Entire Stylesheet

The function call was the hardest part; the rest is almost the same as in the simple example of the last section. We can now show the entire stylesheet. All the work is done, as before, within an `xsl:choose` element that checks the number of rows, and, if there are any, outputs the rows as a table. Following that element, is the HTML form that is passed unchanged to output:

```
<xsl:stylesheet version="1.0"
 xmlns:xsl="http://www.w3.org/1999/XSL/Transform"
 xmlns="http://www.w3.org/TR/xhtml1/strict"
 xmlns:xqd="http://www.jclark.com/xt/java/MyNa.jspUtil.XmlQueryStringDoc"
 exclude-result-prefixes="xqd #default"
>
<xsl:output method="html" indent="yes"  />

<xsl:param name="theSessionID" select="NoHttpSessionIDProvided"/>

<xsl:template match="/">
<html>
<head><title>Weather; you asked for TimeTemp </title></head>
<body>
 <xsl:variable name="rows"
   select="xqd:query-result($theSessionID)//*[name(.)='row']" />
 <xsl:choose>
 <xsl:when test="count($rows)=0">
 Sorry, no weather is happening in your zip-code.
 </xsl:when>
 <xsl:otherwise>
  <p>
  <table border="1">
```

```
    <tr>
     <xsl:for-each select="$rows[1]/*" >
      <th> <xsl:value-of select="@*" /> </th>
     </xsl:for-each>
    </tr>
    <xsl:for-each select="$rows" >
    <tr>
     <xsl:for-each select="*" >
     <td> <xsl:value-of select="." /> </td>
    </xsl:for-each>
    </tr>
    </xsl:for-each>
  </table>
  </p>
  </xsl:otherwise>
</xsl:choose>

  <form method="POST" action="weather.jsp" >
  Zip?<input name="QP1" type="TEXT" size="10" /><br />
   Query?<select name="query" size="1">
   <option selected="yes" value="TimeTemp">Time andTemp </option>
   <option value="all">all fields </option>
   <option value="allForm">all with format result </option>
  </select><br />
  <input type="submit" value="go!" />
  </form>
  </body>
</html>
  </xsl:template>
</xsl:stylesheet>
```

A Stylesheet for WML

Finally, the prize: an XSLT stylesheet that produces WML output. We will show `xslWmlAllTable` in this section, and `xslWmlAllText`, which uses `XSLPrune`, in the next one.

Declarations

This part is more extensive in the WML–targeted stylesheet because of the content–type. This is how it all works out. First, yet another extension namespace, `javaout`, is declared. It is used within the `xsl:output` element to specify the Java class that will serve as the output "method". That Java class is the modified `XMLOutputHandler` that knows how to set the content type to the value of the media–type attribute. The media–type attribute is set to "`text/vnd.wap.wml`", which is what WAP expects:

```
<xsl:stylesheet version="1.0"
 xmlns:xsl="http://www.w3.org/1999/XSL/Transform"
 xmlns:xqd="http://www.jclark.com/xt/java/MyNa.jspUtil.XmlQueryStringDoc"
 xmlns="http://www.w3.org/TR/xhtml1/strict"
 xmlns:javaout="http://www.jclark.com/xt/java"
 exclude-result-prefixes="javaout xqd #default"
>
<xsl:output  method="javaout:MyNa.jspUtil.XMLOutputHandler"
  indent="yes"
```

```
    encoding="UTF-8"
    media-type="text/vnd.wap.wml"
    omit-xml-declaration="no"
    doctype-public="-//PHONE.COM//DTD WML 1.1//EN"
    doctype-system=http://www.phone.com/dtd/wml11.dtd
   />
  <xsl:param name="theSessionID" select="NoHttpSessionIDProvided"/>
```

The Rest of the Stylesheet

Since we have just seen a similar stylesheet, our comments can be brief. The next section is again a block of material to pass through, except it is WML, not HTML:

```
<xsl:template match="/">
 <wml>
 <head>
  <meta http-equiv="Cache-Control" content="no-cache" forua="true"/>
 </head>
 <card id="output" title="AllTable">
  <do type="accept" label="again" >
   <go href="#askCard" />
  </do>
<xsl:variable name="rows" select=
  "xqd:query-result($theSessionID)//*[name(.)='row']" />
```

The `xsl:choose` element is next, as before, but we format the output as two columns:

```
<xsl:choose>
 <xsl:when test="count($rows)=0">
 <p mode="nowrap">
 Sorry, no weather in your zip-code.
 </p>
 </xsl:when>
 <xsl:otherwise>
  <p>
  <table columns="2">
   <xsl:for-each select="$rows[1]/*" ><!-- a row for each header -->
    <tr>
     <td> <xsl:value-of select="@*" /> </td>
     <td> <xsl:value-of select="." /> </td>
    </tr>
   </xsl:for-each>
 </table>
 </p>
 </xsl:otherwise>
</xsl:choose>
 </card>
```

The rest is mostly the entry card in pure WML:

```
<card id="askCard" title="Weather">
<do type="accept" label="Go!" >
 <go href="weather.jsp">
   <postfield name="query" value="$query" />
```

```
    <postfield name="QP1" value="$QP1" />
    <postfield name="target" value="wml-$(query)" />
  </go>
  </do>
<p align="center">Weather Page</p>
<p>
 Zip?<input name="QP1" format="*N" maxlength="10" value="" /><br />
Query?      <select name="query">
      <option value="TimeTemp" > time &amp; temp </option>
      <option value="AllTable" > all fields </option>
      <option value="AllText" > all fields-format </option>
     </select>
</p>
</card>
</wml>
</xsl:template></xsl:stylesheet>
```

This stylesheet produces exactly the same output as the corresponding JSP page. Here is the first screen shot:

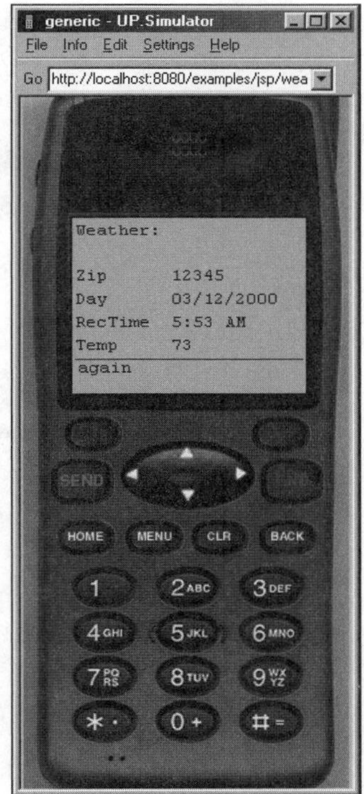

As you can see from the screen shot, the simulated device controls the output, breaking the long table into parts. We can do better by controlling the output ourselves. This is what `xslWmlAllText.xsl` does.

xslWmlAllText and Control of Output

This stylesheet controls the output in two ways. First, it uses `XSLPrune` to control the size of output. Second, it breaks the output into more cards, showing different levels of detail. This stylesheet is an edited copy of `wml/AllText.jsp`; it's more verbose but generates the same output following the same logic.

We are going to skip declarations except to note that there is yet another extension namespace, for `XSLPrune`:

```
xmlns:pruner="http://www.jclark.com/xt/java/MyNa.jspUtil.XSLPrune"
```

Most of the changes are in `xsl:choose`, especially in `xsl:otherwise`, which now outputs several cards. It starts by storing individual values in variables:

```
<xsl:choose>
 <xsl:when test="count($rows)=0">
  ... <!-- as in TimeTemp -->
 </xsl:when>
<xsl:otherwise>
<!-- Zip,Day,RecTime,Temp,DayLo,DayHi,Precip%,Warn,Tomorrow,NextDay -->
 <xsl:variable name="PLim" select="200"/><!-- two hundred characters limit -->
 <xsl:variable name="Zip" select="$rows/*[@*='Zip']"/>
 <xsl:variable name="Day" select="$rows/*[@*='Day']"/>
 <xsl:variable name="RecTime" select="$rows/*[@*='RecTime']"/>
 <xsl:variable name="Temp" select="$rows/*[@*='Temp']"/>
 <xsl:variable name="DayLo" select="$rows/*[@*='DayLo']"/>
 <xsl:variable name="DayHi" select="$rows/*[@*='DayHi']"/>
 <xsl:variable name="Precip" select="$rows/*[@*='Precip']"/>
 <xsl:variable name="Warn" select="$rows/*[@*='Warn']"/>
 <xsl:variable name="Tomorrow" select="$rows/*[@*='Tomorrow']"/>
 <xsl:variable name="NextDay" select="$rows/*[@*='NextDay']"/>
```

Now we output the first card. It shows all the time and temperature data, leaving the rest for the Details and More details cards:

```
<card id="output" title="AllText">
  <do type="accept" label="again" > <go href="#ask" /> </do>
  <do type="accept" label="details" > <go href="#details" /> </do>
<p>
zip:
<xsl:value-of select="pruner:prune($theSessionID,string($Zip),$PLim)"/>
<br/>
temp:
<xsl:value-of select="pruner:prune($theSessionID,string($Temp),$PLim)"/>
<br/>
at
<xsl:value-of select="pruner:prune($theSessionID,string($RecTime),$PLim)"/>
<br/>
day's lo:
<xsl:value-of select="pruner:prune($theSessionID,string($DayLo),$PLim)"/>
<br/>
day's hi:
<xsl:value-of select="pruner:prune($theSessionID,string($DayHi),$PLim)"/>
</p>
</card>
```

The Details card shows more information but saves the potentially lengthy items for More details:

```
<card id="details" title="AllText">
 <do type="accept" label="again" > <go href="#ask" /> </do>
 <do type="accept" label="more" > <go href="#moreDetails" /> </do>
<p>
day:
<xsl:value-of select="pruner:prune($theSessionID,string($Day),$PLim)"/>
<br/>
precip:
<xsl:value-of select="pruner:prune($theSessionID,string($Precip),$PLim)"/>%
</p>
</card>
<card id="moreDetails" title="AllText">
 <do type="accept" label="again" > <go href="#ask" /> </do>
 <do type="accept" label="basics" > <go href="#output" /> </do>
<xsl:if test="$Warn">
<p> Warning:
<xsl:value-of select="pruner:prune($theSessionID,string($Warn),$PLim)"/>
</p>
</xsl:if>
<p>
Tomorrow:
<xsl:value-of select="pruner:prune($theSessionID,string($Tomorrow),$PLim)"/>
<br/>
NextDay:
<xsl:value-of select="pruner:prune($theSessionID,string($NextDay),$PLim)"/>
</p>
</card>
 </xsl:otherwise>
</xsl:choose>
```

The only remaining card is the Ask card, the same as before. This concludes our discussion of XSLT stylesheets for WML output. The remainder of this section presents the technical detail of how query output is fed into the XML parser for XSLT processing. After that, the conclusions will compare the pure JSP and the JSP+XSLT frameworks.

Feeding a NodeIterator into xt

This section describes the background machinery that makes this XSLT line possible:

```
<xsl:variable name="rows"
      select="xqd:query-result($theSessionID)//*[name(.)='row']" />
```

We can rewrite this as two lines, to focus on our topic more precisely:

```
<xsl:variable name="root" select="xqd:query-result($theSessionID)" />
<xsl:variable name="rows" select="$root//*[name(.)='row']" />
```

It is the first of the two lines that we are interested in: it calls a Java method that returns the root of a tree that xt can traverse and transform. What's in that method?

XmlQueryStringDoc

The XPath expression:

```
xqd:query-result($theSessionID)
```

means that the xqd namespace prefix is associated with a Java class that has a static queryResult() method. The class, if you look it up in the XSLT declarations, is XmlQueryStringDoc, within MyNa.jspUtil. Here is its code:

```
import org.xml.sax.*;
import org.xml.sax.helpers.*;
import com.jclark.xsl.om.*;
import com.jclark.xsl.sax.*;

import java.sql.SQLException;
import javax.servlet.http.HttpSession;

public class XmlQueryStringDoc extends XmlStringDoc {
 public static NodeIterator queryResult(String sID)throws SQLException{
   HttpSession hS=(HttpSession)(SessionCache.getInstance().get(sID));
   if(null==hS)return null;
   QBean qB=(QBean)hS.getValue("qBean"); // the bean's name here
   if(null==qB)return null;
   QueryResult qResult=qB.queryResult();
   return stringToNodeList(qResult.toXmlString());
 }
}
```

The queryResult() method spends most of its time getting to qBean; once qBean is obtained, the method packs a lot of action into its last line that actually produces the NodeIterator. In order to get to qBean, we proceed as follows:

- From the sessionCache we request the session via sessionID;
- From the session we request the bean;
- From the bean we request the QueryResult;
- From the QueryResult we request an xmlString.

Reminder: QueryResult and QueryResultTable

As discussed earlier in the chapter, QueryResult is an interface that extends the XmlOb interface, from which it inherits the method toXmlString(). Otherwise, QueryResult expects its implementing classes to have two string arrays, columnHeaders and columnTypes, and a string matrix named rows.

The actual object that is returned by qBean.queryResult() is a QueryResultTable. That class implements toXmlString() by assuming a generic DTD for database tables, dbdata.dtd. Using the given column headers, column types and the rows matrix, the method constructs an XML document that looks like this:

```
<table name='Forecast'>
<headers>
<header name='Zip' fieldType='TEXT'/>
<header name='Day' fieldType='TEXT'/>
 ...
</headers>
<row>
<field name='Zip'>13346</field>
<field name='Day'>Saturday March 10,2000</field>
</row>
 ...
</table>
```

The document (without the formatting white space) is constructed in a `StringBuffer` and returned as one long `String`. At this point, we are in the last line of the `XmlQueryStringDoc.queryResult()` that says:

```
return stringToNodeList(qResult.toXmlString());
```

What happens there?

Reminder: the Resolver class and the InputSource

`XmlQueryStringDoc` extends `XmlStringDoc` where `stringToNodeList()` is defined. Before we look inside, recall the section on XML parsing and the setup steps that are needed before the parser can get to work. The essential lines are these:

```
// Turn the XML input file into an XML "input source" object
input = Resolver.createInputSource (new File (argv [0]));
// Get a parser instance
Parser parser;
parser = ParserFactory.makeParser ("com.sun.xml.parser.Parser");
parser.setDocumentHandler(new Echo01()); // extends HandlerBase

 // Parse the input source
parser.parse (input);
```

For parsing to happen, you need two things, a parser and something to parse: an InputSource. xt has a parser, specified by the `-D` command option. It only needs an input source. In this example, an `InputSource` object is created by the static `createInputSource()` method of the `Resolver` class. This is a very helpful class in Sun's TR–2 package, but the `InputSource` class (defined in `org.xml.sax`) has constructors of its own, three of them. One of them takes a file name, another an `InputStream`, and the third a `Reader`. This last option is the one we exploit. Here is `XmlStringDoc`:

```
import org.xml.sax.*;
import org.xml.sax.helpers.*;
import com.jclark.xsl.tr.LoadContext;
import com.jclark.xsl.om.*;
import com.jclark.xsl.sax.*;

public class XmlStringDoc {
```

```
    public static NodeIterator stringToNodeList(String xmlString){
      try{
       Parser parser=ParserFactory.makeParser("com.sun.xml.parser.Parser");
       XMLProcessorEx proc=new XMLProcessorImpl(parser);
       // create an input source from xmlString
       InputSource in=new InputSource(new java.io.StringReader(xmlString));
       LoadContext lC=new LoadContextImpl();

       // we now have everything to get to the root
       Node root=proc.load(in,0,lC,new NameTableImpl());
       return root.getChildren();
       }catch (Exception e){
         e.printStackTrace();
         return null;}
      }
    }

    private static class LoadContextImpl implements LoadContext {
     public boolean getStripSource(Name name){return false;}
     public boolean getIncludeComments(){return true;}
     public boolean getIncludeProcessingInstructions(){return true;}
    } // end of LoadContextImpl
   } // end of XmlStringDoc
```

Parts of this code will have to remain partly mysterious, but the main outline should be clear. The first two lines create a parser and an `XMLProcessorEx`, an xt interface that declares a `load()` method. That's the method we need. It takes several parameters, the first of which is an `InputSource`. We create an `InputSource` by wrapping our `xmlString` into a `StringReader` and giving it as an argument to the input source constructor.

The remaining two arguments of `load()` would take us too deeply into xt code; what matters is that a call on `load()` returns a `Node` (`com.jclark.xsl.om.Node`, to be precise), and its `getChildren()` method returns a `NodeIterator` that we need. `NodeIterator` itself is an interface that simply declares a `next()` method, but that's all xt needs in order to do its work.

Summary

This chapter has been a long journey that took us several places:

- An architecture for three-tier JSP applications
- WAP and WML
- WML and XHTML content from the same data source using the JSP architecture
- XML parsing
- XSLT and XPath
- WML and XHTML content from the same data source using XSLT for output

We are hoping that the chapter has been useful in bringing up several general design ideas, but its main point has been to create a framework for generating both XHTML and WML content from the same data source. In the actual application of the chapter, the data source is a relational database, but it doesn't have to be: the framework is general enough so that anything wrapped in a `Dict` object or described by an XML document can be a source of data. We did not have time in this chapter to explore that data connection in depth; our task has been to explore and compare the output methods. We have done quite a bit of exploring; is it time for comparisons?

In truth, we don't feel that there is enough accumulated experience as yet to pass definitive judgements. Both JSP and XSLT are extremely powerful tools that can certainly do the job. For applications that are maintained by programmers, JSPs are probably a better choice, if only because they are needed anyway, and why bring in yet another set of tools? However, XSLT enables non–programmers to do very impressive things, and so in an organizational setting in which extensibility by non–programmers is important, the XSLT may prove preferable.

In the meantime, the framework developed in this chapter provides, we hope, a useful testbed for more exploring and experimentation. Enjoy!

J2EE
JSP

20

Case study: Porting ASP to JSP

In this chapter, we'll look at how a content-managed stock-quoting site was ported from ASP to JSP.

In the following sections I will describe:

- The system's original requirements
- The resultant architecture of the original system
- Porting the system from ASP to JSP 0.91
- Porting the system from JSP 0.91 to JSP 1.0

Although this was a real life project, some detail has been omitted in order to focus attention on the actual porting process.

> **This chapter doesn't seek to compare ASP and JSP head-to-head – for that, read Appendix E, *JSP for ASP Developers*.**

The System

In order to explain the port, it is important to understand something of the original project. In this section I will summarize the requirements capture and the analysis portion of the project. Many aspects of these steps have been omitted for brevity.

Requirements

This system is a stock-quoting web site. The site will display:

- Up-to-date stock information
- Financial news
- Company information
- Profiles of individuals, for instance, the chairman of Oracle

Each of the above is called a **content type**. More content types will be needed as the site matures. For example, editorial comment may be needed on the site.

An individual record is called a **content item**. For example, a profile of Bill Gates is a content item. Content items must be capable of display in multiple ways, so that, a summary of a company can be displayed when quoting its stock price but more detailed information can be displayed on the company page.

Live feeds for stock-pricing information will be received regularly and up-to-date information will need to be displayed on the site.

Company information must be proof read by an editor before going live.

Finally, in the future it may be necessary to port the site to other platforms.

Analysis

The site is divided into two areas:

- Main site – accessible to everyone, handles the display of the content
- Administration – area accessed only by authorized users who are password-authenticated

The following actors were identified:

- Live feeds – here we represent live feeds as an actor. This is convenient because they effectively perform actions within the system
- Journalists – users who can add and edit content items. They will typically add company and people profiles
- Editors – take stories that have been entered by Journalists, edit them and publish them onto the live site

- Superusers – superusers add new users with rights to access the administration site.
- Site users – site users are anonymous users of the site and require no logon. They only have rights to access the main site.

Some of the more important use cases are shown below:

Content Entry and Management

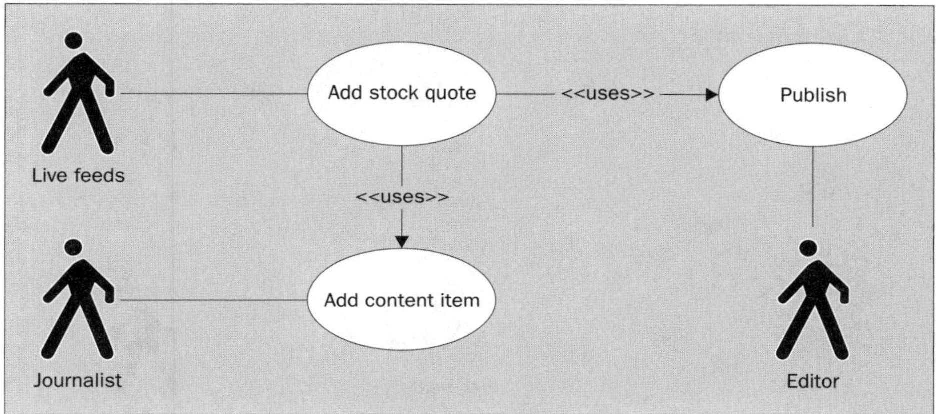

This use case defines how content is added to the system and, from there, how it is published.

A live feed can only add stock quotes to the system. Once these stock quotes have been added they are automatically published to the live site. It is assumed that the source of the feed is correct and that they need no further review.

If a journalist enters content, an editor is required to review it and then publish it.

Content Preview and Display

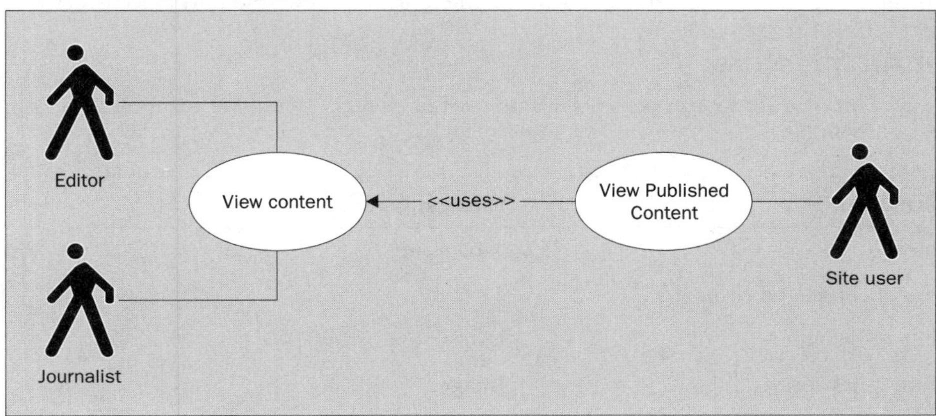

In this section we can see that editors and journalists can view content in either its published or unpublished state but that the site user can only view published content.

In order to display these content items, each content type has a number of **display templates**. This allows the storage of the data to be abstracted from the way that data is displayed. This is important to meet our design objective that content can be displayed in more than one way. For example, we can add WML templates and produce a WAP version of the site without changing any of the content.

User Administration

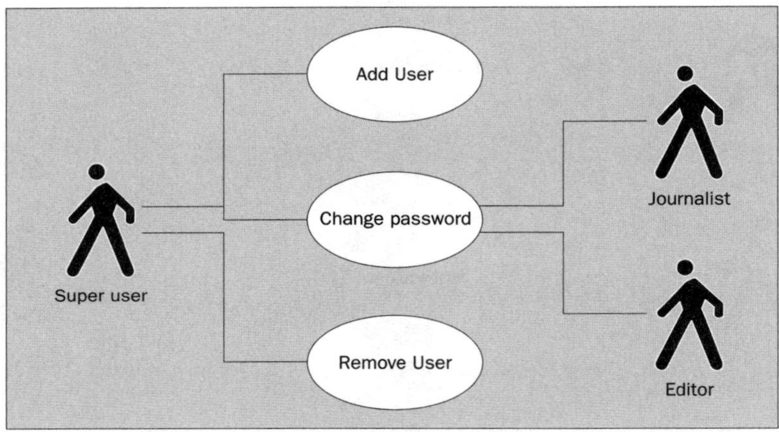

Here we can see a selection of the use cases that are used to administer users.

Architecture

Now that we have captured the requirements from our client, we move onto defining an architecture for the system. At this stage we assumed an object-oriented approach.

I will focus on the content architecture as it has the most impact on the port to follow.

Content Architecture

All the content types can be broken down into a set of element types. For example, a person profile can be broken down into:

Information	Element type
Name	Text string
Name of connected company	Text string
Profile information	Longer text string
Picture of person	Image

The element types are represented in code, as objects. This code defines how to edit, store, retrieve, and validate an element of this type. Content types then become an ordered collection of these element types.

We decided that content types should not be defined in code but rather defined in an XML-based language. In the above example:

```
<ContentType name=PersonProfile>
  <Element name="name" type="shortText">
    Name of person</Element>
  <Element name="company" type="shortText">
    Company</Element>
  <Element name="body" type="longText">
    Profile of person</Element>
  <Element name="picture" type="image">
    Picture of person</Element>
</ContentType>
```

For each element we define:

- A name by which they can be identified
- An element type which represents them
- A description

By making these definitions in XML, we can easily define new content types by simply assembling a set of element types. This effectively allows us to reuse large amounts of code (defined in the element types) across all the content types.

For example, to add support for editing a content item we need only make a generic editing form which can take the XML definition and, from that, produce a specific editing form for this content type. In this case, the generic form merely iterates through the elements and asks the element type code to return the correct editing code for this particular type.

Initial Development

The initial work on the content management system was done for a single site. This was coded in ASP, using exclusively Microsoft technologies.

During the initial development, the team was concerned with delivering the first phase. However, the work took place in the knowledge that the application would shortly be required to run on a pure Java platform. This influenced the development process and a number of design decisions were taken to ensure an easy transition to the second phase.

Over the next few pages, we'll look at the tools and server architecture for the first phase, and their implications for porting to JSP.

Technologies

ASP

The use of ASP for the initial phase was a requirement specified by the client. ASP is a relatively mature technology in the web world and was already in use on the client's sites. The fact that ASP is based on VBScript provided an added bonus, as the client's developers were already familiar with this technology.

These advantages are offset, however, by a number of other factors. Principally, these are:

- ASP does not conform with the developer's future requirement of platform independence
- Error handling is not exception-based. Code is therefore littered with error-checking sequences
- Object support is through Automation – which can't enforce compile-time checks on the objects called from the ASP
- Type safety is not implemented

IIS is used as the web server as it supports ASP and is freely available for the NT platform.

COM Business Objects

It is common practice to split the code into presentation and business logic. Making such a split has many advantages:

- The user experience can be changed without these changes affecting the logic that controls important business processes
- Many people can safely work on the presentation without damaging the business logic
- With all business logic in one layer debugging is made simpler and unit testing of individual business objects is possible
- Porting becomes an easier task as the business object layer can be ported independently of the user interface

ASP is ideal for handling the presentation layer. But Microsoft also provide seductive wizards that tempt developers into putting logic within the ASP. Unfortunately ASP is not a good language for implementing large amounts of complex logic – the page quality gets very messy.

Fortunately, ASP provides a way of importing objects written in other languages through COM (Component Object Model). Objects written in languages such as C++, Java, and even VB can be imported.

In this project we used the Microsoft JVM (Java Virtual Machine) to expose Java classes as COM components. While this is one of the parts of the Microsoft implementation of Java that has upset Sun, it allows us to implement COM objects in Java simply by adding `@com` directives to comments at the top of the class file. In Visual J++ 6 this is made as simple as checking a check box in the file settings.

These classes can be used directly by the ASP with the line:

```
Set object = Server.CreateObject("NameOfDLL.NameOfClass")
```

There were a number of advantages in using Java:

- Meets the future requirement for platform independence
- Clean interface to COM is provided by Microsoft
- There is Java experience in-house
- Java is easier and safer to implement than C++

Against these advantages, there were two negative points to consider. The on-going legal action between Microsoft and Sun posed the threat that Microsoft might remove its support for Java. More quantifiable, was the reduction in performance that was a consequence of the use of Java.

Looking at the COM business objects layer, there are a couple of implementation difficulties:

- Automation in COM has no mechanism to support the overloading of methods.
- Static methods can't be called through Automation. This functionality can only be achieved by calling a static method from a non-static parent created for that purpose.
- COM does not support parameter passing during construction and thus only default constructors can be used. Oyster developed objects with an `initialize()` method that was called after the constructor.

The presence of a business object layer, however, is a huge advantage during a port.

It is obviously an advantage that we decided to use Java as the language for the business object layer. In your port you might not be as lucky as this. But the separation of application functionality into layers, and using COM to communicate between the layers allows your business logic to be ported independently of the presentation layer. In fact individual objects (or object hierarchies if they use a lot of inter-related code) can be ported independently of each other. Using just such an incremental approach, the site can be tested after each object is ported and mistakes spotted and correctly easily.

If you do not have a business object layer in your application do not despair, it is still possible to port the application. As you will see later on in this chapter, you can port all the code that is in ASP to JSP, it will just make it more difficult to track mistakes while you work on the site.

Database Connectivity

SQL Server was used to store and retrieve the content. To connect to the database, we can use either ADO or JDBC, both of which abstract access to the database. These technologies offer almost identical functionality.

The following factors influenced the decision of which technology to use:

- Both JDBC and ADO can be used from the Microsoft JVM. Only ADO is directly supported within the ASP layer of the application.
- Clients using ADO are restricted to a Windows operating system, whereas JDBC clients can exist on any machine.
- Both JDBC and ADO communicate to database servers on any platform, provided that a suitable driver is installed.

For this project, the developers chose to implement the data layer for the application in JDBC. This choice was made with a view to porting it to a 100% Java platform. This meant that no database access could be implemented in our presentation layer, which of course should always be the case anyway.

Once again this decision saved us a large amount of heartache in the port. Unfortunately, ADO is far more likely to be used in ASP sites. This will bring along some more problems that I will discuss later, as part of the port.

Site Server

Site Server is a Microsoft technology based on ASP that includes a suite of helpful tools for creating and managing web sites. In this project we used the search engine that it provides. The search engine can be configured to visit every page on a live site, crawl, and store all the text which it finds. Once a site has been crawled, you can ask the engine to do searches on the content and return references to the pages that contain the words specified.

Using ASP, a full text search of the site can be performed. ASP utilizes the COM interface to the Site Server search engine. In an ASP environment this is a very low cost and easy to implement solution. Unfortunately Site Server only provides a COM interface and is only available on Microsoft platforms.

Initial Architecture

These technologies fit together in the following way:

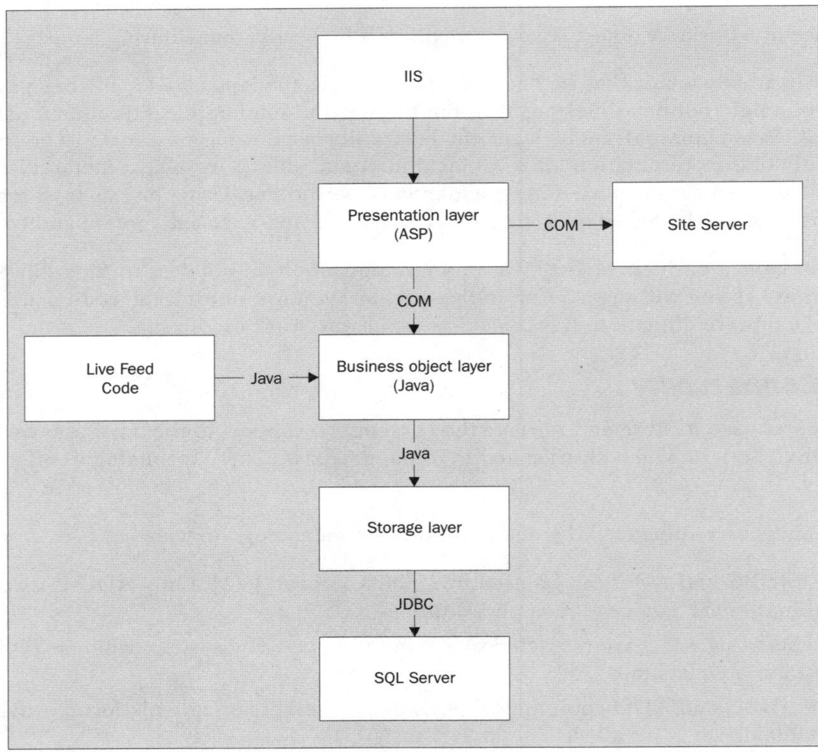

I have added the live feed code to the diagram. This code merely checks a file system directory for new files. If new files are present it processes these files and passes the information into the business object layer and then onto the database. Having a business object layer to communicate with the database is very useful in keeping the live feed code simple.

Site Server is shown being called directly by the presentation layer. This is not entirely true as we made a collection of functions (contained in an ASP include file) which provided some encapsulation for Site Server.

The Microsoft JVM, which allows COM objects to be manipulated directly, could also have been used to talk to Site Server from the business object layer. In this case it was cleaner to call the COM classes straight from the ASP.

Current Status of Initial Development Phase

The developers have produced a site that allows editing and display of stock and company information. The site is based exclusively on a Microsoft platform.

The implementation does include features to ensure easy future portability to Java. The key decisions that will help the developers port this application to Java in the next section are:

- The Java business object layer
- The use of JDBC throughout the application

The next section will include discussion on how to deal with applications that have not been fortunate enough to have these features in place.

The problems that we still have to overcome, and which we'll see soon, are:

- The search engine is a COM-based product. It is unlikely that this code will port.
- The database code contains some SQL Server-specific syntax.

Phase Two

The aim of the second phase of the project was to achieve platform independence. This required changes to be made to the following project areas:

- ASP code to be ported to JSP
- Database code to be ported to support Oracle and potentially other databases
- The search engine support to be changed to allow other search engines to be used

Porting ASP to JSP 0.91

The actual porting of the ASPs to JSPs was relatively straightforward as very little functionality is contained in the ASP code. Most of the functional code is integrated into the business object layer, which makes our work much easier.

Hints on how to use a business object layer that is implemented in a language other than Java are given in the next section.

ASP sites commonly lack this middle layer, without which the porting task becomes significantly more complex. But the same basic guidelines follow.

Much of JSP is very similar to ASP in a more ways than just its name.

Both ASP and JSP:

- Allow HTML and code to mixed
- Use the `<% ... %>` notation to delimit code
- Have session, request, and response objects that represent similar concepts in both frameworks

Thus most of the actual porting task just involves the transcription of each line of code from VBScript into equivalent Java. Of course, there are several small differences that are going to cause problems. I have listed the ones that occurred during our port.

Error Handling

Error handling in ASP is not based on **exceptions**. Thus, after any method call, `Err.number` must be checked and appropriate action initiated if an error is returned. For example, here's a part of an ASP:

```
on error resume next ' Standard ASP code for "Don't just
                     ' report errors to the user, carry on"

Err.Clear            ' Prepare for error handling
                     ' by clearing previous errors
set mailer = Server.CreateObject("MailSender.Mailer")

' Created an object better check it worked
if Err.number <> 0
  Response.write("Failed to send mail")
else
  ' We have our object let's use it
  mailer.send

  ' Check that we managed to send the information
  if Err.number <> 0
    Response.write("Failed to send mail")
  end if
end if
```

As we can see from the above example, this method of error handling is cumbersome and its implementation can make code difficult to read. Many ASP sites allow errors to go unhandled, resulting in SQL errors etc. being shown to the user. The Microsoft site is sometimes guilty of just this error.

An immediate gain from the port to JSP is the availability of exception handling. The entire page can be bounded within a `try-catch` block. This enables errors to be caught globally and 'friendly' error messages displayed to the user. For example, the code we saw above would translate to the following Java code:

```
try {
  Mailer mailer = new Mailer();
  mailer.send();
} catch (Exception e) {
  // Handle all failures in the same way
  reponse.println("Failed to send mail!");

  // Report the failure to the application server log
  e.printStackTrace();
}
```

The `java.lang.Throwable` class' `printStackTrace()` prints the entire call stack, and any other information contained in the `Exception` object, to the error log for the application server (depending on which engine you are using to serve your JSP).

More specific error handling can be applied if a global catch-all mechanism is not appropriate. For example, if our `Mailer` object can throw a `MailerException` if anything goes wrong, we can catch it using the following code:

```
try {
  Mailer mailer = new Mailer();
  mailer.send();
} catch (MailerException e) {
  // tell the user what went wrong during the send
  response.println("Failed to send mail! "+e.getMessage());
} catch (Exception e) {
  response.println("Operation failed, " +
                   "please contact the administrator");
  // give as much information to the log file to aid debugging
  e.printStackTrace();
}
```

Once the code gets more than a few lines long, error handling using exceptions becomes even more useful. It encourages programmers to handle errors correctly by making it easier for them to do so.

Lack of Application Object

In ASP, certain standard objects are provided. These map to JSP v0.91 implicit objects, with the exception of the `Application` object.

ASP	JSP
`Request`	`HttpServletRequest`
`Response`	`HttpServletResponse`
`Session`	`HttpSession`
`Application`	Not available (see note below)

The lack of an `application` object has been addressed in the version 1.0 of the specification. See also Chapter 11, *Global Settings*, for another solution to this problem.

In order to port the existing code, it was necessary for developers to implement their own `application` object.

This was implemented as a singleton (a standard object-oriented pattern which allows one and only one instance of an object to exist). Singletons can be very useful in a port, as a way to implement the behavior of globally available variables. Unfortunately this can lead to them being overused, but to use just the one singleton to emulate the `application` object is ideal.

```
public class WebApplication {
  // instance is a reference to the one and only
  // WebApplication object. It is private so that
  // no one else can access it directly
  private static WebApplication instance;

  // We create the object using a private constructor
  // so that no one can make a new instance using the
  // new keyword.
  private WebApplication() { }

  // We only allow access to one instance of object
  // by calling the method
  //   instanceOf(public static WebApplication)
  instanceOf() {
    if (instance == null)
      instance = new WebApplication();

    return instance;
  }
}
```

More information about singletons and other object-oriented design patterns can be found in the Design Patterns book by Gamma et al. (Addison Wesley, ISBN 0201633612)

We then added a couple of methods that provide the dictionary functionality already provided by the ASP implementation.

```
public class WebApplication {
  // Code as shown above inserted here to implement the
  // singleton behavior

  // Hashtable to contain any global information
  java.util.Hashtable globalHash = new java.util.Hashtable();

  public Object get(String key) {
    return globalHash.get(key);
 }

  public void put(String key, Object value) {
    globalHash.put(key, value);
  }
}
```

Next we have the problem of initializing this object with values which relate to this particular site (assuming that we will reuse the `WebApplication` object for all the JSPs for a site).

We decided to use a configuration file to tell the WebApplication object how to initialize itself. Using the method,

```
getServletContext().getRealPath ()
```

we can find the path of the JSP file. From here we can search up the directory structure to find the root of the web site. There we place a file called Global.cfg that contains initialization information. This global.cfg file can be thought of as similar to the Global.asa used in ASP. Code like this is then inserted into the WebApplication class.

```
import java.io.*

public class WebApplication {
  // Code as before

  private WebApplication(String directory) {
    // Omitting some of the error handling for brevity
    File potentialWebRoot = new File(directory);
    File potentialGlobalCfg = new File(potentialWebRoot,
                                       "Global.cfg");
    // Find the file by running up the directory tree
    while (!potentialGlobalCfg.exists()) {
      potentialWebRoot = new File(
                            potentialWebRoot.getParent());
      potentialGlobalCfg = new File(potentialWebRoot,
                                    "Global.cfg");
    }

    // Now read the file which we have found and
    // use it to initialize the object.
  }

  public static instanceOf(String directory) {
    if (instance == null)
      instance = new WebApplication(directory);

    return instance;
  }
}
```

As can be seen from some of the code above, Java makes it easy to traverse directory trees without having to mention backslashes. This makes our code more portable as we move to UNIX.

If you use this approach, be careful what is stored in the global.cfg file as it is accessible across the web. We typically put the name of a more secure file (a file which is outside the web directory tree) that we can then access to find out more sensitive details such as database connection parameters.

Inline Functions

In ASP you can mix HTML and VBScript within a function. For example:

```
<%function outputStuff()
  response.write("Write this");
%>
  and this.
  And lots more text which is long winded to write in
```

```
   response.write() functions
<%end function

call outputStuff()%>
```

This can be a very useful technique for writing functions which output large amounts of HTML, and which are reused across a site. Unfortunately, this does not port to JSP. When you declare functions in JSP, you can't intersperse the Java code with HTML – there's no way to end the declaration with a tag, put in a bit of template text and open an end-of-declaration tag, as happens in the example above.

In order to support this method of making functions, a class was written that converted the JSP into Java. In effect, it took all the HTML and wrapped it with `out.print`, like a Servlet. The Java output of this class could then be written into a JSP page and successfully integrated into a function.

For example, we converted the above code to the following Java function:

```
<SCRIPT runat=server>

void outputProductType(HttpServletRequest request,
                       HttpServletResponse response,
                       ServletOutputStream out,
                       JSPServlet jspServlet)
         throws IOException {

  out.println("Write this");
  out.println(" and this.");

}
</SCRIPT>
```

File Upload

HTTP file upload functionality was required to enable content with images and sound to be added to the system.

In the development of the ASP site, a component called SA (http://www.softartisans.com) FileUp was used. This component replaced the functionality of the `Request` object provided with ASP and also allowed uploaded files to be handled.

JSP provides direct support for file uploading. This takes the form of a servlet that receives a submitted form. Once the form is submitted, the file is saved to a location named in an HTML hidden field. Unfortunately, this has rather limited functionality and was inadequate, given the much richer features available in ASP.

The developers implemented their own file upload handler, designed to replace `HttpRequest`. In this way, it was possible to support access to all of the form's members and allow full access to the uploaded files from the same object. This method of handling the files mirrored the functionality in use in ASP.

In order to do this, a new object (`HttpUploadRequest`) was implemented. This implements the `HttpServletRequest` interface. It extends the request object that is provided by JSP and delegates most of the functionality to this object. However, it implements the features associated with reading form values to enable files to be handled.

Useful Functions

When implementing an ASP site, it is useful to include files containing frequently used functions. This is standard practice to enforce the reusability of code. These functions allow certain tasks associated with display to be implemented once only and subsequently shared across the site. In the case of this project, functions like `TruncateStringWithEllipsis()`, `RemoveNumbersFromString()`, and `GetContentItemFromID()` were developed.

These functions were stored in a file called `UsefulFunctions.asp` that was imported at the top of each ASP file.

These functions are mostly display-based or designed to give a quick access route to commonly used routines in the business object layer.

In the first phase they were implemented in VBScript and not Java. During the port, the functions were ported to Java. A new class, `UsefulFunctions`, was created to provide these functions as `static` methods. This class was then imported at the top of every JSP file.

For example,

```
Function TruncateStringWithEllipsis(truncate)
  ' I am sure that we could all implement this
End Function

Function RemoveNumbersFromString(remove)
  ' Ditto this one
End Function
```

becomes:

```
public class UsefulFunctions {
  static public String truncateStringWithEllipsis(
                              String truncate) {
    // I am sure that we could all implement this
  }

  static public String removeNumbersFromString(
                              String remove) {
    // Ditto
  }
}
```

This sort of technique is not a good example of object-oriented coding. It is merely a way of porting legacy procedural functions into a Java environment. In many cases it is worth looking at such collections of functions and seeing whether they can sit easily in existing objects or in fact could define an object in their own right.

I mentioned earlier that we made a set of ASP functions that helped us encapsulate Site Server. In this case, a proper Java object should be designed in order to wrap the functionality.

Freeing System Resources

A major difference between ASP and JSP is the method each uses to track objects' references.

In COM, and therefore in ASP, reference to objects is counted using `AddRef` and `Release`.

In the code below, the connection to the database is freed once the database object is set to `nothing`. This prevents problems occurring when connections are held open for longer than required.

```
Set database=Server.CreateObject("ADODB.Connection")

' Use the database for a while

Set database=nothing
```

In JSP, the code below does not have quite the same effect as in the ASP. In this case, it is the garbage collector that decides when to clear the `database` object and close the connection. This could occur much later than the call setting `database` to `null`, depending on the implementation of the virtual machine.

```
Driver database = DriverManager.getDriver(...);

// Use the database for a while

database = null;
```

In order to avoid this trap, code like that shown below will ensure that the database is closed as soon as required access is complete.

```
Driver database = null;

try {
  Driver database = DriverManager.getDriver(…);
  Use the database for a while
} finally {
  if (database != null)
    database.close();
}
```

Case Sensitive Filenames

This is primarily a PC to UNIX issue. However, most of the potential problems can be avoided by adopting a rigorous case convention for filenames. This should prevent problems during cross platform ports.

Where Have We Got To?

Currently we have got to the following architecture.

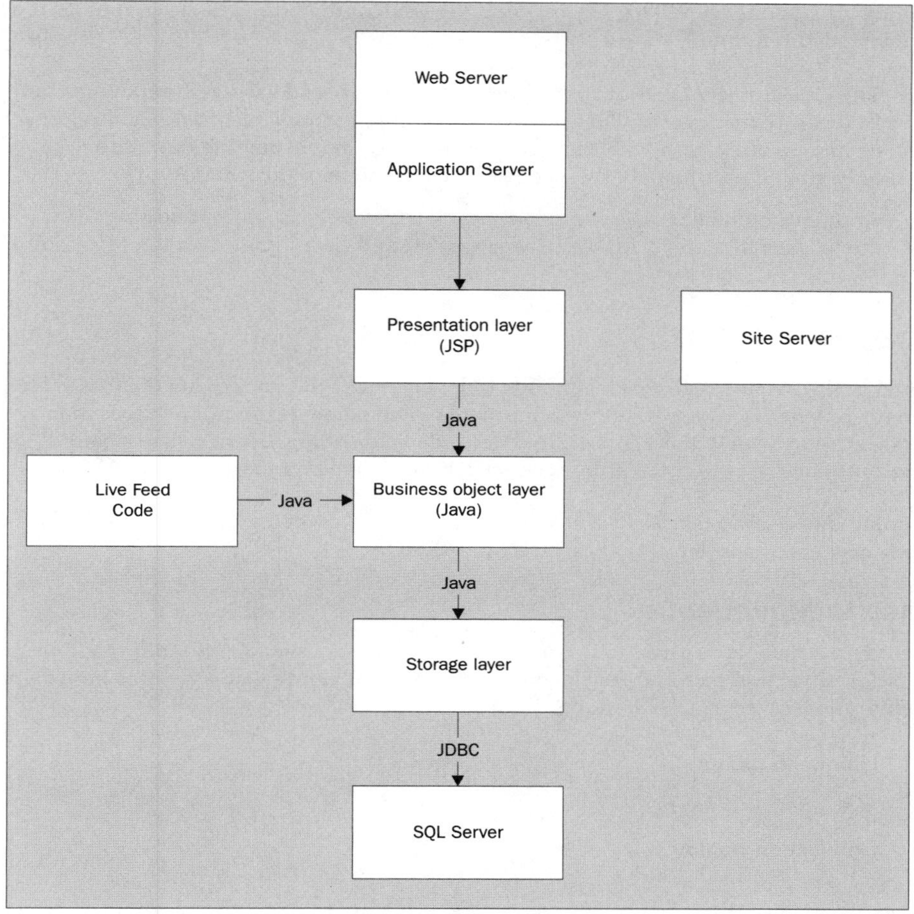

We still have some way to go. As you can see the database is still SQL Server. We will make our code more database independent in the next section.

Site Server is still in the picture and we have no way now of communicating to it.

Before talking about how we tackled these issues I will talk briefly about how you might want to go about porting the business object layer if it's not written in Java.

Porting the Business Object Layer

This layer was written in Java in response to the anticipated future requirement to port the product. Java was chosen from a range of options. The layer could, for example, have been implemented in another language like C++. Had this option been chosen, the layer would still have been functional and could have been ported directly to Java. This process is more or less difficult depending on the language that has been used to implement the business object layer.

The following options are ways to try to avoid the issue of the port. They were not used during this port but are included for completeness:

- The COM object layer could be ported to CORBA and used as components in the JSP layer. In this way the layer would not have to be ported to Java but could be used intact. This is a technique often used with big legacy systems where porting the front end to the web is the only goal. Unfortunately this is outside of the scope of this chapter.
- Another potential solution to reuse legacy COM objects without porting them is to use one of the bridges that are available between COM and Java (other than the Microsoft JVM).

Databases

Our goal in this section is to make our code independent of the underlying database. This means more than merely using JDBC (or ADO) which provide vendor-independent interfaces to most commercial databases. Unfortunately these interfaces don't hide vendor-dependent schemas and SQL. I will give a few examples below as to these differences and how we avoided them.

After going into a few examples I will spend a little time expanding on what can be done if your database access layer is dependent on ADO or ODBC.

Database Independence

To identify the database currently in use, a standard table is used to store information such as database name, schema version etc. This information is retrieved at runtime and governs how the following problems are resolved:

- Unique numbers
- SQL syntax differences
- Connection pooling

This table, called database_values, has three columns called `name`, `value`, `int_value`. The following rows are inserted:

Name	**Value**
`database_version`	Oracle, SQL Server ...
`schema_version`	1

Unique Numbers

In all relational databases, unique numbers are essential. It is only through uniqueness that primary keys can be maintained. The database must be able to supply unique numbers to multiple simultaneous connections.

In practice, databases implement this functionality differently. Oracle, for example, provides sequences. SQL Server provides table auto numbers. By making a standard method of retrieving unique numbers, we go a long way to achieving our goal of database independence.

I will explain how we dealt with SQL Server and Oracle databases. Other databases such as DB2, Informix etc can be treated in a similar way.

Oracle

First we create a sequence in the database using the SQL:

```
create sequence main_sequence
```

A sequence in Oracle is a way of getting unique numbers. They can be obtained using the SQL:

```
select main_sequence.next_val from dual
```

Now that we have the sequence we can obtain a unique number using the following Java:

```
import java.sql.*;

public class UniqueNumberService {

  // Omit error checking and correct resource handling
  // for clarity
  public int getUniqueNumber() throws SQLException {
    Connection conn = getConnection();
    Statement statement = conn.createStatement();
    ResultSet rs = statement.executeQuery(
              "select main_sequence.nextval from dual");

    if (rs.next()) {
      return rs.getInt(1);
    }
  }
}
```

SQL Server

In SQL Server we make use of the identity (auto number) facility in order to get our unique numbers.

First we create a table with the following SQL:

```
CREATE TABLE unique_number (num int IDENTITY (1, 1) NOT NULL, temp_col int NOT
NULL)
```

Then we create the stored procedure that atomically adds a row to this table, checks the identity value, and then deletes the row. As this operation is atomic it is guaranteed that no other user of the database will interfere with this operation.

```
CREATE PROCEDURE GET_UNIQUE_NUMBER AS
 INSERT INTO UNIQUE_NUMBER(temp_col) values (1)
 Delete from UNIQUE_NUMBER where num=@@IDENTITY
 Select @@IDENTITY from unique_number
```

Finally we use the below Java to select the unique number out of the database:

```
// Gets a connection from somewhere
Connection conn = getConnection();
Statement statement = conn.createStatement();
ResultSet rs = statement.executeQuery("get_unique_number");

if (rs.next()) {
  num = rs.getInt(1);
}
```

Syntax Differences

There are variations between different renderings of SQL, dependent upon the various vendors.

As the project now has a standard mechanism for telling which database is being used, it was relatively simple to construct a class to enable the correct syntax for the vendor to be recovered.

Some common examples of syntax difference between SQL Server and Oracle are:

Operation	Oracle	SQL Server
Left outer join	`(+)=`	`*=`
Concatenation	`|`	`+`
Date	`to_date(column_name, 'dd-mm-yyyy hh24:mi:ss')`	`CONVERT(DateTime, column_name, 103)`

In the Java class, we write code to return each of these strings. It determines the database type from the `database_values` table, mentioned earlier, and then produces the correct code.

For example:

```
String getConcatenationOperator() {
  // getDatabaseType() is merely a method which executes
  // the query on the database_values table, and returns
  // the value for database_version
  if (getDatabaseType().equals("oracle")) {
    return "|";
  } else if (getDatabaseType().equals("sqlserver")) {
    return "+";
  }
}
```

Connection Pooling

Connection pooling is a database concept designed to reduce the total number of connections to a database and reduce the number of costly connection creation operations.

It works by stopping a connection to the database being closed when it is not in use. Instead, the connection is returned to a pool. The next time a connection is requested, the pool is checked for a free connection. If a free connection is available from the pool, this is assigned, otherwise a new connection is made.

Code therefore needs to be restructured to request new connections as required and release these immediately once their work is done.

Java 1.1.6 did not have connection pooling as standard in JDBC. The project developers therefore implemented their own connection pooling. The initial version allowed new connections to be made whenever there were no free connections.

Features were subsequently added to limit the maximum and minimum number of connections. A useful feature of this allows the maximum number of connections to be set to 1, thus enabling a full test of the site to check leaking connections.

Connections are remade every time a query fails. This allows for reboots of the database while the service is up. Once the database is restored, the pool reconnects and the remainder of the code is not aware of the problem.

While the above is a recipe for a connection pool, many such pools are available from Sun and other vendors. It is left as an exercise to the reader if he wishes to implement such a connection pool himself. (See Chapter 7 for more details on how to implement connection pools in Java)

Porting Connectivity

If the ASP application uses ODBC or ADO to connect to the database, another problem may be encountered.

In any JSP application you will have to port the database code to use JDBC instead of any other connection mechanism. While JDBC is similar to both ADO and ODBC, they are not compatible. This means that it is harder to port your application in stages. In fact if it is decided to port the application piece by piece you will probably have to decide to maintain two connection pools one in ADO and one in JDBC. This will cause problems for your transactional code. You must make sure that all the code within the same transactional context is all working with the same connection mechanism.

Searching

In the original version of the project, Oyster implemented full text searching using Site Server.

As the interface to Site Server is COM, it is not appropriate for a platform-independent project. In order not be tied to a particular search engine – for example, Excalibur RetrievalWare, Autonomy Agentware, etc., it was decided to invest time in developing an abstraction layer for search engines.

This abstraction layer was modeled on JDBC. It allows multiple drivers to be written, one for each type of search engine supported. These drivers contain all the functionality necessary to parse an arbitrary query. The driver sends the parsed query to the search engine. When the results are returned, the driver parses them and returns a standard response.

This model allows Oyster to quickly change the search engine in use to provide the functionality of full text search. This is important as the content management system is used by a range of clients who each have individual requirements for which search engine they will support.

As most search engines allow results to be returned through a template, it becomes relatively straightforward to make a standard XML template for the returned results from each search engine. Once this is done, the parsing and returning of the results can be put into standard code. This reduces the amount of code stored in the driver.

The query is specified as a tree of terms – string terms, in addition to `and`, `or` and proximity terms.

The functionality for inputting data is usually provided by the vendor. This might, for example, be a web site crawler. It therefore seemed unnecessary to implement an interface to populate the search engine.

Where we're at

Oyster now has a JSP 0.91 application that is platform independent. We've added support for additional database independence that enables the project to move to various vendors. There is also a vendor-independent structure for querying search engines.

We now have this architecture:

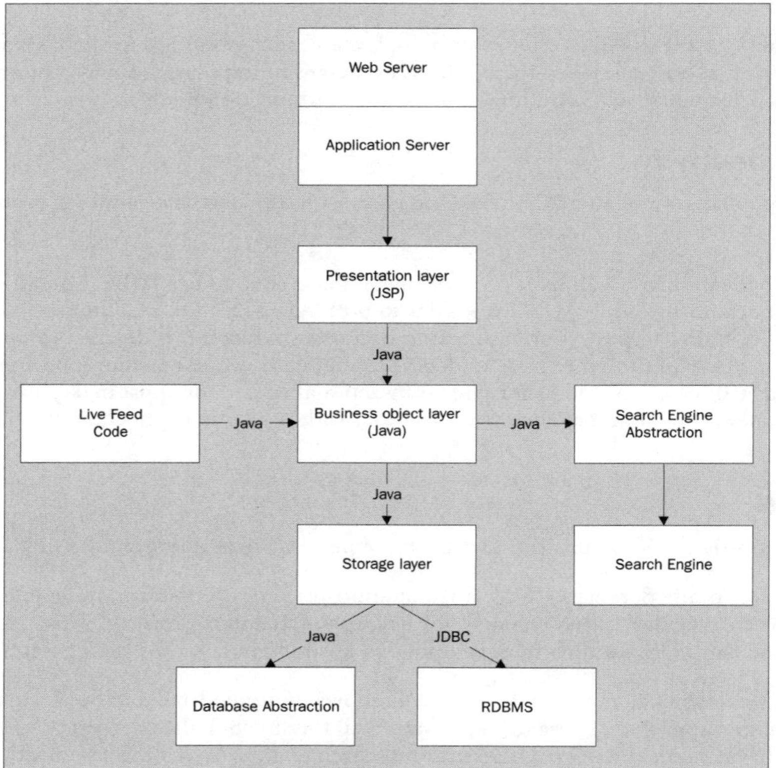

Phase Three

In this phase of the project, we ported the application to JSP 1.0.

JSP 1.0

Changes to the JSP specification have been made, between JSP 0.91 and JSP 1.0, which have meant additional porting is required. This is fortunately not extensive and should not reoccur. The backwards-incompatibility was largely a result of the fact that JSP 0.91, although implemented by many vendors, remained a draft specification.

The main changes required are:

- Imports syntax is now `<%@ page import="..." >` instead of `<%@ import="..." %>`
- `<SCRIPT runat=server>`*`code`*`</SCRIPT>` needs to be replaced by `<%!` *`code`* `%>`
- The `HttpSession` variable, `session`, is now an integral part of the JSP when compiled
- The `ServletContext` variable, `application`, is now an integral part of the JSP when compiled
- The object variable, `page`, is an integral part of the JSP when compiled
- The `HttpServletRequest` interface has changed
- `request` now returns `null` for form fields that were not filled in, rather than an empty string

Changes 1 and 2 guarantee that some code will have to change.

Changes 3, 4 and 5 can result in name clashes. For example, stored information on the current page number within a paginated list was held in a local variable called `page`. This has had to be changed.

Change 6 affects the project in that it implemented this interface in order to handle file upload.

Change 7 means that code had to change in order to deal with `null`s.

Summary

In this chapter, we've seen how a project developed for ASP and the Microsoft platform was ported to JSP and the Java platform. The main goals were platform, database, and search-engine independence for the application.

From this chapter we have seen that:

- Having a business object layer that hides much of the coding from the ASPs, leaving them the job of presenting data, greatly aids porting
- ASP and JSP are very similar – the main differences are in
    - Error handling
    - The use of global configurations
    - The presence of inline functions
    - Grouping helper functions together
    - Freeing resources
    - Case sensitivity
    - JDBC isn't enough for true database independence – extra work is needed to overcome differences in how unique numbers are provided and in SQL syntax
    - The main differences between JSP 0.91 and JSP 1.0

Together with Appendix E, we hope you now know where the differences and similarities between ASP and JSP lie.

J2EE
JSP

Configuring Apache and Tomcat

In this appendix we'll go through a typical installation of Apache and Tomcat, and highlight the interesting bits. We'll cover:

- Installing Apache, Tomcat and mod_jserv.
- Making them work together.
- Setting up the Tomcat server configuration file, `server.xml`.
- Configuring web applications using `web.xml`.
- Web application directory structure.
- The ant tool and `build.xml`.

Installing Apache

Download the Apache binaries from http://www.apache.org, and run the installation program. I used `apache_1_3_12_win32.exe` on a Windows 98 machine. Accept the defaults. Having got the basic installation, you need to edit `C:\Program Files\Apache Group\Apache\conf\httpd.conf` to insert the line:

```
ServerName localhost
```

Try the configuration out by starting Apache (from the start menu) and navigating to http://localhost/ in your browser. Stop Apache when you're ready, again using the start menu.

Installing Tomcat

> **See the Tomcat README (in the `jakarta-tomcat\docs` directory) for more details on installation and configuration.**

Uncompress your download of jakarta-tomcat into some sensible place, like C:\Program Files\Apache Group\.

While configuring the system, bear these points in mind:

- You need to have a Java Development Kit installed (1.1.X, 1.2 or 1.3) – I have used JDK 1.3, Release Candidate 1.
- Set the CLASSPATH environment variable to include the javac compiler.
    - In Java 2, include tools.jar in the CLASSPATH; this is typically somewhere like C:\jdk1.3\lib\tools.jar. Alternatively, set the JAVA_HOME environment variable to the path to your JDK installation, for example, C:\jdk1.3. Tomcat and ant use JAVA_HOME in their startup scripts to find tools.jar.
    - In JDK 1.1.x, the path to the classes.zip file is required instead.
- In Windows 9x, you may get DOS windows that say "Out of environment space". If this is the case, right-click on the offending DOS window, select Properties, go to the Memory tab, and set the initial environment to 4096 bytes.
- If you have multiple JDKs installed, you may need to edit the batch/script files to add full paths to java and other JDK tools.

I added this line to my autoexec.bat file:

```
set JAVA_HOME=C:\JDK1.3
```

although I could have used:

```
set CLASSPATH=C:\JDK1.3\LIB\TOOLS.jar;.
```

Some other things you may want to set are ANT_HOME and TOMCAT_HOME. We'll use these in the build.xml file later, and in the jakarta-tomcat/bin scripts. The startup script for ant tries C:\Program Files\ant or C:\ant and then gives up. I used:

```
set ANT_HOME= C:\progam files\apache group\jakarta-tomcat
set TOMCAT_HOME= C:\progam files\apache group\jakarta-tomcat
```

The startup.bat and shutdown.bat files try TOMCAT_HOME as the current or parent directory and then gives up.

Finally, run the startup.bat batch file found in the jakarta-tomcat\bin directory. If you're running under Windows and the new DOS window that startup.bat starts closes, use the alternative command line tomcat run to run the setup in the same DOS window as your command – this is useful when the configuration isn't quite there.

Test the result by going to http://localhost:8080/ in your browser. Run the `shutdown.bat` script when you're ready.

Installing mod_jserv

> **See the Tomcat+Apache Howto (in the `jakarta-tomcat\docs` directory) for more details on configuring `mod_jserv`.**

Download `mod_jserv`. (The filename for the Windows version is `ApacheModuleJServ.dll`.) Copy it into the Apache `modules` directory (`C:\Program Files\Apache Group\Apache\modules` on my machine).

Next edit your `httpd.conf` (on my machine, in the `C:\Program Files\Apache Group\Apache\conf` directory) and add the following line to the end,

```
Include "C:/Program Files/Apache Group/jakarta-tomcat/conf/tomcat-apache.conf"
```

using the correct path to the `tomcat-apache.conf` file. This file is automatically generated by tomcat from the `server.xml` file, so you need to set tomcat running before Apache, in order to generate the new configuration file to be included in the Apache `httpd.conf`. This setup will set the links to your own web applications, which are configured in `server.xml`, so that Apache can access them. We'll look at the configuration details in the next section.

Alternatively, the static `tomcat.conf` file can also be used; it's configured for the `examples` web application by default. If you want to use this file, include it in `httpd.conf` instead of `tomcat-apache.conf`. Then comment out the line:

```
LoadModule jserv_module libexec/mod_jserv.so
```

and uncomment the line:

```
LoadModule jserv_module modules/ApacheModuleJServ.dll
```

You'll have to add extra web applications by hand.

Test either configuration out:

- Start Tomcat
- Start Apache
- Check it is working (go to http://localhost/)
- Go to http://localhost/examples/jsp/

In order to set up different Apache configurations, simply copy `httpd.conf` to a file called something like `http.conf.tomcat`. Convert `httpd.conf` back to its original version (delete the new line at the end), and copy the **Start Apache** shortcut in the start menu; calling the copy something like **Start Apache with Tomcat**. Finally change the command line by adding to the end `-f "conf\httpd.conf.tomcat"`.

server.xml

The Tomcat server is configured using the `server.xml` file in the `jakarta-tomcat\conf` directory.

In order to set up a new web application for the server, for example, `projsp`, you need to add a new `Context` tag within the `ContextManager` tag. Simple copy the sample used for the examples web application and paste and alter it to the following:

```
<Context path="/projsp" docBase="webapps/projsp" debug="0"
 reloadable="true" >
</Context>
```

The `Context` tag just allows us to alter a few attributes from their default settings. For example, here we:

- Set a `path` after the server name
- Point that to the relative directory in `jakarta-tomcat`, set a debug level (0 the least, 9 providing the most information)
- Set `reloadable` to `"true"`, so that refreshed Beans and other classes are automatically reloaded into a running tomcat instance, speeding up the code-compile-test cycle for JSPs and Beans.

The contexts defined here are translated into `tomcat-apache.conf` when tomcat starts up.

web.xml

Your web application will now be visible to users of the site. The `web-inf\web.xml` file provides the configuration for the web application.

> *There's also one of these files for server-wide configuration, in `jakarta-tomcat\conf`.*

The `web.xml` file defines:

- Display name for general introduction to the application
- Context parameters for information on the deployed web application, for instance the system admin's email
- Servlet names and mappings
- Session configuration
- Tag library mappings (mapping the URL on the page to the actual `.tld` file)
- Supported mime types
- Welcome file list (the default page names that, if present, will be loaded when the URL just points to a path)

The tag library mapping is necessary in Chapter 8. Each tag library has a `.tld` file that describes the tags, their classes, body content type and attributes. This file needs to be available to the JSP container, when it comes across a JSP `taglib` directive. The mapping from `taglib` directive to actual file looks like this:

```
<taglib>
  <taglib-uri>
     /examples/taglib
  </taglib-uri>
  <taglib-location>
     /META-INF/Mylib.tld
  </taglib-location>
</taglib>
```

If you want to use a tag library that's wrapped as a JAR file, just point the URI to the JAR file, either directly from the JSP `taglib` directive URI, or through a `web.xml` mapping. For example, in order to point to the Forms tag library from `bookstore-search.jsp` in Chapter 8, we can use:

```
<%@ taglib uri="/WEB-INF/lib/formtags-0.4-dev.jar" prefix="form" %>
```

or:

```
<taglib>
  <taglib-uri>
    http://localhost:8080/form/taglib
  </taglib-uri>
  <taglib-location>
    /WEB-INF/lib/formtags-0.4-dev.jar
  </taglib-location>
</taglib>
```

The JAR file for the Form tag library has the following format:

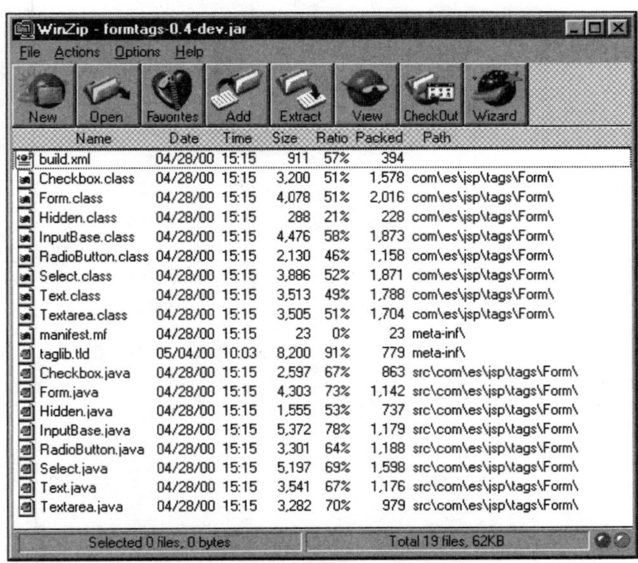

The key points are:

- The tag library descriptor is stored as the file `taglib.tld` in the `Meta-Inf` directory.
- The class packages start from the root of the JAR file, so that classes can be accessed.

It's worth noting that the URI is not the same as the `CLASSPATH` – so, although the JAR files in the `/WEB-INF/lib` folder are automatically added to the Tomcat server `CLASSPATH`, that doesn't mean that the URI can find them. You need to specify a relative URI to the JAR file. It doesn't have to be in any particular directory, but it seems sensible to keep it with the other libraries in your application, rather than with the template content.

Where to Put JSPs and Beans in a Web Application

We'll use the example of the `projsp` web application created for this book.

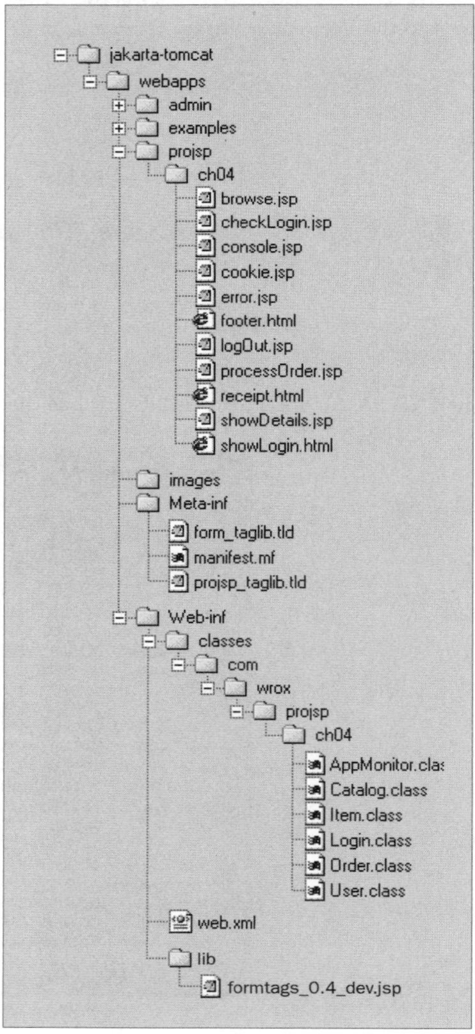

As you can see from the figure:

- JSPs and other template data in the projsp web application live in the webapps/projsp directory or a subdirectory of that folder.
- The CLASSPATH for Beans and other Java support classes starts in the webapps/projsp/WEB-INF/classes directory, so this is where the package names should start.
- JAR files for support classes should go in the WEB-INF/lib directory, where they'll be added to the CLASSPATH.
- The tag library descriptor files typically live in webapps/projsp/Meta-Inf.
- The web.xml configuration file for the web application is in /webapps/projsp/WEB-INF.

Using ant and build.xml

In the previous section we've seen how the web application code should look in position on the Tomcat server. But Tomcat comes with a tool, ant, to help you make the project and put all the files in the right places. In this last section of the appendix, we'll look at how ant and its configuration file, build.xml, work.

Firstly, here's the file structure of the source code for the projsp web application. We'll see how this is mapped to the directories we've just seen in the destination Tomcat server in a moment.

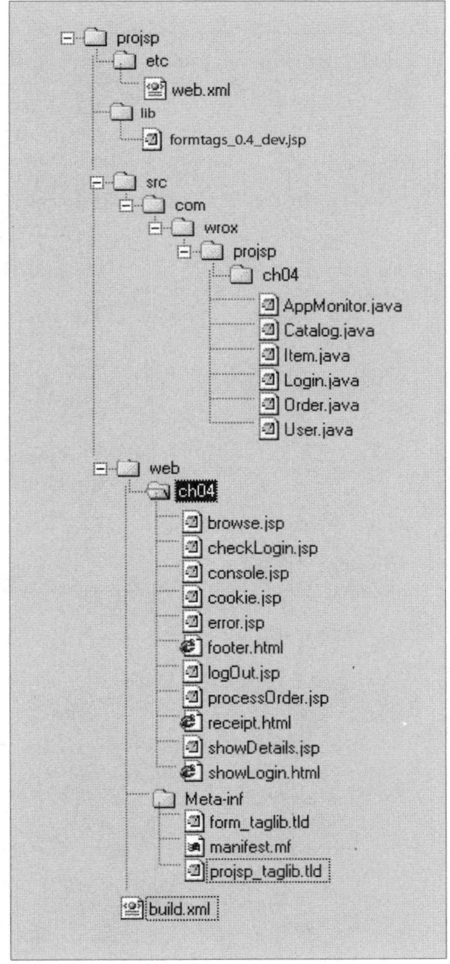

For the projsp web application, we have the following `build.xml` file:

```
<project name="ProJSP" default="compile" basedir=".">
  <target name="init" >
    <property name="build.compiler" value="classic"/>
    <property name="deploy.home"    value="${tomcat.home}/webapps/projsp"/>
    <property name="dist.home"      value="${deploy.home}"/>
    <property name="dist.src"       value="projsp.jar"/>
    <property name="dist.war"       value="projsp.war"/>
    <property name="javadoc.home"   value="${deploy.home}/javadoc"/>
  </target>
```

The `project` tag takes the name of the application, the default action and the base directory from which ant should work. This `build.xml` file is placed at the root of the folders on which it will act, hence the current directory setting for `basedir`.

You need to set the following variables for the `"init"` target to work:

Configuration Variable	Description
`ant.home`	The base directory of the ant installation. We set this as an environment variable earlier, so don't need to redeclare it here. This will normally point to the `jakarta-tomcat` installation.
`tomcat.home`	The base directory of the tomcat installation – also set as an environment variable earlier, so we don't need to set it here.
`build.compiler`	Defines the `javac` compiler
`deploy.home`	The directory where the deployment hierarchy will start – usually `jakarta-tomcat/webapp`.
`dist.home`	The directory where files for distribution are created. See the next two entries.
`dist.src`	The name of the distribution JAR file, created by `ant` to hold the source code for the web application
`dist.war`	The name of the Web ARchive (WAR) file for this application
`javadoc.home`	Directory where JavaDoc information will be created

This configuration assumes that `ANT_HOME` and `TOMCAT_HOME` environment variables have been set.

```
  <target name="prepare" init="init">
    <mkdir dir="${deploy.home}"/>
    <copydir src="web" dest="${deploy.home}"/>
    <mkdir dir="${deploy.home}/WEB-INF"/>
    <copyfile src="etc/web.xml" dest="${deploy.home}/WEB-INF/web.xml"/>
    <mkdir dir="${deploy.home}/WEB-INF/classes"/>
    <mkdir dir="${deploy.home}/WEB-INF/lib"/>
    <copydir src="lib" dest="${deploy.home}/WEB-INF/lib"/>
    <mkdir dir="${javadoc.home}"/>
  </target>
```

As, you can see, we use the "prepare" target to

- Make the web application directory, webapps/projsp
- Copy JSP and other non-Java files from the web folder and folders beneath. This includes the tag libraries in the Meta-Inf folder
- Copy the web.xml file from the etc directory to the WEB-INF folder
- Prepare the Java class, library and JavaDoc folders for other targets

```
    <target name="clean" init="init">
      <deltree dir="${deploy.home}"/>
    </target>

    <target name="compile" depends="prepare" init="init">
      <javac srcdir="src" destdir="${deploy.home}/WEB-INF/classes"
             classpath="${deploy.home}/WEB-INF/classes"
             debug="on" optimize="off" deprecation="off"/>
    </target>

    <target name="javadoc" depends="prepare" init="init">
      <!-- TODO -->
    </target>

    <target name="all" depends="clean,prepare,compile,javadoc" init="init"/>

    <target name="dist" depends="prepare,compile" init="init">
      <jar jarfile="${dist.home}/${dist.src}"
           basedir="." includes="**"/>
      <jar jarfile="${dist.home}/${dist.war}"
           basedir="${deploy.home}" includes="**"/>
    </target>
  </project>
```

The "dist" target builds the WAR and JAR files for the application using the jar tag. The jarfile attribute denotes where the JAR file is written, the basedir is the directory where the jar starts, while includes is set with a comma-delimited list of pattern matches. Note how it uses double asterisks to denote "match any directories, as well as any files" – a single asterisk will only include the files in that directory, and won't recurse sub-directories.

The WAR file can be deployed to servers by placing it in the /webapps root folder. When the Tomcat server starts it will unwrap the contents of the WAR into a folder with the name of the web application.

Summary

In this appendix, we've introduced some of the common configuration issues you'll face in getting Apache, JServ, and Tomcat set up for your web applications.

Further, and more current information can be found in the docs that come with the products, and at http://www.apache.org, http://java.apache.org, and http://jakarta.apache.org.

J2EE
JSP

B

JSP Syntax Reference

This appendix reviews the syntax for JavaServer Pages 1.1. It is intended to provide more information than the syntax card on particular options, while being more compact than the specification.

> **The JSP specifications 1.0 and 1.1 plus PDF syntax cards are available from http://java.sun.com/products/jsp, while the older specifications are archived at http://www.kirkdorffer.com/jspspecs/jsp092.html and jsp091.html.**

A word on the syntax of the syntax:

- Italics show what you'll have to specify.
- Bold shows the default value of an attribute. Attributes with default values are optional attribute, if you're using the default.
- When an attribute has a set of possible values, those are shown, delimited by `|`.

The page Directive

The page directive specifies attributes for the page – all the attributes are optional, as the essential ones have default values, shown in bold.

```
<%@ page language="java"
         extends="package.class"
         import="package.class, package.*, ..."
         session="true|false"
```

```
            buffer="none|8kb|sizekb"
            autoFlush="true|false"
            isThreadSafe="true|false"
            info="Sample JSP to show tags"
            errorPage="ErrorPage.jsp"
            contentType="text/html; charset=ISO-8859-1"
            isErrorPage="true|false"
%>
```

- The errorPage attribute contains the relative URL for the error page to which this page should go if there's an unhandled error on this page.
- The specified error page file must declare isErrorPage="true" to have access to the exception object.
- The contentType attribute sets the mime type and the character set for the page.

```
<%@ page language="java"
            isErrorPage="true" %>

<html>
<body>
<!-- The fully-qualified class that is the exception -->
<%= exception.toString() %>
<br>
<!-- The exception's message to the world -->
<%= exception.getMessage() %>
</body>
</html>
```

taglib Directive

The taglib directive defines a tag library namespace for the page, mapping the URI of the tag library descriptor to a prefix that can be used to reference tags from the library on this page.

```
<%@ taglib uri="/META-INF/taglib.tld" prefix="tagPrefix" %>

...

<tagPrefix:tagName attributeName="attributeValue" >
  JSP content
</tagPrefix:tagName>
<tagPrefix:tagName attributeName="attributeValue" />
```

The tag library descriptor (.tld file) looks like this:

```
<?xml version="1.0" encoding="ISO-8859-1" ?>
<!DOCTYPE taglib
        PUBLIC "-//Sun Microsystems, Inc.//DTD JSP Tag Library 1.1//EN"
        "http://java.sun.com/j2ee/dtds/web-jsptaglibrary_1_1.dtd">
<taglib>
  <tlibversion>1.0</tlibversion>
```

```
    <jspversion>1.1</jspversion>
    <shortname>projsp</shortname>
    <uri>http://www.wrox.com</uri>
    <info>
      Info on the tag library
    </info>

    <tag>
      <name>tagName</name>
      <tagclass>package.class</tagclass>
      <teiclass> package.TagExtraInfoClass</teiclass>
      <bodycontent>empty|JSP|tagdependent</bodycontent>
      <info>
        Information on the tag
      </info>

      <attribute>
        <name>attributeName</name>
        <required>true|false</required>
        <rtexprvalue>true|false</rtexprvalue>
      </attribute>
    </tag>

  </taglib>
```

The teiclass, bodycontent, info, attribute tags are optional. Within the attribute tag, the required and rtexprvalue tags are also optional. The value of rtexprvalue determines whether expressions are allowed to determine the value of the attribute.

Include Tags

There are two include tags – the include directive and the jsp:include tag.

The include directive includes a static file, specified by a relative URL, at translation time, adding any JSP in that file to this page for runtime processing:

```
<%@ include file="Header.html" %>
```

The jsp:include tag includes a static or dynamically-referenced file, so it's handled at runtime:

```
<jsp:include page="relativeURL"
             flush="true" >
  <jsp:param name="parameterName" value="parameterValue"/>
</jsp:include>
```

- The page attribute can be the result of some run-time expression.
- Future releases of the Servlet API will provide some options for the flush attribute.
- The jsp:param tag provides a mapping between a name and a value. The value can be a run-time expression. Here the parameters are appended to the original request, and if the parameter name already exists, the new parameter value takes precedence, in a comma-delimited list.

Bean-handling Tags

There are three tags to instantiate and handle JavaBeans from the page:

jsp:useBean Tag

The jsp:useBean tag checks for an instance of a bean of the given class and scope. If one exists it references it with the id, otherwise it instantiates it. The bean is available within its scope with its id attribute.

You can include code between the jsp:useBean tags, as shown in the second example – this code will only be run if the jsp:useBean tag successfully returns an reference to a bean instance.

```
<jsp:useBean id="aBeanName"
             scope="page|request|session|application"
             class="package.class"
/>
```

```
<jsp:useBean id="anotherBeanName"
             scope="page|request|session|application"
             class="package.class"
>
  <jsp.setProperty name="anotherBeanName"
                   property="*|propertyName" />
</jsp:useBean>
```

Note that the class package must be imported in the page directive

There is a lot of flexibility in specifying the bean. You can use,

- class="*package.class*"
- type="*typeName*"
- class="*package.class*" type="*typeName*" (and with terms reversed)
- beanName="*beanName*" type="*typeName*" (and with terms reversed)

where:

- typeName is the class of the scripting variable defined by the id attribute, that is the class that the Bean instance is cast to (whether the class, a parent class or an interface the class implements).
- beanName is the name of the Bean, as used in the instantiate() method of the java.beans.Beans class.

jsp:setProperty Tag

The `jsp:setProperty` tag we used above sets the property of the bean referenced by `name` using the `value`:

```
<jsp.setProperty name="anotherBeanName"
                 property="*|propertyName"
                 value="newValue" />
```

The property attribute can be any of the following

- ❑ `property="propertyName" value="propertyValue"`
- ❑ `property="*"`
- ❑ `property="propertyName" param="parameterName"`
- ❑ `property="propertyName"`

Where:

- ❑ The `*` setting tells the tag to iterate through the `request` parameters for the page, setting any values for properties in the Bean whose names match parameter names.
- ❑ The `param` attribute specifies the parameter name to use in setting this property.
- ❑ Omitting `value` and `param` attributes for a property assumes that the Bean property and `request` parameter name match.
- ❑ The `value` attribute can be any runtime expression as long as it evaluates to a `String`.
- ❑ The `value` attribute `String` can be automatically cast to `boolean`, `byte`, `char`, `double`, `int`, `float`, `long`, and their class equivalents. Other casts will have to be handled explicitly in the Bean's `setPropertyName()` method.

jsp:getProperty Tag

The final bean-handling tag is jsp:getProperty which gets the named property and outputs its value for inclusion in the page as a String;

```
<jsp:getProperty name="anotherBeanName" property="propertyName" />
```

Comments

Two sorts of comments are allowed in addition to comments in Java code – JSP and HTML:

```
<!-- HTML comments remain in the final client page.
     Can include JSP expressions
-->
<%-- JSP comment which is hidden from the final client page --%>
```

Declarations

The following syntax allows you to declare variables and functions for the page:

```
<%!
  int i = 0;
  char ch = 'a';
  boolean isTrue(boolean b) {
    // Is this true?
  }
%>
```

Scriptlets

Scriptlets enclose Java code (on however many lines) that is translated and evaluated to generate dynamic content:

```
<%
  // Java code
%>
```

Expressions

Expressions return a value from the scripting code as a `String` to the page:

```
<br>My word, is it <%= userName %>? It's been a while...<br>
```

Supporting Applets and Beans

The `jsp:plugin` tag enables the JSP to include a bean or an applet in the client page. It has the following syntax:

```
<jsp:plugin type="bean|applet"
            code="class"
            codebase="classDirectory"
            name="instanceName"
            archive="archiveURI"
            align="bottom|top|middle|left|right"
            height="inPixels"
            width="inPixels"
            hspace="leftRightPixels"
            vspace="topBottomPixels"
            jreversion="1.1|number"
            nspluginurl="pluginURL"
            iepluginurl="pluginURL" >
  <jsp:params>
    <jsp:param name="parameterName" value="parameterValue">
  </jsp:params>
```

```
    <jsp:fallback>Problem with plugin</jsp:fallback>
</jsp:plugin>
```

Most of these attributes are direct from the HTML spec – the exceptions are `type`, `jreversion`, `nspluginurl` and `iepluginurl`.

- The `name`, `archive`, `align`, `height`, `width`, `hspace`, `vspace`, `jreversion`, `nspluginurl`, and `iepluginurl` attributes are optional.
- The `jsp:param` tag's value attribute can take a runtime expression

Forwarding the Request

To forward the client request to another URL, whether it be an HTML file,JSP or servlet, use the following syntax:

```
<jsp:forward page="relativeURL" />

<jsp:forward page="relativeURL" >
  <jsp:param name="parameterName" value="parameterValue" />
</jsp:forward>
```

- The `page` attribute for `jsp:forward` can be a runtime expression
- The `value` attribute for `jsp:param` can be a runtime expression

Implicit Objects

See Appendix C for details of the Servlet and JSP classes, and their methods.

Implicit objects	Type	Scope
`application`	`javax.servlet.ServletContext`	Application
`session`	`javax.servlet.HttpSession`	Session
`request`	`javax.servlet.ServletRequest`	Request
`pageContext`	`javax.servlet.jsp.PageContext`	Page
`out`	`javax.servlet.jsp.JspWriter`	Page
`config`	`javax.servlet.ServletConfig`	Page
`exception`	`java.lang.Throwable`	Page
`page`	`java.lang.Object`	Page
`response`	`javax.servlet.ServletResponse`	Page

J2EE
JSP

C

JSP and Servlet API Reference

This appendix describes the Java classes and interfaces defined in the JSP 1.1 and Servlet 2.2 specifications. These are contained in four packages:

- `javax.servlet` contains classes and interfaces related to Servlet programming.
- `javax.servlet.http` contains classes and interfaces related specifically to Servlets using the HTTP protocol.
- `javax.servlet.jsp` contains classes and interfaces related to JSP.
- `javax.servlet.jsp.tagext` contains classes and interfaces for programming JSP tag extensions.

The javax.servlet Package

A **servlet** is a small Java program that resides on a web server, and listens for and responds to requests from client machines. Servlets do not have a `main()` method, and can be thought of as being analogous to applets, except that they are running on the server side. The most common uses for servlets are processing and storing data submitted from an HTML form, providing dynamic responses to client requests, and managing state information for multiple client requests.

The life cycle of a servlet is governed by three methods defined in the `Servlet` interface. The `init()` method is called when the servlet is loaded into the address space of the server and provides initialization parameters to the servlet. The `service()` method is called when a request is made from a client machine. The `destroy()` method is used when the servlet is taken out of service to release any resources allocated to the servlet.

Servlet Interfaces

RequestDispatcher Interface

```
public interface RequestDispatcher
```

A `RequestDispatcher` is an object that sends requests from client machines to the appropriate resource (servlet, HTML file, etc.) on the server. The server creates the `RequestDispatcher` object, which is used as a wrapper around a particular resource. A `RequestDispatcher` object was intended to wrap servlets, but can be used to wrap any type of resource on a server.

forward() Method

Method	Syntax
`forward()`	`public void forward(ServletRequest request, ServletResponse response) throws ServletException, IOException`

`foward()` forwards a client request to another resource (servlet, HTML file, etc.). This method allows a servlet to serve as a "request processor", performing some preliminary work before sending the request to the resource that will ultimately respond to it. The `foward()` method can be used if the servlet has not already opened a `PrintWriter` or `ServletOutputStream` back to the client machine. If an output stream has been created, use the `include()` method instead.

include() Method

Method	Syntax
`include()`	`public void include(ServletRequest request, ServletResponse response) throws ServletException, IOException`

`include()` allows a resource to be included in the response to a client request. This method is used to include some content to the response after the response has been initiated by opening a `PrintWriter` or `ServletOutputStream` back to the client machine.

Example: Using RequestDispatcher

In this example, a `RequestDispatcher` object is used to include some copyright information, contained in the file `copyright.html`, in a response. The contents of the file are included in the response by having the `RequestDispatcher` object invoke the `include()` method.

```
import javax.servlet.*;
import java.io.*;

public class RDServlet extends GenericServlet {
  public void service(ServletRequest request, ServletResponse response)
          throws ServletException, IOException {

    // A RequestDispatcher object is associated with an html file
```

```
    RequestDispatcher rd =
      getServletContext().getRequestDispatcher("/copyright.html");

    // The ServletResponse object passed to the service() method is used
    // to set the content type of the response and to return a PrintWriter
    // object.  The PrintWriter writes a line of text to the client machine.

    response.setContentType("text/html");
    PrintWriter pw = response.getWriter();
    pw.println("Java Programmer's Reference");

    // The "copyright.html" file is sent to the client machine by having
    // the RequestDispatcher object invoke the include() method.  The
    // include() method is used rather than the forward() method because
    // the PrintWriter object had already been created.

    rd.include(request, response);

    pw.close();
  }
}
```

The `copyright.html` file contains the following code:

```
<BR><BR><BR>
Copyright 2000 Wrox Press, Ltd.<BR>
All rights reserved<BR>
```

Servlet Interface

```
public interface Servlet
```

Every servlet must implement the `Servlet` interface. It declares the methods that govern the life cycle of the servlet as well as methods to access initialization parameters and information about the servlet

destroy() Method

Method	Syntax
`destroy()`	`public void` **`destroy`**`()`

`destroy()` unloads the servlet from the server's memory and releases any resources associated with the servlet.

getServletConfig() Method

Method	Syntax
`getServletConfig()`	`public ServletConfig` **`getServletConfig`**`()`

`getServletConfig()` returns the `ServletConfig` object associated with the servlet. A `ServletConfig` object contains parameters that are used to initialize the servlet.

getServletInfo() Method

Method	Syntax
`getServletInfo()`	`public String getServletInfo()`

`getServletInfo()` returns a `String` containing useful information about the servlet. By default, this method returns an empty `String`. It can be overridden to provide more useful information.

init() Method

Method	Syntax
`init()`	`public void init(ServletConfig config) throws ServletException`

`init()` is called when the servlet is loaded into the address space of the server. The `ServletConfig` object is used to provide the servlet with initialization parameters.

service() Method

Method	Syntax
`service()`	`public abstract void service(ServletRequest request, ServletResponse response) throws ServletException, IOException`

`service()` is called to respond to a request from a client machine. The code representing what the servlet is supposed to do is placed in this method.

Example: A Simple Servlet

This example creates a simple servlet that returns the current date and time. It overrides the `service()` method to write the string representation of a `Date` object back to the client machine. The output from the servlet is set to be interpreted as HTML code.

```
import javax.servlet.*;
import java.io.*;
import java.util.*;

public class SimpleServlet extends GenericServlet {
  public void service(ServletRequest request, ServletResponse response)
          throws ServletException, IOException {
    response.setContentType("text/html");
    PrintWriter pw = response.getWriter();
    Date d = new Date();
    pw.println("<B>The date and time are " + d.toString());
    pw.close();
  }
}
```

ServletConfig Interface

```
public interface ServletConfig
```

A `ServletConfig` object is used to pass parameters to a servlet during its initialization. The initialization paramters are a set of name-value pairs. The `ServletConfig` interface declares methods that can access the parameters as well return the name of the servlet and its associated `ServletContext` object. A `ServletContext` object contains information about the server on which the servlet resides.

getServletContext() Method

Method	Syntax
getServletContext()	public ServletContext **getServletContext**()

`getServletContext()` returns the `ServletContext` object associated with the invoking servlet. A `ServletContext` object contains information about the environment in which the servlet is running.

Methods to Return Information about a Servlet

Method	Syntax
getInitParameter()	public String **getInitParameter**(String *name*)
getInitParameterNames()	public Enumeration **getInitParameterNames**()
getServletName()	public String **getServletName**()

`getInitParameter()` returns the value of the specified initialization parameter or null if the parameter does not exist.

`getInitParameterNames()` returns an `Enumeration` of `String` objects containing the names of all of the servlet's initialization parameters.

`getServletName()` returns the name of the servlet. If the servlet is unnamed, the method will return the servlet's class name.

Example: Reading Initialization Parameters

A servlet is initialized with a parameter read from the servlets.properties file. The parameter represents the name of a file. The `ServletConfig` object passed to the `init()` method is used to access the initialization parameter. If the parameter is read correctly, the file is opened and its contents written back to the client machine

Note that the servlet class name should not be used in the URL, but rather the name that is assigned to the servlet in the Servlet engine configuration file. The initialization parameter is associated with this name. If the servlet class name is written in the location window, the initialization parameter will not be accessed.

```
import javax.servlet.*;
import java.io.*;
import java.util.*;

public class InitServlet extends GenericServlet {
  String file, str;

  // The ServletConfig object passed to the init() method is
  // used to retrieve the value associated with the initialization
  // parameter "filename".

  public void init(ServletConfig config) throws ServletException {
    file = config.getInitParameter("filename");
  }

  public void service(ServletRequest request, ServletResponse response)
          throws ServletException, IOException, FileNotFoundException {
    response.setContentType("text/html");
    PrintWriter pw = response.getWriter();

    // If the initialization parameter was successfully read, its value
    // is used to open a file.  The contents of the file are then sent
    // back to the client machine.

    if (file != null) {
      BufferedReader br = new BufferedReader(new FileReader(file));
      while ((str = br.readLine()) != null) {
        pw.println("<B>" + str + "<BR>");
      }
    } else {
      pw.println("initialization parameter does not exist");
    }
    pw.close();
  }
}
```

The web.xml file includes the following code:

```
<web-app>
  ...
  <servlet>
    <servlet-name>init</servlet-name>
    <servlet-class>InitServlet</servlet-class>
    <init-param>
      <param-name>filename</param-name>
      <param-value>webpages/WEB-INF/names.txt</param-value>
    </init-param>
  </servlet>
  ...
</web-app>
```

Finally, the names.txt file contains:

```
Jackson's birthday is March 21
Zachary's birthday is May 12
```

ServletContext Interface

```
public interface ServletContext
```

The ServletContext interface declares methods that a servlet uses to communicate with its host server. The methods declared in this interface allow a servlet to obtain information about the server on which it is running.

getContext() Method

Method	Syntax
getContext()	public ServletContext **getContext**(String *URLpath*)

getContext() returns the ServletContext object for the resource at the specified path on the server. The path argument is an absolute URL beginning with "/".

getMimeType() Method

Method	Syntax
getMimeType()	public String **getMimeType**(String *file*)

getMimeType() returns MIME type of the specified file or null if the MIME type cannot be ascertained. Typical return values will be "text/plain", "text/html", or "image/jpg".

getRealPath() Method

Method	Syntax
getRealPath()	public String **getRealPath**(String *virtualPath*)

getRealPath() returns a String object containing the real path, in a form appropriate to the platform on which the servlet is running, corresponding to the given virtual path. An example of a virtual path might be "/blah.html".

getServerInfo() Method

Method	Syntax
getServerInfo()	public String **getServerInfo**()

getServerInfo() returns a String object containing information on the server on which the servlet is running. At a minimum, the String will contain the servlet container name and version number.

Initialization Parameter Methods

Method	Syntax
getInitParameter()	public String **getInitParameter**(String *name*)
getInitParameterNames()	public Enumeration **getInitParameterNames**()

getInitParameter() returns a String object containing the value of the specfied initialization parameter, or null if the parameter does not exist.

getInitParameterNames() returns a Enumeration containing the initialization parameters associated with the invoking ServletContext object

log() Method

Method	Syntax
log()	public void **log**(String *message*)
	public void **log**(String *message*, Throwable *thr*)

log() is used to write a message to the servlet's log file. The second version writes an explanatory message and a stack trace for the specified Throwable exception to the log file.

RequestDispatcher Methods

Method	Syntax
getNamedDispatcher()	public RequestDispatcher **getNamedDispatcher** (String *servletName*)
getRequestDispatcher()	public RequestDispatcher **getRequestDispatcher** (String *path*)

A RequestDispatcher object sends requests from client machines to the appropriate resource (servlet, HTML file, etc.) on the server. The server creates the RequestDispatcher object which is used as a wrapper around a particular resource.

getNamedDispatcher() returns a RequestDispatcher object that will be wrapped around the named servlet.

getRequestDispatcher() returns an RequestDispatcher object that acts as a wrapper around the resource located at the specified path. The path must begin with "/", and is interpreted relative to the current context root.

Resource Methods

Method	Syntax
getResource()	public URL **getResource**(String *path*) throws MalformedURLException
getResourceAsStream()	public InputStream **getResourceAsStream** (String *path*)

`getResource()` returns a `URL` object that is mapped to the specified path. The path must begin with `"/"` and is interpreted relative to the current context root.

`getResourceAsStream()` returns the resource at the specified path as an `InputStream` object.

Server Attribute Methods

Method	Syntax
getAttribute()	public Object **getAttribute**(String *name*)
getAttributeNames()	public Enumeration **getAttributeNames**()
removeAttribute()	public void **removeAttribute**(String *name*)
setAttribute()	public void **setAttribute**(String *name*, Object *value*)

`getAttribute()` returns the value of the specified attribute name. The return value is an `Object` or sub-class if the attribute is available to the invoking `ServletContext` object, or `null` if the attribute is not available.

`getAttributeNames()` returns an `Enumeration` containing the attribute names available to the invoking `ServletContext` object.

`removeAttribute()` makes the specified attribute unavailable to the invoking `ServletContext` object. Subsequent calls to the `getAttribute()` method for this attribute will return `null`.

`setAttribute()` binds a value to a specified attribute name.

Version Methods

Method	Syntax
getMajorVersion()	public int **getMajorVersion**()
getMinorVersion()	public int **getMinorVersion**()

`getMajorVersion()` returns the major version of the Java Servlet API that the server supports. For servers supporting version 2.2 of the Servlet specification, this method will return 2.

`getMinorVersion()` returns the minor version of the Java Servlet API that the server supports. For servers supporting version 2.2 of the Servlet specification, this method will return 2.

Deprecated Methods

Method	Syntax
getServlet()	public Servlet **getServlet**(String *name*) throws ServletException
getServletNames()	public Enumeration **getServletNames**()
getServlets()	public Enumeration **getServlets**()
log()	public void **log**(Exception *exception*, String *message*)

getServlet() returns the specified Servlet. This method was deprecated as of Java Servlet API 2.1 and will be permanently removed in a future version of the Servlet API.

getServletNames() returns an Enumeration containing the servlet names known to the invoking ServletContext object. This method was deprecated as of Java Servlet API 2.1 and will be permanently removed in a future version of the Servlet API.

getServlets() returns an Enumeration containing the Servlet objects known to the invoking ServletContext object. This method was deprecated as of Java Servlet API 2.1 and will be permanently removed in a future version of the Servlet API.

This version of the log() method was deprecated as of Java Servlet API 2.1. The version that takes a Throwable argument should be used in its place.

Example: Using ServletContext

A ServletContext object is used to obtain information about the server on which a servlet is running. The ServletContext object is also used to obtain a second ServletContext object that is associated with another resource.

```
import javax.servlet.*;
import java.io.*;
import java.util.*;

public class ServerInfoServlet extends GenericServlet {
  String attributeName;

  public void service(ServletRequest request, ServletResponse response)
          throws ServletException, IOException {
    response.setContentType("text/plain");
    PrintWriter pw = response.getWriter();

    // A ServletContext object is used to obtain information about
    // the server.

    ServletContext sc = getServletContext();

    pw.println("Server info is " + sc.getServerInfo());

    // Two additional attributes are added.

    sc.setAttribute("status", "OK");
    sc.setAttribute("mood", "happy");

    pw.println();
    pw.println("Server Attributes");
    Enumeration e = sc.getAttributeNames();
    while (e.hasMoreElements()) {
      attributeName = (String) e.nextElement();
      pw.println("name: " + attributeName + "  value: "
                 + sc.getAttribute(attributeName));
    }
```

```
      // The original ServletContext object can be used to obtain a
      // ServletContext of another resource

      pw.println();
      pw.println("Other resource info");
      String path = sc.getRealPath("/tmp.txt");
      ServletContext sc2 = sc.getContext(path);
      pw.println("MIME type: " + sc2.getMimeType(path));

      pw.close();
    }
  }
```

Finally, the `tmp.txt` file contains:

```
blah, blah, blah
```

ServletRequest Interface

```
public interface ServletRequest
```

The `ServletRequest` interface declares methods that are used to provide client request information to a servlet. The information can include parameter name-value pairs, attributes, and an input stream. A `ServletRequest` object is passed to the `service()` method defined in the `Servlet` interface as well as the `forward()` and `include()` methods from the `RequestDispatcher` interface.

I/O Stream Methods

Method	Syntax
getInputStream()	public ServletInputStream **getInputStream**() throws IOException
getReader()	public BufferedReader **getReader**() throws IOException

`getInputStream()` returns a `ServletInputStream` object that can be used to read the body of the request as binary data.

`getReader()` returns a `BufferedReader` object that can be used to read the body of the request as character data.

Locale Methods

Method	Syntax
getLocale()	public Locale **getLocale**()
getLocales()	public Enumeration **getLocales**()

`getLocale()` returns the preferred locale of the client that made the request.

`getLocales()` returns an `Enumeration` containing, in descending order of preference, the locales that are acceptable to the client machine.

Parameter Methods

Method	Syntax
getParameter()	public String **getParameter**(String *name*)
getParameterNames()	public Enumeration **getParameterNames**()
getParameterValues()	public String[] **getParameterValues**(String *name*)

Parameters are name-value pairs that can be used to provide request-specific information to a servlet. For instance, they can identify which file the servlet should access.

`getParameter()` returns a `String` object containing the value of the specfied parameter, or `null` if the parameter does not exist.

`getParameterNames()` returns a `Enumeration` containing the parameters contained within the invoking `ServletRequest` object.

`getParamterValues()` is used when a parameter may have more than one value associated with it. The method returns a `String` array containing the values of the specfied parameter, or `null` if the parameter does not exist.

Request Attribute Methods

Method	Syntax
getAttribute()	public Object **getAttribute**(String *name*)
getAttributeNames()	public Enumeration **getAttributeNames**()
removeAttribute()	public void **removeAttribute**(String *name*)
setAttribute()	public void **setAttribute**(String *name*, Object *value*)

`getAttribute()` returns the value of the specified request attribute name. The return value is an `Object` or sub-class if the attribute is available to the invoking `ServletRequest` object, or `null` if the attribute is not available.

`getAttributeNames()` returns an `Enumeration` containing the attribute names available to the invoking `ServletRequest` object.

`removeAttribute()` makes the specified attribute unavailable to the invoking `ServletRequest` object. Subsequent calls to the `getAttribute()` method for this attribute will return `null`.

`setAttribute()` binds a value to a specified attribute name. Note that attributes will be re-set after the request is handled.

getRequestDispatcher()

Method	Syntax
getRequestDispatcher()	public RequestDispatcher **getRequestDispatcher** (String *path*)

A RequestDispatcher object sends requests from client machines to the appropriate resource (servlet, HTML file, etc.) on the server. The server creates the RequestDispatcher object which is used as a wrapper around a particular resource.

getRequestDispatcher() returns an RequestDispatcher object that acts as a wrapper around the resource located at the specified path. The path must begin with "/" and can be a relative path.

Methods that Return Information about the Client Machine

Method	Syntax
getRemoteAddr()	public String **getRemoteAddr**()
getRemoteHost()	public String **getRemoteHost**()

getRemoteAddr() returns a String object containing the IP address of the client machine that made the request.

getRemoteHost() returns a String object containing the name of the client machine or the IP address if the name cannot be determined.

Methods that Return Information about the Request

Method	Syntax
getCharacterEncoding()	public String **getCharacterEncoding**()
getContentLength()	public int **getContentLength**()
getContentType()	public String **getContentType**()
getProtocol()	public String **getProtocol**()
getScheme()	public String **getScheme**()
isSecure()	public boolean **isSecure**()

getCharacterEncoding() returns a String object containing the character encoding used in the body of the request, or null if there is no encoding.

getContentLength() returns the length of the body of the request in bytes, or –1 if the length is not known.

getContentType() returns a String object containing the MIME type ("text/plain", "text/html", "image/gif", etc.) of the body of the request, or null if the type is not known.

getProtocol() returns the name and version of the protocol used by the request. A typical return String would be "HTTP/1.1".

`getScheme()` returns the scheme (`"http"`, `"https"`, `"ftp"`, etc.) used to make the request.

`isSecure()` returns `true` if the request was made using a secure channel, for example HTTPS.

Methods that Return Information about the Server

Method	Syntax
getServerName()	public String **getServerName**()
getServerPort()	public int **getServerPort**()

`getServerName()` returns a `String` object containing the name of the server that received the request.

`getServerPort()` returns the port number that received the request.

Example: Using ServletRequest

This example uses the `ServletRequest` object that is automatically passed to the `service()` method to access information about the request and about the client machine that made the request.

```
import javax.servlet.*;
import java.io.*;
import java.util.*;

public class RequestServlet extends GenericServlet {
  public void service(ServletRequest request, ServletResponse response)
          throws ServletException, IOException {
    response.setContentType("text/plain");
    PrintWriter pw = response.getWriter();

    // The ServletRequest object passed to the service() method is used
    // to obtain information about the request and about the client machine.

    pw.println("IP address of the client: "
               + request.getRemoteAddr());
    pw.println("Name of the client: " + request.getRemoteHost());
    pw.println("Character encoding: "
               + request.getCharacterEncoding());
    pw.println("Length of request: " + request.getContentLength());
    pw.println("Type of request: " + request.getContentType());
    pw.println("Request Protocol: " + request.getProtocol());
    pw.println("Request scheme: " + request.getScheme());

    pw.close();
  }
}
```

ServletResponse Interface

```
public interface ServletResponse
```

The `ServletResponse` interface declares methods that are used to assist the servlet in sending a response to the client machine.

Buffer Methods

Method	Syntax
flushBuffer()	`public void flushBuffer() throws IOException`
getBufferSize()	`public int getBufferSize()`
setBufferSize()	`public void setBufferSize(int size)`

`flushBuffer()` causes any content stored in the buffer to be written to the client. Calling this method will also commit the response, meaning that the status code and headers will be written.

`getBufferSize()` returns the buffer size used for the response, or 0 if no buffering is used.

`setBufferSize()` requests a buffer size to be used for the response. The actual buffer size will be at least this large.

Content Methods

Method	Syntax
setContentLength()	`public void setContentLength(int length)`
setContentType()	`public void setContentType(String type)`

`setContentLength()` sets the length of the body of the reponse.

`setContentType()` sets the content type of the response sent to the server. The `String` argument specifies a MIME type and may also include the type of character encoding, for example `"text/plain; charset=ISO-8859-1"`.

getCharacterEncoding() Method

Method	Syntax
getCharacterEncoding()	`public String getCharacterEncoding()`

`getCharacterEncoding()` returns a `String` object containing the character encoding used in the body of the response. The default is `"ISO-8859-1"`, which corresponds to Latin-1.

I/O Stream Methods

Method	Syntax
getOutputStream()	public ServletOutputStream **getOutputStream**() throws IOException
getWriter()	public PrintWriter **getWriter**() throws IOException

`getOutputStream()` returns a `ServletOutputStream` object that can be used to write the response as binary data.

`getWriter()` returns a `PrintWriter` object that can be used to write the response as character data.

isCommitted() Method

Method	Syntax
isCommitted()	public boolean **isCommitted**()

`isCommitted()` returns `true` if the response has been committed, meaning that the status code and headers have been written.

Locale Methods

Method	Syntax
getLocale()	public Locale **getLocale**()
setLocale()	public void **setLocale**(Locale *locale*)

`getLocale()` returns the locale that has been assigned to the response. By default, this will be the default locale for the server.

`setLocale()` specifies the locale that will be used for the response.

reset() Method

Method	Syntax
reset()	public void **reset**() throws IllegalStateException

`reset()` clears the status code and headers and any data that exists in the buffer. If the response has already been committed, calling this method will cause an exception to be thrown.

Example: Using ServletResponse

This example uses the `ServletResponse` object that is automatically passed to the `service()` method to send an image file back to the client machine. A `ServletContext` object is used to assign the image file to an `InputStream`. The `ServletResponse` object is then used to set the content type of the response and return the `ServletOutputStream` object used to write the image.

```
import javax.servlet.*;
import java.io.*;

public class ResponseServlet extends GenericServlet {
  int c;

  public void service(ServletRequest request, ServletResponse response)
          throws ServletException, IOException, FileNotFoundException {

    // A ServletContext object is used to assign an image file to an
    // InputStream

    ServletContext sc = getServletContext();
    InputStream is = sc.getResourceAsStream("/gardening.jpg");

    // The ServletResponse object passed to the service() method is used
    // to set the content type of the response and to return the
    // ServletOutputStream object that is used to send the image file
    // back to the client machine.

    response.setContentType("image/jpg");
    ServletOutputStream sos = response.getOutputStream();

    while ((c = is.read()) != -1) {
      sos.write(c);
    }
    is.close();
    sos.close();
  }
}
```

SingleThreadModel Interface

```
public interface SingleThreadModel
```

The `SingleThreadModel` interface declares no methods. A servlet that implements this interface will allow only one request at a time to access its `service()` method. The server will achieve this by either sychronizing access to a single instance of the servlet or by assigning a separate instance of the servlet for each request.

Servlet Classes

GenericServlet Class

```
public abstract class GenericServlet extends Object
  implements Servlet, ServletConfig, Serializable
```

```
Object
   GenericServlet
```

Interfaces

Servlet, ServletConfig, Serializable

The GenericServlet class defines a generic, protocol-independent servlet. It provides implementations of the methods declared in the Servlet and ServletConfig interfaces. Because GenericServlet is an abstract class, a GenericServlet object is never created. To create a generic servlet, a class must be written that extends the GenericServlet class and overrides the service() method.

GenericServlet() Constructor

Constructor	Syntax
GenericServlet()	public **GenericServlet**()

This constructor does nothing. The init() methods are used for servlet initialization.

destroy() Method

Method	Syntax
destroy()	public void **destroy**()

destroy() unloads the servlet from the server's memory and releases any resources associated with the servlet.

getServletConfig() Method

Method	Syntax
getServletConfig()	public ServletConfig **getServletConfig**()

getServletConfig() returns the ServletConfig object associated with the invoking GenericServlet sub-class object. A ServletConfig object contains parameters that are used to initialize the servlet.

getServletContext() Method

Method	Syntax
getServletContext()	public ServletContext **getServletContext**()

getServletContext() returns the ServletContext object associated with the invoking GenericServlet sub-class object. A ServletContext object contains information about the environment in which the servlet is running.

init() Method

Method	Syntax
init()	public void **init**() throws ServletException public void **init**(ServletConfig *config*) throws ServletException

`init()` is called when the servlet is loaded into the address space of the server. If a `ServletConfig` object is specified, it can be used to provide the servlet with initialization parameters. The no-argument version is provided as a convenience method and is intended to be overridden by sub-classes.

log() Method

Method	Syntax
log()	public void **log**(String *message*) public void **log**(String *message*, Throwable *thr*)

`log()` is used to write a message to the servlet's log file. The second version writes an explanatory message and a stack trace for the specified `Throwable` exception to the log file.

Methods to Return Information about a GenericServlet

Method	Syntax
getInitParameter()	public String **getInitParameter**(String *name*)
getInitParameterNames()	public Enumeration **getInitParameterNames**()
getServletInfo()	public String **getServletInfo**()
getServletName()	public String **getServletName**()

`getInitParameter()` returns the value of the specified initialization parameter from the `ServletConfig` object associated with the invoking `GenericServlet` object.

`getInitParameterNames()` returns an `Enumeration` of `String` objects containing the names of all of the servlet's initialization parameters.

`getServletInfo()` returns a `String` containing useful information about the servlet. By default, this method returns an empty `String`. It can be overridden to provide more useful information.

`getServletName()` returns the name of the invoking `GenericServlet` object.

service() Method

Method	Syntax
`service()`	`public abstract void service(ServletRequest request, ServletResponse response) throws ServletException, IOException`

`service()` is called to respond to a request from a client machine. The code representing what the servlet is supposed to do is placed in this method. Because this method is declared abstract, a concrete implementation must be provided by a concrete (non-abstract) sub-class of `GenericServlet`.

ServletInputStream Class

```
public abstract class ServletInputStream extends InputStream
```

```
Object
  InputStream
    ServletInputStream
```

The `ServletInputStream` class is used to read binary data from a client request. It provides a method that can read the data one line at a time. Under some protocols (HTTP, POST, and PUT, for example), a `ServletInputStream` object can be used to read data sent from the client.

ServletInputStream() Constructor

Constructor	Syntax
`ServletInputStream()`	`protected ServletInputStream()`

This constructor does nothing. Because `ServletInputStream` is an abstract class, a `ServletInputStream` object is never created directly.

readLine() Method

Method	Syntax
`readLine()`	`public int readLine(byte[] buffer, int offset, int numBytes) throws IOException`

`readLine()` reads data one line at a time and stores the data in a byte array. The read operation starts at the specified offset and continues until the specified number of bytes is read or a newline character is reached. The newline character is stored in the byte array as well. The method returns –1 if the end-of-file is reached before the specified number of bytes is read.

ServletOutputStream Class

```
public abstract class ServletOutputStream extends OutputStream
```

```
Object
  OutputStream
    ServletOutputStream
```

The `ServletOutputStream` class is used to write binary data to a client machine. It provides overloaded versions of the `print()` and `println()` methods that can handle primitive and `String` datatypes.

ServletOutputStream() Constructor

Constructor	Syntax
`ServletOutputStream()`	`protected` **`ServletOutputStream`**`()`

This constructor does nothing. Because `ServletOutputStream` is an abstract class, a `ServletOutputStream` object is never created directly.

print() Method

Method	Syntax
`print()`	`public void` **`print`**`(boolean` *`b`*`) throws IOException`
	`public void` **`print`**`(char` *`c`*`) throws IOException`
	`public void` **`print`**`(double` *`d`*`) throws IOException`
	`public void` **`print`**`(float` *`f`*`) throws IOException`
	`public void` **`print`**`(int` *`i`*`) throws IOException`
	`public void` **`print`**`(long` *`l`*`) throws IOException`
	`public void` **`print`**`(String` *`str`*`) throws IOException`

`print()` prints the specified primitive datatype or `String` to the client without a carriage return/line feed character at the end.

println() Method

Method	Syntax
`println()`	`public void` **`println`**`() throws IOException`
	`public void` **`println`**`(boolean` *`b`*`) throws IOException`
	`public void` **`println`**`(char` *`c`*`) throws IOException`
	`public void` **`println`**`(double` *`d`*`) throws IOException`
	`public void` **`println`**`(float` *`f`*`) throws IOException`
	`public void` **`println`**`(int` *`i`*`) throws IOException`
	`public void` **`println`**`(long` *`l`*`) throws IOException`
	`public void` **`println`**`(String` *`str`*`) throws IOException`

`print()` prints the specified primitive datatype or `String` to the client followed by a carriage return/line feed character at the end. The no-argument version simply writes a carriage return/line feed.

The javax.servlet.http Package

The `javax.servlet.http` package provides classes and interfaces that are used to create HTTP protocol-specific servlets. The abstract class `HttpServlet` is a base class for user-defined HTTP servlets and provides methods to process HTTP `DELETE`, `GET`, `OPTIONS`, `POST`, `PUT`, and `TRACE` requests. The `Cookie` class allows objects containing state information to be placed on a client machine and accessed by a servlet. The package also enables session tracking through the `HttpSession` and `HttpSessionBindingList` interfaces.

HTTP Servlet Interfaces

HttpServletRequest Interface

```
public interface HttpServletRequest extends ServletRequest
```

```
ServletRequest
  HttpServletRequest
```

The `HttpServletRequest` interface extends the `ServletRequest` interface to provide methods that can be used to obtain information about a request to an `HttpServlet`.

getSession() Method

Method	Syntax
getSession()	`public HttpSession getSession()`
	`public HttpSession getSession(boolean create)`

`getSession()` returns the `HttpSession` object associated with the request. By default, if the request does not currently have a session calling this method will create one. Setting the `boolean` parameter `create` to `false` overrides this.

Header Methods

Method	Syntax
getDateHeader()	`public long getDateHeader(String headerName)`
getHeader()	`public String getHeader(String headerName)`
getHeaderNames()	`public Enumeration getHeaderNames()`
getHeaders()	`public Enumeration getHeaders(String headerName)`
getIntHeader()	`public int getIntHeader(String headerName)`

`getDateHeader()` returns a long value that converts the date specified in the named header to the number of milliseconds since January 1, 1970 GMT. This method is used with a header that contains a date and returns -1 if the request does not contain the specified header.

`getHeader()` returns the value of the specified header expressed as a `String` object or -1 if the request does not contain the specified header.

`getHeaderNames()` returns an `Enumeration` containing all of the header names used by the request.

`getHeaders()` returns an `Enumeration` containing all of the values associated with the specified header name. The method returns `null` if the request does not contain the specified header.

`getIntHeader()` returns the value of the specified header as an `int`. This method returns `-1` if the request does not contain the specified header and throws a `NumberFormatException` if the header value cannot be converted to an `int`.

Session ID Methods

Method	Syntax
getRequestedSessionId()	public String **getRequestedSessionId**()
isRequestedSessionIdFromCookie()	public boolean **isRequestedSessionIdFromCookie**()
isRequestedSessionIdFromURL()	public boolean **isRequestedSessionIdFromURL**()
isRequestedSessionIdValid()	public boolean **isRequestedSessionIdValid**()

`getRequestedSessionId()` returns the session ID specified by the client machine or `null` if the request did not specify an ID.

`isRequestedSessionIdFromCookie()` returns `true` if the session ID came in from a cookie.

`isRequestedSessionIdFromURL()` returns `true` if the session ID came in as part of the request URL.

`isRequestedSessionIdValid()` returns `true` if the requested session ID is still valid.

Path Methods

Method	Syntax
getContextPath()	public String **getContextPath**()
getPathInfo()	public String **getPathInfo**()
getPathTranslated()	public String **getPathTranslated**()
getServletPath()	public String **getServletPath**()

`getContextPath()` returns the part of the request URL that indicates the context path of the request. The context path is the first part of the URL and always begins with the "/" character. For servlets running in the root context, this method returns an empty `String`.

`getPathInfo()` returns any additional path information contained in the request URL. This extra information will be after the servlet path and before the query string. This method returns `null` if there is no additional path information.

`getPathTranslated()` returns the same information as the `getPathInfo()` method but translates it into a real path.

`getServletPath()` returns the part of the request URL that was used to call the servlet without any additional information or the query string.

Methods that Return Information about the Request

Method	Syntax
getAuthType()	public String **getAuthType**()
getCookies()	public Cookie[] **getCookies**()
getMethod()	public String **getMethod**()
getQueryString()	public String **getQueryString**()
getRemoteUser()	public String **getRemoteUser**()
getRequestURI()	public String **getRequestURI**()

`getAuthType()` returns the name of the authentication scheme used in the request. Typical return values are `"BASIC"` or `"SSL"`. The method returns `null` if no authentication scheme was used.

`getCookies()` returns array containing any `Cookie` objects sent with the request or `null` if no `Cookie` objects were sent.

`getMethod()` returns the name of the HTTP method used to make the request. Typical return values are `"GET"`, `"POST"`, or `"PUT"`.

`getQueryString()` returns the query string that was contained in the request URL or `null` if there was no query string.

`getRemoteUser()` returns the login of the user making the request or `null` if the user has not been authenticated.

`getRequestURI()` returns a sub-section of the request URL from the protocol name to the query string.

HttpServletResponse Interface

```
public interface HttpServletResponse extends ServletResponse
```

```
ServletResponse
  HttpServletResponse
```

The `HttpServletResponse` interface extends the functionality of the `ServletResponse` interface by providing methods to access HTTP-specific features such as HTTP headers and cookies.

addCookie() Method

Method	Syntax
addCookie()	public void **addCookie**(Cookie *cookie*)

addCookie() adds the specified cookie to the response. More than one cookie can be added.

Header Methods

Method	Syntax
addDateHeader()	public void **addDateHeader**(String *headerName*, long *date*)
addHeader()	public void **addHeader**(String *headerName*, String *value*)
addIntHeader()	public void **addIntHeader**(String *headerName*, int *value*)
containsHeader()	public boolean **containsHeader**(String *headerName*)
setDateHeader()	public void **setDateHeader**(String *headerName*, long *date*)
setHeader()	public void **setHeader**(String *headerName*, String *value*)
setIntHeader()	public void **setIntHeader**(String *headerName*, int *value*)

addDateHeader() adds a response header containing the specified header name and the number of milliseconds since January 1, 1970 GMT. This method can be used to assign multiple values to a given header name.

addHeader() adds a response header with the specified name and value. This method can be used to assign multiple values to a given header name.

addIntHeader() adds a response header with the specified name and int value. This method can be used to assign multiple values to a given header name.

containsHeader() returns true if the response header includes the specified header name. This method can be used before calling one of the set() methods to determine if the value has already been set.

setDateHeader() sets the time value of a response header for the specified header name. The time is the number of milliseconds since January 1, 1970 GMT. If the time value for the specified header has been previously set, the value passed to this method will override it.

setHeader() sets a response header with the specified name and value. If the value for the specified header has been previously set, the value passed to this method will override it.

`setIntHeader()` sets a response header with the specified name and `int` value. If the `int` value for the specified header has been previously set, the value passed to this method will override it.

sendError() Method

Method	Syntax
`sendError()`	`public void sendError(int statusCode) throws IOException` `public void sendError(int statusCode, String message) throws IOException`

`sendError()` sends an error response back to the client machine using the specified error status code. A descriptive message can also be provided. This method must be called before the response is committed. A response is committed when its status code and headers have been written.

The status code will be one of the following. All of these constants are defined in the `HttpServletResponse` interface and are `public static final int`:

- **SC_BAD_GATEWAY**
- **SC_NOT_FOUND**
- **SC_BAD_REQUEST**
- **SC_NOT_IMPLEMENTED**
- **SC_CONFLICT**
- **SC_NOT_MODIFIED**
- **SC_EXPECTATION_FAILED**
- **SC_PAYMENT_REQUIRED**
- **SC_FORBIDDEN**
- **SC_PRECONDITION_FAILED**
- **SC_GATEWAY_TIMEOUT**
- **SC_PROXY_AUTHENICATION_REQUIRED**
- **SC_GONE**
- **SC_REQUEST_ENTITY_TOO_LARGE**
- **SC_HTTP_VERSION_NOT_SUPPORTED**
- **SC_REQUEST_TIMEOUT**
- **SC_INTERNAL_SERVER_ERROR**
- **SC_REQUEST_URI_TOO_LARGE**
- **SC_LENGTH_REQUIRED**

- SC_REQUESTED_RANGE_NOT_SATISFIABLE
- SC_METHOD_NOT_ALLOWED
- SC_RESET_CONTENT
- SC_MOVED_PERMANENTLY
- SC_SEE_OTHER
- SC_MOVED_TEMPORARILY
- SC_SERVICE_UNAVAILABLE
- SC_MULTIPLE_CHOICES
- SC_UNAUTHORIZED
- SC_NO_CONTENT
- SC_UNSUPPORTED_MEDIA_TYPE
- SC_NON_AUTHORITATIVE
- SC_USE_PROXY
- SC_NOT_ACCEPTABLE

sendRedirect() Method

Method	Syntax
sendRedirect()	public void **sendRedirect**(String *newURL*) throws IOException

sendRedirect() redirects the client machine to the specified URL. This method must be called before the response is committed. A response is committed when its status code and headers have been written.

setStatus() Method

Method	Syntax
setStatus()	public void **setStatus**(int *statusCode*)

setStatus() sets the return status code for the response. The status code should be one of the following. All of these constants are defined in the HttpServletResponse interface and are public static final int:

- SC_ACCEPTED
- SC_OK
- SC_CONTINUE
- SC_PARTIAL_CONTENT
- SC_CREATED
- SC_SWITCHING_PROTOCOLS
- SC_NO_CONTENT

To send an error status to the client machine, the `sendError()` method should be used instead

URL Methods

Method	Syntax
encodeRedirectURL()	`public String` **`encodeRedirectURL`**`(String` *`url`*`)`
encodeURL()	`public String` **`encodeURL`**`(String` *`url`*`)`

`encodeRedirectURL()` encodes the specified URL or returns it unchanged if encoding is not required. This method is used to process a URL before sending it to the `sendRedirect()` method.

`encodeURL()` encodes the specified URL by including the session ID or returns it unchanged if encoding is not needed. All URLs generated by a servlet should be processed through this method to ensure compatability with browsers that do not support cookies.

Deprecated Methods

Method	Syntax
encodeRedirectUrl()	`public String` **`encodeRedirectUrl`**`(String` *`url`*`)`
encodeUrl()	`public String` **`encodeUrl`**`(String` *`url`*`)`
setStatus()	`public void` **`setStatus`**`(int` *`sc`*`, String` *`sm`*`)`

`encodeRedirectUrl()` and `encodeUrl()` have been deprecated since Servlet 2.1 in favor of `encodeRedirectURL()` and `encodeURL()`. `setStatus()` has been deprecated in favor of `sendError()`.

Example: Using HttpServletResponse

This example uses the `HttpServletResponse` object that is automatically passed to the `doGet()` to send a response back to the user. A text field in an HTML page asks for a login name. When the Submit button is pressed, the servlet is invoked. If the login name is determined to be valid (in this case if it is equal to the `String "palmer"`), the `HttpServletResponse` object is used to open an output stream back to the client machine. If the login is invalid, the `HttpServletResponse` object is used to re-direct the client back to the HTML login page.

After loading the `HttpServletResponse.html` Web page. Type in any random `String` into the textfield and hit the Submit button. The servlet returns to the HTML login page. Now type in `"palmer"` and see what happens.

```
import javax.servlet.*;
import javax.servlet.http.*;
import java.io.*;

public class HttpResponseServlet extends HttpServlet {
  String login;
  boolean valid = false;

  // The doGet() method is called when the user presses the
  // "Submit" button in the HttpResponseServlet.html Web page.
```

```
    // It reads the login name from the query string and sends
    // a response back to the client.

    public void doGet(HttpServletRequest request,
                      HttpServletResponse response) throws ServletException,
                      IOException {

      // Extract the login name from query string and compare it to
      // a valid entry.

      login = request.getParameter("login");

      if (login.equals("palmer")) {
        valid = true;
      }

      // If the login name is valid (equal to "palmer"), a response is
      // sent back to the client.  If the login is invalid, the
      // HttpSerlvetRequest object re-directs the client back to the
      // login HTML page.

      if (valid) {
        response.setContentType("text/html");
        PrintWriter pw = response.getWriter();
        pw.println("<HTML> <HEAD> <TITLE>HttpRequest Exmaple</TITLE>");
        pw.println("</HEAD><BODY>");
        pw.println("Welcome ");
        pw.println("</BODY></HTML>");
        pw.close();
      } else {
        String str = "/HttpResponseServlet.html";
        response.sendRedirect(response.encodeRedirectURL(str));
      }
    }
  }
```

The `HttpServletResponse.html` code is as follows:

```
<HTML>
<HEAD>
<TITLE> HttpResponse Example </TITLE>
</HEAD>
<BODY>
<FORM METHOD=GET
      ACTION="http://localhost:8080/servlet/HttpResponseServlet">
Enter login name
<INPUT TYPE=TEXT NAME=login ><BR>
<INPUT TYPE=SUBMIT VALUE=Submit>
</FORM>
</BODY>
</HTML>
```

HttpSession Interface

```
public interface HttpSession
```

The HTTP protocol is stateless, meaning that each request is independent and has no knowledge of previous requests. Sometimes, it is desirable to save state information. For instance, the contents of a shopping cart should be known by each request. Http Servlets can maintain this information by way of a session.

The `HttpSession` interface provides methods that define a session between a client and server. The session lasts for a specified time period and can encompass more than one connection or page request from the user. The methods declared by this interface allow the access of information about the session and enable the binding of objects to sessions. The bound object can contain the state information that is intended to be known by every request.

Bound Object Methods

Method	Syntax
getAttribute()	public Object **getAttribute**(String *name*)
getAttributeNames()	public Enumeration **getAttributeNames**()
removeAttribute()	public void **removeAttribute**(String *name*)
setAttribute()	public void **setAttribute**(String *name*, Object *value*)

`getAttribute()` returns the `Object` bound to the specified name in this session.

`getAttributeNames()` returns an `Enumeration` of `String` objects containing the names of all the objects bound to this session.

`removeAttribute()` removes the `Object` bound to the specified name from this session.

`setAttribute()` binds an `Object` to the specified attribute name for this session. If the attribute name already exists, the `Object` passed to this method will replace the previous `Object`.

getId() Method

Method	Syntax
getId()	public String **getId**()

`getId()` returns a `String` object containing a unique identifier for this session

invalidate() Method

Method	Syntax
invalidate()	public void **invalidate**()

`invalidate()` invalidates the session and unbinds any objects bound to it.

isNew() Method

Method	Syntax
isNew()	public boolean **isNew**()

isNew() returns true if the server has created a session that has not yet been accessed by a client.

Time Methods

Method	Syntax
getCreationTime()	public long **getCreationTime**() throws IllegalStateException
getLastAccessedTime()	public lone **getLastAccessedTime**()
getMaxInactiveInterval()	public int **getMaxInactiveInterval**()
setMaxInactiveInterval()	public void **MaxInactiveInterval**(int *time*)

getCreationTime() returns the time when the session was created in milliseconds since midnight Jan 1, 1970 GMT.

getLastAccessedTime() returns the last time a client request associated with the session was sent. The return value is the number of milliseconds since midnight Jan 1, 1970 GMT.

getMaxInactiveInterval() returns the number of seconds the server will wait between client requests before the session is invalidated. A negative return value indicates the session will never time out.

setMaxInactiveInterval() specifies the number of seconds the server will wait between client requests before the session is invalidated. If a negative value is passed to this method, the session will never time out.

Deprecated Methods

Method	Syntax
getSessionContext()	public HttpSessionContext **getSessionContext**()
getValue()	public Object **getValue**(String *name*)
getValueNames()	public String[] **getValueNames**()
putValue()	public void **putValue**(String *name*, Object *value*)
removeValue()	public void **removeValue**(String *name*)

These methods have been deprecated under Java Servlet API 2.2 and should not be used for new code. They have been replaced by the Bound Object Methods described above.

Example: Using HttpSession

In this example, an `HttpSession` object is used to monitor the value of a `Counter` object that is bound to it. The user can increment or re-set the value.

```
import javax.servlet.*;
import javax.servlet.http.*;
import java.io.*;

public class SessionServlet extends HttpServlet {

  // The doGet() method is called when the servlet is invoked.
  // It sends a simple form back to the client containing two
  // buttons, one to add to the count and one to clear the count.

  public void doGet(HttpServletRequest request,
                    HttpServletResponse response) throws ServletException,
                    IOException {

    response.setContentType("text/html");

    PrintWriter pw = response.getWriter();
    pw.println("<HTML> <HEAD> <TITLE> Cookie Example </TITLE>");
    pw.println("</HEAD><BODY>");
    pw.println("<FORM METHOD=POST>");
    pw.println("<INPUT TYPE=SUBMIT NAME=add VALUE=Add><BR>");
    pw.println("<INPUT TYPE=SUBMIT NAME=clear VALUE=Clear><BR>");
    pw.println("</FORM></BODY></HTML>");
    pw.close();
  }

  // The doPost() method is called when either of the two buttons
  // is pressed.
  //
  // This example is set up to run under Java Servlet API 2.1.
  // Under version 2.2, the putValue() method would be replaced
  // by setAttribute() and the getValue() method would be replaced
  // by getAttribute()

  public void doPost(HttpServletRequest request,
                     HttpServletResponse response) throws ServletException,
                     IOException {

    // A HttpSession object is created if it does not already exist.
    // If the client has not yet accessed the servlet, a Counter object
    // is created and bound to the session.  The Counter object is
    // returned using the getValue() method every time the servlet is
    // accessed.

    HttpSession session = request.getSession(true);
    if (session.isNew()) {
      session.putValue("count", new Counter(0));
    }
    Counter counter = (Counter) session.getValue("count");
```

```
    // If the "Add" button was pressed, the count is incremented.
    // If the "Clear" button was pressed, the count is cleared.

    if (request.getParameter("add") != null) {
      counter.addOne();
    } else {
      counter.clear();
    }

    response.setContentType("text/html");

    // Open a character output stream to the client machine and write
    // the current count.  There is also a hyperlink to return to the
    // button page

    char dq = '\"';

    PrintWriter pw = response.getWriter();
    pw.println("<HTML> <HEAD> <TITLE> Session Example </TITLE>");
    pw.println("</HEAD><BODY>");
    pw.println("current amount: " + counter.getCount() + "<BR>");
    pw.print("<A HREF=" + dq);
    pw.print(request.getRequestURI());
    pw.println(dq + ">Return to Buttons</A>");
    pw.println("</BODY></HTML>");
    pw.close();
  }
}

// Counter is a simple class that maintains a count.  Methods are
// provided to increment the count, clear the count, and return
// the current count value.

class Counter {
  int count;

  public Counter(int c) {
    count = c;
  }
  public void addOne() {
    ++count;
  }
  public void clear() {
    count = 0;
  }
  public int getCount() {
    return count;
  }
}
```

Press the Add button a few times and watch the count increment. The Clear button causes the count to be re-set to zero.

HttpSessionBindingListener Interface

```
public interface HttpSessionBindingListener extends EventListener
```

```
EventListener
  HttpSessionBindingListener
```

The methods declared in the `HttpSessionBindingListener` interface are called when an object is bound to or unbound from a registered session.

valueBound() Method

Method	Syntax
valueBound()	public void **valueBound**(HttpSessionBindingEvent *evt*)

`valueBound()` is called when an object is being bound to a registered session.

valueUnbound() Method

Method	Syntax
valueUnbound()	public void **valueUnbound**(HttpSessionBindingEvent *evt*)

`valueUnbound()` is called when an object is being unbound from a registered session.

HttpSessionContext Interface

```
public interface HttpSessionContext
```

The methods declared in the `HttpSessionContext` interface (and the interface itself) were deprecated as of Java Servlet API 2.1 for security reasons. This interface will be removed in a future API version and its methods should not be used for new codes.

Deprecated Methods

Method	Syntax
getIds()	public Enumeration **getIds**()
getSession()	public HttpSession **getSession**(String *sessionID*)

These methods have been deprecated and currently return an empty `Enumeration` or null respectively. They should not be used for new code.

HTTP Servlet Classes

Cookie Class

```
public class Cookie extends Object
  implements Cloneable
```

```
Object
  Cookie
```

Interfaces

```
Cloneable
```

A `Cookie` is an object that resides on a client machine and contains state information. A `Cookie` has a name, a single value and some other optional information. Cookies can be used to identify a particular user and provide information such as name, address, account number, etc. A cookie is sent by a server to a Web browser, saved on the client machine, and can later be sent back to the server.

The optional information that can be attached to a `Cookie` includes an expiration date, path and domain qualifiers, a version number, and a comment. The expiration date specifies when the `Cookie` will be deleted from the client machine. If no date is given, the `Cookie` is deleted when the session ends.

A servlet sends cookies to a browser using the `addCookie()` method defined in the `HttpServletResponse` interface. This method adds fields to the HTTP response header. The browser returns cookies to the servlet by adding fields to the HTTP request header. Cookies can be retrieved from a request by invoking the `getCookies()` method defined in the `HttpServletRequest` interface.

Cookie() Constructor

Constructor	Syntax
`Cookie()`	`public` **`Cookie`**`(String` *`name`*`, String` *`value`*`)`

Creates a `Cookie` object with a specified name and value. The name must consist only of alphanumeric characters. Once the name is set by the constructor, it cannot be changed.

clone() Method

Method	Syntax
`clone()`	`public Object` **`clone`**`()`

`clone()` overrides the `clone()` method from the `Object` class to return a copy of the invoking `Cookie` object.

Comment Methods

Method	Syntax
getComment()	public String **getComment**()
setComment()	public void **setComment**(String *comment*)

A Cookie can contain a comment that is usually used to describe the purpose of the Cookie.

getComment() returns the comment associated with the invoking Cookie object, or null if there is no comment.

setComment() changes or sets the comment associated with the invoking Cookie object.

Expiration Date Methods

Method	Syntax
getMaxAge()	public int **getMaxAge**()
setMaxAge()	public void **setMaxAge**(int *duration*)

getMaxAge() returns the length of time in seconds that the Cookie will persist on the user's machine. A return value of –1 indicates that the cookie will persist until the browser shuts down.

setMaxAge() sets the length of time in seconds that the Cookie will persist on the user's machine. A negative value means the Cookie will not be stored on the user's machine and will be deleted when the browser terminates. A value of zero means the Cookie will be deleted immediately.

getName() Method

Method	Syntax
getName()	public String **getName**()

getName() returns the name of the invoking Cookie object.

Path and Domain Methods

Method	Syntax
getDomain()	public String **getDomain**()
getPath()	public String **getPath**()
setDomain()	public void **setDomain**(String *domain*)
setPath()	public void **setPath**(String *path*)

getDomain() returns the domain name set for the invoking Cookie object.

getPath() returns the path on the server where the browser will return the invoking Cookie object.

`setDomain()` sets the domain name within which the `Cookie` will be visible.

`setPath()` specifies the path on the server where the browser will return the invoking `Cookie` object. The `Cookie` will also be visible to all sub-directories of the specified path.

Security Methods

Method	Syntax
getSecure()	`public boolean` **getSecure**`()`
setSecure()	`public void` **setSecure**`(String` *value*`)`

`getSecure()` returns `true` if the browser will send the invoking `Cookie` object using a secure protocol.

`setSecure()` specifies whether the browser should send the invoking `Cookie` object using a secure protocol. The default is `false`, meaning the `Cookie` will be sent using any protocol.

Value Methods

Method	Syntax
getValue()	`public String` **getValue**`()`
setValue()	`public void` **setValue**`(String` *value*`)`

`getValue()` returns a `String` containing the value of the invoking `Cookie` object.

`setValue()` changes the value of the invoking `Cookie` object.

Version Number Methods

Method	Syntax
getVersion()	`public int` **getVersion**`()`
setVersion()	`public void` **setVersion**`(int` *version*`)`

One optional piece of information a `Cookie` can contain is the version number of the protocol with which the `Cookie` complies.

`getVersion()` returns 0 if the invoking `Cookie` object complies with the original Netscape specification, or 1 if it complies with RFC 2109.

`setVersion()` sets the version number of the protocol with which the `Cookie` complies.

Example: Using Cookies

In this example a `Cookie` is used to store some user data. When the servlet is invoked, the `doGet()` method returns an HTML file containing textfield and a Submit button to the browser. The method first determines if a `Cookie` was attached to the request. If it was, the textfield is initialized with the value of the `Cookie`. If there was no `Cookie`, the textfield is initially blank.

The user can change the contents of the textfield or leave it the way it is. When the **Submit** button is pressed, the `doPost()` method of the servlet is called. This method extracts the contents of the textfield and adds a `Cookie` containing the textfield contents as its value to the response. The response consists of a confirmation of the textfield contents. The `Cookie` is set to live on the client machine for five minutes.

```
import javax.servlet.*;
import javax.servlet.http.*;
import java.io.*;

public class CookieServlet extends HttpServlet {
  String companyName;
  String value = "";

  // The doGet() method is called when the servlet is invoked.
  // It sends a simple form back to the client.

  public void doGet(HttpServletRequest request,
                    HttpServletResponse response) throws ServletException,
                    IOException {

    // see if a cookie exists and if it does extract its value.

    Cookie[] cookies = request.getCookies();
    for (int i = 0; i < cookies.length; ++i) {
      String name = cookies[i].getName();
      if (name != null && name.equals("companyName")) {
        value = cookies[i].getValue();
      }
    }

    // Set the response type to html

    response.setContentType("text/html");

    // Open a character output stream to the client machine and write
    // the response.  If a cookie existed, the textfield will be
    // intialized with its value.  Otherwise, the textfield will be blank.
    // Note that the value passed to the textfield is surrounded by
    // double-quotes to allow for multi-word strings.

    char dq = '\"';

    PrintWriter pw = response.getWriter();
    pw.println("<HTML> <HEAD> <TITLE> Cookie Example </TITLE>");
    pw.println("</HEAD><BODY>");
    pw.println("<FORM METHOD=POST>");
    pw.println("Company Name <INPUT TYPE=TEXT NAME=name VALUE=" + dq
           + value + dq + "><BR>");
    pw.println("<INPUT TYPE=SUBMIT VALUE=Submit>");
    pw.println("</FORM></BODY></HTML>");
    pw.close();
  }
```

```
   // The doPost() method receives the form from the client and sends
   // back a confirmation.  It also writes a cookie containing the
   // String that was written into the textfield.

   public void doPost(HttpServletRequest request,
                      HttpServletResponse response) throws ServletException,
                      IOException {

     // Get the contents of the textfield.

     companyName = request.getParameter("name");

     // Create a cookie that contains the contents of the textfield.
     // The cookie is set to live for 5 minutes and is added to the
     // response.

     Cookie nameCookie = new Cookie("companyName", companyName);
     nameCookie.setMaxAge(300);
     response.addCookie(nameCookie);

     response.setContentType("text/html");

     // Open a character output stream to the client machine and write
     // the response

     PrintWriter pw = response.getWriter();
     pw.println("<HTML> <HEAD> <TITLE>" + companyName
               + " information </TITLE>");
     pw.println("</HEAD><BODY>");
     pw.println("Company: " + companyName + "<BR>");
     pw.println("</BODY></HTML>");
     pw.close();
   }
}
```

The first time the servlet is invoked, no cookie exists and the textfield is empty. Type something in and press the Submit button. Now, exit the Web browser and shut down the server. Restart the server and reload the servlet into the Web browser. A cookie now exists and the text field will be initialized with whatever was previously typed in to the textfield.

HttpServlet Class

```
public abstract class HttpServlet extends GenericServlet
  implements Serializable
```

```
Object
  GenericServlet
   HttpServlet
```

Interfaces

```
Serializable
```

The `HttpServlet` class extends the `GenericServlet` class to provide functionality tailored to the HTTP protocol. It provides methods for handling HTTP `DELETE`, `GET`, `OPTIONS`, `POST`, `PUT`, and `TRACE` requests. Like the `GenericServlet` class, the `HttpServlet` class provides a `service()` method, but unlike the `GenericServlet` class the `service()` method is rarely overridden with `HttpServlets`. The default implementation of the `service()` method dispatches the request to the appropriate handler method.

A concrete sub-class of `HttpServlet` must override at least one of the methods defined in the `HttpServlet` or `GenericServlet` classes. The `doDelete()`, `doGet()`, `doPost()`, or `doPut()` methods are the ones most commonly overridden.

HttpServlet() Constructor

Constructor	Syntax
HttpServlet()	public **HttpServlet**()

This constructor does nothing. Because `HttpServlet` is an abstract class, an `HttpServlet` object is never created directly.

doDelete() Method

Method	Syntax
doDelete()	protected void **doDelete**(HttpServletRequest *request*, HttServletResponse *response*) throws ServletException, IOException

`doDelete()` is called by the server via the `service()` method to handle an HTTP `DELETE` request. A `DELETE` request allows a client to remove a document or Web page from a server.

doGet() Method

Method	Syntax
doGet()	protected void **doGet**(HttpServletRequest *request*, HttServletResponse *response*) throws ServletException, IOException

`doGet()` is called by the server via the `service()` method to handle an HTTP `GET` request. A `GET` request allows a client to send form data to a server. With the `GET` request, the form data is attached to the end of the URL sent by the browser to the server as a query string. The amount of form data that can be sent is limited to the maximum length the URL can be.

doOptions() Method

Method	Syntax
doOptions()	protected void **doOptions**(HttpServletRequest *request*, HttpServletResponse *response*) throws ServletException, IOException

doOptions() is called by the server via the service() method to handle an HTTP OPTIONS request. An OPTIONS request determines which HTTP methods the server supports and sends the information back to the client by way of a header.

doPost() Method

Method	Syntax
doPost()	protected void **doPost**(HttpServletRequest *request*, HttpServletResponse *response*) throws ServletException, IOException

doPost() is called by the server via the service() method to handle an HTTP POST request. A POST request allows a client to send form data to a server. With the POST request, the form data is sent to the server separately instead of being appended to the URL. This allows a large amount of form data to be sent.

doPut() Method

Method	Syntax
doPut()	protected void **doPut**(HttpServletRequest *request*, HttpServletResponse *response*) throws ServletException, IOException

doPut() is called by the server via the service() method to handle an HTTP PUT request. A PUT request allows a client to place a file on the server and is conceptually similar to sending the file to the server via FTP.

doTrace() Method

Method	Syntax
doTrace()	protected void **doTrace**(HttpServletRequest *request*, HttpServletResponse *response*) throws ServletException, IOException

doTrace() is called by the server via the service() method to handle an HTTP TRACE request. A TRACE request returns the headers sent with the TRACE request back to the client. This can be useful for de-bugging purposes. This method is rarely overridden.

getLastModified() Method

Method	Syntax
getLastModified()	protected long **getLastModified** (HttpServletRequest *request*)

getLastModified() returns the time the requested resource was last modified. The return value is the time in milliseconds since midnight Jan 1, 1970.

service() Method

Method	Syntax
service()	protected void **service**(HttpServletRequest *request*, HttpServletResponse *response*) throws ServletException, IOException

`service()` receives HTTP requests and sends them to the appropriate `do()` method. This method is generally not overridden.

Example: An HttpServlet

This example creates a simple servlet that sends a form back to the client machine. When a login name is submitted from the `SampleHttpServlet.html` page, the `doGet()` method of the servlet is called. This method returns a form to the user requesting address information. When the information is entered and the Submit button is pressed, the `doPost()` method of the servlet is called. This method returns a confirmation of the information that was entered.

```
import javax.servlet.*;
import javax.servlet.http.*;
import java.io.*;

public class SampleHttpServlet extends HttpServlet {
  String login, name, address, city, state, zipcode;

  // The doGet() method is called when the user presses the
  // "Submit" button in the SampleHttpServlet.html Web page.
  // It reads the login name from the query string and sends
  // a form back to the client.

  public void doGet(HttpServletRequest request,
                    HttpServletResponse response) throws ServletException,
                    IOException {

    // Extract the login name from query string

    login = request.getParameter("login");

    // Set the response type to html

    response.setContentType("text/html");

    // Open a character output stream to the client machine and send a
    // form back to the client browser

    PrintWriter pw = response.getWriter();
    pw.println("<HTML> <HEAD> <TITLE>" + name
               + " information </TITLE>");
    pw.println("</HEAD><BODY>");
    pw.println("<FORM METHOD=POST>");
    pw.println("Enter mailing address <BR><BR>");
    pw.println("<TABLE>");
    pw.println("<TR><TD> Name </TD>");
    pw.println("<TD><INPUT TYPE=TEXT NAME=name> </TD></TR>");
```

```
    pw.println("<TR><TD> Address </TD>");
    pw.println("<TD><INPUT TYPE=TEXT NAME=address SIZE=20></TD></TR>");
    pw.println("<TR><TD> City </TD>");
    pw.println("<TD> <INPUT TYPE=TEXT NAME=city></TD></TR>");
    pw.println("<TR><TD> <SELECT NAME=state SIZE=1>");
    pw.println("<OPTION VALUE=AZ>AZ</OPTION>");
    pw.println("<OPTION VALUE=CA>CA</OPTION>");
    pw.println("<OPTION VALUE=NY>NY</OPTION>");
    pw.println("</SELECT></TD></TR>");
    pw.println("<TR><TD> Zip Code </TD>");
    pw.println("<TD> <INPUT TYPE=TEXT NAME=zipcode></TD></TR>");
    pw.println("</TABLE>");
    pw.println("<INPUT TYPE=SUBMIT VALUE=Submit>");
    pw.println("</FORM></BODY></HTML>");
    pw.close();
  }

  // The doPost() method is called when the user submits the form.
  // It extracts the address information and returns a confirmation
  // back to the user.

  public void doPost(HttpServletRequest request,
                     HttpServletResponse response) throws ServletException,
                     IOException {

    name = request.getParameter("name");
    address = request.getParameter("address");
    city = request.getParameter("city");
    state = request.getParameter("state");
    zipcode = request.getParameter("zipcode");

    response.setContentType("text/html");

    // Open a character output stream to the client machine and write
    // the response

    PrintWriter pw = response.getWriter();
    pw.println("<HTML> <HEAD> <TITLE>" + name
             + " information </TITLE>");
    pw.println("</HEAD><BODY>");
    pw.println("Current mailing address <BR><BR>");
    pw.println(name + "<BR>");
    pw.println(address + "<BR>");
    pw.println(city + ", " + state + "  " + zipcode + "<BR>");
    pw.println("</BODY></HTML>");
    pw.close();
  }
}
```

The `SampleHttpServlet.html` code is the following:

```
<HTML>
<HEAD>
<TITLE> HttpServlet Example </TITLE>
</HEAD>
<BODY>
```

```
<FORM METHOD=GET
      ACTION="http://localhost:8080/servlet/SampleHttpServlet">
Enter login name
<INPUT TYPE=TEXT NAME=login ><BR>
<INPUT TYPE=SUBMIT VALUE=Submit>
</BODY>
</HTML>
```

HttpSessionBindingEvent Class

```
public class HttpSessionBindingEvent extends EventObject
```

```
Object
  EventObject
    HttpSessionBindingEvent
```

An `HttpSessionBindingEvent` object is generated whenever an object is bound to or unbound from a session.

HttpSessionBindingEvent() Constructor

Constructor	Syntax
HttpSessionBindingEvent()	public **HttpSessionBindingEvent** (HttpSession *session*, String *name*)

Creates an `HttpSessionBindingEvent` object. The session and name are the parameters to which the `HttpSessionBindingEvent` object is bound or unbound.

getName() Method

Method	Syntax
getName()	public String **getName**()

`getName()` returns the name associated with the object that is bound or unbound.

getSession() Method

Method	Syntax
getSession()	public HttpSession **getSession**()

`getSession()` returns the session associated with the object that is bound or unbound.

HttpUtils Class

```
public class HttpUtils extends Object
```

```
Object
  HttpUtils
```

The HttpUtils provides three static methods that are useful when developing HTTP servlets.

HttpUtil() Constructor

Constructor	Syntax
HttpUtils()	public **HttpUtils**()

Creates an HttpUtils object. Since the methods defined in this class are static, they can be called directly so the constructor is unneccessary.

getRequestURL() Method

Method	Syntax
getRequestURL()	public static StringBuffer **getRequestURL** (HttpServletRequest *request*)

getRequestURL() returns the URL the client used to make the request as a StringBuffer object. The return value will not include the query string. A new query string can be appended to the StringBuffer object.

parsePostData() Method

Method	Syntax
parsePostData()	public static Hashtable **parsePostData** (int *length*, ServletInputStream *in*)

parsePostData() parses the form data sent to a server by way of an http POST request. The data sent by the POST method is in the form of key-value pairs. This method returns a Hashtable object containing the key-value pairs. The length parameter is the length of the input stream. The ServletInputStream parameter is the input stream that contains the data sent from the client.

parseQueryString() Method

Method	Syntax
parseQueryString()	public static Hashtable **parseQueryString** (String *str*)

parseQueryString() parses the query string passed from the client to server and returns a Hashtable containing the key-value pairs. The query string should have the key-value pairs in the form "key=value" with each pair separated by the "&" character.

The javax.servlet.jsp Package

The `javax.servlet.jsp` package provides interfaces and classes that support the development of JavaServer Pages.

JSP Interfaces

HttpJspPage Interface

```
public interface HttpJspPage extends JspPage
```

```
Servlet
  JspPage
    HttpJspPage
```

The `HttpJspPage` interface is implemented by the Servlet class representing all HTTP JSP pages. It defines the `_jspService()` method, which is called by the JSP container to generate the page content.

_jspService() Method

Method	Syntax
`_jspService()`	`public void` **`_jspService`**`(HttpServletRequest` *`request`*`, HttpServletResponse` *`response`*`) throws ServletException, IOException`

`_jspService()` provides an HTTP protocol-specific implementation of the JSP `service()` method. This method is generated automatically by the JSP processor based on the contents of the JSP page.

JspPage Interface

```
public interface JspPage extends Servlet
```

The `JspPage` interface provides two methods that are used to initialize and destroy a JSP.

jspDestroy() Method

Method	Syntax
`jspDestroy()`	`public void` **`jspDestroy`**`()`

`jspDestroy()` is called when the `JspPage` object is about to be destroyed.

jspInit() Method

Method	Syntax
`jspInit()`	`public void` **`jspInit`**`()`

`jspInit()` is called when the `JspPage` object is created. It is used to initialize the `JspPage`.

JSP Classes

JspEngineInfo Class

```
public abstract class JspEngineInfo extends Object
```

```
Object
  JspEngineInfo
```

The `JspEngineInfo` class is used to obtain information on the current JSP engine.

JspEngineInfo() Constructor

Constructor	Syntax
`JspEngineInfo()`	`public` **`JspEngineInfo`**`()`

Since the `JspEngineInfo` class is abstract, a `JspEngineInfo` object is not created directly. Sub-classes of `JspEngineInfo` can call this constructor.

getSpecificationVersion() Method

Method	Syntax
`getSpecificationVersion()`	`public abstract String` **`getSpecificationVersion`**`()`

`getSpecificationVersion()` returns a `String` containing the version number, for example `"2.0"` of the JSP engine. The return value is `null` if the specification version is unknown.

JspFactory Class

```
public abstract class JspFactory extends Object
```

```
Object
  JspFactory
```

The `JspFactory` class provides methods for creating or specifying objects that are used to support JSP development, including `JspEngineInfo` and `PageContext` objects.

JspFactory() Constructor

Constructor	Syntax
`JspFactory()`	`public` **`JspFactory`**`()`

Since the `JspFactory` class is abstract, a `JspFactory` object is not created directly. Sub-classes of `JspFactory` can call this constructor.

Default Factory Methods

Method	Syntax
`getDefaultFactory()`	`public static JspFactory getDefaultFactory()`
`setDefaultFactory()`	`public static void setDefaultFactory (JspFactory fact)`

`getDefaultFactory()` returns a reference to the current default `JspFactory` object. The return object can then call the other methods defined in the `JspFactory` class.

`setDefaultFactory()` is used to change the default jsp object. This method can only be called by the `JSP` engine runtime.

getEngineInfo() Method

Method	Syntax
`getEngineInfo()`	`public abstract JspEngineInfo getEngineInfo()`

`getEngineInfo()` returns a `JspEngineInfo` object that can access information about the current JSP engine.

PageContext Methods

Method	Syntax
`getPageContext()`	`public abstract PageContext getPageContext (Servlet requestingServlet, ServletRequest request, ServletResponse response, String errorPageURL, boolean needsSession, int buffer, boolean autoFlush)`
`releasePageContext()`	`public abstract void releasePageContext (PageContext pc)`

`getPageContext()` returns a reference to the PageContext object associated with the requesting servlet. The `errorPageURL` is the URL of the error page of the JSP. This can be set to `null` if there is no error page. The parameter `needsSession` is `true` if the JSP is participating in a session. The parameter `autoFlush` is `true` if the buffer will automatically flush to the output stream on buffer overflow.

`releasePageContext()` releases the specified `PageContext` object. This method results in the `PageContext.release()` method being called. This method should be invoked prior to returning from the `_jspService()` method of a JSP class.

JspWriter Class

```
public abstract class JspWriter extends Writer
```

```
Object
  Writer
    JspWriter
```

The `JspWriter` class provides a character output stream that can be used by a JSP object. It provides overloaded versions of the `print()` and `println()` methods that can handle primitive and `String` datatypes.

JspWriter() Constructor

Constructor	Syntax
`JspWriter()`	`protected` **`JspWriter`**`(int` *`bufferSize`*`, boolean` *`autoFlush`*`)`

The `JspWriter` class is abstract, so a `JspWriter` object is not created directly. This constructor can be used by sub-classes of `JspWriter`.

clear() Method

Method	Syntax
`clear()`	`public abstract void` **`clear`**`() throws IOException`

`clear()` clears the contents of the buffer. This method throws an exception if some data has already been written to the output stream.

clearBuffer() Method

Method	Syntax
`clearBuffer()`	`public abstract void` **`clearBuffer`**`() throws IOException`

`clearBuffer()` clears the contents of the buffer but does not throw an exception is some data has already been written to the output stream.

close() Method

Method	Syntax
`close()`	`public abstract void` **`close`**`() throws IOException`

`close()` flushes and then closes the output stream.

flush() Method

Method	Syntax
`flush()`	`public abstract void` **`flush`**`() throws IOException`

`flush()` flushes the output buffer and sends any bytes contained in the buffer to their intended destination.

getBufferSize() Method

Method	Syntax
getBufferSize)	public int **getBufferSize**()

`getBufferSize()` returns the size in bytes of the output buffer.

getRemaining() Method

Method	Syntax
getRemaining()	public abstract int **getRemaining**()

`getRemaining()` returns the number of bytes still contained in the buffer.

isAutoFlush() Method

Method	Syntax
isAutoFlush()	public boolean **isAutoFlush**()

`isAutoFlush()` returns `true` if the buffer flushes automatically when an overflow condition occurs.

newLine() Method

Method	Syntax
newLine()	public abstract void **newLine**() throws IOException

`newLine()` writes a system-dependent newline character to the output stream.

print() Method

Method	Syntax
print()	public abstract void **print**(boolean *b*) throws IOException
	public abstract void **print**(char *c*) throws IOException
	public abstract void **print**(char[] *charArray*) throws IOException
	public abstract void **print**(double *d*) throws IOException
	public abstract void **print**(float *f*) throws IOException
	public abstract void **print**(int *i*) throws IOException
	public abstract void **print**(long *l*) throws IOException
	public abstract void **print**(Object *obj*) throws IOException
	public abstract void **print**(String *str*) throws IOException

`print()` prints the specified primitive datatype, `Object` or `String` to the client without a carriage return/line feed character at the end. If an `Object` argument is passed, it is converted to a `String` using the `String.valueOf()` method.

println() Method

Method	Syntax
`println()`	`public abstract void` **`println`**`() throws IOException`
	`public abstract void` **`println`**`(boolean` *`b`*`) throws IOException`
	`public abstract void` **`println`**`(char` *`c`*`) throws IOException`
	`public abstract void` **`println`**`(char[]` *`charArray`*`) throws IOException`
	`public abstract void` **`println`**`(double` *`d`*`) throws IOException`
	`public abstract void` **`println`**`(float` *`f`*`) throws IOException`
	`public abstract void` **`println`**`(int` *`i`*`) throws IOException`
	`public abstract void` **`println`**`(long` *`l`*`) throws IOException`
	`public abstract void` **`println`**`(Object` *`obj`*`) throws IOException`
	`public abstract void` **`println`**`(String` *`str`*`) throws IOException`

`print()` prints the specified primitive datatype, `Object` or `String` to the client followed by a carriage return/line feed character at the end. The no-argument version simply writes a carriage return/line feed. If an `Object` argument is passed, it is converted to a `String` using the `String.valueOf()` method.

PageContext Class

```
public abstract class PageContext extends Object
```

```
Object
  PageContext
```

The `PageContext` class provides information on the namespaces associated with a JSP including page attributes and implementation details.

PageContext() Constructor

Constructor	Syntax
`PageContext()`	`public` **`PageContext`**`()`

The `PageContext` class is abstract, so a `PageContext` object is not created directly. This constructor can be used by sub-classes of `PageContext`.

Scope Constants

Syntax
public static final int **APPLICATION_SCOPE**
public static final int **PAGE_SCOPE**
public static final int **REQUEST_SCOPE**
public static final int **SESSION_SCOPE**

These constants are used to define scope.

Attribute Methods

Method	Syntax
findAttribute()	public abstract Object **findAttribute** (String *name*)
getAttribute()	public abstract Object **getAttribute** (String *name*)
	public abstract Object **getAttribute** (String *name*, int *scope*)
getAttributeNamesInScope()	public abstract Enumeration **getAttributeNamesInScope**(int *scope*)
getAttributesScope()	public abstract int **getAttributesScope**(String *name*)
removeAttribute()	public abstract void **removeAttribute** (String *name*)
	public abstract void **removeAttribute** (String *name*, int *scope*)
setAttribute()	public abstract void **setAttribute** (String name, Object obj)
	public abstract void **setAttribute** (String name, Object obj, int scope)

`findAttribute()` searches the page, request, session, and application scope for the named attribute and returns its value as an `Object` or `null` if the attribute name is not found.

`getAttribute()` searches for the named attribute at the specified scope and returns its value as an `Object` or `null` if the attribute name is not found. If no scope is specified, the search is performed at page scope. The parameter `scope` should be one of the scope constants defined above.

`getAttributeNamesInScope()` returns an `Enumeration` containing all of the attribute names in the specified scope.

`getAttributesScope()` returns the scope of the specified attribute.

`removeAttribute()` removes the `Object` associated with the specified attribute name. A scope can also be specified.

`setAttribute()` registers the attribute name and associated `Object` at the specified scope. If no scope is provided, the attribute is placed at page scope.

Exception Methods

Method	Syntax
getException()	`public abstract Exception` **`getException`**`()`
handlePageException()	`public abstract void` **`handlePageException`**`(Exception` *`e`*`) throws ServletException, IOException`

`getException()` returns any `Exception` that was passed to the JSP as an error page.

`handlePageException()` is overridden to process a page-level exception. The exception can be redirected to the specified error page for the JSP or handled inside the method itself.

forward() Method

Method	Syntax
forward()	`public abstract void` **`forward`**`(String` *`relativePath`*`) throws IOException, ServletException`

`forward()` redirects the current `ServletRequest` and `ServletResponse` objects to the target resource at the specified relative URL path.

getOut() Method

Method	Syntax
getOut()	`public abstract JspWriter` **`getOut`**`()`

`getOut()` returns the `JspWriter` object that is being used for client response.

include() Method

Method	Syntax
include()	`public abstract void` **`forward`**`(String` *`relativePath`*`) throws IOException, ServletException`

`include()` causes the resource at the specified relative URL path to be processed as part of the current `ServletRequest` and `ServletResponse` objects.

initialize() Method

Method	Syntax
initialize()	public abstract void **initialize** (Servlet *requestingServlet*, ServletRequest *request*, ServletResponse, *response*, String *errorPageURL*, boolean *needsSession*, int *buffer*, boolean *autoFlush*) throws IOException, IllegalStateException, IllegalArgumentException

`initialize()` is called to initialize a `PageContext` object. The `errorPageURL` is the URL of the error page of the JSP. This can be set to `null` if there is no error page. The parameter `needsSession` is true if the JSP is participating in a session. The parameter `autoFlush` is `true` if the buffer will automatically flush to the output stream on buffer overflow.

popBody() Method

Method	Syntax
popBody()	public JspWriter **popBody**()

`popBody()` returns the `JspWriter` object saved by a previous call to `pushBody()` and updates the `"out"` attribute at the page scope of the invoking `PageContext` object.

pushBody() Method

Method	Syntax
pushBody()	public BodyCount **pushBody**()

`pushBody()` returns a new `BodyCount` object, saves the current `JspWriter` object, and updates the `"out"` attribute at the page scope of the invoking `PageContext` object.

release() Method

Method	Syntax
release()	public abstract void **release**()

`release()` resets the internal state of the invoking `PageContext` object by releasing all internal references. This method is usually called by the `releasePageContext()` method of the `JspFactory` class.

Methods to Return Servlet Components

Method	Syntax
getPage()	public abstract Object **getPage**()
getRequest()	public abstract ServletRequest **getRequest**()

Method	Syntax
getResponse()	public abstract ServletResponse **getResponse**()
getServletConfig()	public abstract ServletConfig **getServletConfig**()
getServletContext()	public abstract ServletContext **getServletContext**()
getSession()	public abstract HttpSession **getSession**()

getRequest() returns the Servlet associated with the invoking PageContext object as an Object.

getResponse() returns the ServletResponse object associated with the invoking PageContext object.

getServletConfig() returns the ServletConfig object associated with the invoking PageContext object.

getServletContext() returns the ServletContext object associated with the invoking PageContext object.

getSession() returns the HttpSession object associated with the invoking PageContext object.

The javax.servlet.jsp.tagext Package

The javax.servlet.jsp.tagext package provides interfaces and classes that support the use of custom tag extensions for JSP.

Tag Interfaces

BodyTag Interface

```
public interface BodyTag extends Tag
```

```
Tag
  BodyTag
```

The BodyTag interface defines methods that are used by a tag handler access its body.

Constant

Syntax
public static final int **EVAL_BODY_TAG**

This constant is used to request the creation of new BodyContent, on which to evaluate the body of the current tag.

doAfterBody() Method

Method	Syntax
doAfterBody()	public int **doAfterBody**() throws JspError

doAfterBody() is invoked every time after the body is evaluated.

doInitBody() Method

Method	Syntax
doInitBody()	public int **doInitBody**() throws JspError

doInitBody() is invoked before the body is evaluated.

setBodyContent() Method

Method	Syntax
setBodyContent()	public void **setBodyContent**(BodyContent *bc*)

setBodyContent() specifies a BodyContent object that will be used in conjunction with the evaluation of a tag's body.

Tag Interface

```
public interface Tag
```

The Tag interface provides methods that connect a tag handler with a JavaServer Page implementation class including life cycle methods and methods that are invoked at the start and end tag.

Constants

Syntax
public static final int **SKIP_BODY**
public static final int **EVAL_BODY_INCLUDE**
public static final int **SKIP_PAGE**
public static final int **EVAL_PAGE**

SKIP_BODY indicates that body evaluation should be skipped.

EVAL_BODY_INCLUDE indicates that the tag body should be evaluated into the existing output stream.

SKIP_PAGE indicates that the rest of the page should be skipped.

EVAL_PAGE indicates that page evaluation should continue.

doEndTag() Method

Method	Syntax
doEndTag()	public int **doEndTag**() throws JspException

doEndTag() processes the end tag associated with a JSP.

doStartTag() Method

Method	Syntax
doStartTag()	public int **doStartTag**() throws JspException

doStartTag() processes the start tag associated with a JSP.

getParent() Method

Method	Syntax
getParent()	public Tag **getParent**()

getParent() returns the parent of the invoking Tag object.

release() Method

Method	Syntax
release()	public void **release**()

release() is called on a Tag handler to release its state.

setPageContext() Method

Method	Syntax
setPageContext()	public void **setPageContext**(PageContext *pc*)

setPageContext() specifies the current PageContext object. This method is called by the JSP prior to calling the doStartTag() method.

setParent() Method

Method	Syntax
setParent()	public void **setParent**(Tag *tag*)

setParent() specifies the parent, or nesting, Tag of the invoking Tag object.

Tag Classes

BodyContent Class

```
public abstract class BodyContent extends JspWriter
```

```
Object
  Writer
    JspWriter
      BodyContent
```

The `BodyContent` class extends the capability of the `JspWriter` class to allow the processing and retrieval of body evaluations.

BodyContent() Constructor

Constructor	Syntax
`BodyContent()`	`protected` **`BodyContent`**`()`

Since the `BodyContent` class is abstract, a `BodyContent` object is not created directly. Sub-classes of `BodyContent` can call this constructor.

clearBody() Method

Method	Syntax
`clearBody()`	`public void` **`clearBody`**`()`

`clearBody()` clears the body associated with the invoking `BodyContent` object.

flush() Method

Method	Syntax
`flush()`	`public void` **`flush`**`() throws IOException`

`flush()` overrides the method defined in the `JspWriter` class. A `BodyContent` object is not allowed to flush.

getEnclosingWriter() Method

Method	Syntax
`getEnclosingWriter()`	`public JspWriter` **`getEnclosingWriter`**`()`

`getEnclosingWriter()` returns an associated `JspWriter` object.

getReader() Method

Method	Syntax
getReader()	`public abstract Reader getReader()`

`getReader()` returns the value of the invoking `BodyContent` object as an input stream. This is performed after body evaluation.

getString() Method

Method	Syntax
getString()	`public abstract String getString()`

`getString()` returns the value of the invoking `BodyContent` object as a `String`. This is performed after body evaluation.

writeOut() Method

Method	Syntax
writeOut()	`public abstract void writeOut(Writer out) throws IOException`

`writeOut()` writes the contents of the invoking `BodyContent` object into the specified output stream.

BodyTagSupport Class

```
public class BodyTagSupport extends TagSupport
  implements BodyTag
```

```
Object
  TagSupport
    BodyTagSupport
```

Interfaces

```
BodyTag
```

The `BodyTag` class extends the functionality of the `TagSupport` class by providing implementation of the methods declared in the `BodyTag` interface.

BodyTagSupport() Constructor

Constructor	Syntax
BodyTagSupport()	`public BodyTagSupport()`

Creates a `BodyTagSupport` object. Sub-classes of `BodyTagSupport` are required to provide a no-argument constructor that calls this constructor.

doAfterBody() Method

Method	Syntax
doAfterBody()	public int **doAfterBody**() throws JspError

doAfterBody() is invoked every time after a body is evaluated. It is overridden to contain any actions that are to be performed after an evaluation is completed.

doEndTag() Method

Method	Syntax
doEndTag()	public int **doEndTag**() throws JspException

doEndTag() processes the end tag associated with a JSP. This method will be called on all Tag objects. The release() method should be called after this method is invoked.

doInitBody() Method

Method	Syntax
doInitBody()	public int **doInitBody**()

doInitBody() is overridden to contain actions that are performed before a body evaluation.

getBodyContent() Method

Method	Syntax
getBodyContent()	public BodyContent **getBodyContent**()

getBodyContent() returns a reference to the current BodyContent object.

getPreviousOut() Method

Method	Syntax
getPreviousOut()	public JspWriter **getPreviousOut**()

getPreviousOut() returns the surrounding JspWriter object.

release() Method

Method	Syntax
release()	public void **release**()

release() resets the state of the tag.

setBodyContent() Method

Method	Syntax
setBodyContent()	public void **setBodyContent**(BodyContent *bc*)

setBodyContent() specifies a BodyContent object that will be used in conjunction with the evaluation of a tag's body.

TagAttributeInfo Class

```
public class TagAttributeInfo extends Object
```

```
Object
  TagAttributeInfo
```

The TagAttributeInfo class provides methods to access information about Tag attributes.

TagAttributeInfo() Constructor

Constructor	Syntax
TagAttributeInfo()	public **TagAttributeInfo**(String *name*, boolean *required*, boolean *rtexprvalue*, String *type*, boolean *reqTime*)

Creates a TagAttributeInfo object. The name is the name of the attribute. The required parameter is true if the attribute is required. The type is the name of the type of attribute. reqTime is true if the attribute can be a request-time attribute.

canBeRequestTime() Method

Method	Syntax
canBeRequestTime()	public boolean **canBeRequestTime**()

canBeRequestTime() returns true if the attribute can hold a request-time value.

getIdAttribute() Method

Method	Syntax
getIdAttribute()	public static TagAttributeInfo **getIdAttribute** (TagAttributeInfo[] *list*)

getIdAttribute() searches an array of TagAttributeInfo objects and returns the one associated with the name "id".

getName() Method

Method	Syntax
getName()	public String **getName**()

getName() returns the attribute name.

getTypeName() Method

Method	Syntax
getTypeName()	public String **getTypeName**()

getTypeName() returns the name of the attribute type.

isRequired() Method

Method	Syntax
isRequired()	public boolean **isRequired**()

isRequired() returns true if the attribute is required.

toString() Method

Method	Syntax
toString()	public String **toString**()

toString() returns a String representation of the invoking TagAttributeInfo object.

TagData Class

```
public class TagData extends Object
  implements Cloneable
```

```
Object
  TagData
```

Interfaces

```
Cloneable
```

A TagData object contains the name-value pairs of the attributes associated with a Tag.

TagData() Constructor

Constructor	Syntax
TagData()	public **TagData**(Object[][] *attrs*)
	public **TagData**(Hashtable *attrs*)

Creates a `TagData` object. The attribute name-value pairs for the `TagData` object can be provided using either a 2-D `Object` array or a `Hashtable`.

getAttribute() Method

Method	Syntax
`getAttribute()`	`public Object` **`getAttribute`**`(String` *`name`*`)`

`getAttribute()` returns the value associated with the specified attribute name.

getAttributeString() Method

Method	Syntax
`getAttributeString()`	`public String` **`getAttributeString`**`(String` *`name`*`)`

`getAttributeString()` returns the value associated with the specified attribute name as a `String`.

getId() Method

Method	Syntax
`getId()`	`public String` **`getId`**`()`

`getId()` returns the value of the `id` attribute, or `null` if it does not exist.

setAttribute() Method

Method	Syntax
`setAttribute()`	`public void` **`setAttribute`**`(String` *`name`*`, Object` *`value`*`)`

`setAttribute()` sets the value of the specified attribute.

TagExtraInfo Class

```
public abstract class TagExtraInfo extends Object
```

```
Object
  TagExtraInfo
```

A `TagExtraInfo` object contains any additional information associated with a custom Tag.

TagExtraInfo() Constructor

Constructor	Syntax
`TagExtraInfo()`	`public` **`TagExtraInfo`**`()`

Since the `TagExtraInfo` class is abstract, a `TagExtraInfo` object is not created directly. Sub-classes of `TagExtraInfo` can call this constructor.

getTagInfo() Method

Method	Syntax
getTagInfo()	public TagInfo **getTagInfo**()

getTagInfo() returns the TagInfo object associated with the invoking TagExtraInfo object.

getVariableInfo() Method

Method	Syntax
getVariableInfo()	public VariableInfo[] **getVariableInfo**(TagData *td*)

getVariableInfo() returns an array of VariableInfo objects containing information on scripting variables defined by the tag.

isValid() Method

Method	Syntax
isValid()	public boolean **isValid**(TagData *td*)

isValid() returns true if the attributes associated with the specified TagData object are valid at translation time. Request-time attributes are indicated as such.

setTagInfo() Method

Method	Syntax
setTagInfo()	public void **setTagInfo**(TagInfo *ti*)

setTagInfo() sets the TagInfo object that is associated with the invoking TagExtraInfo object.

TagInfo Class

```
public class TagInfo extends Object
```

```
Object
  TagInfo
```

A TagInfo object contains any information associated with a Tag.

Constants

Syntax
public static final int **BODY_CONTENT_JSP**
public static final int **BODY_CONTENT_TAG_DEPENDENT**
public static final int **BODY_CONTENT_EMPTY**

These constants denoty JSP, tag-depentent, or empty tag body content.

TagInfo() Constructor

Constructor	Syntax
TagInfo()	public **TagInfo**(String *name*, String *class*, String *content*, String *infoString*, TagLibraryInfo *lib*, TagExtraInfo *tei*, TagAttributeInfo[] *attr*)

Creates a `TagInfo` object. The `name` is the name given to the tag. The `class` is the name of the tag handler class. The `content` provides information about the body content of these tags. The `infoString` is an optional `String` containing information about this tag.

getAttributes() Method

Method	Syntax
getAttributes()	public TagAttributeInfo[] **getAttributes**()

`getAttributes()` returns a `TagAttributeInfo` object containing information on the tag attributes.

getBodyContent() Method

Method	Syntax
getBodyContent()	public String **getBodyContent**()

`getBodyContent()` returns a `String` containing information about the body content of the tag.

getInfoString() Method

Method	Syntax
getInfoString()	public String **getInfoString**()

`getInfoString()` returns the info string, if any, associated with the tag .

getTagClassName() Method

Method	Syntax
getTagClassName()	public String **getTagClassName**()

`getTagClassName()` returns the name of the tag handler class.

getTagExtraInfo() Method

Method	Syntax
getTagExtraInfo()	public TagExtraInfo **getTagExtraInfo**()

getTagExtraInfo() returns the TagExtraInfo object, if any, associated with the tag.

getTagLibrary() Method

Method	Syntax
getTagLibrary()	public TagLibraryInfo **getTagLibraryInfo**()

getTagLibraryInfo() returns the TagLibraryInfo object associated with the tag.

getTagName() Method

Method	Syntax
getTagName()	public String **getTagName**()

getTagName() returns the name of the tag.

getVariableInfo() Method

Method	Syntax
getVariableInfo()	public VariableInfo[] **getVariableInfo**(TagData *td*)

getVariableInfo() returns an array of VariableInfo objects containing information on the object created by the tag at runtime.

isValid() Method

Method	Syntax
isValid()	public boolean **isValid**(TagData *td*)

isValid() returns true if the attributes associated with the specified TagData object are valid at translation time. Request-time attributes are indicated as such.

toString() Method

Method	Syntax
toString()	public String **toString**()

toString() returns a String representation of the invoking TagInfo object.

TagLibraryInfo Class

```
public class TagInfo extends Object
```

```
Object
  TagLibraryInfo
```

A TagLibraryInfo object contains information on the Tag Library associated with a Tag.

TagLibraryInfo() Constructor

Constructor	Syntax
TagLibraryInfo()	public **TagLibraryInfo**(String *libraryPrefix*, String *libraryURI*)

Creates a TagLibraryInfo object.

getInfoString() Method

Method	Syntax
getInfoString()	public String **getInfoString**()

getInfoString() returns the info string, if any, associated with the tag library.

getPrefixString() Method

Method	Syntax
getPrefixString()	public String **getPrefixString**()

getPrefixString() returns the prefix that is assigned to this tag library.

getReliableURN() Method

Method	Syntax
getReliableURN()	public String **getReliableURN**()

getReliableURN() returns a String containing a reliable URN for this tag library.

getRequiredVersion() Method

Method	Syntax
getRequiredVersion()	public String **getRequiredVersion**()

getRequiredVersion() returns the required version of this tag library.

getShortName() Method

Method	Syntax
getShortName()	public String **getShortName**()

getShortName() returns the preferred short name for this tag library.

getTag() Method

Method	Syntax
getTag()	public TagInfo **getTag**(String *tagName*)

getTag() returns a TagInfo object for the specified tag.

getTags() Method

Method	Syntax
getTags()	public TagInfo[] **getTags**()

getTags() returns an array of TagInfo objects containing information about all of the tags contained in this tag library.

getURI() Method

Method	Syntax
getURI()	public String **getURI**()

getURI() returns a String containing the URI from the taglib directive for this library.

TagSupport Class

```
public class TagSupport extends Object
  implements Tag, Serializable
```

```
Object
  TagSupport
```

Interfaces

```
Tag, Serializable
```

The Tag class provides Tag life cycle methods and methods for accessing information about a Tag.

TagSupport() Constructor

Constructor	Syntax
TagSupport()	public **TagSupport**()

Creates a TagSupport object. Sub-classes of TagSupport are required to provide a no-argument constructor that calls this constructor.

doEndTag() Method

Method	Syntax
doEndTag()	public int **doEndTag**() throws JspException

doEndTag() processes the end tag. This method will be called on all Tag objects. The release() method should be called after this method is invoked.

doStartTag() Method

Method	Syntax
doStartTag()	public int **doStartTag**() throws JspException

doStartTag() processes the start tag. This method is called after all set() methods have been called and before the body is invoked.

ID Methods

Method	Syntax
getTagId()	public String **getTagId**()
setTagId()	public void **setTagId**(String *id*)

getTagId() returns the value of the "id" attribute.

setTagId() sets the value of the "id" attribute.

Parent Methods

Method	Syntax
getParent()	public Tag **getParent**()
setParent()	public void **setParent**(Tag *t*)

getParent() returns the parent, or nesting, tag for the current tag.

setParent() sets the sets the parent, or nesting, tag.

release() Method

Method	Syntax
release()	public void **release**()

release() resets the state of the Tag.

setPageContext() Method

Method	Syntax
setPageContext()	public void **setPageContext**(PageContext *pc*)

`setPageContext()` specifies the current `PageContext` object associated with the tag.

Value Methods

Method	Syntax
getValue()	public Object **getValue**(String *name*)
getValues()	public Enumeration **getValue**()
removeValue()	public void **removeValue**(String *name*)
setValue()	public void **setValue**(String *name*, Object *value*)

`getValue()` returns the value of the specified attribute.

`getValues()` returns an `Enumeration` containing all of the values.

`removeValue()` removes the specified attribute from the tag.

`setValue()` sets the value of the specified attribute.

VariableInfo Class

```
public class VariableInfo extends Object
```

```
Object
  VariableInfo
```

A `VariableInfo` object contains information on the scripting variables that are created or modified by a tag at runtime.

VariableInfo() Constructor

Constructor	Syntax
VariableInfo()	public **VariableInfo**(String *varName*, String *className*, boolean *declare*, int *scope*)

Creates a `VariableInfo` object. The `declare` parameter is true if if the variable is new and may require a declaration. The scope must be one of the scope constants defined below

Scope Constants

Syntax
public static final int **NESTED**
public static final int **AT_BEGIN**
public static final int **AT_END**

If a variable is given the NESTED scope, it is visible within the start and end tags. If a variable is given the AT_BEGIN scope, it is visible after the start tag. If a variable is given the AT_END scope, it is visible after the end tag.

getVarName() Method

Method	Syntax
getVarName()	public String **getVarName**()

getVarName() returns the name of the scripting variable.

getClassName() Method

Method	Syntax
getClassName()	public String **getClassName**()

getClassName() returns the name of the class of the scripting variable.

getDeclare() Method

Method	Syntax
getDeclare()	public boolean **getDeclare**()

getDeclare() returns true if the variable is new and may require a declaration

getScope() Method

Method	Syntax
getScope()	public int **getScope**()

getScope() returns the scope of the scripting variable.

J2EE
JSP

HTTP

The Hypertext Transfer Protocol (HTTP) is an application-level protocol for distributed hypermedia information systems. It is a generic, stateless protocol, which can be used for many tasks beyond its use for hypertext. A feature of HTTP is the typing and negotiation of data representation, allowing systems to be built independently of the data being transferred.

The first version of HTTP, referred to as HTTP/0.9, was a simple protocol for raw data transfer across the Internet. HTTP/1.0, as defined by RFC 1945 improved the protocol by allowing messages to be in a MIME-like format, containing meta-information about the data transferred and modifiers on the request/response semantics. The current version HTTP/1.1, first defined in RFC 2068 and more recently in RFC 2616, made performance improvements by making all connections persistent and supporting absolute URLs in requests.

URL Request Protocols

A URL is a pointer to a particular resource on the Internet at a particular location and has a standard format as follows:

```
Protocol Servername Filepath
```

In order, the three elements are the protocol used to access the server, the name of the server and the location of the resource on the server. For example:

```
http://www.mydomain.com/
https://www.mydomain.com:8080/
ftp://ftp.mydomain.com/example.txt
mailto:me@world.com
file:///c:|Windows/win.exe
```

The `servername` and `filepath` pieces of the URL are totally dependent on where files are stored on your server and what you have called it, but there are a standard collection of protocols, most of which you should be familiar with:

- `http`: Normal HTTP requests for documents.
- `https`: Secure HTTP requests. The specific behavior of these depends on the security certificates and encryption keys you have set up.
- `JavaScript`: Executes JavaScript code within the current document.
- `ftp`: Retrieves documents from an FTP (File Transfer Protocol) server.
- `file`: Loads a file stored on the local (Client) machine. It can refer to remote servers but specifies no particular access protocol to remote file systems.
- `news`: Used to access Usenet newsgroups for articles.
- `nntp`: More sophisticated access to news servers.
- `mailto`: Allows mail to be sent from the browser. It may call in assistance from a helper app.
- `telnet`: Opens an interactive session with the server.
- `gopher`: A precursor to the World Wide Web.

This book exclusively deals with the first five of these.

HTTP Basics

Each HTTP client (web browser) request and server response has three parts: the request or response line, a header section and the entity body.

Client Request

The client initiates a web page transaction – client page request and server page response – as follows.

The client connects to an HTTP-based server at a designated port (by default, 80) and sends a request by specifying an HTTP command called a method, followed by a document address, and an HTTP version number. The format of the request line is:

```
Method        Request-URI    Protocol
```

For example,

```
GET   /index.html   HTTP/1.0
```

uses the `GET` method to request the document `/index.html` using version 1.0 of the protocol. We'll come to a full list of HTTP Request Methods later.

Next, the client sends optional header information to the server about its configuration and the document formats it will accept. All header information is sent line by line, each with a header name and value in the form:

```
Keyword: Value
```

For example:

```
User-Agent:    Lynx/2.4 libwww/5.1k
Accept:        image/gif, image/x-xbitmap, image/jpeg, */*
```

The request line and the subsequent header lines are all terminated by a carriage return/linefeed (`\r\n`) sequence. The client sends a blank line to end the headers. We'll return with a full description of each HTTP Header value later on in the Appendix.

Finally, after sending the request and headers the client may send additional data. This data is mostly used by CGI programs using the `POST` method. This additional information is called a request entity. Finally a blank line (`\r\n\r\n`) terminates the request. A complete request might look like the following:

```
GET /index.html HTTP/1.0
Accept: */*
Connection: Keep-Alive
Host: www.w3.org
User-Agent: Generic
```

HTTP Request Methods

HTTP request methods should not be confused with URL protocols. The former are used to instruct a web server how to handle the incoming request while the latter defines how client and server talk to each other. In version 1.1 of the HTTP protocol, there are seven basic HTTP request methods:

Method	Description
`OPTIONS`	Used to query a server about the capabilities it provides. Queries can be general or specific to a particular resource.
`GET`	Asks that the server return the body of the document identified in the Request-URI.
`HEAD`	Responds similarly to a `GET`, except that no content body is ever returned. It is a way of checking whether a document has been updated since the last request.
`POST`	This is used to transfer a block of data to the server in the content body of the request.
`PUT`	This is the complement of a `GET` request and stores the content body at the location specified by the Request-URI. It is similar to uploading a file with FTP.
`DELETE`	Provides a way to delete a document from the server. The document to be deleted is indicated in the Request-URI.
`TRACE`	This is used to track the path of a request through firewalls and multiple proxy servers. It is useful for debugging complex network problems and is similar to the traceroute tool.

Server Response

The HTTP response also contains 3 parts.

Firstly, the server replies with the status line containing three fields: the HTTP version, status code and description of status code, in the following format.

```
Protocol   Status-code   Description
```

For example, the status line:

```
HTTP/1.0   200   OK
```

indicates that the server uses version 1.0 of the HTTP in its response. A status code of `200` means that the client request was successful.

After the response line, the server sends header information to the client about itself and the requested document. All header information is sent line by line, each with a header name and value in the form:

```
Keyword: Value
```

For example:

```
HTTP/1.1 200 OK
Date: Wed, 19 May 1999 18:20:56 GMT
Server: Apache/1.3.6 (Unix) PHP/3.0.7
Last-Modified: Mon, 17 May 1999 15:46:21 GMT
ETag: "2da0dc-2870-374039cd"
Accept-Ranges: bytes
Content-Length: 10352
Connection: close
Content-Type: text/html; charset=iso-8859-1
```

The response line and the subsequent header lines are all terminated by a carriage return/linefeed (`\r\n`) sequence. The server sends a blank line to end the headers. Again, we'll return to the exact meaning of these HTTP headers in a minute.

If the client's request if successful, the requested data is sent. This data may be a copy of a file, or the response from a CGI program. This result is called a **response entity**. If the client's request could not be fulfilled, additional data sent might be a human-readable explanation of why the server could not fulfill the request. The properties (type and length) of this data are sent in the headers. Finally a blank line (`\r\n\r\n`) terminates the response. A complete response might look like the following:

```
HTTP/1.1 200 OK
Date: Wed, 19 May 1999 18:20:56 GMT
Server: Apache/1.3.6 (Unix) PHP/3.0.7
Last-Modified: Mon, 17 May 1999 15:46:21 GMT
ETag: "2da0dc-2870-374039cd"
Accept-Ranges: bytes
Content-Length: 10352
Connection: close
Content-Type: text/html; charset=iso-8859-1
```

```
<!DOCTYPE HTML PUBLIC "-//W3C//DTD HTML 4.0 Transitional//EN"
"http://www.w3.org/TR/REC-html40/loose.dtd">
<html>

    ...

</html>
```

In HTTP/1.0, after the server has finished sending the response, it disconnects from the client and the transaction is over unless the client sends a `Connection: KeepAlive` header. In HTTP/1.1, however, the connection is maintained so that the client can make additional requests, unless the client sends an explicit `Connection: Close header.` Since many HTML documents embed other documents as inline images, applets and frames, for example, this persistent connection feature of HTTP/1.1 protocol will save the overhead of the client having to repeatedly connect to the same server just to retrieve a single page.

HTTP Headers

These headers can appear in requests or responses. Some control how the web server behaves, others are meant for proxy servers and some will affect what your browser does with a response when it is received. You should refer to the HTTP 1.1 specification for a full description. You can download it from:

```
ftp://ftp.isi.edu/in-notes/rfc2616.txt
```

The authentication is covered in a little more detail in:

```
ftp://ftp.isi.edu/in-notes/rfc2617.txt
```

Other RFC documents from the same source may be useful and provide additional insights.

This table summarizes the headers you'll find most helpful. There are others in the specification but they control how the web server manages the requests and won't arrive in the CGI environment for you to access:

Header	Request	Response	Description
`Accept:`	✓		Lists the types that the client can cope with.
`Accept-Charset:`	✓		Lists the character sets that the browser can cope with.
`Accept-Encoding:`	✓		List of acceptable encodings or none. Omitting this header signifies that all current encodings are acceptable.
`Accept-Language:`	✓		List of acceptable languages.

Table Continued on Following Page

Header	Request	Response	Description
`Age:`		✓	A cache control header used to indicate the age of a response body.
`Allow:`		✓	Determines the available methods that the resource identified by the URI can respond to.
`Authorization:`	✓		Authorization credentials. Refer to RFC2617 for more information on Digest authentication.
`Cache-Control:`	✓	✓	A sophisticated proxy-controlling header. Can be used to describe how proxies should handle requests and responses.
`Code:`	✓		Defines an encoding for the body data. This would normally be Base64.
`Content-Base:`		✓	Used to resolve relative URLs within the body of the document being returned. It overrides the value in the Content-Location header.
`Content-Encoding:`		✓	Specifies encodings that have been applied to the body prior to transmission.
`Content-Language:`		✓	This specifies the natural language of the response content.
`Content-Length:`		✓	The length of the body measured in bytes should be put here. CGI responses may defer to the web server and allow it to put this header in.
`Content-Location:`		✓	The actual location of the entity being returned in the response. This may be useful when deploying resources that can be resolved in several ways. The specifically selected version can be identified and requested directly.
`Content-MD5:`		✓	This is a way of computing a checksum for the entity body. The receiving browser can compare its computed value to be sure that the body has not been modified during transmission.

Header	Request	Response	Description
`Content-Type:`		✓	The type of data being returned in the response is specified with this header. These types are listed later in this appendix.
`Expires:`		✓	The date after which the response should be considered to be stale.
`From:`	✓		The client e-mail address is sent in this header.
`Host:`	✓		The target virtual host is defined in this header. The value is taken from the originating URL when the request is made.
`Last-Modified:`		✓	This indicates when the content being returned was last modified. For static files, the web server would use the file's timestamp. For a dynamically generated page, you might prefer to insert a value based on when a database entry was last changed. Other more sophisticated cache control headers are provided in the HTTP specification. Refer to RFC2616 for details.
`Location:`		✓	Used to redirect to a new location. This could be used as part of a smart error handling CGI.
`Referrer:`	✓		The source of the current request is indicated here. This would be the page that the request was linked from. You can determine whether the link was from outside your site and also pick up search engine parameters from this too, if your URI was requested via Yahoo, for example.
`User-Agent:`	✓		This is the signature field of the browser. You can code round limitations in browsers if you know this. Be aware of some of the weird values that can show up in this header now that developers are building their own web browsers and spiders.
`Warning:`		✓	This is used to carry additional information about the response and whether there are risks associated with it.

Server Environment Variables

By and large, the headers in the request correspond with environment variables that are present when a CGI handler executes. Not all headers make it as far as the CGI environment. Some may be 'eaten up' by a proxy server, others by the target web server. Some environment variables are created as needed by the web server itself, without there having been a header value to convert.

Here is a summary of the environment variables you are likely to find available. There may be others if the web server administrator has configured them into the server or if the CGI adapter has been modified to pass them in. You can access them with the `Clib.getenv()` function. These are considered to be standard values and they should be present:

(*Editor's Note: This list is written with respect to ScriptEase CGI scriptwriters. In JSP, the HTTP headers and server variables are accessible via the* `ServletRequest`, `HTTPServletRequest`, `HTTPServletResponse`, `ServletConfig`, `ServletContext` *classes, documented in Appendix C.)*

AUTH_TYPE

The value in this environment variable depends on the kind of authentication used in the server and whether the script is even security protected by the server. This involves server configuration and is server specific and also protocol specific. The value may not be defined if the page is insecure. If it is secure, the value indicating the type of authentication may only be set after the user is authenticated. An example value for `AUTH_TYPE` is `BASIC`.

CONTENT_LENGTH

If the request used the `POST` method, then it may have supplied additional information in the body. This is passed to the CGI handler on its standard input. However, ScriptEase will assimilate this for you, extract any query strings in the body and decode them into variables that you can access more conveniently.

CONTENT_TYPE

The data type of any content delivered in the body of the request. With this, you could process the standard input for content bodies that are some type other than form data. This is relatively unexplored territory and likely to be very much server and platform dependent. If it works at all, you might choose a reading mechanism based on content type and then use other headers to process the binary data in the body. If you are using this just to upload files, then the HTTP/1.1 protocol now supports a `PUT` method which is a better technique and is handled inside the server.

DOCUMENT_ROOT

This is the full path to the document root for the web server. If virtual hosts are being used and if they share the same CGI scripts, this document root may be different for each virtual host. It is a good idea to have separately owned cgi-bin directories unless the sites are closely related. For example, a movie site and a games site might have separate cgi-bin directories. Three differently branded versions of the movie site may have different document roots but could share the same cgi-bin functionality. In some servers, this may be a way to identify which one of several virtual hosts is being used.

FROM

If the user has configured their browser appropriately, this environment variable will contain their e-mail address. If it is present, then this is a good way to identify the user, given the assumption that they are the owner of the computer they are using.

GATEWAY_INTERFACE

You can determine the version number of the CGI interface being used. This would be useful if you depend on features available in a later version of the CGI interface but you only want to maintain a single script to be used on several machines.

HTTP_ACCEPT

This is a list of acceptable MIME types that the browser will accept. The values are dependent on the browser being used and how it is configured and are simply passed on by the web server. If you want to be particularly smart and do the right thing, check this value when you try to return any oddball data other than plain text or HTML. The browser doesn't say it can cope, it might just crash on the user when you try and give them some unexpected data.

HTTP_ACCEPT_LANGUAGE

There may not be a value specified in this environment variable. If there is, the list will be as defined by the browser.

HTTP_CONNECTION

This will indicate the disposition of the HTTP connection. It might contain the value "Keep-Alive" or "Close" but you don't really have many options from the ScriptEase:WSE-driven CGI point of view. You might need to know whether the connection to the browser will remain open but since SE:WSE won't currently support streaming tricks it won't matter much either way.

HTTP_COOKIE

The cookie values sent back by the browser are collected together and made available in this environment variable. You will need to make a cookie cutter to separate them out and extract their values. Which particular cookies you receive depend on whereabouts in the site's document root you are and the scope of the cookie when it was created.

HTTP_HOST

On a multiple virtual host web server, this will tell you the host name that was used for the request. You can then adjust the output according to different variations of the sites. For example, you can present different logos and backgrounds for `www.mydomain.com` and `test.mydomain.com`. This can help solve a lot of issues when you set up a co-operative branding deal to present your content via several portal sites. They do like to have their logo and corporate image on the page sometimes.

HTTP_PRAGMA

This is somewhat deprecated these days but will likely contain the value "no-cache". Cache control is handled more flexibly with the new response headers available in HTTP/1.1. Caching and proxy server activity can get extremely complex and you may want to study the HTTP specification for more info - `ftp://ftp.isi.edu/in-notes/rfc2616.txt`

HTTP_REFERER

This is the complete URL for the page that was being displayed in the browser and which contained the link being requested. If the page was a search engine, this may also contain some interesting query information that you could extract to see how people found your web site. There are some situations where there will be no referrer listed. When a user types a URL into a location box, there is no referrer. This may also be true when the link was on a page held in a file on the user's machine. There are some browser dependent issues as well. Some versions of Microsoft Internet Explorer do not report a referrer for HTML documents in framesets. If you have the referrer information it can be useful, but there are enough times when the referrer may be blank that you should have a fall back mechanism in place as well.

HTTP_USER_AGENT

The User Agent is a cute name for the browser. It is necessary because the page may not always be requested by a browser. It could be requested by a robot or so called web spider. It may be requested by offline readers or monitoring services and it's not uncommon for static page generators to be used on a site that was originally designed to be dynamic. Rather than try to cope with all variants of the browsers, you should focus on determining whether you have a browser or robot requesting your documents. That way, you can serve up a page that is more appropriate to a robot when necessary. There is no point in delivering a page that contains an advert, for example. You can make your site attractive to the sight-impaired user community by detecting the use of a text-only browser such as Lynx. You could then serve a graphically sparse but text rich page instead. When examining this value, be aware that there is much weirdness in the values being returned by some browsers. This may be intentional or accidental, but since the Netscape sources were released, developers have been busy writing customized browsers. Some of these will send User-Agent headers containing control characters and binary data. Whether this is an attempt to exploit bugs in web servers, CGI handlers or log analysis software is arguable. You will encounter e-mail addresses, URLs, command line instructions and even entire web pages in this header.

PATH

This is the list of directories that will be searched for commands that you may try and execute from within your CGI handler. It is inherited from the parent environment that spawned the handler. It is platform dependent and certainly applies to UNIX systems. It may not be present on all of the others.

PATH_INFO

This is a way of extracting additional path information from the request. Here is a URL as an example: `http://www.domain.com/cgi-bin/path.jsh/folder1/file`. This will run the SE:WSE script called `path.jsh` and store the value `/folder1/file` in the `PATH_INFO` environment variable. This can be an additional way of passing parameters from the HTML page into the server-side script.

PATH_TRANSLATED

This is only implemented on some servers and may be implemented under another environment variable name on others. It returns the full physical path to the script being executed. This might be useful if you have shared code that you include into several scripts.

QUERY_STRING

The query string is that text in the URL following a question mark. This environment variable will contain that text. SE:WSE will unwrap it and present the individual items as variables you can access directly.

REMOTE_ADDR

This is the remote IP address of the client machine that initiated the request. You might use this to control what is displayed or to deny access to users outside of your domain.

REMOTE_HOST

It is very likely this value will be empty. It requires the web server to resolve the IP address to a name via the DNS. Whether that would even work depends on the remote user's machine even being listed in a DNS database. It is most often disabled because it imposes significant performance degradation if the web server needs to perform a DNS lookup on every request. You could engineer a local DNS and run that separately, only looking up IP addresses when you need to. Even so, that would still impose a turnaround delay on handling the request and time is definitely of the essence here.

REMOTE_IDENT

This is a deprecated feature. It relies on both the client and server supporting RFC 931 but, since the end user can define the value to be anything they like, the chances of it being useful are quite small. This is probably best avoided altogether and you will be very fortunate if you ever see a meaningful value in it. Of course, in a captive intranet situation where you have more control, you might make use of it.

REMOTE_USER

If the user has been authenticated and has passed the test, the authenticated username will be placed in this variable. Other than that, this variable and `AUTH_TYPE` are likely to be empty. Even after authentication, this value may be empty when the request is made for a document in a non-secured area.

REQUEST_METHOD

This is the HTTP request method. It is likely you will only ever see `GET` or `POST` in here. You usually don't need to deliver different versions of a document based on this value but it might be important to verify that the access was made correctly from your page via the correct method. Apart from the size of the data being larger with a `POST`, there is another more subtle difference between `GET` and `POST`. Using a `GET` more than once should always result in the same data being returned. Using `POST` more than once may result in multiple transactions to the back-end. For example, placing an order more than once due to reposting a form. This is one area where the back button on the browser works against you and you may want to interlock this somehow within your session-handling code to prevent duplicate financial transactions happening. You should be aware that this is happening when the browser displays an alert asking whether you want to repost the same form data.

SCRIPT_FILENAME

This is effectively the same as the PATH_TRANSLATED environment variable. It is the full path to the script being executed. Once you have established which of these your server provides (if any), you should be able to stick with it.

SCRIPT_NAME

This is the logical name of the script. It is basically the Request-URI portion of the URL that was originally sent. It is the full path of the script without the document root or script alias mapping. This would be portable across several virtual hosts where the SCRIPT_FILENAME/PATH_TRANSLATED values might not be. This is also useful for making scripts relocatable. You can use this value to rebuild a form so that it will call the same script again. The result is that the script does not then contain a hard coded path that will need to be edited if it is renamed or moved.

SERVER_ADMIN

If it is configured, the e-mail address of the server administrator is held in this environment variable. You could build this into the security mechanisms to alert the administrator when a potential break-in is detected. Be careful not to mailbomb the server administrator with thousands of messages though.

SERVER_NAME

This is the name of the server and may, on some systems, be equivalent to the HTTP_HOST value. This can be useful for manufacturing links elsewhere in a site or detecting the site name so you can build site-specific versions of a page.

SERVER_PORT

The port number that the request arrived on is stored here. Most web sites operate on port 80. Those that don't may be test sites or might operate inside a firewall. It is possible that ancillary servers for adverts and media may use other port numbers if they run on the same machine as the main web server. Most web servers allow you to configure any port number. In the case of the Apache web server you can set up individual virtual hosts on different ports. This means that you could develop a test site and use this value to activate additional debugging help knowing that it would be turned off if the script were run on the production site.

SERVER_PROTOCOL

This is the protocol level of the request being processed. This area is quite ambiguous in the specifications and previously published books. The browser can indicate a preferred protocol level that it can accommodate. This is the value it puts in the request line. However, the server may choose to override that and serve the request with a sub-set of that functionality that conforms to an earlier protocol level. The server configuration may determine a browser match and override it internally or the request may be simple enough that it can be served by HTTP/1.0 protocol even though the browser indicates that it could cope with HTTP/1.1 protocol. From a CGI scripting point of view, it is unlikely you would need to build alternate versions of a page according to this value. It might determine whether you could provide streaming media but that technique is not currently supported by SE:WSE anyway.

SERVER_SOFTWARE

For example, Apache/1.3.6, but dependent on your server.

UNIQUE_ID

This is available in CGI environments running under an Apache web server that has been built with the `unique_id` module included. You could select the first one of these that arrives in a session, and use it as the session key thereafter, as another alternative way of generating unique session keys. It also might provide some useful user-tracking possibilities.

J2EE
JSP

JSP for ASP developers

If you're an Active Server Page (ASP) developer and you're unfamiliar with JSP and the Java language then you have may have looked at some of the chapters in this book and thought the examples that you have been faced with are pretty complex. You would have been right; Java is a complex language with vast potential for error, but an excellent opportunity to learn if you're prepared to look at a new language with open eyes. For an ASP developer, JSP is an excellent way to get into the Java language, as it is very familiar territory. This appendix aimed to demonstrate some of the real similarities and very confusing differences between the ASP (Microsoft VBScript) language and the JSP (Java based) language. We will concentrate on MS VBScript here – if you are already familiar with JScript then the transition to JSP should be relatively straight forward for you, obviously with some hurdles, but none so high as to hit your chin on. This appendix will not turn you into the ultimate ASP/JSP developer and it is not designed too, it is important to realize that the rest of the book is key in understanding the concepts behind JSP and Java. What this appendix will do is show some of the pitfalls, differences, and advantages in trying out JSP when your experience is firmly bound to ASP.

If we ignore the differences in the underlying language itself for a moment, it becomes clear that both ASP and JSP deliver a very similar type of functionality. They both:

- Reside on the server and are called via typical HTTP or even TCP/IP requests.
- Use a complex set of component objects and third party utilities
- Use tags to allow code to be manipulated to output HTML or XML (or indeed XHTML)
- Have session tracking and database interaction
- Allow for the separation of presentation layers from business and data layers.

Although at first sight ASP and JSP carry many similarities, there are conversely some interesting misconceptions about ASP that are often driven by a complete misunderstanding of the ASP language by people adverse to it, and likewise by hardened ASP fans. ASP is based on ActiveX and COM, and uses components and DLLs that can be developed in any COM-compliant language. The favorites are probably VB, C++, and Delphi, but they can also be developed in Java using the JDK if you know what to do with the Java files to use them as COM objects. In contrast JSP uses JavaBeans at the component layer, based on Java as the component architecture. Both of them come with a plethora of development tools: Visual Café, Visual Interdev, and, my personal favorite, TextPad32. The biggest difference I see between the two is JSPs native handling of the Java API that makes it very extensible in comparison to ASP.

JSP through Java, and ASP via one of its scripting languages, have come with many strengths and weaknesses, but if you're an ASP developer the language comes with a really strong reason not to change. Primarily it is a lot easier to learn and remain skilled in, because it's a loosely defined language based on VBA and COM technology. Microsoft ASP (as opposed to Chili ASP (http://www.chilisoft.com) which runs on a variety of web servers) is also very tightly linked to the IIS server and most ASP developers need a really in-depth understanding of IIS to make the best use of the technology. If you tie that to a high skill level in a COM language and the multitude of pre-supplied ASP native components (such as AdRotator) that JSP does not have, then it becomes a very mature and very powerful integrated tool set. There are still many reasons to look at the Java language and JSP. In particular, from an ASP coders perspective, my favorite reason is the 'learn one language – implement anywhere' approach. The other for me is that Java is low level enough to handle threads very easily: that can be very difficult from ASP. The key reason is that, as a developer, you should always consider the other side of the fence, and looking at JSP when all you know is ASP is without a doubt the best way to approach learning Java.

> **A note to remember before you embark on any JSP programming, and one that often causes a lot of frustration: JSP unlike VBScript is case sensitive. This stems from the need to operate on multiple platforms: if you don't know anything about Unix, it is obsessively case sensitive, hence the need to enforce this requirement in a cross platform language.**

Common Ground

There are some common elements between the two languages that we need to go over to stop any confusion before it begins and show how similar the two languages actually are. Most of the things mentioned here would be familiar to an experienced ASP developer, but they need to be covered for you to understand some of the subtle differences between JSP and ASP in these everyday elements, and these include:

- Scripting elements
- Adding comments
- Doing includes
- The Response object
- The Request object
- The Session object
- The Application object

The appendix will then go on to cover some other essentials that you will need as a migrating ASP developer if you are looking at putting together a comprehensive solution site by looking at:

- JavaBeans
- The different approach to datatypes and type conversion
- Databases

Where possible, simple examples will be provided to enforce the relationship between the two languages, to help you achieve a better grasp of the basics you need to make more use of the Java language.

JSP Scripting Elements

You will probably want to add some programming to your JSP files rather than simply serving up static HTML or JavaScript-driven HTML pages, and like ASP this is done through the use of scripting tags or scriptlets. Like ASP tags, the JSP tags are very flexible, and provide the developer with the opportunity to encapsulate tasks that would be difficult or time-consuming to program. They are designed to save you time, but you will probably still need to use scripting language fragments to supplement the JSP tags. All JSP scripting elements let you insert Java code into the Servlet that is generated from the current JSP page the first time it is requested, or at each subsequent source code change.

The scripting languages that are available to you depend on the JSP engine you are using. With Sun's JSP reference implementation, you must use the Java programming language for scripting, but other vendors' JSP engines may include support for other scripting languages; for example, JavaScript in Cauco's Resin server.

There are three basic types of scripting element that can be used to enable access to either JSP's underlying object model or to the Java language.

Expression Scriptlets

A JSP expression is the same as a `response.write` using the VBScript `<% = Expression %>` shortcut syntax. This is evaluated at run-time and the result inserted into any output, be it HTML, WML, or XML etc. It is used like the VBScript equivalent to insert Java values directly into the output and has the same form as its VBScript older brother, `<%= Java Expression %>`

The Java expression is evaluated, converted to a string, and inserted in the page. This evaluation is performed at run-time when the page is requested. For example, the following shows the date/time that the page was requested:

```
Current Date: <%= new java.util.Date() %>
```

Or, in VBScript:

```
Current time: <%= Date() %>
```

To simplify the level of coding required there are a number of predefined script objects. These objects are discussed in more detail later but, for the purpose of expressions and understanding where they fit in relation to VBScript, the most important ones which you should recognize and need to be aware of are:

Predefined object	Description
request	The HttpServletRequest
response	The HttpServletResponse
session	The HttpSession associated with the request (if any)
out	The PrintWriter used to send output to the client (the response.write command of the JSP world – covered later)

Here's an example of one of the objects that would typically be found in the Request.ServerVariables("") collection of VBScript:

```
Remote hostname: <%= request.getRemoteHost() %>
```

In JSP it is just a property of the request object, which implies that you need to do some homework in identifying where to find the properties and methods in JSP normally available in specific ASP objects you're used to.

As new as it is, JSP goes a little further than ASP in looking to the future when dealing with scripts. With the rapid acceptance of XML, JSP has got a bit of a jump-start over VBScript in that XML authors can use an alternative syntax for their JSP expressions:

```
<jsp:expression>
Java Expression
</jsp:expression>
```

Remember that XML elements, unlike HTML ones, are case sensitive. So be sure to use lowercase.

Code Scriptlets

As in VBScript, these are code sections that may exist between script tags `<% some JSP or ASP code %>`. These are inserted into the servlet, and can be used as methods (or functions) or even to process the whole page. A good example in VBScript of when to use this type of scriptlet would be when we embed scripts within an ASP page between HTML to provide some database data for a drop down list box. The same capability is available in JSP. In JSP, like ASP, scriptlets have the following form:

```
<html>
<body>
<% Java Code %>
</body>
</html>
```

Scriptlets by default have access to the same automatically defined variables as expressions. If you wanted output to appear in the page above, you would use the out variable.

```
<html>
<body>
<%
  String strStringThing = "Hello ASP from JSP" ;
  out.println("A Message to ASP: " + strStringThing);
%>
</body>
</html>
```

Like ASP, the code inside a scriptlet gets inserted into the JSP page, raw HTML outside the scriptlet start or end tag will be compiled to `out.print` commands when it compiles to a servlet. ASP does not do this, the parser ignores information found outside the tags and simply returns the data as part of the response stream.

As in the expressions tag, the XML equivalent is:

```
<jsp:scriptlet>
  String strStringThing = "Hello ASP from JSP" ;
  out.println("A Message to ASP: " + strStringThing);
</jsp:scriptlet>
```

Declaration Scriptlets

A declaration is the VBScript equivalent of `DIM` and has the following form:

```
<html>
<body>
<%! Int myVar = 0; %>
</body>
</html>
```

Declarations do not generate any output and are normally used for scoping variables within JSP expressions or scriptlets. They are also used to pre-declare methods from declared classes and are similar to using an include file in VBScript to get access to a set of common functions.

The XML equivalent is:

```
<jsp:declaration>
Code
</jsp:declaration>
```

What's the Difference?

It is confusing that Declarations, Expressions, and Scriptlets have a very similar syntax and can be used in a very similar fashion. If you are familiar with VBScript already however, the relationship between these tags is less confusing.

Here are some examples of the differences and similarities.

Declarations

These contain one or more variable or method declarations that end or are separated by semicolons:

```
<%! String s = "A String"; %>
<%! int a, b; long c; %>
```

You must declare a variable or method in a JSP page before you use it in the page. There are no on-the-fly declarations as in VBScript without `Option Explicit` set.

The scope of any declaration is usually the JSP file it is called in. If the JSP file includes other JSP files using the include directive (covered later) then the included files come within that declaration scope.

Expressions

These can contain any language expression that is valid in the scripting language of the servlet engine your using. Note the lack of a semicolon when using the `<%=` expression syntax, which is a bit unusual in Java as it normally demands a semicolon on the end of each line:

```
<%= a + b + c %>
<%= new java.util.Date()%>
```

Like ASP, expression are evaluated in left-to-right and you can write any amount of code lines between an expression start and end tags.

Comments

In both ASP and JSP, comments are processed before content is sent to the browser. Unlike ASP, JSP does not use the apostrophe-style comments supported by VBScript; you have to switch to the JScript equivalent, `//`.

The ASP page,

```
<%
'This line is a comment.
'This line is also a comment.
Response.write "This line is not a comment"
'This line is also a comment.
%>
```

converts to this JSP page:

```
<%
//This line is a comment.
//This line is also a comment.
out.print("This line is not a comment");
//This line is also a comment.
%>
```

You can still use HTML comments to add remarks to an HTML page using the traditional html `< -- comment -->` syntax. As in ASP, comments outside the tags are returned to the browser and are visible if the user views the source HTML. Like ASP, you still have to get the `<%` and `%>` tags located correctly to use HTML commenting.

Java comes with a pretty good utility for converting comments to HTML help documents, called JavaDoc; sadly, it's not available for JSP pages. That's not much of a loss really if you are thinking of switching languages, what you don't have already cannot be that much of a loss. It's worth remembering JavaDoc though, for when you need to documents the multitude of class files you're likely to write in the future.

The Include Directive

In ASP, the Include directive is slightly different to the JSP equivalent. To include a file you use the `#include` directive. For example, to insert a file named `header.asp` into an HTML page when it is requested, you use the following directive in the ASP page:

```
<!-- #include file="header.asp" -->
<%
' some other ASP code
%>
```

In this example, the file `header.asp` must be in the same directory as the including file. The HTML file that contains the `#include` directive must be a published file in your Web site.

Of course, contrary to popular belief, it is almost possible in ASP to perform dynamic includes using `if` statements.

```
<% if request.querystring("includechoice")="1" then %>
<!--#include file="1.asp"-->
<% else %>
<!--#include file="2.asp"-->
<% end if %>
```

Just like ASP, JSP has the include directive, but there are two ways to use it. One is with the `include` directive (same as the ASP `#include`), primarily for fixed includes like HTML footers etc.

```
<html>
<body>
<% include file="1.htm"%>
</body>
</html>
```

The other is with the `<jsp:include/>` file directive, but this directive comes with some extra options.

It is possible to perform dynamic JSP includes, with the `<jsp:include/>` element. The included file is specified with the `page` attribute. The `flush` attribute specifies whether or not to flush the output buffer. In the JSP 1.1 specification, however, you cannot have a value of `false` nor can you leave it out, which is a bit odd and the subject of future work.

The following example demonstrates how to perform an include using the `jsp:include` element; it generates a random integer every time the page is accessed. If the number is odd it loads `time.jsp`, which ironically provides the system time; if the number is even, it loads `string.jsp`, which by no feat of real magic gives a string back.

`time.jsp` file contains the following code,

```
<%@ page import="java.util.Date" %>
<%
  Date now= new Date();
  out.print(now.getHours() + ":" + now.getMinutes());
%>
```

`string.jsp` consists of,

```
<%= "Hmm...." %>
```

and the main JSP, `include.jsp`, comprises:

```
<%! java.util.Random random =
      new java.util.Random(System.currentTimeMillis()); %>
<% if (random.nextInt() % 2 != 0) { %>
<jsp:include page="time.jsp" flush="true"/>
<% } else { %>
<jsp:include page="string.jsp" flush="true"/>
<% } %>
```

The Response Object

Any ASP developer with a bit of experience in the language will be familiar with the response object which you would normally use to control the information you send to a user. This includes sending information directly to the browser, redirecting the browser to another URL, and setting cookie values. It is very similar when you are looking at JSP. The language comes with everything you would normally use, although obviously it is syntactically different, and sometimes either located in a different place or called in a different way.

Let us assume for a moment that we are looking to do nothing more than set the Content Type of the page details returned to the browser following a page request.

When the web server typically returns a file to a browser, it tells the browser what type of content is contained in the response stream. This enables the browser to determine whether it can display the contents itself or invoke another application. For example, if the Web server returns a PDF, HTML, or a Word file, the browser must be able to start a copy of Acrobat Reader or Word to display the page, or choose to display it only as HTML or text.

In ASP, you would use the `ContentType` property of the `Response` object to set the HTTP content type string for the content you send to the browser:

```
<% Response.ContentType="text/html" %>
```

JSP, however, is different, because it finds the content object in the `page` directive property, rather than within the `Response` object as in ASP.

```
<%@ page ContentType="text/html" %>
```

This really tells us nothing more than not to assume that we will find everything in JSP where it exists in ASP. Fortunately Sun provide a small PDF file called the Syntax card, that is very useful in determining where some of these methods and properties can be found. The latest version can be found at http://java.sun.com/products/jsp/.

Probably the most noticeable difference occurs with the VBScript `response.write` method, which is probably the most utilized method in VBScript. The relationship to the writer object in JSP is a bit obscure, as it is a property of the `javax.servlet.ServletResponse` object. This object is normally used for sending output from within a servlet. This means that it is typically not used by JSP developers (remember that JSP compiles to a Servlet and you could just write your server code directly into a servlet).

Consequently, what you really need to refer to in place of `response.write` is the `out.print("some text");` method which belongs to the `implicit out` object. It has a number of useful methods available: `clear()`, `clearBuffer()`, `flush()`, `getBufferSize()`, and `getRemaining()`, which all enhance its value.

For the ASP developer, the most useful of course is `out print()` which, while very useful, doesn't really match the equivalent VBScript `write()` method, but is essential nonetheless.

Consider this VBScript example:

```
<%

Dim Str
Str = "Testing Out";

Response.write(Str & 1 & "<br>");
Response.write(Str & 2 & "<br>");
Response.write(Str + 3 + "<br>");
Response.write(Str & 4 + "<br>");

%>
```

Taking account of this, the above VBScript example would become the JSP example shown below. Also notice the difference between the way output is concatenated, with VBScript allowing the mixed concatenation operator, and JSP retaining the C-style + syntax.

```
<%

String str = "Testing Out";

out.print(str + 1 + "<br>");
out.print(str + 2 + "<br>");
out.print(str + 3 + "<br>");
out.print(str + 4 + "<br>");

%>
```

It is also worth noting that the ASP 3.0 VBScript `With` enumerator has no equivalent in JSP.

The Request Object

Form processing in JSP is pretty similar to handling the same type of data in ASP and, like ASP, is very easy. In JSP there are four collections available in the `request` object.:

- Cookies
- Form
- QueryString
- ServerVariables

The ClientCertificate collection is not available. I suggest that you read up on the Java Authentication and Authorization Service (JAAS) for an understanding of Java security at http://java.sun.com/products/jaas.

To cover the request object, we will concentrate on the Form and QueryString collections. Let's work our way through a simple form-processing example consisting of two pages, `formsprocessing.jsp`, which produces a HTML page with an input field, and `faveWordResults.jsp`, which produces some output following a "`GET`" action.

The `Formsprocessing.jsp` file is as follows,

```
<html>
<head><title>JSP Interaction Explanation for ASP Coders</title></head>
<body>
<table border="0" width="500">
  <tr>
    <td width="120">   </td>
    <td width="500">
      <h1>Hello ASP coder. What's your favourite word?</h1>
    </td>
  </tr>
  <tr>
    <td width="120"   </td>
    <td width="500">
      <form method="get" action="faveWordResults.jsp">
      <input type="text" name="faveWord" size="25">
      <br>
      <input type="submit" value="Submit">
      <input type="reset" value="Reset">
    </td>
  </tr>
</form>
</table>
</body>
</html>
```

while `faveWordResults.jsp` looks like this:

```
<html>
<head>
<title>Feedback Results</title>
</head>
<h2>Hey, my favourite word is
<%
```

```
// Get form fields passed in from the form submission
String word = request.getParameter("faveWord");
out.println(word);
%>
 too...how strange </h2>

</body>
</html>
```

Saving and calling the JSP page `formsprocessing.jsp` provides a screen similar to that shown below:

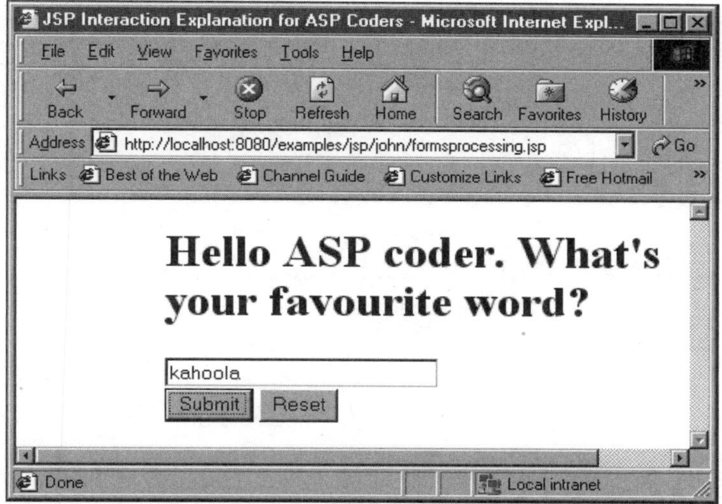

Less than complicated, the screen only requests a single input, as the HTML code shows, and sends the data to the `faveWordResults.jsp` page. The results should be pretty similar to that shown below:

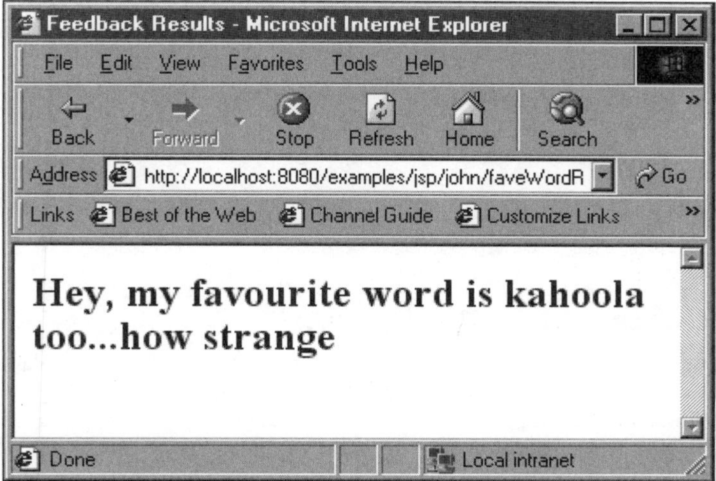

The excellent thing about handling data through the request object in JSP is that it doesn't matter whether the data is sent via GET or POST: the processing method is the same, using the `getParameter("paramName")` method. Unlike ASP, which utilizes two objects (`QueryString` and `Form`), this allows the code to be written using a common syntax that can handle either POST or GET without worrying about whether you are dealing with the `Forms` or `QueryString` collections via the shortcut method `Request("paramName")`. There are some disadvantages to this in that with only one collection to query from you cannot deal with both `QueryString` data and form data submitted via a single post submission together, but it does simplify the management of submitted data.

The JSP request object comes with a set of methods that coincide somewhat to the request.ServerVariables collection in ASP.

Collection Item	Method
Request method	`request.getMethod()`
Request URI	`request.getRequestURI()`
Request protocol	`request.getProtocol()`
Servlet path	`request.getServletPath()`
Path info	`request.getPathInfo()`
Path translated	`request.getPathTranslated()`
Query string	`request.getQueryString()`
Content length	`request.getContentLength()`
Content type	`request.getContentType()`
Server name	`request.getServerName()`
Server port	`request.getServerPort()`
Remote user	`request.getRemoteUser()`
Remote address	`request.getRemoteAddr()`
Remote host	`request.getRemoteHost()`
Authorization scheme	`request.getAuthType()`
The browser you are using	`request.getHeader("User-Agent")`

Calling them is as simple, for example:

```
<html>
<body>
The remote host is <%= request.getRemoteHost() %>
</body>
</html>
```

Session and Application Objects

The `Session` object in ASP is one of the most useful and utilized objects available in creating state in an ASP application. It safe to say it is pretty invaluable in ASP's RAD capability. Traditional methods, like hidden text fields in HTML forms, have been superseded by the ability of ASP to maintain state in this simple object. If you bear in mind what was discussed earlier about the use of loosely defined variables, the ability to simply stuff objects into the `Session` object and maintain state is a very strong feature of ASP.

Well, JSP has its own session object, and it's relatively easy to use, even for an ASP developer. Like ASP, JSP has a number of implicit objects that don't need to be declared, and `session` is just one of them. Like ASP, the session object is useful for applications where several pages have to pass values between each other in order to make the application work.

I don't want to spend a lot of time on the `session` object; it is pretty self-explanatory if you are already familiar with it in ASP. For the sake of clarity we will go through a small example consisting of three pages. The first page, `session1.jsp`, is a simple JSP page consisting only of HTML that displays a form asking for a word. It will submit to `session2.jsp`, and set a session variable containing the word. Here is the first page, `session1.jsp`. (A note of caution – don't forget to enable cookies in the browser.)

```
<html>
<title>
session1.jsp
</title>
<body>
<form method=post action="session2.jsp">
Give Me a word?
<input type=text name="theWord">
<P>
<input type=submit value="SUBMIT">
</form>
</body>
</html>
```

This will result in something similar to this:

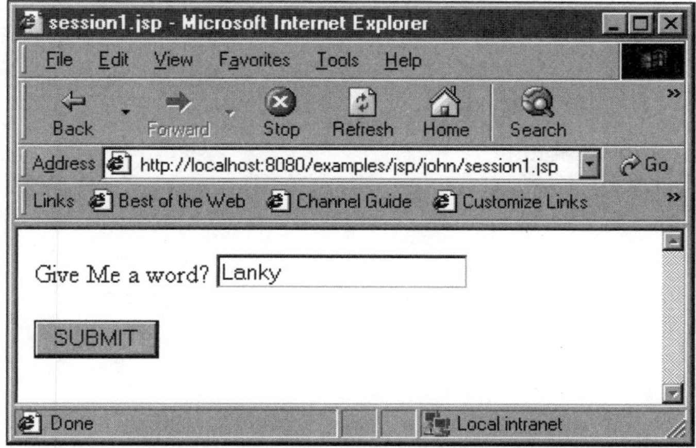

The second page, `session2.jsp`, uses the `request` object we have already covered to set the variable `word` to the value of the `theWord` HTML input text field, and place the value in the `session` object:

```
<html>
<head>
<title>
Session2.jsp
</title>
</head>
<body>
```

```
<%! String word=""; %>
<%
word = request.getParameter("theWord");
session.putValue("theSessionWord", word);
%>

Storing Word <%= word %> to the session object
<p>

</body>
</html>
```

This gives the result:

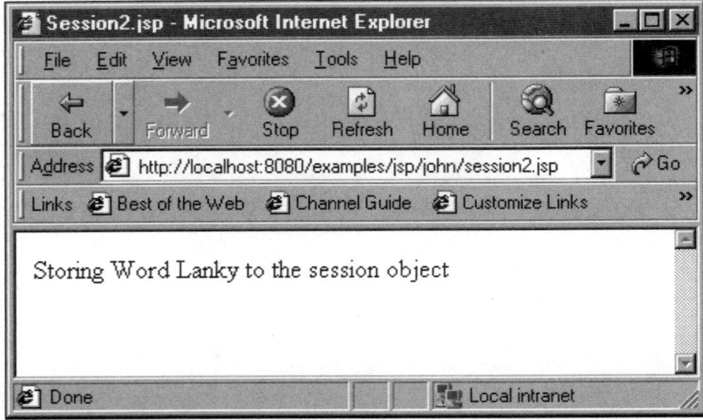

The third page, `session3.jsp`, is a JSP page that simply displays the session value. We will not even link to this; you can just call it directly

```
<html>
<head>
<title>
session3.jsp
</title>
</head>
<body>
<%
String word = (String) session.getValue("theSessionWord");
%>
The Magic Word was <br><%= word %>
</body
</html
```

And you will get:

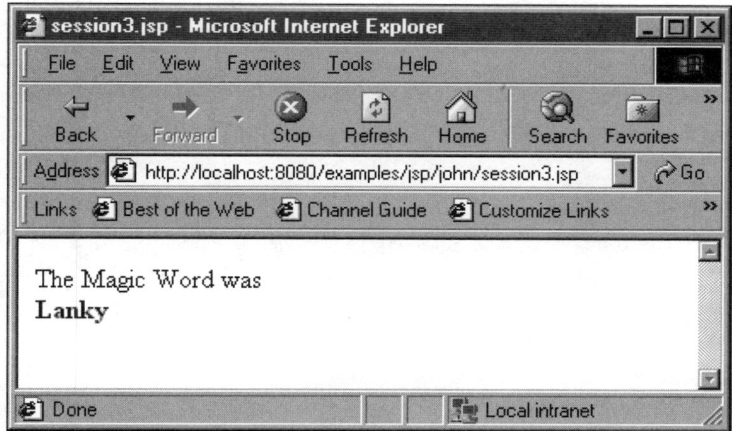

Items that are stored and retrieved from the session object are not allowed to be primitive data types (`int`, `double`, etc.) and must be cast to their true object form (`Integer`, `Double`, etc.).

So we have a `session` object, do we also have an `application` object? Well the answer is no in versions of JSP prior to 1.1. If you're working with those versions, you need to step down another level to make use of the Servlet class.

Application Object

Like ASP, JSP files may need to maintain site-wide application values while each client uses and manipulates the same copy of these values. ASP uses the `Application` object, which is similar to the `Session` object but contains values available to all user sessions, and JSP uses something called the `ServletContext` object that can also contain values available to all sessions.

Consider this JSP, `Application1.jsp`:

```
<%! String Item= new String("MyString"); %>
<%! String appStr = new String(); %>

<%

//set the application value
getServletContext().setAttribute("appstrexample", Item);

// retrieve the application value
appStr = (String) getServletContext().getAttribute("appstrexample");
%>

The value of appStr = <%=appStr%>
```

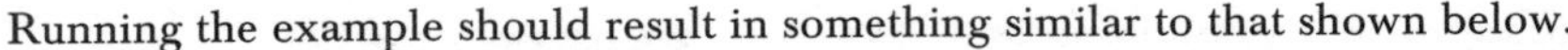

Running the example should result in something similar to that shown below.

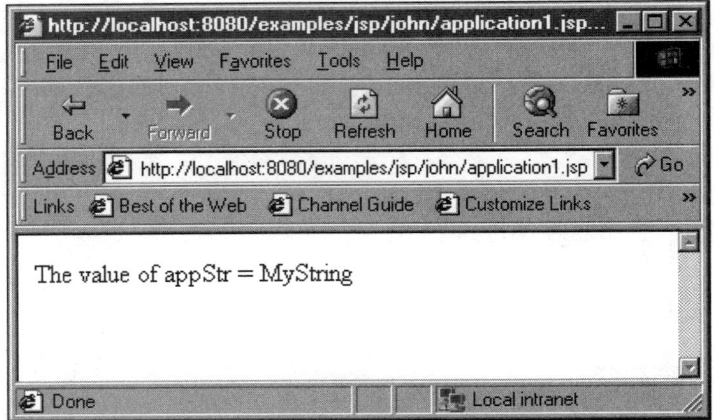

The way application variables are handled is similar to the way sessions are handled: that is, no primitive types. This makes using the application layer quite difficult for inexperienced developers, as you have to become very familiar with type casting, object handling, and exception handling. For a VBScript developer this can be very difficult, given how easy it is to cast type between variant objects. My recommendation is to stick to strings until you are comfortable with casting objects to other types. We cover this to some degree a little later, but until you have experimented a bit with the language the example below will show one way to work with `String` objects at the application layer in dealing with, retrieving and manipulating strings to represent other object types.

The file `application2.jsp` contains the following:

```
<%! Integer IntItem= new Integer(33); %>
<%! String AppValueReturned; %>
<%! Integer AppToInteger; %>

<%
//set the application value
getServletContext().setAttribute("appIntexample", ""+ IntItem);

// retrieve the application value
AppValueReturned = (String) getServletContext().getAttribute("appIntexample");

// convert back to an Int
try {
AppToInteger = Integer.valueOf(AppValueReturned);
}
catch(NumberFormatException e){};

%>

The value of AppToInteger = <%= ""+ AppToInteger%><p>

Consequently, the value of application1.jsp's app variable is
<%= (String) getServletContext().getAttribute("appstrexample")%>
```

The output should be similar to that shown opposite.

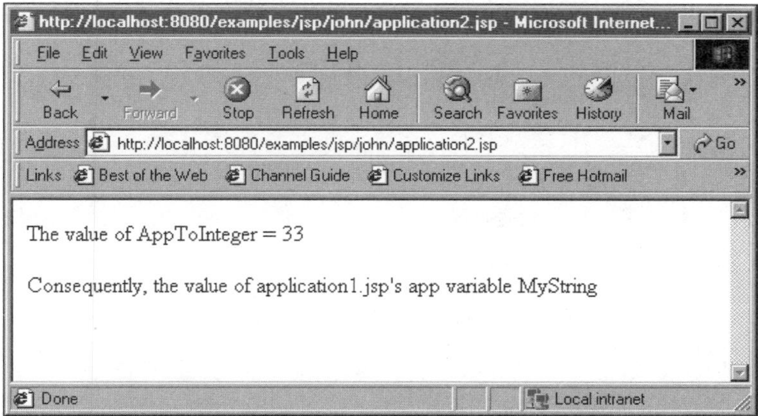

This is where the objects common to both frameworks really ends: the common ground elements may be enough to get you started with JSP producing dynamic pages, but there is more to it than that.

One key thing that you really need to get to grips with subsequently, and which is really likely to confuse you, is the use of JavaBeans.

Making Use of JavaBeans

If you have used VBScript for a while, you are likely to be familiar with COM components. You may have used a set of pre-provided components, or maybe ever written your own. For those unfamiliar with the concept of components, they are used to extend the power of your scripts by providing compact, reusable, and secure means of gaining access to things the ASP scripting language does not provide. Without realizing it, you are probably already using components in ASP. For example, the ADO Database Access component in ASP enables access to databases. COM components are very powerful, as you can call components from any script or programming language that supports Automation.

Java makes use of components in the form of Beans and this includes both visible and invisible beans – the equivalent of ActiveX controls and ActiveX DLLs. It's a good choice for developing or assembling network-aware solutions for mixed hardware and operating system environments, although I feel it takes a lot of management: not all cross platform JSP/Servlet engines use the same versions of the JSP engine, so you need to keep on top of version control. In ASP you normally don't have to worry about that unless you update your scripting language with a new release from Microsoft.

If you are already familiar with developing components, in VB for instance, then you should have a reasonable understanding of ActiveX and COM: I tend to think of Beans as a mix between a VB Class file and a VB ActiveX DLL.

In the ASP environment, it's not that common for developers to integrate Java and ASP unless you are a pretty advanced developer looking to do something a little out of the ordinary. If you are that troubled fellow then it is worth remembering that JavaBean components can actually integrate with ActiveX. Beans can talk to COM via a bridge into other component models such as ActiveX. Software components that use JavaBean APIs are therefore portable to COM compliant applications, including Internet Explorer, Visual Basic, Microsoft Word, Lotus Notes, and others. At the time of writing, a very good explanation of bridging to VB can be found at http://java.sun.com/products/plugin/1.2/docs/script.html, but we are not going to concentrate on that here. We will cover the basics of Beans and help you get up to speed with adding a Bean to your JSP examples.

As a simple example we will create a carCost Bean. It has two simple properties:

- Car
- Cost

Like a VB class, the properties of the bean are set and retrieved by property set and get methods. The Bean will allow you to set the cost for your dream car (if only), and could be used as the database extraction layer. In reality this is where you would add your business logic to feed back to your JSP page that contain, your presentation logic.

Here is the code for CarCost.java:

```
package carbeans;

// the line above is really important, it defines the
// directory where the bean exists

public class carCost {

  // our car cost bean
  String Car;
  double Cost;

  // set the car type
  public void setCar(String carName) {
    this.Car = carName;
  }

  // get back the car type
  public String getCar() {
    return (this.Car);
  }

  // set the car cost
  public void setCost(double carCost) {
    this.Cost = carCost;
  }

  // get back the car cost
  public double getCost() {
    return (this.Cost);
  }
}
```

To use our Bean in a JSP page we will use the <jsp:useBean> tag. When you request a Bean in a JSP page, the runtime engine searches for any existing Beans already instantiated in scope. If none exist it instantiates a new Bean based on the class name of the Bean requested.

To deploy your Bean, you need to put it somewhere that the JSP engine will look to find it. An ActiveX DLL relies on the registry to identify the DLL's location, Beans on the other hand reside where your particular servlet settings dictate. The easiest to configure (and free) engine, and the one I am presently developing with for this example, is the JSWDK from Sun found at http://java.sun.com/products/jsp/. You may be using a different engine, but that's OK, it will still work. I will put my Bean in c:\jswdk-1.0\examples\WEB-INF\jsp\beans\carbeans. You will need to determine where your Beans live in your engine.

Typically, the JSP pages that call a Bean don't live with the Bean as the engine expects them to be elsewhere. I have created a directory called `\cartest` under the `c:\jswdk-1.0\examples\jsp` directory to hold the JSP pages that will demonstrate the Bean working. Also, to confuse the issue slightly, unlike JSPs, Beans have to be compiled. I will assume that you have an appropriate JDK and know how to compile a Java source file, so compile your Bean source and place the class in the `car` directory.

Here is the code for the JSP page `Cartest.jsp`:

```
<html>
<head>
<title>
Bean Test
</title>
</head>

<body>

<jsp:useBean id="carBean" scope="session" class="carbeans.carCost" />

Setting the Car cost and the Car Type:<p>

<% carBean.setCar("Ford");
   carBean.setCost(2000);
%>

Getting the Car cost and the Car Type:<p>
State is: <%= carBean.getCar() %> <br>
Rate is: <%= carBean.getCost() %>

</body>
</html>
```

Calling the JSP page will provide a result similar to that shown below:

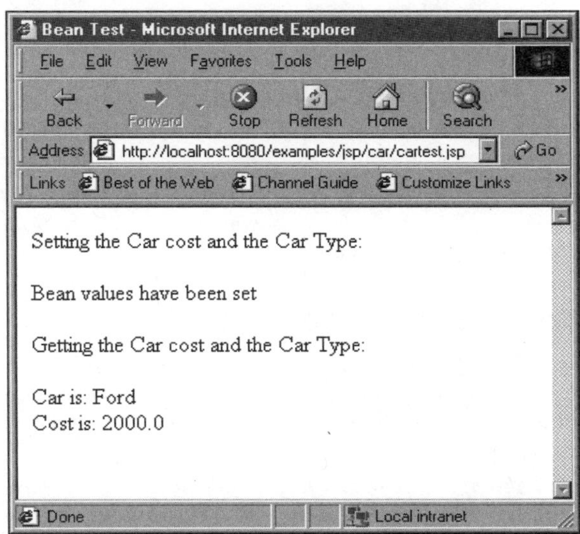

So how does it work?

Within the <jsp:useBean> tag there are several attributes. This is very much in line with VBScript, where you instantiate most DLLs with a fixed Server.CreateObject method, such as:

```
<%
Set ID = Server.CreateObject("myTestObject.MyTestClass").
%>
```

The Bean options are pretty much the same as the ASP options for createObject, insofar as the bean has an ID.

For our carCost Bean, the id attribute is set to "carBean":

```
<jsp:useBean id="carBean"
```

This part of the tag and this id is used to identify the Bean throughout the JSP page.

The scope attribute indicates, naturally, how the Bean remains in scope.

```
<jsp:useBean id="carBean" scope="session"
```

For ASP, you could have assigned the object to the session object, the Application object, or the Page object. In JSP you don't need to explicitly add this to a session variable as you would with ASP, as the servlet engine knows to make this available to the session when it reads the scope attribute:

```
<%
Set Session("ID") = Server.CreateObject("myTestObject.MyTestClass").
%>
```

The class attribute indicates the class file representing the Bean added onto the end of the package name. If you are not familiar with Java packages, it is nothing more than the directory name where the Bean class file lives.

```
<jsp:useBean id="carBean" scope="session" class="carbeans.carCost" />
```

Notice that for the <jsp:useBean> tag we used the XHTML short notation of /> to close the tag instead of the usual </jsp:useBean>. You can use either. In ASP, the class settings are covered by the registry entry in Windows, with the myTestObject.MyTestClass covering the 'package' and the 'class' file which makes the object available via COM.

I would strongly recommend you take a look at the FAQ provided by Sun about Beans, as it covers a lot of information relevant to ActiveX developers looking at using Beans. At the time of writing the URL is http://java.sun.com/beans/FAQ.html.

A Different Approach to Datatypes

One of the things I love about VBScript is that it is a very lazy language when it comes to declaring data types. By lazy I mean it is doesn't force, or even expect, specific declarations of variable types. In fact all variables in ASP if you are using VBScript are of type Variant and you don't even have to name them by default before assigning them.

For those of you reading this appendix from a Java or Perl perspective, a Variant is a special kind of data type that can contain different kinds of information, depending on how it's used. Because Variant is the only data type in VBScript, it's also the data type returned by all functions in VBScript.

At its simplest, a `Variant` in VBScript can contain either numeric or string information. A `Variant` behaves as a number when you use it in a numeric context, and as a string when you use it in a string context (One, Two, Three, etc.). That is, if you're working with data that looks like numbers (1, 2, 3, etc), VBScript assumes that it is numbers and does the thing that is most appropriate for numbers. Similarly, if you're working with data that can only be string data, VBScript treats it as string data. Of course, you can always make numbers behave as strings by enclosing them in quotation marks. This is a very attractive, and easy way to handle data types.

A `Variant` can also disseminate information about the specific nature of numeric information. For example, you can have numeric information that represents a date or a time. When used with other date or time data, the result is always expressed as a date or a time. You can also have a rich variety of numeric information ranging in size from Boolean values to huge floating-point numbers. These different categories of information that can be contained in a `Variant` are called subtypes. Most of the time, you can just put the kind of data you want in a `Variant`, and the `Variant` behaves in a way that is most appropriate for the data it contains. That includes arrays and objects which makes it extremely powerful but not as efficient as native datatypes.

The following table shows the subtypes of data that an ASP `Variant` can contain.

Subtype	Description
Empty	Variant is uninitialized. Value is 0 for numeric variables or a zero-length string `("")` for string variables.
Null	Variant intentionally contains no valid data
Boolean	Contains either True or False
Byte	Contains integer in the range 0 to 255
Integer	Contains integer in the range -32,768 to 32,767
Currency	A value from -922,337,203,685,477.5808 to 922,337,203,685,477.5807
Long	Contains integer in the range -2,147,483,648 to 2,147,483,647
Single	Contains a single-precision, floating-point number in the range -3.402823E38 to -1.401298E-45 for negative values; 1.401298E-45 to 3.402823E38 for positive values
Double	Contains a double-precision, floating-point number in the range -1.79769313486232E308 to -4.94065645841247E-324 for negative values; 4.94065645841247E-324 to 1.79769313486232E308 for positive values
Date (Time)	Contains a number that represents a date between January 1, 100 to December 31, 9999
String	Contains a variable-length string that can be up to approximately 2 billion characters in length
Object	Contains an object
Error	Contains an error number

JSP, on the other hand, retains purity in its declaration and handling of datatypes. While very advantageous, purity sadly is not cheap and the cost comes in the form of a substantial development consideration to migrating VBScript developers in taking you back to a more traditional approach to data types.

The following table shows the type of data that a JSP variable can contain. Notice that these are not subtypes as in the ASP table, but Java **primitives**.

Keyword	Description	Size/Format
Integer types		
`byte`	Byte-length integer	8-bit two's complement
`short`	Short integer	16-bit two's complement
`int`	Integer	32-bit two's complement
`long`	Long integer	64-bit two's complement
Real number types		
`float`	Single-precision floating point	32-bit IEEE 754
`double`	Double-precision floating point	64-bit IEEE 754
Other types		
`char`	A single character	16-bit Unicode character
`boolean`	A Boolean value (`true` or `false`)	True or false

Hence the cost becomes apparent. All variables in the Java language must have a data type declared for them before you (or the server) compile the code, or an error will occur. This is similar to setting `Option Explicit` in VBScript to force declaration of the variables. The primary difference is the lack of primitives in the Java language and of course the slight difference in how you declare the actual variable itself. There are key advantages to being forced down this route: it is a very good plus point in debugging and maintaining code, as it becomes very easy to identify data types and track them through the code, and it increases performance.

```
<html>
<body>

<%
  // the common variables
  byte largestByte = Byte.MAX_VALUE;
  short largestShort = Short.MAX_VALUE;
  int largestInteger = Integer.MAX_VALUE;
  long largestLong = Long.MAX_VALUE;

  // real numbers for handling interesting things like money
  float largestFloat = Float.MAX_VALUE;
  double largestDouble = Double.MAX_VALUE;

  // other primitive types
  char aChar = 'S';
  boolean aBoolean = true;


  // write some output - the equivalent of response.write("output")
```

```
    out.print("The largest byte value is " + largestByte+ "<br>");
    out.print("The largest short value is " + largestShort+ "<br>");
    out.print("The largest integer value is " + largestInteger+ "<br>");
    out.print("The largest long value is " + largestLong+ "<br>");

    out.print("The largest float value is " + largestFloat+ "<br>");
    out.print("The largest double value is " + largestDouble+ "<br>");

    if (Character.isUpperCase(aChar)) {
        out.print("The character " + aChar + " is upper case."+ "<br>");
    } else {
        out.print("The character " + aChar + " is lower case." + "<br>");
    }

    out.print("The value of aBoolean is " + aBoolean + "<br>");

%>

</body>
</html>
```

A variable's data type determines the values that the variable can contain and the operations that can be performed on it. In the above example JSP, the declaration,

```
int largestInteger
```

declares that `largestInteger` is an integer (`int`).

In ASP, the equivalent declaration for an integer variable could contain anything from a string to an int or an object, and the compiler doesn't really care. It's actually very clever at working it out – but it does not encourage good development practice by not giving you the choice to use anything other than variant.

```
<%
Dim largestInteger
%>
```

If you saved the example above as `datatypes.jsp` and called it you will see results similar to this:

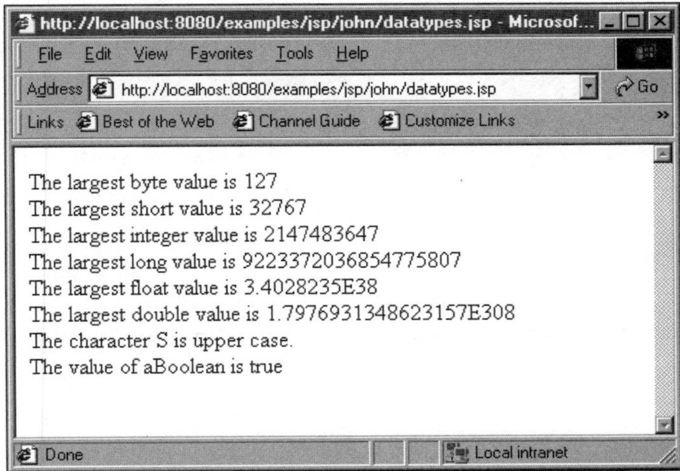

Integers in JSP can contain only integral values that may be positive or negative. Just like ASP you can perform arithmetic operations, such as addition, on integer variables, but only against other integers, so you need to consider how to convert types from one to the other. In VBScript it is very easy as I'm sure you're familiar with the many functions provided for subtype conversion:

```
<%

Dim myStringValue
Dim myIntValue

MyStringValue = "25"
MyIntValue = 25

response.write CInt(MyStringValue) + myIntValue

%>
```

In JSP however, it is an entirely different thing, but some methods are provided to help you out. I'll provide a few simple examples here to help you better understand the differences between how Java handles conversions.

```
<%

// first we'll assign a value to a previously declared int
int i = 50;
// and then to a previously declared but Empty String
String str = "";

// then we can convert between the different types

out.print("integer to String:<br>");
str = Integer.toString(i);
out.print(str + "<br>");

out.print("String to integer:<br>");
i = Integer.valueOf(str).intValue();
out.print(i + "<br>");

out.print("Another Approach for String to integer:<br>");
i = Integer.parseInt(str);
out.print(i + "<br>");

%>
```

The result if you were to run the JSP example should look something like this:

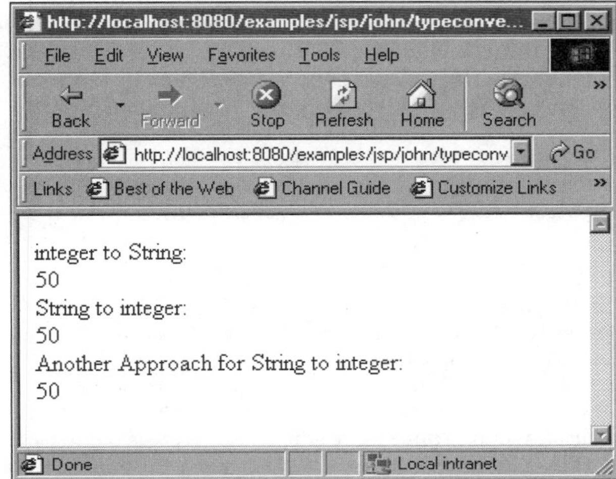

As a last point with regards to data types the Java programming language has two major categories of data types:

- primitive types
- reference types

A variable of a primitive type contains a single value of the correct size and format for its declared type: a number, character, or Boolean value. The value of an `int` is 32 bits of data, the value of a `char` is 16 bits of data formatted as a Unicode character, and so on, as we saw earlier.

In ASP, classes, arrays and objects all exist as variants, while an array, class or interface in JSP is a reference type. The value of a reference type variable, in contrast to that of a primitive type is a *reference* to the value or set of values represented by the variable. A reference is traditionally called a pointer and it relates to the to VB API `addressOf` operator to reference the value in memory. In C++ it would be a pointer, but in JSP (unlike C++) we don't need to go that low level to get to its address. A reference type variable is not the array or object itself, but rather a way to reach it.

Databases

If you have been developing in ASP for a while you have probably used the Microsoft Data Access Components (MDAC) in one form or another. For any ASP developer, ADO or OLEDB components provide a very easy-to-use, programmatic level of access to all types of data located anywhere. The latest version of MDAC in Windows 2000 is very advanced and, given how easy it is to use, could be considered one of the strongest features of ASP.

> *MDAC has reached new heights with Windows 2000 and encompasses a new set of providers for accessing data across multiple platforms and includes the ability to perform LDAP queries. Future releases of MDAC will encourage the migration to a new cross platform access medium known as SOAP (The Simple Object Access Protocol). In case you're interested you can find in-depth information about SOAP at* http://www.develop.com/soap.

> *SOAP combines HTTP and XML into a single solution to provide a whole new level of interoperability. For example, clients written in Microsoft Visual Basic can easily invoke CORBA services running on Linux boxes, web clients can invoke code running on archaic mainframes, and Macs can start invoking Perl objects running on Unix.*
>
> *While some interoperability is achieved today through cross-platform bridges for specific technologies, if SOAP becomes a ratified standard, bridges will no longer be necessary. JSP (at the time of writing) does not use SOAP, it doesn't even use true ODBC which is a problem if you're an ASP developer.*

If you are looking to utilize databases then you are typically going to do two things: use a JDBC/ODBC bridge, or use a pure JDBC driver. We will concentrate on the JDBC/ODBC bridge here as other chapters in the book cover JDBC to a more in-depth level. The other reason is that as an ASP developer you will probably already be familiar with ODBC.

We will start by looking at two simple examples, one for ASP and one for JSP. Both of them do nothing more than extract and display data from a very simple MS Access database called `lazybreak.mdb`. The database has one table called `countries` which has two fields in it, `ID` and `Name`. `ID` is autonumbered, `name` is a char string of 50 length, and there are four records in the database containing four country names.

The `database.asp` file is as follows:

```
<%

set dbConnection = Server.CreateObject("ADODB.Connection")
cnStr = "Provider=Microsoft.Jet.OLEDB.3.51; Data Source=" &
server.mappath("lazybreak.mdb")
dbConnection.Open cnStr

Set rs = dbConnection.Execute("Select * from countries")

        Do while not rs.eof
         response.write  rs.fields("name") & "<BR>"
         rs.movenext
       loop

rs.close
dbConnection.close

set rs = nothing
set dbConnection = nothing

%>
```

If you intend to try and run the ASP examples, you will naturally require an ASP configuration on your server that is capable of executing the code. As this appendix is aimed at existing ASP developers I am making a bit of an assumption that you may already have that. However, if you're a drop in Java developer looking to try the ASP examples alongside the JSP examples you may need a good reference.

The equivalent JSP, `database.jsp`, looks like this:

```
<%@ page import="java.util.*" %>
<%@ page import="java.awt.*" %>
<%@ page import="java.sql.*" %>
```

```
<%
String url = "jdbc:odbc:countrydb";
String user = "";
String password = "";

try {

      Class.forName("sun.jdbc.odbc.JdbcOdbcDriver");
      Connection con = DriverManager.getConnection(url, user, password);
      Statement stmt = con.createStatement();
      ResultSet rs =  stmt.executeQuery("Select * from countries");

      while (rs.next()) {
            String result = rs.getString("name");
            %>
            <%= result %><BR>
            <%

      }
      rs.close();


} // end the try

catch (Exception e) {
      System.out.println(e);
} // end the catch


%>
```

Running either example produces very similar results:

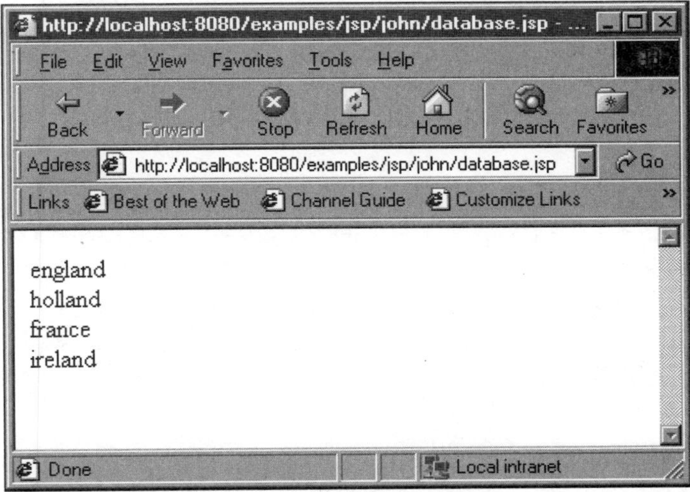

If we look at the two examples they are pretty much the same thing, apart from a modicum of different syntax. However, the biggest difference between them is that the ASP example uses a File DSN defined in the code lines,

```
cnStr = "Provider=Microsoft.Jet.OLEDB.3.51; Data Source=" &
server.mappath("lazybreak.mdb")
```

In JSP you cannot use a File DSN to call an ODBC bridge, because File DSNs are native to ADO under Windows. Instead you have to configure a System DSN for the JDBC driver to invoke the bridge to Access successfully. For this example, the DSN needs to be called `countrydb` and it needs to point to the Access database.

This can be identified by the different setting for the DSN in the JSP page:

```
String url = "jdbc:odbc:countrydb";
```

The other major difference is the `try` and `catch` error trapping that is required for database access in JSP demonstrated below. This is a new feature to VBScript in ASP 3.0, but is a fundamental element of Java and you should take note of it as you'll see it appear a lot in Java code.

```
try {

// do the code

catch (Exception e) {
     System.out.println(e);
} // end the catch
```

The example is hardly taxing: it is intended to demonstrate how easy it is to utilize the JDBC to ODBC bridging capabilities.

Adding a Business Layer

What we will do with the example is include it in a Bean example that simply demonstrates adding a piece of JDBC/ODBC bridging code into a Bean, to separate the presentation from the data extraction. This is the same as moving your business logic into an ActiveX DLL to separate the presentation and business logic in ASP. As an extra step, we will make use of some of the other things we have previously been through:

- The `request` object
- The `out` object
- And type conversion

We will plan the example the way we would use it. The HTML is first, in a file called `DBCallingForm.jsp`. Again we are simply using a `.jsp` extension; `.html` would probably be faster (no initial compile) but it means you typically only need to work in one editor.

```
<html>
<head><title>JSP Bean Business Logic Encapsulation Explanation for ASP
Coders</title></head>
<body>
<table border="0" width="500">
<tr>
<td width="120">   </td>
<td width="500">
<h1>Which Country are you looking for?</h1>
</td>
</tr>
<tr>
<td width="120"   </td>
<td width="500">
<form method="get" action="dbBeanCall.jsp">
```

```
<input type="text" name="dbIDNumber" size="25">
<br>
<input type="submit" value="Submit">
<input type="reset" value="Reset">
</td>
</tr>
</form>
</table>
</body>
</html>
```

Running `DBCallingForm.jsp` gives us something akin to the following:

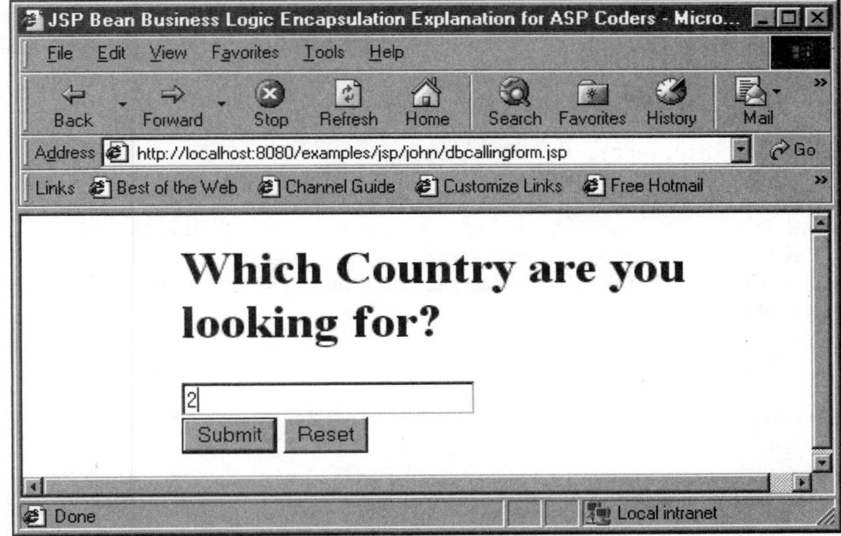

Next we have the form processing page `DBBeanCall.jsp`, which takes the input data, and instantiates and interacts with the Bean.

```
<html>
<head>
<title>
Integrated Database Bean Test
</title>
</head>

<body>

<jsp:useBean id="dbBeanID" scope="request" class="dbbeans.dbBeanClass" />

<%
String myID = request.getParameter("dbIDNumber");
%>

<h3>
Getting the Country for Country ID Number <%=myID%>:<p>
```

```
<%
out.print(dbBeanID.getCountry(Integer.parseInt(myID)));
%>
</h3>

</body>
</html>
```

As you can see, we have included the dbIDNumber from the input page:

```
<%
String myID = request.getParameter("dbIDNumber");
%>
```

We make specific use here of out.print and revisit the need for type conversion to call the getCountry method of the Bean while passing a value to of the Bean using:

```
<%
out.print(dbBeanID.getCountry(Integer.parseInt(myID)));
%>
```

Finally, we will create a suitable package directory called dbbean for the Bean. Then we then take the above database.jsp example and convert it to a Bean, DbBeanClass.java. If you remember the Bean example earlier in the appendix, it was a Java file not a JSP file. You'll need to save it and compile it as you did earlier.

```
package dbbeans;

// this line is really important, it defines the
// directory that the bean exists in

import java.util.*;
import java.awt.*;
import java.sql.*;

public class dbBeanClass {

  // a var for holding values
  String Country = "";

  // get back the country back
  public String getCountry(int countryNumber) {

    String url = "jdbc:odbc:countrydb";
    String user = "";
    String password = "";

    try {

      Class.forName("sun.jdbc.odbc.JdbcOdbcDriver");
      Connection con = DriverManager.getConnection(url, user,
              password);
      Statement stmt = con.createStatement();
      ResultSet rs =
        stmt.executeQuery("Select name from countries where ID ="
                        + countryNumber);
```

```
        while (rs.next()) {
          String result = rs.getString("name");
          Country = result;
        }
        rs.close();

        if (Country == "") {
          Country = "No record Found for " + countryNumber;
        }


      }   // end the try

      catch (Exception e) {
        Country = "There was an error " + e;
      }   // end the catch

      return (this.Country);

    }

  }
```

If we look at the code, the bean wrappers `package dbbeans` and `public class dbBeanClass` are added to the JSP scriptlet. The code is also syntactically different, as we are working in a Java class rather than JSP scriptlet:

The `import` statements,

```
import java.util.*;
import java.awt.*;
import java.sql.*;
```

have changed from the JSP scriptlet statements of:

```
<%@ page import="java.util.*" %>
<%@ page import="java.awt.*" %>
<%@ page import="java.sql.*" %>
```

We are also making a different use of get and set, in fact we aren't even using set, whilst get has changed to take an input parameter of type integer, defined as:

```
public String getCountry(int countryNumber)
```

The code does still use the same DSN defined earlier, thus a call to `getCountry()` with an appropriate integer identifying the ID of a specific country will return a `String` containing the country name.

We have also changed the SQL statement to contain the `countryNumber` being passed from the `DBBeanCall.jsp` page.

```
ResultSet rs =
  stmt.executeQuery("Select name from countries where ID ="
                    + countryNumber);
```

This is the same as you would do it in VBScript, you may however have chosen to use the & operator which is preferred in ASP.

We have also added a simple empty record check to inform the user if they ask for an ID that does not exist.

```
if (Country == "") {
  Country = "No record Found for " + countryNumber;
}
```

In addition to that error trap, we also modified the `try-catch` exception to be user friendly to some degree by changing the returned error message in case there is an error in the database query:

```
Country = "There was an error " + e;
```

As you can probably see, there is not a lot of difference between the Bean and the JSP Scriptlet: the main difference is that you have separated the business logic from the presentation of the results. You could now change the Bean as necessary without affecting what gets presented to the end user.

The initialization parameters for the Bean are self-explanatory and are covered in the earlier Beans section. For this example we have changed the scope of the bean. We don't want it to be so persistent – no specific reason, except that we are passing it a value for a database call and show a different scope choice in action. This would be a good opportunity for you to experiment with scope and see what differences you can create and see how it relates to the creation of database object scope in ASP.

Calling the JSP page, with a value for `getCountry()` of 2 for me returns `holland` as the country that matches that ID.

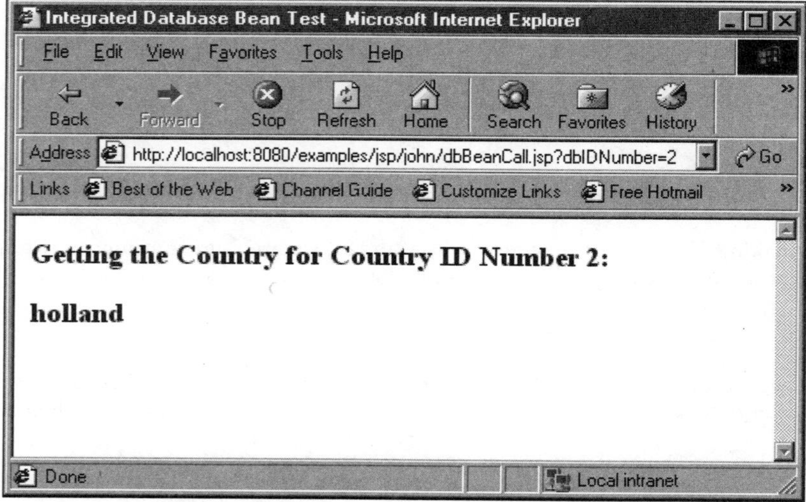

The last thing we included in this example, and have not discussed to any length is exception handling.

Handling Errors in ASP and JSP

ASP, VBScript, and JSP don't look at errors in the same way. If a JSP or Java application is well written and something unexpected occurrs, the code will probably throw an exception and display a suitable error. When IIS encounters an error when it's running VBScript it will generate a 500;100 error. After a 500;100 custom error is generated, IIS will create an instance of the `ASPError` or `Err` object which describes the error condition. Typically, coders had to manipulate the error object with `On Error Resume Next`, and it was a bit limiting. ASP 3.0 however comes with a similar "`try-catch`" type of exception handling as Java does, but you have to drop out of VBScript and drop into JScript. The JScript "`try-catch`" statement provides a way to handle some or all of the possible errors that may occur in a given block of code, while still running code as shown below:

```
function NumberTryCatch(num) {
try { if (num == 20) // Evalute argument.
throw "number equals 20";
else throw "number not 20";
} catch(e) {
}

document.write(NumberTryCatch(17));
```

If errors occur that are not handled by the developer, JScript simply provides its normal `ASPError` object message to a user, as if there was no error handling. This is a very useful capability but it does mean that you have to switch between languages in ASP.

Just like a JScript application in ASP, exceptions that occur while a JSP application is running is called a runtime exceptions. Runtime exceptions are relatively easy to handle in a JSP application. You can use the `exception` object in a special type of JSP page called an error page, where you display the `exception`'s name and class, its stack trace, and a useful message. You use the directive page to set the `isErrorPage="true"` attribute at the top of the JSP page, to tell the page what to do for unhandled exceptions and errors.

```
<%@ page isErrorPage="true" %>
```

By using the Java `exception.getMessage()` method in the error page its possible to display the appropriate message that was caught by the exception handler.

We will modify our database JSP scriptlet to trigger an unhandled runtime exception error in the database call, by modifying the URL `String` to create a badly named ODBC DSN name by removing the letter `b` from the end of `countrydb` and stripping out the `try-catch` elements of the scriptlet.

`exception.jsp` code is as follows:

```
<%@ page errorPage="errorpage.jsp" %>
<%@ page import="java.util.*" %>
<%@ page import="java.awt.*" %>
<%@ page import="java.sql.*" %>
```

```
<%

String url = "jdbc:odbc:countryd";
String user = "";
String password = "";

      Class.forName("sun.jdbc.odbc.JdbcOdbcDriver");
      Connection con = DriverManager.getConnection(url, user, password);
      Statement stmt = con.createStatement();
      ResultSet rs =  stmt.executeQuery("Select * from countries");

      while (rs.next()) {
            String result = rs.getString("name");
            %>
            <%= result %><BR>
            <%

      }
      rs.close();

%>
```

The `errorpage.jsp` file contains the following:

```
<html>
<body>
      <%@ page isErrorPage="true" %>
      <h3> The exception <%= exception.getMessage() %>
      shows there was an error that was handled by errorpage.jsp</h3>
</body>
</html>
```

The result of calling `exception.jsp` should be similar to that shown below:

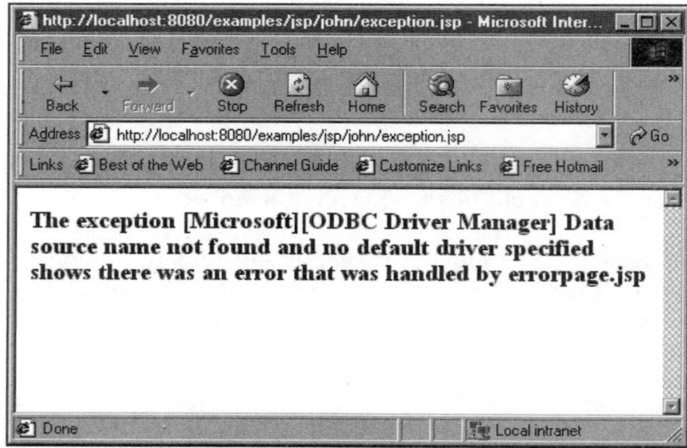

One thing to remember is that some methods demand a `try-catch` and cannot function or compile without one; you need to watch for these. Even when they are not demanded, try to catch your exceptions: it promotes good practice and gets you into the habit of good code management.

Summary

Reading through the examples demonstrated in this appendix, ASP and JSP can seem very similar and, at first sight, they are. That makes it a bit easier for you as an ASP developer to look at how you could make use of the language. However, there are many differences between the two technologies. JSP is still missing a lot of components native to ASP, though some servlet engines (IBM Websphere, for instance) come with a comprehensive set of add in Beans to add additional functionality not offered by standard JSP to address problems like this. The Java language is flexible enough to allow you to bridge most gaps.

For an aspiring VBScript developer, significantly adding to the learning curve of JSP is Java's underlying object-oriented nature. This may well be completely alien to you, given the loosely-defined nature of VBScript as a language. This object-orientation is somewhat responsible for the power and flexibility of the language. JSP also has some fancy features we have not touched on in this appendix, for in reality the topic of JSP for ASP developers is far too much for a single appendix. Hopefully, though, we have managed to get you started.

If you are looking for some additional reading, Sun have written a short white paper *Comparing JavaServer Pages and Microsoft Active Server Pages Technology*, which compares some of the elements of both technologies At the time of writing, this can be found http://java.sun.com/products/jsp/jsp-asp.html.

Some of the other things you might like to look at after this appendix are tag extensions that allow the developer to create custom tags, something you cannot do with ASP (see Chapter 8). Another interesting topic that seems to be gaining some ground is the ability to integrate COM into Java or even use Java in ASP.

J2EE
JSP

Support, Errata, and p2p.wrox.com

One of the most irritating things about any programming book is when you find that bit of code you've just spent an hour typing simply doesn't work. You check it a hundred times to see if you've set it up correctly and then you notice the spelling mistake in the variable name on the book page. Of course, you can blame the authors for not taking enough care and testing the code, the editors for not doing their job properly, or the proofreaders for not being eagle-eyed enough, but this doesn't get around the fact that mistakes do happen.

We try hard to ensure no mistakes sneak out into the real world, but we can't promise that this book is 100% error free. What we can do is offer the next best thing by providing you with immediate support and feedback from experts who have worked on the book and try to ensure that future editions eliminate these gremlins. We also now commit to supporting you not just while you read the book, but once you start developing applications as well through our online forums where you can put your questions to the authors, reviewers, and fellow industry professionals.

In this appendix we'll look at how to:

- Enroll in the peer to peer forums at http://p2p.wrox.com
- Post and check for errata on our main site, http://www.wrox.com
- E-mail technical support a query or feedback on our books in general

Between all three support procedures, you should get an answer to your problem in no time flat.

The Online Forums at P2P.Wrox.Com

Join the Pro JSP mailing list for author and peer support. Our system provides **programmer to programmer™ support** on mailing lists, forums and newsgroups all in addition to our one-to-one email system, which we'll look at in a minute. Be confident that your query is not just being examined by a support professional, but by the many Wrox authors and other industry experts present on our mailing lists.

How To Enroll For Support

Just follow this four-step system:

1. Go to p2p.wrox.com in your favorite browser.
   Here you'll find any current announcements concerning P2P – new lists created, any removed and so on.

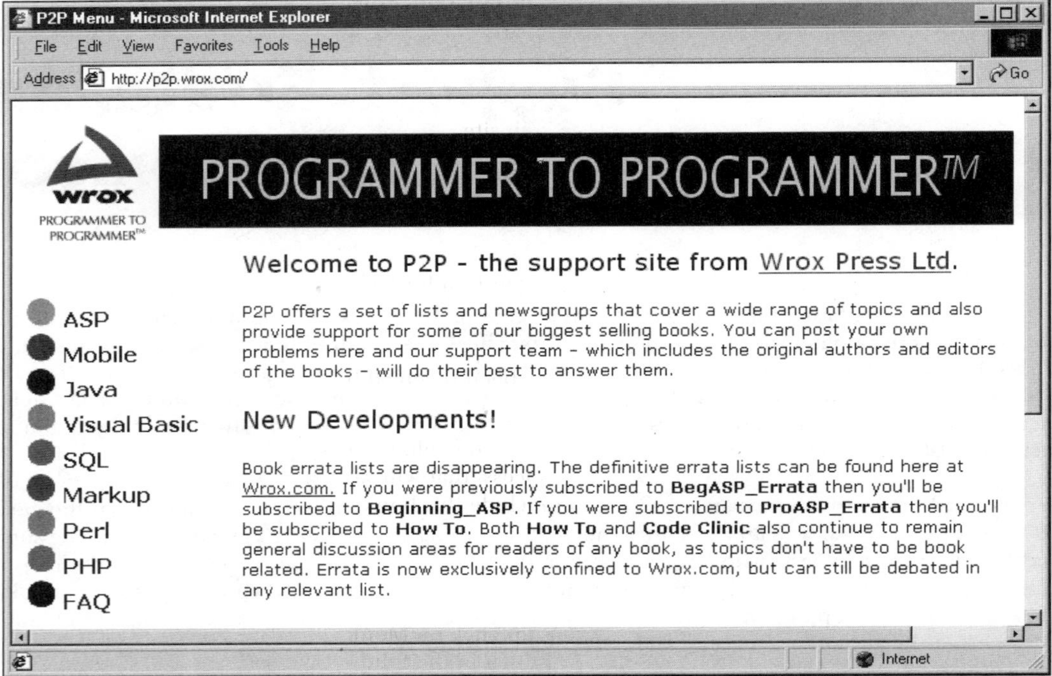

2. Click on the Java button in the left hand column.
3. Choose to access the pro_jsp list.
4. If you are not a member of the list, you can choose to either view the list without joining it or create an account in the list, by hitting the respective buttons.
5. If you wish to join, you'll be presented with a form in which you'll need to fill in your email address, name and a password (of at least 4 digits). Choose how you would like to receive the messages from the list and then hit Save.
6. Congratulations. You're now a member of the pro_jsp mailing list.

Why this system offers the best support

You can choose to join the mailing lists or you can receive them as a weekly digest. If you don't have the time or facility to receive the mailing list, then you can search our online archives. You'll find the ability to search on specific subject areas or keywords. As these lists are moderated, you can be confident of finding good, accurate information quickly. Mails can be edited or moved by the moderator into the correct place, making this a most efficient resource. Junk and spam mail are deleted, and your own email address is protected by the unique Lyris system from web-bots that can automatically hoover up newsgroup mailing list addresses. Any queries about joining, leaving lists or any query about the list should be sent to: moderatorprojsp@wrox.com.

Checking The Errata Online at www.wrox.com

The following section will take you step by step through the process of posting errata to our web site to get that help. The sections that follow, therefore, are:

- Wrox Developers Membership
- Finding a list of existing errata on the web site
- Adding your own errata to the existing list
- What happens to your errata once you've posted it (why doesn't it appear immediately)?

There is also a section covering how to e-mail a question for technical support. This comprises:

- What your e-mail should include
- What happens to your e-mail once it has been received by us

So that you only need view information relevant to yourself, we ask that you register as a Wrox Developer Member. This is a quick and easy process, that will save you time in the long-run. If you are already a member, just update membership to include this book.

Wrox Developer's Membership

To get your FREE Wrox Developer's Membership click on Membership in the top navigation bar of our home site – http://www.wrox.com. This is shown in the following screenshot:

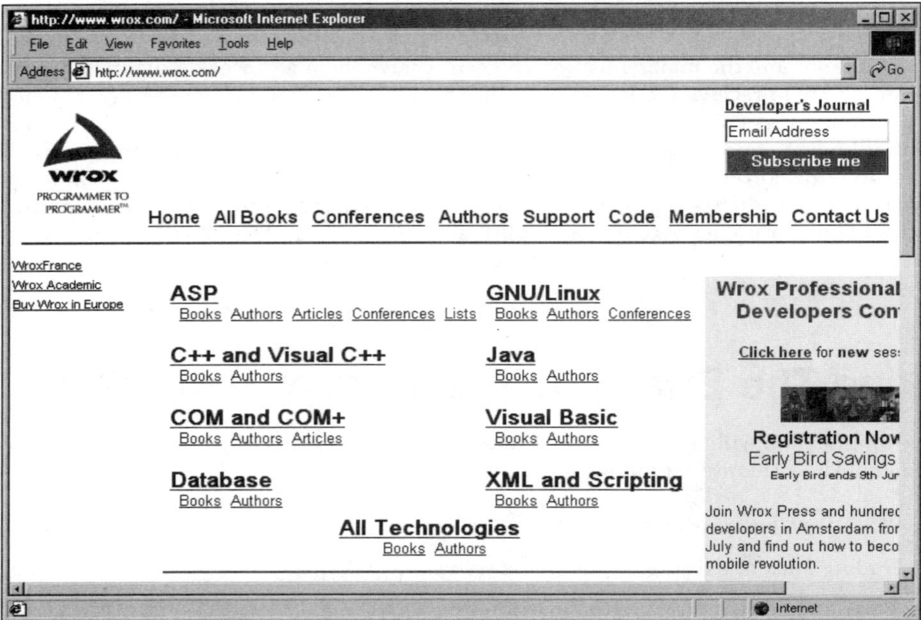

Then, on the next screen (not shown), click on New User. This will display a form. Fill in the details on the form and submit the details using the Register button at the bottom. Before you can say 'The best read books come in Wrox Red' you will get the following screen:

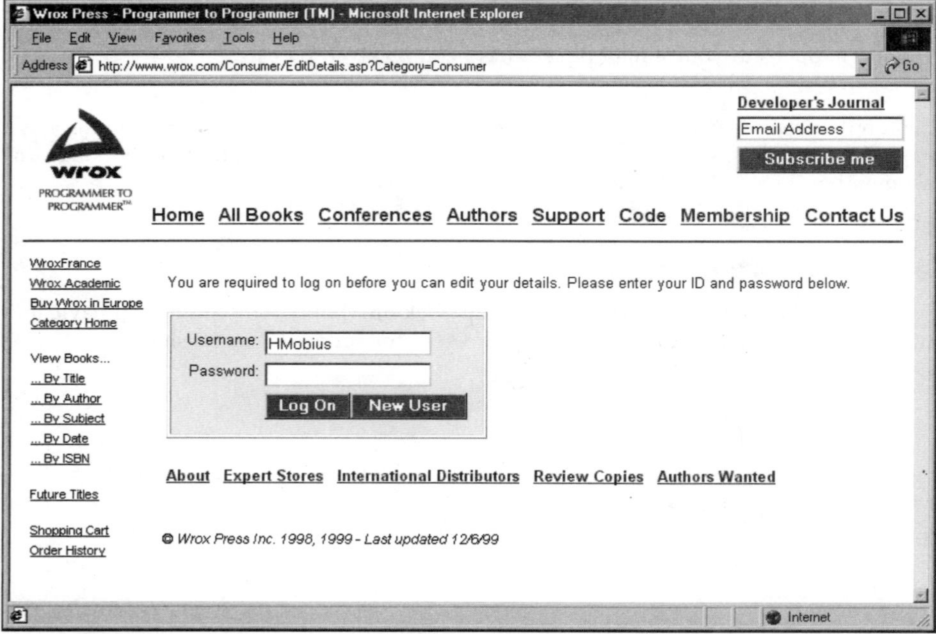

Type in your password once again and click Log On. The following page allows you to change your details if you need to, but now you're logged on, you have access to all the source code downloads and errata for the entire Wrox range of books.

Finding an Errata on the Web Site

Before you send in a query, you might be able to save time by finding the answer to your problem on our web site – http://www.wrox.com.

Each book we publish has its own page and its own errata sheet. You can get to any book's page by clicking on Support from the top navigation bar.

Halfway down the main support page is a drop down box called Title Support. Simply scroll down the list until you see Professional JSP. Select it and then hit Errata.

This will take you to the errata page for the book. Select the criteria by which you want to view the errata, and click the Apply criteria button. This will provide you with links to specific errata. For an initial search, you are advised to view the errata by page numbers. If you have looked for an error previously, then you may wish to limit your search using dates. We update these pages daily to ensure that you have the latest information on bugs and errors.

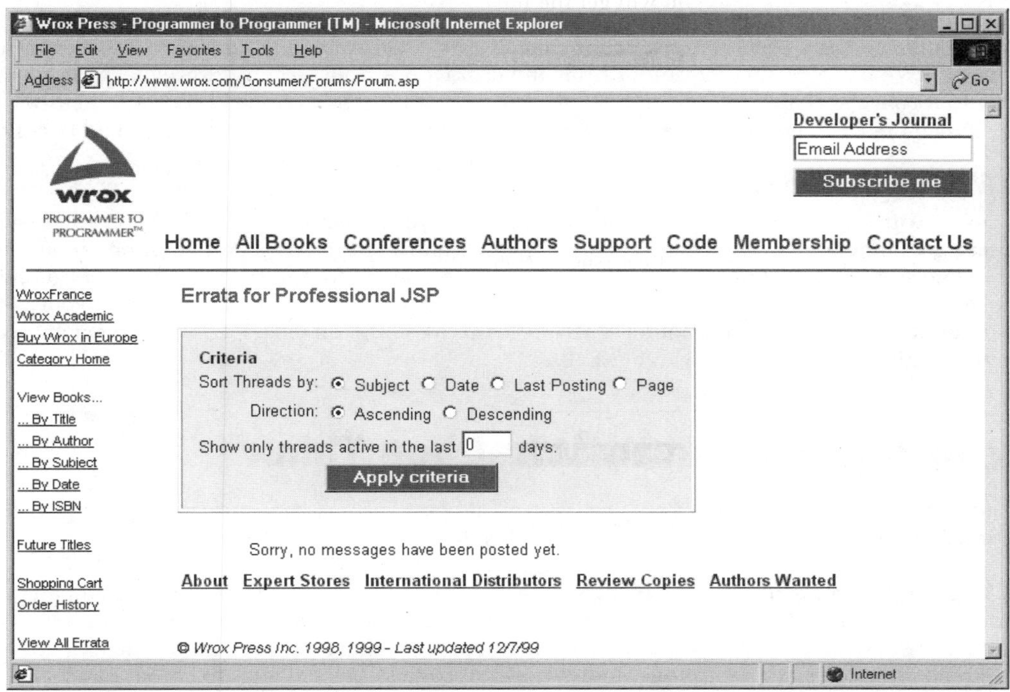

Add an Errata : E-mail Support

If you wish to point out an errata to put up on the website or directly query a problem in the book page with an expert who knows the book in detail then e-mail support@wrox.com, with the title of the book and the last four numbers of the ISBN in the subject field of the e-mail. A typical email should include the following things:

The **name, last four digits of the ISBN** and **page number** of the problem in the Subject field.

Your **name, contact info** and the **problem** in the body of the message.

We won't send you junk mail. We need the details to save your time and ours. If we need to replace a disk or CD we'll be able to get it to you straight away. When you send an e-mail it will go through the following chain of support:

Customer Support

Your message is delivered to one of our customer support staff who are the first people to read it. They have files on most frequently asked questions and will answer anything general immediately. They answer general questions about the book and the web site.

Editorial

Deeper queries are forwarded to the technical editor responsible for that book. They have experience with the programming language or particular product and are able to answer detailed technical questions on the subject. Once an issue has been resolved, the editor can post the errata to the web site.

The Authors

Finally, in the unlikely event that the editor can't answer your problem, s/he will forward the request to the author. We try to protect the author from any distractions from writing. However, we are quite happy to forward specific requests to them. All Wrox authors help with the support on their books. They'll mail the customer and the editor with their response, and again all readers should benefit.

What We Can't Answer

Obviously with an ever-growing range of books and an ever-changing technology base, there is an increasing volume of data requiring support. While we endeavor to answer all questions about the book, we can't answer bugs in your own programs that you've adapted from our code. So, while you might have loved the chapters on file handling, don't expect too much sympathy if you cripple your company with a routine which deletes the contents of your hard drive. But do tell us if you're especially pleased with the routine you developed with our help.

How to Tell Us Exactly What You Think

We understand that errors can destroy the enjoyment of a book and can cause many wasted and frustrated hours, so we seek to minimize the distress that they can cause.

You might just wish to tell us how much you liked or loathed the book in question. Or you might have ideas about how this whole process could be improved. In which, case you should e-mail feedback@wrox.com. You'll always find a sympathetic ear, no matter what the problem is. Above all you should remember that we do care about what you have to say and we will do our utmost to act upon it.

J2EE
JSP

Index

A Guide to the Index

The index is arranged hierarchically, in alphabetical order, with symbols preceding the letter A. Most second level entries and many third level entries also occur as first level entries. This is to ensure that users will find the information they require however they choose to search for it.

Symbols

A

B

C

D

E

F

H

I

J

N

O

P

S

X

Z

J2EE
JSP

Wrox writes books for you. Any suggestions, or ideas about how you want information given in your ideal book will be studied by our team. Your comments are always valued at Wrox.

Free phone in USA 800-USE-WROX
Fax (312) 893 8001

UK Tel. (0121) 687 4100 Fax (0121) 687 4101

Professional JSP - Registration Card

Name ______

Address ______

______

______

______

City ______ State/Region ______

Country ______ Postcode/Zip ______

E-mail ______

Occupation ______

How did you hear about this book? ______

- ☐ Book review (name) ______
- ☐ Advertisement (name) ______
- ☐ Recommendation ______
- ☐ Catalog ______
- ☐ Other ______

Where did you buy this book? ______

- ☐ Bookstore (name) ______ City ______
- ☐ Computer Store (name) ______
- ☐ Mail Order ______
- ☐ Other ______

What influenced you in the purchase of this book?

- ☐ Cover Design
- ☐ Contents
- ☐ Other (please specify) ______

How did you rate the overall contents of this book?

- ☐ Excellent
- ☐ Good
- ☐ Average
- ☐ Poor

What did you find most useful about this book? ______

What did you find least useful about this book? ______

Please add any additional comments. ______

What other subjects will you buy a computer book on soon? ______

What is the best computer book you have used this year?

______

Note: This information will only be used to keep you updated about new Wrox Press titles and will not be used for any other purpose or passed to any other third party.

3625 **Check here if you DO NOT want to receive support for this book** ☐ 3625

NB. If you post the bounce back card below in the UK, please send it to:

Wrox Press Ltd., Arden House, 1102 Warwick Road,
Acocks Green, Birmingham B27 6BH. UK.

Computer Book Publishers

NO POSTAGE
NECESSARY
IF MAILED
IN THE
UNITED STATES

BUSINESS REPLY MAIL
FIRST CLASS MAIL PERMIT#64 CHICAGO, IL

POSTAGE WILL BE PAID BY ADDRESSEE

WROX PRESS INC.,
29 S. LA SALLE ST.,
SUITE 520
CHICAGO IL 60603-USA